Introduction to Human Resource Management

A Guide

3rd edition

Charles Leatherbarrow
Janet Fletcher

The Chartered Institute of Personnel and Development is the leading publisher of books and reports for personnel and training professionals, students, and all those concerned with the effective management and development of people at work. For details of all our titles, please contact the publishing department:

tel: 020 8612 6204

email: publishing@cipd.co.uk

The catalogue of all CIPD titles can be viewed on the CIPD website:

www.cipd.co.uk/bookstore

Introduction to Human Resource Management
A Guide to HR in Practice

3rd edition

Charles Leatherbarrow
Janet Fletcher

Chartered Institute of Personnel and Development

Published by the Chartered Institute of Personnel and Development
151 The Broadway, London SW19 1JQ

This edition first published 2014

Designed and typeset by Exeter Premedia Services, India
Printed in Great Britain by Ashford Colour Press Ltd, Gosport, Hampshire

British Library Cataloguing in Publication Data
A catalogue of this publication is available from the British Library

ISBN 9781843983590

The views expressed in this publication are the authors' own and may not necessarily reflect those of the CIPD.

The CIPD has made every effort to trace and acknowledge copyright holders. If any source has been overlooked, CIPD Enterprises would be pleased to redress this in future editions.

Chartered Institute of Personnel and Development

151 The Broadway, London SW19 1JQ
Tel: 020 8612 6200
Email: cipd@cipd.co.uk
Website: www.cipd.co.uk
Incorporated by Royal Charter. Registered Charity No. 1079797

Contents

List of figures and tables

Preface

The book offers a practical approach to the understanding of human resource management, together with academic underpinning. It is aimed at students on the CIPD Certificate in HR Practice (CHRP) course, but also for those taking higher-level studies – undergraduate or CIPD qualifications. The chapters map against the CHRP qualification.

We have updated the chapters to include legislative changes and some of the latest research and thinking on HR. Chapter 19, 'Handling and Managing Information', has been supplemented by including work on the interpretation of basic statistical concepts and how these are used in the interpretation of survey results.

Good luck with your reading. We hope that the book will be useful to your studies.

Charles Leatherbarrow and Janet Fletcher

June 2014

Overview of the book

Chapter 1: Organisations

This chapter addresses the classification of organisations, HR's role, corporate strategy, policy and objectives, how organisations are structured and concepts such as 'span of control'. The chapter further discusses how organisations are characterised in terms of staff numbers but also in the context of their role in business and society and how organisations interact with their business environment. Consideration is given to the range of what are called 'private' forms of the organisation and the growth of private-public partnerships. Discussion addresses the role of corporate strategy in business development and the use of tools such as SWOT and STEEPLE, which can be used to assess the business environment and the weaknesses and strengths of organisations to compete in commercial markets.

Chapter 2: Aspects of Organisational Culture

The aim of this chapter is to introduce and provide an understanding of the importance of organisation culture and how it is linked to societal culture. Because of the important role that culture plays in most organisations, links are made with other chapters of this book, specifically the chapters that address induction (Chapter 8), reward (Chapter 12), and health and safety (Chapter 14). An attempt is made to demonstrate that culture forms a major characteristic that identifies and distinguishes one, outwardly similar, organisation from another.

Chapter 3: Human Resource Management (HRM)

Chapter 3 offers an explanation and discussion of HRM, its theoretical (or lack of) underpinning, the nature of HRM and the differences between HRM and personnel management. Reference is made to early theories of motivation management, for example the work of Taylor, Mayo, Maslow, McGregor, Herzberg, as well as the early thinking on how organisations should be considered as entities, that is, the work of Weber on bureaucracy and Fayol on the role of management. Further consideration is given to the research of Trist and Bamforth in the context of the socio-technical theories of the organisation and how they impact upon the management of people.

The chapter also addresses the concepts of the 'hard' and 'soft' models of HRM, and the idea of the unitarist and pluralist approaches to the (theoretical) management of people. Consideration is also given to the contributions of Guest, Storey and Ulrich to the understanding of HRM and its role in an organisational environment.

Strategic HRM is also considered, in a limited manner, with discussion of three models of strategic HRM: the best-fit, the best practice and the resource-based view.

In the current climate of the 'customer is king (or queen)', this chapter also addresses the link between HRM and customer service.

Chapter 4: The Role of the HR Practitioner

This chapter covers the roles and responsibilities of HR. The role of the HR practitioner is considered within an organisational context; how the HR department functions and interrelates with the rest of the organisation as a source for advice and support to the line departments. The chapter discusses professionalism and ethics and, linked to this, the

CIPD Profession Map and the expected behaviours of an HR professional. The chapter also discusses HR information systems (these are further discussed in detail in Chapter 19).

Chapter 5: Human Resource Planning

The chapter begins with an explanation of the historical context of human resource planning (HRP). It then proceeds to show how HRP has changed, from what was traditionally called 'manpower planning' – an activity that gave focus to numbers, concentrating on 'headcount' of staff present in an organisation – to one that takes into account both the 'hard' elements of HRM as well as the 'softer' developmental issues of people management when planning for the future. The core mechanisms for human resource planning are addressed:

1 analysis and investigation

2 forecasting

3 planning

4 implementation and control.

Key issues associated with the induction and retention of staff are discussed and details of the way that staff turnover can be calculated and how these figures can be usefully employed are included in the chapter.

HRP in its very broadest sense is discussed, addressing the idea of how HRP is impacted upon by HR supply plans, organisation and structure plans, employee utilisation plans, reward plans, and so on.

Chapter 6: Recruitment

This chapter discusses the importance of 'recruiting for talent' and follows the systematic recruitment cycle. The main objectives are to explain the purposes and the processes of recruitment, such as job analysis, writing job descriptions and person specifications, as well as advertising for the post, including e-recruitment and social media. The chapter also considers how the tools of the recruitment specialist can be used to address the issue of skills shortages.

Chapter 7: Selection

This chapter follows on naturally from the previous chapter on recruitment. The discussion on the search for talent is continued and covers the process of selection: screening applications, shortlisting candidates and the associated administration that surrounds the task. Various selection methods are discussed, including the use of psychometric tests. The chapter pays particular attention to selection interviews and discusses the concept of value-based interviewing. Some of the legal aspects of selection are addressed (additional detail on legislation can be found in Chapter 16, 'Understanding Employment Law').

Chapter 8: Induction and Retention

The purpose of this chapter is to explore the importance and relevance of sound induction processes: why we need induction and what constitutes a good induction programme. The idea of 'employer branding' in terms of attracting and retaining staff is introduced. The notion of 'onboarding' and socialisation is discussed, especially in relation to avoiding the 'induction crisis'. The final part of the chapter examines the problem of retention and what can be done to encourage employees to remain with the organisation.

Chapter 9: Learning and Development – Key Concepts

Chapters 9 and 10 are linked in that Chapter 9 introduces *key concepts* related to learning, while Chapter 10 focuses on learning in organisations and in particular the *practical skills* relating to delivering a learning event. Many of the main terms related to learning are defined, such as 'human resource development', 'talent management', 'human capital' and 'knowledge management'. The chapter discusses learning theories, considers how people learn and concludes with a look at learning styles, continuing professional development and career choice.

Chapter 10: Learning and Development – The Practical Aspects

This chapter starts by exploring the strategic importance of learning and its links with recruitment and talent management. The wider roles of government and government initiatives are discussed in terms of the National Skills Strategy, the Investors in People standard, the use of apprenticeships and 'Time to Train' legislation.

The main focus of the chapter, however, is on delivery of learning events and follows the systematic training cycle, including training needs analysis, planning and delivering training, assessment and evaluation. In particular, there is discussion of training methods, together with an introduction to e-learning and 'blended learning'. The chapter should give the first-time trainer some valuable tips about how to put together a training and learning event.

Chapter 11: Employee Motivation and Performance

The aim of this chapter is to examine performance and to consider how performance can be managed. Definitions and descriptions are given of *performance* (what we do and how we do it), *performance management* (how we manage what employees do) and *performance appraisal* (a means of assessing or measuring that performance).

As performance is so closely related to motivation, the first part of the chapter focuses on exploring a range of key motivation theories.

The chapter then goes on to consider approaches to performance management and discusses performance appraisal, including 360-degree appraisal. In conclusion, the concept of personal development plans (PDPs) is introduced.

Chapter 12: Employee Reward

The aim of this chapter is twofold: first, by considering how people can be rewarded; and, second, by considering how reward fits into the overall business strategy in the context of its role in recruitment and retention and also by focusing the efforts of employees on what the organisation believes is important.

The chapter explains the concept of reward and how reward can be considered from the perspective of total reward, which includes pay, benefits and non-pay-related rewards. The discussion also distinguishes between different types of payment system, approaches to job evaluation, and contribution-related pay in its many guises. It also presents discussion on traditional and HRM approaches to reward (new pay as opposed to old pay), and the role employee benefits play in motivation, recruitment and retention.

Chapter 13: The Employment Relationship

The employment relationship is defined and the notion of the psychological contract is considered. Contracts of employment are addressed, although these are dealt with in much greater detail within Chapter 16, 'Understanding Employment Law'. The unitarist, pluralist and Marxist perspectives of the employment relationship are considered in the context of people management. (These concepts are also addressed in Chapter 3, 'Human Resource Management').

Some of the agencies and organisations which impact upon the employment relationship are examined: the Confederation of British Industry, Business Europe, Institute of Directors, professional bodies and, in particular, trade unions and the Trades Union Congress (TUC), including Unionlearn, the learning and skills organisation of the TUC. The role of Acas (the Advisory, Conciliation and Arbitration Service) is discussed.

The final part of the chapter addresses one of the key areas of employment relations: absence management.

Chapter 14: Health, Safety, Well-being and Work-life Balance

Although not part of the CIPD standards, this chapter is an integral part of the role of any business professional and no less so for the HR specialist. Discussion is made of the legislative framework which underpins the minimum standards of health and safety within the workplace. The Health and Safety Executive (HSE) is introduced and its key role in setting the standards and policing how health and safety is or is not effectively managed in an organisation is discussed.

The essence of effective management of health and safety in the workplace is addressed from the perspective the development of a positive organisational culture towards a healthy workplace. Clear guidance of what employers must do in the context of health and safety management is offered to readers. The chapter addresses managing stress, the issue of stress in the workplace, including employee assistance programmes, relevant law and the idea and practice of risk assessment as well as employee well-being and work-life balance.

Chapter 15: Diversity and Equality

This chapter considers diversity and equality issues in the workplace. It addresses equality from both a legal point of view and a 'business case' perspective. Key terms such as 'diversity', 'equality', 'discrimination' and 'prejudice' are defined and discussed.

The nine 'protected characteristics' named in the Equality Act are examined: age, disability, gender reassignment, marriage and civil partnership, pregnancy and maternity, race, sex, religion and belief, and sexual orientation. The concepts of stereotyping, direct and indirect discrimination and institutional discrimination are addressed, together with the issues of bullying and harassment.

Chapter 16: Understanding Employment Law

The chapter addresses the employment contract, its nature and the obligations it places on the two parties, and how this impacts upon the employment relationship. This chapter has strong links with Chapter 13, which addresses the nature of the employment relationship.

Specifically the chapter considers the essence of a contract and the differences between the various types of contract that are in the employment relationship, including the relatively new shareholder contract. The chapter introduces the requirement to give the employee a statement of their main terms and conditions of employment and also addresses employee rights and how to find information, including the various legislation which underpins how people are managed at work.

The chapter specifically explores the legislation that supports family-friendly policies and rights and employee well-being, such as the right to request flexible working and to whom the right extends. A chapter on employment law cannot be complete without discussion of equal rights legislation, with some discussion about privacy and the need to control information, and the issue of data protection.

An important aspect of life in organisations is how to manage grievance and disciplinary matters. The chapter discusses the nature of procedures, which, after less formal workplace methods have been exhausted, are used to bring closure to discipline and grievance issues. The role of Acas, as a source of information and procedural guidance, as well as mediator in workplace disputes and grievances, is introduced.

New to this chapter is a discussion of the role of the Information Commissioner's Office and how two keys areas of legislation, the Data Protection Act 1998 and the Freedom of Information Act 2000 have impacted upon organisations and those who work within them.

Chapter 17: Ending the Employment Relationship

This chapter discusses why and how the employment relationship can be ended, the issues around fair and unfair dismissal, and how the various types of dismissal can affect both the employee who is about to leave the company as well as those employees who remain, particularly in the case of large-scale redundancies.

Discussion is held on what is fair and unfair dismissal (for example constructive dismissal) and the relevant legislation and guidance that surrounds these issues. As a specific case, the chapter addresses how a redundancy situation should be handled from an HR perspective, for example by addressing how to select for redundancy, against a framework of case law legislation that impacts upon this form of fair dismissal. The chapter also discusses the various options open to management to avoid, or at least moderate, the impact of a redundancy situation. The need to address, after a medium- or large-scale redundancy, the needs of the survivors is also considered from both the perspective of the business as well as from the perspective of the individual who has experienced a traumatic situation, perhaps over a prolonged period of time.

Chapter 18: Change Management

This chapter specifically addresses the need for change, the drivers (triggers) and the types of resistors to change. The organisational development and emergent approaches to change are specifically discussed, showing that different approaches are needed to manage the change process. Included within the chapter are some tools to help analyse and thus to manage the change process.

Change impacts upon people in many different ways. Organisations need to recognise that change, if not managed properly, can lead to negative outcomes for both the organisation and some of its employees. In this context, the role of HR is discussed in relation to how HR interventions can improve the likelihood of the change process being successful, from a business perspective, while mitigating the negative aspects of change on the organisation's people.

Chapter 19: Handling and Managing Information

This chapter relates particularly to the CIPD Level 3 unit, 'Recording, Analysing and Using Human Resources Information', and discusses how information can be identified and used for the benefit of organisations. The chapter is largely based around a case study of a fictitious organisation that has recruitment and retention problems. The reader is taken through, step by step, the process of collating, presenting and analysing data to identify problem areas and develop solutions. There is an introduction to some of the basic techniques of interpreting data using the mean, median and mode, together with examples of how to use these in practice.

The chapter also introduces the role and structure of an HR information system and how this might be configured to serve the needs of the organisation as well as the individual employee.

The content of the CIPD Certificates in HR Practice and Learning and Development Practice are covered as follows:

Unit code	Unit title	Relevant chapter
4DEP	Developing Yourself as an Effective Human Resources or Learning and Development Practitioner	Ch 1, 3, 4, 9, 10, 11
3HRC	Understanding Organisations and the Role of Human Resources	Ch 1, 2, 3, 4
3RAI	Recording, Analysing and Using Human Resources Information	Ch 4, 5, 8, 10, 15, 16, 19
3RTO	Resourcing Talent	Ch 5, 6, 7, 8, 10, 11, 16
3CJA	Contributing to the Process of Job Analysis	Ch 5, 6
3PRM	Supporting Good Practice in Performance and Reward Management	Ch 11, 12
3SCO	Supporting Change within Organisations	Ch 2, 18
3MER	Supporting Good Practice in Managing Employment Relations	Ch 11, 13, 15, 16, 17
3DLA	Delivering Learning and Development Activities	Ch 9, 10, 11
3LNA	Undertaking a Learning Needs Analysis	Ch 9, 10, 11
3PDL	Preparing and Designing Learning and Development Activities	Ch 9, 10, 11
3ELA	Evaluating Learning and Development Activities	Ch 9, 10, 11
3DCS	Developing Coaching Skills for the Workplace	Ch 9, 10, 11
3DMS	Developing Mentoring Skills for the Workplace	Ch 9, 10, 11

Walkthrough of textbook features and online resources

LEARNING OBJECTIVES

After studying this chapter you should understand:

- organisations: what they are for, how they are classified and how classification might change over time
- why organisations are designed in the way they are
- corporate strategy, policy and objectives
- SWOT and PESTLE (STEEPLE) analysis
- the flexible firm.

LEARNING OBJECTIVES

At the beginning of each chapter a bulleted set of learning objectives summarises what you can expect to learn from the chapter, helping you to track your learning.

ACTIVITY 2.8

Reflect upon the comments attributed to Furnham and Gunter above. Do you consider, in reality, that there could be such differences in priorities and ideals within an organisation that this could lead to disharmony and differing agendas which could negatively impact the operation of the whole organisation?

ACTIVITIES

Questions and activities throughout the text encourage you to reflect on what you have learnt and to apply your knowledge and skills in practice.

CASE EXAMPLE 3.6

CUSTOMER SERVICE EXPLAINED

Consider the following scenario: imagine going on holiday. It is 4 pm. The cases are packed, the taxi to the airport is due to leave at 6 pm and you realise that you have insufficient prescription tablets to take with you. You cannot go without them; they are essential to your well-being. You make a frantic phone call to the doctor's surgery, where the receptionist understands your need. She phones back within ten minutes and promises to fax an emergency prescription to the local chemist. She has arranged for the medication to be ready for collection by the time you can drive the six miles to the chemist. Above all, when the receptionist speaks with you, she does not make you think that you are stupid because, as she tells you, 'we all make mistakes when trying to balance a busy life'. She wishes you a good holiday.

CASE EXAMPLES

A number of case studies from different sectors will help you to place the concepts discussed into a real-life context.

PAUSE FOR THOUGHT

Who assesses your performance? Who talks to you about training? If you are given a task that you have never carried out before, who shows you how to do it? Does the HR/personnel department get involved? What is their role in the process? Who would you approach?

PAUSE FOR THOUGHT

Boxes provide questions or facts to keep you thinking about the key themes of the chapter.

KEY CONCEPT: SUBCULTURES

From how Robbins et al (ibid) define subcultures, one may deduce that the subculture on the workshop floor at, say, location A, will be different from that of the marketing department at location B. Furthermore, organisations may have a boardroom subculture, a middle management subculture, a staff subculture and a shop-floor subculture.

DEFINITIONS AND KEY CONCEPTS

Boxes give explanations of key terms and concepts in the book.

REVIEW QUESTIONS

1   What is meant by the following three terms in the context of information management:
   - strategic information?
   - tactical information?
   - operational information?

2   How would you define an HRIS?

3   What is meant by the term wiki?

4   Define the following three terms:
   - mode
   - median
   - average (mean).
   - What is the purpose of the above three measures? What are they indicative of?

REVIEW QUESTIONS

These review questions are aimed at reinforcing what you have learnt in the chapter.

EXPLORE FURTHER

BOOKS

LANDERS, R.L.N. (2014) *A step-by-step introduction to statistics for business.* London: SAGE.

Visit the SAGE website to sample Chapter 1 of the book: **www.uk.sagepub.com/ books/Book237219/title#tabview=samples**

VIDEO LINKS

For some guidance on calculating and understanding *average*, *median* and *mode*, view the following YouTube videos:

www.khanacademy.org/math/probability/descriptive-statistics/old-stats-videos/ v/statistics–the-average

www.youtube.com/watch?v=_gbCPPk1KKY

www.youtube.com/watch?v=NZHPVbRbCAY

EXPLORE FURTHER

Explore further boxes contain suggestions for further reading and useful websites, encouraging you to delve further into areas of particular interest.

ONLINE RESOURCES FOR TUTORS

Visit www.cipd.co.uk/tss

- Lecturer's Guide – Practical advice on teaching an introductory HRM module using this text.

- PowerPoint Slides – Build and deliver your course around these ready-made lectures, ensuring complete coverage of the module.

CHAPTER 1

Organisations

LEARNING OBJECTIVES

After studying this chapter you should understand:

- organisations: what they are for, how they are classified and how classification might change over time
- why organisations are designed in the way they are
- corporate strategy, policy and objectives
- SWOT and PESTLE (STEEPLE) analysis
- the flexible firm.

1.1 INTRODUCTION

The organisation provides the background within which the HR function works, so if you are studying HR for the first time, you need to develop a clear understanding of the context in which it is set. In other words, you need to have a grasp of what organisations are and how they can be considered because the nature and structure of an organisation impacts upon how people are managed. The purpose of this chapter, therefore, is to help you to develop that understanding, so that you can operate efficiently and effectively as an HR practitioner.

1.1.1 USING THIS CHAPTER

This is a chapter that (we hope) you will find yourself dipping into from time to time for information about organisations. Different categories of organisation are explained as well as how their purposes vary from one to another. The explanations of corporate strategy, policy formulation and objective-setting will help you to understand how an organisation assesses and reviews its past performance, how it plans its long-term future and operates in the day-to-day context.

1.2 ORGANISATIONS

1.2.1 WHY ORGANISATIONS EXIST

We live in a society that is dominated by organisations. All of the major factors of our lives – our birth, health, education, marriage, employment, even our death – are influenced or handled by one kind of organisation or another. So why do we create organisations? The fundamental answer is that we do so in order to survive. Unlike other living creatures, human beings are rational in the sense that they are able to reflect upon their past, assess their current situation and make plans for the future. Since we are aware of our survival needs, we are able to create organisations to ensure that those needs will be met. The interdependency of human life makes the need for an organisation an imperative.

Organisations allow us to manage a range of complex activities that result in the provision of a product or service to a customer.

There are therefore vast industries involved in producing our basic needs, such as those for: Food: fish, meat and vegetable canning; Drink: dairy products, brewing, recreational drinks such as colas and fresh fruit drinks; Shelter: construction companies such as Taylor-Woodrow, building material suppliers such as Marshalls; Security providers: G4S plus a host of essential uniformed services. On the lighter side, there are travel and entertainment companies such as the Hilton Hotels and Resorts, SAGA holidays, Sandals luxury holidays. In fact, organisations are set up to serve us, not solely in order to survive, but to survive for longer, in greater comfort, and so that we may lead an interesting and pleasurable life. Organisations are the infrastructure of modern civilised societies.

1.2.2 PUBLIC SECTOR ORGANISATIONS

The UK has a *mixed economy*, which means that some organisations are influenced by central government. For example, government departments and local authorities provide us with essential services such as those for health, education, highways, policing, social services and dealing with emergencies. These organisations are said to be in the *public sector*. The provision of such services as drinking water, drainage, gas, electricity, and public transport used to be in the public sector, but privatisation towards the end of the twentieth century transferred them to what we call the *private sector* (see later).

Ultimately, all public sector organisations are responsible to central government. Those who influence and set policy, 'the politicians', are, in turn, accountable to the public. They, the politicians, derive their authority to make decisions and take actions on our behalf from what we call *public trust*.

Politicians set agendas and develop policy, which defines the framework against which salaried bureaucrats manage the local council or a chief constable manages a police force. If the public is not satisfied with the way that they have done this, the political leaders can be replaced at the next election through the voting system. This concept of public accountability of the police forces in England and Wales was further emphasised by the introduction, in 2012, of the role of 'Police and Crime Commissioner' (Eaton, 2012, p16). Note: The police and crime commissioner is responsible for: how an area is policed, the police budget, the amount of council tax charged for the police and the information about what the local police are doing within a given area (**www.gov.uk/police-and-crime-commissioners**).

Usually, politicians are amateurs in terms of the specific responsibilities they are given, and the policy decisions they make are based upon advice from employed experts, who we have called 'salaried bureaucrats'. These bureaucrats are therefore advisers and also managers who have responsibility for implementing policy decisions.

At the very top of central government, experts who are senior civil servants remain in their positions regardless of any political changes that the electorate makes.

ACTIVITY 1.1

Wolverhampton City Council has 60 elected members, who usually, but not always, have some political affiliation. They are elected by their constituents and so represent a 'ward' or area. Councillors should represent the whole community but clearly they have a specific duty to those people from their ward who elected them to 'office'. Wolverhampton has a mayor who represents the city at major functions and also 'chairs' all council meetings. The council has adopted what they call the 'Leader Cabinet' model of governance. As well as a mayor, the council has a 'leader'. This role is the political head and so drives the council's agenda. Both roles are elected by the councillors, from the 60 councillors voted in by the public. A third of the 60 councillors are elected every four years, thus some continuity is maintained. The cabinet is a group of councillors including the leader who work with council staff to run the council. With some limitations on major policy issues, which have to be referred to the full council, the cabinet can take most decisions.

The council's agenda is turned into reality by the 'head of paid services', who is the council's chief executive, a salaried employee of the council. The role of this position is to run the council on a day-to-day basis with the help of their directors and in co-operation with the leader of the council and cabinet.

Each year Wolverhampton City Council produces an informative document which is called the 'The Constitution'. This document explains how the council is structured and managed. You can find this document by searching for 'Constitution' on the council's website, where you will find a constitution for each year.

Investigate how councils operate

- Using the information above and Wolverhampton City Council's 'Constitution' document, determine how the leader of the council can be removed from position if it is considered that they are not performing in their leadership role.
- Access your local council's website and determine how the council is structured.
  - How, for example, are cabinet members chosen?
  - How does the leader of the council make sure that what the council does is in accordance with good practice and, at the same time, is legally compliant?
- In some councils the mayoral position, such as the mayor of London, is elected by the people and not by councillors. Investigate, using the website for the Greater London Authority:
  - the purpose of the role of mayor
  - how the mayor of London is elected
  - how long the incumbent mayor remains in post before having to stand for re-election.

CASE EXAMPLE 1.1

WHEN IS A PUBLIC SECTOR ORGANISATION NOT A PUBLIC SECTOR ORGANISATION? ANSWER: WHEN IT IS PRIVATISED

Robert Peston, the BBC's Business Editor, discussing the announcement that the UK Government were likely to privatise the Royal Mail by floating it on the stock exchange, points out that, 'it would be the first time in about two decades that a household name nationalised industry will have been sold to investment institutions and retail shareholders' (Peston, 2013). Like many other political pundits, Peston points out that the Royal Mail's profits have soared from a pre-tax loss of £165 million in 2011 to a pre-tax profit of £324 million in the tax year to April 2013 – so here lies a paradox. Why should a profitable, yet government-run, company be sold into the private sector? He suggests that many would see the privatisation as 'harking back to what some see as the glory days of privatisation under Margaret Thatcher and John Major' (ibid).

Royal Mail was sold off into the private sector in October 2013.

> The shares were sold at 330p on 11 October but immediately jumped by 38%, sparking a furore about whether a prime state-owned asset had been sold off on the cheap. The shares closed last night at 532p, still well below the initial offering price but off highs of more than 600p (Treanor, 2014).

Feedback comments

The social and business context within which the Royal Mail operates has changed. Prior to the Internet becoming widely available for business in the developed world in the 1990s and subsequent widespread use by non-commercial users, the Royal Mail's main business was delivering letters. The Internet changed all that: email became 'king'. How we, the British and Irish public, think about mail delivery has changed. Coupled with the growth in email, two further and significant factors have impacted upon the Royal Mail business model. First, there was the removal of Royal Mail's postal service monopoly in 2006. Second, and in response to the change in Royal Mail's position as a monopoly provider of mail, the private sector was stimulated to develop parcel delivery services within the UK. It was accepted that parcels might be delivered by TNT Express (Dutch), DHL (German), FedEx (USA), DPD (French) or Royal Mail's (UK) own parcel delivery service, Parcelforce, to our homes and offices in the UK. Quinn (2012), in the *Telegraph*, noted that TNT Express had, since April 2012, been operating a pilot scheme to deliver letters to cover the 'last mile' in the mail supply chain to residents in west London and had plans to roll the service out into

other large cities such as Birmingham and Manchester.

Coupled with the Government's desire to raise capital, there has been a confluence {*meaning – coming together of*} of political, social, technological and economic pressures to such an extent that, for a capitalist economy such as we have in the UK, the reasoning for maintaining the provision of a service by the state, such as is the case with the Royal Mail, was very debatable.

The growth in the numbers of logistics firms competing for business has been driven by the increase in Internet shopping, which demands a quality delivery service in terms of parcel security, speed and reliability of delivery. So on the face of things, the Royal Mail has moved from a public service monopoly to one where the business landscape offers comparable alternative service suppliers. The Government argued that it was good for Royal Mail to be released from the shackles of government and thus be able to grow its business by going to the 'market' for investment capital. Ministers will also not now have to defend pay rises, pay freezes or changes to postal worker salaries to the general public. There was a compelling case, certainly from the standpoint of the Conservative/Liberal Democrat Coalition Government to move the Royal Mail away from government control.

Assuming that privatisation is always good and holding on to government-provided services is always bad is a limited argument. In terms of the Royal Mail its service was, and is, provided across Great Britain and Northern Ireland *and* is provided at a common cost. Customers do not pay more for a second class stamp if they are situated in Manchester or on one of the Orkney Islands, situated off the north coast of Scotland.

Like other privatised public sector organisations such as British Gas and the water authorities, the Government, through the Postal Services Act 2011 (Great Britain, Postal Services Act 2011), imposed conditions on the newly privatised company. Ofcom, the regulator (**www.ofcom.org.uk**), focuses on the scope and delivery regime of the newly created privatised Royal Mail. For example, there is a legal requirement to maintain the *universal service*, whereby items can be sent to any location within the United Kingdom for a fixed price, not affected by distance. The universal service is enshrined in the Postal Services Act 2011 until 2021.

Prior to the privatisation of Royal Mail it was regulated by Postcomm. Since privatisation, Ofcom has taken over the role. Ofcom is the independent regulator and competitions authority charged with monitoring the UK communication industries and now has added to its role the responsibility for safeguarding the UK's Universal Service Obligation on postal services.

Titcomb in the *Telegraph* wrote a useful set of questions and answers about the then proposed Royal Mail privatisation (Titcomb, 2013).

See what Mike Fallon, MP and Minister for Business had to say about the proposed sale of the Royal Mail. You can view the video at: **www.youtube.com/watch?v=-2wa4oS1ieA**

View also what the general public and employees as stakeholders in the Royal Mail had to say about the plans to privatise Royal Mail (available at: **www.youtube.com/watch?v=cZwKtHOkBbA**).

There is a clear trend in the UK and many other Western countries, which are largely driven by capitalist ideology, to minimise the role of government in business and to open up activities which were previously the role of the public sector. In the 1980s, Margaret Thatcher in her tenure as prime minister (UK) started the trend to privatisation. Similarly, President Ronald Reagan (USA), as a like-minded friend of Margaret Thatcher, energetically drove the privatisation agenda. The European Union, although having a social dimension to its agenda, largely drives capitalist thinking and business ideals. There is no wonder that in developed Western European countries, what thirty years ago would have clearly been the role of the public services is now taken for granted to be provided by private organisations. The bigger and very political debate is which services, currently provided by the state, should be held as sacrosanct {meaning – too special to be changed}.

1.2.3 PRIVATE SECTOR ORGANISATIONS

The *private sector* is made up of industrial and commercial companies that have evolved to respond to the stable and changing demands of the market. Each company exists to make a profit and is owned by its *shareholders*, who are the prime beneficiaries. The members of the *board of directors*, who are responsible for managing the company, are elected to their positions by the shareholders. In the private sector, therefore, it is said that directors' authority to make decisions and take actions is derived from the *ownership* of the organisation.

The directors on the board are employed experts who formulate and implement policy. If the shareholders do not approve of the way the organisation is being managed, they can vote for changes in particular decisions, and when they think it is necessary, they may vote directors out of office. The shareholders' opportunity to vote arises at the organisation's *annual general meeting (AGM)*, where the directors report on the past year's performance, particularly the financial performance, and state their plans for the future. In reality, shareholding has become scattered widely among individuals and institutions, and many shareholders never attend AGMs.

CASE EXAMPLE 1.2

THE WHOLLY OWNED PRIVATE COMPANY – THE CASE OF MARTIN-BAKER

Martin-Baker (Martin-Baker Aircraft Co. Ltd.), a family-owned British company, manufactures ejector seats for fighter aircraft. It does this very well and its products can be found in aircraft built around the world. The Martin-Baker ejector seat in its many forms has saved more than 7,441 lives* since the first prototype seat ejected a test pilot from the cockpit of a Meteor jet fighter in 1946. The company is very successful.

The business has come a long way since those buccaneering days. Martin-Baker's seats, viewed as the industry gold standard, can be found in nearly all the world's leading fighter jets, including the Eurofighter Typhoon (partly built by BAE Systems), France's Dassault Rafale and Lockheed Martin's F-35 joint strike fighter, the world's biggest military programme. Flying with the top guns of the aerospace world brings its pressures. But the septuagenarian brothers are still heavily involved in the running of the business and they have no desire to relinquish control. 'I think that's because we are doing something we enjoy,' said James *[co-founder Sir James Martin – author's comment].* 'It helps if you are successful as well' (West, 2013).

The story, as told by West (ibid) of the Martin-Baker Company (**www.martin-baker.com**), explores how an organisation can leverage its private ownership to grow its talent and view development over the long term; much of course depends upon the principles of the founders and current owners. The Martin-Baker Company has turned down lucrative offers – the company is very attractive to large aerospace organisations because it is technologically advanced and has a range of skills based on both the development in leading-edge safety system technology and the tacit knowledge of its employees.

* Martin-Baker website 30 May 2014.

1.2.4 DEFINITIONS OF AN ORGANISATION

There have been many definitions of organisations, mostly drafted by academics. How an academic defines an organisation is usually determined by why they are defining it in the first place. Economists, management scientists, social scientists and organisational psychologists have produced new and different ways of looking at organisations, while other definitions have been produced by working managers.

Senior and Swailes (2010, p.4, citing Daft, 1989), suggest that a:

> working definition of an organization might say it is: (1) a social entity that (2) has a purpose, (3) has a boundary, so that some participants are considered inside while others are considered outside, and (4) patterns the activities of participants into recognizable structure.

See also later in the chapter how Schein defines an organisation.

CASE EXAMPLE 1.3

 WHAT HAPPENS WHEN A PRIVATE COMPANY FAILS?

Jessops, the photographic retailer which was founded in Leicester in 1935, failed in January 2013. The company became insolvent; it did not have sufficient assets and was unable to pay its debts. Jessops was not the only one to suffer insolvency; its demise came after the collapse of HMV (music), Comet (electrical retailer), Blockbuster (video, DVD rental), Republic (fashion chain), to name but a few. Some, like Jessops, Blockbuster and Republic, have a new life under new ownership.

Peter Jones, the *Dragons' Den* entrepreneur, considers that Jessops still has potential to make money. The following is from *The Times* [online]:

> Jessops, the photography retailer, made a surprise return to the high street today as Peter Jones, the entrepreneur, relaunched the chain 11 weeks after it collapsed Jessops will hire as many as 500 staff and many are drawn from the 1,400 who lost their jobs when it collapsed. 'A lot contacted me on Twitter and asked for a job and

it's great to have them,' said Mr Jones (Bounds, 2013).

Since it was bought in early 2013, Jessops (Jessops Europe Limited) has grown its online business and has a presence in 28 towns and cities within the UK (Jessops website, **www.jessops.com/jobs/ourcompany**, accessed 30 May 2014).

When a company fails, the implications are far reaching and affect a number of other businesses and thus people who work in those organisations. What really happens when a company can no longer service its debts? Specifically, what happens to the:

- monetary stake in the business that its shareholders have by ownership of a number of shares?
- jobs and the salaries owed by the company to employees?
- money owed by the company to businesses from which it has bought goods and services but for which it has yet to pay?
- debts owed to the company for goods and services it has provided but for which it has yet to receive payment?

PAUSE FOR THOUGHT

What do you think is the purpose of a company going into administration? What do you think should happen? Should there be a priority set as to who should get the monies they are owed when the company's assets are finally sold? On what basis would you determine the 'pecking order' of such a priority list?

Feedback comments

Going into administration is but one of several ways a company can manage an insolvency crisis. Once 'into' administration, the company is protected against legal action, preventing individuals or companies attempting, through legal means, to collect debts.

The aim of the administration process can, in effect, be considered a way of trying to achieve one of three possible outcomes:

1   To try to keep the company running as a going concern in some way, as happened with Jessops. This is preferable for the company and also for some, but not all, of its employees and its debtors. One alternative is that the company's assets are liquidated; in such cases the debtors are less likely to receive such beneficial outcomes.

2   Usually, because the process of administration is managed by a 'competent organisation' which has a duty to try to maximise the outcome for the shareholders and employees, it is more advantageous than should the company's assets be liquidated without going into administration.

3   Finally, should all else fail, the administrators will try to obtain the best value for the company's property and other assets it holds.

The administrators have a duty to formally report to the creditors how they intend to manage the company and its debts. If the company has to be 'wound up', that is, closed down, and its assets stripped to realise cash because there are no potential buyers interested in its purchase, the administrators will allocate any money that is owed against a set of legally bound priorities. There are four such categories: employees are ranked second and shareholders are fourth in the list (PwC, 2009).

For more information visit the PwC (PricewaterhouseCoopers) website and download their guide to insolvency, 'Insolvency in brief' (PwC, 2009).

Theorists study organisations through the framework of their own particular science; each will study different aspects and, not surprisingly, they all define them differently. Academics and practising managers have been studying organisations and how they should be managed for more than a hundred years and some of them say that the study of organisations and the study of 'management as an organisational process' are inextricably linked. Indeed Brech's (1965) definition still has relevance. He sees organisations as 'the framework of the management process'.

Schein (1980) defines the organisation as: the planned co-ordination of the activities of a number of people for the achievement of some common, explicit purpose or goal, through division of labour and function, and through a hierarchy of authority and responsibility. Compare his definition with that of Greenberg (2013, p.11), who writes:

> An organization is a structured social system consisting of groups and individuals working together to meet agreed-upon objectives. In other words, organizations consist of structured social units, such as individuals and/or work groups, who strive to attain a common goal.

Schein's definition has stood the test of time and still holds good today. As a preference, Schein's definition is perhaps more appropriate to a business-focused organisation because he introduces the notion of authority and responsibility.

 ACTIVITY 1.2

Using Edgar Schein's definition of an organisation, do you think it adequately describes the activities of:

- a 'food bank', which collects donations of food and distributes it to the less fortunate in society?

- a local nursery?
- FIFA?
- Microsoft?

Would Daft's definition, discussed at the beginning of this section, adequately fit with the operation of the above organisations?

As well as defining organisations, theorists also classify them. Previously we described organisations as *public* and *private* sector undertakings. In 1966, Blau and Scott classified them in terms of who are the prime beneficiaries of the organisation. They proposed four types:

- **Mutual benefit organisations**, in which the members are the prime beneficiaries. A trade union is one obvious example. Others include sports and social clubs, some building societies and professional institutions, such as the Chartered Institute of Personnel and Development (CIPD).
- **Business concerns**, in which the shareholders are the prime beneficiaries. These are commercial and industrial profit-oriented organisations. Examples are motor car manufacturers and supermarkets.
- **Service organisations**, in which the prime beneficiaries are the users, such as customers and clients. Examples of such organisations are health and educational institutions.
- **Commonweal organisations**, in which the public are the prime beneficiaries. Examples are the armed services, central and local government and the United Nations (Blau and Scott, 1966).

When Margaret Thatcher came to power in 1979 (see earlier discussion about the privatisation of Royal Mail), she was, because of her huge parliamentary majority, able to drive through legislation which enabled an ideological shift towards an enterprise culture. Many services which had hitherto been provided by the state were, over time, sold off; for example: Post Office Telephones became BT and the gas, water and electricity utilities moved into private ownership. Moving the ownership into private hands also helped swell the Chancellor of the Exchequer's coffers at a time when the UK economy was suffering.

Charitable organisations in the UK have grown considerably since Blau and Scott proposed their classification. It was claimed then that any organisation would fit into one of their four categories, but it is difficult to see how any of them could accommodate a charitable organisation; perhaps there is room for a fifth category.

An alternative to a charitable organisation is a community interest company (CIC). This is a type of company designed in particular for social enterprises that want to use their profits and assets for the public good. An example of a CIC would be a housing association; the Isle of Skye Ferry would also fall within this category (www.gov.uk/government/case-studies/isle-of-skye-ferry). CICs are easy to set up; with all the flexibility and certainty of the company format, for example they can offer shares, but with some special features to ensure they are working for the benefit of the community (Department for Business, Innovation and Skills, 2013a). A community interest company is not a charity but a charity could convert into a CIC. A CIC does not have the same tax advantages as a charity, but it is not as heavily regulated, can develop a brand identity and, as previously indicated, can offer shares to investors, subject to certain criteria.

Further work by Maltby (2003, cited in Kew and Stredwick, 2013, p.179) suggests that the typology defined by Blau and Scott (1966) is perhaps too simplistic and dated. It is suggested that a continuum of types, ranging from nationalised to private companies, is probably more realistic:

- Nationalised industries.
- Public PLCs, where a company operates as though it is in the private sector (Kew and Stredwick, 2013) . Kew and Stredwick quoted the pre-privatised Royal Mail as an example of this type of company.
- Public interest company (PIC) – these are usually set up to provide a public service; they do not, for example, have shareholders.

- Public/private partnerships (PPP), including privately funded institution (PFI) contracts – the National Air Traffic Services (NATS Holdings) is a PPP, which embodies government and private ownership. NATS provides air traffic control across the UK.
- Regulated private companies – these are typically privatised institutions such as the water and gas boards.
- Private companies (adapted from Kew and Stredwick (2013, p.179) with kind permission of the CIPD).

There are many types of privately owned organisations and they appear in many different shapes, sizes and configurations:

- Public limited company (PLC) – shares of this type of company can be sold on the stock exchange to realise capital and the company can make acquisitions. There are a number of criteria that have to be satisfied, for example, the number of directors and the requirement to hold annual general meetings.
- Limited company – the main advantage is that the personal assets of the investors are protected. The advantages include the ability to restrict who can buy shares – unlike a PLC, whose shares are available to any investor. Also, business expenses can be claimed against tax.
- Partnerships – there are two types of partnership:

  i   In a 'general partnership', the partners manage the company and are responsible for any debts.

  ii A 'limited partnership' has what are called 'general partners', who have a liability for the partnership as explained in (i) above. A 'limited partnership' also has what are termed 'limited partners'. Limited partners do not have any responsibility for debts; they invest in the partnership but not have no control over its operation.

- Sole trader – in this case there is one owner. From a legal perspective there is no difference between the owner and the business. The clear implication from this is that the assets of the owner are also seen as the assets of the business.
- Joint venture (JV) – there are a number of specific types of JV, depending upon how they are set up. Oil and gas companies tend to go into joint ventures when exploring potential underground deposits of oil and gas reserves; by doing so, they share the risk of the exploration costs. The relationship is set up for a finite time; each of the venture partners contributes capital (equity). Each has control but, in the case of an oil exploration JV, one company usually takes the lead as operator. As well as sharing in the costs of the venture, they share in any profits. Once the project has finished the JV can be wound up. In a JV, where the partners own shares, the shares can be sold to others who may wish to buy a stake in the enterprise.
- Franchising – this is where the business model of a successful firm allows the person who has bought the franchise to use the brand logo etc, while the franchisor supplies the goods (for example, in the case of McDonalds, the buns, burgers, fries, etc). There is a cost to buy into a franchise and of course there are the operating costs of purchasing the franchisor's goods. The advantages for the franchisor is that it limits their exposure to losses because, in the example of a food franchisor, they do not have the problem of finding, renovating, equipping and staffing a series of restaurants, sandwich bars, cafes, etc.

CASE EXAMPLE 1.4

FIFA: A COMMERCIAL ORGANISATION, A SPORTS BODY, A CO-OPERATIVE?

Organisations are not always what they appear to be. Consider FIFA – to be precise, The Fédération Internationale de Football Association – the international co-ordinating and managing body of world football. How does this organisation fit into any of the previous typologies? Its origins date back to 1904, when a group of Europeans from Belgium, Denmark, France, the Netherlands, Spain, Sweden and Switzerland came together to create FIFA with the express purpose of developing a unified understanding of the football rules and to create a European competition (FIFA, no date).

FIFA's current mission is embodied in the following three aims: to develop the game, to touch the world and build a better future. It has come a long way since its early beginnings. FIFA is, on the one hand, a commercial organisation selling television rights around the world. It generates revenue through its marketing of the Football World Cup (FIFA trademarked), but on the other hand distributes over 70% of its expenditure back into football (FIFA, no date). Moving its headquarters to Zurich in 2006 also allowed it to take advantage of generous Swiss tax laws which exempt a public benefit business from taxation (Eisenberg, 2006).

Eisenberg (2006), in his analysis of FIFA, determines its nature by defining it as an international non-governmental organisation (INGO), similar to the Red Cross or Greenpeace. The difficulty with this definition arises because INGOs tend not to be perceived as commercial organisations, *per se*, whereas a cursory analysis of FIFA would appear to indicate this to be the case. 'In the world of INGOs entrepreneurial dealings are seen as a legitimate means to raise the level of an organisation's material resources. In this respect FIFA is not a special case amongst INGOs' (Eisenberg, 2006, p.62). A contradiction, which is recognised by Eisenberg (2006), lies in the fact that FIFA is a membership-based organisation; it seeks to achieve its wide aims through its 208-strong global membership associations.

ACTIVITY 1.3

Think about the organisation for which you work or one with which you are familiar. Where does it fit into Blau and Scott's or Maltby's typology? What kind of organisation is it? Who are the prime beneficiaries?

Using Blau and Scott's or Maltby's typology, discuss the nature of the following organisations:

- the Olympic Delivery Authority, which managed the 2012 London Olympics
- G4S, which provided the security for the London Olympics – you will get some insight into G4S by reading Simon Neville's article in either the *Observer* or *Guardian* of 22 July 2012 (Neville, 2012) and a further article in the *Guardian* on 13 February 2013 (Neville, 2013).

1.2.5 MECHANISTIC AND ORGANIC ORGANISATIONS

Burns and Stalker (1966), after extensive research into organisations, defined them according to the degree to which they were mechanistic or organic. The research was related to the marketing function and market forces.

Mechanistic organisations

Mechanistic organisations are those that have been serving a stable market for many years, that is to say that the demand for their products has been consolidated, the assumption is made that things will not change significantly, and therefore the product demand, in terms of quantity and quality, can be predicted with a reasonable degree of accuracy. Internally, the result is a highly structured organisation with centralised policies, rigid hierarchical ranks, a strong emphasis on administration and tightly drawn boundaries between the departments and functions. Mullins and Christy (2013, p.548) suggest that, 'a traditional high-end expensive hotel' would fall into this category.

Organic organisations

Conversely, where customer demands are ever changing, a mechanistic approach would seriously inhibit the organisation's ability to remain in the market. This kind of market situation demands a flattened structure, *colleague* rather than *command and control relationships* as the predominant mode, short-lived and flexible administrative systems and fuzzy departmental boundaries.

This is not to imply that industry is a dichotomy *{meaning – a division into two usually contradictory parts or opinions}*, such that an organisation would fall into one or the other category. It is not a reflection of the real world that some organisations are totally mechanistic while others are totally organic. Organisations may be more or less mechanistic or more or less organic. This is best thought of as a continuum, ranging from mechanistic through to organic, and an organisation may exhibit characteristics of each type depending on the perspective taken:

Mechanistic ←→ movement ←→ Organic

All organisations can be found somewhere on this dimension. Also, as market demands change and new products are developed, organisations are seen to shift to the left or right as they become more organic or more mechanistic.

ACTIVITY 1.4

Although you may not know much detail about the elite British Army Special Air Service (SAS) regiment, you will probably have heard about their anti-terrorism and special operations in the various theatres of war in which the UK armed services have been involved.

Against the Burns and Stalker definitions of organic and mechanistic, how would you categorise the SAS? You should be able to defend your choice in a class discussion.

For some guidance in your discussion you may wish to refer to:

- ARMY (2012) *Transforming the British Army: modernising to face an unpredictable future,* which is available at: **www.army. mod.uk/documents/general/ Army2020_brochure.pdf**.
- COUGHLIN, C. (2013) The SAS: a very special force [online]. *Telegraph.* 31 January. p.21 [cited 13 June 2014]. Available at: **www. search.proquest.com**.

1.2.6 SIZES OF ORGANISATION

Finally, organisations may be classified by their size. They may range from the sole proprietor type of business to vast international and multinational undertakings employing hundreds of thousands of people. Curran and Stanworth (1988) identify three categories of size:

1 **Small to medium-sized enterprises (SMEs)**, which are subdivided by the European Commission (2003) into:

   i   Micro-enterprises – that is, organisations with fewer than ten employees and with a turnover or balance sheet less than or equal to 2 million Euros.

   ii Small enterprises – that is, organisations with less than or equal to 50 employees and with a turnover of less than or equal to 10 million and a balance sheet less than or equal to 10 million Euros.

   iii Medium-sized enterprises – that is, organisations with less than or equal to 250 employees and with a turnover less than or equal to 50 million or balance sheet less than or equal to 43 million Euros.

2 Large commercial enterprises with more than 500 employees.

3 Public sector organisations such as those described earlier in this chapter, for example: health, education, highways, policing, social services.

Within this wide variety of sizes, the way in which HR is managed varies in style and sophistication. In micro-enterprises, for example, HR is dealt with by the owner/manager(s), probably with consultant advice, when and if required. Inevitably, in some cases, professional standards, legal requirements and compliance with employment legislation may be questionable, yet the employee relationship can be positive. In larger organisations, on the other hand, there is a high likelihood of the use of systems and procedures that are based on sophisticated strategies and policies. Usually HR professionals are employed to manage the complex personnel-related policies.

Future growth and the role of small and medium-sized enterprises

SMEs are a dynamic force in any country's economy; they are tomorrow's large organisations. They tend to start up on the basis of a single idea, and those that succeed go on to diversify and grow further. While it is clear that they do not all succeed and grow, many do, which is when they introduce the professional element into their internal systems, such as marketing, management and HR.

The European Union pays particular attention to small and medium-sized enterprises because it perceives this type of organisation to be the future generator of wealth within the EU:

Special attention is given to the needs of small and medium-sized enterprises (SMEs). Supporting SMEs and promoting entrepreneurship is the key to economic recovery. Europe's 23 million SMEs represent 98% of businesses [99% as of July 2013 – Author's note], provide 67% of jobs and create 85% of all new jobs. A range of support instruments is deployed to help such companies deal with administrative and regulatory requirements and formalities, and to support their cross-border activities, access to finance and other business opportunities. (European Commission, 2013)

ACTIVITY 1.5

The European Union is very careful in its literature and legislation in its definition of the small and medium-sized enterprise (European Commission, 2005).

Why do you think the European Commission goes to such lengths to be so precise? Is it because of the perceived bureaucratic nature of the EU or is the reason defined by a realistic business need?

You will find help by accessing the following documents, webpages and videos:

- EUROPEAN COMMISSION (2005) *The new SME definition: user guide and model declaration*. Available at: **http://ec.europa.eu/enterprise/policies/sme/files/sme_definition/sme_user_guide_en.pdf**
- The discussion of the European SME week: EUROPEAN COMMISSION, ENTERPRISE AND INDUSTRY (2013a) *European SME Week*

[online]. Luxembourg: The Publications Office of the European Commission. [Accessed 18 July 2013]. Available at: **http://ec.europa.eu/enterprise/initiatives/sme-week/**
- Watch the video by Antonio Tanjani (Tanjani, 2013), EU Commissioner for Industry and Entrepreneurship, at: **http://ec.europa.eu/enterprise/initiatives/sme-week/**
- And generally you will find useful information on the European Commission's Enterprise and Industry webpage dedicated to SMEs at: **http://ec.europa.eu/enterprise/policies/sme/market-access/internationalisation/#h2–6**
- European Union Press Release (2011), available at: **http://europa.eu/rapid/press-release_IP-11–1513_en.htm?locale=en**

1.2.7 THE PURPOSES OF ORGANISATIONS

The main purposes of all organisations are to provide a service or financial return for those that they serve and to survive and develop. To survive, the organisation must continue to provide the kinds of goods and services demanded by its customers and clients, bearing in mind of course, that to do so will probably demand change. Organisations also stimulate demand by creating and marketing new products and by modifying existing ones. The mobile telephone is an example of continuous modification.

1.2.8 CORPORATE STRATEGY

Everyone wants the organisation to succeed and achieve its purposes of survival and development, and it is the responsibility of those at the very top – the board of directors – to ensure that this happens. Someone has to be at the helm making decisions about the direction that the organisation should take; such decision-making is complex and sometimes involves considerable risk. The people at the helm, making the decisions that shape the future direction of the organisation, are engaged in *strategy*. We discuss strategy in greater depth later in this chapter. Suffice to point out at this stage that strategy exists at corporate and operational/functional levels.

KEY CONCEPT: CORPORATE STRATEGY

Corporate strategy: 'the agreed plan, which would include identified resources, by which the organisation attempts to meet its objectives.' It is the way in which the organisation plans its long-term future.

1.2.9 OBJECTIVES AND POLICIES

For the organisation to reach its strategic goals, *objectives* are set, which are targets that need to be achieved by pre-specified dates. The achievement of objectives is a critically important factor in which appropriate timing is vital. The work that leads to the achievement of objectives has to be carried out within the limits of the organisation's *policies*. Policies are statements of intent about how the organisation proposes to conduct its business and achieve its strategic objectives. The organisation's specialists draft procedures that describe how policy decisions are to be carried out.

 ACTIVITY 1.6

Find a copy of your organisation's policy on matters of health and safety at work. You should also find that there are procedures that describe how the policy is to be implemented.

When the organisation knows where it is going (it has *objectives*), what it has to do to get there (it has a *strategy*) and how it goes about controlling how to make the strategy work (it has *policies and procedures*), attention may be turned to *resources*. The organisation needs resources in the form of money, materials, machinery and, of course, the human resource.

1.2.10 SURVIVAL AND DEVELOPMENT

As we have seen, the main purposes of any organisation are to survive and develop (and to give returns to its shareholders in the case of a company), and to do this it has to continue to supply the types of goods and services demanded by its customers and clients. It is vital for a business to keep a keen eye on the activities of its competitors, changing market demands and the nature of internal and external pressures. The senior managers and specialists, therefore, carry out an annual review of the organisation's performance, and at the review, questions are asked about the internal and external factors and about any situation which might affect the company. The process is analogous to that of a good ship's captain: commanding her sailors to check that the ship is functioning correctly. In this case the first check for threats to the vessel's safety would be external – to turn on the radar and to scan the horizon. Distant ships would pose no immediate threat but vessels in close proximity might cause the captain to change course. Once the captain had an understanding of the external situation, her attention would be turned to check the internal integrity of the vessel by inspecting all compartments to make sure the vessel is watertight and the propulsion and electrical generating equipment is optimally functioning.

In today's fiercely competitive markets and rapidly developing innovation, such monitoring is a continuous, day-to-day process, since the rate of change in today's businesses is greater than ever before. Annual reviews are still held, especially in public limited companies (PLCs), but what is discussed there now is the cumulative product of continuous monitoring. The organisation's current situation is discussed and strategic decisions are made about the future. In short, the process appraises the organisation's past performance and makes plans for the future.

When the Corporate Strategy Section of J.K. Jones Ltd was conducting its annual review of the company's performance, it came to light that while the objectives it had set in the last period had been achieved in principle, there was room for improvement in certain areas. Productivity, for example, had experienced difficulty in keeping pace with sales, so the meeting decided to have the problem investigated with a view to improving productivity for the forthcoming year. The investigative report, which took into account how their competitors had changed their business, showed that investment in new technology would facilitate increased productivity and thereby solve the problem.

1.2.11 STRATEGIC PLANNING TECHNIQUES

Two main techniques have been developed to provide a structure to the strategic planning process, and it is vital for the aspiring HR practitioner to understand and be able to use these techniques.

The first was developed by Ansoff (1987). It focuses on an organisation's *strengths*, *weaknesses*, *opportunities* and *threats* and is usually referred to by the acronym SWOT. The second technique focuses on the internal and external pressures that impinge upon an organisation and these include such factors as political, economic, social, technological, legal-related and environmental pressures. The acronym PESTLE is used to refer to this technique; this has been modified and extended and is sometimes called a STEEPLE analysis (see below).

SWOT analysis

Of the two techniques, this is the most well known. What follows is an analysis of the process that demonstrates the extent of the detail that goes into its application.

Strengths are the valuable and successful aspects of the organisation, such as having ample resources, highly skilled people and appropriate technology for achieving the objectives. Being good at product design, quality assurance and customer care are also examples of strengths, since they help to sustain and improve the organisation's position in the market. The organisation may also be doing well in some particular functions of the business, for example the engineering or finance function; it is a good idea to analyse this to see if lessons may be learned for other functions.

Weaknesses are the organisation's negative features, such as financial or skill deficiencies, out-of-date work systems or poor employee relations. The identification of weaknesses is essential since areas for improvement have to be addressed urgently.

Opportunities are events or openings that may arise from the market or other areas of the business environment. Perhaps the need for a new or modified product is identified, or it may be that the organisation's unique skills can be applied to a new venture or diversification.

Threats can arise from the business environment. For example, an aspiring competitor may be about to invade the market and endanger the business. Competitors are also a threat when they modify standard products to achieve a market advantage. Threats are usually thought to be external, but of course, threats may also arise from poor internal relations; it could be that employees are dissatisfied with the terms and conditions of employment and are threatening to interrupt business progress by taking industrial action.

ACTIVITY 1.7

Examine your own organisation and assess how it would stand up to a SWOT analysis. Make a list of what you regard as:

(i) its strengths and (ii) its weaknesses and think about how they might be capitalised upon and improved respectively.

STEEPLE analysis (PESTLE+E)

Organisations have to keep abreast of, and respond to, the internal and external pressures that impinge upon them.

Social trends occur when market demands change according to changes in cultures, values, fashion, and even mere whim. The rate at which social preferences change can limit or extend product lifecycles and, internally, the need to keep pace will create the need for more frequent changes to be made. For example, the concern for climate change has caused people to think about ecology and ecological issues, which has caused large and small organisations alike to consider how they should respond to reduce their 'carbon footprint' and so become more environmentally friendly.

Technological innovation occurs on two broad fronts. The first is in terms of process innovation, which includes modifying or replacing machinery and the production and administrative systems, because new and better systems have been developed, giving greater productivity, cost-efficiency and effectiveness. The second is in terms of product innovation, in which new products and services are developed and/or modifications to existing ones made. Organisations tend to develop their own product innovation. So far as process innovation is concerned, organisations are largely 'users' of technology that has been developed by manufacturers of capital equipment and computer software.

Economic changes – the influence of regional, national and international economic conditions plays a large part in the fortunes of organisations. Sometimes the economy is buoyant and in a state of boom and plenty, unemployment is low, industrial and high-street spending is high and property values soar. At other times the economy dips and the 'highs' that were mentioned previously go into reverse. These are exactly the 'bust' conditions of an economic recession as caused by the banking crisis that occurred from 2008 and into 2009 in the UK. Organisations have to adjust to the alternate peaking and dipping of the economy and, internally, they must prepare themselves accordingly; sometimes though it is difficult to prepare, especially if the downturn has been caused by an unforeseen crisis, as mentioned. In a global economy, competition is very fierce, and organisations take steps to ensure that they remain competitive. HR specialists should also keep an eye on the changing economy, since in a good economy when the organisation is expanding, there are usually staff shortages, especially of those with rare technical skills, but when it is bad and the organisation has to contract, redundancies may have to be made.

Environmental factors – people are now extremely concerned about the effect that industrial activity is having on the environment, and pressure groups monitor and frequently demonstrate against particular business and scientific activities. Pressure groups such as Greenpeace monitor oil spills, deforestation and a host of other effects upon nature. Animal rights activists apply considerable pressure on organisations that carry out biological and cosmetic tests on living creatures, and sometimes even make physically violent attacks on the premises of such organisations and on the people who work within them.

Political interventions are pressures that appear in the form of new legislation, particularly on business practice in areas such as: employment, health and safety, taxation, etc. In a global market, however, pressures may also relate to overseas trading, for example in the form of European policies on agriculture and regulations relating to commercial fishing. New employment legislation carries implications for the organisation, and these are discussed in Chapter 16, 'Understanding Employment Law'. In the wider overseas trading context, internationally agreed sanctions may curtail, or even outlaw, trading with particular countries that, for example, may be involved in terrorism or human rights abuses. Clearly there is some overlap with the next component – Legal.

Legal-related pressures derive from competition law, government and EU policy, and, in a broader sense, safety issues such as the law on corporate manslaughter. Employment legislation is continually being added to, which makes the life of the HR professional that much more complex, yet interesting. Over the past several years much legislation has been associated with welfare at work, for example:

- The Working Time Directive and the Children and Families Act (2014) – the latter provides, from April 2015, that mothers, fathers and adopters can opt to share parental leave around their child's birth or placement. The Act also extends the right to request flexible working to all employees from 30 June 2014. (**www.gov.uk/government/news/landmark-children-and-families-act-2014-gains-royal-assent**)
- The Agency Workers Regulations 2010, which came into force on 1 October 2011 – the regulations give agency workers the same basic employment conditions after 12 weeks working for the company in the 'same role' as those that would have been applied if they were recruited directly by the hirer.

Ethical considerations cannot be ignored in business. There is a growing expectation from the various stakeholders, employees, shareholders, customers and regulators that an organisation conducts its business against a set of minimum standards, the notion of having a corporate social responsibility (CSR).

Kew and Stredwick (2013, pp.815) give a detailed explanation of the origins and uses of the PESTLE/STEEPLE approach to analysing the internal and external opportunities and threats to an organisation.

1.2.12 USING SWOT AND PESTLE (STEEPLE) ANALYSES

The information that is derived from carrying out SWOT and PESTLE (STEEPLE) analyses, including the data that would have been accumulated as a result of continuous monitoring of internal processes, provides a basis for the decisions that are made about the organisation's future. Where problems have come to light, the strategists look for causes with a view to resolving the problems, and where strengths are identified, they examine the possibilities of improving on those strengths in the future. This results in organisations formulating new policies to respond to the influences of legislation and other pressures.

It has been noticed that some students confuse these two analytical techniques. Consider your own organisation in the light of both, and note the different answers that emerge from your analysis. While both are used to assist the strategic planning process, they should be kept apart conceptually because they serve different purposes. SWOT analysis is a reality check on the organisation's internal situations, its weaknesses, strengths and past performance, while a STEEPLE analysis focuses on the external pressures that impinge upon the organisation. Looking at your own organisation in this way will enable you to remember which is which.

1.3 ORGANISATIONAL STRUCTURES

Most of us are familiar with the conventional shape of an organisation's structure. It has a hierarchical design with descending levels of authority. Viewed laterally (horizontally), we can see how the various departments and specialisms are separated, while vertically, we can see the layers that indicate levels of authority and responsibility.

KEY CONCEPT: CORPORATE STRUCTURE

Commonly referred to as the 'organisational chart', the corporate structure is a hierarchical design (like a family tree), which may be 'tall', meaning that there are many layers of authority and responsibility, or 'flat', meaning that there are fewer layers. Tall structures are generally bureaucratically managed, while with flatter structures managers and employees usually work together in a 'colleague' type of relationship, in which communication is more direct.

The structure shows the relationships that exist between the employees at *vertical* and *horizontal* levels, which are referred to as *vertical* and *horizontal integration*. The structure also outlines what we call *vertical* and *horizontal differentiation*. Vertical differentiation can be seen in the different roles of people within a department or function, such as in the role of the HR director, who has reporting to them the talent development and resourcing managers, who have, in turn, administrative staff reporting to them. The structure not only shows the chain of command but also, in a similar way, the vertical hierarchy of how roles are differentiated. On the other hand, horizontal differentiation can be seen in the way that functional managers take responsibility for separate departments, such as the roles of the marketing, finance, production and engineering directors and so on. (You will find that some writers use the word *lateral* instead of *horizontal*.)

CASE EXAMPLE 1.6

1. SOMETHING AFOOT

Jane Firmstone is a regional sales manager for 'Something Afoot', a company providing tough footwear for agricultural workers, climbers, and so on. Jane has divided the region into three districts and John Glass, Jim Ford and Masha Veretov are her district representatives. Before leaving for home, John telephoned Jane to say that he would be calling in to the regional sales office on his way home to let her have a detailed breakdown of his sales figures for last month. This pleased Jane because she is about to compile the regional sales report for that month and she is anxious that her figures stand up well against those of other regions with which her figures will be compared. The sales figures and current profit and loss accounts are provided by the senior accountant, Jatinder Sandhu, who reports directly to Jane. In terms of the organisation's structure, Jatinder is on a similar level as the three district sales representatives.

Just before finishing her call with John, Jane wished John luck with Grays, an awkward client that she knew he was seeing that day: 'And don't go giving them discounts above the company norm – you know it annoys them at head office.' John is worried about his visit to Grays. It is his district's largest shoe store and at one time was Something Afoot's biggest retail outlet. Over the past year, however, Grays has stocked fewer and fewer of Something Afoot's products and replaced them with imports from Poland. John believes that the problem lies in his company's introduction of a standard discount policy a year ago. Previously, the sales staff had been free to determine the discounts they offered, and major clients were able to obtain larger discounts than are now possible under the company's new standard discounts policy.

John cheered up as he thought of lunch. He had arranged to eat with Masha Veretov. She had promised to bring samples of some of the company's latest designs that John thought would be of particular interest to Grays, whose customers are particularly fashion-conscious. John reflected that working with the sales team was not so bad. They really are a team and their monthly meetings are one of the best parts of the job.

2. TAKING ACCOUNT

Taking Account is a family-run accountancy firm. Jim Jones is the managing director and owner. His intention, with his board's approval, is to maintain the business roughly at the same size. The structure of the business is defined by the nature of its work, which is accountancy services, both corporate and tax, to small and medium-sized enterprises. The business has a turnover (which is the amount of business transacted during a one-year period) of £3 million. The number of staff is kept small in order to maximise profitability. Much use is made of information technology and contracting out of non-core services.

Reporting to Jim is Latif Amir, who is the chief accountant responsible for 'corporate accounts', which is managed by Jane Armitage, Jim's sister. Latif also has reporting to him the 'tax accounts' section, managed by Sukhwinder Singh. Jane has one part-qualified accountant working for her and is also responsible for the development of a trainee accountant who is studying part-time for a CIMA (Chartered Institute of Management Accountants) Certificate in Business Accounting. Sukhwinder has two part-qualified accountants working for him, one to assist in the tax accountancy part of the role and the other to be responsible for accounts payable and invoice chasing.

Supporting the core accountancy services and also reporting to Jim is Peter Etai, internal business manager, who has a varied portfolio of responsibilities. Each manager in the business is responsible for managing their own staff, approving leave, absences, staff development, merit increases, etc. Peter is responsible for corporate HR activities such as policy development on recruitment, selection and development, health and safety compliance, remuneration, absence management, etc. Also in Peter's area of responsibility is managing the monthly salary payment activity. To support him in these activities he has two full-time administrators who share the roles but have complementary expertise, one being a remuneration specialist and the other specialising in recruitment and selection. Unusually, Peter is also responsible for managing the company's information technology systems. To help in this specialist technical area he has one member of staff who he employs on an annualised, part-time contract, which equates to 25% of a full-time contract. Peter, in respect of this role, relies heavily on Zhanara Ibrasheva, both for her practical problem-solving abilities and guidance when deciding upon IT system development.

Peter is particularly struggling to keep on top of his responsibilities because he finds that anything that is not clearly defined as either tax or corporate accounting tends, metaphorically, 'to fall on his shoulders'.

 ACTIVITY 1.8

1   Read the above case examples and list all of the examples you can find of:

- horizontal differentiation
- vertical differentiation
- horizontal integration
- vertical integration.

2   How do the two organisations differ in their approach to differentiation?

3   Using the above two cases, discuss the advantages and disadvantages of the two approaches to differentiation/integration.

4   Explore the options which Jim could adopt to help Peter in his role. Discuss the advantages and disadvantages of each of the possibilities which have been identified.

1.3.1 DESIGNING THE STRUCTURE

Pugh et al (1968, pp.889) produced some ground-breaking work on organisations. Their research:

> …yielded four empirically established underlying dimensions of organization structure: structuring of activities, encompassing Standardization, Formalization, Specialization, and Vertical Span; concentration of authority, encompassing Organizational Autonomy, Centralization, Percentage of Workflow Superordinates, and Standardization of Procedures for Selection and Advancement; line control of workflow, encompassing Subordinate Ratio, Formalization of Role Performance Recording, Percentage of Workflow Superordinates, and Standardization of Procedures for Selection and Advancement; and relative size of supportive component, encompassing Percentage of Clerks, Vertical Span, and Percentage of Non-Workflow Personnel.

Definitions as defined in Pugh et al's work include:

- superordinates – line, chain of command
- workflow – production.

Pugh et al (1968) give us a means of exploring and comparing one organisation with another, especially when an organisation has been in existence for some time and it is perceived that change is necessary. It allows benchmarking to take place by offering a mechanism with which to analyse the organisation and thus compare one organisation with another. Although Pugh et al's (ibid) paper has certain complexities, their paper does offer a number of sub-factors under the above four headings of structuring of activities, concentration of authority, line control of workflow and size of supportive component, which can be used to define an organisation and thus offer a framework for discussion and thus fertile ground for suggestions for organisational improvement and thus change.

Designing a structure is not a simple task. Before embarking upon such a project, the needs of the organisation have to be identified. Child (1988) says that most of the information one needs can be found in the answers to five key questions:

1 Should jobs be broken down into narrow areas of work and responsibility so as to secure the benefits of specialisation, or should the degree of specialisation be kept to a minimum to simplify communication and to offer members of the organisation greater scope and responsibility in their work?

2 Should the overall structure of an organisation be 'tall' rather than 'flat' in terms of its levels and spans of control? What are the implications for communication, motivation and overhead costs of moving towards one of these alternatives rather than the other?

3 Should jobs and departments be grouped together in a 'functional' way according to the specialist expertise and interests that they share? Or should they be grouped according to the different services and products that are being offered, or the different geographical areas being served, or according to yet another criterion?

4 Is it appropriate to aim for an intensive form of integration between the different segments of the organisation, or not? What kind of integrative mechanisms are there to choose from?

5 What approach should management take towards maintaining adequate control over work done? Should it centralise or delegate decisions? Should a policy of extensive formalisation be adopted in which standing orders and written records are used for control purposes? Should work be subject to close supervision?

If these questions are examined, we see that Child presents us with alternatives, implying that each organisation has its own specific structural needs. The questions have very strong human resource implications in terms of 'greater scope and responsibility' (question 1), 'communication and motivation' (question 2) and 'sharing specialist expertise and interests' (question 3). According to the principles of HRM, these advantages are best achieved by introducing a flattened rather than a tall structure, so that managers and employees can work closely together, and the integrity of formal, vertical communication is improved, since information passes through fewer hierarchical levels.

Organisational structures are designed to reflect the roles and relationships of the various positions and employees. The structure should show the logic underlying the division of the organisation's expertise and how functions are placed to work in a co-ordinated way.

Brooks (2009, p.191) writes of the traditional view of organisational structure: 'It describes the way an organisation is configured into work groups and the reporting and authority relationships that connect individuals and groups together.'

Restructuring may be seen as a reflection of the need to make internal changes to continue to complement external changes. In the early twentieth century, academics and practising managers produced theories that have come to be known as classical approaches to management, which were succeeded by the human relations approach, management by objectives, system and contingency theories and, more recently, human resource management (refer to Chapter 3 for further discussion and explanation).

While some of these ideas remain relevant for particular organisations, the adoption of the principles and techniques of human resource management (HRM) has significant implications for structures.

1.3.2 SPAN OF CONTROL

This term relates to the number of employees that fall directly under the control of one manager. Given that the organisation has a particular number of employees, the number of layers in the overall structure will be determined by the sizes of the spans of control within it. Organisations with tall spans of control will have many layers, as in Figure 1.1, and those with flattened ones will have fewer layers (Figure 1.2). Structures are referred to as 'tall', hierarchical {meaning – an organisation which has levels of control/responsibility} structures, or 'flat', that is, those with fewer layers in the structure. The advent of HRM in the 1980s brought with it a tendency for organisations to flatten their structures (see Figure 1.2).

Figure 1.1 A conventional organisational structure (tall structure showing 51 jobs on 5 levels)

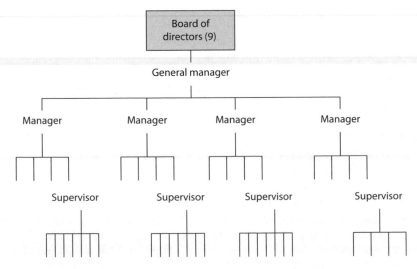

One of the effects of the trend towards flattened structures was to reduce the number of managers and increase the number of employees reporting to each manager. This changed employees' working situations in that in addition to having to adapt to changes in the work itself, they found themselves reporting to different managers and working with different colleagues. Clearly by reducing the number of layers of management within an organisation this has an impact upon how that organisation is managed, how employees work in terms of the range of tasks they are expected to do and how decisions are made.

Figure 1.2 Span of control influencing structure (flat structure showing 55 jobs on 4 levels)

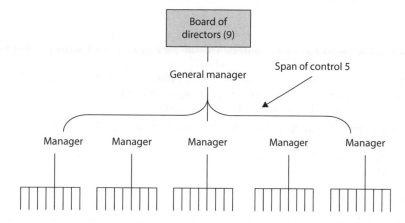

1.3.3 DIFFERENT ORGANSATION STRUCTURES

ACTIVITY 1.9

Using your organisation or one with which you are familiar, consider the impact of flattening the organisation's structure by reducing the levels of hierarchy. Discuss how:

- the way the nature of work is organised may [have to] change within the organisation
- responsibility for decision-making may change
- communication between employees performing different tasks may change
- it would impact upon the overall efficiency of the business

- it would impact upon the effectiveness of the business.

Hierarchical organisations have been much maligned {meaning – spoken ill of}, but they have their advantages. In what ways would you consider that organisations with a formal and hierarchical organisation structure are advantageous to the:

- operation of the business?
- employees within that business?

1.3.4 MATRIX ORGANISATIONS

This form of structure may be introduced where there is a need for teams to work on projects, such as those in the construction industry, civil engineering and other types of commissioning firms. Matrix structures may also be found in an enterprise in which there is a need to set up a temporary unit to carry out a specific project. Managers and specialists are seconded from different parts of the organisation for the duration of the project. On completion, the team may be disbanded and reintegrated into the main structure, or may move on to another new project. A large organisation may have several projects running concurrently. A civil engineering concern, for example, may, *inter alia {meaning – among other things}*, be carrying out such projects as building a bridge in the Midlands, a tunnel in Scotland, a high-rise building in Belfast and a road in East Anglia.

Sy and Kearney (2005, p.40) identify three types of matrix organisation:

1   Functional – employees remain members of a functional department. Processes and procedures are instituted to ensure cross-functional collaboration; project managers are limited to co-ordinating efforts of the functional groups, functional managers are responsible for design and completion of the technical requirements.

2   Balanced – classic model by which the matrix is known. Employees are officially members of two parts of the business, for example a project team and a functional team, at the same time. Strives for equalised power and authority between organising dimensions and pursuit of business objectives; project managers are responsible for defining what needs to be accomplished and when; functional managers define personal staffing and how tasks will be accomplished.

3   Project – employees move between functional departments and projects and respectively maintain membership with those units during the same period; permanent project management overlay; project managers have primary control over resources and project direction; functional managers serve in a support role and retain control over much of the team responsible for carrying out plans and controls established by project managers.

In reality there are adaptations of the above three models, for example, a further refinement of the third model offered by Sy and Kearney would be where the project or business area (unit) has full control over its work: planning, resources, etc. The functional departments would act in a 'staff' capacity offering technical guidance and help when called upon.

A matrix design is typified by a grid that depicts a two-dimensional track of authority and responsibility. Authority and responsibility in the functional departments track downwards, while from the project manager, authority and responsibility track laterally across the main structure. In this way, project managers may look across the organisation to access its resources, a concept that produces economic as well as practical advantages (see Figure 1.3).

In the example in Figure 1.3, the company is split into three business units based on a geographical split of responsibilities. Each business unit can call on the services of HR, finance, technical and marketing as they require. The advantage for the business unit is that they can control their costs and create a sense of competition because it is clear, in the matrix organisation, that HR, finance, technical and marketing are service functions. One could imagine a scenario in which, if it was considered that the finance function was deemed not to be providing an efficient service to Business Unit A, that business unit could go outside the larger organisation and 'buy in' financial services.

The implications of choosing a matrix organisation, the advantages and disadvantages

Managing in a matrix organisation is a complex activity because the asset or project manager has to manage shared resources, human resources, budget and perhaps other capital items. Matrix structures have drawn criticism from employees. They say they become frustrated as a result of working for two bosses: first, the functional heads to whom they report, and second, the project managers who make demands on their services. Such frustrations usually arise from conflicting time constraints and priorities.

Figure 1.3 How a matrix organisation works

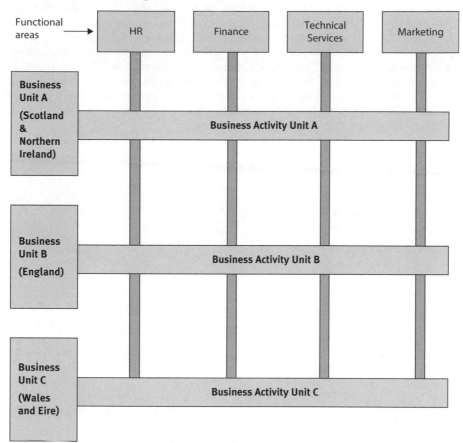

ACTIVITY 1.10

Imagine that you are either a manager responsible for a project activity or an employee in an organisation which uses a matrix structure. What do you consider would be the advantages, disadvantages and frustrations of working in such an organisation?

For help and guidance you may wish to:

- read Sy and Kearney (2005, p.40)

- visit 'YouTube' and view 'Project Organizational Structures Simplified' at: **www.youtube.com/watch?v=iKEpyGhTRmk**
- read Greenberg (2013, p.414)
- read Mullins (2013, p.527)
- read Robbins, Judge and Campbell (2010, pp.437–8).

1.3.5 THE FLEXIBLE ORGANISATION

The need for senior managers to focus on survival and development while remaining competitive in a fierce global market has caused them to review their attitudes towards employment, and *flexible working* (not to be confused with 'flexi-time') is one of the ideas that has emerged. Flexible working was first introduced in the early 1970s, when it was referred to as the *core staff theory*, but did not become widespread until the 1980s and popularised through the work of Atkinson (1984). Within this concept, the notion that the organisation needs to access particular skills 'in-house' no longer applies; neither does it apply that the organisation has to offer a conventional full-time contract of employment to all. Arguably the nature of the contract offered to the person should be determined by the rarity and availability of their skills and the amount of time for which those skills are needed. For these reasons, the terms and conditions of employment would vary from one category of employee to another. Organisations would need to distinguish between *core* and *peripheral* workers (see Figure 1.4).

Figure 1.4 Flexibility in organisations

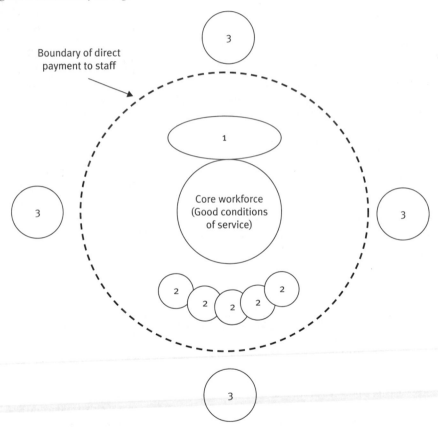

Adapted from Atkinson, 1984.

1.3.6 CORE AND PERIPHERAL WORKERS

Referring to Figure 1.4, the core workers are those who are regarded as critically important to the organisation and who are, therefore, encouraged to stay by virtue of attractive prospects through career development, good rewards and terms and conditions of service. Core staff are recognised as highly skilled and motivated technical, scientific or professional people without whom the organisation cannot optimise performance. They also tend to have a range of skills (functional flexibility) and significant discretion as to how they go about their work. Positive retention planning, therefore, has become an integral part of HR strategy. Core workers would be considered to provide the organisation's talent pool.

Peripheral workers, on the other hand, are not treated so generously and have little scope for discretion as to how they can do their work. In some cases they would not be discouraged in seeking employment elsewhere; they are more expendable. In a similar manner, if extra staff are required in this group, they can be readily recruited. Peripheral groups 1 and 2 sit within the confines of the organisation and members of these groups would be paid directly from the organisation's payroll. Specifically, peripheral group 1, in Figure 1.4, would be those types of worker who would be doing repetitive jobs such as accounts payable or production work. In the context of Atkinson's model, this group would be described as 'numerical flexibility'. Their contracts of work, in respect to working hours and types of hourly contract, can be varied.

The second peripheral group would not be a homogeneous group, per se, but the grouping is associated with how work is managed. For example, this group could be job-sharers or part-time workers; it could even include delayed recruitment or short-term contracts to cover absences or peaks in workload, or work that is of a repetitive nature. This secondary group could also include apprentices, some of whom could, at some time later depending upon individual competence, transfer to the core group of employees and so be part of the 'talent pipeline'.

Finally the flexible firm includes those who are not directly employed by the organisation, the third or tertiary peripheral group – number 3 in Figure 1.4. This group would include the self-employed, contractors, temporary workers and of course outsourced activities.

The idea of having workers who are in receipt of different terms and conditions of service can, of course, create issues between those who have the better conditions of service and those who have not. Interestingly, the Government introduced a bill to harmonise the pay and some conditions of agency workers, called the Agency Workers Regulations 2010, which came into force 1 October 2011. Predominantly, though, agency workers would be working alongside those workers defined as being in periphery groups 1 and 2.

The organisation's attitude towards different categories of worker is reflected in the *reward management* structure. The ideas behind the flexible firm have grown in popularity for several reasons:

- operation of new technology that demands higher skills
- the need for greater economic efficiency
- the need to improve upon and sustain the quality of the organisation's product
- the need for a more flexible and speedy response to external demands
- the need for a greater degree of involvement and, thereby, satisfaction on the part of valued employees.

CASE EXAMPLE 1.7

1. PROCUREMENT PROBLEMS AT THE MINISTRY OF DEFENCE

Becoming more flexible as an organisation can mean different things to different organisations. It could be the adoption of new working practices, for example part-time working, zero-hours contracts, annualised contracts, temporary contracts, the use of agency workers, etc. It could be the introduction of flexible working for its employees. It could also mean a large-scale restructuring of how work is carried out, for example by outsourcing, offshoring or perhaps the contracting-out of an activity. There is no one common approach that would meet the needs of the changing customer demands and how work should be structured to satisfy these demands. It is necessary to review proposals for change against the advantages, disadvantages and risks of carrying these proposals through to fruition.

Consider the following article by Plimmer, Fifield and Blitz, which was printed in the *Financial Times* on 7 May 2013, entitled, 'MoD outsourcing plan stokes US anxiety: Equipment':

> The British Government, under pressure to improve its procurement of military equipment for the three services, Army, Royal Navy and Air Force. The in-house procurement process which the Government operates has been shown, time and again to be slow and also costly to deliver newly specified equipment to front line forces. So in a bid to bring about radical change in the process the UK Government has proposed to contract out key parts of the procurement process to a private sector organisation.

Plimmer et al (2013) write, 'Pentagon worried privatising £14bn budget would endanger security'. The US has raised concerns over the UK's plan to outsource the procurement of military equipment to the private sector. Under pressure to make cost savings, the Ministry of Defence is pressing ahead with proposals to recruit a private company to manage its £14 billion annual procurement budget. If successful, it would be the first time any government with a sizeable military operation has outsourced the purchasing of equipment such as tanks, aircraft and communication technology.

2. THE RAF GROUNDED

The UK Government, as one of its many jobs, is charged with ensuring the security of its people. This term covers many facets of everyday life. We have an effective police force, fire and rescue service, military, etc., as well as the rescue at sea and on land of people who get into difficulties. The RAF and the Royal Navy provide a helicopter rescue and emergency evacuation service for those of us who may get into trouble. The, now well-advanced, plans are to contract out this service to a private contractor.

Predominantly the UK and the USA oil and gas offshore industries have spawned a range of competent and specialist helicopter contract organisations which are used to working in the unpredictable seas around the coasts of the UK and USA. The UK Government has a choice: if it wishes to replace the RAF in its air sea rescue, it does not have to artificially create a private sector organisation to take on the role. Part of the decision to make this change is probably driven by the ideologies of the Conservative and Liberal Democrat Coalition Government, in terms of the role of government and how much it should impinge on the operation of society. Also, pragmatically, if one considers that the primary sea rescue organisation is the charitable Royal National Lifeboat Institute, it becomes logical to consider that the complementary air sea rescue service could also be carried out by a private or not-for profit-organisation; tradition sometimes stands in the way of progress.

Morris and Carrell (2013), writing on *theguardian.com*, capture many of the issues raised by the proposal to contract out air-sea rescue as discussed previously.

3. JLR (JAGUAR LAND ROVER) COME TO A HALT?

Bounds (*Financial Times*, 8 July 2013) writes:

> DHL employees working at Jaguar Land Rover's Halewood plant in the UK have voted in favour of industrial action, threatening output at the crucial factory that runs 24 hours a day to meet demand for its best-selling Evoque car.

Although JLR have outsourced their vehicle delivery logistics to DHL, they cannot ignore the key role the DHL drivers play in providing JLR factories with timely delivery of components so that JLR, in turn, can provide Its customers with timely delivery of their new vehicle.

You may wish to consider what type of relationship JLR needs to have with DHL

and its drivers. The DHI drivers are in a strong 'monopolistic' position *{meaning – exclusive controlling position}*. What type of 'levers' (mechanisms for influencing change) can JLR employ to influence the behaviour of the DHL workforce?

1.3.7 THE VIRTUAL ORGANISATION

A futuristic example of the flexible organisation is summarised by Robbins et al (2010, p.439), in which they describe the 'virtual organisation' as 'typically a small, core organisation that outsources major business functions. In structural terms, the virtual organisation is highly centralised, with little or no departmentalisation.' They describe the American 'motion picture' (film) industry as a prime example of this type of organisation. Many hundreds of specialists, ranging from electrical technicians to camera operatives to catering companies, all come together to create a film then disperse before being called together once again to make another film at a different location under a different production company.

 ACTIVITY 1.11

In this exercise really challenge yourself to think the unthinkable, If you were the managing director/chief executive of an organisation – whether a private company or public sector authority – consider how you might transform the service or manufacturing facility of all, or part, of the organisation so that you and a small team were able to offer the service or product through a virtual organisation.

Once you have some guidelines on how you would provide the service or product, reflect on the advantages and disadvantages of

offering the service or product in this way. In reflecting on the pros and cons of such a way of providing a service, you may wish to consider the advantages and disadvantages both in the long and short term.

Would it be possible, using a virtual organisation approach, to design and manufacture:

- a camera? – high technology
- plastic ties to secure the opening to a plastic bag? – low technology
- a shirt or blouse? – clothing
- a new innovation on the 'Post-it' idea?

1.4 SUMMARY

In this chapter we learned why organisations exist: to provide goods or services to a consumer. We also learned how to classify organisations, whether they are public or private sector and also how they are structured. Organisations can be classified as:

- mutual benefit
- business concerns
- service organisations
- commonweal organisations.

This classification was later modified by Maltby (2003):

- nationalised industries
- public PLCs
- public interest companies
- publicprivate partnerships, including privately funded institution (PFI) contracts
- regulated private companies
- private companies.

As well as classifying organisations by the type of service they offer, we also saw that they can be classified as to whether they are mechanistic or organic, and also in terms of their size, ranging from micro to small, medium and large, rather like the sizes in clothes. Further, the changing nature of the role of government was discussed, whereby more and more services which, traditionally were accepted to be the prerogative of local and central government are, over time, being contracted out into the private sector.

Business can be very precarious and particularly has been seen to be so since the financial crises of 2008; many companies have failed. This chapter explored what mechanisms can be put in place if an organisation is no longer viable and cannot service (pay) its debts.

As well as being able to describe organisations, as above, consideration was also given to how, in a systematic way, it is possible to identify the internal weaknesses and strengths of an organisation using the SWOT analysis technique. It is also possible to identify, looking outwards from the organisation, the immediate issues that the business environment offers or threatens using a PESTLE (STEEPLE) analysis.

Work was discussed in the context of horizontal and vertical integration, and terminology such as 'span of control' was introduced to further extend our understanding of how business is discussed.

Finally, the chapter addressed how organisations can structure themselves, from a strategic perspective, in the form of the 'flexible firm', a concept that was first attributed to Atkinson in 1984.

REVIEW QUESTIONS

1 What are the main purposes of all organisations?

2 Name the four categories into which Blau and Scott classified organisations. Why is it useful to be able to categorise organisations using different typologies, that is, Blau and Scott, Maltby, Burns and Stalker?

3 Discuss the reasons why services which traditionally have been provided by government are progressively being provided by private sector organisations?

4 From where do those who manage public and private sector organisations derive their authority to make decisions and take actions?

5 What are the main differences between the two main techniques (SWOT and PESTLE [STEEPLE]) that senior managers use to assist the strategic planning process?

6 What HR implications arise from the five questions posed by Child (1988) when considering the design of an organisation's structure?

7 What do you understand by the following organisation forms:

- nationalised industries
- public PLCs
- public interest companies

- public/private partnerships, including privately funded institution (PFI) contracts
- regulated private companies
- private companies.

Where would a charity and a university be placed in the above list?

8 Discuss the advantages and disadvantages of a wholly family-owned private company either:

- remaining has a family company or
- converting to a public liability company with shareholders?

9 What happens when a company goes into 'administration'? What is the role of the 'administrators'? What options are open to them?

10 What do we mean by 'flexible working'? Who does flexible working benefit?

11 Has your organisation adopted any flexible working practices? Do you see any real advantages in what management have done? Do you think there are opportunities to introduce flexible working practices?

12 What do you understand by the term the 'flexible firm'?

13 In the context of the flexible firm, in terms of the peripheral groups, where would you position those working:

- annualised hours?
- zero-hours contracts?

14 What is outsourcing? Why would an organisation decide to outsource an activity? For example a college, which has traditionally employed its own security and caretaking staff, decides to outsource (contract out) this service to a security services provider such as G4S. What are the advantages and disadvantages of outsourcing?

15 Why would the first peripheral group in the flexible firm model be more likely to have poorer conditions of service than the 'core' group? Is this unfair? How does HR manage the tensions generated? You may find it useful to refer to the article by Rosemary Bennett in *The Times*, 8 July 2013, entitled 'Part-timers pay price in lower wages and missed promotions'.

EXPLORE FURTHER

BOOKS

KEW, J. and STREDWICK, J. (2013) *Business environment: managing in a strategic context*. 2nd ed. London: CIPD.

Although Kew and Stredwick's book is written for a postgraduate CIPD course, it is very accessible and opens up a broader understanding of the business context, including discussion of the role of government, the European Union and the impact of demographic change.

GREENBERG, J. (2013) *Managing behaviour in organizations*. 6th ed. Harlow: Pearson Education.

A clearly written text appropriately and thoroughly underpinned. It covers a wide range of topics from organisational behaviour to human resource management issues.

MULLINS, L.J., with CHRISTY, G. (2013) *Management and organisational behaviour.* 10th ed. Harlow: Pearson Education.

A good all-round text on organisational behaviour (OB) and management, Mullins is suitable for both undergraduate and postgraduate students who are studying organisations for the first time. In the context of this chapter on the organisation, the Mullins text offers further insight into organisational setting, the structures of organisations, the nature of management and organisation management.

WEB LINKS

SWOT analysis (giving an explanation of what SWOT covers):

The Institute of Directors offers a detailed plan of how to conduct a SWOT analysis in an organisation. Available at: **www.iod.com/guidance/briefings/al-doing-a-swot-analysis**

CIPD factsheet on SWOT analysis: **www.cipd.co.uk/hr-resources/factsheets/swot-analysis.aspx**

Also, using the CIPD's website to access 'Company Profiles', you will be able to get detailed SWOT analysis of 650 companies. To access this service you will need to be a CIPD member. Available at: **www.cipd.co.uk/onlineinfodocuments/companies/byatoz.htm**

Review the YouTube SWOT analysis conducted on the McDonald's organisation by Professor Samur Mathur of McGill University. Available at: **www.youtube.com/watch?v=X5YE06pkt4o**

PESTLE/STEEPLE analysis:

CIPD factsheet on PESTLE analysis: **www.cipd.co.uk/hr-resources/factsheets/pestle-analysis.aspx**

Review the PESTLE (STEEPLE) analysis conducted by Ford before launching the Ford Fiesta into the American market. Available at: **www.youtube.com/watch?v=SykGRZQABlc**

CHAPTER 2

Aspects of Organisational Culture

LEARNING OBJECTIVES

After studying this chapter you should:

- understand the concept of culture, its values and norms
- be able to demonstrate an understanding of how history, corporate climate, managerial style and other factors contribute to the make-up of culture
- understand the importance of culture as a determinant of workplace behaviour
- understand how the 'Cultural Web' model of Johnson, Scholes and Whittington can be used to define organisation culture
- understand and be able to take account of your organisation's culture in your role as an HR practitioner.

2.1 INTRODUCTION

The aim of this chapter is to provide an insight into societal culture and an understanding of organisational culture: what it is, how it develops and its importance as the organisation's most powerful determinant of behaviour. In order for you to develop a complete understanding of what is meant by organisational culture, it will be helpful to provide first an account of how culture is perceived in the societal context. Reading about culture in extra-organisational contexts should help you to understand behaviour that occurs in a diverse workforce.

2.2 WHAT IS CULTURE?

As far back as 1871, the anthropologist Edward Tylor defined culture as 'knowledge, belief, art, morals, law, custom and any other capabilities and habits acquired through membership of society'. In a narrower sense the term is used to describe the differences between one society and another. In this context, according to Giddens:

> . . .a culture is an all-pervasive system of beliefs and behaviours transmitted socially. Specifically, it consists of the sets of values and norms or rules held by a society, together with its material expressions. (Giddens 1989, p.30)

An alternative and similar definition is offered by House et al (1999, cited in Papalexandris and Panayotopoulo, 2004, p.495), '. . .as "shared motives, values, beliefs, identities and interpretations or meanings of significant events that result from common experiences of members of society which are transmitted across generations".'

Values are internalised by young people as they learn what is good and what is desirable. They define for us what is important and worth striving for. Values represent the basic conviction that in a personal or social context, a specific mode of conduct is preferable to any other. Cultural identity is important to individuals. Ethnic- and/or nationality-based origins provide a strong bond between individuals which remains for the duration of their lives.

 KEY CONCEPT: VALUES

A *value* is an ideal to which an individual subscribes. Values are learned during the socialisation process. Individuals adopt them from the values of the society to which they belong; values have an influence on behaviour.

Cultural values, as defined by Schwartz (2007, p.25):

> ...represent the implicitly or explicitly shared abstract ideas about what is good, right, and desirable in a society (Williams, 1970). These cultural values (e.g. freedom, prosperity, security) are the bases for the specific norms that tell people what is appropriate in various situations.

Values in many respects define how we conduct our lives as groups of people. Schwartz (ibid) further reiterates the importance in terms of the way values inform how societal groups develop their institutional systems:

> The ways that societal institutions (e.g. the family, education, economic, political, religious systems) function, their goals and their modes of operation, express cultural value priorities. For example, in societies where individual ambition and success are highly valued, the organisation of the economic and legal systems is likely to be competitive (e.g. capitalist markets and adversarial legal proceedings). In contrast, a cultural emphasis on group well-being is likely to be expressed in more cooperative economic and legal systems (e.g. socialism and mediation).

 KEY CONCEPT: NORMS

A *norm* is a tacit guideline that determines an individual's (or group's) behaviour in particular situations. For example, as a member of a group or team, or of a student group, you learn that there are particular behaviours that conform to the group's expectations, and behaviours that do not. If you breach the code of behaviour, the group will demonstrate its disapproval, usually by applying formal or informal sanctions.

If a norm is breached in a serious way, the sanctions will be more severe. The sanctions are designed to elicit conformity and are a significant feature of controlling overall behaviour and the maintenance of order in a society. Indeed, certain norms are incorporated into law and conformity is enforced through punishment.

2.2.1 THE POWER OF VALUES AND NORMS

The relationship between values and norms becomes clear when a breach of norms defies the group's values; the establishment of behavioural norms reflects its values. This concept extends beyond the group, into larger groups, and out into the whole of society itself: for example, the way people address each other, their table manners and how they conduct themselves in public. People dress according to what is expected of them on special occasions, such as a formal ball, a funeral, an evening at the theatre or visiting a friend in hospital. All such situations demand certain attire and particular ways of behaving.

So, examined through its systems of norms and values, 'The culture of a society is the way of life of its members; the collection of ideas and habits which they learn, share and transmit from generation to generation' (Linton, 1945). At birth, children are totally helpless and dependent on others to provide for their needs. To survive in the longer term, however, children must develop knowledge and skills, and must learn how those around them survive. In other words, children must learn the culture of the society into which they were born.

Culture therefore has to be learned, and for a society to operate effectively, its 'guidelines' must be shared by its members through their behaviour. Learning and sharing a culture is achieved largely without conscious control. It just happens as people develop and become socialised, and even though it directs their actions and thinking, and establishes their outlook on life, most members of a society take their culture for granted. People are hardly aware of their culture, even though their adoption of its values and conformity to its norms demonstrate a mutual understanding of what is and is not acceptable.

2.2.2 DEFINITIONS OF CULTURE

It is difficult to define overall culture since it is an elusive concept. Culture is a dichotomy in the sense that it constitutes, first, visible and tangible factors, and second, abstract and intangible characteristics. For example, it was noted earlier that Giddens summarises culture as consisting of the sets of *values* and *norms* or rules held by a society, together with its material expressions. The term 'material expressions' refers to features of the environment that were put in place by people; this includes such tangible items as bridges, buildings, roads, tools, machinery and equipment. Values and norms, however, are among the abstract and intangible psychological characteristics of individuals and groups.

Herskovits (1948) defined culture as 'the man-made part of the human environment'. Triandis (2002, p.3), citing his earlier work of 1972, further qualified this by pointing out that:

> A broad definition of culture is that it is the human-made part of the environment. It can be split into material and subjective culture. Material culture consists of such elements as dress, food, houses, highways, tools, and machines. Subjective culture is a society's 'characteristic way of perceiving its social environment' (Triandis, 1972, p. viii, 3). It consists of ideas about what has worked in the past and thus is worth transmitting to future generations. Language and economic, educational, political, legal, philosophical and religious systems are important elements of culture. Ideas about aesthetics, and how should people live with others are also important elements. Most important are unstated assumptions, standard operating procedures, and habits of sampling information from the environment.

Papalexandris and Panayotopoulo (2004, p.497) rely upon the work of House et al, defining culture as, '. . .shared motives, values, beliefs, identities and interpretations or meanings of significant events that result from common experiences of members of society which are transmitted across generations'.

Undoubtedly there is a strong relationship between physical and subjective cultures. Subjective perceptions of how things are, how they should be and how they should look do vary from one society to another. For example, the architecture of buildings and the design of particular artefacts are determined by what, within a culture, is regarded subjectively as generally acceptable and right. This is reflected by the obvious differences in the appearance of buildings in different parts of the world. Even cooking utensils are specifically designed to meet idiosyncratic culinary needs, since what people eat and how their food is prepared vary from one culture to another.

It is in these and many other ways that cultures vary from one society to another, and since culture defines what is acceptable and what is not, frequent misunderstandings occur.

KEY CONCEPT: PHYSICAL AND SUBJECTIVE CULTURE

It seems that the physical culture, which is created by people, may be separated from the subjective culture, which is apparent through the values and norms of societies. It is certainly true that academics who have produced *non*-organisational definitions of culture all include the physical culture.

2.2.3 AN EXAMPLE OF CULTURAL DIFFERENCES – PERSONAL SPACE

Personal space, as defined by Beaulieu (2006, p.794, citing Hall, 1959) is '…an invisible three-dimensional zone surrounding a person, which allows that person to regulate his interactions with the outside world.' Beaulieu says of personal space (ibid), 'Most of the time, a person becomes aware of his or her *personal space* by the feeling of irritation or malaise when another person invades the space.' Characteristically the preferred size of the personal space varies with culture. Discussing *personal space*, Beaulieu (ibid, p. 796) writes the following:

> According to Freedman (1975), 'Whites in the United States, Canada, and England stand far apart, Europeans stand somewhat more closer, and South Americans stand closer still' (p.72). Shuter (1977) observed that Italians interact closer to each other than do Germans or Americans. Scheflen and Ashcraft (1976) established that British, British Americans, and Black Americans stand about 36 in. (91.4 cm) apart in a fairly intimate conversation if they have the room to do so…

 SPACE INVADERS

CASE EXAMPLE 2.1

Two men, one from North America and one from South America, are chatting in a hall that is 40 feet long. They begin at one end of the hall and finish at the other end, the North American steadily retreating and the South American steadily advancing. Each is trying to establish the 'customary conversation distance' as defined by his culture. To the North American, his South American counterpart comes too close for comfort, whereas the South American feels uneasy conversing at the distance his partner demands. Sometimes it takes meetings such as this to reveal the pervasive nature of culturally determined behaviour. It is by understanding these types of cultural differences that people can eventually work with those from different societal cultures.

2.2.4 IDENTIFYING CULTURES

Misunderstanding may occur if cultures are treated as discrete entities. Just as there is diversity within indigenous populations, there is also *intra-cultural diversity* created by individual and small-group differences. Within a culture, groups (subcultures) look across at each other and do not always approve of what they see and hear.

2.2.5 ETHNOCENTRISM AND 'IN-GROUPS'

According to Price (1997, p.125), we look at people from other cultures, see that their ways are different and often dislike these ways. Triandis (1990, p.34) supports this view, saying that we use our own culture as the standard and judge other cultures by the extent to which they meet our standard. This is referred to as *ethnocentrism* and is similar to the *in-group* concept, that is, the people with whom we identify.

Studies of ethnocentrism show that everyone tends to:

- define their own culture as 'natural' and 'correct' and other cultures as 'unnatural' and 'incorrect'
- perceive in-group customs as universally valid – what is good for us is good for everybody
- think that in-group norms, rules and values are obviously correct
- consider it natural to help and co-operate with members of one's in-group
- act in ways which favour the in-group
- feel proud of the in-group
- feel hostility towards out-groups

(based on the work of Campbell et al, cited in Triandis, 1990, p.35).

Brewer (2001, p 18) writes, quoting Sumner (1906), that,

> ...ethnocentrism is the technical name for the view of things in which one's own group is the centre of everything, and all others are scaled and rated with reference to it. ... Each group nourishes its own pride and vanity, boasts itself superior, exalts its own divinities, and looks with contempt on outsiders.

The above conveys the power of the notion of the 'in-group' and 'out-group' concept but is, perhaps, over-simplistic because much of the strength of in-group feeling depends, according to Brewer, upon how much an individual is socialised into the in-group, a concept verbalised in what is termed 'social identity theory'. Perhaps one could reflect upon why many organisations spend so much time on inducting new employees into an organisation.

 ACTIVITY 2.1

Watch the 'TED' video by Saba F. Safdar, Professor of Psychology, Guelph, Ontario, Canada on culture and how it is constructed, especially the notion of collectivism and individualism through the lens of how we insult each other in different cultures, at: **www.youtube.com/watch?v=FaOJ71czAGQ**

PAUSE FOR THOUGHT

If you were born and raised in, say, the United Kingdom, but felt in need of a change and wanted to abandon your roots to live elsewhere in the world, in what kind of society would you choose to live: a small tribal island in the Pacific Ocean? A middle eastern country? Central Africa? Spain? Could you survive in another culture? Would you try to continue living like a UK citizen or would you try to adopt the culture into which you had moved? Do you think it would take courage to make such a move? Do you know anyone from an entirely different culture who has moved to the UK? What sort of problems do they face?

Consider the following situations:

- your feelings when you first started work or joined a club as a newcomer
- what can be done to help a newcomer to an organisation to accelerate the feeling of belonging to the society they have joined
- what role a mentor can play in the context of socialising a person into a new organisation.

You will find some useful guidance on the above in Chapter 8, 'Induction and Retention'.

2.3 WHERE DO WE FIND CULTURE?

When people speak and write about the 'English culture' or the 'Spanish culture', we somehow know what they mean. There is an assumption that they are referring to particular idiosyncratic {meaning – something very specific, a particular characteristic} features that may be found only in England, and others that may be found only in Spain, but these might be thought of as *national differences*, as well as cultural differences. All countries have their own particular characteristics, and members of indigenous populations share dominant common values and conform to the accepted norms of their society.

While culture is not nationality – because there can be a range of people who have different ethnic backgrounds within one nation – the two do interact. Within any country, there are groups whose members share additional values, or perceive one of the common values as more important than any of the others, as the following example shows. As Hofstede et al (2010, p.21) write:

> *Nations*, therefore should not be equated to societies. Societies are historically organically, developed forms of social organization. Strictly speaking, the concept of a common culture applies to societies, not to nations. Nevertheless, many nations do form historically developed wholes even if they consist of clearly different groups and even if they contain less integrated minorities.

CASE EXAMPLE 2.2

One can understand the point made by Hofstede et al (2010) by considering the events of March 2014 in the Ukraine. After the overthrow of President Viktor Yanukovych by pro-European protesters, Russia – recognising that in the medium to long term its strategic important Black Sea Fleet base of Sevastopol may be under threat – landed its forces in air bases within the Crimea to secure its national interests. Many, but not all, Crimean citizens see themselves as Russian because of their Russian ethnic ties. Primarily it was those citizens with the ethnic Russian backgrounds who wished to join the Russian Federation, thus breaking the Crimea region away from the Ukraine.

More on this issue can be found by reading 'We fought for mother Russia, but now Putin's invaders are enemies', Donetsk, A. L. *The Times*, 8 March 2014.

2.3.1 DEFINING SOCIETAL CULTURE

 ACTIVITY 2.2

How is societal culture defined? Is, for example, the culture of the English defined by their taste for fish and chips or roast beef and Yorkshire pudding? Are the Scots defined by the male's distinctive attire of kilt, sporran and the skean dhu tucked down the long sock?

Perhaps, though, defining societal culture by food and dress preference is too simplistic.

How would you define societal culture? You may (or may not) find some ideas by reading Mark Eaton's article (Home editor for the BBC) at: www.bbc.co.uk/news/uk-17218635. He writes:

> Britishness, it is often suggested, is ultimately about shared values of tolerance, respect and fair play, a belief in freedom and democracy. This has always struck me as pretty insulting to our friends and relations beyond these shores. Such principles matter enormously, of course, but to claim an international patent on virtue might be seen as a little smug.

> Others try to get a handle on Britishness through its association with institutional abbreviations: the NHS, the BBC, the WI or the RSPCA. This is a more profitable path because our brand of alphabet soup has a distinctly homemade recipe. The complex flavours of our health service, national broadcaster and voluntary sector come from a unique combination of local ingredients. (Eaton, 2012)

Hofstede conducted his first series of studies on the cultural values and identities of IBM employees worldwide in the 1960s and 1970s. As a result of his early work, Hofstede (1980) has developed a typography through which culture can be dissected and studied. He initially defined four values: power distance, individualism, masculinity, and uncertainty avoidance. Since his earlier works he has added and subsequently modified a further two cultural dimensions: pragmatism and indulgence.

He defines the six cultural measures in the following way:

Power distance: is defined as the extent to which the less powerful members of institutions and organisations within a country expect and accept that power is distributed unequally.

Individualism: in individualist societies people are supposed to look after themselves and their direct family only. In collectivist societies people belong to 'in-groups' that take care of them in exchange for loyalty.

Masculinity: a high score (masculine) on this dimension indicates that the society will be driven by competition, achievement and success, with success being defined by the winner/best in field – a value system that starts in school and continues throughout organisational behaviour.

Uncertainty avoidance: the extent to which the members of a culture feel threatened by ambiguous or unknown situations and have created beliefs and institutions that try to avoid these is reflected in the UAI score.

Pragmatism: in societies with a pragmatic orientation most people don't have a need to explain everything, as they believe that it is impossible to understand fully the complexity of life. The challenge is not to know the truth but to live a virtuous life.

Indulgence*: one challenge that confronts humanity, now and in the past, is the degree to which children are socialised. Without socialisation we do not become 'human'. This dimension is defined as the extent to which people try to control their desires and impulses, based on the way they were raised. Relatively weak control is called 'indulgence' and relatively strong control is called 'restraint'. Cultures can, therefore, be described as indulgent or restrained.

(The Hofstede Centre, available at: **http://geert-hofstede.com/united-kingdom**. html)

*Similar, but not identical, to a previous dimension called long-term orientation, which was developed originally in 1991 to reflect the significant influence of China and Confucianism.

(**http://www.worldvaluessurvey.org/wvs/articles/folder_published/article_base_54**)

Hofstede's (1991) concept of culture is *the programming of the mind* and in his view cultures are largely learned by the time a child has reached the age of ten. The following narrative further explores the meaning of the concepts introduced above.

The 'power distance' dimension considers the inequalities within society. For example, it can be expressed and understood from the perspective of those of us who are less privileged or do not hold significant positions in society in terms of how we would perceive those who are more privileged or hold significant/senior positions. Those societies which have a *low power distance* do not revere those in senior positions or who are members of the aristocracy but simply recognise the differences in business or societal position. On the other hand, those in a *high power distance society* would pay deference to those in more senior or privileged positions through birth right.

The 'individualism' dimension considers how societies develop independence as people grow and break links with family. The opposite dimension is *collectivism*, which is an indicator of how close family remains bonded.

Masculinity, opposite of *feminine*, is a measure of competitiveness and assertiveness, while the feminine side considers the importance of relationships.

In the 'uncertainty avoidance' dimension, Geert Hofstede tried to capture how society, not individuals *per se*, thinks about the future and to what extent those individuals, within the society as a whole, can cope with ambiguity and thus withstand levels of anxiety.

The 'pragmatism' dimension deals with how society tries to explain and reconcile events or whether – that is, those societies which take a more pragmatic stance – simply accept the 'norm' and thus what has happened.

The 'indulgence' dimension recognises the influence on childhood in terms of how societal groups restrain and contain emotion. It is a realisation of how the process of induction, in the case of the socialisation of the child, into cultural norms of society allows the outflow or containment of emotion.

 ACTIVITY 2.3

Using the Cultural Tools provided by the Hofstede Centre at *http://geert-hofstede.com/united-kingdom.html* compare the power distance levels and uncertainty avoidance levels for the following countries:

● Germany
● France
● USA

● China
● Japan.

Can you draw any conclusions from the bar chart scores which you have created? Are there similarities or differences between countries?

The narrative on the website will give you some guidance in the interpretation of the results.

Hofstede's approach is just one way of examining cultural differences. It simply gives us a way of explaining how different cultures work. By understanding the factors which cause people to be different, because of the way they were socialised in the world – 'programming' of the mind as Hofstede calls it – we can then better understand how to work together. For example, the European Union is a group of 28 countries that have bonded together founded on political and commercial ideologies; their interdependency now necessitates that countries work together.

There are alternative ways to consider cultural differences and similarities. The work of Inglehart and Welzel (2010) considers a two-dimensional map of world countries, plotting how they lie in terms of cultural proximity.

The dimensions identified in the work of Inglehart and Welzel are those which range from: traditional values *to* secular rational values on one axis; and survival values *to* self-expression values on the other.

Figure 2.1 The world value survey cultural map (2005–2008)

Based on: Inglehart and Welzel (2010, p.554)

Just as Japan and South Korea have been linked, Inglehart and Welzel call this grouping the Confucian group, in respect of the ideological thinking; other groups are linked, such as Russia, Romania and Ukraine as the 'Orthodox' group, in recognition of the predominant religious orthodoxy.

A complete map showing all the countries in the studies and the linkages between them can be accessed at: **www.worldvaluessurvey.org/wvs/articles/folder_published/article_base_54**

The following narrative, explaining the four cultural dimensions, is taken from the above website:

> The Traditional/Secular-rational values dimension reflects the contrast between societies in which religion is very important and those in which it is not. The second major dimension of cross-cultural variation is linked with the transition from industrial society to post-industrial societies—which brings a polarization between Survival and Self-expression values. The unprecedented wealth that has accumulated in advanced societies during the past generation means that an increasing share of the population has grown up taking survival for granted. (**www. worldvaluessurvey.org/wvs/articles/folder_published/article_base_54**)

ACTIVITY 2.4

Using the World Values Survey cultural map of the world, found at the above web address, can you explain:

1   Why Denmark and particularly Sweden should be high, in terms of both secular

rational values as well as self-expression values?

2   Why Pakistan should be high in traditional and low survival values?

2.3.2 DIFFERENCES WITHIN A CULTURE

Sometimes it is useful to regard culture as the personality of the group. In the case of individuals, it is their personality characteristics such as attitudes, values and beliefs that direct their behaviour, and it is not difficult to read this across and into group culture. The relationship between the group and a 'strong-minded' individual member can be quite complex. Sometimes such a member attains the leadership position, and therefore has an element of control over the group's behaviour, but if this does not happen, there might be costs to the individual in the form of reduced freedom of action. William Foote Whyte (1955, p.331) wrote that:

> The group is a jealous master. It encourages participation, indeed it demands it, but it demands one kind of participation – its own kind and the better integrated with it a member becomes the less free he is to express himself in other ways.

PAUSE FOR THOUGHT

The individual and the group

At this point it is important to note that people's group behaviour is often different from their individual behaviour. As we have seen, groups have values and norms to which their members adhere, but such conformity can be misleading. People place a high value on being accepted as group members, and

when the situation demands it, they may suspend their own held values and conform to the group norms in order to sustain their group membership. Conversely, the value in question might be so deeply felt that they might decide not to conform to the norm and to leave the group rather than surrender that particular value.

2.3.3 SOCIETAL CULTURE AND ORGANISATIONS

How does the study of *societal culture* impact upon organisations and the way organisations operate? Ekmekci et al (2013) offer some insight into understanding the link and impact of societal culture on organisations. Their paper (ibid, p.1) 'explores how societal culture influences organizational identity in a global organization'.

Drawing upon a variety of studies, including the works of Inglehart, Basenes and Marino (The World Values Survey), Triandis, the GLOBE studies, Hofstede, etc. (ibid, p.6), Ekmekci and the team of researchers offer some suggestions as to how some of the cultural dimensions defined in those studies quoted and others might impact on organisations and the way they wish to operate.

PAUSE FOR THOUGHT

Many organisations take the view that teamworking is imperative to improving effectiveness, efficiency and worker participation. This concept is supported by the CIPD, which defines the perceived benefits of teamworking in the following manner:

Organisations use teamworking for many reasons, including the desire to achieve the following objectives:

- improve productivity
- enhance quality of products or services
- improve customer focus
- speed the spread of ideas

- respond to opportunities and threats and to fast-changing environments
- increase employee motivation
- introduce multi-skilling and employee flexibility.

There can be benefits for employees too. The most commonly quoted positive outcomes are greater job satisfaction and motivation, together with improved learning. (CIPD, 2013h)

Ekmekci et al (2013, p.9) make the following proposition:

> In a societal culture, where institutional *collectivism* is high, the perceived organizational identity will have more attributes associated with collaborating, team-building, uniting, institutionalizing, bonding, ritualizing, consolidating, and building tradition.

So far so good. For countries such as Thailand, South Korea, Japan, Venezuela, the Philippines – where there is noted to be high power distance and high collectivism – one can imagine that organisations can implement, relatively easily, teamworking. However, in countries such as Great Britain, the USA, the Netherlands, New Zealand, and so on, Hofstede (1991) notes that teamworking might not be that natural and so more difficult to introduce into organisational processes.

ACTIVITY 2.5

1   Reflect upon how, in a country where *collectivism* is low – that is, *individualism* is high, such as Great Britain or the USA – organisations might effectively introduce teamworking.

2   Using the bar chart graph system provided by the Hofstede Centre at **http://geert-hofstede.com/china.html** determine the relative scores for Hofstede's six cultural dimensions of power distance, individualism, masculinity, uncertainty avoidance, pragmatism and indulgence for the following countries: China, the USA, Sweden, Germany and Poland.

3   Using the data of the six cultural dimensions for the five countries above, consider and then discuss how the different levels of these dimensions might impact upon organisations in terms of employee:

- relations with supervisors
- appraisal, especially 360-degree appraisal
- openness at team briefings
- ability to challenge the views of a supervisor when the employee knows that the supervisor is not correct in their understanding of an issue.

2.3.4 SUMMARY OF SOCIETAL CULTURE

Culture may be perceived as *physical*, in the form of bridges, roads, machinery, tools, and so on, and as *subjective,* such as attitudes, beliefs, values and tacit norms. While culture is not religion, sex, race or nationality, they all do interact. History shows that the physical and the subjective elements of a culture change across time as scientific innovation and intellectual advancements replace old structural designs, attitudes, values and beliefs. Cultures relocate themselves and their languages become more complex; they are therefore continuously evolving.

2.4 ORGANISATIONAL CULTURE

Having studied the foregoing section, you should now have a background of understanding of the elements of societal culture. In this section, we examine the degree to which those elements can be 'read across' into the organisational situation. First, however, the following definitions will clarify the concept of organisational culture.

 KEY CONCEPT: ORGANISATIONAL CULTURE

There are many definitions of organisation culture. Some, of course, convey meaning better than others. Stacey (1996) offers perhaps one of the most comprehensive.

> The culture of any people is that set of beliefs, customs, practices and ways of thinking that they have come to share with each other through being and working together. It is a set of assumptions people simply accept without question as they interact with each other. At the visible level the culture of a group of people takes the form of ritual behaviour, symbols, myths, stories, sounds and artefacts. (Stacey, 1996, cited in Campbell and Craig, 2012, p.491)

Robbins et al (2010, p.463) offer the following alternative definition: 'Organisational culture refers to a system of shared meaning held by members that distinguish the organisation from other organisations. This system of shared meaning is . . . a set of key characteristics that the organisation values.' They usefully identify seven characteristics, which they suggest (ibid, p.457) 'in aggregate capture the essence of organisational culture'. These seven characteristics – *innovation and risk-taking, attention to detail, outcome orientation, people orientation, team orientation, aggressiveness and stability* – when taken together, define how employees perceive the organisation. Each characteristic may be more or less dominant in different organisations so defining the perceived prevailing culture.

2.4.1 WHY STUDY ORGANISATIONAL CULTURE?

As a subject of concern for managers and of study for academics working in the field of organisational behaviour, organisational culture emerged in the 1980s. It was always there, hidden in the general atmosphere of the place, and since it was finally teased out and studied, it has achieved an importance that ranks it alongside other principal aspects of management and organisational studies. Understanding culture enables HR practitioners, managers and consultants to understand why people in organisations behave as they do, and enables them to try to alter the culture to make it more conducive to the achievement of section, department and overall objectives.

According to Moorhead and Griffin (1992), organisational culture probably exerts the greatest influence on individual behaviour when it is taken for granted. One of the major reasons that organisational culture is such a powerful influence on employees in an organisation is that it is not explicit. Instead, it is an implicit – meaning it is not written down – part of the employees' values and beliefs. It is for these reasons that managers and academics study organisational culture.

According to Greenberg (2013, p. 370), 'It would be reasonable to think of organizations as unique because of the various cultural forces that shaped them. Indeed, culture plays several important roles in organizations.' Greenberg (ibid) suggests that culture:

- provides a sense of identity
- generates commitment to an organisation
- clarifies and reinforces standards of behaviour.

BP, the oil giant, defines its five values in the following way:

Safety:

Safety is good business. Everything we do relies upon the safety of our workforce and the communities around us. We care about the safe management of the environment. We are committed to safely delivering energy to the world.

Respect:

We respect the world in which we operate. It begins with compliance with laws and regulations. We hold ourselves to the highest ethical standards and behave in ways that earn the trust of others. We depend on the relationships we have and respect each other and those we work with. We value diversity of people and thought. We care about the consequences of our decisions, large and small, on those around us.

Excellence:

We are in a hazardous business, and are committed to excellence through the systematic and disciplined management of our operations. We follow and uphold the rules and standards we set for our company. We commit to quality outcomes, have a thirst to learn, and to improve. If something is not right, we correct it.

Courage:

What we do is rarely easy. Achieving the best outcomes often requires the courage to face difficulty, to speak up and stand by what we believe. We always strive to do the right thing. We explore new ways of thinking and are unafraid to ask for help. We are honest with ourselves, and actively seek feedback from others. We aim for an enduring legacy, despite the short term priorities of our world.

One Team:

Whatever the strength of the individual, we will accomplish more together. We put the team ahead of our personal success and commit to building its capability. We trust each other to deliver on our respective obligations. (BP Corporate Website, [Accessed 15 March 2014]. Available at: www.bp.com/en/global/corporate/about-bp/company-information/our-values.html)

 ACTIVITY 2.6

Access the corporate websites of some other large multinational organisations such as: Exxon, Centrica, Ford, Shell, and so on, and compare and contrast how the different companies have defined their corporate values.

2.4.2 THE RELEVANCE OF PHYSICAL CULTURE

You may have noticed that in the definitions of organisational culture provided by Stacey (1996) and Robbins et al (2010), both include subjective culture, those things that are intangible and untouchable. Even though organisations express culture through uniform, as with the 'uniformed' services (police, ambulance, fire and rescue), or perhaps the style of shops or business premises, it is only Stacey's earlier definition which contains mention of a physical culture, such as uniforms or buildings.

In military terms the uniform plays a very important part in a culture. For example, the wearing of the red beret in the British Army denotes the elite Parachute Regiment. The green beret, on which is mounted a distinctive 'cap badge' of a crowned lion mounted on a crown with a globe of the world above a fouled anchor, embraced by a laurel wreath, identifies and denotes the elite Royal Marine Commando. Similarly, the French Foreign Legion identify strongly with the kepi blanc (white cap); in fact, the Legion's anthem is entitled the 'Kepi Blanc' (white cap); the American elite 75th Ranger Regiment wear the tan beret:

> The distinctive headgear of the 75th Ranger Regiment is the tan beret. The beret is a mark of distinction that brands the wearer as a proven warrior. The tan color is reminiscent of the leather caps worn by the original rangers of American heritage and lore. (**www.army.mil/ranger/**)

See how the UK Government uses the symbol of the green beret in its recruitment advertising at **www.youtube.com/watch?v=66QlFrQeels**

The beret, or cap in the case of the French Foreign Legion, is given to a soldier as a symbol that he or she has attained a standard which permits entrance into an elite club or band of men and women. It represents a 'badge' of 'belonging'; those who wear it have bought into the organisation's credo *{meaning – a set of beliefs that guides the actions of a person or group}* in mind, body and soul. Their future actions will be defined by past endeavours and honours.

ACTIVITY 2.7

Discuss the relevance that the induction process has in the development of an organisation's culture. It may be worth considering induction from the point of view of a 'process of socialisation'. The process is also sometimes known as 'onboarding', which is, in a more transparent way, indicating the part it plays in the overall 'joining' process, the metaphorical linkage to the need to show sailors, in the times of wind-powered ships, the 'ropes', that is, how to do their jobs. Understanding the 'ropes' is and was part of the special language of the seafarer, which has been adopted into general language usage to become a metaphor meaning essentially the same, that is, knowing how to do things.

- See how DHL induct their graduates at **www.dhl-graduates.com/graduate-careers/training-development/**
- The CIPD offers some guidance on induction at **www.cipd.co.uk/hr-resources/factsheets/induction.aspx**
- Volunteering England also have clear views about induction at **www.volunteering.org.uk/component/gpb/inductionandtrainingforvolunteers**

In terms of symbols it is perhaps a company's logo that is the key visible determinant of what its brand stands for. The three-propeller emblem of BMW clearly identifies its technical roots in the development of aero engines. In the case of BP, it has been woven within its company's values, as previously discussed. The BP origins and current meaning of the company's logo are discussed as follows:

> . . .in 2000 BP, now a group of companies that included Amoco, ARCO and Castrol, unveiled a new global brand with a new mark, a sunburst of green, yellow and white symbolizing dynamic energy in all its forms. It was called the Helios after the sun god of ancient Greece. In a press release announcing the change, the group said it had decided to retain the BP name because of its recognition around the world and because it stood for the new company's aspirations: 'better people, better products, big picture, beyond petroleum.' (BP Corporate Website [Accessed 15 March 2014]. Available at: **www.bp.com/en/global/corporate/about-bp/our-history/history-of-bp/special-subject-histories/bp-brand-and-logo.html**)

So the original 'British Petroleum', which over the years has seen its name reduced to BP as an abbreviated version, was fortuitously able to help fully define its international brand as 'BP', with the bonus that the two-letter brand name could also be used in a representational sense of what it stood for: 'better people, better products, big picture, beyond petroleum.'

2.4.3 ORGANISATIONAL SUBCULTURES

The interested parties – managers and academics – tend to talk and write about any single organisational culture as if it is a uniform phenomenon, while in fact organisations are made up of subcultures that represent different professions, locations, functions and levels (Hampden-Turner, 1990). This reduces the number of attitudes and core values that are shared across the whole organisation.

Robbins et al (2010, p.459) define subcultures in the following way: 'Minicultures within an organisation, typically defined by department designations and geographical separations.'

 KEY CONCEPT: SUBCULTURES

From how Robbins et al (ibid) define subcultures, one may deduce that the subculture on the workshop floor at, say, location A, will be different from that of the marketing department at location B. Furthermore, organisations may have a boardroom subculture, a middle management subculture, a staff subculture and a shop-floor subculture.

2.4.4 THE INFLUENCE OF SUBCULTURES

Furnham and Gunter (1993) describe the possible effects of the existence of subcultures at different levels and functions:

> These sub-cultures can assume varying degrees of significance within the organisation, and can be beneficial if they adopt a common sense of purpose, but problems arise where they have different priorities and agendas. Then sub-cultures can clash with each other or with the overall corporate culture, impeding organisational functioning and performance.

ACTIVITY 2.8

Reflect upon the comments attributed to Furnham and Gunter above. Do you consider, in reality, that there could be such differences in priorities and ideals within an organisation that this could lead to disharmony and differing agendas which could negatively impact the operation of the whole organisation?

2.5 CLASSIFYING CULTURAL THOUGHT

Clegg et al (2011) suggest that different perspectives can be taken on culture in respect of how they have been researched and are therefore viewed. They define three different perspectives:

- integration perspective
- differentiation perspective
- fragmentation perspective.

The *integration* perspective is a *managerialist* view of culture as opposed to a *social scientific* view of culture. The *integration* perspective assumes that management can mould and change culture and develop ways of working that, as Clegg et al (2011, p.234) argue, 'promise the dissolution of all that friction and resistance that managers know they often produce routinely. ... In place of conflict is offered integration.' In this way the predominant ways of thinking and doing permeate throughout the organisation; there is a predominant culture that everyone understands. The idea is that an organisation 'has' a culture that management can manipulate. Clegg et al (ibid) point out that 'some analysts refer to the strong cultures model as an integration perspective.'

The *differentiation* perspective is based upon the view that the organisation is made up of a number of subcultures, which both have their own peculiarities and characteristics and will, in all probability, be different from each other (Huczynski and Buchanan, 2013, p.125). In this sense the culture of an organisation cannot be defined in one way but is dispersed, having been built by groups or groupings that have different interests. As Huczynski and Buchanan (2013, p.125) write, there is a 'cultural pluralism'. The idea of the *differentiation* perspective is that taken by the social scientist and so culture '*is*' and is defined by the subcultural groups and so is difficult to change, it being embedded into the deep-seated understanding of how a part of the organisation works.

The *fragmentation* perspective considers that:

> culture is neither clearly consistent nor clearly contested, but likely to be muddled and fragmentary. A fragmentary organisation culture is one that forms around specific issues and then dissolves as these fade or are resolved. The nature of fragmentation is that specific and opportunistic cultural coherencies form at different times around different issues. (Clegg et al, 2011, p.237)

Clegg et al (ibid) go further and argue that:

> The *fragmentation* approach shares very little with the normative *integration* theorists who argue for the benefits of a strong culture, and the *differentiation* proponents, who say that a strong culture equals a dominant culture, and a dominant culture subordinates differentiated cultures. (Clegg et al, 2011, p.237)

It is a theory of the social scientific community, who argue that there is no consensus, even at a subcultural level, as to what a culture can be defined as, since cultural norms may be short-lived. That culture is only constructed because certain methods have been constructed with which to investigate it. In essence the argument centres on how culture is investigated. This does not mean to say that there is not a reality in what is described as a fragmented culture. The fragmentation can be caused by the fact that cultures are confused. One can imagine in an organisation, take a typical school, that there are cultural groupings made up of the functional sections – mathematics, languages, the arts, and so on – that are unique. Within these functional groups there are heads of department (HoDs) who together form a clique or grouping that report into a deputy head. The strength of the bindings will depend upon which 'cultural group' is the stronger and what issues are at play at any one time. Is the departmental head grouping stronger, in terms of allegiance, or could the allegiance be to the functional group of which the HoD is leader and a member? This duality could cause a fragmentation between allegiances.

Becker, cited by Huczynski and Buchanan (2013, p.125) argues that the:

> **fragmentation (or conflict)** perspective on culture assumes the absence of consensus; stresses the inevitability of conflict; focuses upon the variety of interests and opinions between different groups; and focuses upon power differences in organizations. The fragmentation perspective sees organizations as collections of opposing groupings which are rarely reconciled.

2.6 INDIVIDUAL DIFFERENCES WITHIN CULTURES

When you ask people about where they work, they tend to tell you something of the nature of the business, and perhaps its size and location. Then when you go to visit the organisation you see its buildings, the machinery and equipment. None of this tells you what it is like to work there; only the people can tell you that. If you were to ask them, however, you would get a different account from each of them, since they are a diverse group and each will have their own unique interpretation of the place and of its culture. As an outsider, it is only from this combination of perceptions that you begin to get an idea of the kind of culture in which they work.

2.7 ORGANISATIONAL VALUES

The values and norms that make up the culture of the organisation are taken for granted by the employees ('the way things are done around here') and there seems to be a degree of passive acceptance about this.

They – the organisational values and norms – are basic assumptions made by employees, do not necessarily appear in a document and are not transmitted in a training programme, although they can be expressed in written form (McKenna, 1994).

If, however, you undertook to analyse the culture of an organisation to identify and describe it, you would find significant indications of its values in the:

- structure, which demonstrates the lateral layers of authority and decision-making and the vertical patterns of expertise
- documentation, particularly including HR policies such as the systems of performance and reward management
- managerial style, including the formal and informal modes of communication between managers and employees
- condition of the employee relationship, including agreements reached, the absence and staff turnover rates
- nature of the business.

2.8 IDENTIFYING ORGANISATIONAL CULTURE

In the 1970s and 1980s several academics attempted, through analysis, to identify and classify organisational cultures with a view to develop the ability of altering their nature to make them more conducive to the achievement of objectives.

As you will see, the names of the classifications indicate the predominant characteristic of each type of culture. There are strong similarities between some of these classifications; the following describes two that are somewhat different from each other.

Handy (1976) proposed four types of culture as follows:

- **Power culture,** which he typified by the all-powerful head of the gods, Zeus, where power is centralised in the organisation.
- **Role culture** is typified by Apollo, the god of reason. Work is controlled by procedures and rules, and the role, which is more important than the person who fills it.
- **Task culture** is one in which the aim is to bring together the right people and let them get on with it. In this case Handy says that there is no appropriate deity *{meaning – god}* which can represent cultural type. However, Athena, the virgin goddess of reason, intelligent activity, arts and literature, has been associated with this type of culture. Influence is based more on expert power than on position or personal power. The culture is adaptable and teamwork is important.
- **Person culture** is typified by Dionysus, god of fertility. This is a culture in which the individual is the central point. The organisation exists only to serve and assist the individuals in it. This type of culture can be effective in an innovative, entrepreneurial enterprise.

Handy's work is further explored later when the various types of culture are compared in '2.9 Organisation Cultural Typologies'.

CASE EXAMPLE 2.3

THE IMPORTANCE OF ORGANISATIONAL CULTURE – A CLEAR CASE OF THE INTEGRATIVE APPROACH TO CULTURE

Interview with Lise Kingo, Executive Vice-president, Corporate Relations, of Novo Nordisk, by Tim Smedley from *People Management*

Culture is crucial

Staying close to core values as the company grows rapidly matters – to all stakeholders

Over the past 10 years Novo Nordisk has tripled in size, both in terms of personnel and sales. With 30,000 employees in 81 countries and half the worldwide market for insulin, the pharmaceutical firm has certainly earned its global credentials. Yet, despite such rapid growth, the company remains firmly committed to its local heritage. As Lise Kingo puts it, Novo Nordisk is 'a global company, with very strong Danish roots'.

Kingo is executive vice-president, corporate relations, a position that encompasses a variety of responsibilities including HR, corporate communications, public affairs and CSR. She's part of an intimate, five-strong and 100-per-cent-Danish executive management team. And having been with the company for 23 years, she has personally seen it grow from national prominence to international dominance. Today only just under half of the company's employees are based in Denmark, where 'Nordisk Insulinlaboratorium' was founded in 1923.

Such growth brings an acute awareness that, 'this special culture we have needs to be developed and maintained', says Kingo. 'In another 10 years, we expect to have 45,000 employees with one-third of them located in Denmark, two-thirds outside. It's something employees are very concerned about too.'

In 2010, this led CEO Lars Rebein Sørensen to embark on a global tour of the company, talking to employees, which included 350 separate face-to-face interviews. 'He had a dialogue with employees about how they would like the company to be in the next 10 years, what they liked, what should be changed. He also met with stakeholders, patients, key opinion formers and people in the public healthcare sector to update what we call the 'Novo Nordisk Way'.'

The Novo Nordisk Way is a short document distributed to all employees. The company's vision is stated, followed by 10 essentials that all employees have to live by, says Kingo. It includes statements such as 'our business philosophy is one of balancing financial, social and environmental considerations' (see 'The "triple bottom line"', below), and people management commitments such as, 'we focus on personal performance and development'. An internal team even audits every unit in Novo Nordisk on a three-yearly basis for how they adhere to the Novo Nordisk Way, a process Kingo's unit has just been through.

'First, you undertake a self-assessment with your management team, and then two facilitators do a group session with the management team, interview a number of employees and customers and then give a final evaluation,' she says. 'Every quarter, the head of facilitators reports on all the reviews that have been done that quarter, to say where we have become weaker or stronger on particular essentials.'

It's an exhaustive process, but one that underlines to employees and customers how important the culture is to the company. And it will be Novo's most used tool to keep a unified culture as it continues to grow. 'You could say that we handle company culture just as concretely as we handle financial performance,' says Kingo. 'It's a very soft

area that we are trying to make manageable. Because you know you can only manage what you can measure.'

Business ethics

Having had its fingers burnt in the past, now Novo does business ethically or not at all

Kingo arrived at the *People Management* interview carrying a recent copy of the magazine. One article in particular, on the introduction of the Bribery Act, had caught her eye. It's an issue that the company takes very seriously, although Kingo admits that it's been quite a journey to get to where they are today.

In 2005, Novo acknowledged responsibility for improper payments to the former Iraqi government of Saddam Hussein, between 2001 and 2003, to obtain contracts to provide insulin and other medicines. As well as a hefty fine imposed by the US Department of Justice, it proved to be a necessary wake-up call. 'We thought we did [business in Iraq] in a proper way. That was apparently not the case,' says Kingo. 'It was an important learning experience for us, and as management we said, "Now we draw a line in the sand – we will never experience this again."'

It would be wrong to think the company was acting without regard for ethics before the Iraq scandal. Its commitment to the triple bottom line approach to corporate responsibility dates back to the early 1990s. But, following 2005, Novo Nordisk developed specific procedures to apply to all employees across the company covering issues such as bribery and facilitation payments.

A universal training programme was established, implementing a fundamental shift away from following local norms and procedures to adhering to one company-determined way. 'It was a tough job, particularly for our colleagues in countries like China and Russia,' admits Kingo. 'Suddenly we gave them instructions that they had to work according to our business ethics guidelines, which they felt made us the only company in their countries told to act in this way. We had some turbulence until our CEO stood up and said, on several occasions, that we only want business when it lives up to our business ethics guidelines – otherwise forget about it. That was very powerful.'

Five years on, she feels, such resistance has all but disappeared. A combination of engagement, training and strict enforcement has made sure of that. A whistle-blower system, including a 24-hour helpline for people to anonymously report abuses, was also introduced in 2005. Kingo feels a zero-tolerance approach gives the company global advantages that far outweigh any regional disadvantages. 'As I see it, American requirements on business ethics are slowly going to spread to the rest of the world. So we look to our American compliance organisation for the very highest level and we take those same elements to the rest of the organisation.'

The latest stage in this process has seen the creation of a global business ethics board, headed by Kingo, with five senior representatives from global regions of the business as well as the SVP for legal and business assurance.

By keeping the whole company in line with the highest tidemark of ethical standards, Kingo believes it's easier to both spot upcoming trends and be prepared for the unforeseen. 'It's much easier if you start when you have the time, then you can set your own pace,' she says, adding that it helps that 'more and more international companies have business ethics thinking in their veins'.

The 'triple bottom line'

Financial, social and environmental responsibilities

Novo Nordisk 'strives to conduct its activities in a financially, environmentally and socially responsible way'. This is known as the triple bottom line (TBL), an approach to responsible business

practices that first appeared in the 1990s by pioneers of corporate responsibility such as John Elkington, co-founder of consultancy SustainAbility. Indeed, it was with Novo that Elkington originally formulated many of these ideas.

When Kingo joined the company in the late 1980s, genetic engineering and animal testing were top of the agenda of environmental activism. As a pharmaceutical company, Novo dealt in both – and still does. 'We had NGOs from across the world writing letters to us. There were some campaigns against the company,' says Kingo. One of her first jobs was to improve Novo's reputation. She asked Elkington to conduct a full environmental review. In addition, the company invited NGOs in to see for themselves how it operated and it also began environmental reporting. 'We began to develop what turned into the triple bottom line,' says Kingo.

By the mid-1990s, Novo was already ahead of where many UK companies are now with corporate responsibility; in 2011, it's a fundamental part of the business, so much so that Kingo has even advised the Prince of Wales on sustainability. In 2009–10, Novo reduced energy consumption by 0.5 per cent, water usage by 5 per cent and consumption of raw materials by 18 per cent – yet the company grew by 1,154 staff, and net profit by 33.8 per cent, over the same period. Novo has educated more than one million healthcare professionals in diabetes care since 2002, and has a beneficial pricing policy for insulin for the 50 poorest countries in the world.

'We are optimizing business opportunities by balancing being financially responsible with social and environmental responsibility,' says Kingo, who finds the argument that businesses should exist purely for profit very outdated. 'All of our huge shareholders have applauded the TBL at our AGMs,' she adds. 'They can see how it makes this business thrive.'

But do employees understand what 'triple bottom line' means? Kingo laughs: 'I guarantee you could not find one that doesn't know. It's one of our essentials: everyone has to live up to the TBL. We measure it in our annual survey, and being a TBL company is consistently among the three highest rated engagement factors of all – and it's no different if it's people in China, India or Denmark, in the factory or top management.'

When the company signed up to the UN's 'global compact' sustainability charter, it was one of only 50; now there are 8,000 signatories and rising. Yet, despite being a front-runner in this field, Novo is operating in an increasingly competitive environment. 'We have to be on our toes, because there are lots of companies that have seen that this is a very healthy business approach,' Kingo says. 'Employees today want to work for a company that they can be proud of, a company that has an attitude towards human rights or climate change.'

Innovation through culture

Creativity should not only be the preserve of R&D

In 2009 Novo worked with an American consultancy, Doblin, to increase innovation in the company. 'Doblin found that Novo could be stronger on articulating what an innovation culture is, and explaining to all employees what it is we want,' explains Kingo. That began with the leadership team, who, the review found, weren't too sure of what it was either. The top 30 leaders entered a period of self-analysis from which they

only recently emerged, having agreed on five innovation pilot projects, including a project to design the future workplace.

Kingo now leads an innovation culture steering group, with five senior VPs leading one programme each. 'We have a pool of money that people can apply for – wherever you are in the business.' Whether international factory employees will feel intimidated by the prospect of taking an idea direct to the organisation's senior leadership team is yet to be seen. But, says Kingo, 'The five projects we have now would not have survived in our previous development system. We've created a greenhouse where they have slightly different conditions for growing.'

CV highlights

- 2002: Appointed executive vice-president, corporate relations, assuming global responsibility for quality, HR, business assurance, corporate communications, corporate branding, public affairs and corporate social responsibility
- 1999: Appointed corporate vice-president, stakeholder relations
- 1988: Joined Novo Nordisk's Enzymes Promotion, and worked on implementing the triple bottom line
- Pre-1988: Began career in a Copenhagen advertising agency

The above case study is reprinted with kind permission of *People Management*.

SMEDLEY, T. (2011) On my agenda [online]. *People Management*. September. pp.30–33 [Accessed 11 March 2014]. Available via: **http://web.a. ebscohost.com/**

 ACTIVITY 2.9

Consider the following three questions about Case Example 2.3:

1 Although Novo Nordisk has grown through takeovers and acquisitions, how has Lise Kingo tried to develop a 'one culture'?

2 Kingo, together with her co-directors, has also introduced a performance measurement system based upon the triple bottom line (TBL) rather than simply focusing attention on the company's financial outcomes. What advantages do

you perceive this approach has in the context of:

- its people?
- its stakeholders?
- the company?

3   On what basis has Kingo and her management team decided to develop a culture of innovation in the Novo Nordisk Company? As Greenberg (2013, p.389) says, 'Highly innovative companies do not get that way by accident. ... the world's most innovative companies, as identified by *Fast Company* magazine in 2012, engage in a variety of practices to help promote innovation. 'Access the *Fast Company* website at: **www.fastcompany.com/section/most-innovative-companies-2013** and see which companies are listed and on which basis they have innovated.

4   How would you define the values of Novo Nordisk?

Not all acquisitions and mergers go smoothly. Organisational cultural differences can bring about the failure of the integration of two organisations if sufficient attention is not paid to the cultural amalgamation process. Explore this idea by investigating, using the Internet, how the merger of AOL and Time Warner became the most expensive failure in corporate history, costing $183 billion. After reading about AOL, and in light of the article on Novo Nordisk, you may wish to reflect upon whether or not the barriers caused by incompatible cultures can be overcome.

To help you think about mergers and acquisitions you may find the following of interest:

SCOTT, A. (2008) Culture clashes mar mergers and acquisitions [online]. *People Management*. 1 October [Accessed 11 March 2014]. Available at: **www.cipd.co.uk/pm/peoplemanagement**

You can obtain further help by reading:

- the CIPD's 'Practical tool' entitled *Mergers and acquisitions: preparing HR's contribution to success* at **www.cipd.co.uk/hr-resources/practical-tools/mergers-acquisitions-hrs-contribution.aspx**
- in *People Management:* Henri, C. (2008) How to lend HR expertise to mergers. *People Management*, **14**(4). pp.42–3.

2.9 ORGANISATIONAL CULTURAL TYPOLOGIES

Schein (1985) also proposed four types of culture:

- **Power culture** is one in which leadership resides in a few and rests on their ability, which tends to be entrepreneurial.
- **Role culture** is one in which power is balanced between the leader and the bureaucratic structure. The environment is likely to be stable, and roles and rules are clearly defined.
- **Achievement culture** is one in which personal motivation and commitment are stressed and action, excitement and impact are valued.
- **Support culture** is one in which people contribute out of a sense of commitment and solidarity. Relationships are characterised by mutuality and trust.

Typologies such as these provide indications of what happens in organisations according to the ideologies of the top managers and the type of organisation. One could, for example, draw parallels between what is said about:

- *power culture* and what other writers have said about the *unitary perspective* of HRM (refer to Chapter 3)
- *role culture* and what writers have said about *bureaucracy* and the 'bureaucratic control' of F.W. Taylor (Ray, 1986)
- *support culture* and aspects of human resource management, such as commitment, solidarity, mutuality and trust.

Handy (1993) updated his earlier work on cultural typologies, making some minor changes; it is repeated here for completeness and comparison purposes:

- *Power culture* – with this typology there is a strong influential figure who controls what is happening. Decision-making is centralised and so there is little need for rules and procedures, because the person at the centre makes the rules.
- *Role culture* – this type of culture is likely to be present in hierarchical, clearly bureaucratic organisations, where process is important. Equality and fairness of treatment is defined by the overarching procedural blanket.
- *Task culture* – the task, the job to be done, is the over-riding factor. The structure of the organisation is developed to satisfy the needs of task. One could think of an organisation type where managers are given client portfolios to manage, the portfolio representing a client organisation.
- *Person culture* – the control is shared, it is truly a partnership in which the members, together, make decisions about what is and what is not agreed to happen. Huczynski and Buchanan (2013, pp.113–14) suggest this would be typical of 'rock bands and classical chamber music, as well as small, start-up IT firms, architects' partnerships, . . .'.

Consider Figure 2.2, which depicts how a company – let us call it 'FewtureLogistix', which provides logistics, warehousing and stock management services – might manage its relations with three clients. Typically a FewtureLogistix manager will be given responsibility for a portfolio of companies – in the case of Figure 2.2, this would be with three 'client' companies A, B and C. It would be this manager's responsibility to ensure that their three clients receive the service they require. In our case FewtureLogistix provides some logistics, warehousing and stock control services. Another manager within FewtureLogistix will have a portfolio of three or four other companies to service with the internal resources at the disposal of FewtureLogistix. For the portfolio structure to work the portfolio manager needs to have significant influence upon how the company (FewtureLogistix) provides and prioritises services to the three client organisations. The advantage with this model is that there is a strong link between FewtureLogistix, as a service provider, and the client organisations. There is clarity as to where, and with whom, the 'buck' stops.

Figure 2.2 A task oriented organisation

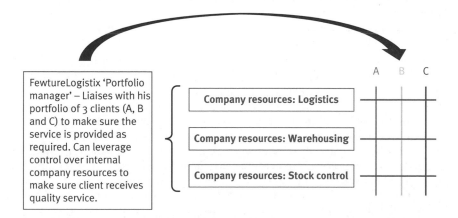

Note: FewtureLogistix is a fictitious name and every effort has been made to check whether there is an organisation operating with this brand name.

This might be confusing to the student who is new to the study of culture, since the typologies say little about values and norms, which are two of the main components of culture. Particular attitudes and beliefs are implied by some of the qualifying descriptions; for example, 'strive to maintain absolute control over subordinates' and 'the role, or job description, is more important than the person who fills it'. If, on the other hand, we examine a perception that describes the dimensions of a single culture, we see it from a different perspective.

Trice and Beyer (1984) proposed an organisational culture consisting of four major dimensions: (1) company practices; (2) company communications; (3) physical cultural forms; and (4) common language:

1   **Company practices** consist of events and ceremonies that help employees to identify with the organisation and its successes. These might include employees attending an extended induction period, attending the ceremonial launching of a new product, or the opportunity to socialise informally at the annual ball or a sports event.

2   **Company communications** consist, *inter alia, {meaning – among other things}* of informal chats such as when long-serving employees tell newcomers about past events and relate the myths and legends that are associated with the organisation. There are also signs and symbols designed to convey positive messages about the organisation, such as the company slogan, its logo, messages contained in the mission statement and in the marketing information.

3   **Physical cultural forms** include the design of the buildings and the nature of the capital equipment, which convey something distinctive about the organisation. It also includes the décor and the layout of the offices and workshops, including the posters, cartoons and even the screensavers that employees choose.

4   **Common language** is probably the most significant indication of overall organisational culture and the nature of the subcultures within it. In any organisation there is a secondary language that is not understood by outsiders. It is based on technical vocabularies and the 'in' jargon of the place.

As you can see, the work of Trice and Beyer (1984) resembles more closely the accounts of culture that are given in the first half of this chapter. References to signs and symbols, myths and legends, and the sharing of a common language indicate that the components and boundaries of ethnic culture can be detected within, and read into, organisational culture.

2.9.1 PUBLIC SECTOR CULTURE

Consider Lawton and Rose's (1994) work, cited in Kew and Stredwick (2013, p.177), which argues that in the public sector there are four different cultures that are prevalent: (1) political culture, (2) legal culture, (3) administrative culture, and (4) market culture. To explain the meaning of these one can consider that the *political culture* is defined by the way local government officials have to engage with politicians. The *legal culture* is defined by how the work of many central and local government offices is controlled by a strong legal framework and there is a requirement to comply. The *administrative culture* is a function of how rules and procedures have been passed down from the time, pre-1980s, when bureaucratic processes were seen as important. Since Conservative Governments of the late 1970s and into the 1990s, the Labour Government of the late 1990s and into the twenty-first century, followed by the Coalition Government, which came into power in 2010, there has been a move to introduce market forces and commercial ways of thinking into how public services go about their work. As Kew and Stredwick (ibid) point out, 'They [Lawton and Rose] argue that the last of these, the market culture, is becoming predominant and that, as a result, running the public sector is becoming an issue of management and much less an issue of administration.'

Lawton and Rose's typology differs from that of Trice and Beyer in as much as they, Lawton and Rose, define culture by the way the public sector carries out work rather than considering the constructs of communication and the organisation's symbols that, as mentioned, have strong links with how societal culture is defined as per Trice and Beyer's approach.

ACTIVITY 2.10

Draw up a list of 15 words, perhaps acronyms, and terms that are taken for granted and used regularly by employees in your organisation (or an organisation with which you are familiar) but would not be understood if you used them at home or elsewhere.

For example:

● The military use the term **AWAC** to mean an aircraft which, through a system of advance electronics, provides airborne early warning and control. The aircraft can detect ships, land vehicles and other aircraft at long range. It has the capacity to command and control other military assets to neutralise a potential threat.

● The process control industry use the term **SCADA**, meaning a control system that gives: **S**upervisory **C**ontrol **A**nd **D**ata **A**cquisition.

2.9.2 ETHNIC OR SOCIETAL CULTURE VERSUS ORGANISATIONAL CULTURE

There is always an element of ethnic culture in the organisational culture, and it is important to take this into account if we wish to prescribe a culture that matches the organisation's core values. Additionally, it is important to understand whether ethnic or organisational culture is the stronger in the organisation. Which culture would predominate in particular situations? Research supports the view that ethnic culture, rather than the organisation's culture, is more influential over employee behaviour (Adler, 1997, pp.61–3). Muslim workers in the UK, for example, will be influenced more strongly by their ethnic culture than by that of the employing organisation.

Organisations that have installations in different parts of the world have to be able to predict, with a reasonable degree of accuracy, the behaviour of their overseas employees. It was noted earlier that culture is the greatest determinant of employee behaviour, but in situations in which the two cultures clash, the ethnic culture will predominate.

2.9.3 CULTURAL FIT

One situation in which the task is that of predicting behaviour is the selection process. What one might call *cultural fit* is the degree to which a prospective employee's attitudes, beliefs, values and customary norms match those of the organisation. Is this something that should be assessed? Robbins et al (2010) write the following about selection and organisational cultural fit when the choice is to be made between two potentially strong candidates for a role:

> When that point is reached [that is, of making the final selection], it would be naïve to ignore the fact that the final decision as to who is hired will be significantly influenced by the decision makers' judgement of how well the candidate will fit into the organization. This attempt to ensure a proper match ... results in hiring of

people who have values essentially consistent with those of the organization, ...
(Robbins et al, 2010, p.465)

PAUSE FOR THOUGHT

From what is said in the above quote, do you think that multinational companies could risk rejecting the right person for the job by focusing on their culture rather than on a prospective employee's suitability in terms of knowledge and skills? Could this develop into a discriminatory policy? How could the 'fit' between employee and employer be improved?

CASE EXAMPLE 2.4

WHAT YOU CAN LEARN FROM FITTLEWORTH MEDICAL

The delivery driver who set off on Christmas Day morning to be certain vital supplies got to a customer in a hospice. The trek up 22 flights of stairs to ensure a parcel reached its destination. The backpack full of sweets and toys staff decided to put together for a customer's sick five-year-old daughter.

Reading *The Fittleworth Way* – a book detailing the myriad ways employees of medical appliance dispensing specialist Fittleworth Medical go the extra mile for their clients – is an inevitably emotive experience. And even HR Director Peter Waller, whose job each day is to crystallise and direct such overwhelming niceness into a functional framework for operational excellence, admits to being moved.

'Someone outside the business asked one of our delivery drivers what his job was,' says Waller, who became the company's first HR director when he joined in 2011. 'He could have said anything but his natural response was "I go to the care centre. I load up my van and I drive home very slowly and call in on a lot of my friends on the way."'

Fittleworth's business is decidedly unglamorous. As a mail order provider of ostomy, continence and wound care products, it deals directly with often vulnerable and critically ill people in need. But, unlike rivals who see their role as fulfilment, the business's USP is its caring touch: unable to compete on price since its orders come via prescription, it has benefited from a self-directed culture of compassion. As Waller puts it: 'Service is our business, and that service is provided by our people and therefore the people are fundamental.

'Every single person we employ has empathy, compassion and understanding and wants to do the right thing for the client because they understand the consequences of getting it wrong. We have people in our care centres who literally spend all day customising stoma bags and they fully appreciate that if they get that wrong, they're going to cause someone pain or irritation. So there is a selfless desire to do the right thing by the client.'

But Fittleworth could have become a victim of its own success. The 30-year-old business has significantly increased in size over the past three years and now numbers 250 employees. The extended care centre network (where goods are handled and dispensed) now covers the entire country, alongside a fresh cadre of in-house drivers and enhanced sales and customer service functions at its head office in Littlehampton, West Sussex.

Waller's job has been to preserve culture through the process – hence the book, with its anonymously submitted stories, which was distributed throughout the company. The low-key project helped give a name to the 'intangible loveliness' of what the business does, and also landed the 2013 CIPD People Management Award for Best SME HR Initiative. For the first time, it has led to discussion of a 'Fittleworth Way' to guide operational decisions, and Waller has helped usher in a new management structure, enhanced communications and training initiatives to underpin the transition.

'There are still some learnings as we mature,' he admits. 'Perhaps we haven't performance-managed, for example, as readily as we should. But we're beginning to address that.' In the meantime, how else has HR helped transform the business?

Paint a picture

The book was a good way to begin a focus on the company's customer-oriented culture. But Waller wanted a clear framework for future initiatives. The not-unexpectedly-named result was Fittleworth Way, a virtual street populated by fictional customers, each with their own back story and life-changing condition. When discussing innovations or training staff on service, it's possible to zoom in on individuals and articulate how the things Fittleworth does affect them.

'As you get into soft skills, for example with the customer service team, you can talk about how you deal differently with Edith rather than Mike,' says Waller. 'One of our nurses can talk about Edith's condition and what we need to understand about her to serve her better.' One home is left empty for a future product area, at which point a 'housewarming' and viral campaign will help drive understanding of the new developments across the business.

Make learning live

In common with many smaller businesses, training has always posed a conundrum for Fittleworth. 'We've relied on supervisors to train and clearly

they've done a good job, but as we've grown and added more sites, that's not appropriate anymore,' says Waller. 'Many of our employees might be in care centres where there might be only three staff – if they're training we can't dispense to the local population.' Drivers and customer service staff face similar difficulties, compounded by constraints on IT equipment.

Waller dismissed e-learning because of the cost and the need for heavy customisation. His solution is an 'academy' suite of timetabled live learning sessions and videos covering everything from induction ('we've had people in tears at inductions when they see what the company is about') through to health and safety, technical knowledge and soft skills. Everything is bite-sized and can include reading, answering questions, watching videos or group discussions – perfect for an operationally focused workforce.

Culture counts

Fittleworth's growth has necessitated a reorganisation of HR, to allow one adviser to be on the road covering remote sites and another to support head office. It means HR can intervene or deliver training as and when it's required, says Waller. And that's particularly important in the recruitment process, where cultural fit is king.

'You're always asking the same three questions,' says Waller. 'Can they do the job (do they have the right skills and qualifications)? Will they do the job (do they have the right attitude)? Will they fit in? The difference with Fittleworth is that the order is reversed: they need the emotional intelligence to put the customer first. If you don't get a feel for that culture, you just don't fit in and we have an intuition about that now [in the recruitment process].'

Reach out for ideas

When Waller saw a presentation on innovation from engineering giant

Alcatel-Lucent at the CIPD's Annual Conference, outlining how the business uses innovation boot camps, it sparked a thought of his own. 'It made me consider how we get ideas, beyond having an idea box or going through a manager. I hadn't thought about putting a structure around things in that way.'

As a result, Fittleworth has introduced its own embryonic innovation process, where employees can fill in a form on the intranet and end up presenting to the business's leaders. It's taught Waller the wider importance of best practice: 'Companies might not be related to us in any sense of scale or sector, but there's sometimes gold dust in what they say.'

Mean it

The search for the Fittleworth Way was also a quest for authenticity, which remains central to the company's communication style. That's why Waller rejected the idea of employee surveys or focus groups and 'absolutely didn't want pillars or a wheel' as a means of disseminating values in a traditional 'corporate' way. Though Fittleworth does have values (dedication, integrity, caring, quality), Waller insists it's more important to 'recognise the wonderful things that happen in our business on an everyday basis. . . the very nature of trying to define and make something tangible means you can inadvertently undermine it.'

As the business has grown, it has moved away from centralised conferences to local, discipline-specific events that are more operationally focused. And there definitely won't be an annual awards programme: 'An award can make things contrived. I wouldn't want anyone to go and drop a parcel off on their way home because they might get an award or a bonus. That is just the stuff we do anyway.'

Source: JEFFERY, R. (2014) What you can learn from Fittleworth Medical. *People Management*. March. pp.43–4.

Reprinted with kind permission of *People Management*.

You can read about Fittleworth Medical at **www.fittleworth.net/about-us/our-story**

 ## ACTIVITY 2.11

From the above article and using the Fittleworth Medical website, discuss:

- the type of culture you perceive Fittleworth Medical tries to nurture
- what processes, which are indicated in the narrative, Fittleworth Medical uses to maintain the culture
- how you consider the culture was developed – did the culture happen or was it engineered?

2.9.4 CULTURE SHIFT

Human beings are the most adaptable creatures on Earth. They quickly acclimatise to unaccustomed conditions, and can move through a variety of different situations dealing with them as they go. People live their lives in stages, and they adopt roles as they move from one stage to the next; through infancy, teens, adulthood, and then middle age to old age. There are also stages in each day: the breakfast scene, the trip to work, the work situation, the trip home, the home scene.

ACTIVITY 2.12

Read again the above paragraph and think about how you behave in each of the stages and in each of the daily situations. Are you aware that your behaviour changes gradually during your life and frequently during each day? Do you speak and treat people differently at home, at work, at study or where you spend your leisure hours?

One of the most important changes is the one that takes place when an employee enters their place of work. As one enters the place of work, much of what is defined as ethnic culture is put aside. The individual slips into the *place* where they spend significant *time* and where the *language* is different. By doing this, the individual and their workplace colleagues become part of a different culture. Without having to make a conscious effort, they all adopt the workplace values and observe the norms. Furthermore, if the individual is a team member, they further adapt to and adopt the team norms.

PAUSE FOR THOUGHT

How many different ethnic backgrounds are there in your team or classroom? Is there mutual understanding about what you have to do? How well do you work together? Is there a bond with your work group or team?

The point that is being made here is that people from a variety of ethnic cultures join together to form a new culture to achieve particular objectives by working harmoniously together. This is not a description of an idealistic situation; it happens for real in all kinds of organisations every day. Indeed, there are times when team members have to close ranks in order to defend their position.

2.9.5 INTEGRATION OF DIVERSE ELEMENTS

The organisation is an ideal venue for integration. It is more disciplined than the external environment and is a space in which the organisation's own values and beliefs can be learned by all, regardless of their backgrounds.

2.10 INDUCTION – THE SOCIALISATION OF A NEW MEMBER INTO THE ORGANISATION

As described earlier in this chapter, and also in Chapter 8, the induction process is vital to socialising the new starter into the organisation because it is through this process that the individual learns what is acceptable and not acceptable behaviour and, with a mentor or through co-workers, quickly learns the norms *{meaning – how things are done around here}* of the organisation's culture. The process of induction is starting the process of familiarising the person into how the organisation works. New employees are selected against a set of standards that managers have agreed. These standards effectively identify those who will 'fit' with the organisation's culture (refer to the previous discussion of 'Cultural Fit'). Because managers are involved in the selection process there is, in effect, some pre-selection that goes on, whether consciously or subconsciously, as to whether people will 'fit' into the organisation. This process of socialisation continues with how senior managers and other key cultural carriers, such as the HR department's staff, engage with the new starter, who soon learns how to behave through a process of adaptation to what is acceptable – the norms. Organisations with strong cultures, as opposed to weak cultures, are likely to expect the new member not only to adapt to the new norms, beliefs and values, but also to adopt them.

> **Strong culture** – 'a culture in which an organisation's core values are widely shared among employees and intensely held by them, and which guides their behaviour.' (Huczynski and Buchanan, 2013, p.130)

The policies and procedures that the HR department has developed further reinforce the culture of the organisation. The policies and procedures, and how they are enforced, say a lot about the running of the organisation, and thus its culture.

How far socialisation occurs depends upon the strength of the organisation culture and whether culture is perceived as a means of control; the concept is called *symbolic management* (see Huczynzki and Buchanan, 2013, p.129). How strong should a strong culture become? Too strong and the socialisation process becomes one of indoctrination and the organisation may lose effectiveness because it lacks diversity of thought.

2.11 CHANGING ORGANISATION CULTURE

Over time both the work practices and the competitive environment in which companies operate changes. How things are done at work can become ritualised and if there has been no significant or major event to create the need to drastically change work practices, business can tend to 'roll on as normal'.

 CASE EXAMPLE 2.5

PENSION LAW REFORMS DRIVE CHANGE IN PENSION PROVISION

On Wednesday, 19 March 2014, George Osborne, the Chancellor of the Exchequer, presented his Budget to Parliament. The Budget was expected to be a vote-catcher, to try to woo the more 'senior citizens', in anticipation of the 2015 general election. The *Guardian* wrote about the 2014 Spring Budget:

> The disillusionment of those aged over 50 with David Cameron's modernising project and the ultra-low interest rates of the past five years are seen by Downing Street as the single biggest force driving the Ukip surge. . . .The chancellor made his pitch for Britain's greying vote in a package for 'makers, doers and savers' designed to complete the repair job after the deepest recession of the modern era. . . . (Elliott and Wintour, 2014, p.1)

In reality, George Osborne's March 2014 Budget was driven by, on the one hand, Conservative political philosophy, that is, a further dismantling of elements of the nanny state, and, on the other hand, smart vote-catching savvy.

George Osborne, though, had a real surprise up his sleeve. As Elliott et al wrote in *The Times* on 21 March 2014, 'Voters back Osborne's pension revolution'. At present people facing retirement, and who have been saving towards retirement in defined contribution pension schemes with the big pension providers such as Prudential, Canada Life, Aviva, Legal and General, etc., were required, after retirement, to transfer the accumulated 'pension pot' into an annuity with a financial institution; this need not necessarily have been with the institution with which they had been saving. The financial institution receiving the 'pension pot' would grow the funds on the stock market, thus securing a steady cash flow for the individual during their retirement years.

The gain for the annuity provider lay in the administration fees for managing the 'pensioners' fund. This has been the case for many years and was a very lucrative business model.

The big problem with annuities, since the financial crisis of 2008, has been the low interest rates which providers have been offering, typically for each £100,000 saved the annual guaranteed pension on a single life at age 65 has been circa £5,900 (March 2014) – not an attractive option. In 2007 the best rates were as high as £7,500 for each £100,000 invested. This represents a fall of 21.3% over a seven-year period. Annuities have, therefore, lost their sparkle and have become unattractive. People have continued to pay into their pension pots because of the immediate tax advantage that one is able to achieve because pension deductions are taken from salaries before income tax is deducted.

Prior to the Chancellor's announcement, individuals could take (draw down) a 25% tax-free lump sum from their pension fund but '...savers would no longer face the current 55% penalty charge if they tried to take the rest of their pension after their tax-free lump sum, but would be taxed at marginal rates – meaning as little as 20% for most pensioners' (Elliott and Wintour, 2014, p.1). In practice this means that, on retirement, the individual can draw their money from the financial institution with which they have been saving and, for example, buy a house or house(s) to rent, go on a cruise or, as was intended, buy an annuity or some other investment which would provide a pension. In practice, it also means uncertainty for the annuity providers.

Already, providers are starting to change the way they manage their annuity business. Costello (2014) wrote the following:

> Standard Life became the first big pension provider to respond to George Osborne's reforms to savings yesterday by making it easier for customers to turn their retirement pots into cash.
>
> In a move to be mimicked across the country, the Edinburgh based insurer reduced the threshold at which savers qualify for its more flexible retirement products. (Costello, 2014, p.7)

Business needs to revitalise itself from time to time; change is inevitable. The problem is that, like life in general, if one feels cosy and comfortable doing what has always been done, the urge, that is, the force to drive change, is simply not there. To cause change to happen, a dramatic event sometimes has to occur to spur movement, in this case the 'spur' was dug into the 'sides' of the financial institutions by the Chancellor of the Exchequer. Initial reaction to the Chancellor's unexpected freeing retirees of the need to buy an annuity was the drop in the share price of some of the large pension providers. Speculation is that the main losers, as a result of the Chancellor's law reforms, will be the large traditional pension providers. Part of the Chancellor's package is that free financial advice will be offered to those who have accumulated pension pots. It is speculated that few people will take an uncompetitive annuity offered by their pension provider but opt, perhaps, for other means of providing for their retirement; some may simply draw down their money as and when required and pay the appropriate tax. Only time will tell the outcome of the massive March 2014 reforms to pensions.

Bringing about a culture change is not impossible but, because it deals with the 'soft' people issues of attitudes and motivations, it is not easy to bring about. Changing organisational culture is dealt with in some depth in Chapter 18.

2.12 DISSECTING ORGANISATIONAL CULTURE

Johnson et al (2012, p. 99) offer a way of analysing organisational culture, which is useful from two perspectives: first, to be able to understand the culture of an organisation and, second, once understood, one can think how and what to change in a culture to bring about better performance or service.

Johnson et al picture culture as a central *paradigm* (a pattern or model of how it works) surrounded by: the *symbols* of the culture, the *power structure*, the *organisational structures*, the *control systems*, the *rituals and routines* and the *stories*:

- The *paradigm* explains, as indicated above, how the organisation is seen to operate. It is about expected and observed behaviours and reflects the organisation's reality to those within and those outside who have some first-hand knowledge of the organisation. It is an expression of the intended and real values of the organisation.
- *Routines* are the way members behave towards each other and make up 'the way things are done around here'.
- The *stories* are perhaps of significant events that help to fix the culture in time and place and give meaning to how the organisation sees itself.
- The *symbols* are the artefacts, logos, the titles of how people within the organisation address each other. They are, as Johnson and Scholes (2002, p231) write, '...shorthand representation of the nature of the organisation'. They could be reserved car parking spaces, preferential office sites, dress codes for managers, and so on.
- *Power structures* are associated with the effective power in organisations. In a car sales operation, power is likely to be with the sales department rather than any of the service functions, such as financial services, HR or maintenance.
- *Organisation structures* reflect how power is devolved within an organisation. A bureaucratic organisation of many layers may see process to be important and that order and discipline, in terms of following procedure, to be key to how it works. This may be relevant and important where quality and safety are wholly dependent on how, for example, a large piece of equipment is put together, such as a jet engine.
- *Control systems* are how the workings of the organisation are focused. The operation of an emergency service control room is controlled by procedure, as is how a pilot flies a commercial airliner. To incentivise either of these activities with bonus payments, for example for the rate of handling calls or time to destination for the pilot, may cause the 'actors in the process' to move away from procedure with disastrous effect.

(adapted from Johnson et al, 2012, p.201)

2.13 SUMMARY – CULTURE

Culture can be considered in two ways. It can be considered as ethnic or societal culture or it can be viewed from the perspective of the organisation as the culture that an organisation has. Organisation culture, according to Clegg et al (2011), can be considered from an integration perspective, differentiation perspective or a fragmentation perspective.

Physical culture is created by people and is represented by cars, roads and bridges of our physical society. There is also the subjective culture, which is apparent through the norms and values of society and is influenced by our upbringing, religion, schooling and so on. The two are very closely tied because both place and time are important; for example, places of religious worship have significance in cultural understanding and being. The physical culture is closely linked to and defined by societal culture. We tend to view other cultures through a lens that is shaped by our own cultural norms and values. In essence we take an ethnocentric view of other cultures and measure and judge others against our own standards, our own 'in' group.

Organisation culture is different from ethnic/societal culture because the focus is on how organisations can be viewed from a cultural perspective; remembering, of course, that organisations operate within different societies. Schein, Handy, Trice and Beyer, Lawton and Rose, and Johnson et al (and many others) all offer a view on how to represent and dissect culture.

From the above discussion one can see that the debate about culture is far-reaching and can be viewed from a number of perspectives. Picking up on the writings of Clegg et al (2011), it is convenient to take a managerialist perspective, if one is in business, because this assumes an organisation *has* a culture that can be moulded and changed, and therefore improved. If, however, one takes the social scientist's perspective – that the culture of an organisation *is* – this implies that it is fixed in time and space and has been developed organically over time and so cannot be changed by managerial processes.

If one considers that an organisation *has* a culture, of course it can be changed, which is part of the discussion that Chapter 18 addresses. The work of Johnson et al is useful as a tool in respect of how to dissect culture.

REVIEW QUESTIONS

1 How would you define organisational culture?

2 What is the relationship between values and norms?

3 Why is culture said to be a powerful determinant of behaviour?

4 How would you distinguish between the physical culture and the subjective culture? How do they influence each other?

5 What is ethnocentrism and why is it important in organisational culture?

6 Why are national boundaries not necessarily the boundaries of societal culture?

7 In what circumstances do members of different ethnic cultures join forces to create a distinctive subculture?

8 What value is there in defining different types of organisational culture?

9 What is meant if one accepts that an organisation *has* a culture compared with the view that the culture of an organisation *is*?

10 How would you define a strong culture?

11 How would you define a weak culture? (You will find answers to this question in Huczynski and Buchanan, 2013.)

12 How does a differentiated culture differ from an integrated culture?

13 Is it useful, when trying to describe cultures, to think of them as Handy or Schein describes them?

14 What role does HR play in the introduction of the individual to the organisation's culture?

15 What is the difference between socialisation as a process and indoctrination?

16 Write down four levels of organisational subculture.

17 What are the positive and negative influences of organisational subcultures?

18 What are the possible consequences of allowing an out-of-date culture to persist at a time of significant external change?

19 What factors might bring about a change in an organisation's culture?

BOOKS

GREENBERG, J. (2013) *Managing behavior in organizations.* 6th ed. New Jersey: Pearson Education Ltd.

As the author points out in the preface to the text, this is not an in-depth account of organisation behaviour. However, it addresses a significant range of issues in a very easy-to-read style supported with diagrams and a range of reference sources.

GREENBERG, J. and BARON, R.A. (2010) *Behavior in organizations.* New Jersey: Pearson Education, Inc.

Greenberg and Baron's text views organisational as well as ethnic/national culture from a number of differing perspectives: its impact upon creativity, decision-making, communication and so on. Their work on culture is not limited to one chapter but is dealt with across the spectrum of organisational behaviour in the way, for example, it impacts upon communication and negotiating across cultures. An easy-to-read and well-illustrated text.

HOFSTEDE, G, HOFSTEDE, G.J. and MINKOV, M. (2010) *Cultures and organizations: software of the mind.* 3rd ed. New York: McGraw-Hill.

Geert Hofstede has revisited and updated his early text and it is well worth reading as a key text in the understanding of societal culture. It is worth dipping into this book to understand how he was able to categorise national cultural attributes, values and meanings to cultural ethnic identity. In this respect both for those who work in international organisations and those of us who work within multicultural groups, the book can help build an understanding of how different cultures approach issues.

SMITH, P., PETERSON, M. and THOMAS, D. (eds). (2008) *The handbook of cross-cultural management research.* Thousand Oaks, CA: Sage.

JOURNAL ARTICLES

HEBDEN, J.E. (1986) Adopting an organization's culture: the socialization of graduate trainees. *Organizational Dynamics [online].* **15**(1), pp.54–72 [Accessed 11 March 2014]. Available via: **http://web.a.ebscohost.com/**

WEB LINKS

Geert Hofstede academic website: **www.geerthofstede.nl/**

World Values Survey: **www.worldvaluessurvey.org/index_organization**

PODCASTS

Listen to the CIPD Podcast 89 – *Rethinking staff inductions* at (it is a long web address, so it might be easier to search for the podcast on the CIPD website!): **www.cipd.co.uk/hr-resources/podcasts/89-rethinking-staff-inductions.aspx? utm_medium=email&utm_source=cipd&utm_campaign=cipdupdate& utm_content=020414_na_textlink_editorial-podcast89**

VIDEO LINKS

Watch and listen to Geert Hofstede talk about societal culture and his insights into defining culture at:

www.youtube.com/watch?v=wdh4okgyYOY

www.youtube.com/watch?v=LBv1wLuY3Ko

A 'TED' video on societal culture – *Wade Davis: Cultures at the far edge of the world* – at: **www.youtube.com/watch?v=bL7vKopOvKI**

A 'TED' video by Saba F. Safdar, Professor of Psychology, Guelph University, Ontario, at: **www.youtube.com/watch?v=FaOJ71czAGQ**

Watch and listen to Edgar H. Schein on his latest ideas (July 2013) about organisational culture at: **www.youtube.com/watch?v=GtV3Jx01BqU**

CHAPTER 3

Human Resource Management (HRM)

LEARNING OBJECTIVES

After studying this chapter you should understand:

- the meaning of the term 'human resource management'
- the difference between modern HRM and personnel management
- the various approaches to HRM, the concept of 'hard' and 'soft' HRM
- strategic HRM and the best-fit, best practice and resource-based view of strategic human resource management (SHRM)
- the impact HRM has had upon organisations' approach to management since the 1980s
- the influence of HRM on the management of people
- why the HR department needs to demonstrate that it adds value to an organisation
- some of the ways HRM's contribution to the organisation can be measured
- the difficulties of developing universally accepted measures of how HRM adds value to an organisation
- how engaging effectively with staff can lead to improvements in the customer experience.

3.1 INTRODUCTION

There is a wide variety of views about HRM. The concept has been variously interpreted, and the style with which its principles and practices are applied varies among academics, practitioners and, indeed, from one country to another. There is neither the space nor the need in a book of this size and level to venture deeply into a discussion of the philosophical pronouncements about HRM, but it is necessary to provide an understanding of how it has influenced not only the management of the employment relationship, but the management of the whole organisation.

This chapter offers some of the insights of academics and practitioners, and we hope you will attain an understanding of HRM that you will be able to take further in later studies. If, however, you wish to look into the concept more deeply at this stage, the references that are cited here will lead you to a comprehensive account of the HRM debate: the philosophies underlying the various interpretations and how the principles and practices upon which HRM is founded are applied.

In addition to developing a sound understanding of HRM, you also need to be aware of the management systems that emerged earlier in the twentieth century. This is because many organisations have not fully adopted HRM and still adhere to the traditional practices of personnel management.

3.2 WHAT EXACTLY IS HRM?

The history of management thought, which began in earnest in the early twentieth century, produced theories that contain allusions to what we now regard as HRM principles and practices (Taylor, 1947; Burns and Stalker, 1966), but they were not introduced into British organisations, as a totally new management system, until the mid-1980s. At the time, people became confused about what the term meant, and this was understandable since the words 'human resource' caused people to think of personnel. Sisson (1995) says that in the late 1980s, there was much debate among practitioners and academics alike about the implications of HRM for the personnel function. He said that even if some found it difficult to understand what the fuss was about, HRM looked very much like the personnel management they thought they were practising. Many practitioners, though, welcomed the new paradigm (Armstrong, 1987; Fowler, 1987).

3.2.1 IDEAL TYPE OF ORGANISATION

The main question became: what is the difference between HRM and personnel management? Indeed, is there a difference or was it just that the term personnel management had lost credibility and needed a new label? A second question that required an answer was: how, in such a dramatic manner, is it possible to introduce a new way of managing the employment relationship without affecting the ways in which the whole organisation is managed? On the basis of studying organisations in a series of case studies, Storey (1992) created an 'ideal type' of organisation in order to clarify and simplify the essential features that distinguish HRM from other forms of people management. His classification shows 27 points of differences in practice between personnel and industrial relations and HRM practice (see Table 3.1).

It has to be understood that the comparative model illustrated in Table 3.1 is purely theoretical and that no single organisation conforms to all of the conditions within it. However, it does give some concrete examples of where 'personnel management' and 'human resource management' differ.

What can be seen from the model is that those who have adopted the principles and practices of HRM have shifted from what was regarded as standard practice in personnel and industrial relations terms (IR, the third column in Table 3.1), to the generally more flexible, open and mutually co-operative standard of HRM (the right-hand column of Table 3.1). However, the legacy of 'personnel management' still remains to haunt the concept of human resource management. It is worth understanding the origins of HRM because one can then better appreciate what are the intended objectives of what we now call HRM.

Research shows that HRM has been *more* or *less* adopted by organisations. Beardwell et al (2004, p.24) and Beardwell and Claydon (2007, p.22) point out, '...in the 1998 Workplace Employee Relations Survey, WERS 98, Cully et al, (1999) investigated sixteen practices commonly associated with HRM, including team working, employee involvement ... The survey found evidence of each of the sixteen practices....' This implied that there was a take-up of HRM practices and that they '...are well entrenched in many British workplaces'. British managers, however, have a record of reluctance to adopt new ideas in the comprehensive sense; they are very financially orientated and change, which is always a costly process, is usually carried out in a cautious and piecemeal fashion. The latest WERS survey (2011) suggests that there has been little change in how far HRM practices have been adopted in UK organisations. There is a more detailed discussion on this topic later in this chapter, in section 3.4.2 'The extent of HRM practices in UK organisations'.

One can draw a distinction between personnel management and HRM by reflecting on the Storey model. Personnel management can be seen to have a focus on the personnel, the people. The personnel department can, metaphorically, be perceived as 'the servant' of the line departments of an organisation, providing a monitoring and largely supportive function. On the other hand, the human resource management function considers people as a strategic asset that can impact upon the bottom line and, at the same time, grow in value. As Francis and Keegan say (2006, p.231), '...research in HRM has focused on the take-up and impact of commitment seeking high performance HR practices that are argued to lead to improved employee and organisational performance'. And Martin, cited in Francis and Keegan (2006, p.231), argues that, 'More recently, attention has been drawn to the potential of e-enabled HRM to reduce costs of HR services and to liberate HR practitioners from routine administration so they can focus on strategic and change management issues.'

Gradually, since the 1980s, 'personnel departments' have become 'HR departments' and the same staff working in those departments have become 'HR specialists', 'HR advisers' or 'HR business partners', regardless, it seems, as to whether or not the organisation has formally adopted the principles and practices of HRM itself. Some of course have hung on to the old title of 'personnel department'.

ACTIVITY 3.1

Storey's '27 points of difference'

Study Table 3.1 and identify the degree to which your organisation conforms (1) to the criteria that typify traditional personnel and industrial relations (IR), and (2), to the HRM criteria.

An important point that should be made here is that the personnel and industrial relations activities that indicated good practice before the 1980s are still practised today using the same methods and techniques, but within HRM a new style of thinking underlies the practices and affects the degree to which the outcomes serve the purposes of overall corporate strategy.

Table 3.1 Storey's 27 points of difference

Dimension		Personnel and IR (industrial relations)	HRM
Beliefs and assumptions			
1	Contract	Careful delineation of written contracts	Aim to go 'beyond contract'
2	Rules	Importance of devising clear rules/ mutuality	'Can do' outlook; impatience with 'rule'
3	Guide to management action	Procedures	'Business need'
4	Behaviour referent	Norms/custom and practice	Values/mission
5	Managerial task vis-à-vis labour	Monitoring	Nurturing
6	Nature of relations	Pluralist	Unitarist
7	Conflict	Institutionalised	De-emphasised

Strategic aspects			
8	Key relations	Labour management	Customer
9	Initiatives	Piecemeal	Integrated
10	Corporate plan	Marginal to	Central to
11	Speed of decision	Slow	Fast
Line management			
12	Management role	Transactional	Transformational leadership
13	Key managers	Personnel/IR specialists	General/business/line managers
14	Communication	Indirect	Direct
15	Standardisation	High (for example 'parity' an issue)	Low (for example 'parity' not seen as relevant)
16	Prized managerial skills	Negotiation	Facilitation
Key levers			
17	Selection	Separate, marginal task	Integrated, key task
18	Pay	Job evaluation (fixed grades)	Performance-related
19	Conditions	Separately negotiated	Harmonisation
20	Labour management	Collective bargaining contracts	Towards individual contracts
21	Thrust of relations with stewards	Regularised through facilities and training	Marginalised (with exception of some bargaining for change models)
22	Jobs categories and grades	Many	Few
23	Communication	Restricted flow	Increased flow
24	Job design	Division of labour	Teamwork
25	Conflict-handling	Reach temporary truces	Manage climate and culture
26	Training and development	Controlled access to courses	Learning companies
27	Foci of attention for interventions	Personnel procedures	Wide-ranging cultural, structural and personnel strategies

Adapted from Storey, J. (1992, p38). *Development in the management of human resources: an analytical review.* Oxford: Blackwell. Reproduced by kind permission of Wiley Publishers.

3.2.2 HRM AND TRADITIONAL MANAGEMENT

So far in this chapter the discussion has been about the history, principles and practices of HRM, without significant reference to the theories of management that were widespread before 1980. Academics and practitioners have been studying organisational management for more than 100 years, resulting in several generations of different approaches (see Table 3.2).

Perhaps F.W. Taylor, the father of *scientific management*, deserves a special mention in this section. His approach to the control of the work process was through the optimisation of worker productivity and the requirement of workers to contribute, in a measurable sense, to the effectiveness of the organisation. Taylor's influence of the work process extended into recruitment and selection as well as job design and efficiency measurements. Taylor's view was relatively simple and common sense; the incumbent of any job should be suited to the job they were doing. The *New York Times* of 22 March 1915 says this of Taylor (Engineer, Inventor and Author) after his death on 21 March 1915. The obituary tells of how Taylor went about the task of improving the efficiency of a production plant, such as steel works and ship yards. The following is an extract from Taylor's obituary:

> A plant that he made over was made over from top to bottom. He laid out the system from the duties of the boy who carried drinking water to the unskilled laborers to the duties of the President, giving his solution to the problems of shop, office, accounting department and sales department, and emphasizing the necessity for the humane treatment of labor.

> ...Some of the big shops into which he introduced his theories of scientific management are the Bethlehem Steel Company, Cramp's Shipbuilding Company, and the Midvale Steel Company... (*The New York Times*, 22 March 1915)

Taylor's methods and approaches to efficiency in the workplace have not gone away. His basic ideas might have been superseded, but his thinking is still influencing the design of industrial, food preparation and administrative processes, from the submarines built in Barrow-in-Furness to the French fries we eat at McDonald's. How work is organised has been overlaid by new approaches to people management.

The *human relations* approach emerged in the 1930s. While the classical theorists were concerned with structures, physical working conditions, work methods, measurement and proposing formal 'rules' of management, it became evident in the late 1920s that attention should be paid to the social aspects of workplace life. It was the study of employees' social interactions, their attitudes and values that gave rise to the human relations approach. One study in particular that stimulated academic and practitioner interest in the motivations of people at work is the Hawthorne study, which took place between 1924 and 1936 at the Hawthorne Plant of the Western Electric Company in Chicago. This was when the importance of people's motivations, in the context of social relationships as well as the technical aspects of being at work, became evident.

3.2.3 BUREAUCRACY

Influential in how organisations should structure themselves for effective and efficient working was the sociologist Max Weber (1864–1920). Weber's most well-known work, *The Theory of Social and Economic Organisation*, published in 1925 after his death, was translated by Talcott Parsons in 1947 (Parsons, 1964). His work was the result of his study of the German civil service. In was in *The Theory of Social and Economic Organisation* he first used the term *bureaucracy* and said that, to some extent, bureaucracy existed in all organisations, in the private as well as the public sector. Weber drew distinctions between three types of organisation in terms of the kinds of authority that existed within them, which he described as *traditional*, *charismatic* and *legal-rational*. Bureaucracy is a frequently found form of organisation. Many writers believe that to some degree, all organisations are bureaucratised. Robbins et al (2010, p.436) say that bureaucracy:

> ...is characterized by highly routine operating tasks achieved through specialization, very formalized rules and regulations, tasks that are grouped into functional departments, centralized authority, narrow spans of control and decision making that follows the chain of command. ... The primary strength of the bureaucracy lies in its ability to perform standardized activities in a highly efficient manner.

Table 3.2 Early management theories and theorists

Classical theorists	Classical theories
Management practitioners H. Fayol (1841–1925) Major work published 1916	**General principles of management** (Administrative model of the organisation)
F.W. Taylor (1856–1915) Major work published 1911 See the *New York Times* at **www.nytimes.com/learning/general/onthisday/bday/0320.html** for a brief biographical history of Taylor's life.	**Scientific management** (The control of the work process, optimisation of worker productivity and the notion of a 'fair day's work')
Frank B. Gilbreth (1868–1924) **Engineer practitioner, Scientific management consultant** Gilbreth helped establish the Management Division of the American Society of Mechanical Engineers (ASME). He is considered to be the 'father of management engineering'. For a biography of F.B. Gilbreth, see Ricci (2012). *and* Lillian Gilbreth (1878–1972) **Academic and Engineer practitioner, Consultant** Continued with the Gilbreth Consultancy company until her death in 1972.	**The science of management** (Systematic management, time and motion study)
M.P. Follett (1868–1933) **Academic, Business management consultant** Follet, M.P. (1918) *The new state: group organization the solution of popular government.* New York: Longmans.	**Democratic management, democratic use of power, the notion of 'constructive conflict'**
E.F.L. Brech (1909–2006) **Academic, Business management consultant** Urwick, L. and Brech, E.F.L (1945) *The making of scientific management Vol. 1.* London: Management Publications.	**The framework of management**

Table 3.3 Twentieth-century theories and theorists

Human relations approach	Systems and contingency approaches
Elton Mayo and the Hawthorne studies (1924–33). Was a founder of what has become known as 'The Human Relations Movement'. Mayo became Professor of Industrial Management at Harvard Business School in 1920. In 1933, Mayo published *The Human Problems of an Industrial Civilization*. Modern society, he wrote, had destroyed 'the belief of the individual in his social function and solidarity with the group.' (Harvard Business School)	Trist et al (1963) *Organisational choice*. Founder member of the Tavistock Institute. His work focused upon the 'socio-technical' field of management and the concept of 'action research'. Major publications: Trist and Bamforth (1951), Trist et al (1963).
A.H. Maslow (1908–70), *Motivation and personality*. In 1943, the US psychologist Abraham Maslow published *A Theory of Human Motivation*, in which he said that people had five sets of needs, which come in a particular order. As each level of needs is satisfied, the desire to fulfil the next set becomes of importance to the individual and the need requires to be satiated. The top of Maslow's hierarchy is what he termed *self-actualization,* of which he said few people ever accede to this level: Mahatma Gandhi and Abraham Maslow to name but two. His theory is still influential today.	Burns, T. (1913–2001). Burns and Stalker (1966). The notion of the *organic* organisation form, which is represented by horizontal as opposed to vertical co-ordination. Also that of the *mechanistic* form, which is appropriate in stable operating markets. Its character is defined by functional specialisation, with a focus on defined task rather than the 'whole' product. The text explores the relationship between an organisation and its market and the technological environment.
F.W. Herzberg (1923–2000), noted for his work on 'job enrichment' and 'motivation hygiene theory'. He co-authored, with Mausner and Snyderman (1959), *Motivation to Work*. See also Herzberg (1966).	Joan Woodward (1916–71). Influential in the development of organisational studies and contingency theory. She wrote *Industrial Organization: Theory and practice* (1965). Her work, amongst other topics, stimulated discussion of the relationship between administrative practices and technology.
D. McGregor (1906–64) psychologist, Professor of Management at MIT. Probably best known work is *The Human Side of Enterprise*, which was published in 1960. His work explored the range of motivational theory and engagement. For an overview see: **www.psgoodrich.com/pc/docs/ARTICLES/HumanSideOfEnterprise.PDF**	

The theories and theorists outlined in Tables 3.2 and 3.3 were all concerned with different approaches to managing, and the theories were based on academic research (for example McGregor, 1960; Weber, 1964) and the experience of practising managers (for example, Taylor, 1911; Fayol, 1949 – translated text). (Note that Fayol's work first appeared in

1916, 'Administration industrielle et générale' in the journal (bulletin) of the *Société de l'Industrie Minérale.*)

Throughout the classical and mid-twentieth-century studies of management the accepted managerial skills were described as planning, organising, directing and controlling; the four functions were linked together through co-ordination (Fayol, 1949; refer also to Pryor and Taneja, 2010, for a discussion of Fayol and his works).

Robbins, Judge and Campbell (2010, p.4), suggest the following as the key managerial functions:

1   **Planning**. This includes setting objectives and making decisions about how objectives are to be achieved.

2   **Organising**. In this context, organising means developing a structure through which the work may be carried out, allocating the work to various staff members, delegating tasks and giving people commensurate authority to have them carried out.

3   **Leading**. Within this function, the manager 'gets things done' through people. It is more than simply directing members of staff. Leadership encompasses a range of skills and the good leader knows how and when to use the skills to their best advantage. The range of skills include the ability to motivate, communicate effectively, coach and counsel staff and to know how best to handle conflict.

4   **Controlling**. The manager monitors and assesses the degree to which predetermined objectives have been met. This involves identifying any shortfalls between the work that was planned and the work that was actually carried out. Decisions then have to be made about how to head off those shortfalls in the future.

3.2.4 CONTROL AND COMPLIANCE

Clearly, from the use of the word 'control' we can see that, before HRM, work was carried out because managers 'controlled' everything and issued orders while employees complied by applying their knowledge and skills to the tasks. As far as history shows, it was not until the Hawthorne study that employees were consulted about their physical working conditions and their attitudes towards their supervisors. Even after that, control and compliance still prevailed.

3.2.5 THE SOCIO-TECHNICAL SYSTEM

An important discovery made by Elton Mayo at the Hawthorne plant was that employees made decisions and took actions that were not planned or in any way determined by the managers. Previously, it had been assumed that productivity levels were the result of managerial exhortation and the fact that the employees were skilled enough to do the jobs. It became apparent that organisations have a social as well as a technical side. It had become clear to Mayo that a work group, which had been put together for technical reasons, also develops socially. It had been thought that variations in productivity at the plant were attributable to problems with the physical working conditions, but Mayo realised that the groups, in the social role, were making productivity decisions that were different from those demanded by the managers. This was a second source of power in the organisation, and the question of what to do about it became important (Mayo, 1933).

What became known as the socio-technical system (the organisation has a social as well as a technical side) was taken a step further by Trist and other researchers (Bamforth), at the Tavistock Institute of Human Relations in London in 1963, by bringing into fuller realisation the interaction between a work group and the task it has to perform. Their research was conducted into the 'long wall' mining techniques introduced into the County

Durham coal fields of the 1940s. Transforming the 'narrow face' mining techniques into 'long wall' faces, and at the same time introducing new, larger and more efficient equipment 'upset' the social balance previously experienced by the miners. Morale suffered and absenteeism increased. Tightly knit social groups had been split up, the new ways of working made communication difficult and differential bonus systems further exasperated matters. The organisation was really a social system and a technical system; the two systems interacted and this had to be taken into account since it was realised that there would always be an interaction between the methods of work, technology and social relationships. Earlier approaches to change had concentrated on either technical aspects (for example scientific management) or social aspects (for example the human relations approach) (see Tables 3.2 and 3.3).

3.2.6 HUMAN RESOURCE MANAGEMENT

A number of factors came together which brought about the right conditions for a change in the way business was run in the UK. British industry was tired. Many companies were operating with equipment which was in use during the Second World War. Competition from foreign manufacturers, for example the rise of the Japanese automobile and shipbuilding industries was strong. If these factors are then coupled with the coming to power of a Conservative Government, which had a massive voter mandate, the conditions were ripe for change. The Thatcher Government of 1979 had a strong ideological stance to reduce the size of the public sector and reassert the right of management to manage.

HRM as a concept was attractive to many organisations because of its unitary perspective by all employed by the organisation, its focus on the bottom line and the focus on the centrality of management. Indeed, according to Goss (1996), it was a little more than that:

> The development of HRM as a body of management thought in the 1980s can be linked to a conjunction of socio-economic factors – in particular, changes in international competition, the restructuring of industrial sectors and organizations, and a rise of a new confidence in the power of managers to manage.

Undoubtedly, the Thatcher* years of Conservative Government in the UK restored managers' confidence, and this was achieved in part by tackling the militant trade unions in the automobile, mining industries and print industries, particularly. All were considerably weakened during the tenure of the Conservative Government during the1980s.

*Margaret Thatcher came to power in May 1979 and served as Prime Minister until November 1990, when she stepped down from office and was succeeded by John Major. See **www.bbc.co.uk/history/people/margaret_thatcher** for further information.

3.2.7 A NEW PERSPECTIVE

Until the 1980s and the advent of HRM as a holistic way of managing the human resources part of the business, most managers had 'cherry-picked' past theories and were managing through an eclectic mixture of ideas drawn from past theories, ideas and concepts. Indeed, some are still doing that today. But there was an urgent need to reorient industry's focus away from the traditional view of management and towards a new perspective. The nature of business was changing rapidly, new technology had increased the speed at which business was carried out and competition had already become fierce in the global context.

KEY CONCEPT: HUMAN RESOURCE MANAGEMENT

Krulis-Randa (1990, p.136) says that in contrast to the 'control and compliance' models (see previous), HRM is typified by the following characteristics:

A focus on horizontal authority and reduced hierarchy; a blurring of the rigid distinction between management and non-management.

Wherever possible, responsibility for people management is devolved to line managers; the role of personnel professionals is to support and facilitate line management in this task, not to control it.

Human resource planning is proactive and fused with corporate-level planning; human resource issues are treated strategically in an integrated manner.

Employees are viewed as subjects with the potential for growth and development; the purpose of human resource management is to identify this potential and develop it in line with the adaptive needs of the organisation.

HRM suggests that management and non-management have a common interest in the success of the organisation. Its purpose is to ensure that all employees are aware of this and committed to common goals.

With regard to the second point, it is not difficult to criticise the notion that devolving responsibility for managing people to the line managers is 'something new'. For example, line managers have been responsible for people management since industry's earliest days, certainly long before personnel management was conceived as a discrete function.

David Guest (1989) defined HRM in a different manner. Guest defines a set of four propositions that he suggests combine to create more effective organisations (refer to Beardwell and Claydon, 2010, p.10, for a more detailed discussion):

1. **Strategic integration:** the way an organisation integrates HRM issues into a strategic plan. Integration is the operative word because there is a need to link with how line management operates, how remuneration policies are developed, and so on, so the individual parts become a holistic whole.
2. **High commitment:** is as much about attitude as the delivering of goals. In terms of the psychological contract the desired outcome would be for staff to work beyond contract.
3. **High quality:** this considers how management behaves and would include management of employees and investment in high-quality employees, which implies high-quality recruitment and selection techniques.
4. **Flexibility** for Guest is primarily concerned with *functional flexibility*.

According to Storey (1992, 1993), human resource management is a distinctive approach to employment management which seeks to obtain competitive advantage through the strategic deployment of a highly committed and skilled workforce, using an array of cultural, structural and personnel techniques. Storey (1993, pp.530–31) identifies

...four key aspects: (i) a particular constellation of beliefs and assumptions; (ii) a strategic thrust informing decisions about people management; (iii) the central involvement of line managers; (iv) reliance upon a set of 'levers' to shape the employment relationship which are different from those used under proceduralist and joint regulative regimes. Using these four categories it is possible to summarize the potential distinctiveness of HRM by contrasting it with 'traditional' personnel and industrial relations.

How these four key aspects can be interpreted and linked to the older 'industrial relations' focused methodology of managing people can be seen by referring to Table 3.1.

David Goss (1996) treats HRM as:

> a diverse body of thought and practice, loosely unified by a concern to integrate the management of personnel more closely with the core management activity of organisations.
>
> Armstrong (1999) defines HRM as:
>
> a strategic and coherent approach to the management of an organisation's most valued assets – the people working there who individually and collectively contribute to the achievement of its goal.

While it is clear that these definitions have similarities in that they all refer to the importance of people, the emphases are different. Goss emphasises the need to integrate people management more closely with the core management activity of the organisation. Armstrong, on the other hand, says that it is an approach to the management of people, whereas Storey says that it is an approach that seeks to obtain a competitive advantage. Armstrong focuses on what the employees do (they contribute to the achievement of goals). Storey, on the other hand, argues what HRM does with the people (it strategically deploys a highly committed and skilled workforce). In Storey's view HRM can be regarded as being ideologically {meaning – a belief system} and philosophically {meaning – the logic of how the concepts are interrelated and the implications of the interrelationships} driven, resulting in a defined set of interrelated principles (Storey, 1992). HRM is concerned with the employment, development and reward of people in organisations and the conduct of relationships between management and the workforce. It involves all line managers and team leaders, but HR specialists exist to make important contributions to the processes involved.

The Guest and Storey models are particularly important because it was they who took the American concepts of HRM, the Michigan (University) and the Harvard (University) models, and sold them to the British market.

However one defines HRM as a concept, it does not have an academic or philosophical underpinning but rather it stands as a belief. There has been much work done over the years to try to demonstrate its effectiveness and contribution to the bottom line but the inescapable fact is it is no more than a concept, but a well-refined concept.

Personnel management, as a profession that offers expert advice and assistance to line managers, is an early twentieth-century phenomenon. What is now the CIPD began life in 1913 as the Industrial Welfare Society. In fact, HRM, along with legislative changes, has added to rather than conferred people responsibilities upon line managers.

 PAUSE FOR THOUGHT

Who assesses your performance? Who talks to you about training? If you are given a task that you have never carried out before, who shows you how to do it? Does the HR/personnel department get involved? What is their role in the process? Who would you approach?

Two principles of HRM which are corollaries *{corollary – meaning proposition that follows from}* of the models and approaches to HRM discussed above are:

- A recognition of the strength of the relationship between human performance and organisational success – this generates the need to develop people to their ultimate potential as contributors to the realisation of the business plans
- The notion that there is a mutuality of interest between the organisation and its managers and employees in the survival and development of the organisation – this is the unitarist perspective.

Pragmatically, that is, dealing with issues sensibly and realistically, doubts may surround both these points, which call for the need for employees to be committed to, and involved in, the success of the organisation. Undoubtedly, there is a 'feel-good factor' that typifies employees' experiences of their organisation's successes and clearly this has a visible and positive effect on them. However, one could suggest that this is due to the enhanced feelings of job security that are produced when employees learn of the organisation's successes or satisfaction of personal achievement, rather than to feelings of personal involvement that might include, say, endorsement of the nature of the organisation's goals *per se*, or its overall achievements.

It is not unreasonable to challenge the notion that there is need to '...develop people to their ultimate potential'. If there is a fair exchange of labour for reward, and the job gets done, why devote further resources in developing an already adequate employee?

Having spread doubt about the viability of HRM as a believable way of managing people, one must be able to defend the position. The cynic would argue why he or she should be committed. A bigger question would be: committed to what? Is it the organisation, its principles or perhaps the line manager? If, however, we review the Storey or Guest models of HRM, then, in Storey's case (see Table 3.1), he suggests that there are some 'key levers' which are used to underpin his model of HRM – careful selection, individual performance-related pay and culture management being three of the processes he identifies. It does not, therefore, take a leap of faith to recognise that there is a subtle sense of control within this thinking. By choosing those (people) who 'fit the mould', there is a high likelihood that they will assimilate the principles and behaviours required of them. Engagement is focused on the individual, so relationship management becomes important and much time and effort is spent developing the 'psychological contract'.

 ### KEY CONCEPT: THE PSYCHOLOGICAL CONTRACT

The psychological contract concerns reciprocal obligations (and hence expectations) between employer and employee (Rousseau, 1989).

The psychological contract is informal; it is not binding legally. It is an understanding between an employer, probably a manager, and their staff of how 'things work'. The understanding is based upon past experiences of both manager and employee. The understanding centres around relationships which have been built over time and so issues of trust and respect feature in the perceived bond.

THE PSYCHOLOGICAL CONTRACT

 CASE EXAMPLE 3.1

Jane is respected by her supervisor Baljinder. Their work is to make sure that gas cylinders, which are filled with oxygen and anaesthetic gases, are delivered to hospitals, ambulance services and doctors' surgeries from one of the company's distribution depots. The task is vital because any delays in supplies may cause the postponement of an operation or worse.

Jane asks her supervisor for permission to leave work two hours early on the forthcoming Friday; she wants to go to her son's school to discuss some concerns. She believes he is being bullied. Both Jane and Baljinder know that, from past experience, the final two hours of the working week are when they receive pleas from some of their less efficient customers for stocks of gas to be delivered early the following week. To respond to these requests, trucks will have to have their loads altered, manifests *{meaning – the record of what a truck is carrying}* for the trucks, which are loaded during the weekend, will have to be amended and delivery routes changed; and that falls to Jane.

Jane offers to Baljinder to come into work on the Saturday morning and to update the manifests with the late orders and to adjust the route schedules. She promises not to leave until the job is done. Because Baljinder trusts Jane she agrees to her request. Baljinder knows then that she can ask a favour of Jane should she require help in the future. This is what is termed reciprocity *{meaning – give and take}* between them.

An alternative scenario, which also explains the concept of the psychological contract, would be if Baljinder agrees to release Jane early from her work and she, Baljinder, covers the final two hours of her shift. Once again there is give and take between the two parties and trust is built because Baljinder would expect Jane to reciprocate if there was an urgent task to be completed. She would strongly believe that Jane would 'go out of her way to help' (reciprocate).

An interesting question on which to puzzle over is, what would happen if Jane said that she was too busy to help Baljinder out, *in her (Baljinder's) time of need*? The psychological contract would be likely to break down. Once broken it becomes very difficult or even impossible to repair.

 KEY CONCEPT: HARD AND SOFT HRM

An analysis of HRM in terms of the style with which it is employed may be regarded in two ways: as hard or soft. According to Clegg et al (2011):

Hard HRM: It is assumed that people do not want empowerment; they simply want to be told what is required of them, be given the resources and training to achieve these requirements and be remunerated if they go beyond these requirements. People will be attracted by good pay, clear objectives and unambiguous job duties.

Further to the definition given above, the consideration is that there is a clear 'fit' between the corporate strategy and goals and the operational/functional objectives of the HRM department. The above approach would sit within the concept of *utilitarian instrumentalism* (see the following discussion of Legge) and has strong links to McGregor's Theory X (the notion that people dislike work and have to be pushed or cajoled into doing their job).

Soft HRM: It is assumed that work is an integral part of life and should provide a fulfilling, empowering and positive experience for people. People will be attracted to jobs that provide opportunity for growth and advancement; they will stay in jobs that invest in them as valued assets.

The above approach would sit within the concept of *developmental humanism* (also see the following discussion of Legge) and has strong links to McGregor's Theory Y (the concept that people are willing to work, thrive on responsibility, will engage with work and enjoy using their intellect to problem-solve).

However, Legge (1995, pp.66–7) points out that the two are not mutually exclusive. Hard HRM is sometimes defined in terms of the particular policies that stress a cost-minimisation strategy with an emphasis on leanness in production, the use of labour as a resource and what Legge calls a 'utilitarian instrumentalism' in the employment relationship. At other times, hard HRM is defined in terms of the tightness of fit between organisational goals and strategic objectives on the one hand and HRM policies on the other. By contrast, soft HRM is sometimes viewed as 'developmental humanism' (Legge, 1995) in which the individual is integrated into a work process that values trust, commitment and communication.

Allusions to these two features of how HRM may be interpreted and applied may be found in the theoretically diverse approaches to management that were expressed earlier in the twentieth century. For example, John Bramham's 1988 version of manpower planning adopts an approach that may be regarded as hard HRM because the demand and supply of human resources is calculated using statistics, employee numbers and costs, while the ideas of the human relations school (Mayo, 1933; Maslow, 1954; McGregor, 1960) may be regarded as soft HRM because they take the human factor into account.

From the employee's point of view, HRM has its disadvantages as well as advantages. Obviously flattened structures, which produce a greater number of employees reporting to each manager, restrict the scope for promotion since each worker has a long line of competitors for the next job up the short ladder of promotion. To some extent, therefore, the message that is communicated to ambitious, career-minded employees has shifted from aspiration to inspiration and the importance of their performance in their current positions. It all throws a challenge to the employer as to how they can motivate staff who have little promotional opportunity.

The challenge for management is, on the one hand, to engage with their staff, which of course is good HR practice, but also to reflect upon the nature of the work their staff perform. How can their roles be so structured such that they are felt to have an intrinsic worth, that is, there are certain qualities and features that make the role interesting, perhaps challenging to the intellect? Thus the work becomes absorbing and appealing to the employee.

ACTIVITY 3.2

1   Assume the role of a manager in an organisation in which there is little opportunity for promotion; the organisation has a very flat and non-hierarchical structure. How could you reward and motivate staff who work for you to maintain a good morale?

2   Now let us assume that your boss has moved on and you have been promoted to her job. What would you do about your newly vacated job that would make it more satisfying to the new junior employee who will be taking over your responsibilities in two weeks' time?

KEY CONCEPT: EMPLOYEE ENGAGEMENT

The CIPD defines employee engagement as 'being positively present during the performance of work by willingly contributing intellectual effort, experiencing positive emotions and meaningful connections to others'.

What does the definition mean in real terms? Helpfully the CIPD (2013n) qualify the above rather complex wording by explaining that there are three dimensions to employee engagement:

- intellectual engagement – thinking hard about the job and how to do it better
- affective engagement – feeling positively about doing a good job
- social engagement – actively taking opportunities to discuss work-related improvements with others at work.

ACTIVITY 3.3

Access the BlessingWhite annual Employee Engagement update for 2013, available at: **www.blessingwhite.com/content/reports/ BlessingWhite_Employee_Engagement_ Research_Report_2013.pdf**

The report contains elements of both 'hard' and 'soft' HRM. Clearly the soft HRM elements are associated with the three recommendations (see page 25 of the report and the accompanying diagram). It is also transparent where managers are asked to review organisational practices in the context of whether 'these help or hinder in our engagement efforts' (BlessingWhite, 2013, p.29).

The notion of soft HRM would not be unexpected since the essence of BlessingWhite is 'employee engagement'. The following is taken from their 'About Us' section on their corporate website:

'We are a global consulting firm dedicated to creating sustainable high-performance organizations. We provide consulting, processes, tools and training to:

- Create high-performance cultures that drive bottom-line results and reinforce your organization's mission and values.

- Develop leaders at all levels who can manage the business and inspire your employees.
- Align employee self-interest, energy and talents with your organization's strategy.' (**www.blessingwhite.com/aboutus.asp**)

They point out and demonstrate that, with their guidance, they can help improve organisation performance. The survey and subsequent report are produced by a company whose job is the provision of consultancy services; their business is to sell a commercial service. We should bear this in mind when interpreting results of their business endeavours and reading their literature, as would be the case when interpreting results from any commercial organisation.

1 Can you find elements of 'hard' HRM? You may wish to refer to the section within the report entitled: 'Disengaged cause drag: coach up or coach out' (p.31).

2 Discuss the table, p.16, 'Satisfaction', with your colleagues or class peers. Do you consider that the elements highlighted in the table are representative of how *you* feel about the workplace? Where and how do your views differ?

Comparisons of the working week

There is at least as much evidence of hard as there is of soft HRM. The culture that is found in some companies is far from benign. Next to Greece and Austria, UK employees work the longest hours in Europe and workplace stress is more widespread than ever before (see Table 3.4). Table 3.4 does not include data for Croatia.

Table 3.4 Working time: average hours worked per week in a main job

Country	All	Men	Women	EU Member?
EU (27) average	41.6	42.6	40.0	–
Greece (EL)	43.7	45.1	41.6	Yes
Austria (AT)	43.6	44.1	42.1	Yes
United Kingdom	42.8	44.2	40.2	Yes
Turkey	52.9	54.2	48.9	No

Source: Eurostat, European Commission, European Social Statistics 2013 edition

On the positive side, HRM is achieving the integration of HR strategy with corporate strategy in many organisations. Perversely, in terms of its unitary perspective, the coming of HRM has signalled the replacement of the *command–compliance* type of manager–worker relationship with a more colleague type of relationship. The new relationship implies that the employee works with, rather than for, the manager.

3.2.8 STRATEGY AND OPERATIONS

The hierarchical nature of the traditional organisational structure may be used to demonstrate the difference between strategy and operations. To the traditionalist, management is strictly a top–down function in which the strategic decisions about the future of the organisation, in terms of what needs to be done in order to survive and develop, are made by those at the top. This implies that an understanding of the purpose of the organisation's strategy need be known only to those at the top – the workforce being a resource to carry out the operational tasks that lead to the success of the strategy.

Modern thinking about management requires that all involved in an organisation should, to some degree, understand what the organisation's key targets are and how they are to be achieved.

3.2.9 STRATEGIC HUMAN RESOURCE MANAGEMENT

Strategic human resource management, on the other hand, integrates rather than separates strategy and operations. In this chapter we have seen that the nature of strategic decision-making has changed in order to remain competitive, with a new and greater emphasis on:

● the importance of having a structure that is flexible enough to respond adequately in a variety of circumstances
● the price and quality of goods and services
● the organisation's speed of response to customer demands.

In fact today, all of the functions within the organisation have to be able to show how well they contribute to the success of the organisation; and this, of course, includes the functioning of the HR department.

The notion that the organisation's activities are contingent upon the strategy, however, is not new. If you read earlier texts on 'management', you could be forgiven for concluding that the functional heads of an organisation were sitting around strumming their fingers awaiting divine inspiration for ideas as to what to do next. One of the CIPD national examination questions that was asked in the 1980s read, 'Is it possible to develop a manpower plan in the absence of a corporate plan?' Thankfully, things are different today. The classic approach to strategic human resource management (SHRM) advocates that HR planning should be integrated with corporate strategy, which as a concept makes more sense. Indeed, academics and personnel practitioners had been campaigning for such integration for decades.

In terms of the management of HR and employment relations, SHRM blurs the distinction between strategy and operations. There is a 'wave of strategic human resource management literature focusing on the link or *vertical integration* [see Chapter 1] between human resource practices and an organisation's business strategy in order to enhance performance' (Golding, 2004). Hsieh and Chen (2011, p.26) argue the following:

> Human resource strategy is designed to diagnose a firm's strategic needs and planned talent development that will be required to implement a competitive strategy and achieve operational goals. Since strategic human resource management links human resource functions with strategic goals and organizational objectives, organizations must carefully plan human resource to improve performance and achieve their intention.

We saw in Chapter 1 that the organisation's strategy is described in its plans, and that all of the activities or operations that are carried out internally and externally by the employees of the organisation are designed to contribute to the success of the strategy. It is, therefore, essential for those at the operational level to understand the strategy. It has long been known that employees derive a great deal of satisfaction from understanding how their work contributes to the achievement of corporate objectives.

3.3 ACHIEVING A COMPETITIVE ADVANTAGE

3.3.1 BEST-FIT MODEL OF STRATEGIC HRM

We saw above that Golding (2004) refers to vertical integration as a means of enhancing performance, but what actually happens? One view of strategic human resource management (SHRM) that is taken by some academics and practitioners is generally referred to as the 'best-fit school of SHRM', which assesses the degree to which there actually is vertical integration between business strategy, policies and practices and activities. This implies 'the notion of a link between business strategy and the performance of every individual in the organisation' (Golding, 2004).

Vertical integration therefore ensures an explicit link or relationship between internal people processes and policies and the external market or business strategy, and thereby ensures that competences are created which have a potential to be a key source of competitive advantage (Wright et al, 1994). Stavrou et al (2010) point out that the: '...'best fit", [is] where the most appropriate [HR] practices are dependent on context and adaptation'.

Figure 3.1 shows the classical *top–down* approach to developing an organisation's strategies: corporate, business and operational.

In Figure 3.1, the corporate strategy deals with the scope of the organisation, for example its prime purpose. It also deals with size and shape, that is, its structural configuration, and questions such as: how much autonomy is given to the different business units which have been created? The corporate strategy will also deal with the market segmentation of its products (high quality v low cost) and the financing plans of a company or organisation. A good example of finance plans would be the strategic decision either to borrow money from banks to finance a business expansion or, alternatively, finance the expansion from the company's own reserves of capital. In terms of possible alternatives to differentiate a product or company (market segmentation choice) consider the car market. One choice could be to enter a high-quality niche market, such as the 'high-end' sports car market. For example, such a choice would be represented by the Pagani Zonda Revolucion (2013), which can be purchased for 2.2 million Euros (approximately £1.8 million) plus taxes (Pagani Zonda website (August 2013) at: **www. pagani.com**). An alternative choice would be to develop and sell a product into the high-volume, low-cost, consumer market. Representative of such a product would be the Hyundai i10, which can be purchased from £8,345 (Hyundai website (August 2013) at: **www.hyundai.co.uk**). Hyundai, like many other car manufacturers, offers products which cover a range of 'market' requirements, but none equivalent to that which the Zonda brand occupies.

Figure 3.1 Classical (top–down) model of an organisation's strategy

CASE EXAMPLE 3.2

The annual reports of large organisations give insight into what is meant by corporate strategy. During the financial crisis of 2008 many motor manufacturers around the world suffered during the downturn. Many nearly went out of business. GM, one of America's largest car manufacturers, was no exception. The company was helped by both the American and Canadian governments (see GM's Annual Report for 2010). D.F. Akerson, the then chairman and chief executive officer of GM, writes, 'I would like to close this letter with sincere thanks, from every one of us at General Motors, to the American and Canadian people and their governments. We will always be grateful for their support in GM's hour of greatest need, and we are determined to prove that this was an investment worth making' (General Motors Company, 2010).

The 2010 corporate strategy focused on three areas:

First, we will remain focused on our top priority: developing and introducing great new products to our valued customers worldwide. . . . second, we will continue to sharpen our focus on how we engage customers. . . . We're doing that by listening to customers, taking a wider view to predict emerging trends, ensuring we have the right features and technologies in our vehicles to set them apart from the rest, and enhancing our advertising and marketing efforts to more effectively connect with customers. . . . our third area of focus is financial discipline. We will maintain a sharp global focus on cost management as we invest in products and technology and expand to meet increasing demand.' (General Motors Company, 2010, pp.4–5)

Using the General Motors Corporation Annual Report for 2012 (pp.4–7), available at **www.gm.com/content/dam/ gmcom/COMPANY/Investors/ Corporate_Governance/PDFs/ StockholderInformationPDFs/Annual-**

Report.pdf, consider how D.F. Akerson has refocused the corporate strategy from that he articulated *{meaning – to speak distinctly about}* in his Annual Report of 2010. What do you consider is the company's attitude to risk as indicated in the 2010 and implied in the 2012 Annual Report?

To obtain a more specific idea about GM's approach to tackling the problem of how to improve Opel-Vauxhall's lack of profitability, read the article by Chris Bryant in the *Financial Times* (11 January 2013) entitled, 'Girsky faces conundrum over Opel's profit and quality mix'.

Vauxhall-Opel has announced a 10-year restructuring plan that,

while acknowledging further tough conditions over the next few years, will have it breaking even by 'mid-decade' and moving on to 'profitable growth.' The plan, dubbed Drive! 2022, was revealed by GM Europe president Steve Girsky* and vice CEO Thomas Sedran. (Bryant, 2013, p.16)

*Stephen J. Girsky, Vice Chairman, Corporate Strategy, Business Development, Global Product Planning, and Global Purchasing and Supply Chain Director since 10 July 2009 (General Motors Corporation, 2012, p.17).

The next layer, below the corporate strategy, is the business strategy. This deals with the competitive strategy of the business and how it would, for example, manage its customer relations. The business strategy would also address development and marketing of its new products.

CASE EXAMPLE 3.3

THE BUSINESS STRATEGY

Consider how the Rainforest Alliance helps companies and organisations such as McDonald's (coffee in the UK) and Mars Galaxy Chocolate (in the UK) with their business strategy when marketing their products.

You will find guidance on how to answer the above question by accessing the Rainforest Alliance website at: **www.rainforest-alliance.org/marketing/examples**

The final layer in the strategic model is the layer that deals with operational strategy. This would be the level where the various functions that make up the business – HR, production, logistics, finance, marketing and so on – all make their contribution to the organisational goals.

ACTIVITY 3.4

Consider the following:

1   Consider how the various airlines market themselves and their services; for

example, explore the websites of airlines such as: Aer Lingus, British Airways, easyJet, Emirates, Flybe, KLM, Ryanair. From what you know of the companies and from what you have read, how do you think that these companies are differentiated? How does the differentiation manifest itself in the customer experience?

2   Similarly, a good example of differentiation in the marketplace is to consider how the main supermarkets compete. Some clearly compete on quality and some on cost. Discuss which ones you consider compete on cost and which compete on quality, and consider how this strategy bears on customer relations.

3   In the above two questions, consider how the company differentiation impacts upon the various human resource processes of: recruitment and selection, training, development, engagement and reward.

Research tip: When researching a company it is always useful to see if your college or university has access to Datamonitor reports, possibly via the EBSCO database. CIPD members have access to these reports by logging on to the CIPD website and clicking through to the 'Resources' section. Datamonitor provides:

. . .company profiles of over 10,000 leading UK, European and US companies including company history, key employees, major products and services, SWOT analyses and top competitors. CIPD has selected over 650 of these (mainly UK plcs, US Incs, and European multinationals) . . . Clicking on a company name takes you to the EBSCO service. CIPD website, available at: **www.cipd. co.uk/onlineinfodocuments/companies/ default.htm**

Clearly, the lower down the chain of corporate, business and operational strategy, the more thought has to go into how strategy melds with the one above or the one above that. For HR the strategy should not only blend with and support those strategies in the chain above but also it should support the strategies developed by other functions that lie in a horizontal line. For example, if the production department aims to develop teamworking or to introduce autonomous working groups, as a key way of improving business efficiency and staff involvement, the HR strategy must support this type of initiative. The HR strategies, policies and procedures would need to be tested to ensure that they either support teamworking or at least do not hinder and thus impair its effectiveness. For example, the HR reward strategy should, in this case, be structured to give focus to team achievement and reward and not to the rewarding of individuals.

    ACTIVITY 3.5

1   Think about the tasks you carry out on a day-to-day basis. Do you know why your job exists and how it fits into the grand scheme of things? How does your section or department contribute to the achievement of the business objectives? Were you involved in the development of your work objectives? Did your manager

explain how your objectives are linked to the overall business objectives?

2   Can you think of where the HR strategy, policies and procedures of your organisation clearly help or hinder the strategic intent of other departments?

3.3.2 THE BEST PRACTICE MODEL OF SHRM

The *best practice* model was originally researched by Pfeffer. Explaining the Pfeffer model, Marchington and Wilkinson (2012, p.55) state, 'The two terms – *best practice/high commitment* HRM – are used interchangeably.' Pfeffer's work has stood the test of time, with some later additions made to his original list, such as work–life balance and harmonisation – referring to conditions of service (Marchington and Wilkinson, op cit).

Distilling the information from Pfeffer (1995, pp.7–9), the following list of desirable attributes when managing people is evident:

- employment security
- selective hiring
- self-managed teams/teamworking
- high compensation contingent upon organisational performance
- extensive training
- reduction of status differences (harmonisation) – as Pfeffer (1995, p.9) writes, '. . .are egalitarian, in both pay practices and in having few status symbols, as in the John Lewis Partnership and in CEO pay,. . .'
- sharing information.

The emphasis is either incorporating all of the above processes into the human resource strategy (HRS) or bundles of say three, four or five of these processes. In this way specific outcomes – say in the development of employee commitment, because the firm will do all in its power to avoid redundancies – would be supported by carefully selecting the *type* of people who are employed and how they are trained.

The questions, of course, that must be asked are:

- How many and what type of organisation can, and do, adopt this model of SHRM?
- If an organisation does adopt these practices, would they do so for all their workforce?
- How does an organisation choose which, out of the list above of the best practices, are best suited to its needs?

Pfeffer and Sutton (2006) argue that business should take a research-based approach to the introduction of people management practices. It should not rely on the fact that, because a specific approach to rewarding people has worked in one company, it should work in another (company). Thus Pfeffer and Sutton recognise that contextual factors impact upon the management of people.

There have been many claims that these high-performance (best practice) approaches to HRM have indeed contributed more to company profitability than, say, research and development, strategy and quality (Marchington and Grugulis, 2000). However appealing these claims are, there is still a problem to prove, in absolute terms, that introducing these practices into a business directly contributes – proportionally when compared with other factors that impact upon profit, such as business climate and product – to bottom-line profits. The difficulty is in determining, in a foolproof manner, the linkage between how the management of someone working in, for example, the 'back office' finance suite of a car sales company has a beneficial impact upon the bottom line. The problem is demonstrating a causal link between the adoption of a 'best practice' HRM strategy, its impact upon behaviour and business outcome. Nevertheless there are companies, particularly public sector organisations, that take the best practice approach to managing their people.

PAUSE FOR THOUGHT

Consider the work practices in the company you work for or in a company that you know. Do you think that they take a best practice human resource strategy to managing their people? Does the company employ all of the seven practices bullet pointed above or a limited number, a *bundle*, of them?

ACTIVITY 3.6

Class discussion:

- Would it be reasonable or practicable in all circumstances for an organisation to engage all seven of the *best practices* from Pfeffer's original list plus harmonisation and work–life balance?
- Which two practices do you consider to be:
  - critical and thus would appear at the top of the list?
  - least important and thus would be pushed to the bottom of the list?
- Did you find it possible to get a class consensus on the priority of the best practices? What factors, when considered between class members, impacted upon their choice of the prioritised list?

3.3.3 THE RESOURCE-BASED VIEW (RBV) OF THE ORGANISATION

Unlike the *best-fit* approach to SHRM, which is a top–down approach, the *resource-based view (RBV)* of strategy is bottom–up. How can this be so? A bottom–up approach implies that it is the HRM strategy that informs, for example, the corporate strategy. This is exactly what happens. There are, though, a number of factors that have to be in place for this to become a reality.

In this scenario it is the human resource strategy that is informed by the type of people involved with the business. For a business to hope to have a sustained competitive advantage, it 'must have four attributes: (a) it must be valuable in the sense that it exploits opportunities or neutralizes threats. . ., (b) it must be rare amongst a firm's current and potential competition, (c) it must be imperfectly imitable, (d) there cannot be strategically equivalent substitutes for this resource that are valuable but neither rare nor imperfectly imitable. . .' (Barney, 1991, p.105). In short, skills have to be rare and not easily imitated or duplicated, nor is there a clear alternative in the marketplace. With these caveats in place, the organisation has a fair chance of being able to develop business and corporate strategies around its workforce. With staff who have rare skills, there is a need to nurture these talents, for without them the business does not have a future. In practical terms one could imagine a research and development (R&D) organisation having the knowledge and skills around which its higher-level strategies can be formed.

In practical terms one can think about an organisation, any organisation, having tangible assets, for example the equipment with which it makes things. An organisation also has intangible assets, things that cannot be touched or sensed – this would be the intelligence and specialist skills of its workforce. Similar companies, which operate in the same sector of business, chemicals, electronics, catering, etc, may, if taken at face value, look the same. However, their profitability may be widely different. The food and, in particular, the restaurant industry is a prime example. It is possible to have a perfectly adequate meal at the local pub, especially if it is a 'gastro' pub. However, the same meal at a Michelin Five Star restaurant would be defined by a quality of customer eating experience difference based upon the knowledge and skills of the resident chef. In basic terms both types of restaurants, the pub and Michelin Five Star, provide a meal which satiates the appetite but there is a quintessential {meaning – *the manifestation or embodiment of class*} difference of quality and so the cost of the meals varies. The word which describes this difference is 'heterogeneous'; two organisations, similar in structure, physical assets, and providing the same service or product will be heterogeneous {meaning – *diverse in character*} because of the way their historical context and developmental path to the present day has brought about different cultures, skill and knowledge sets.

Tastetech employs food technologists and scientists who develop specialist recipes for products which, when added to food, prolong shelf-life. Tastetech markets its products to large multinationals throughout the world. The company was founded in 1992 and by September 2013 had a turnover of £5.8 million (Loizou, 2013).

Key to the success and thus the value of Tastetech is its people, who encapsulate the technical and tacit {meaning – understood or implied without being stated} knowledge about the chemistry and production of food flavouring. As Janis Sinton, the managing director, says, when speaking to Kiki Loizou of the Sunday Times about takeover proposals, 'We get about three a year. . . . we are an independent company and a free spirit and we want to retain that. . .' (Loizou, op cit).

3.3.4 STRUCTURING HUMAN RESOURCES IN THE ORGANISATION

The structuring of HR in the organisation, according to Ulrich (refer to Arkin, 2007), is in the form of a three-legged stool, as below:

- shared services
- centres of excellence
- HR business partners.

Companies have adopted this model in various guises in the past, but as Arkin (2007, p.28) says, the model initially proposed by Ulrich has been transformed: '. . .that to deliver value, the HR function in large organisations needs to consist of the following streams of work:

- Transactional HR. . .
- Embedded HR. . .
- Centres of expertise. . .
- Corporate HR. . ..'

3.3.5 THE ROLE OF THE HR PROFESSIONAL IN THE ORGANISATION

Ulrich and Brockbank (2005) propose a model of how HRM is put into practice premised upon five interdependent roles of the HR professional (performance-specific roles):

HR leader supported by:

- employee advocate
- human capital developer
- strategic partner
- functional expert.

The way that Ulrich and Brockbank arrange the model is as a central circle, representing the HR leader, with the other four roles sited around the periphery. The HR leader is seen as *core* to the five roles because, as leader, the HR professional provides 'leadership to those in the business as well as those in the function' (Ulrich and Brockbank, 2005, p.24) – emphasising the business role of the HR professional or, as the CIPD calls them, the HR business partner.

The remaining four peripheral roles define the task of the HR business partner. *Human capital developer* takes on the mantle of preparing the workforce for the future (Ulrich and Brockbank, 2005, pp.24–5), '. . .often [developing] one employee at a time, developing plans that offer each employee opportunities to develop future abilities, matching desires with opportunities. . .'. As *strategic partner*, 'they partner with line managers to help them reach their goals through strategy formulation and execution'. As *functional experts* the HR business partner has knowledge of the business, they offer expertise in the main HR processes of recruitment, selection, promotions, training development, outplacement and so on, as well as work process design and organisational structures. The role of *employee advocate* is somewhat different because this role requires the HR professional to understand all their customers, including the employee, to be able to see the world through their eyes to best be able to express their views and, '...when the management team discusses the strategy closing a plant ... your job is to represent employees'. It gives employees a voice at the top table. This does not mean of course that the employees' views are paramount but what it does allow is discussion of the issues and perhaps judgements to be made on the best ways to proceed.

3.3.6 HR AND ADDED VALUE

HR, as a process, needs to add value to the organisation; if it does not then it has no place in the organisation. It becomes a drain on resources. There should be a clear line of sight between what HR does and business 'bottom-line' outcomes. 'The business-partner model is to help HR professionals integrate more thoroughly into business processes and align their day-to-day work with business outcomes. This means focusing more on deliverables and business results than HR activities' (Ulrich, 2009, p.6).

The challenge for HR is three-fold:

1   to add value to the organisation

2   to be able to show, to demonstrate, to prove how the function adds value

3   to communicate to its internal customers the value HR contributes to the organisation.

Ulrich (ibid, p.7) points out, 'As business partners, HR professionals will increase their focus on creating value for key external constituents: customers, capital markets, competitors and communities'.

The employee is not forgotten in the Ulrich model. The origins of HR as a welfare department have been buried in the passage of time. However, in today's capitalist society, the improvement in the welfare of employees is achieved through HR's contribution to the wealth of the organisation. As Adam Smith (1776, p.22) wrote in *The Wealth of Nations*, 'It is not from the benevolence of the butcher, the brewer, or the baker, that we expect our dinner, but from their regard to their own interest...'. In other words, by generating and contributing to the generation of wealth, we all benefit.

ACTIVITY 3.7

Priya is an HR officer for a medium-sized logistics and storage company. The company has two operational bases, one in Sheffield and the other in Aberdeen, and employs 200 people, including:

- a senior management team of three (managing director, finance director, operations director)
- four supervisors (Priya, an office manager, two logistics supervisors – one based in each operations base)
- drivers

- warehouse staff, including three apprentices
- accountancy administrators – who pay bills and chase companies who are late paying invoices for services received, and so on
- front-office operations staff – who market the company, liaise with customers, schedule deliveries, and so on
- human resource administrators and apprentice(s).

Priya is responsible to the managing director (MD), who also owns the company, for all the

HR activities within the organisation. She has reporting to her: an administrator who maintains the payroll, pensions and also organises all the training, and a trainee HR apprentice.

She is working in her office one day when Bill, the MD, walks into her office. He clearly has something on his mind. He starts a conversation by saying that he is clear how the accountancy team add value to his company. They pay bills for services received by the business and chase customers for unpaid invoices for such things as storage fees and deliveries. He then poses two questions:

1 How does her HR team add value to the business?

2 Bill has been approached by a local, Sheffield-based company who have offered to take over all aspects of HR for the business; in effect, they have suggested he outsource the activity. He asks Priya to write a paper detailing the arguments for and against outsourcing the HR activity. She should be clear about the risks involved but also the

opportunities that would present themselves. Bill says that he values Priya and she would have a job, in some capacity, no matter the outcome of the final decision.

Putting yourself in Priya's position, how would you respond to the managing director's requests? To help you develop your arguments you may wish to read the following two articles from *HRO Today*, a magazine dedicated to outsourcing:

● Banham (2011) Forecast 2012: HR experts offer their opinion. *HRO Today*. Available at: **www.hrotoday.com/content/5028/artful-predictions**

● Goldstein (2013) The time for outsourcing to move from tactical to strategic is now. So why isn't it happening? *HRO Today*. Available at: **www.hrotoday.com/content/5378/wake-call**

You may find it useful to access Accenture's website at **www.accenture.com/us-en/pages/index.aspx** and read some of the case studies they have in their archives on outsourcing of HR services.

3.3.7 THE SKILLS AND COMPETENCIES OF THE HR PROFESSIONAL

The skills and competencies HR professionals assimilate over time are learned through a mixture of formal education and training perhaps by following a programme of study developed and approved by the Chartered Institute of Personnel and Development or some similar professional organisation. Those of us who are HR professionals are expected to maintain the currency of skills and knowledge through a process of ongoing professional development. The question for those in such a position is how to identify those future skills and competencies because, to become competent, work on developing them has to start today! In our fast changing world, knowing, with some clarity, what is required for the future is a conundrum of the highest order.

 PAUSE FOR THOUGHT

Using a process of logic, think of your organisation or one you are familiar with, and reflect upon how the changing nature of the business might impact upon the type of skills and competencies required from an HR professional.

Use a STEEPLE analysis to help you think of the changes which are happening and might impact upon business and thus the HR function and the HR specialist.

Ulrich et al (2012) and Ulrich (2012) offer a way of thinking about the competency set required of the future HR professional. Ulrich (ibid, p.41) argues that business is driving change. He applies the acronym 'STEPED' to define and contextualise these changes that are impacting upon business:

- Society – urbanisation, family patterns, ethics and lifestyle choices
- Technology – making information accessible, timely and relevant, new industries created, old ones destroyed
- Economic – in the context of the rapid changes in the business cycle (see Kew and Stredwick, 2013, pp.162–3, for an explanation of this term)
- Political – regulations and general political trends, political unrest
- Environmental – how people feel responsible for themselves and the environment – the earth's resources are limited
- Demographic – age, gender and education and the globalisation of talent, income levels affect consumer behaviour (Ulrich et al, 2012, p.11; Ulrich, 2012, p.41).

His research suggests that new competencies are required by the next generation of HR professional. Ulrich et al (2012, pp.50–54) call them 'competency domains' and say these are likely to be defined under six headings:

1   The strategic positioner – which implies that the HR professional will need to be politically 'savvy' to understand the business and political environment and also relate to and take advantage of social changes.

2   A credible activist – which translates into being effective as an organiser, setting and meeting deadlines and, by implication, being recognised as a professional by one's peers.

3   Capability builder – to understand and thus recognise the strengths and weaknesses of the organisation and so, by implication, be in a position to build and also reposition the skills and knowledge base of the organisation.

4   Change champion – this is not new within the Ulrich lexicon {meaning – his vocabulary} – to be in a position to mentor and guide those responsible for change and to build a 'change competency' within the organisation.

5   HR innovator and integrator – here the focus is on understanding the employee, as Ulrich calls it, the 'employee value proposition', to create the environment, culture and positive psychological contract to stimulate employee engagement.

6   Technology proponent – by recognising that there has been a confluence {meaning – a coming together or merging} of social and technological changes to bring about the situation where information is demanded on request and is not constrained by location. The HR professional must understand the technical options and thus be able to maximise their use without comprising sensitive and commercially critical information.

(adapted from Ulrich et al, 2012, pp.50–54)

3.3.8 RESTRUCTURING THE ORGANISATION

One of the most visible features of the introduction of HRM in Britain resulted from the economic decline of the 1980s. The impact of the two forces of economic decline and a strong Conservative Government gaining power (refer to the earlier discussion on this topic) is picked up by Elliot (2012), who writes the following in the *Guardian*:

Margaret Thatcher came to power in 1979 convinced that radical action was needed to reverse Britain's relative economic decline. Interest rates were raised in an attempt to tackle inflation, with the pound – already rising as a result of the UK's booming North Sea oil revenues – allowed to appreciate further on the foreign exchanges. Even so, the annual inflation rate rose to 20% in Thatcher's first year in office and this, together with high borrowing costs and cheap imports drove 20% of manufacturing to the wall. (Elliott, 2012)

To compete effectively in a global market, organisations had to become more flexible and responsive, and one of the approaches to achieving these qualities was the restructuring of the organisation. The objective was to create a 'leaner and fitter' organisation that could achieve similar or even greater productivity using a smaller number of employees. 'Increasingly, organisations have sought to cut costs by reducing the number of employees who are not contributing directly to production or service delivery' (Claydon, 2004, p.138). Behind euphemistic {meaning – a mild term to replace a harsh reality} terms like 'reducing the number of employees' can lie personal upheavals and worry for those employees who have lost their livelihood. This is the hard, 'headcount' side of HRM. Using euphemisms to dress up blunt and perhaps harsh and emotionally weighted truths in milder language, to soften the language of communication, is the domain of corporate spin-doctors. As Pop (2011, p.146) writes, 'Redundancy and dismissal are one area of management practice that particularly suffers from euphemistic jargon.' Such terminology is now well established in the lexicon of business language. The restructuring techniques that are used to achieve the leaner and fitter organisation are as follows:

- **Downsizing**. This means reducing the number of employees at operational levels and reorganising the work system to attain greater productivity. Downsizing and redundancy are used synonymously. How the downsizing is achieved depends upon the organisation. A 'best practice' approach would be to offer voluntary redundancy to employees before compulsory redundancies are introduced.
- **De-layering**. This means reducing the number of staff at managerial levels, including middle managers and supervisors, to reduce costs. The result of this is a flattened structure in which a greater number of employees report to one manager. By doing this, the structure of a small production team might move from that shown in Figure 3.2 to one similar to Figure 3.3.

Figure 3.2 Tall or 'house of cards' structure with 12 employees reporting upwards

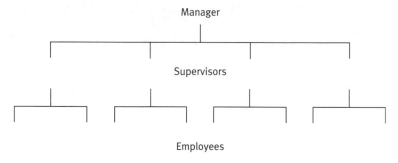

Figure 3.3 Flattened or 'garden rake' structure with nine employees reporting upwards

The structure in Figure 3.3 has only nine employees, since downsizing would also have reduced the number of employees reporting upwards.

If such changes are made, the expectation is that communication between workers and their supervisor flows more freely but with the same types of tasks being carried out. In all probability there would be a need for a training programme or some form of facilitation to ensure that the employees possess all of the necessary interpersonal skills to relate to each other in the new structure. In a larger and/or more complex situation, a programme of multiskilling would have to be introduced and work methods changed to reflect the new reality. Reducing layers has two further effects: it reduces opportunity for promotion and also, in a personal sense, impacts upon the jobs and thus the lives of middle managers.

- **Rightsizing** – '. . .is often used as a euphemism for downsizing, or de-layering, with the suggestion that it is not as far-reaching. . .. The term rightsizing implied that companies should determine and maintain only right employment for its requirements and increase their efficiency and reputation' (Pop, 2011, p.146).
- **Business process reengineering (BPR)** – BPR involves the fundamental rethinking and also a redesign of how a process works. It could be HR, finance or any other business process. The purpose is to achieve dramatic improvements in performance and efficiency and also to ensure that all the processes which have been reviewed are aligned with the organisation's strategy. It requires the active support of the staff who are involved in a process or one or more parts of the business. The aim is not to reduce employee numbers, but usually this is the outcome. How this process is managed, from a people perspective, is crucial to its success.
- **Externalisation** – often referred to as: *business process outsourcing (BPO)*, *outsourcing* or *contracting out*. This refers to activities that the organisation needs to carry out but are not at the core of its business. Outsourcing is a means of reducing employee numbers by having selected activities carried out by external specialist organisations, thus saving on employment costs and work space. The most frequently found examples of 'contracting out' are catering, cleaning, IT services, transport and security. Increasingly, as well as an organisation's administrative tasks, such as computer maintenance and payroll, organisations have outsourced the whole of the HR function.

PAUSE FOR THOUGHT

Significant changes such as those discussed previously have further implications in terms of employment. The instability (ups and downs) of the market means that the organisation has to be flexible enough to vary the size and skills mix of its workforce according to demand. A variety of techniques have to be employed when creating a flexible workforce to meet business demands in terms of customer service and shareholder expectations. We discuss this in more detail in Chapters 5, 7, 8 and 10, which deal with HR planning, selection, induction and retention, and human resource development.

The aftermath of a redundancy exercise can impact upon people in different ways. There will be those employees who have ability, a skill which is in demand, and also recognise that they have a worth in the jobs' market. There will be those who see an opportunity to do something different, because they wish to and can afford to do so – perhaps to take on a role which is less stressful or perhaps more in keeping with personal aspirations. There will, though, be employees who will not easily obtain replacement employment and become reliant upon state aid. They will feel undervalued and therefore will not value themselves; living will, in practical terms, become difficult. Money supply will become restricted yet house rental or mortgage payments, energy bills, food bills, and so on, still have to be paid.

It is worth reflecting upon the moral and ethical questions that arise when an employee has 'given their all' to an organisation and, after 20 years' service, is 'downsized'.

3.4 HRM AND CUSTOMER SERVICE

We all expect good customer service. Salaried employees are both service users and service providers. In our everyday lives we expect good service from the company who provides our mobile phone service, the checkout staff in the supermarket, and so on. In our daily work we are part of the process which provides a service to customers of the organisation in which we work. It is immaterial whether the employee is in a customer-facing role or employed in some form of back-office activity; it is the combination of effort which provides the overall service.

Read (2012) wrote the following in the *Independent* on the subject of customer service, as reported by the Financial Services Authority, by high-street banks in the UK:

> Two weeks ago we published readers' reports of recent experiences with the high-street banks. Almost every story told of woeful service. So I was waiting with some interest to see the results of the latest official figures relating to banking complaints that are published every six months by the Financial Services Authority. They arrived on Thursday and confirmed what readers had intimated, that customer service at banks is getting worse. In fact complaints about banking in the first six months of this year climbed 5 per cent to 828,040.

Read indicates that a 'rough and ready' analysis of the results shows that this equates to 6,215 people complaining every working day

ACTIVITY 3.8

In an organisation the objective is to offer a good service to its customers. The purchaser of faulty manufactured goods is quick to point out a flaw; it will be obvious because a part of the machine may not be working or the product may have been scratched or dented in manufacture or transport. In short, something can be done to put things right. The whole process, of replacing the item or agreeing some form of recompense, requires human intervention on the part of the manufacturer or vendor of the item. This part of the service package is an intangible {meaning – it cannot be seen or touched}.

As pointed out in the Read (2012) article, some organisations do not sell a physical product; they sell a service or experience: care homes for the elderly or infirm, hospitals, banks, cruise liners, and so on. These types of organisations do not provide an article,

something that you can look at and detect a flaw in its structure. The flaw can be pointed out and a refund requested. For those organisations that provide a service, the aim is (hopefully) to provide a good service. This being the case, there is a need to be able to specify, with some clarity, the criteria against which 'good service' is measured. From this starting point it is then possible to work backwards and to develop ideas about how an organisation can equip their staff to be in a position to offer what the customer requires in terms of service.

Working in small groups, consider the following questions in the context of the service you expect from your college, university, bank or retailer which sells you clothes or shoes:

● What constitutes good service?

- How does an organisation know whether it is offering 'a good service'?
- Is good service different from a quality service?
- Are there elements of good service which are generic {meaning – general, not specific} to all industries and sectors?

You will find some useful ideas about customer service on the website of 'The American Customer Satisfaction Index', available at: **www.theacsi.org/**. Particularly visit the 'about us' section, which gives some detail of how the organisation views customer service.

CASE EXAMPLE 3.5

CUSTOMER SERVICE IN THE NHS

Sometimes customer service becomes more than something that is important to an organisation, and of course to its customers, but something which is vital. Consider what happened at Stafford Hospital in 2005 and 2006. The 'Report [known as the Francis Report, 2013] of the Mid Staffordshire NHS Foundation Trust Public Inquiry', chaired by Sir Robert Francis QC, reiterated the findings of an earlier (2009) finding conducted by the Health Care Commission:

'On many occasions, the accounts received related to basic elements of care and the quality of the patient experience. These included cases where:

- Patients were left in excrement in soiled bed clothes for lengthy periods
- Assistance was not provided with feeding for patients who could not eat without help
- Water was left out of reach
- In spite of persistent requests for help, patients were not assisted in their toileting
- Wards and toilet facilities were left in a filthy condition
- Privacy and dignity, even in death, were denied
- Triage in A&E was undertaken by untrained staff

- Staff treated patients and those close to them with what appeared to be callous indifference.'

Francis, R. (QC) (2013, p.13) Report of the Mid Staffordshire NHS Foundation Trust Public Inquiry, Executive Summary

It is worth reading, at least, the Executive Summary of the 'Francis Report' for four reasons. The outcomes of not assessing the level of customer service are clear and extreme: people died unnecessarily. Some of the measures used to assess customer service were flawed, inappropriate and drove unintended outcomes. Thirdly, the impact and thus importance and relevance of an inappropriate organisation culture are highlighted. And finally, Francis offers some guidance on what should be done to improve the specific situation as well as patient care practice in hospitals throughout the NHS.

A summary of events leading to the public inquiry can be found online in the 6 February 2013 edition of 'Mail Online', Robinson, M. and Hodgekiss, A. (2013), available at: **www.dailymail.co.uk/news/article-2274296/Mid-Staffs-report-Families-head-NHS-resign-damning-scandal.html#ixzz2emvYDk4a**

Research evidence, for example the study by Whitman et al (2010), points to the link between higher levels of service quality producing higher levels of customer satisfaction, which leads to increased customer loyalty and, in the case of a commercial organisation, increased sales.

Each organisation needs to reflect upon what service means and thus, by implication, the behaviours required of its employees and at all levels. There are some generic considerations about service, which have been developed by the world of marketing. Schneider's (2004) research suggests the following:

- There is a need to access what the customer wants in terms of service and then to measure, using relevant feedback mechanisms, if the organisation is meeting customer expectations.
- Service quality and experience should not be reliant upon the 'luck of the draw' in terms of the mood or predisposition of the employee to be helpful or unhelpful when a customer has a complaint or query. The customer's experience is affected by the reliability and consistency of how they are treated – whether they call in person or make a telephone query – each time they have cause to contact the organisation. The emphasis is to learn as much about the customer as is practicable, because it is through having a thorough knowledge of the customer that the customer can be served. Important to the customer feedback process is to incorporate a loop which feeds the harvested information on customer perceptions back to those, at all levels in the organisation, involved.
- How the employee engages with the customer is important. The implication is that the employee needs to move from the transactional *{meaning – the employee simply does something without real involvement or care}* to a level which reinforces the type of relationship the organisation wishes to build with those to whom it provides a service – the notion of going beyond contract, having empathy *{meaning – having the power to understand}* with the customer's situation.

CASE EXAMPLE 3.6

CUSTOMER SERVICE EXPLAINED

Consider the following scenario: imagine going on holiday. It is 4 pm. The cases are packed, the taxi to the airport is due to leave at 6 pm and you realise that you have insufficient prescription tablets to take with you. You cannot go without them; they are essential to your well-being. You make a frantic phone call to the doctor's surgery, where the receptionist understands your need. She phones back within ten minutes and promises to fax an emergency prescription to the local chemist. She has arranged for the medication to be ready for collection by the time you can drive the six miles to the chemist. Above all, when the receptionist speaks with you, she does not make you think that you are stupid because, as she tells you, 'we all make mistakes when trying to balance a busy life'. She wishes you a good holiday.

The key to Schneider's hypothesis is that it is the employee experience of a climate of service that is a predictor of good customer satisfaction. What, therefore, constitutes a 'service climate'? The basic ideas that we can distil from Schneider's work are as follows:

1 'Good general management practices (supportive supervision, appropriate training, necessary equipment) provide a foundation on which a service climate can be built;

2 Service climate emerges by management focusing on service quality in all that it does (rewards focus on service quality, planning and goal-setting focus on service quality, measurement *{of outcomes – author's words}* focuses on service quality, employee competencies for delivering service quality are emphasised);

3   Those who deliver service to customers must in turn be served well by those on whom they depend.' (Schneider, 2004, p.146)

Point 3 above begs the question: who is the customer? A customer can either be internal or external to the organisation.

CASE EXAMPLE 3.7

THE INTERNAL CUSTOMER

Perhaps the concept of the internal customer is the most difficult to understand. Consider the HR adviser who, working with the finance manager of an organisation, develops a role profile and person specification for a new accountancy position that has been approved. Having agreed the role profile and person specification, the HR adviser then sets about placing an advertisement on the organisation's website and, because the organisation has a high profile, also in the relevant professional accountancy journals. Applications are received and a first cut shortlisting of the job applicants is proposed by the HR adviser to the finance manager. They then together sift quickly through the applications and agree the shortlist of applicants who will be invited for interview.

In the above example the HR adviser is providing a service to his internal customer, the finance manager. Whether or not the finance manager is formally asked by the HR manager for feedback on the service her HR colleague has provided, she will have made her mind up as to the quality of the HR adviser and whether she is happy to work and thus rely on him in the future.

Some organisations use feedback from internal customers in their staff development exercises using 360-degree feedback and some go as far as to seek feedback from internal customers for appraisal and subsequently remuneration purposes.

ACTIVITY 3.9

Customer care

In either your organisation or one about which you have knowledge, consider a response to the following questions:

● What internal customers does the organisation have?

● How can the HR processes of recruitment, selection, training, reward, and so on be used to improve the service that the organisation provides to its:
  ○ internal customers?
  ○ external customers?

Where does management fit into the whole concept of the service organisation? In the context of providing a 'climate of service', as espoused by Schneider (2004) above, he suggests that it is what management does that has a crucial impact upon service quality. This is supported by the work of Purcell et al (2003), who identified that the role of the line manager was central in the delivery of HR outcomes and the improvement in the bottom-line performance. This is further reinforced by a study focusing upon the link between HRM and performance in the UK health sector by Baluch et al (2013).

Schneider suggests that his research indicates that customer satisfaction is high when contact between customers and employees is high, speed of delivery is important, and there is high interdependence between service deliverers. Further, the nature of what is termed 'good service' is clear to all involved. For example, these circumstances come together when a 'crash team' at an accident and emergency department of a hospital deals with a patient who has suffered a serious trauma: heart attack, stroke or has been seriously injured as a result of a motor vehicle accident. Speed of response and reliance on others is critical. Every team member knows what is expected of them and of each other and, of equal importance, the service levels required. There are no ambiguities because the process has been rehearsed. This of course can only work well if management is supporting these activities with sufficient levels of commitment and resources.

The measurement tools for assessing the 'customer experience' also need to be appropriate. The overweighting on government targets, between 1997 and 2010, within NHS trust hospitals, arguably led some trusts' management to focus on issues such as 'waiting times' and not give due consideration to the quality of patient care, clean wards with available and attentive staff. The metrics {meaning – the type of targets} against which customer care are measured will cause employees to amend their behaviours and to give focus to these measures. This is particularly the case if an employee's appraisal results are to be assessed against these metrics which, in turn, are used to determine the level of the employee's annual bonus. The old adage of 'what gets measured gets done' is very true.

There is a wealth of evidence which points to the link between what is termed organisational citizenship behaviour (OCB), or locus of behaviour, and organisational performance (Purcell, 2003; Boxall et al, 2011). Others (Organ, 1997) argue that there might be a link but the link between OCB and performance is not causal. It is not causal because there is no guarantee that the development of organisational citizenship type behaviours, within an employee workforce, would definitely lead to improved organisational performance, no matter how this is measured. To improve performance other factors need to be at play. However, it is fair to say, the more an employee is willing to contribute through OCB, the greater the likelihood of good organisational performance. In the study by Baluch et al (2013) into the HR-related factors which impact upon patient care in UK NHS trust hospitals, they offer the following when discussing the impact of the carer (doctor, nurse, orderly)–patient relationship:

> By enabling communication and engendering trust, civility in provider–patient interactions is expected to facilitate quicker recoveries, compliance with recommended actions and more effective allocation of resources. Also, patients experiencing civil treatment are more likely to express satisfaction and positive effect than those who are treated disrespectfully... (Baluch et al, 2013, citing Lim et al, 2008)

 KEY CONCEPT: ORGANISATIONAL CITIZENSHIP BEHAVIOUR (OCB)

Organisational citizenship behaviour was defined by Bateman and Organ (1983) as those extra work-related behaviours which go beyond the routine duties prescribed by their job descriptions or required in advance for a given job. They describe OCB by referring to typical behaviours:

> ...that lubricate the social machinery of the organization but do not inhere in [meaning – exist or abide in] task performance. Examples that come to mind include: helping co-workers with a job related problem; accepting orders without a fuss; tolerating temporary impositions without complaint; helping to keep the work area clear and uncluttered; making timely and constructive statements about the work unit or its head to outsiders ... and protecting and conserving organizational resources... (Bateman and Organ, 1983, p.588)

Organ (1997) went one step further by indicating that, because the extra work or activity is not specified within the job description, it is discretionary. Those employees who do not engage in this behaviour cannot be censured or penalised, thus emphasising the voluntary nature of the behaviour.

For information about customer and organisational citizenship behaviour (OCB) refer to:

● CIPD factsheet on Employee Engagement, available at: **www.cipd.co.uk/hr-resources/ factsheets/employee-engagement.aspx**
● Fox, S. and Spectre, P.E. Organizational Citizenship Behavior Checklist, available at: **shell.cas. usf.edu/~pspector/scales/OCB-Cdevelopment.doc**

Schneider offers some measures against which customer satisfaction can be assessed; not all are relevant to all organisations but the following gives some ideas on the type of data which may be harvested:

> . . .total in the customer base, customers who have increased or deepened their relationship, proportion of customers who have rated the service quality as excellent or outstanding, and so on. On the other hand there should be some measure of employee effectiveness, over which HR has control. These could be: 'immediacy with which customer contact jobs are filled when they become vacant, the proportion of employees placed in jobs who are fully trained prior to replacement, results from monitoring customer-contact behaviour of employees (e.g. 'mystery shopper' programs), employee absenteeism and turnover (which is directly linked to customer account turnover). . . (Schneider, 2004, p.148)

As a summary, Schneider (ibid) suggests the following:

● Get marketing, HRM and operations management talking with each other.
● Put in place measurement systems that focus on service quality indicators.
● Do an analysis of the strategic focus accorded to all HRM practices, 'selection procedures (competencies sought), training programs (skills taught), promotion systems . . . performance management systems . . . and mentoring and career development initiatives . . .'.
● At all costs avoid the 'coffee mugs and posters' approach to service quality – this approach has no lasting impact.

What Schneider does not offer in his article is an analysis of what happens if the type of approach he suggests is not adopted. In many respects his approach to obtaining better performance from employees is very unitarist: it does not take into account third-party views, such as those that might be expressed by unions or staff forums.

Managing people to improve performance is not a linear process. Line managers, as the previously discussed research has shown, need to support their staff. In turn they also require support. It cannot be assumed that all people who find themselves in managerial roles have the skills required to fulfil all elements of their role. An individual who has a high level of technical competence would not necessarily make a good line manager. Selection criteria should reflect the requirements of the role and promotion, *per se*, should not be used as a reward for a job well done. This may sound perverse, but if promotion used as a means of rewarding someone for a job well done moves an individual into a role which is completely outside their comfort zone, the organisation needs to rethink its policies and procedures on reward management, perhaps by having a pay spine which reflects technical competence as well as management responsibilities.

Hope Hailey et al (2005), in their longitudinal study of a high street bank (1994 through to 1999), considered organisation performance and HR practices over a period of five years. The analysis of the study was conducted against Ulrich's earlier (1997) model of HR roles:

> ... 'administrative expert', which is process oriented with a day-to-day, operational focus, based on the management of the firm infrastructure ... the other process oriented role, 'strategic partner', which is future-focused, based on the strategic management of people and aligning HRM strategy with business strategy. The operationally focused, people-oriented role of 'employee champion', in which HR is responsible to employees, contrasts with the people-oriented strategic role of 'change agent', which is focused on managing organisational performance. (Hope Hailey et al 2005, p.51)

Hope Hailey et al (2005) found that there was, in their case study, a conflict between the people-oriented role of 'employee champion', which was left to an ill-equipped line management to fulfil, and that of 'change agent' and 'strategic partner'. As a result of this conflict of role (role ambiguity), the employee lost its voice. The focus of the bank on purely bottom-line (monetary) performance measures and cost reduction as a strategic aim can lead over time to both firm economic decline and employee alienation. There need to be incentives to encourage high-commitment strategies, with a focus on delivery of quality training and development, encouraging employee voice and so on.

 ACTIVITY 3.10

Working in groups consider:

1   What is the meaning of the term 'employee voice'?

2   Why it is given significance in organisations?

In practice, how can an employer introduce and sustain this concept in an organisation?

You will find some guidance from the following:

- CIPD factsheet on Employee Voice, available at: **www.cipd.co.uk/hr-resources/factsheet**s
- PURCELL, J. and HALL, M. (2012) *Voice and participation in the modern workplace: challenges and prospects [online]*. London: Acas. [Accessed 8 September 2013]. Available at: **www.acas.org.uk/media/pdf/g/7/Voice_and_Participation_in_the_Modern_Workplace_challenges_and_prospects.pdf**

- CIPD factsheet on Employee Communication, available at: **www.cipd.co.uk/hr-resources/factsheets**
- CIPD factsheet on Employee Engagement, available at: **www.cipd.co.uk/hr-resources/factsheets**
- Read how the Prudential UK and Europe, one of the world's largest insurance companies, has gone about improving its commitment to its customers through enhancing employee engagement and employee voice. You can access the article via:
  - The *People Management* website at: **www.cipd.co.uk/pm/default.aspx** or
  - EBSCO, Business Source Complete: Scott, A. (2012) Dear Prudence. *People Management [online]*, pp.36–9 [Accessed 8 September 2013] Available at: **www.ebscohost.com**

CASE EXAMPLE 3.8

BEING PART OF A TEAM

Consider the following article from *People Management* which depicts how Giraffe Restaurants recruit and manage their staff. Of particular interest is the explicit way that Giraffe involve their people, from all disciplines, in the business. Although the HR role has many generic qualities and many transferrable skills, it is important that the HR practitioner understands the business and becomes integral to delivering, in the case of Giraffe Restaurants, a good service to its external customers.

By: Claire Warren, 'How to work for Darren Cross: "We like people who are a little bit theatrical"', *People Management,* 24 July 2013.

Head of people and communications, Giraffe Restaurants

'You can't work at giraffe if you don't love people as we're a people's business. It goes without saying that you've got to love food and restaurants too. To work in HR or learning and development here you need to have real operational insight and understanding. You need to experience things to really understand them – when you are recruiting chefs, for instance, you have to know what goes on in the kitchen so we have cook-offs every month.

'I look for people who are interested in being closer to the business, who really care about it and who are prepared to get stuck in and help out when necessary on the restaurant floor.

'We like people who are a bit different – maybe even a bit theatrical – at giraffe, so it helps if you recruit HR people who have large personalities. My team needs to be able to identify with the kinds of people we have in the business and if you are one of them so much the better.

'The ability to work in a team is important, especially in a mixed team like ours where you've got HR, recruitment and learning and development. Much of people's time is spent in restaurants talking to and developing our teams so I look for self-starters too: people who like a clear brief but can do their job without having their hand held.

'We're a growing business [giraffe was taken over by Tesco in March, with the first in-store restaurant opening in Watford this month] so there are lots of opportunities for people. I love getting people into roles and then developing them – it's really satisfying to see them change and develop. I always look to give people an opportunity when we open new restaurants and that includes our own staff. Sometimes the best people are already in the business.

'With retail and hospitality being so fast-paced, we need people who are up for the challenge, who are not adverse to change and are resilient and connected to the end goal. I look for drive and real passion and personality, someone who walks in and has a great presence. It's about driven people who want to be a success and who enjoy being part of the daily operation. If people want to sit in an office from nine till five, that's fine – but it's not the right fit for us.'

Reproduced with kind permission of *People Management*.

The problem in essence, for HR, is how to balance the five roles of the 2005 Ulrich model (note: Ulrich updated his four-role model from 1997 in 2005). It is clear though that if line management is to fulfil some of these roles, for example 'employee champion' and 'change agent', that they need appropriate training so that they (line managers) understand both what is required of them and the importance of the roles. And this has to be reflected in the metrics *{meaning – the standards and measures against which performance is accessed}* against which management is measured. In the Hope Hailey case study it was found that line managers were geographically dispersed, their roles had been reduced and all this at a time when people problems were at their most serious. The measurement of their success was by recording the financial performance of their units (sales targets), not by how they managed their people.

In their study, Hope Hailey et al (2005) found that although the HR department, over time, took a strategic perspective, it did not set the conditions nor encourage employee discretionary behaviour. In conclusion the following is offered in the context of HRM and performance:

- The conceptual model of employee linkage needs to be extended by 'bringing employee voice into the equation, observing the processes implemented for creating opportunities for two-way communication'.
- Although the best employee policies (on staff development) may be designed, in the case of the bank it was the introduction of open learning centres. But if these cannot be used, because of pressure of work, their effectiveness is limited.
- High performance is not sustainable unless attention is given to developing innovative HRM policies that develop the firm's human capital.

Kaplan and Norton (1996) offer the 'Balanced Scorecard' as a means of, as its name implies, a 'balanced' way of setting and measuring business metrics *{meaning – a measuring system}*. These metrics are both financial and non-financial, and it is against a variety of outcomes that both the business, and its people within, can be measured. The emphasis on the balanced scorecard is that the mix of measures of business performance should be part of the information system for employees at all levels of the organisation. The balanced scorecard can be both tactical and strategic in nature and consists of:

- **financial measures** – objectives, measures, targets, initiatives
- **internal business processes** – those processes that the organisation must excel at to deliver targets for shareholders (for example increase in return on capital invested by 100%, increase sales by 30%, introduce new products into service)
- **learning and growth** – this could be a focus on mentoring, coaching, employee development, education, but, above all, there must be an effective delivery to relevant staff
- **customer** – how the customer should see the organisation (such as customer service, delivering on promises, dealing with customer queries, handling customer complaints, paying accurate salaries and allowances, handling wage queries and so on – in the latter cases it is the employee as the internal customer).

The above will work only if the agreed measures are effectively communicated to staff at all levels and each level has a chance to air its views and have them recognised. Refer also to the new Valuing your Talent initiative by the CIPD.

The following YouTube video by introfocusUK gives a very clear picture of how the balanced scorecard is supposed to work: **www.youtube.com/watch?v=M_IlOlywryw**

An alternative and detailed view of the use of the Balanced Scorecard can be found at: **www.youtube.com/watch?v=CFkyEi099Zc**

The NHS use the balanced scorecard extensively, led by the NHS Institute for Innovation and Improvement at: **www.institute.nhs.uk/**

'Googling' the above NHS website and then searching for 'Balanced Scorecard' will lead you to a series of webpages which explain its extensive use within the NHS. You may wish to reflect upon whether the NHS usage is somewhat over-complex.

Valuing your Talent and the CIPD, available at: **www.cipd.co.uk/hr-resources/valuing-your-talent.aspx**

3.4.1 MANAGING THE RELATIONSHIP BETWEEN HR AND ITS INTERNAL CUSTOMERS

Regular face-to-face discussions with, for example, the IT department, with whom the HR business partner is providing a general resourcing, reward, leadership and development service, are of immense importance. However, it is useful to move the 'taken for granted service' into a more formal arena. It is at this stage that service level agreements (SLA) can be incorporated into HR practice. The SLA is, in effect, an internal contract for service without the legal binding nature of the formal contract. This sounds a contradiction but the worth of an SLA is in its intention, and also the transparency that it creates.

An SLA covers issues such as who will:

- provide a particular service, for example the developing of a job description to be used as the basis of an advertisement for a position
- take responsibility for framing an advertisement for a position
- 'sign off' on the content of the advertisement
- pay for its placement in a newspaper or professional journal
- physically compile the first shortlist of candidates
- approve the first shortlist of candidates.

The SLA has many advantages. It forms the basis for discussion and in many cases stimulates discussion of and about issues, hopefully leading to clarity of service provision. It does not necessarily systemise the provision of a service but rather states: who is responsible for activities, who is accountable and thus, as mentioned above, signs off an activity, who needs to be aware of an activity and agreed timescales and budgetary responsibilities and, above all, how successful delivery will be measured. In essence, it gives a responsibility to act and accountability for performance.

 ACTIVITY 3.11

Service level agreement (SLA)

Taking the role of an HR business partner, think of an activity – in recruitment, reward, learning and development and so on – for which you could provide a service to a line management function. Working with a colleague, who will take the role of a line manager, develop a draft service level agreement covering the areas mentioned above – and any more you can think of. How 'water-tight' (specific) do you think the SLA needs to be?

It may be useful to think of a service level agreement in the following manner. Imagine that you are the HR director of a medium-sized manufacturing company. You have considered, as a trial, before extending the outsourcing to other types and grades of staff, outsourcing your recruitment and selection activity for machine operator staff. On what basis, that is, against what criteria, would you pay the outsourcing agency for delivering candidates suitable to be recruited by your organisation? Perhaps a mix of measures is more relevant than one simple measurement based upon finding an individual to do the job, for example:

- time to recruit an employee
- how closely the proposed candidate meets the job specification
- the perceptions of line management about the candidate after three months in the job
- whether the candidate remains in the job for more than six months.

You may wish to discuss whether there are any omissions to the above list and how many of the measures are truly reasonable and practicable to implement in a real-world situation but which are simply elements of an idealised wish-list. Perhaps, more importantly, the fact that the question about the type and content of level of service required is the most important part of the story.

A true service level agreement gets to the heart of what measures are important to the customer. Delivering quality service should not depend upon whether the customer is external or internal to the business.

3.4.2 THE EXTENT OF HRM PRACTICES IN UK ORGANISATIONS

How far HRM practices are being assimilated throughout UK organisations is dependent upon how HRM is defined and how it is measured. The Workplace Employment Relations Survey is perhaps a logical place to start when trying to assess the take-up of HRM practices. The survey, which takes place every four to seven years, started in 1980 in its current form, with the 2011 survey being the most recent. The results of the WERS surveys are a 'reasonable' but not absolute indicator of how HR practices are being adopted by UK workplaces. This is largely because of the extent and scope of the research:

> The fieldwork for the sixth WERS took place from March 2011 to June 2012. A total of 2,680 face-to-face interviews with managers were carried out. ... The average length of the management interview was 90 minutes. Some 1,002 interviews were conducted with employee representatives, 797 of which were union representatives. ... In workplaces with 25 or fewer employees, all were given the questionnaire. In larger workplaces, 25 employees were randomly selected to participate. A total of 21,981 employees completed the survey. (van Wanrooy et al, 2011)

The first results from the 2011 survey indicate that large companies, those employing 500 or more employees, tend to have some form of HR representation, over 84% with managers having HR in their title, but the majority of smaller organisations, over 90%, those employing fewer than ten people, do not have formal HR representation. Taken overall, some 45% of the employees represented in the survey had a manager with HR in their title.

The lack of formal HR representation for the majority of small enterprises is not an unreasonable state of affairs when one considers the market and production pressures these types of organisation are under. However, there is evidence to suggest that should a small firm increase its engagement with HR activities by developing performance appraisal, performance-related pay systems, staff development, and so on, profitability would be increased (Patel and Cardon, 2010). It is interesting to note that the major factor which appears to drive the smaller organisation to adopt HRM practices is the nature of group or clan culture within the organisation. The work of Patel and Cardon (ibid) suggests that those small organisations which develop an interdependency of working also stimulate an intensity of relationships and thus the ground is fertile for the introduction and adoption of a number of HR practices. There are a number of factors which mitigate {meaning – to lessen in force} against, especially small firms, adopting HRM practices:

> ...Adopting HRM practices often requires upgrading firm structure, which is a costly investment, and small firms may find adopting such practices prohibitively costly (Klaas, McClendon, & Gainey, 2000). For example, most small firms often do not have detailed performance management systems. This is because developing and implementing such systems require formal controls (which are not always preferred) (Cardon & Stevens, 2004) and require the entrepreneur to invest time (which is at a premium) (Cardon, 2003; Klaas et al., 2000). (Patel and Cardon, 2010, p.268)

Assessing the adoption of HRM as an approach to managing people by organisations is fraught with difficulties. Van Wanrooy et al (2011), in their 'First Findings of the WERS (2011)' survey assess the incidence of the 'strategic role' of HR by polling managers, some with HR in their title to complete the survey questionnaire. They also consider the incidences of: pay for performance (PRP), employee engagement practices, work–life balance, job satisfaction and training, and so on, as a proxy {meaning – substitute} for an absolute measurement of HRM adoption. Marchington and Wilkinson (2012, p.412) dwell on this issue. They do so because the question as to which HRM proxy to take is problematic in itself because of the lack of a formal acceptance of what constitutes the key HRM practices or processes. And, as they go on to argue, simply defining a characteristic which is unambiguous, in its representation of HRM, is a difficult task.

> ...Knowing that a typical employee has been trained for about five days per annum is hardly evidence of high commitment HRM if they are trained to conform to strict rules and procedures. Moreover, problems also arise when compiling scores of high commitment HRM as to whether or not each practice should be weighted equally. (Marchington and Wilkinson, 2012, p.412)

The WERS survey does, though, offer a 'reasonable like for like view of the tapestry of HRM', no matter how it is measured. In terms of the impact of the strategic nature of HRM, the 2011 survey (van Wanrooy et al, 2011, p.13) indicates that there is no significant change from the previous (2004) WERS survey.

> More generally, the percentages of all workplaces in 2011 that were covered by a formal strategic plan covering employee development (55%), employee job satisfaction (38%) and employee diversity (32%) had not altered to a significant degree from 2004. The only notable increase was in the percentage covered by a strategic plan that included forecasts of staffing requirements (42% in 2004, but 47% in 2011). (van Wanrooy et al, 2011, p.13)

ACTIVITY 3.12

Discuss the following:

- What metrics, that is, practices and processes, would you consider to be indicators of the adoption by an organisation of HRM?
- The extent to which you consider HRM is adopted in your organisation.

You will find some guidance by accessing the 'First Findings' of the 2011 WERS survey, available at: **www.gov.uk/government/ uploads/system/uploads/attachment_data/ file/210103/13–1010-WERS-first-findings- report-third-edition-may-2013.pdf**

3.4.3 SUMMARISING HR AND CUSTOMER SERVICE

The above discussions show that time must be given to recruiting people who can add to the organisation and who have the appropriate skills and attitudes. There is also a need to consider how to engage with employees, crucially ensuring that there is both upward as well as downward communication. It is essential that those on the receiving end of the upward communication actively listen to what is being said; failure to do this can have a detrimental effect upon the organisation's effectiveness. Managers need to effectively support staff in customer-facing roles in many ways, some practical by providing training and development and reward, some by providing and maintaining an appropriate company ethos and environment which encourages employees to exhibit organisational citizenship behaviours.

Clearly 'management' of customer and staff expectations is not an easy process to co-ordinate. To use one-dimensional measures of performance, such as company share price, can lead to unintended outcomes: employee stress, disaffected employees and lack of commitment. Organisational success and organisational improvement are very important but it is also important to recognise the need to give employee voice, as mentioned, and to encourage other high-commitment practices for those employees who will eventually deliver the essential organisational outcomes.

3.5 SUMMARY

There is a wide variety of views about human resource management. The concept has been variously interpreted and the style with which its principles and practices are applied varies among academics, practitioners and indeed from one country to another. The history of management thought, which began in earnest in the early twentieth century, produced theories that contain allusions to what we now regard as HRM principles and practices (Taylor, 1947; Burns and Stalker, 1966), but they were not introduced into British organisations as a totally new management system until the 1980s. This was driven by American research at Harvard University, Beer et al (1985) and Peters and Waterman (1995), who arguably created the justification and underpinning to adopt the new approach to people (human resource) management.

British managers, however, have a record of reluctance to adopt new ideas in the comprehensive sense; they are very financially orientated and change, which is always a costly process, is usually carried out in a cautious and piecemeal fashion. Differences between the underlying philosophies and practices in 'personnel and industrial relations' and those of HRM have been postulated by Storey (1992), who clearly outlines 27 points of difference showing how those who have adopted HRM have shifted towards a more open and flexible approach.

Throughout the *classical* and mid-twentieth-century studies of management, the accepted managerial skills were described as *forecasting, planning, organising, commanding, co-ordinating* and *controlling* – which reflects the work of Henri Fayol (1841–1925) (see Huczynski and Buchanan, 2013, pp.545–6, for further discussion of Fayol and his influence on managerial practice). By contrast, HRM engages the employee by changing the nature of the manager–worker relationship away from the *control* and *compliance* model towards a *colleague* relationship, meaning working *with*, rather than working *for*. Indeed, many organisations have adopted the title of *colleague* or some similar term to reflect the nature of the intended relationship between employees, at all levels, within the organisation.

There are a variety of definitions of HRM, each stressing at least one main feature that differentiates it from other approaches to managing the personnel function. These main features range from 'integrating the management of personnel with core management activities', 'moving towards a more flexible organisation in order to achieve a competitive advantage' to 'a strategic and coherent approach to the management of an organisation's most valued assets, the people working there'. The fact that there is no one accepted definition of the term leads to confusion when, for example, trying to define the incidence of how far the practice has been adopted throughout UK and international business.

Distinctions have been drawn between hard and soft HRM, in which *hard* HRM is typified by an emphasis on numbers of people, while little regard is paid to their needs. *Soft* HRM, on the other hand, is typified by a flexible workforce whose talents are nurtured and developed further to enable them to make contributions to the achievement of a competitive advantage.

Strategic human resource management integrates organisational strategy with operations, whereas previously they were regarded as separate entities. In this way employees' understanding of their company's strategy means that they should be able see how the nature of their work contributes to the success of the strategy and thus organisational goals. This, in turn, influences employees' attitudes to their jobs and encourages commitment to and involvement with the all-round success of the organisation.

There are three significant HR strategies: best practice, best-fit and the resource-based view (RBV) of the organisation. Practice shows that no one approach meets the needs of each and every organisation. A heavily research-based organisation or part of an organisation, such as a pharmaceutical laboratory, may adopt the resourced-based view with heavy reliance upon concepts and ideas, leading to strategy, which have been strongly influenced from within its workforce. On the other hand, an organisation which can offer only mundane and repetitive work, for example fruit-picking on a farm, may adopt a simplistic approach by giving staff minimum training and paying the national minimum wage. If an employee decides to leave, the business (HR) strategy accepts that another can be recruited with minimal impact upon the operation. This best-fit approach, as its name implies, takes into account internal as well as external factors, for example the particular example of the fruit farm would work well when the labour market is loose, implying that there are more workers than available jobs and so people can be found who are willing to work for the minimum wage. The best practice, or high road, approach to HR strategy assumes that the organisation has the capacity to invest in its employees, has the capacity to develop sophisticated ways of engaging and involving its people and, as a result, the organisation will reap the rewards by having a staff which is prepared to work 'beyond contract'.

As well as having some idea how to conceptualise a strategic framework, as discussed above, and thus inform policy and practice, Ulrich offers a way in which to structure HRM to be in a position to deliver both at a strategic and operational level and also suggests the essential skills and competencies that an HR professional needs to master to be able to contribute to business success. The work of Arkin further explores how HR needs to consider its role by considering the HR delivery in terms of 'streams of work'.

HR, if it is to be accepted as an essential constituent of any organisation, has to both be able to contribute to business success and also be seen to contribute. The essential tenet *{meaning – principle}* around which Ulrich constructs his thinking on human resource management is how HR can best contribute to the 'bottom line'. He explores this concept by considering how the HR organisation can best be structured and also by reflecting upon the competency sets that the HR practitioner, at all levels within an organisation, needs to master, as described above. One can also explore how HR can contribute by considering what HR does, as a function, from the perspective of its role both as a service provider and functional lead. HR has a role in the development of tools to engage and to encourage staff to 'go beyond' their written contract of service by demonstrating *organisational citizenship behaviours* (Baluch et al, 2013). Key to business success is customer service, which can to be considered in a multi-layered manner. Customers can be internal to as well as external to an organisation. Measuring organisation performance should not simply focus on one measure, such as share price or profitability, but recognise, as Kaplan and Norton (1996) propose, a balanced spread of measures. Schneider (2004) suggests that measures which focus on 'employee contribution' should take account of how employees engage with customers.

REVIEW QUESTIONS

1 If you were asked, 'What is the difference between personnel management and human resource management?' what would be your interpretation?

2 What do you understand by the following terms:

   ● unitarist?
   ● pluralist?

3 How might the introduction of HRM into an organisation affect how the non-personnel functions are managed?

4 Do you consider that it is problematic, from a practical perspective, that there is no one accepted definition of what is meant by HRM?

5 It has been said that the adoption of HRM is not the only way to achieve a competitive advantage. To what does this statement refer?

6 What is meant by the terms 'hard' and 'soft' HRM?

7 Henri Fayol (1841–1925) postulated {meaning – *suggest the existence of*} that the core managerial skills were: forecasting, planning, organising, commanding, co-ordinating and controlling. Consider whether, and by how much, Fayol's nineteenth-century work still has relevance in today's twenty-first-century business society.

8 What is the main reason why an organisation would take up HRM? What factors impact the most on small organisations when considering the adoption of HRM practices?

9 What events brought about the rise of HRM?

10 Why does the 'best-fit school of strategic human resource management' measure the degree to which there is vertical integration within an organisation?

11 Of the three SHRM resourcing strategies discussed within the chapter – *best-fit*, *best practice* and *resource-based view* – which is more likely to be present in British industry? Which type of organisation is likely to have adopted the *best practice* model of HRM?

12 Read Anat Arkin's (2007) article in *People Management* listed in the references at the end of the book and discuss what you understand by, in the modified Ulrich model, the following roles: transactional HR, embedded HR, centres of expertise and corporate HR.

13 What skills and competencies does the twenty-first-century HR practitioner need to develop?

14 What is good practice when considering the link between HRM and customer service? What is meant by *organisational citizenship behaviour*? Why is it important for organisations to consider this concept when recruiting, developing and training people?

15 Discuss how you could use, perhaps in a simple way, the balanced scorecard to measure the way you run your life. What performance measures would you place on yourself?

16 What is a service level agreement (SLA)? What are the advantages of using SLAs?

EXPLORE FURTHER

BOOKS

DESSLER, G. (2014) *Fundamentals of human resource management.* Harlow: Pearson Education.

An American text but relevant in today's business world. It is very well illustrated, contains some good examples of HR practice and self-assessment tests.

LEATHERBARROW, C. (2014) HRM: the added value debate. *in* REES, G. and SMITH, P. (eds) *Strategic human resource management: an international perspective.* London: SAGE.

This chapter explores, in some detail, both the academic and practical debate about the issues and difficulties of measuring the contribution of HR to an organisation's success. However, for the practitioner it does offer some ideas, based upon research, how in a practical sense HR can add value and, importantly, demonstrate how it is adding value.

MARCHINGTON, M. and WILKINSON, A. (2012) *Human resource management at work,* 5th ed. London: CIPD.

A comprehensive text on human resource theory and practice and, although targeted at the postgraduate study market, the text has relevance for those who are just starting their formal education in HR because it offers insights into various elements of HRM. Each of the chapters is standalone so students can 'graze' sections in which they have an interest.

PILBEAM, S. and CORBRIDGE, M. (2010) *People resourcing and talent planning: HRM in practice.* Harlow: Pearson Education Ltd.

Although a postgraduate text, Pilbeam and Corbridge's book is very accessible. Chapter 1 deals with the changing nature of the role of the HR professional and introduces the concept of HR strategy. Chapter 2 deals, in more depth, with the ideas around HR strategy and also offers some critique of the concepts.

JOURNAL ARTICLES

GRUMMAN, J.A. and SAKS, A.M. (2011) Performance management and employee engagement. *Human Resource Management Review [online].* **21**(2), pp.123–36.

GRANT, A. (2013) Givers take all: The hidden dimension of corporate culture. *McKinsey Quarterly [online].* (2), pp.52–65 [Accessed 15 September 2013]. Available at: www.ebscohost.com

The above article is interesting because it considers some practical research into improving how the American secret service works by encouraging sharing information. It has strong links to *organisational citizenship behaviour.*

MURPHY, R.M. (2011) Happy campers. *Fortune [online].* **63**(12) p.71. [Accessed 15 September 2013]. Available at: www.ebscohost.com

The abstract states, 'The article presents information on several companies that were considered among the best 100 companies to work for in 2010 [in the USA] including online retailer Zappos, film production company DreamWorks Animation, and nonprofit education company Teach for America (TFA)....'

WEB LINKS

Watch the video, 'Kellogg's HR Shared Services Transformation Success', available at: **www.youtube.com/watch?v=aOn1PS96p_g** and compare this with the model suggested by Ulrich.

In a similar context as the Kellogg video above, watch and listen to what Dave Ulrich has to say about transforming HR in an organisation, 'Dave Ulrich – HR transformation model', available at: **www.youtube.com/watch?v=Y1sre3ayoJg**

Watch the salutary story of the ant and think about how the moral of the tale relates to effective human resource management, 'The Ant Story' by Shreekanth Dangi, available at: **www.youtube.com/watch?v=ejw9Coycfcw**

Access the Shell Global website at: **www.shell.com/global/aboutshell/careers/ professionals/job-areas/commercial/human-resources.html** and read how Shell has structured its HR organisation to meet the needs of the business. Compare this by accessing the website of the Ford Motor Company at **www.corporate.ford.com/ careers/career-paths/human-resources?&ccode=GB** and similar large organisations to 'achieve a feel' for how they address human resource management.

See how Mark O'Donnell, Director and Practice Leader, Human Capital Advisory Services of Deloitte, addresses 'Defining Value and Measuring HR', available at: **www.slideshare.net/sonyacurley/defining-value-and-measuring-hr**

As above, read what Jamrog has to say about 'The Future of HR Metrics', by J.J. Jamrog of the Jamrog Institute, available at: **www.slideshare.net/Jackie72/future-of-hr-metrics-a-brave-new-world**

CHAPTER 4

The Role of the HR Practitioner

LEARNING OBJECTIVES

After studying this chapter you should understand:

- the varied roles and responsibilities of HR practitioners
- the distinction between operational and strategic HR activities
- the range and scope of the activities of the HR practitioner
- the structure and uses of HR information systems and records
- the performance standards that are expected of an HR professional
- the code of conduct expected of HR professionals
- some of the future challenges for the HR practitioner.

4.1 INTRODUCTION

This chapter examines and discusses what an HR practitioner actually does. You will see that HR covers a wide variety of roles and activities – from 'strategic' (dealing with organisational plans for change, for example closure of a factory or moving the business to another part of the country) to day-to-day sorting out of employee problems (helping staff to settle into a new job as a result of the organisational change perhaps). This calls for a range of skills and in the chapter we look at the performance standards that are expected of the practitioner and the code of conduct to which they are expected to adhere. Historically the role was primarily confined to looking after the welfare of employees – personnel underpinned the whole employee lifecycle while making sure the employment legislation was adhered to. But the role has grown over the years, broadening out into a much wider range of areas – from administration through to organisational strategy. HR has become embedded into the heart of the business, becoming more strategic and thus helping improve organisation performance through people.

In the HR field, practitioners operate at several levels, with the tasks and responsibilities varying according to their level and status. For example, those in senior positions – HR managers or directors – are involved in departmental management, corporate strategy and HR policy formulation, while those in the middle ranks may be specialists in particular areas such as talent management, employee relations or resourcing. Lower down still, HR officers and administrators carry out tasks at operational level, dealing with everyday problems, such as handling disciplinary hearings, interviewing applicants for jobs, and so on. The range and scope of HR activities is wide, and it is possible to become a specialist in one of the main functions, or to operate as a generalist and work in several of the functions.

How HR practitioners operate in this respect determines, to some extent, the structure of the HR department. If practitioners operate as 'specialists', the department is divided into sections according to the main functions and activities, for example recruitment, employee relations, learning and development and so on. Where practitioners are generalists, the structure may mean that each practitioner is responsible for all HR requirements in a particular department or area of the organisation. There are, however, wide variations in the ways that organisations structure their HR departments.

What HR people actually do depends on the needs and HR policies of the particular organisation in which they work, and of course on their own individual capabilities. It is often the case that particularly in small companies HR practitioners are asked to carry out all kinds of roles, from marketing, arranging social activities and events, to buying flowers for someone who is sick! A job in HR is extremely varied – you never know what challenges each day will bring!

'Human resource management covers a vast array of activities and shows a huge range of variations across occupations, organizational levels, business units, firms, industries and societies' (Boxall, 2007, p.48).

ACTIVITY 4.1

Talk to some of the staff in your HR department and find out what activities they undertake. What are some of the most unusual activities they have been asked to perform?

If your organisation does not have an HR function, find out who does the HR-related work, such as recruitment, handling disciplinary hearings, and so on?

In some small companies, of course, there may not even be an HR department. HR may be seen as part of other job roles: line managers, administrators or owners, for example. Some of you reading this book may have responsibility for HR even though your job title does not specifically include it; you may be involved in recruitment, sorting out induction, welfare or training, for example, even though you are not officially classed as 'HR'.

Table 4.1 is an analysis of the levels at which HR practitioners normally operate and their duties and responsibilities.

ACTIVITY 4.2

What is the structure of HR in your organisation? Are there specialists or generalists? Or both? Or none!?

Table 4.1 Example of an analysis of HR responsibilities

Level	Responsibility and specialism
Senior HR managers	Participation in corporate-level strategic decision-making Formulation of HR strategy and policies Advising other managers on the implementation of HR policies and procedures Acting as a figurehead and spokesperson on issues such as redundancy or company changes
Middle-level HR managers and specialists	Managing 'specialist' sections such as: • HR planning • recruitment and selection • employee development • performance and reward • employee relations • health and safety management and welfare/well-being Or – managing an HR department that covers any combination of the above!
HR officers and administrators	Day-to-day administration of the HR department Advising line managers on employee issues Ensuring efficient organisation of events including: interviews, induction and training Dealing with employee problems, grievances, disciplinary issues and so on Giving advice on a broad range of employee issues, for example welfare, pay, conditions, leave, employee rights, and so on Producing data on retention, turnover, absence, and so on Updating and maintaining secure and confidential records
If there is no HR function – HR is often carried out by administrators/owners/ managers.	Usually the welfare-type activities relating to individuals at work, such as absence, annual leave, pay, disciplinary hearings, recruitment and selection, induction, training and performance management

Table 4.1 is, of course, only an example, since organisations differ in how they deploy their HR staff. It does, however, give a broad indication of the kinds of responsibility and tasks that are carried out at each level. The list of activities is long and varied.

 ACTIVITY 4.3

From your answers to Activity 4.1, how does the list in Table 4.1 compare with what HR does in your organisation? Are all of these activities covered? If you don't have HR in the organisation, are all of these activities covered by someone else, such as administration or finance departments? Or are they just 'not done'?

PAUSE FOR THOUGHT

Of course, in reality, the divisions noted in Table 4.1 may not be so clear. Depending on the size and structure of the organisation, HR staff may be involved in both developing strategic direction and also dealing with day-to-day issues, for instance around the employment contract. See Chapter 16, 'Understanding Employment Law', for more on this.

4.2 THE RANGE AND SCOPE OF HR ACTIVITIES

Most people have some understanding of what the HR department does, primarily because a new employee's first contact with an organisation is usually through the recruitment and selection process, which is normally organised by HR. Once in employment the first place for employees to seek advice on problems regarding pay, terms and conditions or training needs is the HR department. But beyond these activities, many people have little understanding of the complex roles played by HR.

In a recession or poor economic climate, much of the job in HR is involved in the 'difficult' areas, such as handling redundancies, redeploying staff and allaying fears about changes in the organisation. These areas require specialised knowledge and skills and, very often, knowledge of the law.

As we mentioned in Chapter 3, Ulrich (2005) and Ulrich and Brockbank (2008) identified the roles of HR specialists as falling into the following categories:

- employee advocate
- functional expert
- human capital developer
- strategic partner
- HR leader.

Employee advocate: This is closely linked with the historical role of the welfare officer, in which HR has its roots. This role focuses on understanding the needs of the employees but also communicating with and on behalf of them. This role might be important, for example, if there are changes happening in the organisation. Staff may worry about redundancies or job changes and HR are seen as a mediator who will ensure 'fair play'. This role can include discipline and grievance as well as discrimination issues.

Functional expert: This is where the HR practitioner will use their expertise and knowledge to undertake specialist HR practices, for example recruitment and selection or performance and reward. It may be an administrative role or one where advice and guidance is given to line managers.

Human capital developer: This role is about training and developing staff to ensure they have the right skills, knowledge and attitudes to do their jobs. It can also encompass knowledge management – the need to develop knowledge, innovation and creativity within the business.

Strategic partner or 'business partner': This is a higher-level role, with involvement in organisational strategy. It is about ensuring that HR has an input into how the business runs and that HR policies and procedures are in line with where the business is going. Having an HR director on the company board who can advise on where HR can help the organisation to achieve its objectives can be important here.

HR leader: This involves leading the HR function, setting goals and working with all parts of the business on HR. This role is not just at the top of the organisation – *all* HR managers should be leaders.

Ulrich and Brockbank (2008) suggest that 'the HR profession as a whole is quickly moving to add greater value through a more strategic focus'. Ulrich et al (2012) have added to the competences of HR and list these as:

- strategic positioner
- credible activist
- capability builder
- change champion
- human resource innovator and integrator
- technology proponent.

Rather than repeat the descriptions here, see Chapter 3, 'Human Resource Management', for further details.

Armstrong (2014) offers a slightly different model, describing the roles as follows:

- **General role:** helping to improve organisational capability, acting as facilitators, formulating integrated HR strategies, giving guidance on core values and ethical principles.
- **Service delivery role:** emphasis on transactional activities, such as recruitment, training, employment law and day-to-day employment matters. Often seen by line managers as more important than the strategic role.
- **Strategic role:** a transformational role. This involves formulation and implementation of HR strategies based on the needs of the organisation, aligned to business objectives and integrated with each other. This includes contributing to development of business strategies (such as advising on best use of human resources and talent) and supporting line management on strategy implementation.
- **Business partner role:** this involves sharing responsibility with line managers for the success of the enterprise. It means adding value through HR initiatives that make a contribution to organisational success.
- **Innovation role:** introducing new processes and procedures to increase organisational effectiveness.
- **Change agent role:** facilitating change by providing advice and support on its introduction and management.

(adapted from Armstrong, 2014)

As we can see, there are some similarities between the two models. The roles will be carried out differently, depending on the context in which HR are working (for example size and type of organisation, the organisation culture, values, and so on).

Table 4.1 showed the ideal situation in which senior HR managers are involved at the top level. They formulate HR strategy and policies, ensure that these are integrated into the overall corporate strategy and they offer guidance to other senior managers on the implementation of policy. The aim of the business partner model is to help HR professionals align their work with business outcomes and to integrate more thoroughly into business processes.

Top-level managers rely on the expertise of HR managers for guidance on such matters as the availability of particular knowledge and skills in the internal and external labour markets (see Chapter 5), since the employment of people with appropriate knowledge and skills is essential for the achievement of objectives.

Historically HR has been perceived as a service provider: such as recruitment and selection, human resource planning, training, health and safety, employee relations, reward, and so on. HR should focus on providing an efficient and effective service to managers to help them run the business and should include services to individual staff such as counselling and welfare.

However, the actual management of human resources and employee relations is primarily the responsibility of line managers. It is increasingly line managers who enact the HR policies and procedures – hopefully with the advice and assistance of HR specialists – recruiting staff, managing and leading people, allocating work, assessing performance, guiding and counselling, making decisions about training and development, and handling employee relations problems such as matters of grievance and discipline. A large part of what a line manager does is HR! The growth of 'business partnering', where the HR function closely supports the business, demonstrates the need for HR to help managers with their people management practices.

KEY CONCEPT: LINE MANAGER

A line manager is a senior employee who is responsible for ensuring that all of the tasks necessary for the achievement of the objectives of an operational department or section are carried out on time and to the required standard.

However, line managers may often have little knowledge or expertise of HR issues and thus it is vital that HR is able to provide this to support them.

ACTIVITY 4.4

Talk to some line managers and see what aspects of HR they undertake in their daily jobs. How much need do they have for HR guidance and support?

Line managers turn to HR practitioners when they need guidance on such matters as policies and procedures in relation to pay, absenteeism, grievance and discipline, redundancy, bullying, and so on. Often this advice is in relation to employment legislation, for instance adhering to discrimination laws. Then there will be advice given to employees – on a variety of issues, such as career development, grievances, stress or personal problems.

4.3 ALIGNING HR TO CORPORATE STRATEGY

HR strategy should always fit with the corporate strategy – the goals and priorities of the HR department should be steered by, and be in harmony with, the organisation's goals and aims. To provide a good service, HR needs access to a vast amount of information: absence records, labour turnover figures, recruitment data, pay structures – these are just a few areas where accurate data can impact on important decisions to be made by the organisation. If the organisation wishes to expand, data about effective recruitment will be vital. If cost-cutting is paramount, data on pay, staffing numbers and expenditure on training may all be key to achieving the organisation's goals.

While 'soft' HR approaches can help with improved productivity, motivation and discretionary behaviour, the 'hard' approach may be essential in achieving cost savings vital to the survival of the business. HR practitioners need to keep their eye on the ball with regard to finance – all too often the criticism is made that HR does not understand the financial side of the business – and today, that is just not acceptable. Whatever we do in HR must be financially viable. If we want to gain the support and 'buy-in' of line managers (and of senior managers), we need to show the value of our work. To be fully effective and add value to the organisation, HR must have influence at board level and be able to influence things at a strategic level. It is important that managers see the value of HR and how HR can help the business.

4.3.1 PROFESSIONALISM AND ETHICS

All those working in HR need to act professionally and ethically. The CIPD has a code of conduct which covers four specific areas:

- professional competence and behaviour
- ethical standards and integrity
- acting as a representative of the profession
- stewardship.

All CIPD members must commit themselves to adhere to this Code of Professional Conduct, which sets out the standards of professional behaviour. This is important because HR are often powerful people – responsible for making decisions that affect lives at work – they need to be trusted, have integrity and be able to deliver.

ACTIVITY 4.5

Read the CIPD's Code of Professional Conduct (**www.cipd.co.uk/cipd-hr-profession/about-us/code-professional-conduct.aspx**). Which areas do you think are hardest to adhere to?

Can you think of examples where you have demonstrated professional conduct at work? What are the advantages of having a set 'code of conduct'?

PAUSE FOR THOUGHT

Are there ever times when you have found it hard to act professionally – perhaps due to pressure from a boss to do something quickly or to save money?

4.4 CIPD PROFESSION MAP

The CIPD Profession Map covers the *technical elements* of professional competence required in the HR profession as well as *behaviours* that an HR professional needs in order to be able to carry out their activities. It describes what you need to do, what you need to know and how you need to do it within each professional area within four bands of professional competence. It is organised around areas of professional competence, rather than organisation structures, job levels or roles.

The Map is a comprehensive view of how HR adds the greatest sustained value to organisations, now and in the future. It combines the highest standards of professional competence with the closest alignment to organisational goals, to deliver sustained performance.

It captures what HR people do and deliver across every aspect and specialism of the profession and explores the underpinning skills, behaviour and knowledge that they need to be successful. It also creates a clear and flexible framework for career progression, recognising that HR roles and career progression can follow many directions.

4.4.1 PROFESSIONAL AREAS

If we look at the CIPD Profession Map at **www.cipd.co.uk/cipd-hr-profession/hr-profession-map/** we can see the ten professional areas in which the CIPD expects practitioners to be competent in order to carry out the various roles involved in HR:

- strategy, insights and solutions
- leading HR
- organisation design
- organisation development
- resourcing and talent planning
- learning and talent development
- performance and reward
- employee engagement
- employee relations
- service delivery and information.

For each of these roles, there are four bands (or levels) of professional competence that define the contribution that professionals make in the following key areas:

- the relationship that professionals have with clients, such as support, adviser, consultant or leader
- the focus of the activities performed by professionals, such as support, advising or leading
- where professionals spend their time, such as providing information, understanding issues, understanding the business or understanding organisational issues
- what services are provided to clients, such as information-handling issues, providing solutions or challenging hard issues
- how their contribution and success is measured.

The behaviours are as follows:

- **Curious:** shows an active interest in the internal and external environment and in the continuous development and improvement of self and others at both organisation and individual levels. Is open-minded with a bias and willingness to learn and enquire.
- **Decisive thinker:** demonstrates the ability to analyse and understand data and information quickly. Is able to use information, insights and knowledge in a structured way, using judgement wisely to identify options and make robust and defendable decisions.
- **Skilled influencer:** demonstrates the ability to influence across a complex environment to gain the necessary commitment, consensus and support from a wide range of diverse stakeholders in pursuit of organisation benefit.
- **Driven to deliver:** demonstrates a consistent and strong bias to action, taking accountability for delivery of results both personally and/or with others. Actively plans, prioritises and monitors performance, holding others accountable for delivery.
- **Collaborative:** works effectively and inclusively with colleagues, clients, stakeholders, customers, teams and individuals both within and outside of the organisation.
- **Personally credible:** builds a track record of reliable and valued delivery using relevant technical expertise and experience and does so with integrity and in an objective manner.
- **Courage to challenge:** shows courage and confidence to speak up, challenge others even when confronted with resistance or unfamiliar circumstances.
- **Role model:** consistently leads by example. Acts with integrity, impartiality and independence, applying sound personal judgement in all interactions.

(Taken from the CIPD website at **www.cipd.co.uk/hr-profession-map/**)

The CIPD itself encourages its members to adopt continuing professional development (CPD) and urges organisations to encourage their employees to engage in personal development planning. See Chapter 10 for more on CPD.

ACTIVITY 4.6

Do you keep a log of your activities and what you have learned from them? Do you have a plan outlining your future development? Why not start now? How would you go about keeping a log?

4.5 THE STRUCTURE AND USES OF HR INFORMATION SYSTEMS (HRIS)

The need for information has been steadily increasing over the past 20 years. With the advent of the Internet, the world's advanced economies have now entered the information age and the basis upon which management decisions are made has become more systematic, factual and information-based. The HR practitioner needs to have all kinds of information at their fingertips. Records on sickness absence, turnover, ages, race and gender of staff, number of those with disabilities are some of the information kept by organisations, either to inform them in making policy decisions or to fulfil government requirements. Inability to provide information at an employment tribunal can, for example, lead to the loss of a case, which might have seemed 'cut and dried'. Legislation also demands that certain information is kept by organisations. Much of this information is confidential and needs to be treated carefully. The amount of research carried out by educational and industrial organisations grows larger by the day and provides an increasing amount of data for HR to consult.

The amount of information that HR has to deal with, therefore, has grown considerably.

(See more on HRIS in Chapter 19, 'Handling and Managing Information' and also Chapter 5, as HR information systems are also used in HR planning.)

4.5.1 MANUAL VERSUS COMPUTERISED SYSTEMS

Most documentation nowadays is held in electronic format. There may still be some paper-based items such as employees' original CVs, contracts of employment and any other documentation – letters, references, and so on – that relate to employment. Such records should be systematically filed for security purposes and ease of access to authorised users.

4.5.2 COMPUTERISED HR INFORMATION SYSTEMS

Taylor (2014, p.98) comments on the growth of human resource information systems in recent years, which allow more data to be stored about jobs, employees and applicants and which enable HR practitioners to improve their ability to monitor what goes on in the business. Not only can absence, turnover, pay and training be monitored easily, but specific information on human resource planning, psychometric testing, employee development and appraisals can be used to help make relevant decisions. Databases containing employee details can be a real time-saver when it comes to working out pay awards, or retrieving statistics on how many people have been trained, who is working flexible hours and so on.

A well-maintained, up-to-date and accurate computerised HR information system has many advantages. It:

- provides a reliable basis for strategic decision-making
- supports services to line managers
- can provide information to assist guidance and advice given to line managers on HR matters
- gives immediate access to policy statements
- provides information when decisions need to be made about the future of an individual employee
- ensures that information required by law is readily available.

At the strategic and policy-making level, managers turn to the HR department when they need particular information, for example information about numbers and locations of staff, pay structures, or skills audits, which might be useful in a staff development or, alternatively, a redundancy situation.

4.5.3 USING AND MAINTAINING HR RECORDS

One of the most important administrative duties of the HR practitioner is keeping records. Acas, the Advisory, Conciliation and Arbitration Service, suggests that all organisations, however large or small, need to keep records of their employees. Some records are kept to comply with the law and others are useful for internal administration. For example, keeping records of pay rates will help employers to check they are complying with the National Minimum Wage Act 1998 (**www.acas.org.uk**). From the records, the HR department can provide strategic planners and other managers with information that will enable them to make good-quality decisions about people. In fact, it is continuously necessary as a basis for decisions affecting major HR functions at an organisational level, such as human resource planning, recruitment and selection, performance management, succession planning and health and safety.

(Maintaining records is also discussed in Chapter 19, 'Handling and Managing Information', and Chapter 16, 'Understanding Employment Law', which focuses on the issue of the security of sensitive data held under the Data Protection Act.)

HR records should be seen as a useful tool of management, and maintaining them can be a full-time job. Well-maintained records are up to date, accurate and secure, yet easily accessed. If they are neglected, especially in terms of keeping them up to date, they do not become merely useless, they can become dangerous. Sending someone a letter about their 'long service award' when they died in service six months ago is something to be avoided! Clearly, poor decision-making will result from the use of out-of-date records as a source of information for matters of importance.

Information about its human resources is vital to the successful management of the whole organisation. If we don't have information about how high our staff turnover is, for instance, how can we do anything about it? Such information can give an insight into problem areas in the organisation and point to where changes can be made for the better. A detailed examination of labour turnover may show high turnover in certain areas of the business that is costing the organisation very dearly. The 2013 CIPD/Hays *Resourcing and Talent Management* survey gives a figure of £2,000 as the cost of filling a vacancy. For replacing managers the median cost rises to £5,000. Multiplied up, this can mean enormous costs for the business – so it is essential to know what our turnover figures are and then decide what can be done about it. A lack of such information can mean we are spending money unwisely or are wasting money – so HR information of this kind can be extremely important in increasing the profitability of the business.

What the records contain

The HR department keeps and maintains records that include the personal details of all employees and the events and activities in which they become involved during their period of employment. For example, a personal history is kept on every individual employee from when they first joined the organisation. The details that are held could include:

- the employee's original application form or CV
- copy of the contractual arrangements, terms and conditions of service
- job title on joining (updated with any changes) and, if possible, job description
- date on which employment commenced
- background and previous employment history
- department in which the employee works
- employee category (staff or hourly paid, and so on)
- National Insurance number
- date of birth
- gender
- ethnic origin
- marital status
- salary/wage details and other rewards
- hours of work
- record of attendance and absences
- personal contact details
- academic achievements
- training and further education undertaken before and since joining
- performance assessments
- suitability for transfer and promotion
- career interviews with managers and HR staff
- pension contributions
- trade union membership
- disciplinary record.

ACTIVITY 4.7

If you work in HR, have a look at the records and see the variety of information that is held. Is it stored in a way that is easily retrievable – and useable? Are there any serious gaps? Is it held securely and confidentially? If you don't work in HR, or work in an organisation without an HR function, ask a manager what information they keep about their staff.

4.5.4 USES OF INDIVIDUAL INFORMATION

It can be seen that when individual information is held on all employees, it represents an extremely useful data bank for management and for planning purposes when viewed collectively. But records about individuals in themselves are also valuable. If, for example, a case arises that concerns an individual's current employment or future position, their personal history will provide background information that will assist in managerial decision-making. Similarly, when people are being considered for further training and development, promotion or special assignment work, their personal records provide an ideal basis upon which good-quality decisions can be made, which would be to the benefit of the individual and the organisation. And on a more negative note, records relating to disciplinary hearings and absence may be used in redundancy selection.

4.5.5 STATISTICAL INFORMATION

Organisational statistics serve two very important functions:

- They provide essential information about main areas affecting the general state of the organisation at a particular time.
- They also indicate trends that need to be made apparent so that timely measures may be taken to improve conditions of work and performance.

HR-related statistics can be drawn from accumulated individual records that have been collated, such as those for attendance management, accident rates and wages and salaries. Statistical information may also be drawn from accumulated records relating to staff turnover, workforce stability, sickness absence, skills inventories, deployment, job analyses, recruitment trends and employment costs. Externally gathered data may also be added to provide information on the availability of labour, including special or rare skills, local, regional, national and international employment trends, and average earnings. Information of this type and quantity is indispensable to senior managers and HR strategists, especially in relation to aspects such as HR planning.

4.5.6 LEGAL ASPECTS OF RECORD-KEEPING

On the one hand, many managers are reluctant to allow employees access to the information about themselves that is on record, while on the other, most employees feel that they are entitled to have access, even if only to check that the information is correct. The Data Protection Act 1998 (DPA98) provides a legal entitlement for employees to access their own personal records and, indeed, any information about themselves. Visit The Information Commissioner's Office to find out more on data protection: **http://ico.org.uk/** or see Chapters 16 and 19 for more on data protection laws and the legal requirements to collect and keep information.

 PAUSE FOR THOUGHT

Where do you think the dangers lie in record-keeping? Do you think it is always a good thing to keep records? Do you know what records are kept about you? How do you feel about that?

4.6 THE FUTURE OF HR

The Next Generation HR research project by the CIPD in 2010 led by Lee Sears prompted the profession to start thinking about what it needs to look like in the future.

The three main challenges highlighted by the research showed that:

HR professionals need to be 'Insight-led', that is, to have 'real business savvy and a deep appreciation of the people, political and cultural factors that determine 'what really goes on around here'.

We should future-proof our organisations to ensure their long-term, sustainable performance. HR has a unique role to play in helping an organisation succeed today in a way that lays the foundations for future, sustainable success. HR should help to create engaged employees and develop trust.

HR should act as 'architect, facilitator, provocateur and guardian', to encourage new ways of doing business or new areas of strategic focus. In other words, not to just act in a 'corporate policeman' role, but to be proactive in making a difference to organisations – informed by deep organisational insight.

(*Time for Change – Towards a next generation for HR [online].* Available at **www.cipd.co.uk/binaries/5126nextgenthoughtpiece.pdf**)

Sears (2011) sums it up in stating that 'HR needs a deep understanding of business, contextual and organisational factors'.

The Boston Consulting Group research (Strack et al, 2013) lists five areas that present a challenge for HR in Europe to 2015:

1   Managing talent – assessing the need for talent in the light of business and strategic requirements. Attracting, recruiting and retaining talent.

2   Managing demographics – dealing with the loss of capacity and knowledge through retirement and an aging workforce.

3   Become a learning organisation – investing in a wide variety of learning initiatives to arm workers with the skills for a global economy.

4   Managing worklife balance – offering flexible working such as opportunities to work from home, job-share, and so on.

5   Managing change and cultural transformation to cope with increasing globalisation.

The report suggests that the way to achieve these is to make HR a strategic partner, employing HR staff with a business background and by using qualitative and quantitative metrics to measure performance.

PAUSE FOR THOUGHT

Do you think HR will still exist in the future? Will it have a name change? Do you think the title of 'human resource management' is accurate and appropriate?

HR MORE WORRIED ABOUT THE LONG TERM THAN LEADERS

CASE EXAMPLE 4.1

The CIPD's *HR Outlook: A variety of leader perspectives* (2013) found a close alignment between what HR and leaders considered to be the top five business priorities. Their main concern was cost management, with 64% of business leaders and 71% of HR professionals citing it as their top business priority.

However, when asked what keeps them awake at night, HR respondents said they were more likely to be worrying about longer-term people issues. This was most notable in the areas of leadership development (41% of HR respondents versus 18% of business leaders) and talent development in line with future skills needs (27% HR versus 18% business).

The report said: 'It appears that HR is focused not just on what needs to be in place now, in a time of belt-tightening and frugality, but what the organisation needs to face future scenarios. For example, HR is looking at leadership development and considering whether they have the capabilities needed for the workplace of the future as organisations will require different skill sets than have been needed before.

'A key issue for HR here is its ability to challenge and influence the board to think beyond the short term, and encourage it to plan for the future. For example, continuing to invest in leadership of the future, even when attention is largely focused on immediate cost management priorities.'

Peter Cheese, CIPD Chief Executive, said: 'This is a time of real opportunity for HR. In what is often called the current economic climate, but would more accurately be called the new normal, businesses face many conflicting priorities, such as reducing costs at the same time as trying to increase employee engagement. This puts HR issues at the heart of the business agenda now more than ever.

'Business leaders are looking to HR for creative solutions to the challenges the business faces – but there still needs to

be a solid and robust business case for action. Using metrics effectively to inform business decision-making is essential.'

However, the research also found that many business leaders remain unconvinced about HR's contribution to business performance, suggesting they are not currently demonstrating their strategic value as strongly as they could.

HR is perceived by business leaders to be more involved in implementing strategy than in devising it. And worryingly, almost a fifth of business leaders say they don't know what HR's contribution to strategy is.

'It is clear that HR still has work to do in terms of increasing its visibility and impact and ultimately in demonstrating the organisational value they deliver,' Cheese added.

'HR needs to make better use of metrics to look forward, support and inform the business agenda, but HR leaders must also have the courage, and the business savvy, to effectively challenge and influence business leaders and strategies.'

(Churchard, C. (2013) 'HR more worried about the long term than leaders. *People Management*. 22 January)

ACTIVITY 4.8

What do you think about the future of HR? Where do you think the future of HR lies in terms of its role or even its survival? Does HR deliver a worthy contribution to the business?

4.7 SUMMARY

In this chapter we have discussed the varied functions and roles of HR. We have seen that HR responsibilities can take on many forms, depending on what level the HR practitioner is working at in the organisation. Most practitioners are involved at the 'coal-face' – they deal with the everyday issues and problems of people management in organisations, such as grievance and disciplinary hearings, selection interviews and induction activities. According to Ulrich and Brockbank (2005), there are several roles to play: those of employee advocate, strategic partner and human capital developer, as well as HR leader and functional expert. Ulrich et al's work of 2012 suggests that those working in HR need to have six competences, namely: strategic positioner; credible activist; capability builder; change champion; human resource innovator and integrator; and technology proponent.

The activities within these roles are again wide and varied – carrying out job analysis, advertising vacancies, training staff, supporting the performance management process, monitoring absence, to name but a few. The average day of someone in HR is full of variety, from sorting out pay queries and making someone redundant, to delivering an induction programme and then handling a disciplinary interview. You never know what the day will hold in store – and that is part of what makes it exciting to work in HR.

The CIPD Profession Map reflects the variety of the HR role, the essential competences and responsibilities. It identifies the behaviours required in an HR professional, from being curious and possessing the ability to challenge, to acting as a role model and being personally credible. Being able to deliver is important, as is the need to work collaboratively. Being in HR means you will need knowledge as well as many skills and talents – hopefully reading this book will help you in developing some of them.

REVIEW QUESTIONS

1 What is the difference between an HR specialist and an HR generalist?

2 Who is responsible for managing, leading and developing people?

3 How can HR contribute to business success?

4 Why are good HR records important?

5 How can computerised HR records help the HR practitioner?

6 What are the four areas covered in the CIPD Code of Professional Conduct?

7 How is the CIPD Profession Map relevant to a career in HR?

8 Name the ten areas covered by the CIPD Profession Map.

9 Using the CIPD Profession Map, what behaviours are HR professionals expected to display?

10 What legislation do we need to be aware of when keeping employee records?

11 What kind of records should HR keep?

12 What are some of the most important challenges for HR in the future?

EXPLORE FURTHER

BOOKS

There are many books on HR, but one of the most practical is:

ARMSTRONG, M. with TAYLOR, S. (2014) *Armstrong's handbook of human resource management practice*. London: Kogan Page.

This is a down-to-earth book that covers most aspects of HR.

WEB LINKS

The CIPD's own website has a wealth of information about HR – visit it at **www.cipd.co.uk/**

For anyone considering a career in HR, the CIPD Profession Map makes essential reading: **www.cipd.co.uk/hr-profession-map**

The CIPD's Code of Professional Conduct can be found at: **www.cipd.co.uk/cipd-hr-profession/about-us/code-professional-conduct.aspx**

The Advisory, Conciliation and Arbitration Service provides excellent HR information and their website is well worth a visit: **www.acas.org.uk**

For employment legislation, which is a key part of HR today, go to: **www.legislation.gov.uk/**

The Information Commissioner's Office is worth checking for issues relating to data protection: **http://ico.org.uk/**

CHAPTER 5

Human Resource Planning

LEARNING OBJECTIVES

After studying this chapter you should understand:

- the elements of human resource planning in the traditional and modern contexts
- how human resource planning relates to the overall business strategy
- the make-up of the various elements of human resource planning which contribute to the human resource plan
- the process of forecasting HR supply and demand
- the concept of the internal and external labour markets
- the approaches to and processes associated with carrying out a job analysis.

5.1 INTRODUCTION

More than ever before, human resource planning plays an essential and integral role in the achievement of the overall business strategy. The purpose of this chapter is to explain and discuss the techniques that are applied to human resource planning (HRP) and to demonstrate how the HR plan relates to the organisation's overall business plan. First, there is a brief history of its background, including definitions of traditional and modern systems. Second, we detail the ideas and theoretical concepts that form the basis upon which traditional and modern HRP activities are founded. Third, we examine and discuss the activities with which the HR planner must involve themselves. Fourth, there is guidance on how the activities themselves may be carried out.

The chapter contains case studies and activities for you to work through and to aid your understanding. There are examples based on organisational situations, some of which are hypothetical, while others have been taken from real life.

5.2 A BRIEF HISTORY

From the very early days of industrial activity, organisations have tried to ensure that they have people 'coming up through the ranks' or indeed recruited fresh talent into the organisation to replace longer-serving skilled and knowledgeable employees.

Apprenticeships, for example, traditionally within which young people learn the skills that will be needed in the future, date back to the 'cottage industries' that preceded the Industrial Revolution. It made sense for master craft workers to take on apprentices and train them in their crafts.

It is important to bear in mind that these arrangements for continuity of the crafts were made in the days when change was slow; the craft workers could rely on their skills remaining useful, long into the foreseeable future, and they could safely pass their industrial knowhow down to the rising generation. With the Industrial Revolution came the development of factories and larger-scale industries, which created a demand for a more organisation-wide approach to planning of the future workforce. The craft guilds also provided a certain amount of 'job protection' for those lucky enough to be members.

By the twentieth century, apprenticeship was widespread across a broad range of skills and crafts. Post the Second World War there was concern over the economic performance of the UK economy and its links to poor training quality. Industrial Training Boards (ITBs) were set up in 1964, under the Industrial Training Act. The ITBs represented different sectors of UK industry: construction, engineering, electrical installation, and so on. The focus was on quality provision, funding was provided by a levy on the respective industries which benefitted from the output of the training programmes, which were usually a mix of work and college-based training. This system remained until it was abandoned by the Conservative Government which was in power during the 1980s. Following the abandonment of the ITBs the subsequent neo-liberal approach {meaning – unregulated, capitalist approach} to training was perceived to have failed to deliver a sufficient quantity of skilled workers. Government saw wealth creation to be in the banking sector and UK industry was not a priority.

5.2.1 THE GROWTH OF PLANNING FOR THE FUTURE WORKFORCE

Governments past and present, in the UK, see the imperative to increase the uptake of apprenticeships. This is a double-edged sword. One side of the blade is aimed at incentivising business to increase its potential skills and knowledge base by training young people to be ready to take on future roles. The other edge of the blade reduces youth unemployment, which has always been a concern for successive governments.

Ian Powell, chairman and senior partner at PwC, writes the following in the *Daily Telegraph*:

> At a time when the international economic environment is tough and the world has never been more competitive, there are no quick or easy solutions to boosting economic growth in the UK, especially given the fiscal constraints the Government faces. However, I believe there are three priority areas for the decade ahead, specifically in relation to infrastructure investment, the re-shoring of manufacturing and support services, and skills. ... Last, but by no means least, the skills of the workforce will determine whether the opportunities for growth are taken up. Investment is needed in talent to acquire the necessary skills for a 21st century economy, and a focus on vocational training including apprenticeships will be important. (Powell, 2013)

Apprenticeships, which fall within the Government's vocational and education initiatives (refer to Chapter 10, 'Learning and Development'), are for those 16 years of age and over, eligible to work in the UK and not in full-time education. Currently there are three levels of apprenticeship in England (refer to: **www.gov.uk/apprenticeships-guide** for information about Scotland and Wales).

- **Apprenticeships** – the apprenticeship gives the equivalent to five GCSE passes. Apprentices work towards work-based learning qualifications such as an NVQ Level 2, Key Skills and, in most cases, a relevant knowledge-based qualification such as a BTEC.
- **Advanced apprenticeships** – the apprenticeship gives the equivalent of two A-level passes. Advanced apprentices work towards work-based learning qualifications such as an NVQ Level 3. Candidates are required to have five GCSEs at grade C or above.
- **Higher apprenticeships** – higher apprentices work towards work-based learning qualifications such as an NVQ Level 4 or a foundation degree.

(Guide to Apprenticeships, Available at: **www.gov.uk/apprenticeships-guide**)

Key to the success of national apprenticeships is funding. At the moment (October 2013) funding is available from the National Apprenticeship Service.

Employers can apply for funding to cover training costs for apprentices. This is paid directly to the organisation that provides and supports the apprenticeship – in most cases the learning provider. The National Apprenticeships Service says the following about apprenticeships in England. Scotland, Wales, and Northern Ireland have their own similar systems:

> The Apprenticeship Grant for Employers of 16- to 24-year-olds (AGE 16 to 24) supports businesses that would not otherwise be in a position to do so, to recruit individuals aged 16 to 24 into employment through the Apprenticeship programme. Department for Business Innovation and Skills. (National Apprenticeship Service, 2014)

Employers can receive, if their apprenticeship qualifies, £1,500 per trainee with a cap of ten payments over the life of the government initiative. The target of the scheme is employers who have less than 1,000 employees on their payroll.

For more detailed information on the current scheme (May 2014), go to: **www.apprenticeships.org.uk/employers/steps-to-make-it-happen/incentive.aspx**

 ACTIVITY 5.1

1   Access the National Apprenticeship website to read about and watch what the organisation can offer in terms of apprenticeships at: **www.apprenticeships.org.uk/about-us.aspx**

2   What are the current concerns about apprenticeships?The Government commissioned an independent review, which was carried out by Doug Richard, 'The Richard Review of Apprenticeships'. The review focused on what an apprenticeship should be, and how apprenticeships can meet the needs of the changing economy.

What were the key findings of the Richard (2012) review? You will find some useful information at **www.gov.uk/government/publications/the-richard-review-of-apprenticeships** and also by accessing the report, written by Richard (2012), available at: **www.gov.uk/government/uploads/system/uploads/attachment_data/file/34708/richard-review-full.pdf**

In response to the Richard review the Government published 'The Future of Apprenticeships in England: Next Steps from the Richard Review', March 2013. This document is available at: **www.gov.uk/government/uploads/system/uploads/attachment_data/file/190632/bis-13–577-the-future-of-apprenticeships-in-england-next-steps-from-the-richard-review.pdf**

As a first step to implementing the recommendations the Government has published 'Future of Apprenticeships in England: Guidance for trailblazers (version 2)', which can be found at: **www.gov.uk/government/publications/future-of-apprenticeships-in-england-guidance-for-trailblazers**

3   What happens if someone is too old to apply for an apprenticeship and their employer will not agree to retrain them in a professional discipline? What opportunities are open to them? What rights have they to ask for training? You will find some useful guidance and a short survey by accessing the following government website: **www.gov.uk/training-study-work-your-rights**

Caterpillar Articulated Trucks has worked with the Institution of Mechanical Engineers to accredit their Advanced Apprenticeship programme. Read the following article from the *Professional Engineering Magazine*, September 2013, p.69.

Caterpillar Apprenticeship on Track for Professional Registration

The Institution of Mechanical Engineers has formally accredited the Advanced Apprenticeship programme of Caterpillar Articulated Trucks at Peterlee in the North East of England.

The accreditation was announced at the Peterlee plant by Denis Healy, the Institution's Business Development Manager for the North East region, who presented apprentices and Phil Handley, the Managing Director of Caterpillar Articulated Trucks, with a certificate at Caterpillar's Learning Centre of Light. The recognition included apprentices from disciplines such as fabrication and welding, auto electrical, maintenance and tool room.

Among the presentation party was auto electrical apprentice Vicky English, who is Caterpillar Peterlee's first female apprentice. In June, she had been one of the apprentices from leading manufacturing and construction companies who met the Prime Minister at Downing Street, when he announced a new initiative to create 100,000 registered engineering technicians by 2018 and fill a shortage in the industry.

Representing Caterpillar's commitment to developing engineering excellence, Vicky said: 'I believe that getting young people into apprenticeships and giving them knowledge of job opportunities is essential for the country to excel. I also believe that young people are the future and therefore need to be invested in.'

'The Prime Minister was very friendly and very interested in all of the apprentices and their positions. The experience of Downing Street is one I will never forget.'

Vicky was so inspired by this experience and by David Cameron's description of apprenticeships as being 'at the heart of the mission to rebuild the economy,' that she has joined the Institution as an affiliate EngTech member, and has recently registered to become an apprentice ambassador for the National Apprenticeship Service.

After the formal presentation of the accreditation certificate Jill Dwyer, the Institution's Business Development Executive who supports apprentices working towards professional registration, did a presentation about Engineering Technician (EngTech) status for 15 apprentices from Caterpillar who have completed their apprenticeship and who are now submitting their approved route EngTech applications.

Caterpillar is a strong advocate of apprenticeships with long-standing and successful schemes employing hundreds of apprentices across its UK businesses. Caterpillar Peterlee's current apprenticeship programme has been active for seven years. In 2012, the National Apprenticeship Service recognised Caterpillar Peterlee as having the best apprenticeship programme in the North East region. Caterpillar Peterlee apprentice Andrew Price was also recognised in 2012 as one of the top three apprentices in the North East Region Advanced Apprentice of the Year category. Accreditation by the Institution of Mechanical Engineers now gives the company professional backing and reinforces the high standard of the advanced apprenticeship programme.

Fred Felton, Caterpillar's Apprentice Manager, said: 'It is a fantastic achievement to be formally recognised by the Institution of Mechanical Engineers. It's an endorsement of the apprenticeship scheme we run here at our Peterlee plant and is recognition for all the teams involved in delivering first-class training and development to aspiring young engineers of the future.'

'From the apprentices' perspective, this is an opportunity for them to further develop their career and demonstrate professional expertise. The apprentices now have the additional benefit of professional recognition, career progression, information and resources, life-long support.'

Chris Fairs, HR Manager, said: 'Developing skills in our region is critical for our continued success as a strong contributor to the UK manufacturing base and export markets. Diversity is equally important to our continued success – Vicky is our first ever female apprentice and is developing into a great role model for others to follow.'

'Being formally recognised by the governing body now gives our apprenticeship programme the credibility it deserves and provides our apprentices with the opportunity to develop with the first-class support of the institution.'

Summing up the significance of the achievement, and the company's support for its employees' commitment to professional registration, Denis Healy said: 'Caterpillar is a fine example of the best of North East engineering, producing superb articulated trucks which are exported all over the world. The company is fully committed to professional registration, and the apprentice scheme complements the graduate MPDS scheme

that has been in place for a number of years. There is masses of enthusiasm from the young apprentices, and they all now have a clear pathway to professional registration as engineering technicians.'

Reproduced with kind permission of: *Professional Engineering Magazine* (Caspian Media)

Questions

1   How does Caterpillar Articulated Trucks benefit from having its own apprentice scheme? Refer to the National Apprenticeship website for ideas.

2   How does the Advanced Apprenticeship scheme fit into the talent pipeline of Caterpillar Articulated Trucks?

3   See how Caterpillar in North Carolina, USA, has started a youth apprenticeship programme at: **www.caterpillar.com/cda/layout? x=7&m=629215&id=3844080**

4   What are the nature of the external 'pull' and internal 'push' factors which may encourage apprentices to leave?

5   What measures can Caterpillar take to retain its apprentices once they have qualified? Refer to Chapter 8 for ideas.

5.3 MANPOWER PLANNING

The manpower planning process first appeared in the 1960s. This was the first attempt to develop a systematic method of ensuring that an organisation would have a continuous supply of the people it needed for current and future needs in order to carry out the tasks that lead to the achievement of objectives.

When manpower planning was first proposed, manufacturing represented 60% of jobs and the planners relied on the availability of traditional skills. The process was analytic, and it was comprehensive in the sense that it set out to provide the staffing needs of the whole organisation. This approach was fine for the purpose it served, since the demand was for traditional knowledge, skills and competence across the total spectrum of organisational activities. By today's standards, change was still relatively slow, large-scale change was rare, and innovation was limited to little more than the modification of the then current methods and techniques.

Few organisations developed and maintained manpower plans. In the absence of computers the related tasks were found to be cumbersome and time-consuming, and many organisations thought of it as an unwarranted cost. It was a paper exercise in which the need to maintain and keep the plan up to date included a set of tasks that could be likened to painting the Forth Bridge.

 ACTIVITY 5.2

The Department of Employment defined human resource planning in 1974 as:

'A strategy for the acquisition, utilisation, improvement and retention of an enterprise's human resources.'

The HR Council of Canada is part of the Communities Foundations of Canada (CFC), a not-for-profit organisation, and is part of the national network for Canada's community foundations. You can access the CFC website at: **www.cfc-fcc.ca**

The HR Council of Canada offers the following definition of Strategic HR planning.

'The overall purpose of strategic HR planning is to:

- ensure adequate human resources to meet the strategic goals and operational plans of your organisation – the right people with the right skills at the right time
- keep up with social, economic, legislative and technological trends that impact on human resources in your area and in the sector

- remain flexible so that your organisation can manage change if the future is different than anticipated' (HR Council of Canada, **www.hrcouncil.ca/hr-toolkit/planning-strategic.cfm**).

1   Do you think that the 1974 definition, as defined by the Department of Employment, has maintained a currency over the passage of time, especially when enterprises have become smaller, more have become global and times have become more uncertain? What would you add to or subtract from the definition?

2   Does the definition offered by the HR Council of Canada offer any significant advantages over that defined by the Department of Employment and the additions you might have suggested?

3   Do you detect any significant differences between what we, in the UK, might consider to be relevant to HR planning that are specific to and can be explained by our culture compared with that of Canada?

5.3.1 MANPOWER PLANNING AND HUMAN RESOURCE PLANNING (HRP)

The term *human resource planning* (HRP) came into being in the 1980s, when human resource management (HRM) first appeared. Around the same time, political correctness was introduced and thus it was inevitable that an alternative term to *manpower* planning would have to be found. However, modern *human resource planning* is different from manpower planning. Attempts to define both concepts show there are areas that are common to both, but they differ markedly in the strategic approach and purposes. Definitions of processes, however, say more than simply what a process is; they also indicate the thinking that underlies the approach to its implementation.

For example, the original thinking behind defining manpower planning was that it was a strategy that '*secured the enterprise's human resources*', which amounted to acquiring the right number of appropriately skilled people when they were needed. The central idea was to achieve a match between manpower demand and manpower supply. *Demand* means the organisation's current and future human resource requirements, while *supply* refers to the degree to which the demand may be met, both from the current workforce and the external labour market. Cost and statistical analysis was central to the whole process. HRP is more than this; see the next section (5.3.2), where a number of definitions of HRP are analysed.

5.3.2 DEFINITIONS

Beardwell and Claydon define modern HRP as 'the process for identifying an organisation's current and future human resource requirements, developing and implementing plans to meet these requirements and monitoring their overall effectiveness' (Beardwell and Claydon, 2007). According to Bulla and Scott (1994), it is the process for ensuring that the human resource requirements of an organisation are identified and plans are made for satisfying those requirements.

Manpower planning focused on the numbers of people required to fulfil an organisation's strategic objective, but human resource planning (HRP) gives due regard to the softer skills that people would need to have to effectively fulfil the needs of a role. Therefore consideration has to be given to the process of developing these softer skills.

Armstrong (2011) prefers the term 'workforce planning'. He writes (ibid, p.223) that workforce planning:

> . . .is based on the belief that people are an organization's most important resource. It is generally concerned with matching resources to business needs in the longer term, although it will be concerned with shorter-term requirements. It addresses people needs both in quantitative and qualitative terms. This means answering two basic questions: (1) How many people? and (2) What sort of people? Workforce planning also looks at broader issues relating to how people are deployed and developed in order to improve organizational effectiveness. . .

Consider the following definition, offered by Doving and Nordhaug (2010, p.293):

> A firm's human resource planning (HRP) comprises the strategies and routines it has elaborated in order to be better prepared to analyze and develop its human resources, and depends on the extent to which it invests attention and effort in elaborating these strategies and routines.

It is of interest because, although it is not specific, unlike the bullet-pointed definition offered by the HR Council of Canada (op cit), Doving and Nordhaug offer a moderating comment by saying, '. . .and depends on the extent to which it invests attention and effort in elaborating these strategies and routines.' In essence they are pointing to the fact that an organisation may have developed the most detailed strategy and processes for managing HR planning, but the outcomes of *effective planning* are a function of the time, effort and money an organisation is prepared to expend.

In very practical terms human resource planning is not just about making sure that the organisation has identified the numbers and types of people it requires to fill current and future roles. In many respects the definition offered by Armstrong is the most comprehensive. As Armstrong (op cit) mentions above, it is also about the quality, skills, competencies and behavioural traits that people need to have to be able to effectively fill roles. Planning, as its name implies, must also address the changing needs of the business by predicting where there might not only be deficits but also surpluses in the future workforce.

5.3.3 THE IMPACT OF THE FLEXIBLE FIRM AND NEW TECHNOLOGY ON HR PLANNING

The concept and meaning of the 'flexible firm' is introduced in Chapter 1, 'Organisations'. Students are recommended to read about the flexible firm and what it means in terms of how organisations can be structured and organised from a people skills perspective.

Technologies change and therefore ways of working change to reflect the introduction of new technological processes and methods of communication. Staff, whose skills were once at a premium within an organisation, may find that their skills base has become obsolete and may require, if they have the capacity to do so, retraining. Technological change has also driven how work can be done and so the process of HR planning must also focus upon the utilisation of people by introducing more flexible systems of work.

Many large organisations have adopted the 'flexible firm' approach and have outsourced and/or contracted out parts of their operation or operations (refer to Chapter 1, 'Organisations', for a detailed discussion of the 'flexible firm'). By doing so this creates, to some extent, a dependency relationship of the outsourcing organisation on the contractor agency. Consider a large organisation which, for example, makes bricks, decorative paving slabs, and so on. Its competency is in the manufacture of bricks; it does not have a special competence in IT. A decision to outsource the organisation's information technology section could be driven by the desire to give its 'back office work', such as its IT services – which are not core to its operation – to a competent contractor. An IT contractor would be both competent and better prepared for changes to what is its core business (information technology) and so is better prepared to maintain a currency of this type of skill within its workforce.

Although there are advantages in outsourcing activities, there are also disadvantages. In the example discussed, the brick manufacturer would become solely reliant on the IT provider for maintenance of telephones, computer systems and websites. The brick manufacturer would, by necessity, have to develop an IT competency in a few key staff so that the complex contract with the IT provider can be effectively managed.

Outsourcing or 'contracting out', as it is sometimes called, is not a one-off activity. It brings with it a whole new range of problems to an organisation because, although work has been contracted out or outsourced, there is still a need to proactively manage the relationships with the external agency (contractor) and to understand their business. Clearly, therefore, although a conscious effort may have been made to outsource a large, but not core, activity, there are still implications for competency requirements and skills sets for the outsourcing organisation, as was explained in the example of the brick manufacturer. There is a need for the outsourcing organisation to maintain some core roles which are responsible for contract management. This implies that those people employed in those roles must have both contract management skills and have a currency of knowledge and skills to be able to manage the contract for outsourced activity – in the example used this would in the IT field.

From a common-sense perspective, it is important to understand what the outsourcing agency or contractor does in some detail, and thus be able to judge whether or not they are effectively doing their task. It is also important to understand to what extent they are proactively preparing for the future. Many organisations struggle with the dilemma of how to resource and develop staff to manage contracts in which they no longer have a core skills base.

Once an activity has been outsourced, the future success of the contractor's business as well as the outsourcing organisation become almost inexorably {meaning – it cannot be stopped} intertwined.

 KEY CONCEPT: HUMAN RESOURCE PLANNING

Human resource planning (HRP) is a strategic management function, the aim of which is to ensure that the organisation will have the quality and number of human resources it needs currently and in the future in order to realise its strategy and achieve its business objectives. This definition owes much to the thinking of Armstrong (2011).

5.4 THE NATURE OF PLANNING

Before giving in-depth consideration to such a specialised area of planning as HRP, it is essential to develop a clear understanding of what we mean by the term. All organisational processes are designed to serve and support the corporate strategy.

5.4.1 AN IMPRECISE PROCESS

Organisational planning is not a precise activity. Indeed, the question has been asked, 'If it is an imprecise process, then why do it?' Truly, the predictions and demands that form essential components of a plan are seldom precise, but having some information with which to work is better than having no information. The rigorous application of related skills can produce a plan that is manageable and, in terms of precision, at least has a working chance of coming close to defining real needs and thus guiding future decisions on staffing. In fact, all of business planning is like that; after all, few strategists would try to predict the precise nature of the business environment in the medium or long term.

This is not to say that the future is a complete mystery to the strategist, since the organisation itself, by developing and marketing new products and new and creative ways of serving its customers, does have an influence on what happens in the future. There are, however, many external factors that are beyond the organisation's control; competitors' activities and the vagaries {meaning – *a change that cannot logically be explained*} of the economy are two examples of this.

5.4.2 PLANNING PERIODS

Plans are normally divided into short, medium and long term. The period over which business plans extend varies from one organisation to another, depending on the type of organisation, the type and state of market it serves (see Case Example 5.2), the rate of internal change and its financial situation. Since we cannot predict all of the future, long-term plans have to be fairly vague in their content and direction. Medium-term plans, on the other hand, are slightly easier to specify; clearly, we can forecast more accurately what will happen in the forthcoming, say, two to five years. Short-term plans, which might range from the present day to two years hence, need to be precise and crystal clear; they are plans that demand more or less immediate action.

  FACTORS INFLUENCING PLANNING TIMESCALES

CASE EXAMPLE 5.2

Consider the following: Concrete is a *stable product*, a product for which the demand is steady and long term. There is some but no significant *product innovation* and there are few companies in the industry at a primary level. The equipment to grind the rocks and to heat the powdered products is large and is a considerable capital expenditure. With such a dependable market, the companies can draw up marketing plans that stretch far into the future and invest in capital equipment, confident that since there will not be a significant reduction in demand, they will get a return on their investment.

The manufacture of communication devices – computers, laptops, handheld devices – on the other hand, is an *unstable product*, the demand for which changes rapidly and continuously as does the demand for popular software applications. Product innovation is the main route to survival, and there are many companies in the industry. Few such companies have a long-term plan. To them, the medium term might be 18 months and the short term is in real time, depending on the rate at which the specifications of their products change and the innovation of the competitors.

The issues for this type of market are exemplified by considering how Nokia and BlackBerry have been affected by changing consumer demands driven by product innovation of competitor companies such as Apple. Nokia has been thrown a lifeline by Microsoft's takeover. Microsoft, in turn, has had to innovate because it can no longer rely on computer retailers packaging Windows with their hardware because the nature of personal computing is changing. Rushton and Warman (2013) write the following in the *Daily Telegraph*:

> If Dell or HP wanted their PCs to have any traction in the market whatsoever, they had to ensure they came with Microsoft's software pre-installed. But the world eventually changed around it, and gadgets rather than software became the key to success. Apple had spent years snapping at Microsoft's heels, but it pulled into the lead by launching a string of sleek devices – the iPod, the iPhone, the iPad. Apple knew that if the hardware was good enough, it could persuade users to accept its own, newer operating system and leave Microsoft far behind.
>
> Meanwhile, Google steadily chipped away at other parts of

Microsoft's business, using its free Android operating system and its Chrome web browser to woo hardware companies such as Samsung, knocking Microsoft yet another rung lower. (Rushton and Warman, 2013)

The handheld BlackBerry, the device which drove the success of Research in Motion (RIM), the Canadian multinational company which owns BlackBerry, is at the time of writing – like Nokia – struggling in a very competitive and fast-moving market. It already has plans to reduce its workforce by 40%, totalling 4,500 people worldwide, and was on track in 2013 to post a loss of $4.4 billion. Fairfax Financial Holdings, a large Canadian insurance and investment company, showed some initial interest in buying the remaining shares in BlackBerry, but at a price. 'The $4.7 billion offer from Fairfax, which already owns about 10 percent of BlackBerry, is a powerful symbol of the phone maker's decline. In June 2008—a time when BlackBerrys defined smartphones—the company had a stock market value of $83 billion' (Austen and Gelles, 2013).

The current share price of BlackBerry (May 2014) is circa $7.90; in June 2008 its share price was $149.90. This means that the share price, in a period of six years, has fallen to 5.3% of its peak value.

5.4.3 THE PLANNING PROCESS

All types of planning have a set of features in common.

CASE EXAMPLE 5.3

PLANNING A VISIT

A simple analogy: planning

All four of these stages are interrelated, and in the simplest of terms, the process is no different from that of planning a holiday. You decide that you need a week away from work.

Scoping the holiday:

● **Phase 1** would include questions such as how long to take for the actual

vacation, where to go on holiday – the UK or overseas. If the decision is made to stay in the UK, consideration would have to be given as to where to go and how to get there.

Once a decision has been made about the destination, data would be collected about accommodation availability, transport, and so on. For example, data on train times or route planning information, if a journey by car is contemplated; this would equate to:

- **Phase 2**, which would entail the collection and review, for example, of the cost versus the facilities offered by different hotels, as well as the costs against time benefits of the various methods of travel. In essence, much of the work associated with this phase is associated with what is termed a 'cost-benefit analysis' of the options.
- **Phase 3** heralds the decision stage, where – based upon the outcome of the Phase 2 assessment – decisions are made on where to stay and how to get there.
- **Phase 4** is the implementation phase, where hotel accommodation is booked, train tickets are bought, bags are

packed and you are ready to go on holiday! The enjoyable part is putting all the plans into practice and to actually go on holiday. This, though, is not the end of the process. All good projects should have a review phase – some organisations call this a 'lessons learned process': assessments are made of where mistakes had been made and, importantly, how they could have been avoided. This information gleaned from the review is recorded for future access.

Certainly, business planning is more complex than planning the holiday as described in this example, but the simplicity of the analogy is intended to clarify the nature and sequence of the stages in the process.

Figure 5.1 The classic planning process

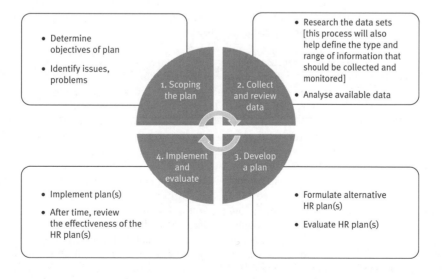

CASE EXAMPLE 5.4

THE IMPORTANCE OF PLANNING

Two weeks ago, Alan submitted an assignment report and was glad to have seen the end of it; he had found the research and writing process about his topic particularly arduous. Subsequently, he was notified of the grade; it was much lower than he had anticipated. Reflecting upon how he went about this task, Alan concluded that his poor performance was due to his lack of planning:

1   He failed to clarify his true goal.

2   In terms of other commitments, he had not assessed his position in terms of time management before he had started.

3   He had launched himself in at the deep end without considering alternative methods of approach to the task.

4   He could not, therefore, select an appropriate method.

5   He carried out the work randomly, as and when he felt like it.

Your task: Draw up a plan for carrying out your next assignment.

Reflection: What have you learned from Alan's experience? How will you approach your assignments in the future?

Plans are a very important part of business and have a number of uses:

● They give an opportunity for individuals to give serious thought to what they want and not be panicked into quick and sometimes irrational decisions. Because the process is systematic, most, if not all, relevant factors are considered, such as resource requirements, for example financial demands, logistics needs, time schedules, and so on.
● Goals are more likely to be achieved in full.
● Relevant people who may be able to 'throw more light' on the subject can be involved.
● Planning saves time in the long run because many of the issues that may arise will have been tabled for discussion and decisions approved.

5.5 TRADITIONAL AND MODERN HRP

At this stage it is necessary to draw a distinction between what many writers refer to as *traditional* and *contemporary* (or *modern*) HRP. In Chapter 3 we drew a distinction between hard and soft HRM. Traditional HRP largely follows the 'hard' approach to planning. Hard HRM is concerned with assessing the numbers of roles that are likely to be vacant or, alternatively, overstaffed and also the range of skills required of those who are employed to fill a vacancy. Contemporary HRP equates with both the 'hard' and 'soft' approaches to HRM. In this sense, as well as collecting the hard, measurable data, due consideration is also given to the need to assess the attitudes, motivation and teamworking skills that the organisation wishes to encourage within its staff.

It is important to note that although 'modern HRP' has found a firm foothold in British industry, one should not assume that it is widespread. Many HR planning specialists are still using traditional systems, largely because their organisations have not adopted the principles and techniques of HRM. In the rest of this chapter, therefore, it is necessary to explain and discuss traditional and modern approaches to HRP.

Beardwell and Claydon (2007) argue that for modern human resource planning (HRP), consideration should be given to both hard and soft factors of the process. This is because it is not just the hard factors alone, that is, primarily the numbers of different skilled positions required, that should be considered. In a world where customer service is king (or queen), the soft issues of planning such as the behaviours and attitudes that staff exhibit, as previously mentioned, should be considered at the forefront of the process.

HRP has grown in importance in recent years, and in well-run organisations it is firmly integrated with business planning. Advances in information technology (IT) have eased the pain of the traditional and tedious methods of HR planning. With appropriate software, the computer has eliminated the tedious pen-pushing element and turned HRP into a dynamic, interesting and, at times, exciting function. Many HR information systems (HRIS) have bolt-on HR planning modules (refer to Chapter 19, 'Handling and Managing Information' for further discussion of HRIS systems).

ACTIVITY 5.3

In today's turbulent times, following the recovery from the 2008 recession, it would not be unreasonable for the busy HR manager to consider that HR planning is a luxury, rather than necessity.

Discuss whether or not you consider it is a worthwhile activity or whether time would be better spent on more pressing HR activities.

You will find some useful information by accessing the following documents:

- CIPD (2013a) *Workforce planning*. Factsheet. Available at: **www.cipd.co.uk/hr-resources/factsheets/workforce-planning. aspx**
- CIPD (2013b) *HR outlook: winter 2012–13*. Available at: **www.cipd.co.uk/hr-resources/survey-reports/hr-outlook-winter-2012–13-views-profession.aspx**. This survey report reviews HR capacity in organisations and also gives some indication of the type and time spent on activities by HR professionals.

5.5.1 HR PLANNING AS A COMPETENCE-CENTRED FUNCTION

In modern management terms the human resource is the most important resource in the organisation. Arguably, therefore, HRP is one of the most important processes. Human resource planning is a *competence-centred* activity, since its central purpose is to match the knowledge and skill *supply* to the organisation's knowledge and skill *demand*. To this end, HR specialists study and analyse business plans, consult the business's managers to obtain information about their HR needs, make decisions about the nature of the HR requirement in terms of competence, and identify the most appropriate sources of supply.

5.5.2 SHADOWING THE BUSINESS PLAN

The best HR plans are produced by those who understand how their particular organisations interact with their total business environment; this enables an understanding of the thinking that underlies the business plans. It is essential for the HR plan to complement the business plan. To meet the needs of an ever-changing business environment, business plans are continuously monitored and updated to ensure that the organisation competes effectively and continues to serve the needs of its customers and clients. By implication this means that those who create, maintain and update the HR plan appreciate that both business and HR plans are interdependent entities that are continuously changing. The business plan changes in an attempt to continually reflect external market demands and competitor threats, while the HR plan, in a classic sense, changes to complement the business plan. The HR planner therefore has to shadow and keep pace with the business plan to maintain this complementary and supportive relationship.

5.5.3 TRADITIONAL APPROACHES TO HRP

Pilbeam and Corbridge (2010) adapted Bramham's (1994) HRP process (see Figure 5.2). According to the model, the HRP process goes through four main stages:

1   analysis and investigation

2   forecasting

3   planning

4   implementation and control.

5.6 ANALYSIS AND INVESTIGATION

This first stage is concerned with analysing and investigating the condition of the internal and external labour markets and the current capability of the organisation in terms of knowledge, skills and competence. The corporate strategy also has to be scrutinised for details of any future changes that would affect the HR requirement. For example, in its simplest terms, if a product expansion is expected, clearly more staff would be required. The sooner this is known the better, because new employees would have to be recruited and trained to the required competency levels.

Figure 5.2 Stages in the process of human resource planning

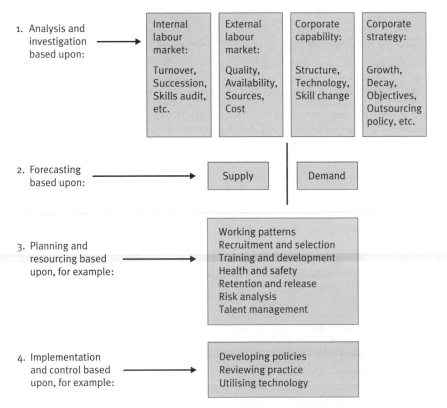

Adapted from Pilbeam and Corbridge (2010) and Bramham (1994) and reproduced with kind permission of the CIPD.

5.6.1 INTERNAL LABOUR MARKET

Qualitative and quantitative information has to be gathered about the current workforce in terms of the kind of work that is carried out by each individual or teams: the qualifications, experience, skills and competence they need to do the job and the level at which they operate: administrator, team leader, supervisor, manager, and so on. When assessing the current workforce as a source of supply for retraining, development, and promotion, it is necessary do so within the context of continuous movement and activity. It may be that a large proportion of the employees will remain in their present positions, but there are always people leaving and joining the organisation, being promoted, transferring, and so forth. From an organisation's HR records it should be possible to assess:

- how many employees there are
- the nature of the skills and other qualities of employees
- the level or status in the organisation of employees
- the standards of employee performance
- employee attitudes and versatility
- employees' potential for promotion, development or other movement within the organisation
- employees' likely time-frame for retirement.

5.6.2 EXTERNAL LABOUR MARKET

Where the results of the HR demand analysis produce shortfalls in staff numbers and required competences, we then gather and assess information about the external pool of potential future employees. The nature and levels of the jobs that are, or will be, affected by the shortfall means that the HR planner may have cause to search the labour markets at three levels: locally, nationally and internationally.

It also has to be borne in mind that competitor organisations will be searching within the same three levels of the labour market and competing for similar people. To compete effectively with other organisations, there is a requirement to understand how competitor organisations attract potential recruits and to research the terms and conditions of employment they offer. This – in terms of salary but could also reflect benefits and perquisites – is often referred to as the *going rate*.

CASE EXAMPLE 5.5

Foy and Murray Brown (2013) write the following about the announcement by Jaguar Land Rover (JLR) to invest in an engine plant near Wolverhampton and a new aluminium body shop at a new facility in Solihull.

The health of the quality car producer, since it was bought from Ford Motors by the Indian TATA group, has gone from strength to strength. It is one example which highlights and exposes the critical skills shortages in the engineering disciplines in the UK as the country comes out of recession, rebalances its economy from heavy reliance on financial services to a more balanced and mixed economy.

Jaguar Land Rover is in the process of investing £1.5 billion into the West Midlands and thus creating a voracious appetite for engineers at all levels.

The scarcity of trained engineers is a 'critical issue' that represents a 'serious problem at all levels' of the automotive industry, Vince Cable, business secretary, has warned, as the recent surge in recruitment bleeds the skills pool dry. JLR and other carmakers with factories or research centres in the UK are frequently being forced to recruit engineers from their suppliers to make up for the shortfall in available trained labour, or else rely on overseas recruitment. 'There is a massive skills gap. From apprentices, to technician level, to graduate level, to engineers ... there are shortages across all areas,' Mr. Cable told the *Financial Times* during a recent trip to a Midlands automotive research centre. (Foy and Murray Brown, 2013)

The Murray Brown article illustrates how the external labour market can quickly change when a large organisation decides to invest in plant, equipment and thus jobs. The small to medium-sized businesses, which are likely to benefit as suppliers to JLR, are likely to be impacted upon by the 'pulling power' of the JLR brand, its conditions of service and pay rates. There will be a local war for talent.

From a national perspective the Office for National Statistics (ONS) offers a range of useful statistics that can, in a *hard HR* sense, be incorporated into the organisation's macro planning activities. NOMIS*, which is part of the ONS data resource, offers a range of useful statistics.

*Note: The NOMIS acronym originally stood for National Online Manpower Information System. However, because the term 'manpower' is deemed now to be politically incorrect, the initials now are not taken to 'stand for' anything. A video promoting the original NOMIS service, circa 1990, can be found at: **www.youtube.com/ watch?v=M8ZiUeUfPE8** Although the video is dated, it is worth viewing.

The set of statistics in Table 5.1 were taken from the ONS website and depict the range of unemployment rates for all people and males for the West Midlands and the UK.

Table 5.1 Local unemployment rates in the West Midlands compared with the whole of the UK

	West Midlands (Millions)	West Midlands (%)	United Kingdom (Millions)	United Kingdom (%)
All people				
Economically active	2.73	76.8	32.3	77.7
In employment	2.46	69.1	29.8	71.6
Unemployed	0.27	9.8	2.49	7.7
Economically inactive	0.80	23.2	8.96	22.3
	West Midlands (Millions)	West Midlands (%)	United Kingdom (Millions)	United Kingdom (%)
Males				
Economically active	1.48	83.0	17.4	83.5
In employment	1.32	74.0	15.9	76.4
Unemployed	0.16	10.5	1.43	8.3
Economically inactive	0.29	17.0	3.13	16.5

The above data was accessed on 25 September 2013 and is adapted from NOMIS at: **www. nomisweb.co.uk/reports/lmp/gor/2013265925/report.aspx#tabempocc**
Age range: 16–64 years; Time line: May to July 2013, seasonally adjusted.
Equivalent data is also available for females.

Using the NOMIS data, it is possible to build up a picture of employment and unemployment rates over time, which allows analysis of how changes have occurred as technologies, global pressures and political pressures have caused movements in the labour market. It is also possible to compare different regions within the UK.

This type of information would be useful to companies who may be considering expansion activities and so would be searching for areas where there is a source of available labour, that is, where there is a *loose* labour market. *Loose* refers to the type of labour market where there are more people for jobs than there are jobs for people. A *tight* labour market would be one where there are more jobs than there are skilled people for those jobs.

ACTIVITY 5.4

NOMIS offers data on a variety of social and labour force indicators:

- resident population
- headline indicators – *{means labour supply}*
- employment by occupation – unadjusted
- qualifications – that is, the numbers and percentage of individuals with given qualifications in a geographical area
- earnings by residence
- out of work benefits
- workforce jobs
- Jobcentre Plus vacancies.

You will find the following useful: **www.nomisweb.co.uk/home/newuser.asp#find**

1 Using the NOMIS website determine, for your area in the UK, the following information:

- the headline indicators
- the qualifications
- the Jobcentre Plus vacancies.

2 Discuss how this information can be used from an HR manager's perspective.

5.6.3 CORPORATE CAPABILITY

To establish corporate capability, information is gathered about the performance of the organisation, its structure, the technology it uses and what it might intend to use in the future. Information about the organisation's strengths and weaknesses are gathered; the results of a SWOT analysis would provide much of this data (see Chapter 1). The data is assembled and assessed and decisions can be made about the organisation's strengths and its weaknesses.

5.6.4 CORPORATE STRATEGY

This is where the focus is on the organisation's future direction. Strategy is seldom a 'more of the same' process; in today's business environment strategic planning, for most organisations, spells change. The organisation's current capability, therefore, may not totally match up to the requirements that are laid down in the business strategy, which is a document that specifies the approach that will be taken by the organisation to meet the future business goals.

The corporate strategy cannot be enacted unless the organisation has the number and type of people it requires for its future needs. The HR plan will compare current profile of skills and competencies with the predicted future capabilities. This information is then fed back into the corporate strategy.

ACTIVITY 5.5

Obtain a copy of your organisation's annual report (or one of an organisation that you know) and look at what is said about the degree to which past objectives were achieved and compare this with what is said about how potential problems with achieving future objectives might be overcome. Investigate how these predictions were developed.

5.7 FORECASTING HR DEMAND

Looking again at Figure 5.2, you will see that at the second stage, the planner studies the data gathered from the analysis and investigation to identify, and thereby forecast, the HR demand and supply.

Forecasting HR demand is, in part, a data-gathering process. It involves identifying the kinds of knowledge, skills and competences that will be required, where in the organisation the requirements exist, when they are needed, and in what quantities. The data should be gathered in an organised and systematic way.

According to Armstrong (2012, pp.644–6), there are four basic demand forecasting methods for estimating the numbers of people required:

- managerial judgement
- ratio-trend analysis
- work study techniques
- use of spreadsheets – modelling the workforce levels against known and expected demand.

5.7.1 MANAGERIAL JUDGEMENT

This is a subjective technique and is not renowned for its accuracy. It is, however, the most commonly used. It is most effective in small organisations and those where the structure, technology and productivity remain relatively stable. The organisation's managers estimate their future workloads and decide how many people they will need. Their decisions are based upon what they know about past trends and forthcoming changes. Managers sometimes do this under the guidance of their seniors who, in turn, are probably acting on the advice of specialists, such as those in the HR department.

To help managers consider, in meaningful ways, what the future might hold, in terms of the requirements for staff, they will probably request, from various departments and functions within the company, the following types of information:

- replacements for retirements, leavers, transfers and promotions
- possible improvements in productivity
- the impact of technological changes, which will probably cause new ways of working or even make current processes and thus people redundant
- redeployment of existing staff
- planned changes in output levels
- planned reorganisation of work
- the impact of changes in employment law or collective agreements
- downsizing, which may cause a requirement for a redeployment of staff and therefore upskilling for some individuals.

With the above information and a manager's or group of managers' experience, it is possible that they are able to build a number of scenarios. Usually there will be a best-case scenario, where the organisation is required to expand, perhaps because it is considered that the company might win a large contract. On the other hand, the worst-case scenario is considered, where the company loses a large contract and so fewer people are required. Usually, reality will be somewhere in the middle.

PAUSE FOR THOUGHT

The task of working methodically through a set of business scenarios is not easy. It is both tedious and time-consuming. Questions arise about the time horizons to use *{meaning over what period of time the plan should consider, 2, 5, 10 or 20 years in the future?}* and the level of detail to consider. However, because it is difficult and time-consuming, it does not mean that it should not be done. For the HR professional involved in the process, the learning is invaluable. Working with colleagues from other disciplines, an essential component of the process, a tremendous amount of information can be gleaned about the business, workforce requirements and trends, thus decisions about the organisation, which involve HR plans, are likely to be better informed.

Armstrong (2012, p.214) refers to this *top-down* approach to HRP and suggests an alternative and additional *bottom-up* approach, in which the line managers submit staffing proposals for agreement by senior managers. He further suggests the use of both approaches in which, in addition to being given guidelines, line managers are encouraged to seek the help of the *HR (and in large organisations [authors' comments]), the organisation and methods (O&M) or work study)* departments. Staffing targets are usually set and while the line managers are producing their departmental and functional forecasts, HR, work study and O&M get together to produce an organisation-wide HR forecast.

The use of this technique draws on the contents of the business plan in that guidelines are issued to the managers indicating which of the organisation's future activities will be most likely to affect their departments.

Both forecasts (the line managers' and the HR version) are then reviewed by an HRP committee consisting of functional heads. This committee reconciles, with departmental managers, any discrepancies between the two forecasts. The process introduces alternatives and provides checks and balances by offering alternative perspectives.

5.7.2 RATIO-TREND ANALYSIS

Perhaps to understand what is meant by 'ratio-trend' analysis it is appropriate to consider an example where the process can be used. Ratio-trend analysis is a simple ratio between the number of products an organisation produces and the number of employees it needs to produce the product. Consider the example of a small primary school, which has:

> Children – 210, Head Teacher – 1, Teachers – 7, Teaching Assistants – 2, Administrators – 2

Relevant ratios:

- ratio of teachers to children = 7/210 (1:30)
- ratio of teaching assistants to children = 2/210 (1:105)
- ratio of administrators to children = 2/210 (1:105).

A builder buys a plot of land, half a mile from the school, and plans to put 600 houses on the land. Once the houses are occupied a survey would indicate how many children there are of, or near to, primary school age. Let us assume the houses have been built and a survey is conducted, which shows that there are 90 children requiring primary education in the immediate area. The head teacher, together with the education authority, would then be able to assess that there would be a requirement for the following number of extra staff, assuming all of the children came to the school:

- number of extra teachers required: 90/30 = 3
- number of extra teaching assistants = 90/105 = 1 (we cannot have 0.86 of an administrator!)
- number of extra administrators = 90/105 = 1.

The previous is a very simple example. It does not take into account the need for extra cleaning staff, classrooms, furniture, and so on. It does, however, give some idea of the process. How much detail to consider depends upon what information is available and how much confidence there is in the projected future. It is the level of confidence in the projections of children that will need educating that the head teacher and the education authority would have to weigh in their minds because the outcome of their deliberations would trigger a release of funds to recruit staff and purchase buildings.

If the process is considered from a business perspective, the effectiveness of this technique is determined by the future stability of the relationship between (if the example of a manufacturing facility is taken) the productivity volume and the number of employees (explained in the previous example of predicting staff numbers for a school). Clearly the risk is to assume that relationships remain constant. Few organisations would survive without at least some element of growth and enrichment and this is the problem with the 'ratio-trend analysis' technique; it does not emphasise the need to allow for foreseeable changes. The effectiveness and efficiency with which the technique is managed relies upon the planner's ability to handle (juggle with) changing ratios, a task that is made somewhat easier when the changes are planned, or at least foreseen.

One could imagine that for a fruit-growing farmer in the south of England, he or she will require a workforce that reduces in winter to a level that is commensurate with the seasonal needs of the business. The winter work centres on preparing the land, maintenance work on, for example, poly-tunnels and preparatory work, such as ploughing – in general, all the work required to get ready to produce the summer crop. At harvest time, larger numbers of people are required. In this relatively stable environment the farmer could trend his usage of labour over the seasons and so, in a timely manner, recruit and release staff.

The use of the ratio-trend methodology is appropriate so long as, as indicated previously, stable conditions prevail. A number of factors can trigger change and the kinds of change they bring about. If, for example, the organisation plans to introduce new technology into the picking process, the demand forecasts would have to be based upon knowledge of the new processing technique, probably reducing the demand for human resources or perhaps changing the skill requirements of the human resources employed. In essence, managerial judgement would have to be introduced and incorporated into the planning process.

5.7.3 WORK STUDY TECHNIQUES

Work study techniques are used much less frequently than they were in the twentieth century, largely due to the decline in manufacturing. They are used to measure work in terms of how long it takes for operators to carry out particular tasks and how many operators would be required to carry out a total work schedule. The work study approach is most effective when it is used to forecast requirements on the factory floor and in administrative sections where the tasks are repetitive. Its origins of work and motion study lie in the work of F.W. Taylor and F.B. Gilbreth (see Chapter 3, 'Human Resource Management').

5.7.4 MODELLING

This refers to mathematical modelling techniques in which spreadsheets are used in the preparation of demand and supply forecasts. Modelling can be a very powerful tool, especially in large organisations, such as manufacturing and process industries where productivity levels can be equated to head count. Factors such as projected retirement dates, wastage – in terms of staff turnover rates, reduction in head count caused by the introduction of new technology – can all be factored into and 'tweaked' within a spreadsheet. The timelines for which the model is operated can be both stretched and compressed *but the output is only as good as the data inputted and the premises on which the model is run*. This type of technique can be used to supplement other methods of planning to try to 'home in' on a realistic solution that can stand scrutiny.

5.8 FORECASTING HR SUPPLY

Forecasting HR supply involves using information from the internal and external labour markets. HR planners keep a monitoring eye on the staff turnover and workforce stability indices. The staff turnover index informs us of the turnover that is likely even when discounted to reflect any major or minor planned changes. The stability index gives an indication of the degree to which long-serving employees remain with the organisation. The understanding of and use of these ratios is important to the work of the HR practitioner.

5.8.1 FORECASTING INTERNAL SUPPLY

Many of the employees who will be needed in the future are already in the workforce and many of them will stay in their current positions. Staff movements, however, have to be taken into account.

5.8.2 CALCULATING STAFF TURNOVER

Staff turnover refers to the rate at which people leave the organisation. The turnover index is expressed as a percentage and is calculated as follows:

$$\frac{\text{Number of leavers in a period }(\text{year})}{\text{Average number of employees in that period (year)}} \times 100 = y \text{ \% turnover}$$

CASE EXAMPLE 5.6

1 If the organisation employs an average of 2,200 people, and 88 leave during the year, the staff turnover is:

$$\frac{88}{2200} \times 100 = 4\%$$

2 An organisation employs five people and one leaves during the year. Then the turnover, if a replacement employee is found very quickly and

so the average employed remains at approximately five people, is:

$$\frac{1}{5} \times 100 = 20\%$$

In example (2) the mathematical analysis is correct, but because of the small numbers involved the meaningfulness of the value has to be questioned. Consider the following scenario:

In four departments – A, B, C and D – of an organisation, each employing, in turn: (A) 200, (B) 300, (C) 150 and (D) 5 people, turnover figures are calculated for the previous 12 months as, respectively: 4%, 8%, 7%, 40%. Taken as headline figures, that is, without delving into the detail of how the statistics were calculated, a senior executive could jump to the conclusion that there was something seriously wrong with department D. It would not be unreasonable for her to demand, 'why are so many people leaving this department?' The detail, however, would show that a turnover of 40% equates to two people, one who had retired and the other promoted into another department! Chapter 19, 'Handling and Managing Information', deals with staff turnover statistics that can be used to good effect.

5.8.3 DEPARTMENTAL OR SECTIONAL DISTRIBUTION OF TURNOVER

The simple calculation in the example above, the 'overall or 'headline figure', is of some use if the HR practitioner wishes to benchmark the 'overall' staff turnover rates in their organisation with that of other organisations in the same industry, or against national trends. The planner also needs to identify staff turnover figures by section or department. To achieve this, they may decide to calculate the turnover for *every* department and function in the organisation.

Calculating the sectional distribution of staff turnover is vital if projection of future HR needs is to be useful in building a picture of how the organisation works from a human resource planning perspective. If, as in example (1) in Case Example 5.6, the past turnover trend of 4% is likely to continue, the HR department will need to recruit at least 88 new employees in the forthcoming year. Furthermore, having completed the calculation in other departments and functions, a picture will have emerged of where and how many replacement staff will be needed. More importantly, the data will also provide information on the kinds of disciplines, skill sets and other qualities required. This type of information is useful when determining the projected workload for the HR department.

Understanding the various profiles of staff turnover across the organisation may unveil problems that are unrelated to the immediate task, which was to understand the nature of staff turnover trends within the organisation.

CASE EXAMPLE 5.7

ONE PROBLEM LEADS TO ANOTHER

The organisation has a staff turnover problem. In Department A, turnover is 2%, in Department B it is 3% and in Department C it is 10%. Calculating an average value produces a figure of 4.1% across all three departments. (Note percentages cannot be averaged; the raw turnover and average number of staff figures have to be used to calculate the overall turnover.)

Clearly, there is a greater staff turnover problem in Department C when compared with the low turnover figures for Departments A and B. Rather than simply allowing for such a high figure when she was projecting HR requirements, Julie, the HR manager, decided to investigate the possibility of reducing it. She wanted to know why it compared so unfavourably with the figures for the other two departments, not only because a high staff turnover is costly in recruitment terms, but because Julie suspected that there might be a deeper problem.

She assigned the task to Jack, who discovered that people were leaving because they were fed up with the communication style of the manager. This triggered a further investigation, after which the manager agreed to receive counselling and development training in interpersonal and basic people management skills.

This is an example of how a problem in one area of HR can uncover an entirely different kind of problem. Rather than being a problem simply based in hard HRM terms, it was one with its roots in soft HRM.

Staff turnover figures vary considerably between different kinds of organisation and between different industries. Figures for national turnover averages are collected by the CIPD. They are characterised by public and private sector and by type of organisation.

In Case Example 5.7, the point is made that recruitment is costly and a staff turnover that is too high can cause financial problems. Equally, however, a staff turnover that is too low may also cause problems. An organisation needs to maintain objectivity when it is assessing the efficiency and effectiveness of its operations and new people coming into the organisation bring new ideas; they can, perhaps, see things more objectively than those who have been with the organisation for many years.

Long-serving people fall into work routines that they perform out of habit; the habits become *activity ruts* and they fail to notice areas in which improvements could be made. New people will bring in a fresh perspective influenced by different experiences in other organisations. If a too-high or a too-low staff turnover rate can be problematic, the aim is to achieve a healthy balance of in-house experience and incoming fresh ideas.

 ## ACTIVITY 5.6

From the 2013 CIPD/Hays *Resourcing and Talent Planning* annual survey report (p.40), the median figures for staff turnover for the private and public sector are given as follows:

Sector/Year	2009	2010	2011	2012	2013
Private	16.8%	14.6%	13.8%	16.1%	16.3%
Public	12.6%	8.6%	8.5%	10.1%	9.4%

1 Taken year on year, the median turnover rates for the private compared with the public sector are higher. Can you suggest whether there might be an underlying reason why this should be so?

2 Why do you think the CIPD/Hays use median rates rather than average rates of turnover? You will get some ideas as to why the median, as opposed to the average or mean, is used by reading Chapter 19, 'Handling and Managing Information'.

3 Calculate the average rate of turnover for the organisation in which you work and compare these figures with the figures found in the above CIPD survey. How does your organisation compare?

5.8.4 CALCULATING THE WORKFORCE STABILITY INDEX

Just as important as staff turnover is the workforce stability index (WSI). This is also expressed as a percentage and is calculated as follows:

$$\frac{\text{Number of employees with more than one year's service}}{\text{Number of employees employed one year ago}} \times 100 = \text{WSI (\%)}$$

Experience shows that people who are going to leave do so in their first year of employment, and that those who stay for a year will probably stay for much longer. The WSI, therefore, is useful in that it provides an indication of the percentage of people who will be unlikely to leave in the forthcoming year. In the above form, however, it does not take account of the number of people joining the organisation during the past year, nor does it account for exact length of service, although there are techniques that can be used to obtain such information.

The problem with turnover statistics is that they only give numerical data. They say nothing about the quality of staff who may have left. This is why it might also be worth considering some technique which tracks particular groups of staff who are key to the organisation. Cohort analysis is one method of tracking what happens to staff which the organisation can ill afford to lose.

5.8.5 COHORT ANALYSIS

A cohort is a group of people who have some characteristic which is common to all. Examples of cohorts could be: for a hi-tech organisation, the number of technician apprentices recruited in one year; for a logistics company, the number of long distance lorry drivers; or for a train company, the number of engine drivers.

The workforce stability index can also be used in an innovative way to calculate information about identifiable and specific groups (cohorts) of staff who join the organisation, for example, graduate recruits.

As part of the talent management process, it is a common-sense approach to track groups of staff who have been targeted with the specific purpose of becoming the organisation's future management or technical elite. Significant expenditure both in time and money has gone into the selection and recruitment of these people, or groups of people, so their progress should to be monitored both from a personal development point of view and also as a group to assess the effectiveness of the selection – induction – development – reward process.

Consider the following analysis of graduate intake as recruited by a large supermarket chain:

Graduates recruited:
Cohorts: 2005 (10 graduates); 2006 (15 graduates); 2007 (15 graduates); 2008 (6 graduates); 2009 (4); 2010 (4); 2011 (6); 2012 (9); 2013 (10)

In 2013 the records for the previously recruited cohorts were analysed and the following was found:

Cohort leavers: 2005 (7); 2006 (7); 2007 (8); 2008 (1); 2009 (1); 2010 (2); 2011 (3); 2012 (4); 2013 (7)

From the above information the retention ratio, let us call it the cohort stability index (CSI), for the seven cohorts was calculated using the stability index method but over the time they had been working for the company.

$$\frac{\text{Number of graduates from cohort in employ } 31^{st} \text{ Dec. } 2013}{\text{Number of graduates recruited in cohort}} \times 100 = \text{CSI } (\%)$$

Cohort stability index (retention ratio): 2005 (30%); 2006 (53%); 2007 (47%); 2008 (83%); 2009 (75%); 2010 (50%); 2011 (50%); 2012 (56%); 2013 (30%)

Clearly something is amiss with the retention of graduate recruits. Retention is poor, with the exception of the 2008 and 2009 intakes, which could possibly be explained by recessional pressures causing a general reluctance of people to leave jobs. Of some concern is that from 2010 onwards, the stability index drops below an acceptable level. Research shows that the first 12–18 months of a graduate's time with an organisation is crucial in the building of a bond between the organisation and the individual, so some turnover is expected in this type of group. However, something is amiss, and further detailed analysis is required.

You will glean some explanation of the possible causes of the turnover problem by reading Chapter 8, 'Induction and Retention' and Chapter 2, 'Aspects of Organisation Culture'.

ACTIVITY 5.7

Taking the role of the group HR director, in the above supermarket chain, what steps would you take to determine why a significant number of the graduates recruited by your organisation decide to leave?

- How would you determine what is an acceptable number of leavers from any one cohort over, say, a five-year period?
- What may cause a graduate to move from one organisation to another?

5.8.6 ANALYSES OF LABOUR TURNOVER

As early as 1955, Hill and Trist identified three phases in labour turnover, the *induction crisis*, *differential transit* and *settled connection*. The induction crisis was alluded to above by saying that people who are likely to leave their organisation do so in the first 12 months or so of employment. The reasoning behind the induction crisis is explored further in Chapter 8, 'Induction and Retention'.

According to Beardwell et al (2004), 'the major drawback with all quantitative methods of turnover analysis is that they provide no information on the reasons why people are leaving. ... Quantitative analyses can help to highlight problems, but they give those responsible for planning no indication about how these problems might be addressed.'

5.8.7 EXIT INTERVIEWS

In addition to quantitative methods of calculating turnover and stability, data using qualitative research methods may be gathered, for example, from exit interviews. These are most frequently carried out when the departing employee is leaving to join another employer. The main purpose of carrying out exit interviews is, as its name implies, to gather information about the reasons for leaving. For example, it may be that pay and other entitlements and benefits may be more attractive elsewhere, or the prospects of training and promotion are better. Analysis of responses from the exit interviews may be valuable in the sense that information could be fed back into the organisation to make improvements or change practices.

It should be remembered, however, that the responses to an exit questionnaire or a face-to-face interview may not be totally reliable, bearing in mind that the person leaving will be aware that their next employer might request a reference. The interviewee's responses may therefore be couched in terms designed to ensure that nothing is said that might diminish the value of the reference, or the chance of re-employment at some stage later. It is not obligatory for a departing employee to submit to an exit interview, but most leavers will agree; if only on the grounds that a refusal might negatively influence their 'reference'.

ACTIVITY 5.8

Considering the practicalities of conducting exit interviews:

● Who do you think is best positioned to conduct the interview in respect of obtaining the *real* reason why someone has decided to leave the company?

● What other options does a company have to obtain this type of information from leavers?

5.9 PLANNING

5.9.1 DEALING WITH DEFICITS AND SURPLUSES

Referring to Figure 5.2, the third stage in the planning process involves the planner in identifying imbalances between demand and supply. While this would have implications for recruitment, in terms of the geographic scope of the search for talent; it would also trigger a *skills audit* of the current workforce. The audit would probably give consideration as to whether there is some capability within existing staff to retrain or up-skill. The planner has to take numerous factors into account, including future developments, work patterns, planned changes to organisation structure, and policies and procedures such as those for managing reward, diversity, training and development.

 KEY CONCEPT: SKILLS AUDIT

This is a way of identifying the competence gap at departmental and sectional levels. The skills needed to carry out all of the tasks on time and at the required standard are listed and placed against the skills possessed by all of the members within a section or department. Where deficits are found, arrangements can be made for the gaps to be filled.

A skills audit is a reconciliation process in which problems, and the solutions to problems, may be hard or soft. Piercy (1989), writing about strategic planning in the general context, suggests a set of tools to help managers to work through the issues that may arise.

On the hard (HRM) side, the feasibility of the plan may be focused on the supply forecast being less, in available numbers of employees, than the demand forecast. For example, the forecasts may have revealed a shortage of a particular skill in both the internal and external labour markets, to the extent that it might be difficult to fulfil parts of the demand. There is currently (May 2014) a recognition that certain professional technical skills, for example first degree qualified mechanical, electrical and electronics engineers, are in short supply within the UK (external) labour market and companies are having to stretch their recruitment net into other EU countries to source staff.

Piercy (1989) recommends that:

● Alter the demand forecast by considering the effect of changes in the utilisation of employees, such as training and productivity deals, or high-performance teams.
● Alter the demand forecast by considering using different types of employees to meet the corporate objectives, such as employing a smaller number of staff with higher-level skills, or employing staff with insufficient skills and training them immediately.

- Change the company objectives, as lack of staff will prevent them from being achieved in any case. Realistic objectives may need to be based on the staff who are, and are forecast to be, available.

When the demand forecast is less than the internal supply forecast in some areas, departments or sections of the organisation, the possibilities are to consider four options:

- Consider and calculate the costs of overemployment over various time spans.
- Consider the methods and cost of (losing) reducing staff numbers.
- Consider changes in utilisation: work out the feasibility and costs of retraining, redeployment and so on.
- Consider whether it is possible for the company objectives to be changed. Could the company diversify, move into new markets, and so on (Piercy, 1989)? This has links to the resource-based view (RBV) of the firm (see Chapter 3, 'Human Resource Management').

It is worth a reminder at this stage that HRP is a continuous and circular process: 'Because of unpredictable events, the implementation of action plans does not always run smoothly. It is necessary to monitor progress carefully, evaluate the effects and, as required, amend the action plan' (Armstrong, 2012, p.215). Staff movements and changes to other organisational plans trigger amendments to the HR plan. The HR plan is never fixed but is dynamic in nature. On the soft side, however, there are factors that need to be taken into account, such as the degree to which the changes are acceptable to the senior managers who have their sights set on the vision of the future for the organisation. There is a need to reflect the needs of employees and to manage the culture of the organisation and the psychological contract. Sometimes HR planners will find themselves 'selling' the plan within the organisation. They need to have the political and emotional awareness and 'streetwise savvy' to tap into the thinking of senior colleagues and managers from other disciplines within the organisation and to be aware of the factors that could facilitate or hinder implementation of a well-thought-through HR plan.

5.9.2 WHAT MAKES A HUMAN RESOURCE PLAN?

Students often ask, 'What does the HR plan actually look like?' The answer is that it is virtually impossible, and not really advisable, to draw up a grand plan containing all of the necessary features. With the demand and supply situations reconciled, and feasible solutions decided upon, specific action plans are designed to include all of the organisational areas and activities. Rather than a single HR plan, therefore, there are a number of action plans.

The following is adapted from Torrington and Hall (1998) and Torrington et al (2007):

1 **Human resource supply plans:** Plans may need to be made concerning the timing and approach to recruitment or downsizing. For example, it may have been decided that to recruit sufficient staff, a public relations campaign is needed to promote the company image. Internal movement plans would also be relevant here. Serious consideration should be given to succession planning.
   Talent management and mentoring plans are important. The focus on talent management is important in so much as thought and due consideration should be given to the available stock {meaning – *quantity and quality of talented people*} and necessary developmental routes to ensure that there is a reservoir of competent people, with the appropriate experiences, to move into the positions of senior members of the management team as they move or retire.

2 **Organisation and structure plans:** These plans may concern departmental structure and the relationships between departments. They may also be concerned with the hierarchy within departments and the levels at which tasks are carried out. Changes to organisation and structure will usually result in changes in employee utilisation.

3   **Employee utilisation plans:** Any changes in utilisation that affect human resource demand will need to be planned. Some changes will result in a sudden difference in employees' tasks and the numbers needed. Managers need to work out the new tasks to be done and the old ones to be dropped. Other plans may involve the distribution of hours worked: for example, the use of 'annualised hours' contracts or the use of functional flexibility, where employees develop and use a wider range of skills. All of the employees involved will need to be consulted about the changes and be prepared and trained for what will happen. A final consideration is: if fewer employees are needed, what criteria will be used to determine which jobs should be made redundant and who can be redeployed and retrained, and into which areas?

4   **Training and management development plans:** There will be training implications taken from both the HR supply and utilisation plans. The timing of the training can be a critical aspect. For example, training for specific new technology skills loses most of its impact unless it is carried out immediately after installation, or even before, using process simulators.

5   **Performance plans:** These directly address performance issues: for example, the introduction of an objective-setting and performance management system, setting performance and quality standards, or culture change programmes aimed at encouraging specified behaviour and performance.

6   **Appraisal plans:** The organisation needs to make sure it is assessing the important aspects of work. For example, if customer service is paramount, employees need to be assessed on relevant aspects of customer service. Linking appraisal to pay reinforces the importance of customer service and provides a mechanism for improvement in this area.

7   **Reward plans:** It is often said that what gets rewarded gets done, and it is key that the rewards reflect what the organisation sees as important, as indicated in point 6 above.

8   **Employee relations plans:** These plans may involve unions, employee representatives or all employees. They include any matters that need to be negotiated or areas where there is the opportunity for employee involvement and participation.

9   **Communication plans:** The way that planned changes are communicated to employees is critical. Plans need to include methods for informing employees what is expected of them, and methods that enable employees to express their concerns and needs if implementation is to be successful. Means of eliciting employee commitment are also important: for example, communicating information about the progress of the organisation.

5.9.3 UNDERSTANDING WORKFORCE CHARACTERISTICS

An HR manager should understand the characteristics of the organisation's workforce. This means collecting data on skills, competencies and also gender, ethnicity and age, etc. From a workforce planning perspective equality issues are important but also, by understanding the demographics of the organisation, the HR manager/planner can identify issues which might impact upon the effectiveness of the organisation.

This year [2013] HM Revenue and Customs won a well deserved prestigious award from the Employers Network for Equality and Inclusion (ENEI) for the approach it has taken to ensure a balanced workforce age profile. Like most other civil service organisations and UK plc, it is characterised by a workforce 'broadly' reflective of the ageing demographics of the UK. However, workforce analysis showed a disproportionate number of employees aged over 50 – at 35% of the organisation, in comparison with 28% of the UK working population – while only 13% were aged under 30, compared with a UK-wide figure of approximately 19%. This age-skewed profile presented HMRC with a challenge that needed attention to protect its capability to deliver its business aims and objectives. (Worman, 2013, pp.36–8)

Equality legislation prevents positive discrimination to redress a skewing of the age profile caused by an ageing workforce. It is important to investigate and understand the age profile of an organisation and how this has impacted upon absence, sickness and the progressive skills depletion and loss of knowledge as people ask for flexible working patterns or go on partial and eventually full retirement. By addressing, rather than ignoring, the challenges and also opportunities of the changes in workforce demographics, the organisation is better equipped to consider the impact upon its ability to meet both current and future objectives.

You can read the full Worman (2013) article at:

WORMAN, D. (2013) Is the age of your workforce in shape to deliver your business objectives? *CIPD Impact Magazine*. Issue 44, pp.36–8, at: **www.cipd.co.uk/ impactmagazine**

5.10 JOB ANALYSIS

As a practitioner, the effectiveness in carrying out HR planning procedures will be influenced by the degree to which they understand the jobs: for example, in terms of their content, the required competences, where in the organisation they are situated, the degree to which they are subject to change and many other details. This information is obtained through the process of job analysis.

5.10.1 WHAT IS JOB ANALYSIS?

Job analysis is an operational, data-gathering process that involves reducing every job to its constituent parts, including the nature of the activities, the task-related responsibilities that the job entails, the knowledge and skills that are required to carry out the work, the reporting responsibilities and the level of the job. Work methods sometimes change, perhaps through the introduction of new technology and, when this occurs, parts of the job need to be updated, which means that the future job-holder might use different work methods to achieve the same or modified ends. If the tasks and the skills needed to carry them out in the future are integrated into the final analysis, the process is referred to as *job modelling*.

5.10.2 PURPOSE

On the grounds that the products of job analyses are job descriptions and person specifications, books on this subject often discuss job analysis in a chapter on recruitment and selection. Pilbeam and Corbridge argue that:

In addition to recruitment and selection, job analysis information is fundamental to many other HR management activities, including establishing the job requirements for appraising performance development needs; making reward comparisons between jobs; considering the implications of legislation relating to health and safety, . . . disciplinary matters or the negotiation of job changes. (Pilbeam and Corbridge, 2010, p.160)

It is worth noting that job analyses that have been competently carried out are prerequisites for many decisions and activities that have a crucial influence on the lives of employees, including:

- designing systems of payment
- designing work systems

- designing and remodelling the jobs themselves
- assessing the competences that are required to carry out the job effectively
- training and longer-term career development needs
- building health and safety policies and procedures, and auditing health and safety practices.

Although not always evident in practice, there is an important distinction between *job descriptions* and *roles*. A *job description* defines a series of tasks which have to be done, whereas a *role profile* defines the outcomes.

 ACTIVITY 5.9

First, analyse your own job or a job that you have held in the past and arrange the tasks and responsibilities in order of importance. Compare how you have described the job with the contents of your actual description. Secondly, do the same with a colleague's job. How do they compare? What are the key differences?

5.11 JOB DESCRIPTIONS AND ROLE DEFINITIONS

According to Armstrong (2012, p.534), '...a job description is more concerned with tasks than outcomes, and with the duties to be performed than the competencies required to perform them...'.

5.11.1 FLEXIBLE APPROACH

Many academics and managers take a flexible view of what a job actually involves. Some even regard the job description as redundant and say *role profiles* should be used to replace the traditional job description. The *role profile* defines the outcomes of the job rather than the detailed content of the job. The reason for this is that the rate at which organisations are changing and developing is still increasing, and many line managers feel that job descriptions inhibit the flexibility that is needed to respond adequately to customer demands. The case they make is that:

> inflexible definitions of jobs place limitations on change and development because they do not allow for changes in deployment or for multi-skilling and a wide variety of other factors that describe the reality of the ways in which the talents of the human resource need to be maximised in today's organisations. (Currie, 2006)

5.11.2 DEFINING THE 'ROLE'

One approach to resolving this dilemma is for the organisation to reach an agreement with the employee in which the role is loosely defined and there is mutual agreement that within the limits of the individual's capabilities, and trainability, the role may be flexible and subject to change. The role defines both outcomes and behaviours of the individual and so is quite *loose*, when compared with the idea of a *rigid* job description. Bratton and Gold (2012) further discuss the introduction of *performance contracts*: they suggest that the performance contract contains details of what the job-holder agrees to accomplish within a given time and also includes, in a summary format, the purpose (objectives) of a job, and how the achievement of the objectives will be met. This type of approach, which focuses on outcomes rather than the content of a job (see also Chapter 6, 'Recruitment') has implications for the kinds of people the organisation prefers to recruit: those people who are sufficiently willing and motivated to accept the challenge of change. This also implies that the traditional approach to analysing jobs may, in some organisations, be inappropriate.

PAUSE FOR THOUGHT

Job versus role

Stop and think for a moment. Would you prefer to have a job, which is described by Armstrong as a 'fixed entity, part of a machine that is designed like any other part of a machine', or would you prefer to have a role in the organisation, which means playing a flexible part in the changing organisation?

While working in Kazakhstan the author was the HR manager for an international oil and gas operating company. Many of the indigenous staff, who had previously worked under the old Soviet regime, where everything was highly regulated, wanted tightly specified job descriptions. Culture impacts upon the way people think and behave.

5.12 INFORMATION FROM A JOB ANALYSIS

The information that you obtain from a job analysis may be summarised as:

- **The overall purpose of the job:** what the job is for and how it contributes to the achievement of the organisation's objectives.
- **The type of job:** the nature of the tasks and responsibilities; the duties to be carried out and the expected outcomes.
- **The essential skills, knowledge and attributes** required of the job-holder.
- **Professional jobs:** does the job-holder need to be a member of a recognised professional institution such as those for law, accountancy, HR, and so on?
- **Exclusivity:** is the job the only one of its kind in the organisation, or are there other similar jobs or jobs to which this one is related?
- **The location of the job:** in which department or functional area does it exist?
- **The status of the job:** where does the job stand in the departmental structure?
- **Reporting responsibilities:** to whom does the job-holder report, such as to a line manager for their work performance and to an appropriate senior manager for specialised responsibilities such as IT, marketing or finance?
- **Motivation:** the degree to which motivational factors and/or demotivators are built into the job.
- **Movement:** is the current job-holder likely to move upwards or laterally in the organisation in the foreseeable future?

5.13 GATHERING THE INFORMATION: FOUR STEPS

As much relevant information needs to be collected as is practicable and, above all, the information has to be accurate. To achieve this the following four steps are suggested:

Step 1: Examine documents that provide information about the job. These include the existing job description. Relevant information about the job may also be obtained from training manuals and other job-related records.

Step 2: Interview the job-holder. Here, you seek information about the activities that are involved in carrying out the job.

Step 3: Talk to the manager to whom the job-holder reports about the purpose of the job and to confirm the information that was provided by the job-holder.
Step 4: Observe employees while they are doing their jobs.

Using a range of techniques and collating information from multiple sources, as suggested above, is more likely to deliver a quality analysis of the job.

5.13.1 EXAMINING DOCUMENTS

The important features of the existing job description are the date on which it was last reviewed and why it was reviewed. The existing job description can be compared with the data collected from the job-holder. As previously mentioned, training manuals will contain information about the knowledge and skills required to carry out the job effectively. Individuals' records include data about their performance standards and the training to which they have been exposed. The task of defining the job description is detailed, laborious and time-consuming.

5.13.2 INTERVIEWING THE JOB-HOLDER

Depending on the scope and complexity of the job, it may be advisable, two or three weeks in advance, to ask the job-holder to keep a diary or an activity record of the tasks that they perform. Since this is done on a daily and weekly basis, as the job is being carried out, it avoids problems associated with faulty memory and the current incumbent 'talking-up' their job (see 'Conducting the interview' below). Again this may be difficult at times and time-consuming.

As a matter of courtesy, the job-holder's line manager should be informed. In addition, it is essential to tell the interviewee the exact purpose/reason for conducting the interview. If this is not done the employee may become uneasy, thinking perhaps that the job is going to be redesigned or, even worse, that they might be made redundant.

5.13.3 PREPARING FOR THE INTERVIEW

It is advisable to prepare for the interview by drafting a questionnaire that includes not only the basic elements of the job, as described above, but also further supplementary questions. The questionnaire will act as a checklist and enable a logical sequence to be built into the interview (see Table 5.2). Good practice is to prepare a semi-structured interview, with some pre-prepared questions, yet leaving gaps for the job-holder to give their own personal slant to the interviewer, and so perhaps offer some insights into elements of the job that were not obvious to the unskilled eye.

The questions listed in Table 5.2 are not exhaustive. Most of the questions included in the table may be asked about any job. It is an obvious advantage if the job has been analysed previously. The information that was gathered then, the questions asked and the answers given, should have been archived with the HR department. HR information systems (HRIS) usually have this basic type of data-capture facility built in.

By comparing the previously gathered information with the freshly gathered information, it is possible to assess the degree to which the job has changed.

5.13.4 CONDUCTING THE INTERVIEW

While common sense tells us that the job-holder should be able to give a good account of the information about the activities involved in the job, some caution needs to be exercised, since it sometimes happens that information obtained in this way conflicts with that provided by the manager. For example, when a job is first created it is the organisation that prescribes its content in terms of the order of importance in which the tasks and accountabilities are arranged. Experience shows that after individuals have settled into their jobs, they unconsciously alter the task priorities to suit their own liking and abilities, favouring some tasks above others. Job-holders have also been known to give an inflated account of the importance of what they do. Despite this, the job-holder can provide some useful information, but it is always advisable to 'check back' with the line manager after interviewing the job-holder.

Interviewees are sometimes inclined to offer more information than you have asked for, and some of this may not be relevant. On the other hand, answers may be lacking in sufficient detail, especially when answering questions about items that the job-holder appears to be unsure about or perceives to be at the bottom of their priorities. In such cases there is a need to probe more deeply to get the information required.

Table 5.2 Job analysis interview – questionnaire

Questions
What is your job title?
What is the job title of your manager?
What is the purpose of your job?
Does anyone in the organisation do a similar job and, if so, how many?
What do you actually do? (Here you ask the job-holder to list the job-related duties, tasks performed, measurements taken, recording of information, types of communication with others: verbal, electronic, written, and so on.)
Did you require training to enable you to do your job?
Would anyone require training regardless of their qualifications and experience?
What knowledge and skills are needed to do your job?
What qualifications and experience do you need to carry out your job?
Do you have people reporting to you and, if so, how many?
What are their job titles?
How would you describe your responsibilities?
Do you have authority to make decisions and, if so, what types of decision?
Do you have contact with others within the organisation and externally?
Does your job involve travelling and/or working unsocial hours on behalf of the organisation?
What problems do you encounter in your job?
What performance standards are required of you in your job?

 ACTIVITY 5.10

First, think of the ways in which the information from a job analysis may affect people's lives at work. Second, think about how any significant changes made as a result of the job analysis and incorporated into the job description might affect the status of the job itself.

5.13.5 INTERVIEWING THE LINE MANAGER

The interview with the line manager should cover two main areas:

1   First, it is to discuss the answers given by their staff member. For example, the manager may help to sift out any irrelevant material, such as responsibilities that may have been inflated, or help with the technical detail that was not fully explained by the employee.

2   Second, it is to discuss what the manager knows about the future of the job. For example, technological change might be on the horizon that may have implications for the design of the job, including changes in the necessary competences required of the incumbent employee.

It may be clear from the job analysis that a similar task is duplicated elsewhere in the organisation. It may be that the job would be better incorporated with another to improve the way work is carried out and perhaps be more rewarding, financially and in terms of the quality of the work.

5.13.6 USING OBSERVATIONAL METHODS

For this, *structured observational techniques* (see below) are used and those being observed should be advised that they are observed while they work and why the observation is taking place. The fact that they are aware of why you are observing them may cause them to modify what they would do in a normal unobserved situation, but it is still possible to gather useful information in this way from, say, office or factory floor workers.

KEY CONCEPT: STRUCTURED AND PARTICIPANT OBSERVATION

Observation may be *structured*, in which the observer simply watches and notes what the person does, or it may be *participant observation*, in which the observer works with the person and gathers *qualitative* rather than *quantitative* information. In both cases the person being observed must be told the purpose of the observation.

5.14 MODERN APPROACHES TO HUMAN RESOURCE PLANNING

This section of the chapter focuses on the principles of human resource planning in terms of the modern approaches that are taken by many organisations. It reflects how traditional HRP has been revised to produce differences in the aims of HRP and the thinking that underlies modern practices.

Key to successful HR planning (HRP) is management involvement and explicit agreement to the project. It is a business process, not simply an HR process. In this sense the politically astute HR manager will involve senior management at an early stage in the planning process to explain why a review or partial review of part of the business is required. HR can gather data on skills, skills shortages, skills surpluses, age profiles, and so on, but how the changes are handled is a management, not HR, prerogative. HR can and should advise and facilitate the changes.

The aims of HRP are to:

● identify the number of people required with the appropriate skills, expertise and competences (that is, the mix of hard and soft elements of the planning process)

- anticipate problems of potential surpluses or deficits of people
- develop a well-trained and flexible workforce, thus contributing to the organisation's ability to adapt to an uncertain and changing environment
- reduce dependence on external recruitment when key skills are in short supply by formulating retention and development strategies
- improve the utilisation of people by introducing more flexible systems of work
- identify and put in place succession plans for key roles
- develop talent management plans for key technical and managerial roles.

(after Armstrong, 2006)

As can be seen from the first two of these aims, they are similar to those of traditional HRP. However, the overall thrust of modern HRP redirects the focus away from the practices of traditional manpower planning and towards an emphasis on internal workforce flexibility. Problems of deficits and surpluses in the HR demand and supply situations are dealt with first through the development and redevelopment of the internal workforce. Where recruitment is necessary, part-time workers may be brought in and short-term contracts are offered to people whose skills are needed for limited periods. See also the discussion of the concept of 'core and peripheral workers' in Chapter 1.

The underlying thinking here is that a more flexible workforce, with a broad repertoire of skills and competences available when needed, is more likely to be able to respond appropriately to the volatile demands of today's turbulent market.

5.15 SUCCESSION PLANNING AND TALENT MANAGEMENT

Succession planning is a process which focuses on key senior management and other critical positions within an organisation. For example, let us consider how an international organisation might seek to identify who will replace the HR director when she retires or perhaps moves on to another organisation.

Plans and individual programmes of development have to start well in advance of the need to appoint the replacement. Graduates will have to be recruited, trained in the core skills of the profession, perhaps by following a CIPD advanced course of study. They will also require exposure to the various HR disciplines – recruitment, reward, employee relations, and so on – as part of their training. They will also have to be exposed to the management of people – common sense suggests both in the UK and overseas. This could be achieved by a cross posting, for example into the HR function within a UK subsidiary company and perhaps overseas to one of the organisation's operations. In this way the person being developed can accumulate and assimilate the skills, competencies and experiences to take on a very senior role. With a cadre of talented candidates 'in the wings', final plans can be put in place to hone the development of one or two people who could 'step into the shoes' of the HR director.

As the CIPD (2013c) says, succession planning 'may be broadly defined as a process for identifying and developing potential future leaders or senior managers, as well as individuals to fill other business-critical positions, either in the short or the long term.'

Talent planning has close links to succession planning. Talent planning is the process of identifying the key roles within an organisation and recruiting, developing, retaining and placing competent individuals into those roles. The title is, perhaps, pertinent to 5% or perhaps 10% of the workforce. As well as the identification of talent, it also includes the development of a pipeline of talent that can supply people into these roles.

The CIPD (2013c) defines talent and talent management in the following way:

Talent consists of those individuals who can make a difference to organisational performance either through their immediate contribution or, in the longer term, by demonstrating the highest levels of potential.

Talent management is the systematic attraction, identification, development, engagement, retention and deployment of those individuals who are of particular value to an organisation, either in view of their 'high potential' for the future or because they are fulfilling business-/operation-critical roles.

Talent planning is a process with a 'long lead time' and involves proactive interventions to identify and develop links with reservoirs of talent – schools, colleges, universities – to nurture these relationships. It may involve providing summer placements for students, which are more than a 'summer job', because the placement has a purpose and so is structured, and involves training and interesting experiences. Talent has to be nurtured, so once recruited into the organisation care should be taken by developing and delivering:

- induction programmes which seek to go beyond the basics of explaining about reporting relationships, salary, holiday entitlement and health and safety, but rather to consider deeper relations through a structured process of building cultural bonds
- professional programmes of training with planned stages of experience and roles
- challenging tasks that offer the opportunity for people management and business management roles which are both financially and emotionally rewarding.

How individuals feel about belonging to an organisation is important and so talent management has strong links with the concept of the employer brand. Refer to Chapter 6, 'Recruitment' as well as to Torrington et al (2011, pp.170–71) for a more detailed discussion of employer branding.

ACTIVITY 5.11

Consider whether a small organisation of 150 employees should involve itself in talent management. Would this be a pointless luxury leading to nowhere?

You will get help by reading the CIPD (2010a) survey, *The Talent Perspective: What does it feel like to be talent managed?* Available at: **www.cipd.co.uk/binaries/5262_Talent_Perspective.pdf**

5.16 IMPLEMENTATION AND CONTROL

Once the planning process has been completed and budgets developed, the HR department's staff start to put the well-developed plans into action. This could mean:

1 promoting and training existing staff
2 retraining and perhaps redeploying employees whose jobs are no longer required
3 recruiting and training people from outside the business
4 making redundant employees who are surplus to the needs of the organisation.

It is not inconceivable that points (3) and (4) could potentially occur simultaneously.

However, assuming that new plans have been put into place, the planning process will be revisited after a period of time. The period of time could be as little as 12 months for a micro plan, where a department or section is concerned, but could, for a full-scale planning activity, be undertaken after two to three years. The frequency will depend upon the type of sector and market that the organisation operates within.

5.17 THE INFLUENCE OF BUSINESS STRATEGY

The degree to which an HR strategist can operate effectively is determined by the clarity of the business strategy. In a previous era business strategies worked because the market was more stable than it is today; this is a recurring theme of discussion. The objective is to achieve a competitive advantage, and the ability of business strategists to be precise about their requirements is governed by market forces that, in turn, govern the degree to which the HR strategists can be precise. Whittington (1993) points out that strategies may be deliberate or emergent.

Deliberate strategies assume a rational evaluation of external and internal circumstances and an identification of the best way to achieve a competitive advantage.

Emergent strategies, on the other hand, 'emerge on the basis of a series of decisions, a pattern in which, becomes clear over time ... not as a "grand plan", but as a developing "pattern in a stream of decisions"' (Johnson et al, 2011, p.404).

'The most appropriate strategies ... emerge as competitive processes that allow the comparatively better performers to survive while the weaker performers are squeezed out' (Legge, 1995, p.99).

An *emergent strategy* is one that, as its name implies, emerges as the business trades. For this to work senior managers must be scanning their business for signs of an emerging trend on which a strategy can start to be formed. Text messaging was designed as a by-product of mobile telecommunications; there was initially no expectation, and therefore no strategy, to build it into the multi-million-pound business it is today.

ACTIVITY 5.12

1   How does the content of the teaching on your course match up to the ideas that are expressed above? Is the teaching, for example, emergent and does it develop as the course progresses, with the lecturer taking advantage of opportunities for learning in the class? Or is it deliberate and focused on a prescribed plan and delivery process?

2   How has your organisation's approach to home or remote working changed as the development of new information technologies become both available and robust in operation?

3   Is the HR strategy in your organisation deliberate and focused on prescribed business goals and business strategy or is it emergent in nature? Can you think of examples in the workplace when issues have arisen that have caused policy to be changed?

5.18 SUMMARY

Those involved in early industrial activity, even before the Industrial Revolution, tried to ensure that there would be people feeding through businesses to succeed longer-serving skilled employees. With the Industrial Revolution came the development of factories and larger-scale industries, which eventually demanded a more organisation-wide approach to planning the future workforce. By the twentieth century, apprenticeship schemes were widespread and the demand was for the continuation of traditional skills to serve the purposes of a largely manufacturing economy.

In more recent times the recession, which started in 2008, has caused the Government to consider a move away from total reliance on the financial sector of the economy to developing a more mixed economy where manufacturing is seen as a key part of the country's turnaround strategy. This has caused a renewal of interest in apprenticeships, in all sectors, as a way to improve the quality of the workforce.

Manpower planning, now referred to as HR planning (HRP), appeared in the 1960s, and a modified version of it is still practised. Information technology has eased the activities related to HR planning. In the 1980s HR planning was revised to enable organisations to meet the demands of a rapidly developing and fiercely competitive global market. Many of the traditional practices are still used for HRP purposes, but new HR resourcing strategies have been introduced.

Planning itself was always an imprecise process, but the rate of change that was necessary to sustain a competitive advantage shortened planning periods and altered strategic emphases. The degree to which HR planners can be precise in their forecasts is determined by the business strategy, which, in turn, is strongly influenced by market forces. The ideas underlying modern strategic developments in the management of employment and employee relations call for a workforce that is flexible and able to respond appropriately. Planning needs to access the *soft* as well as the *hard* dimensions of HRM.

Staff turnover is an issue for many organisations. Using analytical means to calculate staff turnover rates can lead to insights into why turnover may be high in certain parts of the organisation.

HR planning can consider the whole or part of an organisation and is relevant to organisations of all sizes. Specific elements of planning such as succession planning and talent management justify separate consideration because they are concerned with the development of people into key roles within the organisation.

Successful HR planning must be seen as core to the business process and so must involve senior managers if it has any chance to succeed.

REVIEW QUESTIONS

1 What are the purposes of HR planning?

2 Why were organisations slow to adopt manpower planning when it was first introduced?

3 How would you define HR planning?

4 What is meant by *soft* and *hard* HR planning?

5 What factors influence the length of planning periods?

6 Why is HRP said to be a 'competence-centred' function?

7 What are the four main elements in the process of HR planning?

8 What is meant by the terms 'top-down' and 'bottom-up' in terms of approaches to HRP?

9 Find out from your HR manager how frequently your organisation engages in a full-scale planning activity that covers the whole firm. How often do micro planning activities take place where departments or sections are reviewed?

10 How would you calculate staff turnover rates? Why is it an important activity?

11 How would you calculate the organisation's workforce stability index?

12 What is 'cohort analysis'? What cohorts or groups can you recognise in your organisation (or an organisation that you know) that would be worth tracking in terms of their turnover rates? Explain and justify why you have chosen these particular groups or cohorts.

13 How might imbalances between HR demand and supply be reconciled?

14 What are the four steps you can take to gather information when carrying out a job analysis?

15 How would you distinguish between deliberate and emergent strategies? Why is it important to recognise that some strategies are emergent?

16 Referring to Figure 5.2, discuss the limitations of the data provided. What (external type) statistics would be more meaningful for an HR planner working in a medium to large organisation?

17 Using information from the Office for National Statistics website (**www. statistics.gov.uk/elmr**), find out how many people are employed in the following occupations:

- agriculture and fisheries
- energy and water
- manufacturing
- construction
- distribution
- transport
- finance and business
- public sector.

EXPLORE FURTHER

BOOKS

BRATTON, J. and GOLD, J. (2012) *Human resource management: theory and practice* 5th ed. Basingstoke: Palgrave Macmillan.

Bratton and Gold address the fundamentals and the historic trajectory of HRP and also deal with the metrics used to measure issues of absenteeism and turnover. They also consider specific and specialist issues of human capital management, diversity and the impact of 'e-HR' on the subject of human resource planning.

JOHNSON, G., WHITTINGTON, R. and SCHOLES, K. (2011) *Exploring strategy* 9th ed. Harlow: FT Prentice Hall.

This text, although aimed at the postgraduate student, is useful when trying to understand business strategy. The book is written in a clear style and supported by examples of practice. It is available as an ebook via Dawsonera.

MARTIN, M. and WHITING, F. (2013) *Human resource practice*. London: CIPD.

A very practical text, as its name implies, designed for the person meeting the theoretical underpinning of human resource management studies for the first time. Well supported by examples and case studies.

ONLINE SOURCES

CIPD (2010b) *Workforce planning: right people, right time, right skills [online]*. Guide. London: CIPD. [Accessed 25 September 2013]. Available at: **www.cipd.co.uk/ binaries/5219_Workforce_planning_guide2.pdf**

CIPD/Hays (2013) *Resourcing and talent planning [online].* Annual survey report. London: CIPD. [Accessed 27 September 2013]. Available at: **www.cipd.co.uk/ binaries/6226%20RTP%20SR%20WEB.PDF**

STEWART, J. (2007) *Developing skills through talent management: SSDA catalyst report [online].* UK: UKCES. [Accessed 18 October 2013]. Available at: **www.ukces. org.uk/assets/ukces/docs/publications/ssda-archive/ssda-catalyst-issue-6- developing-skills-through-talent-management.pdf**

WEB LINKS

Deloitte University Press at: **www.dupress.com/?icid=duplg**.

1   Read what John Hagel III has to say about *Three lessons about talent from Tibetan Buddhist monks* at: **www.dupress.com/articles/three-lessons-about- talent-from-monks/?top=7**

2   Read and listen to what the American Government is thinking of in terms of attracting the brightest and the best into government roles at: **www.dupress. com/articles/govcloud-and-generation-y-video/?top=7**

National Apprenticeship website: **www.apprenticeships.org.uk**

Office for National Statistics: **www.statistics.gov.uk**

Office for National Statistics (Economic and Labour Market Review): **www.statistics. gov.uk/elmr**

UK Commission for Employment and Skills: **www.gov.uk/government/ organisations/uk-commission-for-employment-and-skills**

PODCASTS

CIPD (2007) Talent Management – Podcast 4. Available at: **www.cipd.co.uk/ podcasts/_articles/article4.htm?link=title**

CIPD (2010) Workforce Planning – Podcast 46. Available at: **www.cipd.co.uk/ podcasts/_articles/_workforce-planning-podcast-46.htm**

CIPD (2011) The Business Case for Employing Young People – Podcast 58. Available at: **www.cipd.co.uk/podcasts/_articles/ _thebusinesscaseforemployingyoungpeople.htm?link=title**

Recruitment

6.1 INTRODUCTION

The main objectives of this chapter are to explain the purposes and the processes of recruitment. Recruitment and selection are seen as one of the key areas of HR. In fact, in the 2007 CIPD survey report *The Changing HR Function*, recruitment and selection was rated as the highest priority (CIPD, 2007). Taylor and Collins (cited in Redman and Wilkinson, 2009, p.64) give recruitment as the most critical human resource function for organisational survival or success. With the growth of 'talent management', attracting the right people with the right blend of skills and abilities is becoming ever more important. Recruitment is expensive – according to the CIPD/Hays (2013) *Resourcing and Talent Planning Survey*, the average recruitment cost of filling a vacancy per employee is £2,000, with the median cost for filling a management vacancy being £5,000. With high labour turnover, it is easy to see that recruitment and selection will be costly for the organisation and an area in which HR can add value to the business.

6.2 DEFINITIONS

Recruitment and selection are frequently seen as one entity – recruiting and selecting are all part of the same thing – filling a vacancy with the best talent available. Selection begins where recruitment ends. We have seen from the previous chapter on human resource planning how important it can be to assess demand for staff and to consider how to fill that demand. Once we have identified that there is a genuine vacancy and that we need to fill it with a certain type of person, we can begin to consider how to go about finding them. So *recruitment* is about 'attracting in a suitable pool of candidates' from which we can then *select* the best candidate available by 'shortlisting applicants and using techniques to choose the best one'. The selection process ends when a suitable candidate has accepted an offer of employment and is often seen to include the induction process, which is the final stage of establishing the new recruit into the organisation. In practice, recruitment and selection are a continuous process – one cannot take place without the other – and the relevant HR practitioners need to be skilled in both.

 KEY CONCEPT: RECRUITMENT

Taylor (2014, p.135) defines recruitment as 'actively soliciting applications from potential employees ... requiring employers to sell themselves in the relevant labour markets so as to maximize the pool of well-qualified candidates from which future employees can be chosen'. Beardwell and Claydon (2010, p.165) state that the 'recruitment process involves identifying the skills and abilities required and then choosing the most effective recruitment methods to attract a pool of suitable candidates'.

6.3 THE CONTEXT OF RECRUITMENT

If we consider people as the organisation's main means of achieving competitive advantage, recruitment and selection are critical. Whether in a recession (where survival of a firm may depend on having competent staff who perform to a high standard) or in a boom (where competitive advantage depends on having talented workers), attracting and appointing the right staff is crucial. As Douglas McCormick, a commissioner at the UK Commission for Employment and Skills (UKCES), says, 'Whilst the rise in the number of vacancies is a good sign that the economy is recovering, there's a real possibility that businesses might not be able to make the most of the upturn because they don't have the right people' (BBC News, January 2014).

Pfeffer (1998) suggests that selective hiring is one of the important areas of HR that can affect the success of the business and Purcell et al (2003) include recruitment and selection as one of the key areas of HR that make a difference to performance.

Businesses today require skilled, talented workers in order to help achieve competitive advantage. Talent management may mean moving away from the traditional 'person-job match' to recruiting suitable people whose attitudes match the organisation's culture and then developing jobs around their skills and capabilities. Organisations such as Google use this approach to attract the right kind of people to the organisation and then let them develop the role.

6.3.1 RESPONSIBILTY FOR RECRUITMENT

Most organisations (69%), according to the CIPD/Hays (2013) *Resourcing and Talent Planning* survey, carry out recruitment and selection activity in-house. The survey states that just 3% outsource it completely, which demonstrates the importance with which recruitment is seen. Twenty-eight per cent combine an approach which involves in-house and outsourcing. Often this will mean that an agency takes responsibility for advertising, but the actual selection process is carried out by HR professionals within the company, together with the line managers relevant to the post being filled.

6.3.2 DIVERSITY AND FLEXIBILITY

The idea of diversity in the workforce has increased in importance over the past 40 years – partly because of the influence of equality legislation, but also because of the increasing recognition of the business case for a diverse workforce. Businesses should not only adhere to legislation on equality, but also understand that having a diverse workforce adds to the flexibility of an organisation and can improve its competitiveness. You can read more on this in Chapter 15, 'Diversity and Equality'.

6.3.3 INTERNAL AND EXTERNAL LABOUR MARKETS

When recruiting, we might consider applicants from the internal environment (staff who already work for the organisation) as well as the external environment (which may include candidates from outside the organisation and even outside the UK), both of which offer constraints and opportunities. (There is more discussion on internal and external labour markets in Chapter 5, 'Human Resource Planning'.)

Internal labour market

When a vacancy or a new position arises, should we look firstly at the internal labour market? Promoting from within the organisation offers opportunities to existing employees, and thus acts as a motivator. Internal opportunities for promotion can be attractive to those who like working for the company, but who also want to further their career. Using the internal labour market demonstrates to the workforce in general that internal promotion is encouraged and career progression is possible – thus increasing motivation and morale. This is important if we are to recognise and reward the 'talented' employees already within our workforce. In fact, some organisations are well known for 'promoting from within'. Employees in the public sector often see their lifelong career path as being within the same organisation. In the Civil Service, for example, long service may also be a factor in achieving promotion.

If an organisation is going to develop its talented staff in order to promote them, there is always the danger that these employees will leave and go to a competitor; however, if there is a visible career path and opportunity for promotion, the likelihood of employees leaving once they are qualified or when they have come to the end of their training is much lower.

From the organisation's point of view, recruiting from the internal labour market is much cheaper (no advertising costs, for example) and applicants are 'known' so are less of a risk in terms of whether they will make a good 'fit' to the organisation. Additionally, it is useful for filling vacancies when the organisation is in a redundancy situation and needs to redeploy staff rather than making them redundant.

The down side of recruiting only from within the organisation is that the pool of potential recruits may be small and so choice is limited. It may be better to take on 'fresh blood', who will bring new ideas and different approaches to the business. External recruitment may be vital if you are seeking new talent who can add creative new ideas to your competitive edge.

External labour market

The external labour market can be viewed on four different levels: local, regional, national and international. The size and location of the area from which you need to recruit is determined first and foremost by the nature of the job in terms of its level in the organisation, its technical complexity and degree of specialism, the qualifications, competences and experience required. You may have vacancies with particular skill requirements. Engineers, nurses and certain teaching disciplines, for example are difficult to fill and you may need to think carefully about where you can find people to fill these posts.

In reality, there is usually a mix of both internal and external recruitment. Restricting recruitment to one or the other leads to a lack of choice, lack of opportunity for current staff and is likely to decrease the diversity of your workforce. The internal and external labour markets as sources of recruitment both have their own advantages (see Chapter 5, 'Human Resource Planning', for more on this).

PAUSE FOR THOUGHT

Should all vacancies be advertised outside the organisation? How do internal employees feel if they don't get the chance for promotion? How do people outside the organisation feel if they never get an opportunity to apply? Does this work against the idea of equal opportunity?

6.3.4 FACTORS AFFECTING SUCCESS

There are a variety of factors that can inhibit or facilitate an organisation's recruitment success rate:

- **Unemployment:** Unemployment fluctuates with the state of the economy. Since the recent recession the number of redundancies has been high and job vacancies have been hard to find for many people. But having a large pool of unemployed people does not necessarily mean that there will be people with the right skills for your organisation. When unemployment is high, job applications abound and the selection process has to be handled with great care if the organisation is to employ the kind of people it needs. Even in times of low unemployment there may still be a lack of the 'right' or 'talented' people for your business.
- **Diversity:** The increase in immigration rates in recent years has had a positive effect on recruitment in that it has raised the level of the availability of required knowledge and skills. In a moderate way, this has helped to alleviate the skill shortage. Among the overseas applicants for UK residency there are doctors, nurses, dentists, engineers and all of the trades and crafts.
- **Skill shortages:** The existence of a 'talent war' in the external market means that organisations are competing with each other to 'capture' people who possess exceptional knowledge and rare competences.
- **Employer branding:** Employers need to be attractive to applicants and the concept of employer branding is becoming more important. The CIPD/Hays (2013) *Resourcing and Talent Planning* survey found that nearly three-quarters of organisations had made efforts to improve their employer brand – through activities such as employee surveys, developing an online careers site, attending graduate careers fairs, working with charities, or by extending flexible working practices.

ACTIVITY 6.1

Visit The UK Commission for Employment and Skill's website at **www.ukces.org.uk/ourwork/employer-skills-survey** and see their Employer Skills Survey. Where are the UK skills shortages? How do they compare with skill shortages in your own organisation?

6.3.5 SKILL SHORTAGES

Not only are there specific shortages of particular skills, such as in manufacturing, construction and plumbing, health and social care, but employers also struggle to find employees with the 'core generic skills' of communication, literacy and numeracy. Three in ten vacancies are reported to be hard to fill, and shortages in suitably skilled, qualified and/or experienced workers are the main reason for this. Skill-shortage vacancies represent more than one in five of all vacancies (22%) (the UK Commission's Employer Skills Survey, 2014). The CIPD/Hays (2013) *Resourcing and Talent Management* survey found that 60% of employers had experienced recruitment difficulties, with managers and professionals/specialists and technical positions being the most difficult vacancies to fill, followed by senior manager/director posts.

ACTIVITY 6.2

Have a look at the Migration Advisory Committee Review (February 2013) of the recommended shortage occupation lists for the UK and Scotland. Available at **www.rsc. org/images/mac-report_tcm18–227964.pdf**

This lists occupations where there are skills shortages in the UK. The report contains a lot of information, but have a browse through to see which jobs are on the current list and

which are now not considered as skill shortages (pp.51–3).

See pages 41–42 of the report:

● What are the alternatives to employing immigrants in response to perceived staff shortages?
● Are these alternatives feasible, and do you think employers have explored them fully?

PAUSE FOR THOUGHT

The growth in the EU has enabled an influx of Eastern European workers into the UK. There have, however, been issues as to whether it is unfair that in a recession, UK jobs should go to non-UK workers. An alternative view is that

migrant workers are taking jobs in which UK workers have no interest anyway. Having looked at the report in Activity 6.2, you should now have a more informed view of the matter.

6.4 RECRUITMENT PROCESSES

This section explains the systems of recruitment and offers guidance on the related skills. Once a genuine vacancy has been identified, the recruitment process can be activated.

6.4.1 SYSTEMATIC RECRUITMENT CYCLE

The stages of the recruitment process may be seen as the 'systematic recruitment cycle':

● Stage 1 – Identify genuine vacancy. This may involve the human resource planning process (see Chapter 5).
● Stage 2 – Obtain authority to recruit.
● Stage 3 – Carry out job analysis or check that previous analysis is still applicable.
● Stage 4 – Write or revise job description and person specification/job profile.
● Stage 5 – Make the vacancy known (write the advert and decide on relevant media).
● Stage 6 – Place the advert in the appropriate media.

The first stage is to identify that the job exists: how has the vacancy arisen? Then, in most organisations, there is a need to get approval to fill the post. Next there is a need to find out about the job (job analysis), followed by ensuring that there is an up-to-date brief of what the job is about and what kind of person is sought and what skills they need (job description and person specification). Then, finally, attract the right kind of people to the job (making the position known by advertisement).

Identifying the vacancy

If someone has left the organisation or has retired, a vacancy will have occurred. Or there may be a restructure, which means a new post has arisen.

Gaining authority to recruit

Often, once a line manager has identified a vacancy, they need to make sure that they have authority to recruit. This means deciding whether the post needs filling at all – there may be no budget for filling jobs at the current time. The decision may be taken by senior management or, in the public sector, approval may need to be given by a committee and consequently the process may take some time. In some organisations the process may be an informal one, while in others there will be 'approval to fill a vacancy' forms that require justification: do we need the job? Does the job need to be filled on a full-time or part-time basis? Can the work be done by any other means (overtime, casual labour, the introduction of new technology or machinery)? Again, we can see where human resource planning is an essential part of the recruitment and selection process.

Job analysis

The following factors are identified from a job analysis (see Chapter 5) and they are used to write up a job description or role definition (see Table 6.1) and a person specification:

- the nature of the tasks that make up the job
- how the job has changed (if it has) since it was last analysed
- the priorities of the job and the key tasks
- the knowledge, understanding, skills, competence and other personal qualities needed for the job.

In practice, these documents are usually stored on a computer, but it is recommended that the HR practitioner and the line manager get together to agree on their contents in case there have been any changes since the documents were last drafted. For more on job analysis, see Chapter 5, 'Human Resource Planning'.

The job description

Every opportunity should be taken to keep job descriptions up to date. The fact that a specific vacancy has been identified provides an opportunity for the HR practitioner to make a further update, in consultation with the relevant line manager, who will be aware of any changes to the job. In addition to their use in recruitment, job descriptions have a key role in other activities, such as identifying training needs, and introducing or reviewing a job evaluation scheme and other systems of payment.

A job description should include the following:

- job title
- location
- responsible to
- main purpose of job
- responsibilities/duties
- working conditions
- any other duties/requirements/special circumstances.

Table 6.1 A typical job description

Organisation	'NewYou' Recruitment Company
Location	Administration Head Office, Wolverhampton
Job purpose	Management of administration team
Job title	Senior administrator
Main duties and responsibilities	1 Ensure the efficient running of the administration office, including accounts and customer service. 2 Supervise and monitor the performance of administration staff, offering advice and guidance where necessary. 3 Work with management to ensure all customer requirements and key performance indicators are met. 4 Attend monthly meetings alongside the management team where required. 5 Research and provide reports for management on various projects. 6 Maintain customer records and set up new customers and contracts on the dedicated service software. 7 Ensure all invoicing is completed on time. 8 Train new administration staff as well as existing members. 9 Co-ordinate holidays and working hours to ensuring adequate staff levels are maintained. 10 Instigate new and effective methods of working. 11 Any other duties commensurate with the grade of the post.
Salary and other main terms and conditions	Salary £22,000–25,000 p.a. Relocation allowance, well-appointed office, situated in Wolverhampton city centre. A six-month probationary period applies.

In some organisations, job descriptions are seen as too rigid. 'Role profiles' may be used instead, which are more generic and outline key result areas, rather than actual tasks (that is, outputs, rather than inputs). These would show the job applicant what they would be responsible for and may give some flexibility in how the job is carried out, providing results are achieved.

The person specification

The purpose of this document is to detail the particular qualities that match the profile of the ideal person for the job, and these may include education, qualifications, experience, competences, attitudes and any specific requirements that are exclusive to the job in question. Fundamentally, it outlines the *knowledge, skills* and *abilities* required to do the job.

While the job description tells us about the *tasks* of the job, and what the work involves, the person specification is about what kind of *person* we want to fill the job. The contents of the job description (see Table 6.1) provide the basic criteria for the person specification.

Models that have, in part, stood the test of time are:

- the seven-point plan (Rodger, 1952)
- the fivefold grading system (Munro-Fraser, 1966).

Rodger's model is the most well known and most frequently used. This covered seven areas:

- physical attributes
- attainments

- intelligence
- special aptitudes
- interests
- disposition
- circumstances.

Munro-Fraser's fivefold grading system covers the following:

- innate abilities
- qualifications
- impact on others (physical make-up, appearance, bearing, speech, manner)
- adjustment (emotional stability, ability to withstand stress, ability to get on with people)
- motivation.

While the ideas behind Rodger's and Munro-Fraser's models still hold good, the *contents* in their original form are not recommended for use today. They reflect the values that were held at the time of publication, which was long before discrimination laws came into being. For example, items such as 'physical make-up' and 'circumstances' are potentially discriminatory as they may contravene disability discrimination or sex discrimination laws. Marchington and Wilkinson (2008) comment, 'Although the broad framework may still be valid, it is now unethical, inappropriate and potentially too discriminatory to probe too deeply into some of these areas.' The model, however, provided a structure or 'checklist' that can be useful in placing the requirements against the appropriate categories on the specification. It is important to make sure that all items can be objectively justified – particularly as such criteria will be looked at in some detail if there is a case of unfair discrimination which goes to an employment tribunal.

Armstrong (2014, p.226) suggests using the following headings:

- knowledge
- skills and abilities
- behavioural competences
- qualifications and training
- experience
- specific demands.

You might add in other categories but you must make sure that they can be justified and will not be classed as discriminatory. Outlined in Table 6.2 is a possible person specification for the job description mentioned earlier.

Table 6.2 A possible person specification for senior administrator at 'New You'

'New You' Recruitment Company	Job title: Senior Administrator	
Job requirements	Essential	Desirable
1 Qualification	A-level or equivalent	Degree in Business Studies/Management
2 Knowledge	Good understanding of administrative processes	Knowledge of the recruitment business and its administration
3 Skills	Ability to work efficiently and instigate new processes and procedures to improve effectiveness Ability to motivate staff	Ability to work in a team and on own initiative

4 Experience	Experience of being a team leader or in a supervisory role	Some experience of a relevant team leadership role Accustomed to dealing with problems and staff issues
5 Personal qualities	Polite manner Good oral and written communicator	Good leadership skills and accustomed to pressure

Even qualities such as 'mature' or 'youthful' can be seen as age discrimination. Personal/domestic or family circumstances should not be pertinent to the job and questions at an interview about such would also be seen as possibly discriminatory. However, with care, person specifications are still useful.

ACTIVITY 6.3

Draft a person specification for your own job, or one that you have held in the past, and another for a colleague's job that is different from yours. How do they differ?

KEY CONCEPT: COMPETENCIES

Competencies are 'underlying characteristics of a person, such as a motive, skill, trait, social role, self-image or a body of knowledge, which results in effective and/or superior performance in a job' (Boyatzis, 1982, p.21). The CIPD's (2013t) *Competence and Competency Frameworks* factsheet defines it as 'the behaviours (and, where appropriate, technical attributes) that individuals must have, or must acquire, to perform effectively at work. . . . A competency framework is a structure that sets out and defines each individual competency (such as problem-solving or people management) required by individuals working in an organisation or part of an organisation.'

6.5 COMPETENCY FRAMEWORKS

Similar to person specifications, competency frameworks outline a list of characteristics which are required by the job-holder. These may be *organisation-wide competencies*, such as 'communication skills', 'customer-focused', 'teamwork', which we would want everyone in the company to possess; or *specific to the job*, such as 'attention to detail', or 'numeracy' perhaps for an accountant. To set up a competency framework, it is necessary to analyse, not the job, but the people, who provide superior performance. What are the qualities we want people to have in order to do a particular job well? Once we have a list of the competencies we are looking for, we can use them as a means of attracting the right kind of employees, much in the same way as we would use a person specification; the framework can be made available with the job description, so that applicants can self-select and decide whether the vacancy is for them. The framework can also be used as a means of selection, by matching the candidates to the list of competencies to see who is a good fit. They are often used as a base for interview questions, where candidates need to provide evidence relating to each competency.

6.6.1 INFORMAL RECRUITMENT METHODS

Many organisations use employee referral schemes, whereby they ask current staff to put forward any friends or acquaintances for positions. This is a cheap and relatively easy way of recruiting to the organisation. They are one of the most effective recruitment methods for the private sector, according to the CIPD/Hays (2013) *Resourcing and Talent Planning* survey. Information can be placed on noticeboards or the company intranet, so that all employees are encouraged to tell people they know about job vacancies that have arisen. There may be a financial incentive offered so that the employee gets a bonus payment if the person they recommended is successful. Usually this is after a period of six months to ensure that the new recruit has stayed with the company. The payment may vary – from £50 as a token thank you, to a generous £1,000. If the company is saving on advertising fees, the cost of the incentive is worthwhile.

There are advantages to this form of recruitment. Recruits will have some knowledge of the organisation in advance and will have a supportive network once they arrive at work. Research by Blau (1990) and Iles and Robertson (1989) showed that informal methods produce a better selection of suitably qualified applicants than formal methods. These applicants, once employed, also have lower turnover and better performance.

The drawbacks of this method are that there is a limited target audience and it can mean that the workforce are clones – all members of a family, neighbourhood or with similar backgrounds. It may also mean nepotism, where staff may favour friends and thus fairness is compromised. If large numbers of staff come from one family, for example, there could be issues if one of them is disciplined or has a grievance – all the rest may gang up to support them. Managing this kind of scenario can be difficult.

6.6.2 ADVERTISING THE VACANCY

Once you have all the detail about what kind of recruit you are seeking, the next stage is to advertise the vacancy. There are various ways of doing this, depending on what type of vacancy you are offering. For example:

- **Advertise internally** on noticeboards, on the company website and in the company magazine, but check the frequency of the magazine, find out its closing date for the acceptance of advertisements and see how this matches up to the target date for filling the vacant position.
- **Search the HR records** for suitable internal candidates and scan the files on people who have previously sent in CVs on speculation. The internal advertisement should still appear, since everyone should have an equal opportunity to apply for the post.
- **Advertise in national newspapers or professional journals:** for specific posts, such as HR, architects, engineers, and so on, there are specialist professional journals where such types of staff are likely to look for job vacancies. *People Management* is one for HR posts.
- **Advertise in local newspapers:** these tend to be used for routine or lower-paid jobs where applicants live locally and will not want to travel far to work.
- **Use general and specialist selection consultants (headhunters):** consultants are brought in when the organisation would benefit from their expertise in recruiting for positions in the higher levels of the organisation, and when vacancies occur in key specialisms, such as in certain aspects of engineering, IT, chemicals – whatever the organisation needs.

- **Use employment agencies:** people associate employment agencies with temporary and part-time staff, but most of them are extremely good at finding people for permanent positions in other areas of the workforce. Their reputation is for finding administrative and clerical workers, but many specialise in particular kinds of function, such as finance, catering, the building trades, HR and IT.
- **Invite applications from 'work experience' students:** this can be quite a good source, especially since the managers have already met the candidate and seen something of their work.
- **Contact schools, colleges and universities,** support their career conventions and maintain good relations. These are opportunities to meet prospective employees and 'sell' the benefits of working in your organisation. Often organisations recruit their graduates from students who have done their placement year with them – and this can act as a good way of finding the right person who will fit in with the organisation.
- **Use Jobcentre Plus:** people who register with Jobcentre Plus are usually unemployed, and therefore the Jobcentre can produce applicants very quickly and cheaply. Employers can use 'Universal Jobmatch' to advertise jobs and search for jobseekers whose CVs match their needs.
- **Use e-recruitment:** advertise on the company website or use a website that specialises in recruitment advertising. Many supermarkets, for instance, recruit using only online methods.

According to the CIPD/Hays (2013) *Resourcing and Talent Planning* survey report, by far the most commonly used methods for attracting candidates are through an organisation's own corporate website (62%) with recruitment agencies (49%) second most popular.

6.6.3 SOCIAL MEDIA

Facebook, Twitter and LinkedIn are the most commonly used social media sites for resourcing. Eighty-six per cent of employers use it for attracting candidates and 74% use it for brand building. It is also seen as being useful in keeping in touch with future applicants – 49% use it for this purpose. Only 6% use it for screening applicants' profiles online – or admit to it! The advantage of social media, according to three-quarters of organisations, is the great reduction in cost (CIPD/Hays, 2013).

6.6.4 RECRUITING ELECTRONICALLY

E-recruitment has grown substantially in the last few years. The CIPD/Hays *Resourcing and Talent Planning* survey (2013) states that 62% of companies used their own corporate websites for advertising. Thirty-one per cent use professional networking sites such as LinkedIn. Use of national newspapers has declined to just 12%, although this is more popular amongst the public sector organisations. Traditional and electronic activities can be combined at almost any stage. For example, a press advertisement may direct readers to a website providing further information or may require applicants to request an application form via email or telephone that will then be processed manually.

Advantages and disadvantages of electronic recruitment

E-recruitment gives access to a large number of people at a very reasonable cost. Indeed, if using the organisation's own website, the actual advertising cost is minimal, as the site exists anyway. Using a job vacancy site such as Monster (**www. monster.co.uk**), Reed (**www.reed.co.uk/recruiter**) or Totaljobs.com will incur a cost but is more likely to reach those who are actively in the job market seeking a position (charges generally start from £99 at the time of writing). The sites will advertise the job for you, but usually offer other services as well, such as emailing candidates or shortlisting. You can target certain areas of the country if you so wish, or request CVs of applicants who are on the recruitment agency's books already. There are large numbers of these sites – see 'Explore Further' at the end of the chapter for more links.

If you use your own corporate website for advertising your vacancies, this is a good opportunity to publicise the company and to make a positive impact. Employer branding comes in here – the recruitment process is an ideal way to showcase the organisation and to make a good impression to the prospective applicants.

The downside of e-recruitment can be that you may be overwhelmed with responses. It is easy for an applicant to send their CV to many jobs with a few clicks of the mouse – so it is important to be specific about wording and requirements so that applicants can self-select (or deselect) easily. It's vital, too, that the technology works well, or applicants may become frustrated and be put off.

CASE EXAMPLE 6.1

MegaSite are a small IT company who build commercial websites. They have a small team of expert technical staff and want to expand, but don't have enough capacity. They want to build a bigger business, but need employees with specific computer skills. They know there is work out there and demand for their kind of business, but without enough employees with the right skills, the company cannot consider any kind of expansion. They have tried advertising locally but with little success – although they received lots of replies, none were what they really wanted.

Task

What options could you offer to MegaSite to help them find suitable applicants? Where could they look for staff? (See CIPD/Hays (2013) *Recruitment and Talent Planning* survey, p.9, for ideas.)

6.6.5 RECRUITMENT ADVERTISING

If you are using newspapers and magazines to advertise your jobs, you may wish to use 'display' adverts – often a quarter or half a page in size, with borders and artwork that are designed to project the organisation's corporate image, usually including a logo. Large adverts of this type are costly, but have an impact on the eye and are good for advertising more senior technical and professional jobs. They also create an image with which readers will eventually become familiar.

There is a need to do some research before committing to an advertisement. It is important to check details about how much an advertisement will cost, the date the advert will appear, how many insertions you will be given, and so on. This advice applies when advertising online, too, if you are using a job vacancy website.

It is important to be brief (as more space costs money), but to include all the details of the job, so that people are attracted to it. Beware of having too much text that looks cramped and is off-putting. Handling a full display advertisement is best left to the experts. Few individuals have the capacity to produce good copy, artwork that will be indicative of, and reflect well on, the organisation, or lay out an advertisement that will compel the attention of a serious potential candidate. Most display advertisements are designed and placed by advertising agents.

An agency can provide expertise in copywriting, producing artwork and eye-catching captions and other forms of visual impact. The agency can advise on all aspects of advertising including the legal aspects (discrimination), media selection, placing the advertisements as well as working with you on response analysis. Agencies can also provide anonymity, in which your advertisements appear under the name of the agency. The organisation may decide to do this when it is carrying out confidential marketing or developing a new product and does not wish the job titles in the advertisements to reveal the nature of its plans. All of this has a cost, of course, but the benefits should outweigh it.

6.6.6 WHAT THE ADVERTISEMENT SHOULD CONTAIN

Whether you are advertising online, in a newspaper or a professional journal, there are certain things that all good adverts should contain. There needs to be a caption; this is usually the job title. On the other hand, there may be something about the job that is more likely to 'draw the eye', such as the salary, prospects or the location. 'Come and work in the sunny Cornwall', for example, would make an attractive caption, perhaps with a background picture of sea and sand. On the question of the job title, it should be remembered that people who scan the recruitment adverts are looking for something familiar, so keep job titles simple and recognisable – otherwise you may lose candidates because it is not what potential recruits are looking for.

From an ethical point of view, it is better to be honest about the job. The clearer you are in the advert, the more likely you will get a candidate who fits the job as they will be able to 'self-select'; only those who meet the criteria will apply and you will not waste time with dozens of applicants who don't stand a chance of getting the job.

When placing an advert, make sure that the copy you have written conforms to the provisions of the equality legislation. Don't ask for a 'mature lady' or a 'young man', for instance.

Include also a brief synopsis of the job content, its requirements, reporting responsibilities and benefits. Use the job description, person specification and/or competency framework to guide you – these should contain the information you need. You may say something about the organisation itself, its status in the industry, employment policy, promotion prospects, and so on. Obviously, advertising space is expensive and limited, so keep it as brief as possible!

Salary should be included where possible, as it is one of the things everyone looks for when scanning for jobs. It will give some indication of the level of the job. If it's flexible, you may want to say so, but a rough indication is helpful to those who want to know whether it's a waste of time applying because they are already on a higher salary.

Location is also important and will often be a 'deal-breaker', so if your vacancy involves travelling throughout the UK, or is based in London, say so. It will stop anyone applying who doesn't want to move house, or dislikes being away from home, for example. You do not want to waste your time (or company money) on someone who really wants to stay in their current location and is not prepared to move. Better to say what is required and let people make their own decisions.

Finally, the advertisement should inform the reader how to apply for the job. This might be by submitting a letter of application, CV, by writing or telephoning for an application form. This last is seen by many organisations, especially those in the public sector, as an opportunity to send out 'further details' about the job, which may include a job description and person specification. Alternatively, many advertisements refer the reader to an application form on the organisation's website. Some companies ask candidates to write a letter as to why they believe they are right for the position.

PAUSE FOR THOUGHT

Should adverts include the salary? What do you consider to be the drawbacks of this? Do you think that knowledge of new starters' salaries cause issues at work amongst current staff?

ACTIVITY 6.4

Look through some recent job advertisements in professional magazines or on a job vacancy website. See what job titles are used. Do they actually describe what the job does? Which jobs would attract you? Do you think the jobs will actually be like they say they are in the advert?

ACTIVITY 6.5

Draft the copy of an advertisement for your own job and one for the job of a colleague. When writing the advertisement, think of those aspects of the job which would attract you to apply for it.

6.6.7 OTHER MEDIA

Large organisations, such as the armed services, the National Health Service and government departments, use television, often as part of a campaign that includes displayed advertisements in newspapers and magazines. These are usually part of a big campaign to attract large numbers, for example for teachers or for recruits to join the RAF. Television is the most expensive medium to use, and advertisements in spoken and written media are transitory and therefore have to be repeated, but the impact cannot be matched through any other medium.

PAUSE FOR THOUGHT

Graduate recruitment

Graduate recruitment substantially reduced following the 2008 recession. However, the latest research from the High Fliers Research Limited report on *The Graduate Market in 2014: Annual review of graduate vacancies & starting salaries at Britain's leading employers* finds that the outlook for 2014 is significantly better than it has been in the previous four years. The UK's leading employers expect to hire a total of 18,300 graduates; 8.7% more than in 2013. Thirty-seven per cent of vacancies, though, are expected to be filled by undergraduates who already have experience with the organisation – for example as interns, vacation work or through work placements, which indicates the importance for employers of having such schemes as a means of recruitment, rather than solely relying on advertising for graduates.

6.6.8 APPLICATION FORMS

The advantage of using application forms is that they set out the information you need in a standardised format. This speeds up the pace of manually sifting applications since, unlike CVs, which may take many forms, you know where on the form to look for each successive item of information. With online recruitment, forms are completed electronically, which may speed up the process even further (see Chapter 7 for more on shortlisting).

6.6.9 RECRUITMENT DIFFICULTIES

We saw earlier in the chapter that many employers suffer difficulties in finding suitable candidates. So, if we cannot find applicants, what can we do? The CIPD/Hays (2013) *Resourcing and Talent Planning* survey asked organisations what initiatives they undertake in response to recruitment difficulties. The most popular reaction is to upskill existing employees (68%), or to resource candidates from another sector or industry (just over half of employers do this). Sponsoring relevant professional qualifications was also popular (54%) – which will be welcome news to any CIPD students out there! Forty-two per cent develop apprenticeship schemes and 43% recruit candidates with potential for development but who have not got the experience. Recruiting from overseas was the least likely option; only 30% of respondents use this option.

ACTIVITY 6.6

Foxley Retail, a medium-sized company, is seeking staff to manage its chain of retail outlets, but is struggling to find suitable candidates. They have come to the conclusion that there just aren't the right people out there in their locality. They are a good employer and employ keen, motivated staff. If they want to expand they need more managerial staff at a number of levels: managers, assistant managers, supervisors.

What suggestions can you make to them to help overcome their recruitment difficulties? What options might be available to them? (Hint – see CIPD/Hays (2013) *Resourcing and Talent Planning* survey, page 18, for ideas. Available at: **www.cipd.co.uk/hr-resources/survey-reports/resourcing-talent-planning-2013.aspx**)

CASE EXAMPLE 6.2

EDF ENERGY 'BRIGHT FUTURE PROGRAMMES'

EDF Energy is one of the UK's largest energy companies and the largest producer of low-carbon electricity, producing around one-sixth of the nation's electricity from its nuclear power stations, wind farms, coal and gas power stations and combined heat and power plants. The company supplies gas and electricity to more than 5.5 million business and residential customer accounts and is the biggest supplier of electricity by volume in Great Britain.

EDF Energy has developed several programmes to develop the talent pool available within the UK:

● Industrial placements – a 12-month sandwich placement for students currently on an undergraduate degree course. Twenty-nine students joined the EDF Energy industrial placement programme in 2012 and 56 in 2013.

● Summer internships – a placement for students to intern over the summer. Seventy-five students joined the EDF Energy summer placement programme in 2012.

● 'STEM (Science, technology, engineering, and mathematics) Ambassador' programme – the company has identified 'STEM Ambassadors' who actively go out to schools and encourage students to see the value in continuing with studying STEM subjects. In February 2012, 179 STEM Ambassadors were active.

- Graduate schemes – in 2012, 87 graduates joined EDF Energy and 83.
- The company also offers a range of apprenticeships in areas such as Engineering Craft, Energy Field Services and Business.

(Published with kind permission of EDF)

The company is proactive in not only recruiting talent, but also in developing employees so they are ready for a future career with the organisation. Their investment in recruitment demonstrates the good sense of attracting and recruiting good staff.

6.7 SUMMARY

This chapter has considered the various elements of the recruitment process – one of the key areas of HR. Being able to resource talent is vital if we want to compete and succeed in the business world. The various stages of the systematic recruitment cycle are outlined as:

- Stage 1 – Identify genuine vacancy.
- Stage 2 – Obtain authority to recruit.
- Stage 3 – Carry out job analysis or check that previous analysis still holds good.
- Stage 4 – Write or revise job description and person specification.
- Stage 5 – Make the vacancy known (write the advert and decide on relevant media).
- Stage 6 – Place the advert in the appropriate media.

We have examined in more detail job descriptions, person specifications and competency frameworks and have seen the importance of these when recruiting. The growth of e-recruitment and use of social media have also been discussed, together with the impact of this on the recruitment process. We have also considered what options are available if we face recruitment difficulties.

Recruitment can be a costly process – so getting it right is one of the most important things HR can contribute in adding value to the organisation.

REVIEW QUESTIONS

1 How would you define recruitment?

2 What are the factors that can inhibit or facilitate an organisation's recruitment success rate?

3 What types of job are the most difficult to fill in the UK?

4 What are the six stages of the recruitment cycle?

5 What should typically be included in a job description?

6 What is the purpose of a person specification?

7 Why should we be careful if using Rodger's seven-point plan?

8 What is a competency framework?

9 What are the advantages and disadvantages of an employee referral scheme?

10 When making a vacant position known, what are the alternatives to advertising jobs in newspapers and magazines?

11 What are the benefits of using e-recruitment?

12 In what ways can social media be used to help with recruitment?

EXPLORE FURTHER

BOOKS

Most HR textbooks have a section on recruitment and selection. Try:

ARMSTRONG, M. with TAYLOR, S. (2014) *Armstrong's handbook of human resource management practice*. 13th ed. London: Kogan Page.

BEARDWELL, J. and CLAYDON, T. (2010) *Human resource management – a contemporary approach*. 6th ed. Harlow: Prentice Hall

TORRINGTON, D., HALL, L., TAYLOR, S. and ATKINSON, C. (2014) *Human resource management*. 9th ed. Harlow: Pearson.

Another good text covering a range of resourcing-related issues in an easy-to-read style is by Stephen Taylor:

TAYLOR, S. (2014) *Resourcing and talent management*. 6th ed. London: Chartered Institute of Personnel and Development.

WEB LINKS

The CIPD/Hays annual *Resourcing and Talent Planning* survey report is an essential read for the latest trends in recruitment and selection. The 2013 survey is available at: **www.cipd.co.uk/hr-resources/survey-reports/resourcing-talent-planning-2013.aspx**

EDF website for information on careers: **http://careers.edfenergy.com/careers**

If you want to find out more about skill shortages in the UK, see Report on Migration Advisory Committee Review (February 2013) *Skilled Shortage Sensible*. Available at: **www.rsc.org/images/mac-report_tcm18–227964.pdf**

For information on the graduate market see High Fliers Research Limited's research on *The Graduate Market in 2014: Annual review of graduate vacancies & starting salaries at Britain's leading employers*. Available at: **www.highfliers.co.uk/**

A selection of recruitment sites:

TotalJobs: **http://recruiters.totaljobs.com/**

Reed: **www.reed.co.uk/recruiter/**

Fish 4 jobs: **www.fish4.co.uk**

Jobsite: **www.jobsite.co.uk/recruitment/?src=tab**

Monster: **http://hiring.monster.co.uk/**

CHAPTER 7

Selection

LEARNING OBJECTIVES

After studying this chapter you should:

- understand traditional and modern approaches to selection
- be able to organise a selection event
- identify and choose appropriate selection methods
- understand different approaches to interviewing
- be aware of the legal aspects of selection.

7.1 INTRODUCTION

As we have seen in the previous chapter on recruitment, attracting the right calibre of people is vital for the success of the business. The selection stage is where we make the decisions about who to appoint from those who have applied. Hopefully, if the recruitment stage went well, you will have a good pool of talent from which to choose.

Selection is one of the most important tasks of the HR practitioner, since it is vital to fill vacant positions with people who are not only suitably skilled for specific jobs, but are also flexible, and willing and able to cope with change.

Those involved in selection include both HR practitioners and line managers, in the sense that HR tend to actually organise the selection events and participate in them all the way through to the final selection decisions, offering advice to the line manager throughout the process.

7.2 THE SEARCH FOR 'TALENT'

The search for talent is paramount in gaining the competitive edge and so it is important that the selection process is effective, reliable and cost-effective. Appointing the wrong person is costly and problematic, so we need to find a way of appointing the most likely 'best person for the job'. To achieve this, there is an increased emphasis on the use of complex selection techniques, such as assessment centres, which may include a variety of activities such as presentations and in-tray exercises as well as interviews. Selectors may also use occupational tests that are designed specifically to identify in candidates the necessary skills and competences that are required to carry out the work. Or they may use psychometric tests that identify candidates' personality characteristics, intelligence, values and attitudes that will fit with the organisation's culture as well as specifically for the job itself.

The job interview, which was once the central feature of the selection process, still has an important part to play, but the use of more sophisticated techniques means that we can now have more data upon which to make a selection decision. Research studies on the effectiveness of different selection methods in predicting whether a person will be good in the job, such as those by Robertson and Smith (2001), found the techniques often used in assessment centres, for example ability tests and structured interviews, are more accurate in predicting future success in the job than the traditional one-to-one interview. They researched various selection methods in terms of assessing the 'predictive validity' of the process, that is, how well a selection technique can predict a good performer in the job. Ideally we would like a selection technique that will definitely predict whether someone will fit into the job and do well. But unfortunately, such a test has yet to be devised! It is probably better to use a variety of methods because it is far more likely that there will then be enough information on which to base a sound decision.

ACTIVITY 7.1

Read Robertson and Smith (2001), Personnel selection, *Journal of Organizational Psychology*, 74, pp.441–72.

They discuss the concept of *'predictive validity'*, that is, how well does the selection method predict whether a person can do the job? This is expressed as a co-efficient, where 1 relates to a perfect prediction (that is, the method of selection works perfectly in predicting whether a candidate will be good at

the job) and 0 means there is no correlation between the method of selection and the person's performance in the job.

- What do they say are the best selection methods in terms of high 'predictive validity'?
- Which are the 'worst' methods? Would you agree with what they say?
- Why can we never have a perfect prediction of 1?

7.2.1 TRADITIONAL METHODS

All of this is not to say that traditional methods of selecting new employees have been completely abandoned. Organisations often use the 'classic trio' – application form, interview and references – as their means of recruiting and selecting staff. Most people would not wish to appoint someone if they have not spoken with them at an interview – but nowadays there are such a wide variety of other methods; it would make sense to incorporate more than one of these methods in the selection process in order to make a better informed decision. Bearing in mind that the CIPD/Hays (2013) *Resourcing and Talent Planning* survey report states that it costs an average of £2,000 to replace a member of staff who leaves, it is crucial that selection is undertaken in a cost-effective and reliable manner. It is better not to appoint someone, rather than appoint using insufficient evidence and then have them leave fairly soon afterwards, thus meaning you have to start the whole process over again. And possibly even worse – appointing someone who stays in the job but who does not perform well. It becomes more and more vital that selection is done as carefully as possible in order to have a successful outcome. And what is better, in terms of job satisfaction for an HR practitioner, than to see someone you have selected doing well in the company and to think 'I appointed that person'!

The use of complex and perhaps lengthy selection procedures can mean that line managers are unwilling to use them. Often the attitude is just to replace someone as quickly as possible, and while this is obviously a good thing to aim for, it is far more important to appoint a good-quality candidate. The old phrase 'marry in haste, repent at leisure' could well be applied to selection! Better to spend time doing it properly and end up choosing the 'right' person – a talented and successful employee who will add value to the organisation and who is more likely to stay for a number of years.

7.2.2 SELECTION POLICY

Most organisations have a policy stating how the organisation intends to go about the selection of new staff. The actual processes, therefore, should be designed specifically to bring in people with knowledge, skills, competences and attitudes that will enable them to make appropriate contributions to the organisation. We have seen in the previous chapter how we can match the candidates to a person specification and so attract people whose attributes are exactly what we need in that job.

Sometimes we may see a candidate who is not right for the job we are filling, but who does have abilities and qualities that we think would be useful in the organisation. In these cases, should we appoint them anyway and help them to develop a job around their skills? The idea of 'job sculpting' is an excellent way of developing staff and fits in with the adage of 'recruit for attitude, train for skill'. Unfortunately, not many companies have the luxury of being able to do this and usually we have a specific job in mind when we are selecting staff. The approach of moulding a job to a candidate works well when taking on graduates, for instance, when we have some leeway in the specific job we have in mind. Recruit a talented individual and then see in which area of work they perform best, before placing them into a final job.

7.2.3 EQUALITY AND DIVERSITY

The selection policy should also state the approach to selection in relation to ensuring equal opportunities. Organisations vary in their approaches to formulating ethical and legitimate strategies and policies on discrimination. This is an extremely important section of the recruitment and selection policy statement and is dealt with at greater length in Chapter 15, 'Diversity and Equality'. The main thing to bear in mind is that all selection procedures must adhere to legislation and must be seen to be fair and equitable. It is a good idea to ask yourself throughout the process, 'Would this be acceptable if it went to an employment tribunal?' Phrasing of interview questions, use of some tests, for instance, can all be seen as being unfairly discriminatory if care is not taken. And this is where HR advice to line managers can be essential in averting a tribunal case.

7.3 THE SELECTION PROCESS

As we have said earlier, selecting new employees is a critically important task. It is about predicting potential and in-job performance. Final decisions should be based on data from reasoned and systematic assessment of the candidates.

Successful recruitment will have produced applications from qualified and experienced people from whom the best person for the job can be selected. The next stage is to screen the applications, develop a shortlist of candidates, and organise and conduct interviews and other selection activities.

7.3.1 SELECTION STRATEGY

So, what selection strategy should you use? A selection strategy incorporates which methods should be used, how much should be spent on the process, who will be involved, how candidates will be evaluated, and so on. The selection strategy should be flexible enough to accommodate the variety of jobs that exist in the organisation. For example, the strategy that might be adopted to select, say, a factory operative will be different from that for selecting a senior manager. It may be seen as worthwhile to have a lengthy (and costly) selection process for a management post, whereas not so important for the factory operative. Some organisations, however, carry out assessment centre activities for most jobs – perhaps taking the view that all selection decisions are important.

7.3.2 SCREENING APPLICATIONS

In many organisations this is still carried out manually, but computerised systems are available for use if applications are made online. Used mostly by recruitment agencies and where large numbers of application forms are received, the forms can be processed electronically using specific programs designed to select candidates with the required attributes. When screening is carried out systematically, all of the applicants are subject to exactly the same process and are therefore all treated equally. However, the danger of having such automated and clinical processes with very little human intervention is that some very good candidates may be missed because they have used different phrases from the ones programmed. For example, if the computer is looking for leadership qualities and therefore picks out any applications that mention the words 'leader' or leadership', it may miss someone who has written about their experience of being 'head of a group', just because the applicants have used different terminology. The human mind will notice and pick up on different experiences and terminology and see their worthiness, whereas a computer will not.

Some organisations use short tests to help to sift out the better-quality candidates. A questionnaire may be completed online and only those who pass will continue on to the next stage of the process. This has the added advantage of helping to reduce the number of 'timewasters' – as only those who are really interested in the job will put the effort in and will complete the test.

7.3.3 PRODUCING THE 'LONG' SHORTLIST

After making a list of the basic details of all of the applicants (name and contact details), you should read through the applications, comparing their contents with the demands of the person specification and make a prioritised list under the headings of 'rejections', 'possibles' and 'probables'. Possibles are those who could do the job perhaps with some training, while probables are those who meet most or all of the criteria and therefore are a close match with your requirements. A courteously worded letter or email should then be sent to the rejected applicants and the 'long' shortlist is made up of the remaining possibles and probables.

If, at the advertising stage, a large number of applications is anticipated, a line may be inserted in the advertisement saying that only those who reach the minimum standard will receive further correspondence, thus heading off the need to spend time and money on written replies. Or even better would be to say that if candidates have not heard by a certain date, they can assume they have been unsuccessful. There is a dilemma here – should unsuccessful candidates be notified, as part of common courtesy, or is the cost saving justified? Even if replying by email, there is a cost incurred in the time it takes to reply to everyone. However, remember that any recruitment exercise is an opportunity to expose the business to the public – and any unprofessional behaviour will reflect badly on the organisation.

7.3.4 EQUAL OPPORTUNITIES

A word of warning here: the whole selection process can be prone to claims of discrimination. You may wish to use equal opportunities monitoring forms as a means of reducing the risk of illegal discrimination. Some companies now prefer to incorporate equal opportunity forms as part of the application form and remove them before shortlisting. When producing a 'long list', the use of numbers on documentation, with names withheld, reduces even further the chances of discrimination based on foreign sounding names or whether the candidate is male or female – though this will obviously become apparent at interview stage.

7.3.5 SHORTLISTING

The next step is to re-screen the 'long' shortlist, and it is important to involve the line manager at this stage. They should have had a hand in the development of the person specification and will understand the purposes of the job, the meaning and importance of any technical aspects, and how the job might develop in the future.

The process begins by re-reading through the 'possibles', studying applications that most closely match the demands of the person specification and deciding, with the line manager, whether any could be moved into the 'probables' file. With this task, it is best to err on the side of caution and the rule is: *if in doubt, retain.*

Once we have a pool of candidates that we wish to take further, the question now is, which methods should we use in order to select the best person for the job?

PAUSE FOR THOUGHT

Think about jobs that you have applied for. What methods were used in the selection process? How did you feel about the whole procedure? Was the selection process carried out professionally? Did you feel you had been treated fairly? How could the experience have been improved?

7.4 SELECTION METHODS

While interviews are the most popular method of selection, there are a number of other possibilities open to us in choosing our 'best candidate', some of the options are outlined below.

7.4.1 PSYCHOMETRIC TESTING

Research by Anderson and Shackleton (1993) and Robertson and Smith (2001) suggest that the use of tests can add to the accuracy of the selection decision. Tests are one way of gathering data to supplement our knowledge of the candidates and there are a variety of these available. According to the British Psychological Society:

> objective measures such as tests and questionnaires provide more accurate assessments of individuals than subjective approaches such as interviews or evaluating CVs. While these subjective approaches can provide useful information, particularly in skilled hands, the reliability and precision of objective measures is difficult to match.
> (British Psychological Society: **www.bps.org.uk**)

KEY CONCEPT: PSYCHOMETRICS

Psychometrics is the measurement of psychological attributes, including testing mental attributes such as intelligence and personality, usually in the form of questionnaires.
Such tests might include *personality tests*, which are concerned with identifying a person's disposition to behave in certain ways in certain situations. Components of intelligence, such as verbal, spatial and numerical ability, are measured through *cognitive tests* or *aptitude and ability tests*. Cognitive and personality tests are available commercially.

7.4.2 TYPES OF PSYCHOMETRIC TESTS

Some examples of psychometric tests are as follows (though there are many more):

Cognitive tests

> **Numerical reasoning:** measures the ability to analyse and comprehend numerical data and perform calculations, for example, working out percentages, ratios, trends or currency conversions.
> **Verbal reasoning:** comprehension and reasoning, usually by reading a passage and then answering questions with a 'true/false/cannot say' answer.
> **Inductive reasoning tests or abstract reasoning tests:** these might involve a set of shapes or diagrams and working out which is next in the sequence.
> **Situational judgement test (SJT):** a test used to assess a candidate's approach to solving work-related problems.
> **Aptitude tests:** these are used to measure a person's ability or knowledge level in a certain area or to ascertain a candidate's general level of intelligence and ability.

Personality tests

> **16-PF (16 personality factor model, Cattell, 1946):** a multiple-choice format test that is used to ascertain 16 dominant personality traits: warmth, reasoning, emotional stability, dominance, liveliness, rule-consciousness, social boldness, sensitivity, vigilance, abstractedness, privateness, apprehensiveness, openness to change, self-reliance, perfectionism, and tension.
> **Big Five profile:** measures five core personality traits, based on the Big Five personality traits of openness, conscientiousness, extroversion, agreeableness and neuroticism.
> **Myers-Briggs Personality Indicator/Jung Typology:** used to get an overview of personality traits based on four dichotomies: extraversion/introversion, sensing/intuition, thinking/feeling, and judging/perceiving.

 ACTIVITY 7.2

Visit **www.practiceaptitudetests.com/situational-judgement-tests/** and assess yourself using some of the free online tests.

How well did you do? How daunting would it be to have to do these in a job application situation?

7.4.3 USE OF PSYCHOMETRIC TESTS

Selection tests are ideally designed by psychologists who are experts in the field. Tests should be *valid*, which means that they measure what they purport to measure (do they measure intelligence or ability, for example?), and *reliable*, which means that they produce consistent results (if you took the same test repeatedly, you would get the same results).

It is important that the interpretation of results and feedback to candidates is done professionally and by someone qualified to do so. The British Psychological Society has defined standards of competence that a person should meet before being able to purchase and use psychometric tests and questionnaires. The International Test Commission has produced international guidelines on test use (available from their website: **www.intestcom.org**) that have been endorsed by the Society. Tests can be carried out only by an organisation's own Human Resources officers if they hold the Society's qualifications in test use and have a current entry on the Register of Qualifications in Test Use (RQTU).

Alternatively, tests can be administered by using the services of an independent qualified occupational test user.

The Data Protection Act regards test results as personal information and therefore anyone taking a test has a right to receive information on their results.

7.4.4 WHY USE PSYCHOMETRIC TESTS?

There has been a steady growth in the use of psychometric testing in recent years, partly because of the view that interviewing is unreliable and open to bias, and partly because of the importance of appointing the right people as the means of achieving a competitive advantage. Such emphasis has caused selectors to use the best means available to achieve this. Also, the use of evidence from tests supports the organisation's drive for fairness and equal opportunities, since all applicants for any one particular job undergo exactly the same test, and it is not a test that has been devised by the selectors, so is free from any intended bias. Problems with bias and discrimination in interviews, for example, is minimised by using a test that is seen to be fair and equitable to all candidates. The advantage of using psychometric testing techniques is that they produce corroborative and objective evidence, although an employment decision should never be made on the sole basis of test results. Some objective evidence, however, is better than none, especially if it supports what you subsequently learn about the candidate during the interview. However, even tests can discriminate unfairly (with possible gender or cultural bias), so it is wise to be careful with their use.

ACTIVITY 7.3

Visit the British Psychological Society's website at **www.bps.org.uk** and download their Code of Good Practice on the use of tests. What are the key areas to be aware of when using tests?

7.4.5 CULTURAL DIFFERENCES

It is necessary to be careful with selection tests because they may contain cultural bias. Those undertaking such tests need to have a reasonable command of the English language. Use of sayings and phrases that are understood by one culture may not be understood by another. For example, the phrase 'you scratch my back and I'll scratch yours' would be understood by most native English speakers to mean 'I will do you a favour if you do one for me', but may be read literally by anyone for whom English is not their first language. In addition to language barriers, the different cultures may have very different interpretations about what is expected or is appropriate behaviour and this may lead to poor test results.

7.4.6 OTHER TYPES OF TEST

You may of course just want to see how well a candidate fares in simple tasks related to a job, without resorting to psychometric testing. This might include using job simulation or work sampling or giving the candidates an ability test.

Tests add an element of objectivity and clarity to the selection decision. It is unlikely that we would appoint someone based purely on test results, but the additional information gleaned about the applicants helps us to make a more informed decision.

7.4.7 JOB SIMULATION

This is an exercise in which the candidate is required to deal with situations that typically represent the job for which they have applied. Often, in-tray exercises and role-plays are involved. For example, asking a lecturer or a training officer to give a short talk or presentation would be a valid means of testing out their abilities in this area. It is what they would be expected to do in their everyday job if they were appointed. The candidate is observed throughout the process and the observers should mark against a set of pre-agreed criteria.

7.4.8 WORK SAMPLING

This involves placing the candidate in the role or giving them work tasks to carry out for a predetermined amount of time and assessing their performance. This has the advantage of allowing the candidates to see whether they can do the job and whether they will enjoy it.

When selecting a lorry driver, for example, you might first assess the candidates in a simulator (*job simulation*, as discussed above) and then take them out on the road in a real truck for assessment on the job (*work sampling*).

7.4.9 ABILITY TESTS

These might be used to find out how good a candidate is at a particular skill. For example, a typing test for a data input clerk would be a valid and reliable test as it would test for accuracy and speed on an activity that is relevant to the job.

 ACTIVITY 7.4

You are recruiting for a college lecturer in human resource management. Devise some possible activities and tests that could be used when selecting for the post. (Note that the job involves marking, planning, dealing with students' problems and certain

competences in IT systems as well as just teaching in class.)

You could try these out on a real college lecturer and see whether they think the activities are a valid means of testing their ability!

7.5 FURTHER MEANS OF SELECTION

Apart from tests, there are several additional sources of information about candidates: *biodata*, *references* and *graphology*.

7.5.1 BIODATA

Biodata is data about the candidate that is collected from the application form and/or from a biographical questionnaire. The data relates to criteria such as qualifications, background and experience. Large organisations gather information (biodata) about their successful employees and form a profile of 'the desired employee'; they then try to match the candidates' biodata to this. So the profile of a good performer might be a white male, aged 27, firstborn, with a first-class honours degree in computing from Bath University. We would then seek applicants who have a similar profile. As we can see, this may be seen as discriminatory, as information on a person's background (gender, age, race, and so on) might be used as part of the selection decision, rather than on their skills and abilities.

7.5.2 REFERENCES

References may be obtained with permission from the candidate from several sources including previous employers and academic tutors; personal character references may also be obtained from independent parties. The reliability of references is sometimes questionable; opinions about character and suitability are less reliable. If you write someone a bad reference, you may be in trouble if they are subsequently not successful in their job application. Can you justify the things you say about the person? Best to be factual and stick to the nature of the previous job, time in employment, reason for leaving, salary and academic achievement. Robertson and Smith (2001) suggest that they are one of the least reliable means of selection. Many companies now will only provide the very briefest of references (based on confirming that the person was employed, the dates of the employment and the employee's job title), rather than be taken to court for defamation of character. The opposite may of course be true – would you write someone a good reference just to get rid of them? An employer owes a duty of care to both the employee and the recipient for the content of a reference and should provide one which is true, accurate and fair; the best advice when writing a reference is to stick to the facts. Note that you are no longer able to ask questions on sickness absence and health until after the job offer has been made because this may discriminate on the grounds of disability.

If you do use references, make sure you use them carefully and only as a small part of the whole selection process. References can be important in certain circumstances: in the Soham murders case in 2002, where Ian Huntley, caretaker at the local school, was convicted of the murder of two young girls, references had not been checked correctly. If they had been, the school would have found that Huntley had not worked in the schools and places where he had said that he had worked. It is part of the security checking and ties a person to a time and place. See also 'Disclosure and Barring Service' (criminal records check) at the end of this chapter for more information.

For a useful guide, see the 'Employment Practices Code', which gives advice on collection and use of data from job applicants and is available on the website of the Information Commissioner's Office at **www.ico.gov.uk**.

7.5.3 GRAPHOLOGY

Graphology is the study of a person's social profile through their handwriting. Its use in selection is based on the idea that handwriting reveals something about the individual's personality, which provides the basis for making a prediction about work behaviour. It is used in Europe, especially France, more than in the UK. According to Robertson and Smith (2001) it has very low predictive validity.

PAUSE FOR THOUGHT

Think about your organisation. Does it use tests? Should it? What is your opinion? How successful is your selection process – do you feel it could be improved? In what ways?

7.6 ORGANISING INTERVIEWS AND TESTS

The approach to this is determined by the selection strategy. In this context, the word 'interview', colloquially, can refer to all of the selection process, which may, of course – depending which strategy has been adopted – include psychometric tests and assessment centres, which can include job simulation/work sampling and/or group selection methods. The interviews may be held in one-to-one or two-to-one situations, panel interviews, selection boards or a combination of these models.

7.6.1 SCREENING INTERVIEWS

Sometimes the competition for the job is particularly tight, making it difficult to distinguish clearly between the 'possible' and 'probable' candidates. One approach to this problem is to hold preliminary interviews to clarify specific points with the candidates, with the final interviews following at a later date. Those that are not rejected at that stage make up the shortlist. Rejection letters are then sent to all of the remaining applicants and interview invitations are sent to the applicants who have been shortlisted.

7.6.2 TELEPHONE AND 'SKYPE' INTERVIEWS

Screening interviews may be held by telephone – a cheap way of screening candidates – or, increasingly, by use of Skype. Using Skype is becoming more common because it offers remote audio and visual communication. There is no guarantee that an interview with a person on a telephone is with a bona fide candidate. Skype offers the same advantages of a telephone conversation but has the advantage that a whole panel can be involved in the conversation and is able to see some visual cues too.

Those that are successful would then be invited in for second interviews and further selection procedures. A telephone interview may enable you to cut your list down from 'probables' to 'definites' for the rest of the selection procedure. The remaining applications are then studied and finally checked to ensure that they all meet with your selection criteria. There is the potential for individual prejudices and biases to creep in when only one person speaks to a potential employee. This is something to be aware of: having a structured set of questions to follow will help. Telephone interviews can be just as daunting as the real thing. Give candidates plenty of warning so they have time to prepare themselves.

7.6.3 ASSESSMENT CENTRES

An assessment centre is usually at least a full day of selection tests and activities, designed specifically to test out the skills and abilities of the candidate in relation to the job. Assessment centres take a lot of planning. It is important to think of which skills and qualities are required (gathered from the person specification) and then to devise exercises that will test out those qualities. For the post of a learning and development officer, for example, where presentation skills, organisation and interpersonal skills are required, the day might involve doing a presentation, taking part in a group problem-solving discussion, undertaking some in-tray exercises and a panel interview. Each exercise will relate to a specific skill needed for the job and it is useful to draw up a matrix showing which exercises will test which skills. For example, giving a mini-lecture will test for presentation skills, confidence and organisation, while a group activity might test problem-solving, interpersonal skills, time-keeping and ability to work under pressure. Candidates are assessed by trained observers in each activity and scored accordingly. At the end of the day, a sound decision can be made by comparing the performances of each candidate.

Where assessment centres or group selection methods are used, more time has to be allowed and the process may last more than one day, in which case candidates should be given advance warning of this.

If we are to select the best talent available, assessment centres which include a structured interview and some tests may be the best way of ensuring that we achieve this.

 ACTIVITY 7.5

Think of your job – what exercises would you include in an assessment centre that would test whether you have the ability and skills necessary to do your job? Draw up a matrix of skills required and then match suitable exercises to test for these.

You will find information to help you at the Prospects website: **www.prospects.ac.uk/ interview_tips_assessment_centres.htm**

7.6.4 ADMINISTRATIVE PREPARATION

Whatever methods you use for selection, you need to be professional in their execution. The arrangements, including the venues, timing and all who are to be involved, need to be carefully co-ordinated. The answers to the following questions make a reasonable administrative checklist:

- **Timing:** Have all relevant dates been set and agreed by everyone involved?
- **Venues:** Has all of the necessary accommodation been booked for:

  ○ the waiting area?
  ○ selection testing?
  ○ interviewing?

- **Reception:** Have the staff on reception been given a list of the candidates, the title of the job, the times and dates of their arrival, where they are to wait?
- **Personnel:** Has everyone who will be involved in the process been briefed on the timing and sequence of events?
- **Testing:** If testing is included, is a qualified test administrator available?
- **Candidates:** Have all shortlisted candidates been advised of the relevant times and dates, and has their availability been confirmed?
- **Refreshments:** Have drinks and lunch been arranged – coffee, tea, water? Any special requirements – vegetarian, gluten-free?
- **Technology:** Are there computer and screen facilities available for any presentations?
- **Special needs:** Have appropriate arrangements been made for candidates, and members of your own staff, who have special needs? This should include access to the premises, car parking and physical assistance where required. Did your invitation letter make it clear what assistance would be available?

7.6.5 ARRIVAL AND WAITING

When candidates arrive, they should be shown to the waiting area and told approximately how long they will be waiting, which should not be so long as to give the impression of a poorly organised event. This stage can be handled by the receptionist, but some organisations, especially for important jobs, have one of the selection team ready to go out, greet the candidate and make them comfortable.

Reasonably comfortable chairs, coffee tables and relevant company literature may be placed in the waiting area. Candidates will be keen to learn as much as they can about the organisation before the interview process starts. Perhaps some information on the structure of the day can be provided so that the candidates know what lies ahead for them during the process.

PAUSE FOR THOUGHT

Have you ever been for an interview and felt that it was carried out badly? What went wrong? What could have been done to make it a better experience?

7.7 INTERVIEWING

No selection process is complete without an interview. Depending on the interview strategy, sufficient time has to be allowed and the interviews have to be organised so that every candidate is allocated the same amount of time. It is important to plan what questions will be asked and who will cover which areas. One-to-one interviews, while perhaps more informal, may have problems in that if there is an accusation of discriminatory behaviour by the interviewer, it is difficult to refute, being only the word of the interviewer against the word of the interviewee. Panel interviews are generally safer for this reason. They also allow several members of the panel to discuss their decisions at the end and to justify their choice.

Armstrong (2014, pp.236–7) defines the aim of the selection interview as being 'to elicit information about candidates that will enable a prediction to be made about how well they will do the job and thus lead to a selection decision'. He notes criticisms of interviews as being that they can 'lack validity and reliability' and may 'lead to biased and subjective judgements by interviewers'. Research by Anderson and Shackleton (1993) and Robertson and Smith (2001) tends to support this by casting doubt on the power of unstructured interviews to be able to predict competence in the job. By their very nature, interviews are subjective, although the need to treat all candidates equally has encouraged selectors to structure interviews, which also goes a little way towards reducing subjectivity. Having said all that, the absence of the interview from the selection process would be regarded as unusual and it is still widely used as a selection method.

7.7.1 STRUCTURED AND UNSTRUCTURED INTERVIEWS

It was mentioned above that interviews may be structured, semi-structured or unstructured. Much of the criticism mentioned above is levelled at unstructured interviews, in which the interviewer enters into a free-flowing conversation with the interviewee. Truly, there are some experienced people who can derive a considerable amount of information about a candidate in this way, but where this method is used, it is unlikely that all candidates will be treated in exactly the same way and this may lead to claims of unfair discrimination.

To avoid this, interviews should be standardised and 'structured' as much as possible, so that all candidates are asked the same questions. This is where advanced preparation is important – decide with the other interviewers which areas will be covered and by whom. Use the job description and person specification as a basis for your questions, or a competency framework if you have one.

Table 7.1 Candidate's interview performance form

Interview Assessment Sheet						
Candidate name	Job title					
Grade	Department					
Criteria	Poor	Fair	Adequate	Good	Excellent	Evidence and comments
Qualifications						
Experience						
Previous relevant training						
Education						
Knowledge and skills						
General rating						
General comments						

If you prepare a separate form in respect of each candidate, such as the one in Table 7.1, you can record any new information that came to light during the interview, and jot something down that will enable you to remember which candidate is which – some distinctive feature or something they were wearing. When you have interviewed ten candidates in a row, it is difficult to recall who said what. Remember you are going to have a discussion with your interviewing colleagues afterwards, and you will want to make a sensible and meaningful contribution. Be careful about making personal comments, however. If there is a case that goes to an employment tribunal for, say, sex discrimination, all your notes, private or not, will be made public. So writing 'the candidate wore an awful yellow cardigan – no fashion sense!' will not add to your integrity when read out at the tribunal!

7.7.2 USING THE APPLICATION FORM

Some interviewers recommend basing the interview structure on the contents of the application form, so that the form acts as a kind of checklist. This is not always a good idea: the completed application form contains factual information, but it may also include information that the applicant wished to present to you. It is important to identify gaps on the CV or application form – be prepared to ask questions on these to ensure you have the full story.

The main aim of the interview is to select the best person for the job, which is achieved through predicting the 'in-job' performance of each candidate. An interview structured around the job description and the person specification can be a safe method of ensuring that the person can do the job. This, coupled with the factual information on the application form in addition to information that was gathered from tests, other assessment methods and references should give sound data on which to base a decision.

7.7.3 PROBLEMS WITH INTERVIEWING

Be aware of some of the dangers of interviewing. Bias towards a favoured candidate that you like the look of as soon as they enter the room and from the first few minutes of the interview (the 'halo effect') or against one whom you dislike (the 'horns effect') can affect your objectivity when making a rational decision. Make sure you listen to all that your candidate has to say throughout the interview and don't make snap decisions based on the answers to the first few questions. We sometimes make our minds up too early and then seek confirmatory evidence to support that view, rather than remaining open and unbiased throughout.

There are other forms of bias – for instance if we have a very poor candidate followed by a good one, we tend to overestimate how good the second candidate is. The recency effect can come into play here – we remember the last candidate we see and forget the ones seen earlier, perhaps resulting in making a decision on a relative measure rather than on a measurement against the job and person specification. Note-taking is important to help us recall who said what and use of a grid such as the one in Table 7.1 is helpful.

There is also a danger of stereotyping (see below) and of choosing someone who is 'like me'; we tend to want to appoint people we will like and with whom we identify. But unless we want an organisation full of clones of ourselves, it makes more sense to make our decision based on the person specification and the competences for the job, rather than on personal liking. Be aware of discrimination: remember that you should always be able to justify your decision and be able to confirm that you have appointed the 'best person for the job, on job-related grounds' – assessments of candidates should focus on their abilities in relation to the job.

7.7.4 COMPETENCE-BASED INTERVIEWS

The questions in an interview should be closely related to the job, either by linking them to the job description and person specification as noted above, or by relating them to 'competencies' – 'a set of behaviours that individuals demonstrate when undertaking job-relevant tasks' (Whiddett and Hollyforde, 2003). There may be 'core competencies' that apply to all employees whatever their job (for example, teamworking) and 'job-specific competencies' (for example, analytical ability) that are the specialised attributes necessary for the job in question. If you have a set of competencies for the job, questions can be linked in to those, thus providing a valid structure to the questions asked. Answers are then scored and comparisons between candidates can easily be made. There is less likelihood of bias and justification of decisions is far more transparent.

7.7.5 VALUE-BASED INTERVIEWING

The Francis Report (2013), which examined the causes of the failings in care at Mid Staffordshire NHS Foundation Trust between 2005 and 2009, made recommendations that emphasised the need to 'foster a common culture shared by all in the service of putting the patient first'. Obviously, one way of achieving this is to appoint staff with the right attitudes.

Organisations such as the NHS and National Society for the Prevention of Cruelty to Children (NSPCC) now use 'value-based interviewing' (VBI), where the emphasis is on appointing people with the right attitude and values, rather than *just* qualifications and experience. It is particularly relevant for jobs where there is a high importance on appointing someone who cares for people, say in a hospital, or working with children.

Examples might be: 'Give me an example of a time when you were particularly perceptive regarding a patient's (or customer's) feelings and needs?' Or: 'Tell me about a time when you went the extra mile to meet the needs of a patient.'

CASE EXAMPLE 7.1

NSPCC VALUES-BASED INTERVIEWING

The NSPCC sees VBI as a way of helping organisations to recruit the most suitable people to work with children. It helps employers assess the values, motives and attitudes of those who are applying for jobs. It focuses on 'how' and 'why' an applicant makes choices in work and seeks to explore reasons for their behaviour.

The VBI method builds on good recruitment and safeguarding practice. It is not a substitute for good pre-employment checks or sound general recruitment. It relies on an organisational commitment to high standards of safer recruitment and staff training from the top and a culture where children's safety and well-being are paramount.

The need to improve training around the selection of candidates to work with children has been highlighted by a number of official reports, including the Bichard Inquiry (following the murders by Ian Huntley of Holly Wells and Jessica Chapman), Choosing with Care (Warner, 1992 – an inquiry into the abuse of children in residential homes), and the serious case review into abuse by nursery worker Vanessa George.

What are the benefits of VBI?

Managers who use VBI have more in-depth information on which to make decisions about candidates' suitability. It provides managers with a true understanding of, and insight into, candidates' values and behaviours and how they are aligned with those of the organisation.

By appointing people using VBI an organisation is demonstrating its ongoing commitment to the values and behaviours which help create a safer environment for children. VBI helps select candidates who have positive safeguarding attitudes and values, and who are therefore likely to be more effective in identifying and addressing safeguarding issues at work.

How does a VBI work?

The value-based interview forms part of safe recruitment processes but should never be used as a substitute for other recruitment methods in making recruitment decisions. Value-based interviews are held separately from standard panel interviews by two VBI-trained interviewers.

The VBI interviewers will select four to five questions that allow them to use the organisation's values and behaviours to explore a candidate's suitability to work with children. They use active listening skills and a range of questioning and probing techniques to explore a candidate's answers in depth during the interview, which normally should take 45–60 minutes. Interview rooms should be set up in a more relaxing, less formal style for conducting a VBI.

Reproduced with kind permission of NSPCC.

(Source: NSPCC Inform. Value based interviewing: keep children safer through recruitment. Online, available at: **www.nspcc.org.uk/Inform/research/briefings/Value-based-interviewing_wda95721.html**)

PAUSE FOR THOUGHT

Analyse your own approach to interviews. Are you aware of any bias? How easy is it to remain completely neutral? What can you do to ensure impartiality? Are values of importance in your organisation or, for example, in a bank or building society?

7.7.6 TYPES OF INTERVIEW

Interviews may be held as one-to-one, two-to-one or panel interviews. Where there are several interviewers, the person who takes the lead should be a good interpersonal communicator, have a sound knowledge of the job for which the selection is being made, and be capable of controlling the track of the interview and of establishing and maintaining a healthy rapport with the interviewee throughout. Plan the structure before the interview – who will ask what? And have the same set of questions for each candidate. Inevitably, you will want to perhaps follow up and ask probing questions that will differ slightly for each candidate, but the basic set should be the same for all, as this avoids claims of discrimination, as we saw earlier. A professional approach will leave the candidates feeling that they have been treated well, and even if they are not successful in getting the job, they will at least feel they have had a fair trial.

7.7.7 INITIAL EXCHANGES

Start the interview with some easy to answer questions to enable the candidate to relax. It is important to establish rapport to encourage the interviewee to open up and answer freely. A nervous interviewee will give you less information about themselves than will one who is relaxed. From that point on, the interviewee should do most of the talking. Allowing them to talk for 70% of the time, while you talk for 30% is the recommended balance; the longer you talk, the more you will deprive the candidate of the opportunity to tell you things about themselves. It is helpful, though, to allow discussion and two-way communication, so rather than leaving questions from the candidate to the end (in the typical 'Have you any questions you would like to ask us?'), try to make them feel able to ask throughout – as you would in any normal conversation. Interviews are not meant to be interrogatory, but should form an exchange of information in as relaxed a way as possible. The interview is a two-way process and the interviewee may want to find things out about the organisation.

7.7.8 QUESTIONING TECHNIQUES

How you ask a question is every bit as important as what you ask. Questions should be framed in a way that invites the candidate to reply in full. Questions may be closed or open. A closed question is one that invites a short but informative answer, often used to check and confirm facts: for example, 'How many years did you work there?', answer: '15'. They can be useful to clarify information, perhaps where there are gaps on the CV or application form. Open questions are those that begin with 'why' or 'how did you...?' Such questions should not be too long or convoluted, and you should ensure that there is only one question at a time. If you ask more than one question in a single statement, you will only get an answer to the last one. Here is an example of the difference between open and closed questions:

> *Closed version*: 'Do you like working in HR?'
> *Open version*: 'What do you like about working in HR?'

The answer to the open version allows the candidate to explain the outcomes of the work and why it is enjoyable, while the answer to the closed version could just be a 'yes'. The more relevant information you have about the candidates, the more able you will be to make a good-quality selection decision. Questions are best linked to competencies. Ask for examples where the candidates have used a particular competency: can they tell you how they have demonstrated leadership qualities, or worked as part of a team? If you have a list of competencies, you can frame a question for each and this will give you sound evidence of what a candidate has done. This is far better than asking loose, vague questions about 'what would you do' and focuses them on 'What have you actually done to demonstrate this skill?'.

Be careful to avoid 'leading' questions. Questions such as, 'So you agree that leadership is about controlling people?' are likely to make a candidate think this is what you are looking for and they will therefore go along with what you say. After all, the candidate is trying to appear to be the person you want – and this may inhibit them from giving their true feelings. If you ask instead, 'What do you feel are the main components of leadership?', you are giving nothing away, and the candidate is more likely to say what they really think. A better question would be to ask, 'Can you give an example of your leadership style?' as you can see from this whether they meet the leadership competency.

Questions such as 'Can you cope with pressure?' are also likely to elicit a response of 'yes'. Who would answer differently, if they want the job? A better way would be to ask, 'Tell me about a time when you have dealt with pressure,' which forces the candidate to rely on their past experience and actually say how they have dealt with it. If you ask questions that make candidates draw on their actual experience, you are more likely to get a truer response, rather than one they might make up. Again, this style of question links back to competencies.

Replace hypothetical questions such as, 'How would you deal with a difficult customer?', where they have to invent a scenario, with 'How have you dealt with difficult customers?', which should elicit a more realistic and reliable answer. As we saw earlier, basing your questions around the competencies necessary for the job makes for a much more relevant interview, focused on the real attributes required.

 ACTIVITY 7.6

Devise a set of questions that you might ask if you were recruiting for a replacement for your own job. What are the key things you would want to find out about the person in terms of skills and experience?

7.7.9 QUESTIONING AND EQUAL OPPORTUNITIES

Be careful to avoid stereotyping – make sure you base your decisions on reality. Stereotyping involves making assumptions about the group to which people belong, such as 'English people drink tea and eat fish and chips', or 'all students like to drink and party'! Obviously a large proportion of people in these groups do not fit this description. Making assumptions about people based on their gender, age or ethnic origin, for instance, or about what a disabled person is capable of, is both shallow and risky. The general position is that it is unlawful for an employer to ask any job applicant about their health or disability unless and until the applicant has been offered a job. If an employer asks questions about disability and health and then uses the information gained to discriminate against the person, that person can take a disability discrimination case to an employment tribunal. If an employer asks unlawful questions but does not use the information to discriminate against the person because of disability (for example the disabled person is nevertheless offered the job), no discrimination has occurred and there is no case to bring.

There are certain specific situations in which health or disability questions are allowed to be asked during the early stages of the recruitment process.

1   To establish whether the applicant can take part in an assessment to determine their suitability for the job.

2   To determine whether any reasonable adjustments need to be made to enable a disabled person to participate in an assessment during the recruitment process.

3   To find out whether a job applicant would be able to undertake a function that is intrinsic to the job.

4   To monitor diversity among job applicants.

5   To support 'positive action' in employment for disabled people.

6   If there is an occupational requirement for the person to be disabled.

(Source: Government Equalities Office: **www.gov.uk/government/uploads/system/ uploads/attachment_data/file/85013/employment-health-questions.pdf**)

When questioning candidates, always bear in mind that their domestic situation and personal circumstances have no bearing on the case for employment. If the recruitment process has been handled according to good practice, the shortlisted candidates will only have proceeded with their applications if they are sure they could meet the demands of the job. One approach is to ensure that all questions relate directly to the job, its technicalities, duties, responsibilities and the performance required. Again, a set of competencies for the job will provide a useful format on which to base your questions, ensuring that they all relate specifically to the job.

 CASE EXAMPLE 7.2

A distribution warehouse wants to appoint a warehouse operative. The job involves a lot of lifting and manual handling. It is legal to ask candidates whether they are capable of lifting and handling goods because it is an intrinsic part of the job.

7.7.10 CLOSING THE INTERVIEW

When you have all the information you need, the interview is almost at its end. It is then that you should give interviewees the opportunity to make any points or ask questions. Candidates may have studied the job requirements and come to the interview hoping to put across several points that they feel are in their favour. During the course of the interview, they will have taken any opportunities that arose to express these points, but there may be something they wish to say that they feel would complete their case for being appointed.

7.8 MAKING THE DECISION

Selection decisions are seldom made by just one person sitting alone, and while HR people do contribute with information and legal guidance, they should make such decisions only if the position is in the HR department.

The objective is to select the best person for the job, and the decision has to be made fairly and legally. To achieve this, you have to be sure that all of the candidates received exactly the same treatment, that the selection process (including any selection tests) was structured in the same way for everyone, and that they all received an equal opportunity to make a case.

The whole process has to be fair, and be seen to be fair. A structured decision-making process that focuses upon how each of the candidates rated throughout the selection process, in which evidence from tests and interviews is seriously considered, has the hallmarks of a fair system. Notes can be compared and agreements reached about the performance of each individual.

Having borne in mind the demands of fairness, legality and the provision of equal opportunities, it is up to the decision-makers to select the candidate they think is the best person for the job. This is a difficult decision to make, not least because the very idea of selecting just one person makes the whole process discriminatory.

7.9 MAKING AN OFFER OF EMPLOYMENT

Making an offer of employment 'subject to satisfactory references' should be avoided. If you make the offer and then receive poor references, it is a difficult and awkward task to retract it. References should be received prior to offers being made if possible. This may be problematic in that sometimes people do not want their employer to know that they have applied for another job, so do not want to ask for a reference before they have a firm offer. As we discussed earlier, references may not offer any real insight into the candidate's suitability but do give important information about the candidate's employment history. However, most employers do use them, and it is worth making sure that you have followed correct procedures. If there is more than one possible choice of appointment, it is wise to wait until the offer has been accepted in writing before communicating the final decision to the rest of the candidates.

7.9.1 MEDICAL EXAMINATION

It is unlawful under the Equality Act 2010 to ask candidates to complete a medical questionnaire before being offered a job or for employers to ask about a candidate's health, except in certain circumstances (see 'Questioning and Equal Opportunities' above).

The CIPD's factsheet on *Recruitment* (CIPD, 2013o) states that 'employers should also take care before making selection decisions relating to a candidate's mental or physical health. They need to think creatively and innovatively about where they can make reasonable adjustments, such as flexible working, where someone has a disability.'

7.9.2 OTHER CHECKS TO CARRY OUT

Criminal records checks

For certain posts you may need to carry out further checks. If you are recruiting to certain jobs in vulnerable areas – for example working with children or in healthcare – you may need to get a criminal records check processed through the Disclosure and Barring Service (DBS) as part of the recruitment process. The DBS provides a list of posts which can be checked. As legislation changes, it is worth visiting their website for the latest advice on the process (**www.gov.uk/government/organisations/disclosure-and-barring-service**).

Right to work in the UK

With workers coming from the European Union to work in the UK, it is important to check that your candidates have the right to work here. The Asylum and Immigration Act 1996 made it a criminal offence to employ those who do not have permission to live or work in the UK. This was updated by the Immigration, Asylum and Nationality Act 2006, which came into force on 29 February 2008. Basically employers must ask for and take copies of original, acceptable documents showing that the person is allowed to work, before they are offered employment. If a person has a restriction on the type of work they can do and/or the hours they can work, the employer must make sure the job does not break those conditions. HR monitoring and recording systems must be in place. Penalties for organisations employing illegal workers can include fines of £20,000 for each illegal worker. If an employer is found to have 'knowingly employed' an illegal worker, there can be an unlimited fine or a prison sentence of up two years.

As legislation changes fairly frequently, make sure you are up to date; see the UK Visas and Immigration website (**www.gov.uk/government/organisations/uk-visas-and-immigration**).

ACTIVITY 7.7

Go to the Disclosure and Barring Service (DBS) at **www.gov.uk/government/publications/dbs-check-eligible-positions-guidance** and download their Guide to Eligibility. What are the main areas which can be checked? Are you surprised at any of the categories?

7.9.3 MAKING APPOINTMENTS

Appointments should be handled sensitively, as there may be a number of internal candidates who did not get the job. Reasons for appointing the one candidate you have chosen must be sound – and *be seen to be* sound – if you wish to avoid staff being demoralised because they didn't get the job.

PAUSE FOR THOUGHT

There are many things to be aware of in the selection process: discrimination, legal obligations, behaving professionally and ethically, giving the candidates a good experience, choosing the right candidate, one who has the right skills, abilities and attitudes. . .. Having read the chapter, do you now feel confident about being able to select staff?

7.9.4 COST BENEFITS

Recruitment and selection can be costly processes. But while tests, interviews and assessments can be expensive and consume a great deal of time, the costs to the organisation of selecting the wrong candidate are high. Having to start all over again is something to be avoided, especially as we noted earlier that, according to the CIPD, it costs around £2,000 to replace someone (£5,000 if it's a senior manager's post) (CIPD/ Hays, 2013). Not only is there a financial cost: when staff have to cover while a post is vacant and then the new recruit doesn't fit in, or does not perform effectively, or leaves soon after appointment, this can have an impact on the remaining staff's morale. This might have a knock-on effect on employees' ability to cope with extra work and may lead to sickness absence through stress, making the organisation even more short-staffed. Time and effort spent on selecting the right person, who has the skills needed, the right attitude and will fit in with the organisation's culture will be worthwhile.

If the right selection procedures are used, you should find that you can select talented employees in an effective and cost-efficient way (which will also help to convince line managers of the usefulness and value of HR). A professional approach will impact not only on the business internally, but also on those outside it who have contact with you in the selection process. Poor selection processes reflect badly on the organisation's image. A good employer should have transparent selection procedures that are fair and equitable.

7.9.5 FINAL WORD

The last stage in selection is induction. This process establishes the appointed candidate in the job. If induction is poor, the likelihood of a new appointee leaving is higher, and you may have to start the whole recruitment and selection process all over again. See the next chapter for more detail on induction.

7.10 SUMMARY

In this chapter we have moved on from recruitment to selection and have considered a wide variety of selection techniques that can be used in the search for talent. These include traditional methods such as the classic trio of application form, interview and references, but also more modern techniques, such as assessment centres and psychological tests that identify candidates' personality characteristics, intelligence, values and attitudes.

The need to avoid discrimination is imperative – the whole selection procedure must be fair, ethical and equitable. The selection process reflects on the organisation, so it needs to be handled as professionally as possible, so that both employer and candidate are satisfied.

Interviews are an integral part of the selection process, with structured interviews being seen to be a better predictor of eventual performance in the job. Some hints and tips have been given on how to interview, with discussion of questioning techniques together with some of the pitfalls of interviewing, such as stereotyping. The competence-based interview is a modern approach that can help the interviewer to focus on the job and helps to alleviate some of the discrimination traps where candidates are asked about their private lives, which have nothing to do with the job in question. Another more recent approach in value-based interviewing, which is useful in areas of work that need people with the right attitude and who share the values of the organisation – used particularly in the NHS.

This chapter has covered the entire selection process and has given practical advice on how to select candidates so that we can identify talented people who will be a credit to the organisation and who will perform well once appointed. A key part of HR, selection must be carried out professionally and efficiently – if you follow the advice in this chapter, you will be well versed in how to tackle this major HR activity.

The final stage of selection should be induction, as this finalises the whole process. Induction is the subject of our next chapter.

REVIEW QUESTIONS

1 Name three different methods of selection.

2 Why are psychometric tests so useful?

3 How much does the CIPD say it costs to recruit someone every time an employee leaves?

4 Why are references an unreliable source of data on a candidate?

5 What are the advantages of a Skype interview?

6 What activities might you include in an assessment centre for a lecturer's post? Or an administrator in the surgery of your local family doctor?

7 Why are competence-based interviews a good idea?

8 What are the benefits of using value-based interviews?

9 Name three things that are a cause of bias in an interview.

10 What percentage of the time should you allow an interviewee to talk?

11 Why is it good practice to structure a selection interview?

12 What is the difference between an open and a closed question?

13 In which situations might we be able to ask questions about a candidate's health?

14 What checks should you do before confirming an offer of appointment?

EXPLORE FURTHER

BOOKS

TORRINGTON, D., HALL, L., TAYLOR, S. and ATKINSON, C. (2014) *Human resource management*. 9th ed. Harlow: Pearson.

There are many textbooks on selection interviewing, but this is a sound textbook on HR that has a good section on selection decision-making.

ARMSTRONG, M., with TAYLOR, S. (2014) *Armstrong's handbook of human resource management practice*. London: Kogan Page.

Another good text, with a chapter on selection interviewing skills.

WHIDDETT, S. and HOLLYFORDE, S. (2003) *A practical guide to competencies*. London: Chartered Institute of Personnel and Development.

Despite its age, this is a sound textbook on using competencies in selection.

WEB LINKS

See the 'Equality Act 2010: What do I Need to Know? A quick start guide to the ban on questions about health and disability during recruitment' for information on what is and isn't legal when interviewing in relation to health and disability. Available at: **www.gov.uk/government/uploads/system/uploads/ attachment_data/file/85013/employment-health-questions.pdf**

The British Psychological Society has lots of information on testing – see **www. psychtesting.org.uk/the-ptc/guidelinesandinformation.cfm**

Guidelines on test use can be found at the International Test Commission (ITC) (2000) *International Guidelines for Test Use [online]*. Available at: **www.intestcom. org/itc_projects.htm** (Accessed 23 March 2014).

The Acas website has good advice – especially on references – see **www.acas.org.uk**

As advised in Chapter 6, the annual CIPD *Recruitment, Retention and Turnover* survey report makes essential reading. The 2013 survey is available at: **www.cipd. co.uk/hr-resources/survey-reports/resourcing-talent-planning-2013.aspx**

Disclosure and Barring Service: **www.gov.uk/government/organisations/ disclosure-and-barring-service**

UK Visas and Immigration website: **www.gov.uk/government/organisations/uk- visas-and-immigration**

The Home Office's Guidance Documents for Employers on Preventing Illegal Working are available at: **http://webarchive.nationalarchives.gov.uk/ 20140110181512/http://www.ukba.homeoffice.gov.uk/sitecontent/documents/ employersandsponsors/preventingillegalworking/**

The Francis report can be accessed at **www.midstaffspublicinquiry.com/report**

Information Commissioner's Office: **www.ico.gov.uk**

See the NSPCC factsheet for more on value-based interviewing at: **www.nspcc.org. uk/Inform/research/briefings/Value-based-interviewing_wda95721. html#References**

For free online examples of tests, visit **www.practiceaptitudetests.com/**

Some very useful and practical information on assessment centres can be found at: **www.prospects.ac.uk/interview_tips_assessment_centres.htm**

CHAPTER 8

Induction and Retention

LEARNING OBJECTIVES

After studying this chapter you should understand:

- the purpose of induction and the variety of approaches that are used in today's organisations
- the concept of employer branding
- the concepts of onboarding and socialisation
- the typical causes of the induction crisis and the steps that may be taken to prevent it
- the importance of retaining key employees
- the measures that may be put into action to achieve effective retention and be able to contribute to the retention plan.

8.1 INTRODUCTION

The purpose of this chapter is to discuss the systematic induction of new employees into the organisation after recruitment checks have been carried out and they have been appointed to their positions. The notion of employer branding is introduced in the context of attracting and retaining staff and the concept of 'onboarding', or organisational socialisation, is discussed. We also look at retention issues and what can be done to encourage employees to remain with the organisation.

Induction is often considered to be the final part of the recruitment and selection process. Indeed, if induction is not carried out correctly, it is likely that the new recruit will leave and the whole recruitment process will have to start all over again. The concept of an 'induction crisis', where new starters feel that they don't 'fit' with the organisation and leave the job in the first few weeks, is all too common. Without an effective induction programme, the likelihood that an employee will leave a company within the first 12 months is increased.

 KEY CONCEPT: INDUCTION

Induction is the process through which new employees become familiar with an organisation, learn its norms and begin to share its values. Taylor (2014, p.243) defines induction as 'a general term describing the whole process whereby new employees adjust or acclimatise to their jobs and working environment.'

KEY CONCEPT: ONBOARDING

'The process through which new employees move from being organizational outsiders to becoming organizational insiders'. . . . The mechanism through which 'new employees acquire the necessary knowledge, skills, and behaviours to become effective in their new organizations' (Bauer and Erdogan, 2011). Induction is about how we get new staff 'on board' with our organisation and give them a 'sense of belonging'. Methods to achieve onboarding might include using meetings, lectures, videos, printed materials or computer-based programmes to introduce new starters to their new jobs and organisations. Research by Ashford and Black (1996) and Kammeyer-Mueller and Wanberg (2003) has demonstrated that these socialisation techniques lead to positive outcomes for new employees, such as higher retention, job satisfaction, better performance, greater commitment and a reduction in stress.

Induction, as a process, has strong links to how an organisation's culture is enforced. Further discussion of this facet of the importance of 'induction' is discussed in Chapter 2, 'Aspects of Organisational Culture'.

8.2 EMPLOYER BRANDING

The CIPD (2013p), in its factsheet, *Employer Brand,* defines employer branding as 'how an organisation markets what it has to offer to potential and existing employees'. The CIPD/Hays *Resourcing and Talent Management* survey report (2013) states that 'positioning as an employer of choice plays an important role in attracting the best talent'.

The idea of employer branding is twofold: to attract good candidates but also to create a culture that will retain them in the business. The CIPD (2013p) comments that:

> in the wake of the global financial crisis, many organisations are recognising the business benefits and opportunities that can develop from embedding a responsible and sustainable ethos into the organisation and employer brand – this makes it attractive to potential employees.

Clearly for the large national or multinational organisation, there are advantages in developing an employer brand because there is already likely to be in existence a recognisable consumer brand, but for the smaller business this may present more of a challenge. However, there are paybacks in terms of recognition of the brand by local communities, which increases the likelihood of becoming an employer of choice with its links into recruitment and employee retention.

Carrington (2007) describes the pitfalls of employer branding in terms of the difficulty of putting a value on the effectiveness of the branding process. Making the link between cause and effect between employer branding and its impact upon recruitment, quality and quantity is like trying to determine the effectiveness of HRM as a process; both pose problems of quantifying and measuring success.

Allied to employer brand is the notion of the **employee value proposition** (**EVP**): the balance of the rewards and benefits that are received by employees in return for their performance at the workplace. The value proposition describes what an organisation stands for, requires and offers as an employer. It is important to find out what the employees want from their employment and for the employer to be able to deliver it.

KEY CONCEPT: EMPLOYER BRAND

The CIPD defines the **employer brand** as a set of attributes and qualities – often intangible – that makes an organisation distinctive, promises a particular kind of employment experience, and appeals to those people who will thrive and perform best in its culture.

Specifically, organisations that have a strong and attractive employer brand:

- can use it to help them produce in turn a more engaged workforce who 'live the brand' and in turn reduce the costs of employee turnover
- are likely to perform better, have higher attendance levels and deliver a more positive customer experience.

(CIPD/Mercer, 2010)

8.3 THE IMPORTANCE OF INDUCTION

Acas (2012a) suggest that 'induction is an essential part of onboarding your new recruits and familiarising them with your organisation. Getting the induction process right can help you get new employees up to speed and productive as quickly as possible.' Being able to understand and manage the process of socialisation will help to provide competitive advantages to an organisation.

Induction is usually a formal process, whereby new employees are introduced to co-workers and managers, given a tour of the workplace, and told about rules and procedures. Sadly it is sometimes the case that new starters are 'thrown in at the deep end', given a hurried chat about the job and main rules and regulations, given a few standard company documents to read and are then expected to be ready to work. It is important to ensure that new staff are not 'overloaded with information' but that they receive everything they need to settle into the job easily and that they feel welcome. The process of induction begins before the employee is appointed to the job. Impressions are formed by how well the company responds to requests and queries from the new starter, and how the invitation for interview and the subsequent recruitment and selection process is handled. The organisation's external publicity, as well as all of the events mentioned above, have an impact on the potential future employee. The importance of employer branding becomes apparent.

Many organisations now recognise that a good induction helps an individual to become effective in the job more quickly and therefore is more likely to stay with the organisation. How the organisation handles the process is determined by what emphasis it places on induction, the level of resources the organisation will commit and the expertise available to carry out the process.

ACTIVITY 8.1

Think about when you started work. How did it feel on the first day? How long did it take for you to feel settled? What contributed to you feeling 'a part of the organisation'? What hampered this process?

8.3.1 THE PURPOSE OF INDUCTION

The purpose of induction is twofold. First, it is to help make new employees become effective in their job, and second, to achieve onboarding or socialisation of individuals into the organisation, that is, to help give them a better understanding of what the company expects from them and what it is prepared to offer in return.

Michael Armstrong (2014, p.257) proposes that induction serves four purposes:

- to smooth the preliminary stages when everything is strange and unfamiliar to the new starter
- to establish quickly a favourable attitude to the company in the mind of the new employee so that they are more likely to stay
- to obtain effective output from the employee in the shortest possible time
- to reduce the likelihood of the employee leaving quickly.

It has to be borne in mind that when people first come to the organisation to work, they will be keen to gather as much information about the place as possible, to begin to build their internal map. In doing this, they go through the process of 'socialisation'. Without a formal induction process the individual will learn about the organisation by default; their work colleagues will present their own interpretations of 'the way things are done around here', which may not match the way the organisation would like things done, nor the culture the organisation intends to create and maintain. Refer to Chapter 2 for a description of culture and its importance to the organisation.

Induction, at its extreme, is the first opportunity to introduce the individual into the company's culture, its norms, standards (values) and expected behaviours. This is particularly so with large corporate organisations where there are strong cultural identities. The intention here is to start the process whereby external expectations (of the company) are slowly internalised by the new employee (Poulter and Land, 2008). The level of effort and thought put into how we get people 'on board' is crucial.

The Ritz-Carlton organisation in the United States even goes so far as having a training institute where they not only train their own staff in the fundamentals, general and specific requirements of customer service, but they also market their training to other organisations. It is worth reading Paul Hemp's (2002) article in the *Harvard Business Review*, where he, as senior editor for the *Harvard Business Review*, spent two days of induction and four days working in the Ritz-Carlton, Boston. The induction covers everything from the 'appropriate language' to use when addressing a guest to the uniform worn by a member of staff. The induction programme is key to carrying the culture into new employee generations.

PAUSE FOR THOUGHT

When you seek a new job, what attracts you to the company? How much do you find out about the organisation before you make your decision? What do you consider in addition to the job and the salary? How much do you really know about what it will be like to work there?

8.4 INDICATIONS OF A SUCCESSFUL INDUCTION PROCESS

- New employees become effective in their jobs quickly.
- An increase in the rate at which employees adapt to their surroundings.
- Good interpersonal relations between new and longer-serving employees.

- A reduction in staff turnover, thus reducing recruitment costs and disruption to workplace productivity.
- A satisfactory staff retention rate and stability index.

ACTIVITY 8.2

Read the article by Lashley and Best (2002) in the *International Journal of Contemporary Hospitality Management*, entitled 'Employee induction in licensed retail organisations'.

The article explores the extent and scope of induction in the licensed retail trade just to see how hit and miss the induction process

can be, although they do indicate 'that some form of induction does take place in most firms' (Lashley and Best, 2002, p.8). They also argue that 'best practice suggests that induction should be an ongoing process starting before the employee joins and extending through a period of weeks and months' (p.12).

KEY CONCEPT: SOCIALISATION

Socialisation is the process through which individuals become familiar with their environment and learn about the kind of behaviours that are expected of them. It is experienced in our early development years and what we learn then stays with us for the rest of our lives. When we enter an organisation, we go through a process of finding out about the culture, how things are done in the organisation; we learn all about what is acceptable behaviour, both formally (for example the disciplinary procedures) and informally (for example jokes, banter). The sooner we do this, the quicker we adapt to our new situation and feel comfortable in it.

8.4.1 THE INDUCTION CRISIS

As the new employee begins to get to know the job and the organisation, they may have second thoughts about the original decision they made to join the organisation and consider leaving. The job and the organisation may not match up to the employee's expectations and, in some cases, the employer's promises; the psychological contract may be broken. This is why employer branding is so important – companies need to make themselves attractive to prospective employees and to live up to those images. Additionally, the decision to stay or leave may be determined by other factors, such as pay, working time and the possibility of finding another job. If the strength of the crisis is not enough to justify leaving, the employee may decide to 'put up with it for now', and hope that things will improve. In this case a period of accommodation may follow, in which they begin to adjust to their role and situation.

In a survey by Harvey Nash (2012) entitled 'Onboard and upwards: How an executive's first 90 days make or break the ones that follow', it was found that 'less than a third of executives (28 per cent) felt the organisation they joined was represented very accurately in the recruitment process' and '39 per cent of executives considered walking away in their first three months'. Perhaps the best argument for having a good induction process comes from 50% of the respondents in the survey saying 'they could have been on average 50 per cent more productive if their start in the business had been better organised'.

8.4.2 INFLUENTIAL FACTORS

The new employee's co-workers can influence how they feel about the job, especially if they have negative feelings because, for example, they had built up a close rapport with the previous incumbent and the new person's behaviours differ significantly from what they had previously experienced and liked.

It may be that there is a discrepancy between what the new employee had been told to expect about the job and working atmosphere. This mismatch between expectation and reality can cause doubts in the mind of the individual as to whether they wish to stay with the organisation. They may feel let down and disillusioned.

Recruiters are key culture carriers for the organisation and, if they have not fully understood the nature of the job and have passed on, inadvertently, false information, this may build unrealistic expectations in the new employee and so becomes a key area to be addressed – to prevent the problem from recurring in the future. At the recruitment stage all documentation and briefings should reflect, as accurately as possible, the reality of the job and working environment.

Van Dick et al (2004, p.352) argue that the:

> research suggests that social identification in organizational contexts is a powerful concept to explain individuals' performance, well-being and turnover intentions. . . . Organizational identification contributes to levels of self-enhancement, . . . self continuity, and reductions of uncertainty. In addition, the more an employee identifies with an organization, the more this employee's self image incorporates the organization's characteristics. Thus the more I identify myself with my organization, the more I define myself in terms of this particular membership and the more is my own future determined by the organization's future.

8.5 PURPOSE

The purpose of the induction process can be seen as twofold. It is about providing the inductee with a thorough understanding of the organisation, its mission, history, products, current situation and its plans for the future. For the larger organisation a complete corporate picture will include details of the organisation's main policies, its status in the industry, photographs and short biographies of the board and senior managers, along with charts of the organisation's structure. Second, the induction process starts the process of passing on the culture of the organisation to the individual in terms of work ethic and values: for example, how the organisation views work-life balance issues, or how it views health and safety – does it pay lip-service or does it take safety issues very seriously?

For a smaller organisation the induction process will be of no less importance but the scope may be reduced. The company history may be shorter but still relevant; the senior managers and their roles and the company structure will be discussed. Introducing the new starter to members of the management team, where they can listen, first-hand, to a manager speaking about the organisation, is key to the socialisation process.

8.6 APPROACHES TO INDUCTION

Attitudes towards induction differ widely from one organisation to another. Issues can range from the important aspects of knowing the name, status and reputation of the new employee's manager, what work they will be involved in and payment arrangements. There are also the more trivial, but still important, questions of when to take a break and the location of the toilets. Good inductions help the new starter understand what makes the organisation 'tick' and what it stands for in terms of principles and values.

The differences in senior managers' attitude to induction determine the level of resources that are invested in the process; the quality and effectiveness of the induction will vary according to the time, effort and money devoted to it. Well-run organisations will have several different induction systems that are relevant to each type and level of employee. For inducting large numbers of employees it may be advantageous to have common elements (for example discussion of health, safety and welfare issues, pay and conditions of service and so on) and to run the induction process for participants from several departments together. This is both cost-effective and ensures that there will be an intermingling of staff that may bear fruit at a later time by generally improving communications within the organisation. However, there will be a need to have job- or role-specific elements conducted within specific departments, tailored for their new staff, or presented by department specialists.

The following gives some examples of induction. You may wish to reflect which type would be more effective for yourself:

- **Induction pack:** this may include a 'company handbook' that gives the main terms and conditions of service (salary, holiday entitlement, disciplinary and grievance procedures), a copy of the corporate structure, a brief history of the organisation and a site map of the building with the main facilities identified, and perhaps something about company plans for the future. For senior management the induction pack may also include a copy of the annual report. In general, care should be exercised to ensure that the materials included reflect the level of the job and new recruit. Generally today, much of this information will be available on the company website and new starters will be directed to look at this. As well as being always accessible, the information will be updated when things change (or should be updated!).

- **Induction tour**, in which the new employee is shown around the site and is given explanations about each work activity on the way around the facilities. Towards the end of the tour the department in which they will work is visited and more detailed explanations of what happens are given. This is a good time to introduce new employees to their new colleagues.

- **Induction training event:** this is the most successful and effective form of induction and a large number of organisations have adopted this practice. The approach takes the form of a number of training sessions, each of which deals with a particular aspect of work and each is usually delivered by a specialist in that subject area. The duration of the induction is usually staggered over a period of days or even weeks, depending on the amount and complexity of the information to be delivered. However, there are problems with this, as by the time the induction event happens, the new starter already may know much of the information and may feel that their time is being wasted.

- **Coaching, mentoring and buddying** are also used in many organisations to help the new starter over the longer term. Having a mentor to answer questions and give advice is comforting. The mentor will need training in 'how to mentor' and keep up to date with company requirements. Acas (2012a) suggest 'employing a "buddy" system for a new employee's first week can help answer practical questions and deal with any problems in an informal way'. Perhaps someone to have lunch with and who will 'show you the ropes'. There is more on buddying later in the chapter. Social media can be used to assist the onboarding process. Telecom's company O2 use the social network tool Yammer so that co-workers can collaborate on ideas, share feedback and ask questions.

When inducting employees into the organisation it is important to be aware that new recruits may have special needs caused by a disability, for example sight or hearing impairment or learning difficulty. The induction process must, therefore, take account of any special requirements to help them become part of the team.

ACTIVITY 8.3

Think back to your first few days at work in your organisation. Try to recall how you were treated. Which of the approaches, listed above, most closely matched your experience? Did you find it:

- friendly and satisfactory?
- hurried or well planned?
- timely or out of date?
- mystifying?

How could it have been improved?

8.7 STAGES OF INDUCTION

People may be inducted at two main levels: corporate and department. At the corporate level, people learn about the size and shape of the business, for example in which countries it operates, where the corporate head office is located, how many branches it has, its values and beliefs. Second, they will learn some information about their terms and conditions of employment and, third, perhaps most importantly, they will want to see their place of work, meet their new work colleagues and learn about the job itself.

8.7.1 INITIAL BRIEFING

It is the HR practitioner who usually receives new employees and who will explain to the new starter the main points, which includes the kind of information that is in the 'induction pack', as previously discussed. Security passes and passwords should be sorted at this stage, so that the employee can function in the job immediately. The initial briefing should be short, keeping the information to the essential 'need to know' and 'interesting to know' materials. Detailed information is not appropriate at this stage and departmental managers can fill in the salient points of what happens at the workplace. The HR practitioner who greets the new starter should be prepared to create an appropriate atmosphere right from the first 'hello'. There have been instances of new starters turning up on the first day and no one expecting them – not the best beginning to a new job!

Most of us when we start a new job feel nervous. Being fed with streams of information is likely to create information overload and we will not remember most of what has been said.

From the HR practitioner who has done the initial 'meet and greet' and obtained the essential regulatory information, for example to input into the payroll system, the new starter will probably go on to meet the department manager, who will continue with the induction. Once again, being prepared is essential.

8.7.2 INDUCTION TRAINING

The simplest, but probably least effective, way is to load or overload people with information, sending them home at the end of their first day carrying an armful of documents – which they may get down to reading one day. Using the induction pack and laboriously working through it is not an effective way of communicating, although it is vital to ensure that the key points are covered – for health and safety reasons, for instance – and it should not be left to chance that the new starter accesses and understands its content. A more effective approach to induction is through a dedicated training event or series of events, where the information is delivered in a more controlled manner. In this way the information will have a better chance of being remembered. A problem with this type of programme is that it becomes boring and individuals will switch off. One large supermarket chain gives its new starters a series of 12 videos to watch in one day – and while this gets the same message across to all participants, it also becomes draining and tedious.

New starters who are key specialists, for example people who have been recruited into managerial positions, are usually inducted on a one-to-one basis and may not undergo an induction training course as such. When numbers of people are recruited at the same time, a formal induction event is usually organised. The programme will normally be led by an experienced HRM or HRD practitioner, with some of the event being delivered by departmental or subject specialists.

The drawback of having a formal event is that it may occur several weeks after the employee has started. Induction, by its very name, should occur as soon as possible after the new person commences work. Leaving matters until a quorum of several people have arrived will nullify its effect because people will have already settled into the job and may not see its significance and see the event as being 'too late'. Timely delivery of the induction materials is critical if the event is to have a positive effect on the new employee.

8.7.3 METHODS AND MEDIA

Some induction courses can be lengthy events that take place over a number of days. The training programme may consist of a number of discrete sessions enlivened with a variety of media presentations, PowerPoint, DVD, and other visual aids such as actual photographs used to illustrate, for example, bad or good practice in the workplace. In this way the main points of each subject can be delivered and emphasised. Using a variety of delivery methods (as with any training event), is advisable.

A session or seminar with a senior manager, whose presence will emphasise the importance of the induction activity and at the same time convey a message about what the company sees as important, is vital to the effectiveness of the event. Managers, as well as HR, are key cultural carriers of the organisation and for one to take time out of their busy day sends a strong message about what is important to the company. Having a senior management team representative present to answer questions about the company – for example its approach to and philosophy of managing people and, of course, company values – significantly increases the weight and importance of the messages transmitted and received.

8.8 INDUCTING MINORITY GROUPS OR THOSE WITH SPECIAL NEEDS

Acas (2012b) have an excellent guidance booklet entitled *Recruitment and Induction* which gives sound advice and includes a section on induction for those who need special attention – those with disabilities, minorities, people returning from a break, graduate starters, for example. They state:

> Employers may need to be aware and take account of any particular cultural or religious customs of new employees who are part of an ethnic or religious minority so that misunderstandings do not occur. Acas' Equality Service can assist employers with free advice on the development and implementation of policies and practices for greater equality among the workforce. (Acas, 2012b, p.29)

Induction should be properly planned and consistently delivered to ensure that all new employees are treated fairly and receive the same information.

Care needs to be taken when inducting employees who have special needs, perhaps because of a disability or those who have special educational needs. Specialist advice is available from the Disability Employment Adviser and the Disability Service Teams of the Department for Work and Pensions. The Department for Work and Pensions also operates the Access to Work Scheme (see weblinks at the end of the chapter), which can offer assistance in meeting the cost of any aids and adaptations required. These services can be contacted via the Jobcentre network.

When inducting employees who are new to this country, the speed and type of delivery or even lack of understanding of the English language may seriously impair the effectiveness of the induction process. This is especially important where the programme is addressing health and safety matters and there is a clear requirement for the inductees to go away with a clear understanding of how the company views health and safety in the workplace. Equally, inductees should understand the company's discipline and grievance procedures.

Minority groups, especially from overseas, may have come from a culture far removed from the UK culture and so will, on the one hand, be socialising themselves into the UK's societal culture and, on the other hand, be trying to come to terms with the company's organisation culture. They may have to settle into a job, learn or consolidate a new language, be socialised into the local community, and find schooling for their children, all concurrently and in strange surroundings. Having a buddy might be especially helpful here in making the new employee feel at home.

ACTIVITY 8.4

How would you structure the induction process to meet the needs of a:

- partially sighted person?
- a non-native English speaker?
- someone with special education requirements?

8.8.1 DURATION OF INDUCTION PROGRAMMES

Induction programmes vary in their complexity and duration. There are programmes that last for no more than a day and yet are effective. Others may last several days, or even weeks, although a new employee would benefit from no more than one day during their first week. There is no set pattern or universal blueprint for an induction programme; the content and process of it is determined by the varying needs of the new employees and the complexities of different organisations.

Some parts of induction need to be the same for everyone: health and safety, the discipline and grievance procedures and the presentation of the company structure and how it is organised, for example. But other aspects, such as the job itself, finance, or company procedures, are likely to be of different value depending on the job and therefore are delivered to different depths.

However the induction programme is structured it should be revisited on a frequent basis to make sure that the material and structure has not become obsolete. Acas suggest possible items to cover in their *Recruitment and Induction* booklet (2012b), which serves as a useful a checklist.

8.8.2 WHO MIGHT BE INVOLVED

A number of staff may be involved in an induction training programme:

- **HR:** welcomes the new recruit and deals with the paperwork – security, gathers bank details for payroll, information on next of kin, and so on.
- **Line manager/supervisor:** explains about the departmental organisation, the job itself, any probationary period and performance management.
- **Senior manager(s):** gives an overview of the organisation, its history, products and services, quality system and culture. Also their presence adds gravity and importance to the process.
- **Health and safety officer:** explains health and safety issues.

- **Training officer:** describes available training services, then helps to develop a personalised training plan. Provides details of other sources of information during induction, such as the company intranet or interactive learning facilities.
- **IT department:** to discuss the IT systems (and possibly expected behaviours – is personal email allowed? Are employees allowed to access the Internet during work time, and so on?).
- **Trade union representative:** gives details of membership and its benefits.
- **Workmate or 'buddy':** a colleague who is there to offer help during those first few weeks to help the new employee to settle in. For more senior jobs, this may be a *mentor*, who will give advice and guidance.

8.9 TERMS AND CONDITIONS OF EMPLOYMENT

The induction training environment is an ideal place in which to provide new employees with a copy of the particulars of their main terms and conditions of employment. It is advisable to make this a discrete event, rather than issue this type of information along with a sheaf of other documents which may be filed away in the induction pack never to be opened.

KEY CONCEPT: TERMS AND CONDITIONS OF EMPLOYMENT

To serve as evidence that a contract exists between employer and employee, the Employment Rights Act (ERA96) requires an employer to issue a statement of terms and conditions to all employees who are employed for one month or more. This is an important document that should be issued as soon as possible after the person commences work and, in any case, within two months of the start of employment. This is a legal requirement.

The minimum terms and conditions of employment, which the employer must specify, are together called the 'principal statement' and must include: the employer's and employee's name; employee's job title; the date of commencement of employment; the date on which any continuous service commences; the notice period; the rate and scales of pay and how often the employee will be paid (for example hourly, weekly, monthly); normal hours of work; places of work; and holiday entitlement.

In addition to the principal statement covering the above, the employer must also give the following: how long a temporary job is expected to last; the end date of a fixed-term contract; notice periods; collective agreements; pensions; who to go to with a grievance; how to complain about how a grievance is handled; and how to complain about a disciplinary or dismissal decision.

If an employee has to work abroad for more than a month, an employer must state: how long they will be abroad; what currency they will be paid in; what additional pay or benefits they will get; and terms relating to their return to the UK.

If the employee will be working in another country in the European Economic Area (EEA), they must get the terms and conditions that are the legal minimum in that country for: working hours and rest breaks; holiday entitlement; minimum pay (including overtime).

(Guide to Employment Contracts: **www.gov.uk**)

For more on the legal side, see Chapter 16, 'Understanding Employment Law'.

8.10 THE COMPANY HANDBOOK

In addition to the legal statement of terms and conditions, most organisations refer employees to the *company handbook*, which gives the expected rules of behaviour in the workplace. These will be presented either as a paper hard copy or in a link to the company website. There is no legal requirement to have a handbook, but it is a useful repository for procedures and regulations. The company handbook will include the following type of information:

- the payment systems, including the frequency of payments and the deductions that are made, for example tax, National Insurance, pension deductions
- holiday entitlement
- holiday and sick pay arrangements
- sickness absence procedure and attendance policy
- promotion policy
- discrimination and equal opportunities policy
- health and safety policy
- disciplinary rules, including conduct policies on sexual harassment, alcohol and drug use
- grievance procedures
- rules concerning mail; use of the telephone, company equipment, Internet and email; and employee use of motor vehicles for work
- confidentiality rules
- education and training policy
- provision for employees' well-being
- available benefits and facilities: canteen, crèche, and so on
- trade union and joint consultation arrangements
- special working arrangements overseas (if applicable).

ACTIVITY 8.5

Does your employer issue a handbook? If so, read through it and see how its contents compare with the previous list. What type of circumstance in your organisation may cause you to read the handbook?

For further information on handbooks, go to the Acas website and access their advisory handbook, *Employing People: A handbook for small firms*. Available at: **www.acas.org.uk/ index.aspx?articleid=924**

8.11 DEPARTMENTAL INDUCTION

When all of the main points have been explained and questions answered in the companywide context, the new employees are moved on to the *departmental induction*, which is more directly concerned with the new employee's role in their immediate work area. The departmental induction, as well as forming a first and formal introduction to colleagues and supervisor, is also concerned with the technicalities and other details of the job itself. The new employee's expectations are founded upon the job description and person specification, and so it is at this time that expectation is turned into reality. The idea is to settle the new starter into their new place of work and to try to make them feel welcome.

A new entrant will be interested in the departmental environment, including: working relationships, what the supervisor and departmental manager are like (for example, are they approachable?), where the wash facilities are, when breaks and meal times are taken, and where their place of work is. It is normal to show the person around and to introduce everyone. As for information about the job, this will come from the department manager and, in somewhat more detail, the supervisor or team leader. Some manufacturing organisations have 'process trainers' whose role is to teach new starters their job. It is important that the department manager be present at this time so as to be seen as an active colleague. As previously mentioned, the supervisors and managers are key culture carriers for the organisation. They should affirm and reaffirm what is expected of the new employee, in terms of behaviours, so as to commence the socialisation of the individual into the expected norms of the organisation.

Once the new employee becomes accustomed to the workplace, the job can be explained in terms of how it can contribute to the department's objectives. Clearly this should be done in a manner that arouses interest by explaining how the role played by the employee fits into the overall department task and, ultimately, the company. For example, an invoice clerk in the finance department has a role that is key to chasing late or unpaid invoices. This is a task that impacts upon company cash flow, which, in turn, is critical in reducing company borrowing. The level of involvement and enthusiasm of whoever is providing the information will be communicated verbally and non-verbally to the newcomer, and thus, depending upon how it is done, can have either a motivating or demotivating effect. The information given should include details of performance standards and also training and career prospects.

At a department level it is an opportunity to start the process of building the psychological contract between supervisors, team leaders, managers and the new employee. As Armstrong explains (2014, p.420):

A psychological contract is a system of beliefs that encompasses the actions employees believe are expected of them and what response they expect in return from their employer, and, reciprocally, the actions employers believe are expected of them and what response they expect in return from their employees.

Induction is an ideal opportunity for employers to define their expectations and thus start to establish a positive psychological contract.

8.12 SPECIAL CASES

We tend to think of induction as being for new employees starting a new job. However, there are other times when induction back into the workplace might be useful. Those returning to work after a period of sickness or from maternity/parental leave may find it helpful to have a session on what changes have been made in their absence. Or those moving to a different department might need information on the new environment and culture.

See the Acas (2012b) *Recruitment and Induction* booklet for more on induction for special cases.

8.13 FOLLOW-UP

Once the job-holder has gone through the main induction and has started to settle into the job, it is important that their manager watches their progress and checks that all is well. New employees need ongoing support, from a buddy or a mentor and from their line manager.

8.14 BUDDY SYSTEMS AND MENTORS

When the new person starts work on the job itself, the line manager should introduce them to a 'buddy' – a work colleague who understands the organisation, can be trusted to carry out the role professionally, who will act as a kind of guide and to whom the new starter can relate. Alternatively, the new employee may have a mentor, who is usually someone more senior in the organisation and who will assist in the development of the new employee.

In their article, Lau et al (2009) indicate that having a buddy system can offer significant advantages to a business. They argue (p.27):

> The buddy can make the new employee feel welcome, answer questions and help the new person navigate the organisation's culture. This leads the new employee to feel comfortable more quickly and to achieve a sense of acceptance and belonging. For example, new employees may be uncomfortable asking questions for fear of appearing incompetent.

According to Lau et al (2009), the 'buddy' system should be focused on the needs of both the buddy and the new starter. There should be a clarity about '...the knowledge which should be imparted to increase productivity and performance' (Lau et al, 2009, p.27). Further, there should be empathy with and clear understanding about the needs of the new employee and some form of feedback system to check that the process is in fact delivering the intended outcomes. The overall aim is to bring about an assimilation of the new starter into the organisation as quickly as is practicable while building upon the psychological contract, which in turn should reduce the probability of the person leaving. The buddy system should not be entered into lightly. As previously mentioned, the buddy should be professional and should fully understand their role, which implies a degree of personal development on their part, which, in turn, implies commitment to the development process by the company.

8.15 RETENTION, WORK AND WHY PEOPLE WORK

Once an organisation has spent a great deal of time and effort in recruiting, selecting and inducting an employee, the last thing it wants is for that person to leave. In order to encourage staff to stay with the company, it is useful to consider what motivates people at work. Early theories on motivation focused on money as a motivator, as espoused by people such as Henry Ford and engineers such as F.W. Taylor (1911). There was, as Matthewman et al (2009) suggest, a focus on the instrumentality of work; work was purely and simply a means to an economic end, the bills were paid at the end of the month with some money left over for entertainment. As Arnold et al (2010, p.336) point out, pay and other material rewards often signal that a person is successful. So from this perspective pay *is* a motivator if and when it indicates that the person has succeeded in their work tasks. Performance pay is popular in many companies today.

There is much academic discussion about whether money is a motivator. (See Chapter 11, 'Employee Motivation and Performance', for a greater discussion of motivation theory.)

Herzberg et al (1959), in their *two factor theory model*, consider that pay is a 'hygiene' factor and would contribute to work *dissatisfaction* but will not actually *motivate*. Motivators are things such as growth, recognition, responsibility, work itself and achievement. As Herzberg et al suggest, to have fulfilment at work, the nature of the work we do and responsibility for our work all contribute to the feeling of satisfaction. There are many factors to take into consideration when trying to understand why people work. For example, those who have a vocational calling will occupy positions in caring professions, despite the comparatively low rewards for doing so. This of course does not mean that all vocational callings are not well rewarded; one can cite examples of well-rewarded occupations in the legal and medical practitioner sectors.

How effective are we at motivating people in the workplace? Critical to business success is how effective people are engaged with their work and would be inclined, for example, to recommend where they work to family and friends. The Towers Watson Global Workforce survey of 32,000 workers (2012) found that only 35% of employees are highly engaged in their work. Twenty-two per cent felt unsupported (engaged but lacked enablement and/or energy), 17% were 'detached' (lacking in a traditional sense of engagement) and 26% were 'disengaged'. The inference is that employers are losing out, with the estimated cost to industry of disengagement going into the tens of millions of pounds.

PAUSE FOR THOUGHT

Why do you go to work? If you are a student on a degree or professional course, why did you choose that particular subject? Are you drawn to it as a way into an occupation that you think you are likely to enjoy in the long term? Do you have a vocational calling?

8.16 RETAINING STAFF

There is no unequivocal answer to how we can get employees to stay loyal to the company. However, it is clear that success in bringing in and retaining the right people is determined not only by ensuring that they are indeed the 'right' people in terms of knowledge and skills, but, additionally, by their attitudes to work. The time, money and other resources spent on recruiting, selecting and inducting the right people is only a worthwhile investment if they remain with the organisation in the medium to long term. An implication for staff retention is that the recruitment and selection process should have a degree of sophistication and should use a range of selection processes (see Chapter 7, 'Selection').

Retention became an important issue when organisations recognised that human resources are just that – key resources – which, if managed effectively, can grow in value. Talent should be nurtured and developed; it is vital to the success of the business. Talent is hard to find and sometimes hard to keep. Kets de Vries (cited by Williams, 2000, p.28) states: 'Today's high performers are like frogs in a wheelbarrow: they can jump out at any time.' The message is clear: organisations that wish to retain their core staff should take positive steps to ensure that they do so.

According to Maund (2001, p.192):

Many organisations are of the opinion that, once employed, individuals will remain with them, unquestioningly believing that a wage or salary secures their loyalty and long service. However, the strategy involved in recruiting new employees should be progressed into plans for their retention, and failure to do so is likely to result in demotivated staff and a high labour turnover.

The CIPD/Hays (2013) *Resourcing and Talent Planning* survey showed that the median rate of labour turnover has declined steadily since the 2008 financial crisis, standing at 11.9% for 2012, down from 18.3% in 2006. But according to the survey, 88% of organisations experience some difficulty in retaining staff, with higher-skilled categories of staff – managers and professionals/specialists – particularly in the public sector, being the most difficult to retain.

According to research by Scott et al (2012), the top reasons that key staff leave organisations are:

- opportunity to earn more pay elsewhere
- lack of promotional opportunities
- feelings that pay levels are unfair relative to others outside the organisation
- dissatisfaction with job or work responsibilities
- feelings that pay levels are unfair relative to employee's performance and contribution.

As we saw above, money may not be enough to secure an employee's services for a long period of time – we need to think of other means of keeping our 'frogs in the wheelbarrow'!

8.16.1 RETENTION PLAN

An increasing number of organisations have heeded this message, or have learned by experience. Organisations that succeed in keeping their key staff have a retention plan that is based upon the results of staff turnover analysis. Retention measures can include some or all of the following:

- **Pay and benefits:** competitive rates of pay, deferred compensation – for example share option schemes, retention bonuses, flexible benefits, a benefits package that improves with service.
- **Improve induction process:** as we have seen earlier in the chapter, this makes a difference, especially in preventing the 'induction crisis', where people leave soon after starting a new job.
- **Recruitment and selection:** set appropriate standards, match people to posts, provide an accurate picture of the job. Using value-based interviewing can help to ensure people with the right attitudes are appointed (see Chapter 7).
- **Learning and development:** increased learning and development opportunities, good induction processes, provision of development opportunities to meet the needs of the individual and the organisation, structured *career paths*.
- **Coaching and mentoring:** these, together with learning and development, will help employees to feel valued and will give them a sense of having a career in the organisation, rather than just 'a job'.
- **Management:** improve line managers' people skills, so that employees feel valued and listened to. Poor relationships with managers can push employees to leave, so training managers in people management is essential.
- **Make changes to improve work-life balance:** flexible working, homeworking, offering part-time work. Together with *improving physical working conditions*, these make life at work better for employees and may encourage them to stay.
- **Job design:** provision of interesting work, as much autonomy and teamworking as possible, opportunities for flexible working to meet the needs of the individual (this fits in with the need for work-life balance).
- **Improved employee involvement:** allowing workers to have their say and get involved in decision-making will mean that they feel more valued and 'a part of the organisation'.
- **Better promotion of the employer brand:** as we saw earlier in the chapter, employer branding and an improved *EVP* can help to create a culture that encourages retention of staff in the business.

(adapted from CIPD/Hays (2013) *Resourcing and Talent Planning* survey report)

It is interesting to note that the most popular method of combating retention problems is to *improve induction processes* (45% of respondents in the CIPD/Hays survey) as it is seen as a low-cost way of preventing new employees from leaving within the first few months and is likely to have additional benefits in terms of aiding orientation and early productivity. While better induction processes are a sound strategy for retaining *new* staff, other strategies are more useful for retaining those with *longer* lengths of service. The most effective method of retention is considered to be to improve line managers' people skills (31%), followed by increased learning and development (29%). There is mixed opinion about pay, with 27% of responses saying that pay is one of their top three preferred methods of retaining staff, but 21% saying it is their *least* preferred method.

In turbulent times the CIPD/Hays (2013) suggests that the approach should be no less rigorous; just because it is more difficult for staff to move when the jobs market becomes 'tight' in times of recession, it does not mean that less stringent efforts should be made to retain staff when times improve. Employees, once the job situation gets better, will start to vote with their feet and leave the business; the employer cannot become complacent. Employers need to nurture and develop their talent pools so that they will stay with the business.

ACTIVITY 8.6

Positive action can make a difference. See Brockett's article (2009), which discusses how employer branding can still make an impact on retention when economic pressures begin to challenge: **www.cipd.co.uk/pm/ peoplemanagement/b/weblog/archive/ 2009/03/12/employer-branding-still-makes- its-mark-2009-03.aspx**

The article lists the top big companies to work for in 2008.

Now for comparison, visit *The Times* top 100 companies to work for in 2014, at **http:// features.thesundaytimes.co.uk/public/ best100companies/live/template**

- Where are the differences?
- Who is still in the list in 2014? Who has dropped out?
- How well would your own company (or companies that you are aware of) fare in terms of being 'good to work for'?

ACTIVITY 8.7

Employee turnover

The CIPD/Hays (2013) *Resourcing and Talent Planning* survey report gives the average cost to replace an employee as £2,000, and for a manager this increases to £5,000. How would

you go about costing employee turnover? What factors would you include?

Are there other 'non-financial' costs to the organisation?

8.17 RETENTION AND HRM

While positive retention planning has become an integral part of HR strategy, the activities that are implied by typical retention plans in organisations that have adopted the principles and practices of HRM are aimed largely at key staff. Peripheral workers (part-timers, casual workers or agency workers, for example), by definition, are often not treated so generously, albeit legislation ensures parity for their salaries and conditions when they are doing similar work to company core staff. The underlying rationale here appears to be that 'there is a talent war going on out there and if we are lucky enough to get the high-fliers, we should make every effort to keep them; we can pick up the rest whenever we need them'.

This is a pragmatic and practical view, and few would argue with the facts that all organisations need highly talented staff at the core, but it can create a visible class system between and among employees. However, the consequence of not identifying and nurturing talent is equally fraught with problems because if we fail to identify and develop potential, at an early stage, they may leave. The talented staff are exactly those who, in a 'tight jobs market' (when jobs are not easy to come by), can still move from one employer to another. Actively managing the career paths of the company's talented few is crucial for the smart employer.

A complete retention plan should include arrangements for ensuring the retention of peripheral staff as well as key talent, since the replacement of any employee is expensive and counterproductive (see Activity 8.7). Additionally, care needs to be taken to ensure that equality, fairness and compliance with employment legislation are maintained when benefits and facilities are on the retention agenda.

8.18 MANAGING CONTRACTOR ORGANISATIONS

In a wider context, if the organisation relies upon a significant number of contractor organisations for services, the quality of their staff can and does have a significant impact upon the level of service that your organisation can supply. High turnover and poor retention in the contractor become as much an issue for your organisation as they do for the contractor themselves. The quality of the HR processes that the contactor applies to its own staff can, to some degree, be controlled through the tender document, with clauses that sanction regular auditing by the contracting organisation. In this way vigilance over key contract operations can be maintained so that timely interventions can be managed. How the contractor manages its business can be influenced by the nature and length of the contract awarded and how the contract manager engages with the contractor.

8.19 RECORDING AND ANALYSING INFORMATION

It may sound obvious but there is a need to monitor the amount of labour turnover in an organisation. However, only 16% of respondents in the CIPD/Hays (2013) *Resourcing and Talent Planning* survey reported that their organisation calculates the cost of labour turnover. Sixty-three per cent said they do not, while a further 21% did not know whether they do so or not! If we want HR to add value to the business, perhaps this is one area in which to begin.

The CIPD recommends that staff turnover is calculated on an annual basis as follows:

$$\text{Turnover} = \frac{\text{Average no. of staff who left in a period}}{\text{Average no. employed in the period}} \times 100$$

The staff turnover values can be calculated as an average for the whole organisation or by department. With the quality of HR information systems (HRIS), this calculation, once set up, becomes routine and figures for different departments and the organisation as a whole can be provided regularly. Data should also be kept for key groups of staff, graduates and managers – in essence, those who have been identified as talented or key employees. However, keeping statistical information is no good unless it is accessed and analysed for 'hotspots', that is, where there are high turnover rates.

Refer to Chapter 19, 'Handling and Managing Information', and Chapter 5, 'HR Planning', for more on labour turnover.

The following case study comes from the CIPD/Hays (2013) *Resourcing and Talent Planning* annual survey report.

Which? – recruiting the right people for the growing areas of business

Which? – the largest consumer body in the UK – has been expanding into new areas of business, including the recently launched and quickly expanding mortgage advice business. As Which? stands for making individuals as powerful as the organisations they deal with in their daily lives, it was essential that this new business area, essentially built from scratch, fits under the Which? brand. One of the biggest challenges was in recruiting people who understood the desire to build a successful commercial business, but would also live the values of integrity, independence and bravery espoused by the organisation.

Kim Brosnan, Director of Talent, argues that despite a fierce war for specialist talent, even smaller-sized organisations must select candidates for their cultural fit, as well as for their skills. 'When we launched the Which? mortgage advice business, many of the individuals we were interviewing would talk about customer service, but, in many instances, it was just lip service. We interviewed lots of people, and they just weren't right. And it's about being brave enough to say they are not right for us because they do not share our values, and not hire them.'

To ensure that they attract the right candidates, Which? aims to clearly articulate what they stand for at all recruitment stages. The company has undertaken a thorough review of their brand as an employer, consulting with internal and external stakeholders. Being clear about the deal you are offering, Kim says, helps the person in front of you reflect on whether their values align with yours, enabling them to self-select to some extent. 'Successful recruitment is critical to the success of an organisation, and if you don't get that bit right, you can

spend a lot of time and effort trying to put it right.'

Talent management continues even after the right people are secured into the organisation. Which? employs 500 staff, with many different types of skill-sets for a fairly small organisation to respond to various business needs. Kim emphasises that due to internal silos and lack of understanding of professional areas around the organisation, Which? used to lose employees that they wanted to keep but who thought they had hit the development ceiling in the organisation. The company reviewed and harmonised their reward structure, opting for job families rather than job roles, and gave its people an interactive reward and career management tool to navigate their way around the organisation and plan their internal career.

This was also supported by career planning workshops and training for managers on how to get the best from their teams.

Kim estimates that since Which? have brought in a clearer employer proposition, it has been easier to attract talented people, including those from senior jobs in high-powered companies. The change in the turnover rate is positive on the whole, and there has been a 300% increase in internal rotations and secondments. Staff engagement levels are at an impressive 80%. An ongoing challenge is to get the business – specifically managers – comfortable with taking on more junior people and growing and developing them. This way, Kim believes, Which? can provide people with greater career opportunities and retain people for longer.

'If you are someone like Accenture or PwC, you've been around for so long, you've got a strong brand that people have a greater understanding of what it might be like to work for you. For a smaller organisation it is hard to compete with that. But why can't we be the

> Accenture of the social enterprise world? We can't compete on all levels and are unable to provide international career opportunities, but we offer other things which make Which? a brilliant place to work. And it's being clear about what the other things you have to offer are, and articulating it well. Not overselling, but being real with the person in front of you.'
>
> (Source: CIPD/Hays (2013) *Resourcing and Talent Planning* survey)

8.20 SUMMARY

8.20.1 INDUCTION

The purpose of induction is twofold:

- to help the new employee become effective in the job as soon as possible
- to assist the 'onboarding' process of the new employee by helping them to orient themselves in the organisation and thus improving the likelihood of retaining them in the organisation.

New employees are in a learning situation as soon as they join: they need to attain a sense of identity in their new place of work and a true perception of the role. They need to understand the organisational and departmental cultures and the expectations that others have of them. If the job fails to match up to expectations (that is, breaking the psychological contract), it may lead to employees leaving fairly soon after starting – creating an induction crisis. A frank job description or role profile and honest depiction of the job at interview is important so that the picture (of the job) that the potential employee builds in their mind is not too far removed from reality.

An effective induction system is handled through training and contains corporate and departmental induction processes. Indications of a successful induction programme are:

- new employees quickly becoming effective in their jobs
- an increase in the rate at which employees adapt to their surroundings
- good interpersonal relations between new and longer-serving employees
- a reduction in staff turnover
- a satisfactory retention rate.

The use of employer branding is important in attracting new staff to the organisation and also in keeping them. Building an effective employee value proposition (EVP), outlining what is expected from employees and what the employer can provide in return, can strengthen the employer brand and help to improve the psychological contract and employee engagement.

8.20.2 RETENTION

Lack of good induction together with poor recruitment and selection decisions, both on the part of the employee and employer, are often to blame for retention problems. If, during recruitment and selection, promises are made which then are not kept, an employee finds the job doesn't match up and so they start looking for a job elsewhere.

The CIPD/Hays (2013) *Resourcing and Talent Planning* survey showed that the median rate of labour turnover is 11.9% for 2012, with 88% of organisations experiencing some difficulty in retaining staff.

The top reasons that key staff leave organisations, according to Scott et al (2012), are:

- opportunity to earn more pay elsewhere
- lack of promotional opportunities

- feelings that pay levels are unfair relative to others outside the organisation
- dissatisfaction with job or work responsibilities
- feelings that pay levels are unfair relative to employee's performance and contribution.

Retention became an issue when organisations realised that the success of the business depended on its ability to attract and retain people who were capable of making contributions that would give an organisation a competitive advantage. To achieve this, organisations formulate a *retention plan*, the components of which are designed to encourage people to remain with the organisation.

Strategies for improving retention include:

- pay and benefits
- improved induction
- recruitment and selection
- learning and development, career paths, coaching and mentoring
- job design
- improve line managers' people skills
- make changes to improve work-life balance, together with improving physical working conditions
- improved employee involvement
- better promotion of the employer brand and improving the employee value proposition (EVP).

Retention plans need to be aimed at all new employees, whether they are recognised as a high-potential graduate recruit or staff who have been recruited to fill routine roles. There is a cost to staff turnover for all grades of staff. The average cost of replacing a member of staff is over £2,000 (CIPD/Hays, 2013).

REVIEW QUESTIONS

1 What are the main purposes of induction?

2 What do we mean by 'onboarding'?

3 Why is employer branding useful to an organisation?

4 What is meant by the term 'induction crisis'?

5 How would you advise the organisation that wishes to reduce the prospect of having an induction crisis?

6 What are the main elements that should make up an effective induction programme? Write a brief description of each.

7 How can we tell if induction has been successful?

8 What is the advantage of having a mentoring or buddy system in the organisation?

9 What help is available for disabled people starting a new job?

10 What elements would you expect to find in a company handbook?

11 How are induction and retention related?

12 How can we calculate labour turnover?

13 What are the main reasons why key staff leave an organisation?

14 What, according to CIPD/Hays (2013), is the cost of someone leaving the organisation?

15 What strategies can be used to help retention?

EXPLORE FURTHER

BOOKS

TAYLOR, S. (2014) *Resourcing and talent management*. 6th ed. London: CIPD.

Most HR textbooks offer some discussion on induction, although not necessarily in any great detail. Taylor gives a practical overview in his book with some useful ideas for good practice.

WEB LINKS

Induction and retention

Acas guidance booklet *Recruitment and Induction*, designed to assist anyone dealing with, or who is affected by, the processes of recruitment and induction. Available at: **www.acas.org.uk/media/pdf/l/e/Recruitment_and_induction_%28October-2012%29-accessible-version-may-2012.pdf**

The Acas main website (**www.acas.org.uk**) also offers advice on all employment matters and has a helpline (Tel: 08457 47 47 47). They also have a useful booklet: *Employing People: A handbook for small firms*, which can be downloaded from: **www.acas.org.uk/index.aspx?articleid=924**

The CIPD factsheet on induction gives introductory guidance dealing with the purpose, advantages and disadvantages of formal workplace induction programmes. It also considers the role of HR in the induction process and gives some practical advice in the form of a checklist. The factsheet can be found at: **www.cipd.co.uk/hr-resources/factsheets/induction.aspx**

Article on onboarding with company examples: **www.hrmagazine.co.uk/hr/features/1020702/onboarding-fast-track-staff-productivity**

The Harvey Nash report on executives' first 90 days in an organisation makes interesting reading and gives an insight into what makes senior executives stay in or leave their new jobs. Download it from: **www.harveynash.com/group/mediacentre/2012/10/a_third_of_executives_consider_quitting_in_their_first_90_days/index.asp**

For small businesses it is worth looking at Gov.UK. The site offers advice on employing staff – especially if this is your first time recruiting (**www.gov.uk/employing-staff**) – plus general useful advice on a number of topics: **www.gov.uk/government/organisations/department-for-work-pensions**

Access to Work is a specialist disability service from Jobcentre Plus that gives practical advice and support to disabled people, whether they are working, self-employed or looking for employment. The Access to Work guide for employers can be found at: **www.gov.uk/government/publications/access-to-work-guide-for-employers**

UK legislation can be found at: **www.legislation.gov.uk/**

Employer branding

Informative factsheet from the CIPD on employer branding can be found at: **www.cipd.co.uk/hr-resources/factsheets/employer-brand.aspx**

The CIPD/Mercer (2010) research report on *Employer Branding and Total Reward* is worth reading to help HR, reward and branding professionals develop their own employer branding. Download it at: **www.cipd.co.uk/hr-resources/research/employer-branding-total-reward.aspx**

For an easy-to-read and practical article on 'Employer Branding: Building your EVP', see HRZone at: **www.hrzone.com/blogs/oasis-hr-findings-hr-think-tank-series/employer-branding-building-your-evp/140964**

CHAPTER 9

Learning and Development – Key Concepts

LEARNING OBJECTIVES

After studying this chapter you should:

- be able to define the concepts of human resource development, talent management, human capital and knowledge management
- be aware of the concept of a 'learning organisation'
- understand who benefits from learning
- be able to define and understand the principles of learning
- understand the different ways in which people learn
- consider your own learning style
- start thinking about planning your career.

9.1 INTRODUCTION

In this chapter and Chapter 10 the subject of learning and development will be explored. In this chapter we concentrate on *individual* learning (how you learn and your learning style) and consider some of the *key concepts* related to learning, while in Chapter 10 we focus on *learning in organisations* and on the more *practical skills* of running a course or a learning event. So in this chapter we introduce some of the key concepts of *human resource development*, *talent management*, *human capital* and *knowledge management* and look at the idea of the *learning organisation*. We also define and explain the principles of learning and examine some early and more recent theories. We consider who benefits from learning and development – why is so much time and effort spent on learning? Finally, as learning is so important to careers, we consider career planning.

You will see that there are a plethora of terms – some of which are used interchangeably. Let us start by looking at some of these to see what we mean.

9.2 TERMINOLOGY

You may come across various terms, such as:

- **education:** broadly based 'training for life' and society
- **training:** usually relates particularly to work, or specific tasks
- **development:** personal growth, where employees develop skills and knowledge to help them in their career.

However, distinctions have become blurred, and terminology changes. Underlying all of the above is the concept of *learning*. We will look at these terms in more detail below.

KEY CONCEPT: LEARNING

Learning is about the acquisition of new knowledge or skills. It often results in a change in our behaviour. In the workplace, we use learning to help us improve how we do our job, and to learn new things that will enable us to progress in our careers.

Rees and French (2013, p.199) suggest that learning 'results in a relatively permanent change in behaviour and comes about through the acquisition of knowledge, skills and attitudes'.

KEY CONCEPT: TRAINING

Noe (2010) defines training as: a 'planned effort by a company to facilitate employees' learning of job-related competencies'. In short, this means that training is the means by which employees acquire the competences they need to carry out their work to the required standard.

Purcell et al (2003), in their research on 'the people and performance link', list training and development as one of the 11 key HR factors in encouraging 'discretionary behaviour' that leads to higher productivity in the workplace.

9.2.1 TRAINING AND HUMAN RESOURCE DEVELOPMENT

In the workplace the training function is often referred to as 'human resource development'. This is where learning and development is designed and delivered for employees, in order to increase their skills and abilities, for the benefit of both the individual and the organisation. There has been a move away from the term 'training', which suggests 'being taught a skill', to 'learning and development', which implies that the learner takes more responsibility for their own learning.

Whereas 'training' is needed in the shorter term to carry out tasks that are needed now (for example induction training), the term 'development' has broader connotations. It relates to the future, to the longer-term development of people throughout their careers, providing them with the kind of confidence, maturity and stability that enables them to adopt greater responsibility. Training produces competence while development produces continuous *psychological growth*. It could be said, therefore, that training is for *now*, while development is for *the future*. Human resource development tends to imply a more strategic approach to learning.

KEY CONCEPT: HUMAN RESOURCE DEVELOPMENT (HRD)

As early as 1970, Nadler discussed HRD and defined it as 'organised learning experiences provided by employers, within a specified period of time, to bring about the possibility of performance management and/or personal growth' (Nadler and Nadler, cited in Gold et al, 2010, p.14).

From this we can see the link between human resource development and performance. Employers generally see the need to develop their staff in order to achieve competitive advantage. For without development, the organisation stagnates and competitors will overtake it. Human resource development (HRD) encompasses a range of organisational practices that focus on learning: training, learning and development; workplace learning; career development and lifelong learning; organisation development; organisational knowledge and learning (Mankin, 2009).

9.2.2 SELF-DEVELOPMENT

'All development is self-development' (Drucker, 1977). In this context, Drucker was saying that people can teach, train and coach you, but nobody can learn for you. Learning is a 'do-it-yourself' activity. If you are currently studying at college, you will identify with this – you can attend classes and listen to excellent lecturers, but no one else can do your learning for you. And now that for the majority of people there is little opportunity to have a 'job for life', learning is crucial for an individual's employability. Information technology facilitates learning as never before, since it has broadened and deepened the available range of methods and media through which learning may take place, but the actual learning process is still down to the individual.

In the workplace today, the development of *competence* is a critical factor; your employability depends on it. Traditional ways of working are changing and new ways are continually evolving; these demand more than just competence: they require new knowledge and skills, creativity, flexibility and commitment. With such a fast pace of change, we need to be up to date with the latest ways of doing things – and this can only be achieved by learning.

9.3 HUMAN CAPITAL

Organisations today rely very much on 'human capital' – the knowledge and skills that their people possess which will enable the organisation to function and be competitive.

KEY CONCEPT: HUMAN CAPITAL AND INTELLECTUAL CAPITAL

Intellectual capital relates to the collective value added to an organisation by the employees' knowledge and expertise. This includes *human capital* – knowledge and competences that are required for particular jobs and that can be developed by learning to achieve higher performance – and *social capital* – the value that comes from networking and customer relationships, for example. Human capital includes the flexibility of individual employees that turns them into valuable assets when, through learning, they find themselves able to make high-performance contributions to the organisation. Human capital 'creates value by investing in the development of individuals' (Stewart and Rigg, 2011, p.186).

ACTIVITY 9.1

When you first started at college (or senior school), you probably knew very little about the subjects you were about to study. By the end of your studies, what knowledge had you gained? What skills had you learned? How much more did you know as a result of studying on the course? Are you now a more 'valuable' asset than you were before you started? Hopefully so. You have increased your 'human capital' value.

PAUSE FOR THOUGHT

When you first started your job or a course at college – you probably knew no one. After a while you build up networks of people who can help you and have answers to your queries. For instance, in the workplace, you may have built up a rapport with staff in payroll when you have to sort out salary problems. Knowing who can help you to do your job makes it so much easier and saves a lot of time. Having these kinds of networks, where there is trust and a common bond, is part of 'social capital'. Who are the people you network with, who add to your social capital?

9.4 TALENT MANAGEMENT

Talent management encompasses a much broader spectrum than just learning and development. It covers the whole process of recruiting, developing and promoting talented employees in an organisation so that they can contribute to the best of their ability. Managing talent involves having an overall plan and a strategy for identifying who the 'talented' are, and then developing their knowledge and skills to benefit both the business and the employee. If an organisation can develop its talented employees, it adds significantly to its 'human capital' and thus it can increase its competitiveness. It will have staff whose knowledge can be used to benefit the business.

KEY CONCEPT: TALENT MANAGEMENT

The management consultancy, McKinsey, adopted the term 'the war for talent' in the 1990s to describe the need for businesses to find and keep the best workers as a means of attaining competitive advantage.

Tansley et al (2007, p.xi) define talent management as 'the systematic attraction, identification, development, engagement/retention and deployment of those individuals with high potential who are of particular value to an organisation'.

There is an argument about who constitutes 'talent' in an organisation. It could be argued that all employees should be developed and treated as 'talent', that is, 'everyone at all levels working at the top of their potential' (Redford, 2005, p.20). In general we tend to think of 'talent' as the elite – the staff who have expert knowledge, skills and attributes which are essential to the business. As Goffee and Jones (2009, p.57) put it, 'highly talented individuals with the potential to create disproportionate amounts of value from the resources that the organisation makes available to them'. These are often people who are the 'knowledge workers' – the ones who use their knowledge and ability to make a difference to the organisation and give the business its competitive edge. (There is more on talent management in Chapter 10.)

In the UK we have moved away from being a 'traditional economy', based on making or manufacturing goods, to being a 'knowledge economy', where ideas and innovation are important to success. This brings a need for 'knowledge management'.

9.5 KNOWLEDGE MANAGEMENT

Many businesses rely on knowledge as the main means of staying ahead. Without knowledge, our competitors will gain advantage by having better ideas and better strategies, and will achieve better success. 'Knowledge is the main distinguishing factor of business success and is seen as the foundation of competitive advantage' (Carlucci et al, 2004). In a traditional economy, companies make money by converting raw materials into items: metal into cars, for example. However, in a knowledge economy, the added value comes from taking good ideas and developing them into services. 'Company value has come to be increasingly dependent on intangible assets, knowledge assets, intellectual capital and intellectual property. In 1996, 94% of Microsoft's market value (US$119 billion) came from intangible assets' (Quintas, 2001), which means its value came from knowledge and ideas, not from machinery, buildings, factories or materials. Without innovative new ideas, Microsoft would not be the success that it is today.

 KEY CONCEPT: KNOWLEDGE MANAGEMENT

Knowledge management is about identifying, capturing and developing knowledge in the organisation. It involves building on 'human capital' to make the most of everyone's knowledge and skills and thus has close links with 'talent management'. Noe (2010) defines knowledge management as 'the process of enhancing company performance by designing and implementing tools, processes, systems, structures and culture to improve the creating, sharing and use of knowledge'.

Think about the computer games industry. The successful companies are those who come up with the best ideas, not the ones who sell the cheapest games – it's about having staff who can be innovative, who can use their ideas and knowledge to keep the company ahead of its competitors. Google might be another example. Its success comes from providing a service, not from converting raw materials into goods. Without intelligent staff who develop ideas, Google would not exist.

 PAUSE FOR THOUGHT

Twitter has only $500 million in revenue, no major physical assets, and makes no profit but is vastly successful – the *Wall Street Journal* valued it at between $38 billion and $45 billion in January 2013. Twitter's staggering valuation is based on one thing: a great innovation that is changing the way the world communicates. What other organisations can you think of that have very few assets but are successful and valuable companies? Where does their value come from?

 ACTIVITY 9.2

What organisations can you think of that rely particularly on knowledge? Obvious ones might be law firms, architects, universities. What other businesses could not function without specialist knowledge?

In Activity 9.2, you might say that all organisations need and use knowledge – and you would, of course, be right. Garages, supermarkets, shops, for instance, all need to have knowledge of their customers, of products, of their competitors, and so on, so that they can stay ahead of the game. Knowledge is essential to all businesses to some extent. In today's world, knowledge is becoming more and more crucial if the business wants to survive.

 ACTIVITY 9.3

What knowledge is crucial to the survival of your own organisation? Are there specialists who add value to the business, just by possessing expert knowledge that helps to keep it competitive? If that knowledge became out of date, what would happen?

 KEY CONCEPT: LEARNING ORGANISATION

If a business wants to develop the knowledge of its staff, it may strive to be what Pedler et al (1997, p.3), describe as a 'learning organisation', that is, an organisation 'that facilitates the learning of its members and continuously transforms itself'. A learning organisation is an organisation that encourages learning among its people, promoting exchange of information between employees, hence creating a more knowledgeable workforce.

This produces a very flexible organisation where people will accept and adapt to new ideas and changes through a shared vision.

Senge (1990, p.3) suggests that a learning organisation is one 'where people continually expand their capacity to create the results they truly desire, where new and expansive patterns of thinking are nurtured, where collective aspiration is set free, and where people are continually learning how to learn together'.

Learning organisations therefore believe that learning is a good thing for the business and that it should be continuous and never ending. It should be something that is on the conscious agenda of the organisation.

9.6 WHY IS LEARNING SO IMPORTANT? WHO BENEFITS FROM LEARNING?

Who are the main benefactors from learning? Certainly the individual, as they gain new knowledge and skill that will help them in their job. The newly learned skills will also improve their employability and assist them in gaining promotion or a new job elsewhere.

In addition, the organisation benefits. It gains more highly qualified and competent staff who will do a better job. More tenuously, you might say that the Government benefits because when you get a better job, you will earn more money – and thus pay more tax! As a result, the whole of society benefits.

 ACTIVITY 9.4

Who benefits from training that you undertake? What are the benefits to the organisation? And to you? What skills have you learned recently? Does this impact on your job?

9.6.1 THE BENEFICIARIES OF LEARNING

'Who should pay for training and why?' – a good question.

Since there are three parties who benefit from training – the state, the employer and the individual – it can be argued, perhaps, that all three should be responsible for funding learning.

The individual

Individual employees benefit from training and development in several ways. First, if they understand how their tasks should be carried out, they are more motivated to do them well and thereby experience satisfaction from what they do. If they know they are good at what they do, they feel valued and respected. Training gives people skills, which in turn makes people competent, gives them confidence and feelings of security, and they feel that that their presence in the organisation is worthwhile.

Secondly, people who seek a career and plan their own future development will regard training sessions as important opportunities to extend their repertoire of knowledge and competence. This enhances their employability and their promotion prospects. Studying for CIPD qualifications can, for example, add to your employability and enhance your career prospects considerably in the professional field of human resource management. Many employees, with the support of their employers, have created their own personal development plans (PDP) in which the identification of their developmental needs forms an integral part of the performance management system.

PAUSE FOR THOUGHT

Continuing professional development (CPD)

Do you have a personal development plan? The CIPD defines CPD as a personal commitment to keeping your professional knowledge up to date and improving your capabilities throughout your working life. It is about knowing where you are today, where you want to be in the future, and making sure you get there.

The organisation

HRD is a strategic approach to investing in human capital. The organisation benefits when the knowledge and competence of its employees, combined with their commitment and involvement, are specifically geared to the achievement of business objectives and, thereby, the realisation of strategy. Most of those who lead today's organisations have grown to understand the strength of the relationship between human performance and organisational success, which is why they now see HRD as a critical factor in the organisation's future.

There are, however, those who need convincing and still view learning and development as a cost to the organisation and who fail to see the benefits of investment in learning. Advancing technology removes the requirement for traditional jobs and creates jobs that demand the application of new knowledge and skills. An organisation that keeps pace with change, by anticipating technological advances and preparing its workforce in good time, will suffer least from the effects of a recession in the economy. For as long as technology continues to advance, organisations that fail to prepare their workforce will always experience the detrimental effects of the skills gap.

The State

The State benefits when organisations perform well in the home market and compete effectively with their overseas industrial counterparts. A knowledgeable and skilled workforce contributes enormously to the economy of the nation, creating wealth from which the whole of society benefits.

Note: There is more on the role of government in learning and development in Chapter 10.

9.7 THE PRINCIPLES OF LEARNING

9.7.1 SOCIAL LEARNING

We often learn from others. It is part of our natural development. We learn to conform to societal, group and family norms by observing and copying the behaviour of others and through a system of reward and punishment. If, for example, in childhood, we behave in a way that invokes the disapproval of parents or teachers, they express that disapproval and we may receive a punishment. On the other hand, good behaviour will be rewarded. As time goes by we develop patterns of behaviour based around the societal norms (a norm is something that is usual, typical, or standard) that we have learned, many of which we have internalised as habits, so that much of what we do is done without conscious thought. In the 'Bobo doll' experiments conducted by Bandura in 1961, children who observed adults being aggressive with a doll learned that this behaviour was acceptable and replicated the behaviour themselves. Learning the right habits from good role models is important. If we see bad habits when watching other people when we start a new job, we may learn these habits ourselves. Being taught correctly at the beginning is key to doing a good job.

The CIPD's 2013 *Learning and Talent Development* survey suggests that interaction with the job, the organisation, colleagues, customers and suppliers will be an increasing feature of learning, enabled by social learning technology. There is some disparity about what is interpreted as social learning: more than two-thirds of respondents in the CIPD survey included group webinars and mentoring/peer-to-peer learning in their definition. Almost as many consider learning around the water cooler to be social learning. Half of the survey respondents include 'learning on the job' to be social learning, while just a third included using collaborative platforms such as Jive or Salesforce Chatter or online forums. Revans' action learning sets could be seen as examples of social learning (see later in this chapter).

PAUSE FOR THOUGHT

Think about how you dress, how you speak and how you behave generally when you are out with your friends. Compare that with how you behave at work, in the classroom or at home with your family. What is it that determines the nature of your behaviour? *How do you know* how to behave in those very different situations? You were not born with such social skills and therefore you must have learned them.

9.7.2 EXPERIENTIAL LEARNING

In a sense, what has been described above as social learning is *experiential learning*. This is learning from our experience – from 'doing' things in our everyday lives and learning what is the best way of completing them (or not!). This might be through 'trial and error' or from watching other people (often our parents or family members). In the workplace this might translate into having good mentors or coaches to make sure good habits (practices) are encouraged and bad habits discouraged.

PAUSE FOR THOUGHT

How did you learn to tie shoe laces? Or a tie? We can be shown how, but we don't learn properly how to do it until we have a go ourselves. We learn not to touch hot things, often from the experience of doing so! The 'experience' teaches us to avoid them. What else have you learned from 'experience'?

Transferable skills

Is it possible that your non-work learning could turn out to be useful in the workplace? If you reflect on this, you might conclude that what can be learned from carrying out such tasks as maintaining your home, arranging your social life and observing other people becomes useful in all areas of life. Those who are involved in sports teams, voluntary groups or parent-teacher organisations, for example, may all gain skills that are transferable to the workplace. Fundraising, organising others and motivating group members are all skills which might be useful at work.

When the term 'experiential learning' is used in a professional context, it generally refers to learning from organisational situations. If you are undertaking a new task, you may learn as you go along. Sometimes such situations occur unexpectedly, as for example when there is an emergency and you have to find a way of dealing with it. By its nature, it may be something that you have never previously encountered, so you have to analyse the situation, diagnose the problem and find and implement a solution. Usually you will apply your previous knowledge of similar situations to help you to find an answer to the new problem.

When we start a new job, we learn as we go along. We may have been appointed to the job because we have the potential and the skills to do the job well, but in the first few months, we will learn as we go; we pick up tips for improving our performance on the job just from our experience of doing it.

CASE EXAMPLE 9.1

Maysam is an HR assistant in a busy office. She deals with very different activities every day, from recruitment to the management of disciplinary cases. One day, she is asked to run a short training session on induction. She has never delivered any training before and is nervous about the new experience. She has, however, been on lots of courses and watched how it's done. She has also performed presentations at college as part of her course. She applies her previous knowledge together with her observations and devises an interesting and engaging session. Although this is important because it means that she is well prepared, she learns more from the experience of actually *performing* the training presentation. Next time she is not as nervous because she has learned so much from the experience; she knows what went well and what to avoid next time. Soon she is delivering excellent sessions and does not worry about them at all. She has become an experienced trainer on the induction course.

9.7.3 PERSONAL CHARACTERISTICS

The motivation to learn plays a significant role. If the learner lacks interest in the subject and is therefore unwilling or reluctant to learn about it, learning will not take place. The trainee must be *motivated* to complete a course, for example, and must see some benefit from it (for example pay, promotion, and so on).

The learner also has to be *able* to learn. The learner may be highly motivated, but if their intelligence is such that they are unable fully to grasp the ideas or achieve the necessary performance standards, the likelihood is that *sufficient* learning will not have taken place.

PAUSE FOR THOUGHT

Think about your own studies. What motivates you to learn? Would you enrol on a course in advanced chemistry? Or undertake a Master's in mathematics? Only if you felt that the subject was within your capability. A learner has to feel that they are able to achieve the skills and understand what is being taught. Expectancy theory is relevant here – we must value what is on offer (the degree must have 'valence', or 'value to the individual'), we must expect that we are able to achieve it (that is, we have an 'expectancy' we are able to understand the concepts being taught) and that by learning, this will lead us to the reward (that learning is instrumental in getting the degree). See more on motivation in Chapter 11.

ACTIVITY 9.5

Identify a concept that you have found difficult to learn. How did you eventually learn it? What contributed to your success? Make a list of the factors that help you to learn. What stops you from learning?

9.7.4 SYSTEMATIC LEARNING

This is the learning that is experienced through formal education, or through training and instruction in the organisation or externally in a local college or university. Whereas social learning occurs naturally and teaches us the norms of our society, *systematic* or *organised learning* occurs when something specific is to be learned and is developed within you with instruction and guidance from others, usually through the processes of *formal* education, a training course, or coaching and counselling sessions. The CIPD's *Learning and Talent Development* survey 2013 suggests that learning is increasingly focusing on counselling and 'on the job' learning, and less on formal 'training' courses.

9.7.5 THE LEARNING SITUATION

This refers to the physical environment in which the learning takes place, the ambience of the location and the shape and size of the training room. All of these factors have to be conducive to learning and appropriate and suitable in the light of the subject to be learned. We have all sat in warm, stuffy classrooms, where we just want to fall asleep, or bundled up in coats because the room is too cold. If the session is too long or the environment is not right, learning is less likely to take place. As we shall see later in this chapter, there are a variety of situations in which learning typically takes place.

9.7.6 PLANNED EXPERIENCE

Much of our learning comes from 'planned experience'. It may be that, as a result of your appraisal, or a promotion, you are lacking certain skills or knowledge which is necessary for the job. You may thus plan to undertake an activity or experience in order to gain these skills or knowledge. For example, if you have never been involved in recruitment and selection, you may perhaps plan to participate in some interview panels in order to gain some experience and learn from it. Or you may be assigned a new task, such as performing an exit interview with a leaver. Your manager may then ask you to report back what you have learned from the experience. As we saw above, reflection following the event is important here to complete the learning process

CASE EXAMPLE 9.2

Jackie has just gained a promotion to a new job in a college, dealing with student recruitment interviews. On paper she has all the required skills and knowledge and she was by far the best candidate for promotion. But on the first day she realises that the interview procedures are different from those in her previous job as a student guidance adviser. She feels overawed with the amount of things she doesn't know. To cope with this lack of knowledge she arranges to sit in on some student interviews with a colleague and makes notes on the procedures.

Afterwards she reflects on the process and thinks about how she can apply what she has learned in future interviews. As she gets into the job, she realises that she has lots of transferable skills from her previous job – she is good at talking to students, sorting out problems and keeping calm in a crisis. She approaches the new job by calling on her previous experience and she soon finds that her new job is not so different from the old one. Both involve very similar skills. She just needed to learn the new procedures and to gain some experience.

Planning some experiences so that she can gather the missing knowledge and then reflecting on these is very helpful in getting Jackie up to speed with the job. Soon she is confident and feels like she has been doing the job all her life!

9.7.7 DEVELOPMENTAL DELEGATION

You may learn through tasks being delegated to you. There are times when a task has to be completed quickly to meet a customer's delivery deadline. At such times, the manager will select an employee who is fully competent to do the job, with all the required knowledge and skills. When things are not so urgent, however, a manager might select an employee who would have to learn something to complete the task successfully. This might be referred to as *developmental delegation*; it provides the employee with vital experience and concurrently gets a necessary job done. Delegation of this kind needs to be undertaken with care; the manager should offer support and guidance and not just 'dump' the task on the employee. Sometimes it can feel easier to 'do the job yourself' rather than take the time to teach someone else by way of delegation. But the effort expended if delegation is properly carried out can pay dividends: the delegate will feel good about having acquired a new skill and will have improved their employability, plus they can take on similar tasks in future, thus saving the manager more time.

ACTIVITY 9.6

Identify a time when a task was delegated to you. What support did you need? How did you approach it? If you were delegating a task to someone, how would you go about this? What process would you follow?

9.7.8 THE TRAINER

Despite the trend of moving away from 'instruction' and 'classroom-based' learning, much workplace-related learning relies on us being taught or 'trained'. This, in turn, relies on having a good trainer or teacher. Training is a skill in itself. You may be brilliant at understanding physics or mathematics, but not very good at passing this understanding on to others.

So a good trainer, in addition to their own competence in the subject, needs particular skills in being able to teach others and pass on their own knowledge.

 ACTIVITY 9.7

Identify the skills needed to be a good trainer. It may help to consider the tutors who have taught you in the past. What made them so good? . . . or so bad?

A good trainer also needs credibility. If, for example, you announced that you were going to deliver a talk on the finer points of football, you would be lucky if just two or three people turned up for the event. Conversely, if you announced that you had managed to get David Beckham to deliver such a talk, he would have a full house. Someone who is known to be an authority on a subject has credibility. They may also gain credibility as a result of their style of delivery – an enthusiastic trainer will pass on their passion for the subject. A monotone delivery of PowerPoint slides will not engage anyone!

 KEY CONCEPT: KNOWLEDGE AND TRAINING – TWO SEPARATE SKILLS

The fact that someone is regarded as an expert in a particular subject area does not necessarily mean that they have the ability to *develop* those qualities within others. The ability to *teach* or *train* people is a separate skill altogether.

Reflection

After we have had a learning experience, it helps to reflect on what we have learned. What did we do that helped to achieve success? How can we use this knowledge or skill in future? If we don't stop to reflect, we may lose the opportunity to learn from the experience. We can so easily forget what we have done in the rush to move on to new tasks. Reflection means that we gain the most out of our experience.

KEY CONCEPT: REFLECTION

Reflection is the active process of mentally summarising what you have learned from a particular experience. Its purpose is to increase your awareness of the knowledge and skills that you have added to your repertoire. It also helps you to be able to *apply* what you have learned to future tasks.

PAUSE FOR THOUGHT

Think about a time when you had to perform a task at work that you have never done before. What previous knowledge did you use to help you perform it? Afterwards, did you stop to think about the experience and reflect on it? What went wrong? What worked well? What could you do differently next time?

9.8 EARLY THEORIES OF LEARNING

In this section, we will examine the theories of learning that were proposed in the early part of the twentieth century. The early theorists were mostly interested in learning as a psychological process, while the later theorists took the psychological aspects into account, but tended to focus upon the practicality and effectiveness of deliberately created learning situations.

Since the concept of learning is so important, it is important to develop an understanding of learning theory, which includes *behaviourism* (including the concepts of *classical conditioning* and *operant conditioning*) and *cognitive learning*.

9.8.1 BEHAVIOURISM

Behaviourism is a theory of learning first proposed by John B. Watson in 1913 and is based upon the idea that all behaviours are acquired through *conditioning*. Conditioning occurs through interaction with the environment. Behaviourists believe that our behaviour is shaped by our responses to environmental stimuli. While behaviourism is less popular today, it still remains an influential force in learning psychology.

Classical conditioning

The first theory of classical conditioning was propounded by the Russian physiologist Ivan Pavlov, who published his theory of 'conditioned reflexes' in 1927. He was interested in internal reactions to external stimuli, and he used dogs as the subjects of his experiments. He fed the dogs at the same time every day and as he gave them the food, he rang a bell. One day he rang the bell but did not feed the dogs, and he discovered that they were salivating, obviously not at the sight or the smell of food, but at the anticipation of it. They were reacting automatically to the sound of the bell, an indication that they associated it with the food. They had become 'conditioned' to salivating at the sound of the bell. It is important to note that in 'classical' conditioning, the subject of the experiment always has a passive role.

Operant conditioning

The American psychologist E.L. Thorndike, a contemporary of Pavlov, was the founder of operant conditioning (sometimes referred to as *instrumental conditioning*). The subjects of his experiments were cats. 'Operant conditioning' differs from 'classical conditioning' in that the subject is not passive and has to make a response before the reward is given. It involves learning from the consequences of our behaviour.

In Thorndike's experiments (1913), a hungry cat was placed in a cage from which it needed to escape, usually by pulling on a wire or pressing a lever, in order to get food. At first the cat knocked against the lever accidentally, but then after successive attempts, it learned that the lever led to the door being opened. These experiments differ from Pavlov's in that the animal played an active role. Thorndike maintained that any behaviour that is followed by pleasant consequences is likely to be repeated; he called this the 'law of effect'.

Today, the researcher mainly associated with operant conditioning is the American B.F. Skinner, whose work (1953) is really an extension of the work of Thorndike. Experiments involving animals typified the work of both researchers, although Skinner, after researching mainly with rats and pigeons, went on to research human learning to produce what he called *stimulus-response psychology*. The main idea here is that we react to a stimulus with a response. For example, the stimulus of hunger will prompt us to respond by seeking food. He, like Thorndike, thought that we will act according to the consequences of our behaviour: that how we act depends on the result of what happened previously when we took that action. If we do something that has bad consequences, we won't do it again. If we are rewarded for our action, we are likely to repeat it. This is the principle of reinforcement. So if I want you to deal with a customer in a pleasant way, I need to praise you afterwards in order to reinforce this behaviour. You are then likely to repeat this behaviour. If, however, I tell you off for insulting a customer, you will probably avoid behaving like this again.

9.8.2 COGNITIVE LEARNING

Cognitive theorists are mainly interested in changes in individuals' knowledge, since they regard this as more important than changes in what the learner does. Cognitive learning includes all of the elements of human consciousness that the behaviourists ignore: imagination, creativity, problem-solving, human intuition and perception. The cognitive approach has two components: *insight learning* and *latent learning*.

Insight learning

Having an understanding of what is being learned is an important feature of cognitive learning. To take a problem-solving exercise as an example, experience of working with children has shown that when a person is given a problem to solve, they sometimes study it, analyse and think about it and then, after a period of time, during which an onlooker might think that the person was stumped, the solution is suddenly produced. You might have a sudden revelation – an 'aha!' moment – where you realise what the answer might be. Wolfgang Koehler (1959) carried out experiments with chimpanzees after which he claimed that such insight was not exclusively human behaviour.

Latent learning

According to cognitive theorists, learning may also be latent. This means that something can be added to someone's knowledge and then used only as and when needed, that is, at a later time. An interesting feature of latent learning is that the learner does not always appreciate that they have gathered something new and added it to their knowledge. Trainees, for example, sometimes come away from a course complaining that they have learned nothing. It is not until a later time, perhaps at work, that they find that they can solve particular problems or carry out tasks that they could not do prior to the training about which they had complained – realisation that the training was useful after all.

9.9 MODERN THEORIES OF LEARNING

Most of the modern theories of learning have their roots in the theories explained above. Indeed, the psychological aspects of some of the older theories still exercise a degree of influence over current practice. Modern theorists, however, are not so keen on developing hard and fast rules of learning. They are more inclined to empower individuals over the means through which they are developed.

9.9.1 ACTION LEARNING

Revans introduced the idea of 'action learning sets', which accepts that learning is participative – groups of learners meet together and discuss real problems that exist in the workplace. Revans used action learning sets as a means of developing managers. He got them to work together on issues to help them learn and develop new ideas and solutions (Revans, 1982). The idea fits in well with the concepts of 'social learning' and 'experiential learning'.

9.9.2 KOLB'S LEARNING CYCLE

The *experiential learning cycle*, developed by David Kolb in 1979, is probably the most well-known model in modern theory (Kolb, 1985). Kolb distinguished between 'teacher-centred' (being instructed) and 'student-centred' learning (focus on the student finding out things for themselves). He regarded the classroom situation as a necessary function; his main criticism was that insufficient attention was being paid to other forms of learning such as problem-solving. When developing his experiential learning cycle, he incorporated the features of both the classroom and problem-solving situations.

Kolb explained this cyclical process with the following analysis:

Stage 1 – 'Concrete experience' is the first point of the cycle, in which the learner practises a skill for the first time, for example, using a machine.
Stage 2 – This is followed by a process of 'reflection', in which the learner makes observations and thinks about the experience.
Stage 3 – From there, the learner 'formulates abstract concepts and generalisations'; they begin to make sense of the structure of the machine. In other words, they begin to realise how the machine functions – what it is for and to grasp a proper understanding of it.
Stage 4 – The final stage is 'testing concepts in a new situation'. The learner then returns to the machine. This produces a new situation because it includes prior learning, which is then tested in the new situation and includes using the machine, bringing the learner back to the first point in the cycle, in which the use of the machine provides a new experience.
Learning improves as the cycle continues. Kolb emphasises that this whole process is driven by the individual learner, thus empowering the individual to strive towards their own internally motivated needs and goals.

9.9.3 LEARNING STYLES

Learning is a psychological event and since individuals are all different from each other, they all learn differently. In other words, everyone has their own *learning style*. Some learn best from experience, while others prefer to study or hear about the subject and reflect upon what they have learned. Yet others are dependent on being shown or taught, requiring detailed coaching and real-time feedback, while others again prefer not to be coached but to be given time to learn alone.

In light of this, a good trainer will construct the course to reflect the learning styles of the trainees. Additionally, trainees benefit, first, from understanding their own learning style and, second, from knowing how to learn. It is helpful to identify your own learning style and to consider how you learn best.

Honey and Mumford have one of the best known models of learning styles. They took Kolb's cycle of experiential learning and related each stage to a particular style of learning. They state that learners are one of four types: *activist*, *reflector*, *theorist* or *pragmatist* (Honey and Mumford,1982).

> **Activist:** someone who learns best by 'doing' or having a 'concrete experience'. Enjoys practical tasks.
> **Reflector:** learns by observing and thinking more deeply about that experience. Likes to reflect and ask questions.
> **Theorist:** enjoys finding out more about the 'whole concept' of the experience. Learns best through reading and gathering detailed data.
> **Pragmatist:** likes to try out the learning in a new situation. Learns by relating the learning to 'real-life' examples.

Several learning styles inventories (questionnaires) have been produced, most of which were based on Kolb's (1985) experiential learning theory.

ACTIVITY 9.8

What is your learning style?

Think of a skill you have learned recently. For example, how to operate a new mobile phone, a new laptop or use a tablet computer. Now consider how you went about learning the skill.

A   Did you just play about with the device and press a few buttons? Did you disregard all the detailed instruction and just go for the hands-on approach? Did you think you will just 'work it out' as you use it? Are you impatient to 'get on with it'?
These are most like an *activist* style of learning.

B   Did you read all the instructions carefully before using the device? Did you watch a YouTube video of how to use it? Did you go online and read extra instructions there? Did you ask other people questions about how to use it, then go away and try these ideas out for yourself?
If so, you probably use a *reflective* learning style.

C   Did you look into all the reviews before you bought it so that you could understand how well it works and what it actually does? Did you buy a 'user's guide' and read it thoroughly beforehand? Did you research into all aspects of the device so that you have a thorough, in-depth knowledge of its capabilities?
This type of behaviour is probably indicative of a *theorist* learning style.

D   Did you give careful thought to what you wanted to use it for and how it will help you to do other things in life? Did you try it out to see if it is practical and can do the things you need it for? Did you see who else uses one and have a go with theirs?

These are activities most closely associated with a *pragmatist*.

A: Activists value the opportunity to take an active part in their learning. They like high-profile activities, such as giving talks.

Strengths

- keen to try out new ideas
- flexible
- open-minded

Weaknesses

- act without thinking
- take unnecessary risks
- get bored with implementation

B: Reflectors are people who learn through watching things and thinking them over. They enjoy opportunities to mull over their ideas in an unhurried way and then produce carefully thought-out conclusions. They learn little when they are forced into activities at short notice with inadequate information. They do not enjoy having to take shortcuts to a solution.

Strengths

- careful
- thoughtful
- methodical

Weaknesses

- slow to make up their minds
- too cautious
- not very forthcoming

C: Theorists like to understand the concepts underlying what they are learning and to explore the implications. They dislike unstructured situations where emotions run high.

Strengths

- disciplined approach
- rational
- objective

Weaknesses

- intolerant of anything subjective

D: Pragmatists learn best when they can link the content of their learning to a real problem. They dislike theoretical ideas but like ideas leading to practical outcomes.

Strengths

- business-like
- straight to the point
- realistic
- practical

Weaknesses

- tend to reject that which does not have an obvious application

Bear in mind that learning styles are not rigidly fixed – they may change over the space of time. You may dislike theoretical study in your youth, but find it more interesting as you grow older and enjoy learning about things in more depth. Alternatively, you may be an activist who, with age and experience, becomes more reflective. Or you may find that when you study at college, you need to develop your 'theorist' side – by reading and researching although you prefer to learn 'by doing', in your preferred 'activist' style. We have a blend of styles but with preferences for particular ones.

9.9.4 CONTINUING PROFESSIONAL DEVELOPMENT (CPD)

When we first start out in a career, we may have knowledge that is relevant and useful to our job; indeed, we may be appointed to the job because of our superior knowledge and skills over the other candidates. But as time goes on we need to update our knowledge and skills in order to stay current. Technology advances, current thinking may change, methods of working become outdated, new legislation is introduced – these are all reasons why we may need to update our skills. We need to learn new things to keep ourselves abreast of the best practices and new ways of performing our work. Only by continually developing ourselves can we stay ahead of the game and retain our professional knowledge and skills.

In most professional careers, there is a requirement to update skills on an annual basis. So if you are a doctor, for example, you will be expected to learn new skills and knowledge related to medical practice: this is part of your professional development. For HR practitioners, the CIPD's policy on CPD states that members must 'maintain professional knowledge and competence' and 'ensure that they provide a professional, up-to-date and insightful service'. So continuous learning is paramount. The CIPD sees regular investment of time in learning as an essential part of professional life.

The process involves assessing what needs to be learned, planning how this can be achieved and reflecting on the learning afterwards to see how it can be applied in practice. Development is the responsibility of the individual. And learning can be from any means – not just training courses, but from all manner of experiences. Activities such as watching a DVD, taking part in an event, observing a colleague, volunteering for a difficult task and attending a conference can all be a part of CPD, providing we can reflect on it and see how it can help us to perform better in future.

9.10 TRANSFER OF LEARNING

Where learning results from specific training, *learning transfer* is the most important aspect of training programmes. Bearing in mind the amount of money spent by employers and individuals on training and learning, it would be considered a waste if the knowledge and skills acquired are not successfully transferred back to the workplace. The CIPD 2013 *Learning and Talent Development* survey says that UK employers have a median spend of £303 on each person on training every year. It is vitally important this money is well spent.

Barriers to learning transfer may include participants who are afraid of change and are lacking in confidence; managers who do not provide support; and HRD practitioners who are suffering from work overload (Gilley et al, 2002, cited in Mankin, 2009, p.269).

Much of this may be related to the organisational culture – if the organisation does not value training and realise its importance, employees who attend training events will not be encouraged to put their newly found skills into practice when they return to the workplace.

 PAUSE FOR THOUGHT

Think of a training course you have attended. What did you learn from it that you could actually use? Did you come back to work and put your new knowledge and skills into practice? Or did you forget what you learned within a few days because you were not able to practise what you had learned? Consider how much that course cost the employer – not only in training fees, but also in lost time while you were away. If we don't want to waste our training budget, transfer of learning into the workplace is crucial.

9.11 CHOOSING A CAREER

While learning and development are critically important at work, they are also predominant in your mind when you are at the stage of choosing a career for yourself. Many students have made this choice before entering university or college and, obviously, it is a choice that has helped them to decide on the nature of the course they will take. Others, however, use the university course to learn about particular subjects that, in turn, will help them to decide what they would like to do as a career. With the increase in university fees, it becomes more important to choose a degree that is going to be useful and worth the investment.

When researching a career, there are lots of options and it may seem overwhelming. It can be helpful to talk to an experienced careers adviser, who should be able to give direction and guidance. Most colleges and universities have their own careers service and it is well worth paying them a visit for some professional advice.

Additionally there are careers websites that can offer help. Some allow you to complete a questionnaire and identify which careers you would be suitable for. 'Prospects' is the UK's official graduate careers website (**www.prospects.ac.uk**).

As career choice is so important – we spend a large part of our lives at work – it is worthwhile choosing carefully and spending time in researching what the profession involves and how to enter it.

If you are reading this book with an intention of having a career in HR, you have perhaps already made up your mind. It is worth looking at the Profession Map on the CIPD website to see what skills you need in order to progress. A career in HR is varied and rarely dull!

CASE EXAMPLE 9.3

LEARNING AND CAREER PLANNING

Bharti Patel is just about to complete a degree in business and management. So far, she has studied many aspects of organisational behaviour, change and globalisation, and the influence of HRM. The business subjects she has taken include HR, finance, marketing and business planning.

She took her degree because she was interested in the subject, but really she has no idea about what she would like to do for a career. The university has an excellent careers service run by Bob Garner, an experienced careers adviser.

After some discussion, Bob gave her some exercises to complete to assess her strengths and weaknesses, preferences and prejudices, likes and dislikes. He also recommended that she write a summary of her knowledge, skills and competences: he encouraged her to think about her transferable skills – things she had learned outside of her studies, but which might be useful in a job; these included her hobbies, participation in sporting teams, voluntary work and other activities.

In addition, Bob advised Bharti to visit the Prospects website, which specialises in advising graduates on their careers. The site included a whole directory of employers and possible jobs for graduates. By reading this, she gained some ideas of possible career openings for someone with her qualifications and interests. It also gave her an idea of future prospects and salaries. She used their online career planner to help her to decide what might suit her.

By taking time to do all of this, reflecting on what she was good at, what she enjoyed doing and also what she disliked doing, Bharti learned more about herself and what she wanted to do. The investment was worthwhile because she now felt confident in choosing a suitable career.

9.12 SUMMARY

In this chapter we have defined some important terms, such as *human capital, talent management, knowledge management* and the concept of the *learning organisation*. Some of the terms are used interchangeably. People talk of going on a 'training course' at work, that this is part of their 'development', and that the managers see this as being included in the 'talent management' strategy or as being part of knowledge management in the organisation. In practice, many people still refer to the term 'training' in the workplace and use it to encompass all manner of workplace learning, while the term 'human resource development' suggests a wider approach with a strategic viewpoint.

We have discussed learning in detail, including early learning theories such as those of Pavlov, Skinner and Thorndike. We have also introduced Kolb's learning cycle, Honey and Mumford's learning styles and Revans' 'action learning sets'. There has been an opportunity to think about your own particular learning style. The chapter concludes with a look at career choice.

REVIEW QUESTIONS

1 Why is learning important to organisations?

2 How would you define learning?

3 What is meant by 'human capital'?

4 How can we define 'talent management'?

5 What is the difference between a traditional economy and a knowledge economy?

6 What do you understand by a 'learning organisation'?

7 What is meant by the term 'social learning'? Describe a situation in which this might take place.

8 Why is reflection such an important skill?

9 Who are the beneficiaries of training and how might they reap such benefits?

10 Name the four stages of Kolb's Learning Cycle.

11 What are the four learning styles according to Honey and Mumford?

12 According to the CIPD Learning and Talent Development survey 2013, how much do employers spend on training, on average, per employee?

13 Name one way of finding out more about a career in HR.

14 If you have read this entire chapter, you should have a fairly sound understanding of learning. How would this understanding help you to design a training course? For more help on this, read the next chapter.

EXPLORE FURTHER

BOOKS

Some useful textbooks on learning and development:

STEWART, J. and CURETON, P. (2014) *Designing, delivering and evaluating L&D: essentials for practice.* London: Chartered Institute of Personnel and Development.

BEEVERS, K. and REA, A. (2010) *Learning and development practice.* London: Chartered Institute of Personnel and Development.

NOE, R.A. (2010) *Employee training and development.* New York: McGraw-Hill.

REES, G. and FRENCH, R. (2013) *Leading, managing and developing people.* London: Chartered Institute of Personnel and Development.

STEWART, J. and RIGG, C. (2011) *Learning and talent development.* London: Chartered Institute of Personnel and Development.

For something a bit more in-depth and with more theory, interlaced with some good case studies, try Harrison's book:

HARRISON, R. (2009) *Learning and development*. London: Chartered Institute of Personnel and Development.

MEGGINSON, D. and WHITAKER, V. (2007) *Continuing professional development*. 2nd ed. London: Chartered Institute of Personnel and Development.

This is a comprehensive text on CPD and has lots of practical ideas for your own continuing professional development.

WEBSITES

The CIPD's annual *Learning and Talent Development* survey report: **www.cipd.co.uk/research/_learning-talent-development**

Prospects website for careers advice for graduates: **www.prospects.ac.uk/careers.htm**

CIPD Profession Map for information on skills needed for a career in HR: **www.cipd.co.uk/cipd-hr-profession/profession-map**

For the Honey and Mumford Learning Styles Questionnaire, visit: **www.peterhoney.com**

Learning and Development – Practical Aspects

10.1 INTRODUCTION

In the previous chapter we approached the subject of learning, by setting the context of learning and explaining some of the related concepts, focusing particularly on 'how individuals learn' and your own learning style. In this chapter we move on to look at learning from an *organisational* viewpoint and focus on 'learning in relation to work'. The first part of this chapter discusses the current status of learning and 'human resource development' (HRD) and the strategic importance of learning. One of the key aims of this chapter, however, is to explain the practical aspects of learning and development and offer some advice on how to deliver training and learning. If you are involved in training delivery, you will find some useful ideas that you can use. We also discuss e-learning and consider the pros and cons of its use.

10.2 THE STRATEGIC IMPORTANCE OF LEARNING AND TALENT DEVELOPMENT

The growth of global competition has brought the importance of learning and development to the forefront of strategic thinking. In times of recession, it becomes even more important to have highly skilled staff (the 'talented' workers) who will give the organisation a competitive edge and help it survive the difficult times. The president of the Chartered Institute of Personnel and Development (CIPD) in the 2000 annual report said, 'People are our only source of differentiation and sustainable competitive advantage' (Beattie, 2002). The director general of the CIPD maintained that: 'Staff management and development will become the primary weapon available to managers to generate success' (Rana, 2000). The retention of talent is crucial to business competitiveness. In the 2013 CIPD *Learning and Development* survey report, 57% of organisations report they undertake talent management activities with a focus on 'high-potential' employees. Other organisations adopt a more inclusive view of employee development and have a 'whole workforce' approach. This emphasises the importance of developing employees and growing future senior managers/leaders in organisations. The survey states that learning and talent development 'is gradually becoming less about instruction and more about interaction', which emphasises the change in approach to learning today. On-the-job training, in-house development programmes and coaching by line managers have ranked among organisations' most effective learning and talent development practices for the last five years. In this chapter we will look in more detail at in-house delivery and how this can best be achieved.

10.2.1 THE RELATIONSHIP WITH RECRUITMENT AND TALENT MANAGEMENT

If we remember the adage 'recruit for attitude, train for skill', we can see the importance of human resource development. It is vital for organisations to recruit and select the right kind of people to work for them, but once they are employees, it is just as important to ensure they are not only trained to do their *current job*, but also to develop their skills, to prepare them for *promotion* within the organisation. If we see talent management as being crucial for the success and survival of the business, training, learning and development are key to this. We need to employ the best talent we can and to *develop* that talent to retain our competitive edge.

The term 'human capital' (defined in Chapter 9) suggests that we are all valuable resources, which can be invested in and can grow in value. If we take on a new graduate, for example, they will have the potential to become a successful employee, but unless we train them and give them the opportunity to improve their skills and abilities, they will become bored, demotivated and will eventually leave. We should, then, ensure that our staff are treated as valuable assets and allow them to develop and grow accordingly.

So, should we see our 'talent' as the top employees – those with special skills, who are our 'elite'? Or does the term 'talent' apply to everyone? We need *all* our employees to work to their full potential, so does it make sense to only develop 'the chosen few'? With the rising importance of flexibility and multi-skilling, the need to have well-trained workers becomes essential. In the previous chapter we looked at the idea of the 'learning organisation' – where learning is constantly on the agenda of the business. Talent development fits in well with this concept.

 ACTIVITY 10.1

Think of a time when you have been into a shop and wanted to buy something quite technical – a computer or a DVD player, say. What was your experience like? Was the shop assistant well informed about the product? Or were you frustrated by their lack of knowledge and ability to answer questions? Does training in product knowledge – or lack of it – make a difference to whether you might buy the product?

10.2.2 'TIME TO TRAIN' LEGISLATION

Legislation introduced in April 2010 gave employees working in organisations that employ 250 or more people the legal right to request time off for studying or training. It is only applicable to employees who have worked for their employer continuously for at least 26 weeks. As with a request to work flexibly, the employer must consider the request to train and can only turn it down if they have a good business reason for doing so, which may include the cost.

10.3 NATIONAL SKILLS STRATEGY

As the UK competes in a global economy (an economy in which competitor countries are investing in their people), the Government understands the need to keep pace with developments in learning and development and invest in its people similarly. Lord Heseltine's review, *No Stone Left Unturned in Pursuit of Growth* (October 2012), identified the importance of skills in supporting local economic growth. To enable employers to play a greater role in shaping skills provision going forward, local enterprise partnerships (LEPs) have a new strategic role over skills. The Skills Funding Statement 2012–2015, issued by the Skills Funding Agency and the Department for Business, Innovation and Skills, lays out some of the key areas of importance in achieving a highly skilled workforce, with emphasis being laid on improving apprenticeships and identifying and supporting skills for growth.

The Employer Ownership Pilot (EOP) continues to offer employers the opportunity to shape training provision for themselves and to invest in their current and future employees. This was introduced as an attempt to strengthen the link between training and employment, allowing businesses to design their own training programmes so that they are closely aligned to industry needs. Government focus and policy are constantly changing, so it is likely that by the time you read this book, things will have moved on. To keep abreast of the latest in government policy on skills, visit the **gov.uk** website.

10.3.1 APPRENTICESHIPS

There is currently great emphasis on apprenticeships, which provide work-based learning and experience tied in with gaining a qualification. Apprenticeships bring considerable value to organisations, employers, individuals and the economy. The National Apprenticeship Service (NAS) has responsibility for apprenticeships in England and has been designed to increase the number of apprenticeship opportunities. It provides a dedicated, responsive service for both employers and learners. Apprenticeships provide a means of achieving a qualification in a wide range of areas, including engineering, agriculture, arts, business and construction.

Chapter 5, 'HR Planning', also tackles the issue of introducing apprenticeships as part of workforce planning.

10.3.2 INVESTORS IN PEOPLE (IIP)

The Investors in People (IiP) standard provides a practical framework for improving business performance and competitiveness through good people management practice in people. Investors in People is owned by the UK Government and managed nationally by the UK Commission for Employment and Skills (UKCES).

IiP has been taken up by over 40,000 organisations across the UK (32% of employers) and covers 8 million employees (UKCES, 2012). Generally these organisations report that achieving the required standards for recognition as an Investor in People is extremely beneficial. Sixty per cent of Investors in People accredited firms predict business growth, compared with the UK establishment average of 47% (UKCES, 2012).

IiP recognises that organisations use different means to achieve success through their people and does not, therefore, prescribe any one method for doing this. Instead, it provides a framework to help organisations to find the most suitable means for achieving success through their people. It is 'more than an accreditation process – it involves a cultural shift – an organisation-wide approach to doing business that leads to empowerment, ownership and improved productivity at every level' (Investors in People,

2013). The main outcome of the review of the standard is the provision of a simplified structure to provide a better fit with how organisations operate. The focus is on helping employers to:

PLAN, by developing strategies
DO, by taking action, and
REVIEW, by evaluating and improving performance.

ACTIVITY 10.2

Your organisation, or an organisation with which you are familiar, would like to be recognised as an IiP organisation. Have a look at a copy of the IiP Framework summary (**www.investorsinpeople.co.uk/about-iip/ framework**). What areas do you think the organisation needs to focus on to help it work towards achievement of the standard?

10.4 SYSTEMATIC TRAINING

In corporate terms, the ultimate purpose of training is to improve the performance of employees, and thereby the whole organisation. Individuals, however, may regard training as one of the means by which they can improve themselves to enhance their career prospects. Viewed in this way, training may be driven by both the organisation and by its employees.

10.4.1 LEARNING AND DEVELOPMENT (OR TRAINING) POLICY

With the growth of knowledge management and the importance of talent development, a policy which outlines the strategy for training and development is essential. It is in an organisation's best interests to formulate a clear and cost-efficient statement of intent to provide resources for a human resource development strategy that is accessible to all areas of the enterprise.

Growing future senior managers/leaders and developing high-potential employees remain the key objectives of talent management activities.

It is HR's responsibility to develop a training policy that meets the needs of the business and to have it accepted at the top level. Additionally, a training needs analysis (TNA) should be carried out that links the needs of the business and of individuals, the findings of which will determine the specification of the training programme.

ACTIVITY 10.3

Visit the Eddie Stobart website and view their learning and development policy: **www. eddiestobart.com/careers/the-academy/ group-learning-and-development-policy** Could you now come up with something similar for your own organisation, or an organisation with which you are familiar?

10.4.2 DEVELOPING A TRAINING COURSE

The professional expertise in training resides in the HR department, and in particular with the learning and development (L&D) specialists (the 'learning and development manager' or 'HRD manager' – assisted by HR practitioners or 'trainers'). Although L&D staff may design and deliver training, they may not always have the expertise themselves and may buy in training courses from a consultant. Their role is also to offer guidance to line managers who may deliver coaching to their own staff, for example. However, one of the biggest roles for L&D practitioners is to deliver training courses, and this is where we will now concentrate.

Developing a training course involves the practitioner in a well-known sequence of activities. The activities form a cyclical process that is generally referred to as the *systematic training cycle* (see Figure 10.1).

Figure 10.1 The systematic training cycle

10.5 THE COMPONENTS OF THE SYSTEMATIC TRAINING CYCLE

From Figure 10.1, you will see that the *systematic training cycle*, sometimes referred to as the *systematic approach to training*, is made up of six interdependent and interrelated components. It has been used successfully in industry and the public sector for many years and is regarded as a sound basis for cost-effective training.

10.6 STAGE 1: IDENTIFY TRAINING NEEDS

The most objective and effective approach to this task starts at job level. Carrying out a *job analysis* forms the basis for the production of job descriptions and specifications. The knowledge and competences that a job-holder needs to meet the required standards, and the standards themselves, are clarified in a completed job analysis. The next stage is to identify the *competence gap*. By performing a 'gap analysis' we should be able to determine the difference between what the job-holder *is* able to do and what they actually *should* be able to do. In behavioural terms this can be expressed as what the job-holder is *expected* to do and what they *actually* do. Where there is a gap between actual and required performance, it may be filled by training.

There can be a danger that training is seen as a panacea – the answer to all performance problems. This may not be the case; the employee may possess the ability, but the gap between actual and required performance may be caused by lack of motivation or opportunity to perform. Training may be a possible answer, but there may be times when there is a need for disciplinary action, for example where an employee has the right skills but just does not perform well owing to their attitude. There may, of course, be other reasons why someone may not perform well – perhaps through being poorly managed or owing to lack of support from the rest of their team.

10.6.1 HOW TRAINING NEEDS ARE IDENTIFIED

There are several ways in which training needs may be identified:

- *Performance appraisal:* managers identify training needs in their day-to-day monitoring of staff performance and when they carry out formal performance appraisal sessions. For example, the manager identifies a training need when an employee's standard of performance needs to be raised.
- Individuals may notice their own lack of knowledge of techniques or systems, or they may identify gaps in their skills when asked to carry out particular tasks.
- Training needs may also be identified during the selection process. The 'best person for the job' rarely possesses every single item of knowledge, skills and competence that the job demands.
- A mentor or coach may identify a training need – especially in relation to the employee's personal development.
- *Assessment or development centres:* employees may go through tests and exercises that identify areas where they excel, are competent or where they require extra training.

PAUSE FOR THOUGHT

Who is best placed to determine what training and development and individual should receive? The trainee? The manager? HR specialists? Can you think of anyone else?

10.6.2 TRAINING NEEDS ANALYSIS

The technique for identifying training needs at individual, group and corporate levels is known as a *training needs analysis* (TNA). This may be carried out through a formal training survey that is conducted across the whole organisation. Typically, this is needed when a company-wide change is taking place, such as when new technology is being introduced, or when restructuring occurs. In such cases, new competences need to be learned and tasks and responsibilities are redistributed. A company-wide training survey is a massive undertaking and its effectiveness will be maximised if it is started well in advance of the anticipated change.

10.7 STAGE 2: SET TRAINING OBJECTIVES

The next stage is to set the training objectives. In general, the objective of training is to develop in people the knowledge and understanding, skills and competence that they need to meet required performance standards. The training objectives, therefore, should be set out in behavioural terms, specifying what the trainee should know and be able to do as a result of the training. As an example, if you look at the box at the beginning of every chapter in this book, you will see how the learning objectives are set out.

10.7.1 SMART OBJECTIVES

The acronym SMART is often used as a mnemonic to aid those who regularly set objectives for others. SMART means that objectives should be: **S**pecific, **M**easurable, **A**chievable, **R**ealistic and **T**ime-related.

Specific means making a clear statement about the knowledge or skill that the trainee should be able to do and actually demonstrate at the end of the course. This includes the level of operation, such as, 'After the training, the trainee should be able to use the machine safely and efficiently to produce the product at the specified quality.'

Measurable means that the standard of the trainee's performance after the training can be measured in terms of, for example, quality and number of items in a specified period of time.

Achievable means that it should be possible for the trainee to achieve the objectives in the light of the situation, the practicability, and the intelligence and motivation of the trainee.

Realistic means that the objectives should be obviously useful and clearly related to the type of work that the trainee carries out.

Time-related means that the trainee should be able to develop understanding, attain concepts and demonstrate skills within a pre-specified period of time. For example, you might be able to type a letter perfectly if you took an hour to do it, but not if you only had five minutes. A skilled typist would be able to achieve the objective in the shorter time.

10.8 STAGE 3: PLAN THE TRAINING

Bearing in mind the nature of the subject matter in which the employee needs to be trained, decisions have to be made about how and where it is to be carried out. There are several choices. Most training, however, falls into one of two categories:

1 *On-the-job training*, which, as the term implies, takes place while the trainee is actually working. This can include:

   - E-learning (electronic learning), using the Internet or the organisation's own intranet – e-learning may also be done 'off the job'.
   - 'Sitting by Nelly', in which the trainee is taken through the steps of the job by a colleague – you may see this in supermarkets when new checkout operators are being trained, for example.
   - Use of instruction manuals – this may rely on the trainee teaching themselves the required skills by reading the manual.
   - Completing a project or assignment related to the job.
   - Coaching – usually performed by a line manager.

2 *Off-the-job training*, which may be external training, when, for example, an individual or a small group is sent out to a local college or training centre, or to a higher education institution to undertake a professional qualification. Off-the-job training may also include in-house training, for example when the trainee undertakes a short course (for example a health and safety course) or carries out an assignment supervised by the manager. This might include undertaking role-plays, discussing case studies, attending workshops, and so on.

One way of offering training, especially where it is expensive if mistakes are made, is to use simulations. Most of us are aware of flight simulators, used to train pilots, but simulators are also used in training lorry drivers (most notably at Eddie Stobart), where a mistake may also cost lives.

PAUSE FOR THOUGHT

Eddie Stobart run apprenticeships in conjunction with System Training. The Eddie Stobart Training Academy is a state-of-the-art training academy that includes an £80,000 simulator giving apprentices the chance to sit behind the wheel of the truck and master the skills of taking it out onto the road.

Look at the information on the Eddie Stobart website at: **www.eddiestobart.com/careers/the-academy**
What do you think of such an investment in training? What message does it give to staff? And to customers?

10.8.1 TRAINING STRATEGIES

It is important to consider the best way of fulfilling the training need. Questions to think about include:

- Should the training be carried out in the organisation's own training facility by one of the managers or specialists, or by an external trainer? Cost may be a factor to consider here.
- Is it a subject that would be best handled externally, perhaps by a college or a private training establishment? Do you have experts in-house with the right knowledge to deliver the training?
- Is there a government training initiative that would serve the purpose?
- Could the employee's competence gap be filled by coaching, on-the-job training or counselling?
- Could the organisation sponsor the employee to undertake a course that bears a qualification?
- Could the manager give an assignment to the trainee who could then be coached by either the manager or another suitably qualified person? In this way, the employee may emerge from the assignment having learned enough from it to fill their competence gap.
- Could the training objectives be achieved through e-learning, in which the employee uses the Internet or the organisation's intranet to gather the knowledge, understanding and competences they need?
- How is the training to be funded?

The advantages and disadvantages of all of these options have to be weighed carefully, since training can involve considerable cost and commitment on all sides. While cost is an important factor, the nature of the training objectives is the key to the answer. Cheap training may not be the best – 'cost-effectiveness' would make a better criterion. If we want to teach interview skills, for example, e-learning is probably not the best option, as we want people to be able to try out these skills in practice – so a course that includes some role-play might be more effective.

10.9 STAGE 4: IMPLEMENT THE TRAINING

If it is decided that external training would be the most appropriate way forward, the HR practitioner becomes involved in administering the event: for example, securing the trainee's entry to the course, ensuring that the fee is paid and monitoring the trainee's progress. The trainee's manager, however, should be involved in a different way, as the following case example shows.

CASE EXAMPLE 10.1

Claire wants to study for her professional exams and become CIPD-qualified. Her manager, Pam, is keen to support her and is willing to let her have the afternoon off, once a week, to attend class, as well as paying her course fees.

Pam asks Claire what she has learned every week and goes through the topics with her, discussing how the subject might be applied in the organisation. When she studies 'People Resourcing', Pam allows her to sit in on the assessment centre and observe candidates. For the 'Investigating a Business Issue' module, Claire talks through with Pam what she has found and how it will benefit the company. Pam is able to offer advice about the project and give valuable help.

Claire feels she is not alone in studying and feels valued because Pam is willing to spend time supporting her. The fact that Pam considers the course to be useful to the company means that the training is seen to be worthwhile. All of this helps Claire to complete the course and to gain high marks. She is motivated to learn because she knows it will be a good investment for both her and the organisation.

Commentary

It has to be pointed out that not all managers take such an interest in the development of their staff, as in this case. This is evidenced by the fact that at enrolment in colleges for part-time and short courses, you will often find that it was the student's, rather than their employer's, idea to take the course.

ACTIVITY 10.4

Think about a course you are on, or have been on. Where did the idea come from to attend the course? Was your manager supportive? Did they take an interest in what you learned? Were you able to put the learning from the classes into place back at work?

PAUSE FOR THOUGHT

Why should managers take an interest in what their staff learn? In what ways do you think this has broader implications for the organisation?

10.9.1 RUNNING AN IN-HOUSE COURSE

If it is thought that in-house training would be the best way forward, the HR practitioner becomes involved in organising and administering the course. This includes setting the date and organising the venue for the training, and ensuring that the prospective trainees and their managers receive sufficient notice of the times and dates of the training events. Where the subject matter is HR-related, such as training managers in a new system of appraisal or in selection interviewing, the HR practitioner is often expected to be able to deliver it. Otherwise, a trainer who is an expert in the subject should deliver the course, especially if it is a technical subject. For this purpose, it may be possible to enlist the services of a manager or specialist from within the organisation. If not, you may have to buy in the services of a training consultant.

10.9.2 TRAINING CONSULTANTS

Some HR departments have a register of external specialists who come in to the organisation to deliver the training. When this happens, the HR practitioner will have made the consultant aware of the training objectives and the consultant will have developed an appropriate course that they will bring to the training area. It is necessary to be certain, however, that the course meets the needs of the trainees precisely, and this may involve meetings with the consultant.

It is important at such meetings not to allow the consultant to dominate the proceedings. With the appropriate managers, the HR practitioner will have set the training objectives, and it is only by these objectives that the training must be driven. While the views of an experienced consultant might be valuable, they cannot know the organisation and its training requirements as well as its staff do, so do not allow the training to be driven by what the consultant would like to deliver – make sure it is exactly what your organisation needs and that it fits the objectives.

10.9.3 COST-EFFECTIVENESS

Earlier we alluded to the cost of training, and while we almost instinctively relate cost to college fees, engaging external trainers, travel expenses and so on, it can still be costly to run an in-house course. Cost-effectiveness may also be related to the number of trainees on the course at any one time, since many organisations calculate the cost per head.

There is a balance to be achieved here in the sense that while the number of trainees has to justify the cost of the course, it also has an influence on the event. Too few trainees may not provide a suitable mix or allow for group work, while too many may make it difficult for the trainer to deal with questions. A large number of trainees may also influence your decisions about the methods and media to be used (see below) and the duration of the course. If, for example, you decide to use group work, you have to consider the amount of time it is fair to allocate to delegates when they return from their discussions to present their findings.

Costs do not just relate to paying for the course, but also the 'opportunity costs' of people not being at work and doing their job while they are attending the training course, which can be significant.

10.10 COURSE DEVELOPMENT

Let us now assume that the subject matter of the training is HR-related and that you are going to organise and deliver the training. Firstly, the course objectives have to be studied carefully and you have to decide how they are going to be achieved. Secondly, therefore, you decide what the course should contain and what methods and media would be most likely to achieve the objectives.

Table 10.1 Training methods

Method	Usage
Lecture	Presenting information, particularly to a large number of people. Keep lectures as brief as possible as attention spans are short. Making lectures interactive by encouraging or asking questions throughout is advisable as it generates good rapport with the trainees.
Seminar	Ideal to discuss a topic or concept. The trainer may introduce the subject and run a group discussion on it. Trainees can present their views on which the trainer may comment.
Case study	These may describe hypothetical situations, while others are based on reality. They are a useful way of exposing trainees to organisational situations that are relevant to the subject and are current.
Role-play	This is a case study in which the trainees adopt the roles of the characters in the situation. Usually, it is a problem-solving situation related to the subject of the course. Ideal for exercising interpersonal skills and for training in recruitment and selection interviewing, for example. Where necessary, the trainer intervenes to offer guidance.
Group work	Normally a problem-solving session in which the trainees are given a problem based on an organisational situation. The course members are divided into small groups and asked to try to find a solution to the problem. When they return to the main training area, they present their findings to the group.
Exercises	These are suitable for trainees to learn and practise skills for the first time. This might be to complete a questionnaire or a quiz, to work out answers to problems, or to do a physical activity, such as playing a game.

10.10.1 TRAINING MEDIA

Information technology has extended the range of training media, especially in the area of visual aids. These include PowerPoint and DVDs. Other visual aids include overhead projectors (OHP, now rather old-fashioned and rarely used), electronic whiteboards, flipcharts, videos and YouTube clips. Handouts may also be used to get your message across.

There are occasions when the media you use are determined simply by what is available in the training facility, and sometimes therefore you just have to make do. Having said that, each of the media mentioned above lends itself to particular subject matter. You should always make sure you have a back-up plan. If the electronic technology fails, you need to have written handouts, to work through, or to convey your points on a flipchart. A trainer should always be ready for things that may go wrong. Technology may be a wonderful thing, but you do not want to face a room of eager trainees and not be able to teach them just because the computer isn't working! Beware – this happens far more frequently than might be imagined.

Meanwhile, Table 10.2 lists the most commonly used media and the purposes for which they are suitable.

Table 10.2 Commonly used visual training aids

Medium	Usage
PowerPoint	Everything is prepared on the computer. It is usual to run off copies of the PowerPoint slides to hand out to the trainees as aides-memoire. With this medium you can use colour and animation. Be wary of getting carried away with fancy tricks, though – it is the content of your PowerPoint slides that counts, not whether your text flies in with a whooshing sound!
Smartboards	These are whiteboards on which you can play PowerPoint slides, write down points as you go along, or access Internet sites – all of which will enhance your presentation. You may for example be discussing Investors in People and then be able to click on a web link that takes you straight to the IiP website.
Whiteboard and flipchart	Handy for summarising findings, trainees' answers to your questions and for laying out the main points of a talk.
DVD, video, film, YouTube clips	There is an infinite selection of these. Some are made specifically for training purposes in which actors adopt roles in case studies and problem-solving situations. Others are well-known feature films in which there are leadership and motivation issues.

10.11 PREPARING THE COURSE

Thorough preparation is the key to delivering a successful course, and there are several factors to be considered. You need to do the following:

- Assess the training venue and see what media hardware is available and in good working order (note the warnings above about the unreliability of technology!). Is the venue accessible and suitable? A noisy room may interfere with delivery and affect the ability to concentrate.
- Create the course structure – refer back to the course objectives. How will you achieve these in the time available?
- Decide what methods and media you are going to use. Decide on activities, role-plays, case studies, and so on.
- Draft your presentation notes.
- Develop the visual aids.
- Select the DVDs, videos, films, YouTube clips (if any) you intend to use.
- See what you can find out about the trainees. You may have someone with a disability who needs special equipment to help them hear or see the presentation. Or who needs to lip read. If you know in advance, you can adjust your training methods to take this into account. It is worth finding out if anyone has special dietary needs, if you are providing refreshments.

10.11.1 ASSESSING THE VENUE

It is important to take the time to visit the training facility. You need to know:

- The size and layout of the place – will it accommodate your trainees comfortably? From which point in the room will you deliver the course? What visual and other training aids are available and are they all in working order? How do you operate the computer and screen?
- How many syndicate rooms are there (if any)?

- How does the place 'feel' in terms of its ambience? In other words, is it conducive to a pleasant and successful experience for the trainees? Is the room warm enough (but not so warm that they will be encouraged to sleep!)? How does the lighting work? Are there blinds on the windows to keep out the sun?
- What are the catering facilities like? Are you providing coffee, tea, biscuits, lunch? Are there any special dietary requirements? It's a good idea to have coffee at the start as it encourages people to mix and chat before the course starts and is thus good for helping to establish rapport.

These may all sound like common sense, but it is worth checking so that you can deliver with confidence and not have to worry about appearing incompetent in front of the class.

10.11.2 CREATING THE COURSE STRUCTURE

Having decided on the duration of the course, you now have to decide how much of the time to allocate to each of its elements. Here, your priorities are governed partly by the importance of the elements in relation to each other, and partly by their detail and complexity, the latter implying that the trainees will need time to understand and internalise them. You also have to create a logical sequence in which they are to be delivered, allowing for reasonable breaks between each session.

10.11.3 METHODS AND MEDIA

These are listed in Tables 10.1 and 10.2, and bearing in mind the course objectives and the nature of the material you need to deliver, you have to select the methods and media that you regard as the most suitable in terms of purpose and clarity. Some subjects seem naturally to lend themselves to particular methods and media.

CASE EXAMPLE 10.2

PLANNING AND DELIVERING A COURSE

Lee Chang is an HRD manager who delivers some of the in-company training courses. The company are introducing a new recruitment and selection procedure and they want everyone involved to receive some training on the process.

Lee finds out that 100 people need the training. He investigates costs and decides that a consultant would be too expensive and that he has the skills and knowledge to be able to deliver it himself. He plans exactly what needs to be taught, what the key points of the training are and writes some learning objectives. He decides that 100 people is too large a group to train all together, so he splits them into five groups. He will deliver the course each day to one group of 20. He thinks this will be an ideal size if he wants to do practical skills with them.

Lee designs a one-day course that will give everyone the basic knowledge about the process and will also include some skills practice exercises, starting with a few slides to set the context and explaining why the training is taking place. Then he will use an icebreaker activity to get everyone relaxed and to encourage rapport in the group, followed by an interactive talk on the procedure, with handouts reiterating the main points.

He has found some YouTube clips to illustrate bad practice – to introduce some humour to the talk.

In the afternoon, he wants the group to do some skills practice so he writes a role-play exercise for them to perform. He will observe the groups and give them feedback. Hopefully by this time the group will feel at ease with each other and will enjoy taking part.

He will finish with a final summary and build in a question and answer session at the end to ensure that everyone has a chance to ask for guidance.

10.11.4 WRITING YOUR TRAINING PLAN

This involves working out the detail of the training session and also drafting your notes of what you are going to say. Go through each element of the course carefully, draft a separate set of notes for each element and place them in a file in the order of delivery. On the right of each page, leave a margin that is wide enough to make 'reminder' notes, such as when a PowerPoint slide should be shown or when the trainees may need a slight pause while they absorb a particular point or concept. It is also useful to have the plan to hand, so that you can refer to it if you get lost – you may come to the end of a set of slides and then panic about what comes next. A quick glance at the plan will show you what exercise or activity you need to deliver. You need to get to know your plan so well that you hardly ever have to refer to it; just take it in as your security blanket!

10.11.5 DEVELOPING VISUAL AIDS

Some visual aids come ready-made, such as DVDs, videos and films. Others, such as PowerPoint presentations, you have to make yourself, although many textbooks now have PowerPoint slides that you can use.

Flipchart

This is quite a versatile tool. One of its main advantages is its portability. You may have to run a session in an area that is not customised for training, and if it is off-site, the flipchart will fit into the back of your car. Alternatively, syndicate groups can make presentations on a flipchart, having prepared them during the session. In this way, different people's conclusions and recommendations may be compared, contrasted and discussed in a subsequent plenary session. When using the flipchart yourself, as a trainer, try to develop the skill of writing and speaking while facing the audience as much as possible. Talking into the flipchart should be avoided.

PowerPoint

In order not to bore your trainees to death, it is important to use PowerPoint sensibly. Keep slides to a minimum and do not clutter them with unnecessary detail. Make sure the font size is large enough to read from the back of the room. Use each slide to give the key points – as an aide-memoire for you, as presenter. Avoid using too many effects; flying images and sounds will detract from the content. Keep it simple.

Talk about each slide, giving additional information, to keep the delivery interesting. Most students hate a trainer who 'just reads from the slides', so don't fall into this trap. Have some entertaining examples to share to add to the content of the slide. This will make your talk more memorable and enjoyable. And as with the use of flipcharts, direct your speech to your audience, not the screen. It is also useful to give a copy of the slides as handouts so that people can take them away for later perusal. It also means they don't have to make copious notes while you are delivering your talk and can thus concentrate more easily on what you are saying.

10.11.6 RUNNING A TRAINING SESSION

In advance of actually running a session, a good trainer will go through their notes thoroughly and learn them so well that they seldom need to refer to them. If you have never done it before, practise your delivery as if you are in the real situation. Performing in front of a mirror, or in front of a friend or colleague, is a good idea as they can give you feedback. Be careful to choose someone who will be constructive, though – someone who is destructively critical is not a good idea! (For this reason, avoid asking your partner/wife/husband to do this!)

To run a session effectively, you have to be skilled in the use of visual aids. You may be able to develop and practise the skills if you are on an HR course. Many universities and colleges offer a short course in the use of media and training aids generally. Try to get accustomed to the technology before you start.

Establishing rapport

Before introducing the subject matter, you need to develop a friendly but business-like atmosphere that is conducive to learning. If you have a class of students or trainees whom you have never previously met, you may wish to tell them something about yourself (although without sounding too self-important). Putting name cards in front of the trainees is a good idea, not only so that the trainer will know who they are, but for other participants to know each other's names.

Icebreakers

At this early stage, you can run a brief interactive session. The idea is to get the trainees talking to each other and to relax. People can be quite intimidated at courses, especially in front of a big group, so the more you can get them to relax and enjoy it, the more readily they will learn. Using the following as an icebreaker can be very entertaining. Lengthy introductions can become boring – so if the course is a short one, you don't need to spend too long on this. If you are running a longer course, perhaps where the trainees will be together for a number of sessions or weeks, it is worth spending longer on letting them get to know each other.

 CASE EXAMPLE 10.3

ICEBREAKER

Ask each of the trainees to tell the group one thing they have in their pockets or handbags that means something to them. They may have a photo of a child or partner, a memento from a parent or it may just be their credit card without which they can't function! The aim is to get everyone used to saying something to the group and to 'break the ice'.

Introduction

It is vital for you to arouse the immediate interest of your audience with a good introduction of the subject. Without going into too much detail, tell them what you have planned for the session and the order in which each part of the course will be delivered. Providing them with an agenda or programme is helpful as they know what to expect regarding breaks and finishing times.

Main sections

At this stage you start to deliver the first section of the course. Speak fairly slowly and clearly (without boring the audience) to make sure you are getting your points across. Use simple, everyday language and avoid using a monotonous tone – be natural in your delivery. Avoid jargon and specialised terms, unless it is absolutely necessary, in which case explain what is meant. Round off one idea or concept, pause, and then introduce the next. Use examples as this will illustrate your ideas more clearly.

There is a limit to the amount of information you should express verbally; good visual support material is essential. Focus your attention on concepts rather than detail; you can always provide detail on handouts at the end of the session. If you have included citations or web links on your PowerPoint slides, leave them on show long enough for the trainees to jot down; otherwise include them on your handouts.

It helps to build and maintain rapport with the group if you can use people's names. It is also a good tip to refer back to any comments they have made during the course. For example, if you say, 'As Bernadette mentioned earlier, role-plays are an excellent method of training,' it shows that you have remembered what they said and reinforces that they made a worthwhile comment. This can make people feel valued – and helps to build up their confidence.

PAUSE FOR THOUGHT

If you are on a course, observe your lecturer; see how they deliver the material and, at the end of the session, think about the planning that must have gone into it. Well-delivered training should appear effortless – we should all be aware that it is not!

Handling questions

Keep a close eye on the clock! If you over-run you may not have time to answer questions. It is wise to lay the ground rules for questions from the beginning of the session. There are several ways of handling this. First, are you willing to take questions at any time? Second, would you prefer to take them at the end when you can see how much time you have left? (As your experience of training grows you will become adept at timing the sessions.) Third, you may decide to ask for questions at sectional points when, for example, you have just finished explaining a concept. There are advantages and disadvantages to all of these options.

If you allow the interruptions you may decide to turn these to your advantage. They may allow you to focus upon particular points of interest and engage your audience by encouraging them to participate with their thoughts and to change the pace and direction of your delivery. It is not unusual to be interrupted by someone who wishes to have a point clarified. This can be useful, since the understanding of what follows may depend on this. It may be that others in the group also feel they would like this point clarified but have not had the confidence to ask. It takes courage for people to speak out in front of a group, so if someone asks a question, it is better to give an answer, even if a brief one.

If you take questions at the end you can be sure of a free run throughout your delivery, which would allow you to focus exclusively on what you are doing, while avoiding any digressive discussions. The danger of this is that people do not feel able to question throughout – and this may mean that they stop concentrating because they have failed to understand a point. If trainers tell trainees to keep that question to the end, it is unlikely that the question will ever get asked.

You may find that one person hijacks the session by asking too many questions about their own personal circumstances, for instance; it may be worth asking them to chat to you over the coffee break, where you can speak to them in more detail. You do not want to lose the interest of the group by concentrating on one particular issue. On the other hand, sharing that one person's experience may be invaluable to the rest and this opportunity should not be overlooked. If possible, it is best to give a quick answer at the time without getting too 'off track'.

Always allow some time for questions, otherwise people may go home feeling they haven't really understood the session. Time management of the session is important. Too many questions may mean you over-run, which is something to avoid. It is better to have a session's structure planned with time for questions, but with an optional activity available if the group does not ask questions and you are left with time to spare. As a trainer you will need to build in flexibility to allow for things such as this. If you invite questions intermittently, this is an opportunity to engage the audience and give them a sense of participation. Also, it provides you with on-the-spot feedback: first, on how you are being received and, second, to check the trainees' understanding.

PAUSE FOR THOUGHT

Think of a time when you have attended a course and wanted to ask a question. How did the trainer handle it? If you were told to wait until the end, did you have the courage to ask it at the end? Or did the question get forgotten in the meantime? How do you feel about not having your question dealt with?

10.12 STAGE 5: EVALUATE THE COURSE

Running and participating in a training session – perhaps a one- or two-day course – should prove to be an interesting and exciting event for the trainer and the trainees. It is a socially interactive process after which the participants should feel confident that they have all learned from the experience. Additionally, it should also be effective in terms of achieving the training objectives; and it should be cost-effective.

PAUSE FOR THOUGHT

For developmental and financial reasons, evaluation is a vitally important process and yet most organisations pay little attention to it. They have ineffective systems of evaluation, or they ignore the need completely. Do you think that training without evaluation is a risky investment? Why?

Training evaluation is often criticised for only taking account of whether the trainees enjoyed the course and not whether they actually learned anything that they could apply back in the workplace. Since 1975 the most commonly espoused model of evaluation has tended to be that of Kirkpatrick, who developed a four-level framework consisting of:

- **Level 1, reaction:** This is where trainees state what they thought of the course, whether they enjoyed it and whether it was useful.
- **Level 2, learning:** Has the trainee actually learned anything? Have the learning objectives been achieved?
- **Level 3, behaviour or performance:** Has the training actually made any difference to the trainee at work? Can they do their job better as a result?

- **Level 4, results:** Has the training had any impact on the organisation? Have sales increased? Are things being run more efficiently? Are there fewer accidents? Is there less waste or fewer errors?

The higher the level, the more difficult it is to relate the results back to the training. For example, how do we know whether sales have increased because of the training, or whether it is as a result of our competitors closing down? Is the manager better because they attended a 12-month course, or because they now have an extra 12 months' experience of managing staff? Russ-Eft and Preskill (2005, p.71) reviewed training evaluation practices worldwide and concluded that there was little formal evaluation of training, little rigour and evaluation did not focus on the organisational/corporate level. As employers are currently spending an average of around £303 per employee (CIPD *Learning and Development* survey report, 2013), it seems ridiculous that we do not monitor how well that money is spent!

10.12.1 HOW TO EVALUATE

So with this in mind, *how should* we evaluate? Let us take Kirkpatrick's four levels:

- **Level 1** is relatively easy. We can ask trainees to complete a questionnaire at the end of the course (a 'happy sheet') to see whether they enjoyed the course and felt it was worthwhile. It may be that they did indeed enjoy the training, that it was good fun, a day off work, and so on, but that they did not actually learn very much at all that would be useful.
- At **Level 2**, learning can be assessed by giving tests, assignments and projects, much like you will be used to as students on educational courses such as the Certificate in HR Practice, or even for a degree.
- **Level 3** evaluation looks at whether performance or behaviour has changed. So we could use performance appraisals to see whether there has been any marked difference in how the person does their job. Or we could observe the person both before the training and then again afterwards and see if there have been any changes in behaviour. Can the trainees deal with issues better than they did before?
- **Level 4** evaluation needs to use data relevant to the type of course: for example, figures such as accident rates in the case of health and safety training, customer complaints in the case of customer care training. But it can become difficult. If we run recruitment and selection training, we may need to look not only at retention levels (on the assumption that a good recruitment process will appoint people who will stay with the organisation), but also at things such as a drop in the number of discrimination cases taken as a result of better interviewing, or an improvement in the induction crisis. This data may be hard to come by and even then may not prove whether the training was actually the cause of the improvements.

With the emphasis on cost, it is useful to try to do an analysis of return on investment. This means analysing the cost of the training and comparing it with the expected returns as a result. So if the training costs £3,000, are we getting an improvement in service worth at least that amount? This might be easy where we know the costs before training, but it is not always easy to quantify. Do we know how much loss of production costs? Can we say how much sickness absence costs? And can we quantify how much money we have saved as a result of the training? If our sales increase in December, is it as a result of our sales training course, or just the fact that it's nearly Christmas and everyone is out spending money on presents? Being able to say whether the success is a direct result of the training is difficult to do – and even more difficult to attach costs and savings to it.

CASE EXAMPLE 10.4

Accidents caused by fork lift trucks cost Walker Factories at least £28,000 per annum in lost production, absences and injury. The HRD manager decides to put all the fork-lift truck drivers through extra training, which costs £10,000. This is expensive, but he believes it will be worth it. The following year, the number of accidents reduces substantially, with only minor incidents occurring. The £10,000 cost of the training set against the £28,000 annual cost of accidents means an overall saving of £18,000 – a worthwhile return on investment in training and a demonstrable cost saving. While this may seem simplistic – and it is advisable to be aware of other reasons for the reduction – it can be argued that the training has been worthwhile. Keeping data to justify the value of training is always worthwhile – we don't want to spend money on training courses unless we can demonstrate their worth. Information on absence reduction, accidents and increased productivity are useful indicators of whether training has had an impact or not.

10.13 STAGE 6: ANALYSIS AND REVIEW

It is rare for a training session that is being run for the first time to achieve every single aspect of every objective, and even more rare for it to fail completely. Analysis and review is the final stage of the systematic training cycle. The task is to review how the course was received and to examine its effectiveness. An analysis of the results of evaluation will reveal areas that need to be improved. Evaluation, analysis and review are components of a continuous process, so after a course has been run a second time, it is reviewed again and re-evaluated to achieve improvements. Are there things we need to change? Can we do things better, cheaper, faster?

10.14 ONLINE OR E-LEARNING

This is a growing area and involves using software so that you can study on your computer without attending a class. Online learning may be *synchronous*, where everyone learns at the same time, for example taking part in a real-time lecture that you can participate in at the same time as others – this has the advantage that you can comment and take part via video link. It is rather like being in class because you can ask questions and receive answers from the tutor immediately. The alternative is *asynchronous*, whereby you can watch the lectures in your own time and at your leisure. This is not 'live' and is like watching a video. You can watch as many times as you like, pause and go back over areas you don't understand and skim through bits that you have already grasped. It may also use resources such as email, electronic mailing lists, threaded conferencing systems, online discussion boards, wikis, and blogs.

Usually there will be online exercises to complete and you can monitor your progress through the course. Online courses may use virtual learning environments, such as Moodle or Blackboard, for example.

10.14.1 ONLINE DELIVERY

Online learning can be very isolating for the student. There are no classmates with whom you can sit and chat or discuss issues. The tutor is only available in a virtual classroom environment and it is hard to ask questions or generate open discussion in the same way that you might in a real-life situation. It can be a lonely experience and may make learning difficult to sustain. Attending a class where you can be in direct contact with a tutor who is available to answer questions can be invaluable to your learning. Also, having friends on the course who can share and support your learning experience is extremely helpful and can help keep your motivation and momentum going. Making time to sit down at your computer can be far harder than attending a class at college. Other tasks get in the way and we struggle to prioritise in order to study.

To try and overcome this, it is important to make all learning materials as interactive as possible. The work should be engaging and able to keep the student's interest. Just reading a set of PowerPoint slides will be boring and although slides may contain useful information, they should only be seen as part of the learning. The tutor should be available to do live lectures, which also include time for questions. This personal contact helps the student to feel supported and not so isolated. Lectures can be recorded so that anyone who misses the live version can catch up at a later date.

Interactive exercises, quizzes and activities should be used to allow students to test their learning as they go along. This also helps them to see what progress they are making.

Message boards and chat rooms should be included so that students can communicate with each other – and with the tutor. Feedback from the tutor is essential in encouraging the student to continue and keep up their motivation, as well as enabling the student to see how they are doing.

A danger with online learning might be that no actual learning takes place. It is all too easy to click through the assessment activities and not really take on board the actual information. A quick skim through a set of slides and then answer a multiple choice quiz will not ensure that the information has been assimilated or will be remembered. Classroom discussions are far more memorable and give the student an opportunity to question and reflect – all part of the process of embedding the learning.

Formative assessments, which offer guidance and support, are useful tools, which will keep a student engaged and will also help towards gaining success in the final assessments. Summative assessments are marked pieces of work which form the basis of the final result for the course. An advantage of online learning is that assignments can be uploaded from anywhere and there is no necessity to hand in a paper copy. A student can be on holiday in Cyprus and still hand in their work on time!

Many courses are not restricted solely to online study and take a 'blended learning' approach.

 KEY CONCEPT: BLENDED LEARNING

An approach to learning that includes electronic means, such as online study, but also includes learning in a classroom with a tutor. There is a balance of e-learning and classroom-based study.

So with blended learning you may attend class with a tutor and other students, but also complete additional exercises or assignments online. There may be lectures or extra notes to read or supplementary activities to perform in your own time on the computer. Blended learning has the advantage of being able to be done at your own pace and convenience, but has the support of a tutor and some face-to face contact, which overcomes some of the problems of isolation and motivation.

10.15 OTHER TYPES OF E-LEARNING

With the general acceptance of the need for learning to be available online, the growth of 'massive open online courses' (MOOCs), the move towards online courses and the use of technology to support learning, it is worth understanding more about the concept of e-learning. In the CIPD's 2013 *Learning and Talent Development* survey, only 15% of employers see e-learning as one of the most effective methods of learning – a slow but sure rise over the past few years – but the vast majority believe that e-learning is more effective when combined with other types of learning – that is, in a blended learning approach. Interestingly, nearly three-quarters of respondents agreed it is not a substitute for face-to-face or classroom learning – but do see it as an important way of supporting learning.

Use of social media (Facebook, LinkedIn, and so on), 'gamification' (the application of fun elements of game-playing, for example point-scoring, competition with others, rules of play, to other areas of activity, such as training); bring your own device (BYOD) (whereby employees can bring their own computing devices – such as smartphones and laptops – to the workplace or training course to use and connect on the corporate network); and 'cloud computing' (delivering hosted services over the Internet) are all part of today's learning environment.

KEY CONCEPT: MASSIVE OPEN ONLINE COURSES (MOOCS)

These are free courses aimed at unlimited participation and open access via the web. They make use of traditional course materials such as videos, readings and activities and also provide an online community for the students and tutors. A key advantage of MOOCs over traditional classroom-based learning is their convenience: they allow students to work at their own pace and according to their own schedules. However, the drawback is that students lose motivation and drop out; completion rates are currently poor – *The Times* Higher Education supplement (9 May 2013) quotes figures as low as 7%.
(See Activity 18.4 in Chapter 18, 'Change Management', for more on open source programmes.)

PAUSE FOR THOUGHT

Have you ever done online training – perhaps a fire safety course or diversity training? How much do you remember from the course? Were you tempted to just click through without really absorbing the information? Did you learn much? How could the course have been improved? Would it have been better to attend a 'real' course?

10.16 SUMMARY

We have seen in this chapter how important human resource development can be to an organisation. Whether we are in a recession or boom times, development of its human resources can add to an organisation's competitive edge. Developing people is not only beneficial for individuals in that it adds to their employability and furthers their career prospects, but it is essential for businesses today by helping to ensure an organisation's survival in a global economy. Appointing people with talent is important – *developing* that talent is essential if we want to retain good people in the organisation and achieve a competitive edge.

The chapter outlines the systematic training cycle and gives some useful tips on delivery of learning events. The chapter ends with a look at e-learning and MOOCs, which are a growing concept but which need to be delivered carefully to avoid isolation and demotivation. A better approach is to use blended learning, which brings together e-learning and classroom contact.

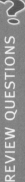

1 According to the 2013 CIPD Learning and Development survey, what are the most effective learning and development practices?

2 What was the key finding of Lord Heseltine's review, *No Stone Left Unturned in Pursuit of Growth* (October 2012)?

3 What is an Investor in People? What are the advantages?

4 What are the components of the systematic training cycle?

5 Name three ways of identifying training needs.

6 What is meant by the acronym SMART and how would you explain each of the elements?

7 Give an example of off-the-job training.

8 Suggest suitable methods for imparting factual information to a large group of people.

9 Why do we use 'icebreakers'?

10 What are Kirkpatrick's four levels of training evaluation?

11 Why is return on investment in training so difficult to calculate?

12 What can be done to ensure e-learning is not an isolating experience?

13 Why is blended learning an improvement on e-learning?

14 What is a MOOC?

BOOKS

STEWART, J. and CURETON, P. (2014) *Designing, delivering and evaluating L&D: essentials for practice.* London: Chartered Institute of Personnel and Development.

HACKETT, P. (2003) *Training practice.* London: Chartered Institute of Personnel and Development.

This is an excellent book on the practicalities of training.

SIMMONDS, D. (2003) *Designing and delivering training.* London: Chartered Institute of Personnel and Development.

This book provides a solid introduction to the subject.

TRUELOVE, S. (2006) *Training in practice.* London: Chartered Institute of Personnel and Development.

The above books, although slightly dated, still offer sound advice and practical help on how to design and deliver training.

For more depth on learning and development, see STEWART, J. and RIGG, C. (2011) *Learning and talent development.* London: Chartered Institute of Personnel and Development.

WEB LINKS

Apprenticeships: **www.apprenticeships.org.uk**

Government policy – **www.gov.uk** – the gov.uk website houses the Department for Business, Innovation and Skills, the Skills Funding Agency and the UK Commission for Employment and Skills

For statistics on educational initiatives visit: **www.thedataservice.org.uk/statistics/ statisticalfirstrelease/sfr_current** The site shows information on learner participation and achievement for further education and skills from 2008/09 to 2012/13. It includes information from the Labour Force Survey on the level of highest qualification held in England and information on vocational qualifications awarded in the United Kingdom.

Investors in People: **www.investorsinpeople.co.uk**

System Training is a training provider working with Eddie Stobart, amongst others. Visit **www.system-training.com/case-studies/** for some case study examples.

UK Commission for Employment and Skills (UKCES): **www.ukces.org.uk** (is being incorporated into the gov.uk website as we go to press).

CHAPTER 11

Employee Motivation and Performance

LEARNING OBJECTIVES

After studying this chapter you should:

- be able to define performance, performance management and performance appraisal as separate concepts
- understand the factors that motivate individuals and the main theoretical concepts underlying work motivation
- understand performance management as a process through which the organisation achieves its ultimate goals
- be able to explain how particular organisational factors may influence performance
- understand modern performance assessment systems
- be able to create your own personal development plan.

11.1 INTRODUCTION

The aim of this chapter is to examine performance and to consider how performance can be managed. To clarify your understanding of this, we consider separate definitions and descriptions of *performance* (what we do and how we do it), *performance management* (how we manage what employees do) and *performance appraisal* (a means of assessing or measuring that performance). One of the key contributors to performance is 'motivation' and the first part of the chapter focuses on some of the main motivational theories. For without motivation, few of us can perform!

11.2 BACKGROUND

We all understand the term 'performance' – it relates to whether we are fulfilling our objectives – whether as an organisation or as an individual. If someone is 'under-performing', we take it to mean that they are not as good as they could be, or that they are not meeting expected standards. However, if an *organisation* under-performs (and especially if its competitors are doing well), this has serious connotations for its continued survival. So it is important to ensure that organisations perform effectively and for us to understand how this can be achieved. Organisations are, of course, made up of individuals, so we need to know how we can get the best performance from everyone in order to achieve the best performance for the organisation.

11.3 WHAT IS PERFORMANCE?

First, let us look at what is meant by performance. There is a need to define 'good performance'. Can we agree what is meant by this? What constitutes 'poor' performance? We cannot define performance without relating to some kind of measurement.

11.3.1 DEFINITION: PERFORMANCE

When we talk about performance, we usually mean how well we do something. We might say, 'I performed well,' or 'My performance wasn't as good as it usually is.' Thus we are measuring a behavioural or physical quantity such as: 'accuracy, speed, or standards against set criteria'. At work, this might mean whether you achieved targets or how well you dealt with situations. In college, it might mean whether you passed an assignment – did your performance meet the set criteria?

11.3.2 PERFORMANCE AS BEHAVIOUR

In fact, performance is behaviour – because when you perform, you are doing something, that is, you are behaving in a certain way. It may be the cause of an outcome, but it is not the outcome itself. In the organisational context, performance is about doing the job.

KEY CONCEPT: THE PEOPLE AND PERFORMANCE LINK

Purcell et al (2003), in their study *Understanding the People and Performance Link: Unlocking the black box*, suggested that performance is a function of ability, motivation and opportunity. Discretionary behaviour (the willingness to 'go the extra mile') happens when capable people are motivated to work hard and are also given the opportunity to do so.

You can, therefore, talk about the level and the quality of performance, and clearly an individual can only do a job if they possess the necessary knowledge and skills. However, the fact that a person possesses knowledge and skills does not guarantee that they will use them to the organisation's advantage; people have to be motivated. People only ever do what they are motivated to do.

CASE EXAMPLE 11.1

THE INFLUENCE OF MOTIVATION

Two people are doing similar work and both are equally competent, yet one of them is putting in a better performance than the other. Since you know that neither one is better qualified or experienced than the other at doing the job, you have to ask yourself, what could be the cause of the difference in performance?

The answer is a difference in their motivation. Perhaps the poor performer is unwell or distracted by a personal problem, in which case they are motivated to focus on that, rather than on the job. Alternatively, they might not like doing the job.

ACTIVITY 11.1

Think about tasks at work that you have to complete. Which ones do you enjoy? Are these the ones that get done first? What happens to the tasks that you don't like? Is your motivation lower in doing these tasks? Is your performance affected by your motivation?

11.4 FACTORS INFLUENCING PERFORMANCE

Appointing the right people in the first place is important – remember: 'recruit for attitude, train for skill' – but once good staff have been appointed, we need to make sure that they are motivated to perform and that they have the opportunity and support they need to perform well.

Table 11.1 Organisational factors influencing motivation

Factor	Effect
Learning and development	Raises morale and brings about feelings of competence, visible changes in the employee's behaviour and tangible benefits in terms of performance improvement. An important outcome of learning and development is that it increases the versatility of the employee; multi-skilling and sharing complex tasks inspires confidence and mutual respect.
Employee relations	Sound and fair policies and procedures sustain an individual's motivation to work. If relations are good, motivation levels are likely to be higher.
Reward	Financial reward is seen by employees as a return on the investment of their time, skills and efforts. If, therefore, they see reward as fair and reasonable, they will continue to be motivated to work. However, there is a lot of academic argument about the role of reward in motivation.
Leadership style	Many employees still see themselves as 'working for', rather than 'working with', their managers. The style with which managers communicate with their staff, therefore, has a significant effect on the effort that the employee is prepared to put in. Transformational leaders are those who inspire and motivate staff to want to do well.
Organisational culture	All of the above will be affected by the culture of the organisation. Culture has an impact on behaviour, or 'the way we do things'. It can affect commitment and sense of identity.

The motivation to perform, however, is influenced by many factors, some of which are organisational, while others are related to the individual's attitudes and other personality factors.

Organisational factors relate to the work environment, such as the state of the employee relationship, the leadership and communication style of the managers and the general organisational culture (see Table 11.1).

11.4.1 MOTIVATION

While there is no universal definition of motivation, it is generally accepted to be 'the willingness to apply one's efforts towards the achievement of a goal that satisfies an individual need'. It is a natural human response to a stimulus. The response involves action designed to satisfy a need or attain a particular goal.

Work motivation is 'the willingness to apply one's efforts towards the achievement of the organisation's goals, while concurrently an individual need is satisfied'.

 ACTIVITY 11.2

Activity 11.1 asked you to think about your motivation at work. In this context, consider how much is pay a motivator for you? Most people say they would not come to work if they were not paid – but does pay make you want to work harder? Or does it just ensure that you attend?

Managers need to achieve their objectives by maximising their resources, including human resources. Their goal, therefore, is to elicit a performance from their staff that will lead to the achievement of their business objectives. Managers often look to motivation theories for clues of how to do this, on the grounds that 'a motivated workforce is a high-performing workforce'. As we saw above, Purcell et al's research (2003) might support this, as they suggest that performance is a function of ability, motivation and opportunity. The manager's aim, therefore, should be to align the employee's motivations with what the organisation requires. If an employee's wishes and needs are in line with those of the organisation, it is likely that the employee will be motivated to perform satisfactorily.

CASE EXAMPLE 11.2

Nathan wants a good career, with promotion for working hard, a good salary and a challenging job. He works hard but never gets promoted as there are few vacancies. His motivation declines because he cannot see a future in the company. His hard work will never get him a better job.

He is successful in applying for a new job in a larger company which prides itself in promoting keen, enthusiastic staff. The work is interesting and there are lots of opportunities for getting on. Nathan's motivation increases as he can see that reward for hard work exists. The company wants talented employees and Nathan has the ability that the company is looking for. Their needs are in alignment and performance is assured.

11.5 SCIENTIFIC MANAGEMENT

One of the earliest and best-known studies on 'performance measurement' was Frederick Winslow Taylor, a US steel engineer, who worked as a management consultant at the Bethlehem Steel Corporation. He developed a set of principles that formed the core of a system that was later referred to as *scientific management* (Taylor, 1911, 1947) (refer also to Chapter 3 for more on Taylor). His central principles were:

1 Apply scientific methods to management by using work measurement as a basis for accurate planning and production control.

2 Establish the best work methods: give each worker a clearly defined task.

3 Select, train and instruct subordinates scientifically.

4 Pay people fairly: high pay for successful completion of work.

5 Obtain co-operation between management and men and divide responsibility between them.

Taylor studied the capabilities of the human body and the length of time it took to carry out particular tasks. In other words, he invented what we now call *work study*. He then tied the pay of the workers to their performance. Today this is referred to as *payment by results*, or PBR schemes, which are now far more sophisticated. Taylor's development of scientific management is one of the most well-known studies in the history of management thought. He was concerned that industry was afflicted with problems that were rooted mainly in a severe lack of knowledge. 'Management,' he declared, 'is ignorant of what men can produce ... and they make no effort to find out or even define what a day's work is.' The workers took it for granted that there would be delays, 'down time' and other problems because they did not realise that there might be a better way of doing things; nor did they know how to improve their performance because they had not been shown.

Taylor's aim was to remove the guesswork from management and replace it with facts. He showed the men how to use their physiques to the best effect to increase their productivity, and he motivated them to do this by tying their pay to their performance.

 PAUSE FOR THOUGHT

Reflect on your organisation, or one with which you are familiar. Do you think Taylor's principles apply today?

It was Taylor's belief that people worked to obtain financial rewards rather than because they were interested in what they were doing. His main objective was to increase productivity, and it seemed logical to him to simply show the workers how they might increase their rewards: 'The more you produce, the more you will earn.' The notion that the labourers with whom he dealt would benefit psychologically from job satisfaction and involvement probably did not occur to him. Taylor's philosophy was that money was the motivator.

 PAUSE FOR THOUGHT

Is money a motivator? Consider your own situation. Would you still go to work if you won the lottery? Does money actually make you work harder? What about voluntary work? Think of examples where people go to work without being paid: life boat crew, the Olympic Games 'games makers'. What makes people work in that situation – where they are not paid?

11.6 HAWTHORNE STUDIES

It was not until the Hawthorne Studies conducted in the 1920s and 1930s that people started to realise that money might not be the only motivator at work. The first experiments tried to find out what might improve production, such as increasing light levels – the illumination experiments. The outcome was that production went up even when conditions returned to normal. It was deduced that the workers were more motivated as a result of being observed and of the interest being shown in them, rather than any change in physical environment. This has been termed the 'Hawthorne effect'. A later set of experiments by Elton Mayo – the 'relay assembly tests' – involved a group of women who worked together, away from the rest of the workers, and who were observed daily. Their supervisor listened to their suggestions and made changes in shortening shifts, giving breaks, and so on. Mayo concluded that having a sympathetic supervisor, being treated as 'special' (that is, away from the rest of the workers) and being able to form a cohesive, friendly workgroup contributed to their increase in productivity. The inference that Mayo drew from his experiments was that pay was not the only important factor to them.

A further set of experiments – the bank wiring room experiments – was set up to find out how payment incentives would affect productivity. The men involved in the experiment formed tightly knit informal groups who put pressure on each other to conform to their norms – they limited output, for instance, to a level that suited them. The results showed that workers responded to the social force of their peer groups rather than to the control and incentives of management. There has since been criticism of the Hawthorne experiments, but it is clear that pay is not the only motivator at work and that in HR we need to consider other factors in the motivation of staff.

11.7 THEORIES OF MOTIVATION

Two main approaches to motivation were proposed in the twentieth century. The first is based on *content theories*, in which people are said to have basic needs that provide the motive for their actions (that is, *what* actually motivates them). Second are *process theories*, which explain the cognitive (or mental) processes whereby people make decisions on how to act (that is, *how* people decide on what to do). This is based on our experience, which has taught us that certain behaviours produce particular outcomes and we will act in the expectation of achieving desired outcomes. In this way, motivation is generated through a mental process, rather than as a response to particular job factors.

11.8 CONTENT THEORIES OF MOTIVATION

By far the most well-known of these theorists is Abraham Maslow (1954, 1972). He proposed a *theory of growth motivation*, in which he classified five human needs and said that we behave in ways that are designed to have those needs met in a particular order of priority. The classification, which is referred to as a *hierarchy of needs*, is as follows:

1 **Physiological:** these are the basic biological needs that lead to our survival. Things such as:

   - thirst
   - hunger
   - fear
   - fatigue
   - sex.

   So, for example, we need money to buy food and drink for us to survive. This means that pay is going to be a motivator here in order to satisfy these needs.

2   **Safety and security:** the need for a danger-free, non-threatening and secure environment. At work, that might mean having job security and not being threatened by redundancy.

3   **Belongingness:** the need to feel part of humanity; attached to other individuals and groups. In the workplace, that could mean being part of a supportive, friendly team.

4   **Love and esteem:** the need to know where we stand in our relationships with others; how we are seen in terms of respect, especially by those whom we ourselves value. So, we need a job that offers us a chance to gain the respect of others, one where people look up to us perhaps and give us a feeling of worth.

5   **Self-actualisation:** the need to be self-fulfilled by developing our capacities and expressing them through our behaviour. This would be fulfilled by reaching our full potential at work and being in a job that stretches us and gives us the opportunity to show our expertise.

Maslow maintained that we progress through the hierarchy so that when we are sure that our physiological needs are or will be met, we will move up and turn our attention to safety and security. Next we turn to love and esteem needs and so on until we reach self-actualisation. He further classified the first, second and third levels as *lower-order needs* and the fourth and fifth as *higher-order needs*.

Other motivation analysts have proposed content theories similar to that of Maslow: for example Clayton P. Alderfer, whose research and publications took place between the 1940s and 1980s.

11.8.1 ERG THEORY

Alderfer (1972) proposed three categories of need that were similar to Maslow's classification. Essentially, he drew a parallel between Maslow's five categories and three categories of his own, which he referred to as *existence*, *relatedness* and *growth*. However, Alderfer did not believe that his needs were hierarchical but could be considered on a continuum.

Existence needs are concerned with physiological, safety and security needs and cover all needs of a material nature that are necessary for human survival. *Relatedness* needs mean those for love, esteem and belongingness, while *growth* needs are represented by achievement, recognition and the realisation of potential: what Maslow called self-actualisation.

11.8.2 MCCLELLAND

McClelland (1961) suggests that people have three possible needs:

● need for achievement (for example to achieve challenging goals) (nAch)
● need for affiliation (for example to belong to a group) (nAff)
● need for power (for example to influence and control others) (nPow).

Similar to Maslow and Alderfer, McClelland sees the importance of the need for friendship and to have our social needs met – that is, the need for an 'affiliation' with other people.

We can also see similarities to Maslow's need for self-esteem and self-actualisation in McClelland's need for achievement. The need for power may manifest itself in things such as teaching – demonstrating a need to encourage and help other people.

11.8.3 MOTIVATION-HYGIENE THEORY: F.W. HERZBERG

Herzberg (Herzberg et al, 1957) was principally interested in job satisfaction and proposed a two-factor theory of motivation.

He identified factors which might cause dissatisfaction at work (which he termed as 'hygiene' factors, or 'dissatisfiers'), which are different from the factors that motivate us ('motivators'). For instance, hygiene factors may be things such as pay, which we might not be happy with. We might feel that we are not paid enough, which will make us *dissatisfied* about work. But if we then receive a pay rise, Herzberg suggests that the pay will make us *satisfied*, but not necessarily more *motivated*. He says that there are a different set of factors – motivators – which are things that will make us work harder.

He thought that even if the hygiene factors were satisfied, it wouldn't necessarily make people motivated – it would just reduce their dissatisfaction. If we want people to be motivated to work harder, we need to ensure that the motivators are in place.

The most frequently occurring *hygiene* factors were:

- company policy and administration
- supervision – the technical aspects
- salary
- interpersonal relations – supervision, relationships with peers
- working conditions.

The most frequently occurring *motivators* were:

- achievement
- recognition
- the work itself
- responsibility
- advancement
- personal growth.

So according to Herzberg, if we want people to be more motivated, we need to increase the motivators – perhaps by making the work more interesting, by giving people praise, or by offering them chances for promotion.

PAUSE FOR THOUGHT

Having thought earlier about whether money motivates you, think now about what else might motivate you at work. Do you identify with any of Herzberg's factors?

11.8.4 EXTRINSIC AND INTRINSIC FACTORS

Herzberg's motivating factors are seen to be 'intrinsic' to the job. Intrinsic means that they are 'part of the job itself'. Having a challenging job that is fulfilling and enjoyable means that it is 'intrinsically satisfying' and is therefore likely to motivate you to work harder. (We tend to work hard and put more effort into things we enjoy.) Herzberg believed that it was important to improve the intrinsic job factors to motivate people. He suggested using job rotation and job enrichment to make the work more interesting and thus increase workers' motivation and performance.

Intrinsic job factors relate to things that actually make up the job, for example the tasks, the responsibilities of the job. They are an integral part of the job (see Table 11.2).

Table 11.2 Intrinsic job factors

Authority	The right amount for what I do and for the position of the job in the organisation/department
Responsibility	For my own productivity and quality of my work
Autonomy	Freedom to be a 'self-starter'; to make decisions about how the job might be carried out
Variety	The opportunity to exercise a variety of skills, removing boredom from the job
Recognition	For the quality of my work and general performance standard

PAUSE FOR THOUGHT

Is your own job intrinsically satisfying? Do you enjoy all aspects of the work? What do you look forward to when you come into work every day?

Extrinsic job factors might be described as those things that are not a part of the job itself, but that do impact on the job. Extrinsic job factors tend to be Herzberg's 'dissatisfiers' and might include:

- company policy
- health and safety
- managerial style
- working time
- culture
- holiday entitlement
- peer relationships
- pension scheme.

Note that none of the above factors is a *central feature of the job itself*.

'Extrinsic' motivation is related to tangible reward: salary, fringe benefits, the work environment and conditions of work, for example. Tangible rewards can cause people to focus on the reward, rather than on the task, whereas verbal rewards appear to keep people focused on the task itself and encourage them to want to do better.

PAUSE FOR THOUGHT

Would you work harder because there is a good health and safety policy? Or better holiday entitlement? Or because your boss gives you praise and recognition? Which do you think motivates you more? Extrinsic or intrinsic factors?

ACTIVITY 11.3

Think of some examples of jobs in your workplace? Can they be redesigned to increase intrinsic satisfaction?

11.8.5 THEORY X AND THEORY Y

McGregor (1960) claimed that managers may have a view of their staff that may affect how they treat them. Managers who have a *Theory X* viewpoint see the individual as having an inherent dislike of work, lazy and who will avoid work whenever possible. Continuous prodding, coercion and even threats are needed to get this kind of person to work. Managers who are authoritarian by nature tend to treat people in that way.

Managers who adopt a *Theory Y* view believe workers do not need to be coerced or threatened. They see workers as being self-motivated, willing to do their best and who can be trusted to work hard.

In other words, it is said that there are 'Theory X managers' and 'Theory Y managers'. A manager's attitude to their workers may thus influence how they treat them and this, of course, may impact on workers' motivation.

11.8.6 CRITICISMS OF NEED-BASED/CONTENT THEORIES

There are criticisms of these theories. In the case of Maslow, for example, the structured progression through the lower-order to higher-order needs seems not to occur for many people. Research has shown (Rauschenberger et al, 1980) that a significant number are happy to accept the satisfactions provided by the lower-order needs. People do need to fulfil themselves, but in many cases that fulfilment is achieved by pursuing interests *outside* the workplace. There is also criticism that little evidence supports its strict hierarchy; people may find that social needs, for instance, are more important than physiological needs – especially in some cultures (Adler 1986, pp.128–9). And often we don't address only one need at a time.

PAUSE FOR THOUGHT

What is your opinion of the theories mentioned above? Do you know managers who have a 'Theory X' viewpoint? What is your own view? Consider Maslow's theory – does your experience of workers' motivation fit in with this?

11.9 PROCESS THEORIES OF MOTIVATION: EXPECTANCY THEORY

This theory was first proposed by Vroom (1964) and is based on the idea that there is a relationship between effort and performance. We will exert effort if we expect it will result in an outcome that we value. We are motivated to do things because we believe they will lead to outcomes that we want.

Expectancy theory has three components:

- **expectancy:** the belief that effort will lead to desired performance
- **instrumentality:** the belief that the performance will lead to a reward
- **valence:** whether the reward is something the person actually wants and values.

We therefore choose to take a course of action based on the 'expectancy' (the probability that our efforts will lead to the desired outcome, such as better performance), the 'instrumentality' (whether we think our performance will *actually lead to* the outcome or reward) and the 'valence' (how much we really *value* the results of the outcome, is it a reward that we really want?).

If there is no *valence*, you won't be motivated, because you are not interested in achieving the outcome – that is, you have no *desire* for it (for example, if you are not able to drive, you will not be interested in a company car as a reward). With *expectancy* you might ask whether working harder will actually make you *perform* better (you may not have the skills necessary to improve your performance). With regard to *instrumentality*, you would consider whether your efforts will actually lead to getting a promotion. It may be that there are no opportunities for promotion in the company and so, however hard you work, you will never get promoted.

For managers seeking to motivate staff, it is important to bear all these in mind:

Expectancy: Do employees have the resources to perform well? Are they receiving the necessary training and support to help them succeed?
Instrumentality: Are there opportunities for promotion for those who do perform well? Is there budget funding to pay incentive bonuses to those who achieve their work targets and goals?
Valence: Are the rewards offered things that employees actually want (pay, extra holidays, responsibility)?

11.9.1 PORTER AND LAWLER'S EXPECTANCY THEORY

Porter and Lawler (1968) further develop Vroom's ideas. They point out that effort alone is not enough to produce a good performance; the individual has to be equipped with the right knowledge and skills. So good performance depends on having the right *ability* as well as believing that efforts will lead to the outcome and that the outcome is actually achievable and likely. They suggest that a further factor impacting on performance might be the lack of *role clarity*; if the individual doesn't understand what they are supposed to be doing, this will inevitably affect their performance.

CASE EXAMPLE 11.3

John works in marketing. He feels that he puts in a lot of effort at work, but does not possess the right skills to do the job well. He is not very creative and struggles with the job. His aptitude lies in doing detailed administrative work, rather than coming up with innovative ideas. It is unlikely that he will achieve the outcome or required performance, as he does not possess the right qualities for the job.

David works in accounts. He, too, puts in a lot of extra hours and effort, but because he has not been trained to do the job properly, his performance is poor.

Ken works in HR and feels completely overworked. He *does* have the right skills to do the job, but there are other factors outside his control that stop him from achieving the required performance – there is a lack of management support and his colleagues are overworked and are not willing to help him out.

Peter works in admin. He is well qualified and works hard. However, the job is unstructured and lacks proper organisation. Peter never really knows what he should be doing, or where he should prioritise. He spends a lot of time doing tasks but is never sure why he is doing them, or how they fit in with organisational objectives. Much of the day is spent rushing round trying to sort problems that should have been dealt with at an earlier stage. His job feels like a big muddle – and he never feels satisfied with his performance.

All four employees would like promotion and want a career with a good salary.

They know that the company offers high salaries for good performers. *Valence* of the rewards is high.

They also know that the company offers promotion to employees who do well and who achieve their work objectives: *instrumentality* is high.

However, in all four cases, *expectancy* will be low, as it is unlikely that, despite their efforts, a good performance will be achieved. However hard they work, they will not gain promotion. Motivation, then, will be low, as the employees know that they cannot expect to gain the rewards, despite all their efforts. However hard they work, they will not achieve success. This then becomes a real de-motivator and their eventual efforts may decrease.

ACTIVITY 11.4

After reading Case Example 11.3, what advice might you give to the managers of these employees? What can be done to improve their motivation? Use what you have read about expectancy theory to help you. Check your answers below. Did you think of the same suggestions? Or do you have different ones?

Some possible answers to Activity 11.4 include the following:

If management want to improve motivation for these employees, it will be necessary to change things. For example, John could change jobs so that he is working in an area that matches his aptitudes. David needs some training in accountancy so that he can become competent at the job. Ken needs a supportive manager who takes better control of his workload. Peter needs a proper job description and a chat to his manager about the role he is trying to fulfil. These solutions would increase expectancy as performance would be achievable and thus John, David, Ken and Peter would feel that the rewards are available to them.

PAUSE FOR THOUGHT

To apply the principles of expectancy theory, think about your motivation in relation to studying. Why do you work hard? *Valence* might relate to how much you want to gain the qualification – is it something you value (for example perhaps you study because you think a CIPD qualification is worthwhile)? You have an *expectancy* that by attending classes, reading books and working hard, you can attain a pass (the reward of the qualification is available to you if you put the effort in). *Instrumentality* means that you think a CIPD qualification will actually lead to a better job. If you want promotion to a job with a higher salary and believe that better qualifications will lead to that job, you will be motivated to study hard.

11.9.2 EQUITY THEORY

Adams' equity theory (1961) is based on the concept of fairness or, more accurately, a *fair exchange*. (See Chapter 12 for more on equity theory in relation to reward.) We know that people expect certain outcomes from their behaviour, but what is their perception of those outcomes in terms of value? In the work situation, for example, how does the value of the worker's input compare with the value of the related outcome: for example, 'a fair day's work for a fair day's pay'? This is a question of *perceived* value. Individuals might ask themselves: is the reward worth the effort I put in, compared with that of other people who I work with? How does our pay compare? This might arise when two people are doing what they perceive to be similar work but one gets paid less than the other. Of course, if this really was the case, and one person is male and the other female, there could be a case for an equal pay claim.

Adams' central theme is that it is the quest for perceived equity that motivates the work effort. If there are inequities, we will change our behaviour accordingly:

- Where reward values are perceived to exceed input values (that is, we are paid more than we think we are worth), the work effort will increase because of feelings of guilt or inadequacy. This may be the case where we feel that because we receive a very good salary, we should work harder (or, as is often the case, longer hours!) to earn it.
- Where the input values are perceived to exceed the reward values, the work effort will decrease in an attempt to redress the balance. So, if we think we are not being paid enough, we might not work as hard in future.
- A more constructive response to the feeling that we are not paid enough might be to ask for a pay rise, which would then remove the inequity.
- An alternative reaction to decreasing our work effort when we perceive the value of the work to be greater than the reward (for example when we feel we are not being paid enough for what we do, in comparison with what others get paid) might be that we feel constantly aggrieved (perhaps that others are 'getting away with less work') and act like a martyr.
- We might choose to compare ourselves with a different comparator, where we feel the comparison is fairer. We may 'count our blessings' that we are being paid more than others, even if we are not being paid as much as we would like.
- If we feel very strongly about the inequitable situation, eventually we may leave the job and go elsewhere, where perhaps we might feel our work effort will be rewarded more fairly.

It is likely, however, that the individual's perception of fairness, or a *fair exchange*, in the above respects will influence their *behaviour* rather than exclusively the work effort. An alternative to feelings of guilt or inadequacy, for example, could be fear – especially where the perceived value of the reward is considerably greater than the value of the worker's input. The worker may decide to look busy, as if they are overloaded with work, without actually putting in any extra effort.

RELATIVE VALUES

CASE EXAMPLE 11.4

Cathy works in an office as a clerical assistant with lots of people of her age. They all do similar work, completing administrative tasks, filing, answering queries, staffing reception – all the usual work associated with admin jobs. They are all on the same grade and work the same hours.

One day a new clerical assistant, Julie, is appointed and everyone is very friendly and keen to help her settle in. They answer her questions and support her in the new job, often taking on extra duties themselves to allow Julie time to learn the work. However, after a few days, Cathy finds out that Julie has been appointed at the top of the grade – she is earning more than everyone else in the office. Cathy tells her colleagues that Julie is on higher pay than all of them. The attitude then changes towards Julie – 'why should we help her when she is being paid more than us for doing the same work?' The offers to help cease, and although people are friendly, they are less likely to take on any extra support work or do anything outside of their own role to assist her. A manager then asks Cathy to take on some extra work. Cathy's response is that she is busy – 'give it to the new starter. She is being paid for it!' Resentment abounds amongst all the staff and relations are not as good as they were.

Question

Considering the ideas within the motivation theories discussed above, which theoretical ideas do you think can be applied to this situation? What can management do about the situation? Do you recognise Cathy's feelings? Have you ever had a similar experience? Would the explanation by management that 'Julie has more qualifications' help to ease the situation?

11.10 SUMMARY OF MOTIVATION THEORIES

Content theorists stress the importance of environmental and in-job factors and say that employees are more or less motivated by the presence or absence of desired factors. Process theorists, on the other hand, say that people *choose* to behave in particular ways because they expect to achieve desired outcomes. It is a *mental process* that motivates us towards a particular course of behaviour, and we speculate or predict the outcomes before we act. It is important for managers and HR practitioners to have a sound understanding of what motivates people to work. Motivation leads to performance, and the degree to which a knowledgeable and skilled individual will apply their best efforts to a task is determined by the degree to which they are motivated. (Performance itself is, of course, also dependent on the ability to do the job and the opportunity to practise skills or use knowledge.)

Despite the criticisms of content theories, there is no doubt that many employees are motivated by such extrinsic rewards as money, friendly relationships with team members and a managerial attitude that offers recognition, respect and consideration. It is also true that when people are faced with a number of alternative courses of action that might lead to the achievement of their desired outcomes, they go through the mental process of choosing the most appropriate behaviour. For example, 'Should I apply for the new job that pays more money even though it means working more hours?' or, as in the case above, 'Should I help someone who is paid more than me, or do I think that they are paid to work harder and I am not?'

Additionally, it is important to bear in mind the element of individual differences. People have their own unique attitudes to work, the job and the organisation, and they are not all driven by the same motivators or possible types of outcome.

 ACTIVITY 11.5

Think carefully about the theories you have just read about. Which ones do you think are particularly relevant in your workplace?

PAUSE FOR THOUGHT

So now that we understand more about motivation, how can we apply this knowledge to help improve performance in the workplace? How do we motivate people to work harder in practice? How do we measure how they are performing? How do we manage people's performance at work? The rest of the chapter will look at this in more detail.

11.11 PERFORMANCE MANAGEMENT

Performance management and performance appraisal are often confused as being the same thing. But they are not. Performance management is a holistic process that includes many activities that together contribute to the effective management of people at work, such as development, talent management, and even disciplinaries. Performance appraisal is just one of these activities.

KEY CONCEPT: PERFORMANCE MANAGEMENT

Performance management is a systematic and *strategic* approach to ensuring that employees' performance enables the organisation to achieve a competitive advantage by the achievement of objectives and the ultimate realisation of strategy. In order to do this, performance management needs to be integrated, aligning people policies and organisational objectives. It is a means of ensuring that we are all working towards the same goals. It is also a means of providing employees with information on what is expected of them, giving them feedback on their performance and offering them support and development so they can achieve their work objectives and ultimately contribute to the organisation's objectives. Performance management may encompass issues relating to the setting of objectives and measurement of standards, pay, development and feedback. One of the main means of managing performance is through performance appraisal.

11.11.1 DEFINITION: PERFORMANCE MANAGEMENT

Armstrong and Baron defined performance management in 1998 as:

> ...a process which contributes to the effective management of individuals and teams in order to achieve high levels of organisational performance. As such, it establishes shared understanding about what is to be achieved and an approach to leading and developing people which will ensure that it is achieved.

Armstrong and Baron's later work in 2004 provides evidence for performance management as a means of integrating a number of activities relating to individual contribution, such as talent management, career planning, and learning and development. They see it as an important way of managing people effectively. It involves a continuous cycle of assessing how people perform and seeing how that performance can be improved.

The CIPD (2009) survey of 507 organisations, *Performance Management in Action*, found 'a surprising degree of agreement that performance appraisal, objective-setting, regular feedback, regular reviews and assessment of development needs are the cornerstones of performance management'. It found that:

Appraisal, objective-setting and review and development still top the list of activities most commonly carried out under the banner of performance management. ... There is a trend of integrating performance management more firmly with other HR processes to manage talent, develop potential, plan careers or support individuals through coaching or mentoring.

It seems that performance management is indeed an important tool for managers today in increasing engagement, communicating with staff and integrating individual effort and goals with those of the business; as we stated above, 'aligning people policies and organisational objectives'.

11.11.2 PERFORMANCE MANAGEMENT THROUGH DEVELOPMENT

In order to achieve the right standards of performance, employees need to develop the right skills and capabilities to do their job. Even if we appoint someone with excellent skills, they will still need to develop their capabilities in the job. It is rare to get a candidate who can do the job to 100% perfection from day one. There should be relevant development opportunities that allow employees to improve their skills and knowledge, so that they can do a good job that meets (and exceeds) our standards.

Improved performance is also achieved through encouraging individual employees to create their own personal development plans (PDPs) so that they can build on their repertoire of competences and monitor their own performance. In a 2004 CIPD survey, *Managing Performance: Performance management in action* (Armstrong and Baron, 2004), 87% of organisations surveyed used a formal performance management process – for 83% of these, the focus was developmental.

Employees need to understand what is required of them in terms of standards and competence, in order to perform. And managers should communicate these standards, so that employees not only know what is expected, but also what they must do to improve.

We will return to the very important 'development' aspects of performance management later in the chapter.

11.11.3 PRINCIPLES OF PERFORMANCE MANAGEMENT

The principles of performance management are summarised by Armstrong (2014, p. 335) citing the research of Armstrong and Baron (1998, 2004):

- it's about how we manage people, it's not a system
- performance management is what managers do: a natural process of management
- a management tool that helps managers to manage
- driven by corporate purpose and values
- to obtain solutions that work
- only interested in things you can do something about and get a visible improvement
- focus on changing behaviour rather than paperwork
- based on accepted principle but operates flexibly
- focus on development, not pay
- success depends on what the organisation is and needs to be in its performance culture

 ACTIVITY 11.6

Think about what you have just read. Do you think you now know what performance management is? Is this how performance is managed in your organisation? If not, what are the differences?

11.11.4 PRINCIPAL COMPONENTS OF A PERFORMANCE MANAGEMENT SYSTEM

Marchington and Wilkinson (2012) outline the main components of performance management – see Figure 11.1.

Figure 11.1 Principal components of a performance management system

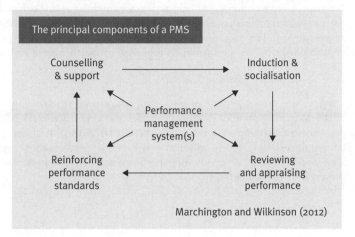

(Reproduced with the kind permission of the CIPD.)

Marchington and Wilkinson maintain that a good system of performance management should start at *induction*, where new starters should be told what their tasks are, and also how they fit into the organisation. They say that performance should be reviewed through daily interactions with managers and also through formal *reviews of performance*, as these are means of motivating employees and gaining their commitment. (As we saw earlier in this chapter, motivation and performance are closely linked.) From this, it can be established as to how well the employee is doing.

The third stage is to *reinforce performance standards*, which is about rewarding and developing those employees with good performance. It is also about dealing with poor performance issues, such as absence, lateness or poor attitude. If there are problems, these may be helped by the final stage of *counselling and support*, perhaps in the form of support from the line manager, or from professional help, such as occupational health or counselling services.

11.12 PERFORMANCE ASSESSMENT SYSTEMS

First, this section discusses and critically reviews the traditional approaches to managing individual performance that are still widely used in the UK. Following that we shall move on to discuss more recent approaches.

Performance management activities are designed to assess and improve employees' performance. How the activities are carried out has undergone considerable review since the 1980s, when HRM drew attention to the importance of performance as a means of achieving a competitive advantage. Some organisations, however, have either ignored or only partially adopted the principles and practices of HRM, and in the UK today there are a variety of assessment systems.

11.12.1 REWARD AND POTENTIAL

Many organisations use systems that base a person's pay on their past or current performance. Systems of this nature often involve the use of complex calculating mechanisms designed to culminate in 'grading' the appraisee. How they are treated thereafter in terms of pay and promotion prospects depends upon the level of the grading given. Clearly, such systems should be fair and assessment should be based on valid evidence. Most organisations use an analysis of individuals' performance when assessing suitability for promotion. The most commonly used system for assessing performance (whether related to pay or not) is 'performance appraisal' or 'performance review'.

11.12.2 DEFINITION: PERFORMANCE APPRAISAL

Performance appraisal is one of a range of tools that can be used to manage performance. As we saw in the Marchington and Wilkinson model above (Figure 11.1), appraisal is a part of performance management. According to the CIPD (2013q), it is 'an opportunity for individual employees and those concerned with their performance, typically line managers, to engage in a dialogue about their performance and development, as well as the support required from the manager'.

11.12.3 PERFORMANCE APPRAISAL

Appraisals are usually carried out as an interview between a manager and their subordinate. Normally your immediate boss will meet with you and discuss your progress and performance. Appraisals may or may not be linked to pay. If they are, it is usual for performance to be rated and assessed against previously set standards. Has the person achieved the targets set, and can this be linked to their incentive bonus, or salary rise?

But Armstrong and Baron's survey (2004) showed that many appraisals are carried out mainly with development in mind, rather than as a means for assessing past performance to pay a salary or bonus.

The results of performance appraisal may be used for a variety of purposes. In addition to those mentioned above, they may be any of the following:

- to reinforce performance standards
- to agree future standards
- to motivate the appraisee
- to identify training needs
- to address any problems the appraisee has encountered
- to assist in writing and progressing the individual's personal development plan.

11.12.4 ESTABLISHING ASSESSMENT CRITERIA

If we want to measure someone's performance, we need to set clear criteria about what is expected. This may be by comparing performance against the job description. Usually when a job description is drawn up, the job is analysed and the key criteria and tasks are identified. We might then set rating scales against each one. The factors on the list may include such job-related features as the knowledge and skill requirements, competences required for the job – for example leadership, teamwork, and so on – and perhaps several personal qualities such as initiative, intelligence, social skills, and so on, depending on the nature of the job and its requirements. Employees are then rated on the degree to which they possess these factors.

PAUSE FOR THOUGHT

Some organisations try to appoint good staff and then fit the job around the person, instead of matching the person to a specific job description. This might occur particularly with senior staff, graduates or very talented individuals. Do you think this would work in your organisation? How feasible do you think it might be?

11.12.5 TRADITIONAL SYSTEMS

There are several approaches within the traditional models of performance appraisal, but the one that is familiar to most managers and employees involves the manager in an annual interview with each individual employee to carry out a review of the employee's performance. The stages involved in this model are as follows:

1   About two weeks prior to the interview, the employee is given a self-assessment form that is designed to give the employee a measured way of assessing the key points in the job. The underlying idea is that the questions on the form will focus the employee's attention on to the various features of the job, and cause them to try to make an objective assessment of their own performance.

2   The manager also has a form that they complete in advance of the interview. It is important that the manager assesses the employee in the light of valid and verifiable information. The manager will rate the employee against a set of measurable criteria (behaviours or targets) or outcomes.

3   The two then get together to reach agreement over the degree to which the employee has met the required standards and targets.

11.12.6 RATING SCALES

There are a number of ways of rating people. We can use numbers: from 1 to 5, where 1 is 'poor' and 5 is 'excellent'. Or we can use words to rate them, such as 'poor', 'fair', 'good', 'very good', 'excellent'. Or even 'low', 'average', 'high'. Some may use a Likert scale, where statements are made, such as 'the employee works hard', to which the response is '1 – strongly agree', '2 – agree', '3 – neither agree nor disagree', '4 – disagree' or '5 – strongly disagree'. The drawback with ratings such as these is that it is very subjective. And not very scientific – what one person rates as 'very good' may be seen by someone else as merely 'good'. Bias can creep in too, where personality clashes can impact on the rating. If you and your manager don't see eye to eye, this will have an effect on your rating. If the appraisal rating is related to your salary increase or bonus, this can be of serious concern.

11.12.7 BEHAVIOURALLY ANCHORED RATING SCALES (BARS)

BARS attempts to measure performance in terms of behaviour. This focuses on what the individual actually does, rather than the person's capabilities or other qualities, although personal qualities such as initiative are deduced from what the individual actually achieves. Scales for this model are devised after discussion, observation of behaviour and analysis, usually by managers, HR practitioners and sometimes external consultants. Job analysis is critical to this process, since the first objective is to identify the key categories of performance in each job or *job family*.

With BARS, it is usual to have statements relating to performance in the job. For example:

- deals with customers in an expert way, always going beyond the call of duty
- deals with customers in a satisfactory way, so that the customer receives good treatment
- deals with customers in a slapdash way, leaving them barely satisfied
- deals with customers badly, leading to complaints.

There may be a rating scale applied to each statement, in order to add up to a total for each area of work. This process can be quite costly and time-consuming, as statements need to be given for all of the relevant job tasks, and examples of good and poor behaviour found. This can be a tedious process. However, the BARS approach reduces the effect of bias through a consensus, since several people establish the performance criteria. It can be useful in achieving credibility in that specific behaviours are cited, and calls for evidence, which can be justified much more easily than just rating someone as 'good' or 'poor'.

11.12.8 OBJECTIVE-SETTING

Some appraisals will not necessarily rely on a rating system, but will assess the employee against whether they have met targets. This approach might lead to a more fruitful discussion on performance, where employees do not feel they are being rated, but are merely discussing what they have (or have not) achieved. This process can be less confrontational and therefore more productive. It still requires both manager and employee to provide evidence as to whether the objective has been met. It also depends on both parties agreeing goals and objectives to be met for next time. And, of course, objectives may not be met for a variety of reasons, such as lack of resources, failure of colleagues to provide support, change of focus within the organisation, and so on.

CASE EXAMPLE 11.5

Paul has his appraisal and is worried about it as he doesn't feel that he has achieved the objectives that were set at his last appraisal meeting. There are several reasons for this: he has been overloaded with extra work due to a colleague being off sick and he hasn't had the opportunity to spend as much time as he would like on developing his own job. He has asked for support from other colleagues, but none has been forthcoming as everyone is so busy. Paul doesn't like to create a fuss, so has just 'got on with things' without complaint, but now is worried because he hasn't completed everything he should have.

He had also been promised some training to help him learn new techniques, but budget cuts and lack of time have prevented Paul from attending the course.

He feels that in view of the circumstances, it is unrealistic to expect him to accomplish all the objectives set.

In the appraisal interview, Paul discusses this with his manager and puts his side of the story. The manager has been under pressure himself and didn't realise that Paul had been experiencing such problems, nor that he needed help and support. As a result, the manager acknowledges Paul's efforts, offers Paul some additional help and agrees that the objectives were unachievable, given the circumstances.

The two of them discuss and agree a new set of objectives that are less ambitious for the coming six months and also agree to set some specific dates for the training course he was promised. Paul feels much better after the appraisal, having been able to discuss the issue, and now feels that something will be done about it. He is both relieved and re-enthused about the job, as he feels that the new objectives are achievable. The appraisal has also been useful in allowing both parties to get together and discuss the problems and achieve a satisfactory outcome.

11.12.9 CRITICISMS OF APPRAISAL SYSTEMS

It has to be borne in mind that all appraisal systems are susceptible to subjectivity on the part of the manager and the employee. As we saw above, when discussing rating scales, bias is often inherent in the appraisal system. It is very difficult to appraise someone totally objectively.

On the question of subjectivity, Roberts (2001) says that 'the inherent subjectivity of the assessment process may lead to claims of favouritism, bias and arbitrariness'.

A further problem is indifference or lack of interest, in which the process becomes a kind of form-filling exercise: an annual ritual in which the manager and the employee meet primarily to complete the forms, which end up gathering dust in a cabinet in the 'HR office'. If nothing comes out of the appraisal, people soon lose interest in its credibility and pay no attention to it. If, during the appraisal, an employee asks for training in a new area, and it is agreed, but then this does not happen, the employee will become disillusioned with the whole process.

There is also the danger that managers underestimate the importance of the role of appraisals in motivating staff and thus improving their performance. They see it as too time-consuming, instead of acknowledging the benefits of talking to their staff about their jobs. Appraisal should be a tool of good management.

11.13 MORE RECENT APPROACHES

Since the 1980s the attitudes of many organisations to people management have changed. In organisations that have adopted the principles and practices of HRM, with its lean and flattened structures, the manager and the employee have a close working relationship. The old-fashioned 'boss-subordinate' relationship has been replaced by what is more like a working partnership.

11.13.1 PERFORMANCE AGREEMENT AND PERSONAL DEVELOPMENT PLANS

In the situation described above, it is easier for the manager and the employee to reach agreement over the performance requirements and the job's key result areas. This can be turned into a *performance agreement*. The agreement, therefore, is based on the assumption that the employee is clearly aware of what is expected in terms of performance and of how their performance will be assessed. This may then be linked in to the employee's personal development plan (PDP), which outlines what skills need to be developed and how this might be achieved. Training plans, time off and financial assistance for courses or qualifications, or acquiring a mentor, may all be part of the support the employee needs.

11.13.2 360-DEGREE FEEDBACK

360-degree feedback has grown in popularity and is used for development purposes as well as for performance appraisal. What happens is that the people with whom the individual has day-to-day contact provide measures of their performance by completing a questionnaire that includes a rating scale designed to measure competences. Their data is fed into the process to be collated.

These may include, for example, the person's immediate boss, peers such as team colleagues and individuals, internal and external customers and suppliers, other work colleagues and subordinates. Clearly, in advance of the formal assessment, the manager and the employee already possess much of the criteria-related information that will be used, but it is equally clear that the manager will not always be present when the employee encounters others in the course of the job.

Figure 11.2 A model of 360-degree feedback

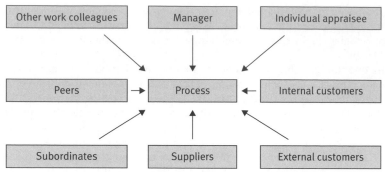

In Figure 11.2, you can see that all of the stakeholders feed their assessment data into the process. This shows the range of possibilities of who may be involved in the process.

Use of the outcomes

360-degree feedback is a versatile model, serving the purposes of the organisation and the individual. Organisations use it primarily for appraisal, but also for career management and resourcing purposes (Handy et al, 1996). The outcomes are also used for decisions on promotion and pay.

However, the advantage is that there is less chance of bias and it is seen as being a fairer means of assessment. There could still be a danger of responses being untruthful – how do you choose who to ask to complete the appraisal? Would employees only choose those who are likely to give them a good rating?

It is quite a cumbersome process and is very time-consuming, which also means it is more costly.

11.13.3 THE PERFORMANCE APPRAISAL INTERVIEW

An appraisal interview has many purposes:

- to review the employee's performance over the past appraisal period
- to identify development/counselling needs when discussing shortfalls in performance and future development
- to motivate the individual and set and agree future objectives and performance standards
- to identify support that the employee may need in achieving these objectives – this might be in terms of help from the manager, other staff, or extra resources required
- to agree arrangements for future development, career plans and, in particular, discuss and exchange ideas about the employee's personal development plan.

PAUSE FOR THOUGHT

How would you feel if, after taking so much trouble, you entered the interview room to find that the manager was short of time, rushing through the forms and – the most crushing factor – appears to be thinking about something else when you are talking? How can we make sure this doesn't happen – which all too often is the case?

Preparation

Particular attention should be paid to the venue. It should be held where both parties can be certain they will not be disturbed (for example, in a quiet room). Mobile phones should not be checked during the interview. The review itself should be planned well in advance, and an appropriate amount of time reserved for it. All of the relevant documentation and information should be fully completed in advance so that each party can see what has been written. While forms will be kept electronically, it may make sense to take notes during the interview and transfer the information at the end so that full attention is on the discussion rather than typing. It should, however, be done as soon as possible, before things are forgotten. Both the manager and the employee should agree the outcomes.

Outcomes to aim for

At the end of the interview, the employee should leave the room:

- believing that the manager is aware of their total job situation and any barriers that they face
- knowing exactly what lies ahead in terms of the standards and objectives to be achieved and that they are attainable
- being aware of any training and development that will be provided to help them achieve the objectives and to fill in any gaps in knowledge or skills
- with a general feeling that the perceptions, decisions and agreed action were fair and reasonable
- motivated to perform well.

Interviewing style

The interview has been defined as a conversation with a purpose. The purpose here is to exchange views and information about the employee's performance. Clearly, the manager is running the interview, but they should allow the employee equal participation. As we saw in the chapter on selection, interview technique is important and it is important to remain as unbiased and open as possible.

11.13.4 MANAGING POOR PERFORMANCE

It is important to see the benefits of appraisal as a means of encouraging better performance and as a tool for motivation. However, there may be times when the employee's performance is poor and the manager will need to have a conversation with them that addresses that performance: instruction should be given in very straightforward terms about how they must improve. This, of course, can be difficult – none of us like having to give negative feedback. It is much easier to be able to tell an employee that they are doing well and to give praise than to tell them that they are not doing as well as is expected.

In this case, it can be useful to ask the employee to say which areas they think they are not performing well in – often the employee will be aware of their own weaker areas and will voice their concerns. It is far easier to pursue this if the employee raises it first. Being told that they are not doing well can lead to the employee becoming defensive and can turn the whole appraisal process into a negative experience and one that can be a real de-motivator. Be careful, however, not to turn the appraisal interview into a 'disciplinary interview'. If there are serious issues relating to performance (incapability, irresponsible behaviour, being late for work, and so on), these should be addressed at a separate disciplinary interview and not in the appraisal.

ACTIVITY 11.7

It has been said that 'performance appraisal looks like a good idea on paper but seldom works well in practice'. Do you think there is any truth in this statement? If you do think so, why?

11.14 PERSONAL DEVELOPMENT PLAN (PDP)

As we saw earlier, one of the main focuses of performance management is development and part of the appraisal process is to elicit a personal development plan (PDP). Personal development planning (PDP) can be seen as an essential component of performance management, and the CIPD encourages its members to develop themselves and take responsibility for their own continuing professional development (CPD).

PAUSE FOR THOUGHT

Does everyone need to be a high-flyer? What do we do about those people who just want to come to work and do their job, without wishing to be developed or get promoted? Should we let them just do their job?

KEY CONCEPT: PERSONAL DEVELOPMENT PLANNING

Personal development planning is a dynamic process and is a useful part of continuous professional development. It is a means of reflecting on learning and identifying what you need to work on in the future. The plan itself is a draft describing how you propose to learn and develop yourself and your achievements to date. You need the active co-operation of your line manager or an HR practitioner to guide you through the process, although you are responsible for your own further development.

11.14.1 WHO BENEFITS FROM PDP?

There are two main considerations in PDP. First, the organisation needs you to develop yourself to enhance your performance and thus aid the business in achieving its objectives. Second, there are your own needs in terms of career development: you develop transferable competences, increase your repertoire of knowledge and skills, and thereby enhance your flexibility and employability. These considerations are not mutually exclusive, since you may centre your planning on your current job (to enhance your performance) and future aspirations (to improve your own career prospects). You can achieve these aims concurrently by:

- identifying your developmental needs and setting learning objectives
- costing and time-scaling your plan (most employers will underwrite this)

- using a wide range of developmental methods
- making yourself aware of your own learning style and using it to advantage
- identifying suitable sources of relevant information and practical support
- maintaining a comprehensive record of your current activities and plans for future development.

A PDP is made up of your past, present and future learning. First, this involves reflecting upon your past and current experiences and writing down what you have learned from them. Second, clarify your current position by reviewing and recording the competences you now possess. Third, you can then identify the point at which your future planning commences and have some ideas about what things might be part of your future development. This might include attending a course, researching a particular subject, improving a skill or gaining a qualification. For example, at the end of a course such as the Certificate in HR Practice, you may decide you want to continue with further CIPD qualifications to enhance your career prospects – this could go into your plan for the future.

11.14.2 LEARNING ACTIVITIES

You cannot go through a day without learning something:

- all of your experiences of listening to what others have to say
- observing what they do and how they do it
- solving problems at work and at home or in your local community
- helping others to develop by coaching them
- reading good-quality material and watching TV documentaries.

Traditionally, many people initially turn to training courses to develop themselves and, undoubtedly, if you are motivated to learn and careful about your choice of course in terms of its relevance to your needs, your knowledge and competences will increase. There are, however, several additional learning sources:

- **E-learning (electronic learning):** information technology makes it possible for you to learn sitting at the computer.
- **Project and assignment work:** this is learning from experience. Usually it involves problem-solving and training. You have to learn to complete the work satisfactorily.
- **Learning from others:** see how other people go about their work. You need to find those people who are generally regarded as being good at what they do. Talk to them and find out why they do things in the way they do.
- **Mentoring:** identify someone who is prepared to coach or mentor you.
- **Studying job descriptions and role definitions:** choose more senior-level jobs or jobs that you aspire to. Study them to identify the knowledge and competences that are required to do the work.

11.14.3 SELF-APPRAISAL

As you make progress, write down the details of your development and review your situation intermittently. This involves studying and updating your plan, noting your recent learning and deciding on the best way forward. A good time to do this is immediately after your appraisal interview at work, when you have all of your manager's comments to hand along with the suggestions they have made for your future development. It is worthwhile revisiting the plan at frequent intervals to see how you are progressing.

ACTIVITY 11.8

In your organisation, or one with which you are familiar, analyse the performance appraisal system with a view to updating and improving it. Prepare yourself to answer questions on why your proposed changes would improve the system.

11.15 SUMMARY

We have looked at the differences between performance, performance management and performance appraisal.

Performance management is wide-ranging and can involve such things as managing absence or handling disciplinary issues, but from a more positive viewpoint it is about improving performance – most commonly by the use of appraisal interviews. This may mean looking at past performance or setting targets for the future. To improve performance, employees need to be motivated to work harder or more effectively and, with this in mind, the chapter has discussed a number of motivation theories.

The appraisal interview has its critics and, to be effective, it needs to be executed professionally and with care. If the appraisal uses a rating system, there is a danger that bias may creep in and the process may be discredited, leading to disenchanted and demoralised staff. Carried out correctly, performance appraisal can be a useful tool in motivating staff and improving the performance of individuals and, consequently, of the business. One way of reducing the effects of bias is to use 360-degree appraisals, though these are costly and time-consuming to do.

A major way of improving performance is to undertake training and development and this should be a key focus of appraisal. Appraisal should be about agreeing joint objectives, with support given to help an employee to develop their skills and abilities, to enable them to perform more effectively. One way of doing this is to write a personal development plan as a result of the appraisal, which summarises the learning required to achieve the objectives set.

REVIEW QUESTIONS

1 How would you define performance management?

2 What is performance?

3 What factors influence performance?

4 What is a 'content' theory of motivation? Give two examples.

5 What are the similarities between Maslow's and Alderfer's theories?

6 How would you differentiate between intrinsic and extrinsic job factors?

7 How does McGregor's X-Y Theory describe managers' attitudes to employees?

8 What are the four components of performance management according to Marchington and Wilkinson? How do they link together?

9 What are the advantages and disadvantages of using 360-degree feedback as an appraisal process?

10 What criticism can be made of appraisals?

11 How would you define personal development planning?

12 Who benefits from personal development planning and in what ways?

EXPLORE FURTHER

BOOKS

ARMSTRONG, M. and BARON, A. (2004) *Managing performance: performance management in action*. London: Chartered Institute of Personnel and Development.

This is a major text on the subject.

ARMSTRONG, M. (2009) *Handbook of performance management: an evidence-based guide to delivering high performance*. London: Kogan Page.

This is a more recent text that covers the entire subject of performance management in some depth.

Or try HUTCHINSON, S. (2013) *Performance management: theory and practice*. London: Chartered Institute of Personnel and Development.

HOLLYFORDE, S. and WHIDDETT, S. (2002) *The motivation handbook*. London: Chartered Institute of Personnel and Development.

This book makes a worthwhile read and covers key motivation theories.

There are many books covering motivation and organisational behaviour. These include:

HUCZYNSKI, A.A. and BUCHANAN, D.A. (2013) *Organizational behaviour*. Harlow: Prentice Hall.

MULLINS, L.J., with CHRISTY, G. (2013) *Management and organizational behaviour*. 10th ed. Harlow: Prentice Hall.

WEB LINKS

The CIPD factsheet on performance management gives a good overview of the subject. Available at: **www.cipd.co.uk/hr-resources/factsheets/performance-management-overview.aspx**

Also see the CIPD factsheet on appraisal: **www.cipd.co.uk/hr-resources/factsheets/performance-appraisal.aspx**

Employee Reward

12.1 INTRODUCTION

This chapter introduces the concept of reward, including monetary and non-monetary rewards. Payment is seen as a component of the 'exchange' element of a contract (consideration) between employer and employee. Also, by some academics, it is seen as a motivator and as an indication of how employees are valued by the organisation in terms of their contribution to the achievement of objectives.

The concepts of *incentive* and *equity* systems of payment are explained, including job evaluation, payment by results, performance-related pay and non-cash rewards. Reward also has strong implications for equal treatment, that is, paying equal value for equal worth. The subsequent discussion deals with the issues raised both in legal and business terms.

The chapter includes explanations of the management philosophies, strategies and policies that lead to the choice and development of reward systems, and an examination of the factors that determine pay levels. The discussion also includes new and traditional systems of payment.

12.2 PERCEPTIONS OF REWARD

The terms *reward* and *reward management* are relative newcomers to the managerial vocabulary. Before the 1980s, references were made to 'money', 'pay' and 'systems of payment'. Today the word 'reward' is often used to refer to payment.

12.2.1 DEFINING REWARD

It is not possible to define reward in a single statement because perceptions of it vary from one person to another and from one situation to another. A manager, for example, might define reward as 'the payment that an employee receives in accordance with the value of his or her work contribution to the organisation'. An employee, on the other hand, may say that it is 'the return that he or she receives on the investment of his or her time, knowledge, skills, loyalty and commitment'. Non-financial factors such as some benefits and also the facilities that the organisation offers to its employees are also regarded as reward, as are recognition, praise and career development.

In fact, reward literally means something that is given or received in return for a service or for merit. It is often financial. There are differences in terminology between the UK and the USA. In the USA the word *compensation* is used instead of *reward*. The term compensation sounds more like the outcome of a lawsuit than payment for a valued performance. 'Pay' or 'payment' in the forms of wages and salaries are what spring to mind first when one thinks of reward in the organisational context, but since 'reward' entails more than just money, 'reward' is the word that will be used throughout this chapter. When dealing with the detail, however, we shall call things what they are, such as *wages*, *salaries* and *payment*.

12.3 HRM AND REWARD

According to Pointon and Ryan (2004), 'reward management' has often been viewed as the 'poor relation' of HRM, concerned with 'systems, figures and procedures'. A poor relation it might be, but, as Cox et al (2010) point out, an organisation's reward strategy is central to the employment contract. Central it may be to the employment contract, but there are concerns about the low incidence of organisations which have a written and active reward strategy. The CIPD (2013e, p.8) *Reward Management* survey indicates that only 'three in twenty organisations currently issue total reward statements to employees, with another one in ten planning to introduce them in 2013.'

Organisations that have adopted the principles and practices of HRM can legitimately argue that their reward philosophies are consistent with and act in support of other HRM principles; for example, they reward 'good performance' because this adds value to the organisation. An organisation which has adopted the 'best practice' or 'high road' HRM strategy sees its employees as its most important resource. Investing in that resource through the development of knowledge and skills enhances employees' performance. The improvement in performance thus generates an increased return on the investment (see Chapter 3).

12.3.1 THE NEW PAY

Since 1990, when E.E. Lawler coined the phrase *new pay*, there has been a great deal of activity in industry and commerce concerning the fitness of the older and more traditional pay systems to serve the needs of modern organisations.

The managers of such organisations rightly believe that the success of the organisation is ultimately determined by the performance of its employees. It follows, therefore, that an organisation needs to recruit and retain people who are appropriately skilled and flexible in their outlook. Ideally an organisation would wish its employees, or future employees, to be prepared to become involved with, and committed to, its purposes and share the belief that the achievement of the organisation's objectives is a good thing, not only for the organisation, but also for the employee. This is the idea of the unitary approach (refer to Chapter 3 for further detail). It is rooted in the philosophies of HRM.

It follows that the reward strategy and systems must support the overall business strategy, indeed that they should flow from it, and that pay should be commensurate {meaning – *corresponding with and in proportion to*} with an employee's contributions.

KEY CONCEPT: THE 'NEW PAY'

The underlying philosophy that follows the principles of HRM brought a fresh strategic approach to reward management; reward is firmly linked to actual performance. According to Heery (1996), new pay, which reflects a unitary approach, is often contrasted with 'old pay', which reflects a pluralistic approach in that it (old pay) uses job-evaluated grade structures, payment by time and seniority-based financial rewards and benefits. New pay is focused on paying for contribution and not paying for time served in the role.

Schuster and Zingheim (1992), who further developed Lawler's concept of 'new pay', state that:

> The new pay view provides that organizations effectively use all elements of pay – direct pay (cash compensation) and indirect pay (benefits) – to help them form a partnership between the organization and its employees. By means of this partnership, employees can understand the goals of the organization, know where they fit into those goals, become appropriately involved in decisions affecting them, and receive rewards to the extent they have assisted the organization to do so. New pay helps link the financial success of both the organization and its employees.

PAUSE FOR THOUGHT

How would you like to be paid for the work you do? Figure 12.1 is an edited table of results from a survey conducted by the CIPD in 2011. It depicts the views of employees about how they are paid.

For people working in the *private sector*, personal performance (54%) is the most important basis on which employees would like to be paid, followed by inflation/cost of living increases (41%) and experience (31%). The *public sector* employee offers a different perspective. Inflation/cost of living increases (59%) is the most significant factor which they believe should be considered when determining pay, followed by personal performance in the job (41%). The emphasis

on trade union negotiated pay deals also plays more of a significant role for those in the public (21%) compared with the private sector (6%) (CIPD, 2011).

Consider the following questions:

● Why do you think that significantly more people in the public sector consider that having a union-negotiated pay deal is the best way to determine what employees should be paid?

● What does 'being paid the going rate for the job' mean?

● On what basis would you wish to be paid? Would it be on the basis of time served in a job or how you contributed to the performance of the organisation?

12.4 NON-FINANCIAL REWARDS

The total range of what might be classified as 'reward' is considerable and may reach beyond the workplace. Few firms provide the complete range of what is possible, and others prefer to provide only the rewards which are specified in employment rights statutes, such as, for example, a healthy and safe work environment, the minimum provision of annual holidays and leave associated with maternity, paternity and adoption rights, and access to some form of pension scheme.

Figure 12.1 Basis on which employees would like to be paid

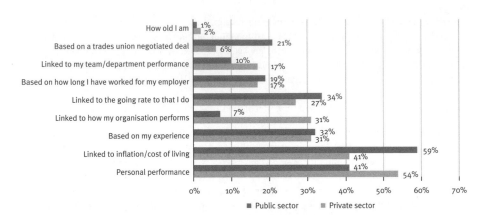

CIPD (2011) *Employee Attitudes to Pay*. Annual survey report. Printed with kind permission of the CIPD.

12.5 BENEFITS – A MIX OF FINANCIAL AND NON-FINANCIAL REWARDS

There are, however, a range of benefits and facilities that are designed to demonstrate to employees that the organisation values them and is therefore prepared to enhance the quality of their life at work. An organisation's managing philosophy will be influential in defining its 'benefits package' as also would be the need to match those (benefits) offered by similar organisations. The concept has strong links to employee retention and attraction. Typically a 'benefits package' might include:

● An attractive pension scheme. Many organisations used to provide a pension scheme which gave employees a pension that was a percentage of their final salary, depending upon years served with the organisation. Increasingly, though, this type of pension provision is being phased out because of financial cost reasons. The schemes are either being closed to new employees or closed altogether. In the latter case, existing members are transferred to an alternative, less costly, but not as attractive scheme. Information about the prevalence of pension schemes can be found in the CIPD (2013e), *Reward Management* annual survey report, which is available from: **www.cipd.co.uk/hr-resources/survey-reports/reward-management-2013.aspx**
● Life insurance
● Access to private medical care
● Help with long-term sickness
● Assistance with family matters, such as bereavement, crèche facilities, help with schooling and transport and supported housing for families who are moved around geographically
● Counselling services
● Access to occupational support schemes (OSS) and employee assistance programmes (EAP)
● Staff restaurant and social and recreational facilities
● Preparation for redundancy and retirement
● Loans for season ticket transport costs
● Car parking
● Advisory services for contemporary welfare issues, such as HIV/AIDS and sexual health generally; problems with drugs and alcohol and the formulation of policies on smoking in and around the workplace and stress management.

PAUSE FOR THOUGHT

The cost of getting old

Getting people to prepare for old age by saving for retirement is one of the most significant problems for the UK Government. How much income would you wish to receive each year when you retire? The Government provides some help but will not fund a preferred lifestyle. The following are some of the factors that would need to be considered when deciding how to fund a chosen style of retirement living.

Accommodation is a significant cost in anyone's life. If you started to buy a house in your early working life you may have paid the mortgage {meaning – the money you borrowed from a bank or building society to pay for your house or flat} by the time you retire; but you may not have. So you will have mortgage payments to fund or rent to pay – if you have never bought property.

The cost of energy – gas, electricity and oil – is averaging at over £1,000 per year for homes. And then there is transport, food, entertainment, and so on, to build into your annual retirement budget.

The maximum state pension (May 2014) is £113.10 week for a single person. This does not go far towards meeting the costs of living listed above. Let us assume that you would like £20,000 per year income on which to live. The money from a workplace or other personal pension could make it much easier for you financially when you are retired. Consider the following example: for a man born in January 1990, his state pension age is 68 years. Let us be pessimistic and assume that he only lives another 12 years, that is, until he is 80. The following gives some idea of the amount of money required to fund his retirement:

Annual income from the state pension (taking 2014 values) = £5,881

Annual 'top-up' required from personal savings or pension fund = (£20,000 – £5,881) = £14,119

The total 'draw-down' fund required to sustain the 12 years of retirement = £14,119 x 12 = **£169,426**

However, the £169,426 does not allow for any contingency expenditure {meaning, in this case – extra unplanned expenditure} that he might have need of to meet in an emergency, such as a roof repair or repairs to his car. Also the amount of a pension received which is greater than £10,000 per annum (basic tax rate, May 2014) would be subject to income tax of 20%.

The state pension is subject to income tax, but not taxed at source, so any tax due is taken from the private pension fund. The implication of this is that £10,000 of the £14,119 would be taxed at 20%. In real terms, therefore, it is worth £8,000 to the pensioner, per annum. The 'effective pension', that is, the amount that the pensioner has available to spend, is £18,000 per annum, a shortfall of £2,000 on the desired amount.

To receive a £20,000 'in-hand' pension per annum when retired, the employee would have to save at the rate of approximately £16,619 per annum. Thus the size of the required 'pension pot', to support the desired standard of living becomes:

Pension pot = 12 years x £16,619 per year = **£199,428**

The big question is: how do you fund a retirement which provides a reasonable lifestyle? What provision do you intend to make?

The state pension age is the age at which an individual receives a pension from the state until the time that they die.

From an employment perspective the default retirement age, which was previously set at 65 years in the UK, has been phased out (October 2012) (refer to Chapter 16, 'Understanding Employment Law', and Chapter 17, 'Ending the Employment Relationship', for further discussion on this topic). Therefore, unless the employing organisation can, on some objective grounds, set a default retirement age, the majority of employees can work for as long as they wish.

Dismissing an employee on age-related grounds would be seen as 'unfair' on the grounds of age discrimination. The Government offers further guidance on this topic at: **www.gov.uk/retirement-age**.

To find out at what age you will receive a state pension, go to: **www.gov.uk/calculate-state-pension**

 ## ACTIVITY 12.1

Funding retirement – government support for pensions

One way for an employee to fund their retirement is to join either a company or personal pension scheme. The Government, through part-funding of a workplace pension scheme, is encouraging people to plan for their retirement. The Government gives the following example (the detail is available at: **www.gov.uk/workplacepensions**):

John puts in £40, his employer puts in £30, and the Government adds £10 tax relief.

A total of £80 will be paid into John's pension.

You have recently transferred into the payroll section of your company. Your new supervisor, who is a member of the Pensions Management Institute, asks you, as part of your professional development, to make a presentation on the 'relatively' new Government-initiated 'auto enrolment' scheme for workplace pensions. The presentation is intended as an update for company employees who will be affected by the changes. Particularly, she asks that you include in your presentation details about the following:

- Identify who will and will not be automatically enrolled.
- Explain whether employees have to opt into the scheme.
- Explain if an employee can opt out of the scheme.
- Define the age at which employees become eligible to be enrolled.
- Explain if there are any criteria which relate to the annual salary received by an employee.
- Discuss the issues related to location of work, that is, does the scheme apply if the employee is working at an overseas location for the company?
- Explain how the law applies to foreign nationals.

Sources of information:

- Acas: **www.acas.org.uk/index.aspx?articleid=3965**
- The perspective and advice from Age UK: **www.ageuk.org.uk/money-matters/pensions/**
- Government website: **www.gov.uk/retirement-age**
- The NHS view on the default retirement age and pensions: **www.sept.nhs.uk/Equality-and-Diversity/Workforce-Sub-Sections/Information-for-Equality-Groups/~/media/SEPT/Files/Equality/Workforce/QA%20Regarding%20Retirement.ashx**
- Pensions Management Institute: **www.pensions-pmi.org.uk/home/**

12.5.1 CAFETERIA, OR FLEXIBLE BENEFITS

Some organisations offer a range of benefits from which an employee may choose from a mixture of cash and benefits. Organisations, through leverage of size, can get good deals against costs of benefits, which they can either offer to employees at no cost or at a substantially reduced cost. This allows employers to offer choices geared to their employees' lifestyle needs and changes, such as marriage, the arrival of children and even divorce. Wherever an employee receives a benefit there can be a tax liability, so employers need to consider this carefully before making promises that may be expensive to keep.

Flexible benefits are also associated with the employee value proposition (EVP) in terms of the type of person the organisation wishes to recruit. By getting the reward mix correct, the organisation is more likely to be able to recruit successfully the type of person it seeks. Hutchinson (cited in CIPD, 2007) states: 'Flexible benefits, as a concept, gives focus to investments and empowers employees to choose for themselves the benefits that best suit their needs.' As a suggestion the report (p.16) advises that employees can '. . .buy and sell benefits to achieve personal aims'. 'Stand-alone' benefits include:

- salary sacrifice schemes that buy enhanced pension benefits, childcare vouchers and so on
- holiday buying and selling plans
- voluntary contributions to buy higher levels of cover for certain benefits
- cycle purchase schemes.

12.5.2 THE TOP BENEFITS GIVEN TO STAFF

The top benefits given to staff, according to the CIPD (2013e) *Reward Management* survey report, are shown in Table 12.1.

Table 12.1 Top benefits given to staff, by sector

Universal Benefit	Manufacturing	Private Sector	Public Service	Voluntary, Community not-for-profit
Allow internet purchases to be delivered to work				✓
Car parking (onsite, free or subsidised)	✓			
Childcare vouchers				✓
Christmas party/lunch	✓	✓		
Death in service/life assurance		✓		
Enhanced maternity/ paternity leave			✓	
Paid leave for bereavement	✓	✓	✓	✓
Paid leave for military service			✓	
Paid leave greater than 25 days	✓		✓	✓
Pension scheme	✓	✓	✓	✓
Tea/coffee/cold drinks – free		✓		
Training and career development	✓	✓	✓	✓

Data reproduced with kind permission of the CIPD.

Further information from the CIPD survey (2013e) indicates that one-fifth of organisations use flexible benefits schemes and a further one in twenty planned the introduction of flexible benefits for 2013, that is, prior to publication of the CIPD report. Three in twenty organisations offer voluntary/affinity benefits, with a further one in thirty introducing them during 2013.

Affinity benefits are voluntary benefits which are products and services that are available through an employer for purchase by employees, usually at a discount. It is the employee who pays for them out of their own taxable income. These schemes differ from flexible benefits schemes as the employee, rather than the employer, pays for the cost of the benefits. The type of benefit this might involve could be, for example, membership of a fitness centre. Given that sufficient employees are interested, the employer would negotiate a preferential membership fee for their staff. The cost to the employer would be the administrative time costs, that is, the opportunity costs, associated with setting up the arrangement with the fitness centre.

 ## ACTIVITY 12.2

Given the opportunity to start with a clean sheet, what would you include in a benefits system and why? What criteria would you use to guide you in your decision-making? You may find some help within the CIPD's factsheets on:

● Employee benefits: **www.cipd.co.uk/hr-resources/factsheets/employee-benefits.aspx**

● Strategic and total reward: **www.cipd.co.uk/hr-resources/factsheets/strategic-reward-total-reward.aspx**
● Flexible and voluntary benefits: **www.cipd.co.uk/hr-resources/factsheets/flexible-voluntary-benefits.aspx**

12.6 REWARDS WITH FINANCIAL VALUE

People might receive special rewards, perhaps for performance, such as the successful conclusion of a particular project, or for making a useful suggestion or delivering on targets set over the previous year. One of the most important aspects of such rewards, however, is the influence of the element on individual differences. Porter and Lawler (1968), for example, point out that it is just that type of performance that produces job satisfaction. It is of importance that it is understood by managers where an expected reward stands in an individual's value system. The reward has to be valued; it has, in other words, to have a positive 'valance'. The level of values that people place upon types of rewards differs from one individual to the next.

 ## A REWARD WORTH STRIVING TO ACHIEVE (VALANCE)

CASE EXAMPLE 12.1

The wrong prize and the wrong message

Sathi enjoyed his job and he was also very good at what he did; and, what is more, he was a 'company man'. He had been with the firm for ten years. He started in the office and over time, through hard work and commitment, he had progressed to become one of the company's best sales representatives. He

understood the company's products, which were specialist sensors: weight sensors, temperature sensors, humidity sensors, and so on. Basically, the company could provide high-quality sensors to measure just about any physical quantity. He regularly achieved and sometime bettered his sales targets.

Sathi's 'sales patch' stretched from Stoke-on-Trent to the far north of

Scotland. He regularly visited his clients and provided a good first-stop contact for them should they experience a problem with the products he had sold.

Although Sathi had a large area to cover, he did so either by taking the train or driving his company car. He could fly to visit his more distant clients but he chose not to because he was terrified of flying. His boss knew this. He found that he could cope with the travelling part of his role so long as his feet were not too far off terra firma.

The past year had been good. Sathi had won some very lucrative long-term contracts with the Ministry of Defence and also with a large crane manufacturer. He felt that he was in with a good chance of winning this year's sales prize and was excited by the prospect, because normally the prize reflected the value of contracts won.

On 21 December at the company's annual Christmas party, the winner and runner-up for the sales prize was announced. Sathi had won the prize: a two-week, all-expenses paid holiday to North America. Sathi was happy that he had won, and he was sure that he would be able to change the holiday, but … the nature of the prize took the sparkle off the event for him.

12.7 FACTORS THAT INFLUENCE REWARD

Reward systems are founded upon the organisation's strategies and policies for compensating employees for their performance, and the investment of their time, knowledge, skills and competence. The level of rewards employees are given is based on the perceived value of the individual to the organisation, the nature and rarity of their skills on the employment market, the industry sector and the financial health of the organisation.

The availability of labour rises and falls with the economy, and the intensity of competition for the appropriate staff to fill vacancies fluctuates accordingly. The new millennium brought with it a 'talent war', fuelled by the skill demands of ever-advancing technology and the fierceness of global competition. Obviously, the size and nature of the rewards that are offered to those who possess the required skills will determine the organisation's ability to compete effectively for, as well as retain, staff. The recession in the UK, which commenced in 2008, saw a reduction in turnover in staff, that is, fewer employees left their current employment voluntarily; they preferred to remain in their jobs and not actively seek alternative employment (CIPD/Hays, 2013, p.39). Many reasons influence a person's decision to change jobs: an increase in pay, opportunity for promotion, types of benefits, being nearer to home or the chance of a new lifestyle. However, during times of recession there is a natural tendency for employees to remain with an employer. A job held might not pay as well as a potential alternative but a perception of job security is likely to influence a decision to leave.

There is always a tension between internal and external market forces. There is the need to pay the 'going rate' for people with particular and sought-after skills, but on the other hand there is a need to maintain internal pay consistencies. For example, paying a newcomer to the organisation, perhaps someone who has potential for development and is seen as a future talent, more than those who are already in employment with the organisation may create dissatisfaction in staff already in employ. Tensions clearly can arise, so there is a requirement upon the remuneration specialist to maintain a watching brief over the changes that may occur in external remuneration practices. This can be achieved by either joining a 'jobs club', where local employers get together to benchmark jobs in terms of pay and benefits offered, or paying a commercial organisation, such as Towers Watson, and so obtain access to their pay and benefits survey data.

The strategy adopted by the organisation should address its need to obtain, retain and motivate committed, competent, experienced and loyal employees.

12.7.1 DETERMINING REWARD STRATEGY

The organisation has to be *financially able* to provide the levels of reward that enable it to compete with other organisations for staff. When formulating a reward strategy, therefore, decisions have to be made about how much of the financial resource can be allocated to reward. Such decisions are influenced by the current and expected future profitability of the organisation, the negotiating positions of the relevant parties and the percentage of overall costs that are represented by pay.

The organisation's freedom to formulate reward strategy and set salary and wage rates is constrained by internal and external influences and obligations. The main pressures may be summarised as follows:

- the organisation's values and pay stance
- the organisation's ability to sustain pay levels
- comparisons with what other organisations pay
- national and industry-wide trends
- trade unions'/employees' demands
- current and expected productivity levels
- legislation on pay, for example the minimum wage levels
- UK government and European policies on pay
- stakeholder and shareholder influence
- changes in technology, the economy and the labour market
- cost of living increases
- the availability of particular skills
- levels of knowledge and competences required
- the evaluation of employee performance
- the relative values of the jobs, as defined by job evaluation.

The reward strategy should support the business strategy. HR strategy is usually derived from the business strategy and the reward strategy flows from the HR strategy. The reward strategy can be very influential in the business because it can impact upon the ways people work and also whether or not individuals wish to remain with or come to work for the organisation. Reward can affect:

- Resourcing, attracting and retaining people
- Development of employees by linking development to skill or competence-related pay
- The employee relations environment because the way in which reward is seen to be developed and operated affects the climate of trust, fairness and involvement with employees; it is key to the notion of employer branding (Allen, 2008). The findings of research by Biswas and Suar (2013, p.100) indicate that 'employer branding can be affected by four employees' values, namely, social value, interest value, developmental value and economic value'. The economic value 'being the degree to which an individual is attracted to an employer that provides above average salary, an attractive overall compensation package, and job security and promotion opportunities' (Ibid, p.95).

One cannot think about the above in isolation but these factors must be reviewed within the framework of other HR strategies, policies and procedures.

Key to developing the reward strategy is consideration of the aims and objectives of reward. One could consider that reward is about: encouraging adoption of the organisation's values and required behaviours, ensuring that the workforce is skilled and competent to do its job, supporting the culture of the organisation and, of course, contributing to the competitiveness of the organisation.

 ## ACTIVITY 12.3

Read the following *People Management* article, 'No rise, no problem', by Claire Churchard and consider the questions and references to articles and websites which follow. By exploring the various websites and responding to the range of questions, you should be able to understand that there are many strands to reward and how different organisations think about how they can and wish to reward their employees. One size does not fit all.

Keeping staff happy in an era of wage freezes means rethinking the way you engage. But are organisations really playing fair?

Not everybody is underpaid in the current economic malaise. Take Herbert Stepic, chief executive of Austria's Raiffeisen Bank, who felt sufficiently comfortable to hand back around £1.7m of his salary on the grounds that 'remunerations can turn out to be too high'.

To most British employees, such altruism is admirable but entirely alien. Median pay increases of 2.5 per cent are lagging inflation, macroeconomic indicators offer little reason for optimism and a simmering sense of unfairness in the way they are remunerated can quickly turn into a disastrous case of disengagement among staff. But awarding rises when the business is not performing creates unrealistic expectations, say the experts, and only has a limited effect on satisfaction. How can HR square the circle?

The pain on pay has been felt most widely in the public sector, where the news that a 1 per cent cap on rises would be extended into 2016 prompted union fury. Louise Tibbert, Public Sector People Managers' Association (PPMA)

pay and reward lead and head of HR and OD at Hertfordshire County Council, knows she has a key role to play in explaining the new reality. 'Looking after employee engagement has come to the fore,' she says. 'A big issue for us is how we engage with employees and involve them with budget pressures.'

Similar conversations are taking place across a huge variety of sectors. Research by recruitment agency Robert Walters found half of all financial services staff received no pay rise in 2012. Post Office employees walked out in April this year, partly in protest at a pay freeze that has run since April 2011. And at local media giant Newsquest, four of the past five years have seen a standstill on wages.

It's a situation Kerry Smith, head of HR at the Royal Horticultural Society, knows intimately. 'There's no money for pay rises,' she says. 'But that's always been the case for us, even in good times. We've had to look creatively at our reward policy to motivate staff.' RHS gives staff the opportunity to make a business case for an individual raise if they feel they are being underpaid. 'We tell staff: "If you are unhappy with pay, we will look at it,"' she says. HR professionals help staff to build their cases, backed by a wider communications strategy on pay.

With 400 unique roles among 750 employees, a career progression path for each individual helps them see their place in the wider picture. 'We also remind people it's a great environment to work in, and that you're working with lovely, motivated people. In fact, that's mentioned in our reward strategy,' says Smith.

Tim Fevyer, director of reward and policy at Specsavers, adds: 'You have to get the basics right first. You can't ignore money when it comes to motivation, engagement or retention. But once you have got it right, it can be overrated in what you do. Get it too low and you will struggle to get good people and keep them. You need to be at a point where you can take it off the table.'

We understand the psychology of workplace motivation better than ever before, and most employers now offer a wider and more inclusive range of benefits. But has that translated into a more effective way of explaining and contextualising benefits and mitigating pay freezes?

Alan Measures, head of HR reward at engineering firm Moog, says a staff survey showed employees valued the workplace culture more strongly than pay, a fact borne out by the long service records of many at the company. As a result, a global profit share scheme has helped place the emphasis on collective achievement, rather than individual bonuses. Staff can gauge the likelihood of a good payout from the quarterly business performance plan.

In the past, Measures says, 'we've had pay increases where people have questioned why they are below the retail price index. So we've gone through a process of explaining that we're not gauging it against RPI, but against market movement. Although that doesn't guarantee people will accept your argument, at least you can explain that you're trying to pay the going rate.'

Moog, he adds, has had to hold down pay increases when the business has faced lean times: 'Most people take a long-term view: they know we would do what we could to prevent laying people off. Job security is important to our staff. We have a particular skills base, so we need to hold on to talent. We have a value here that "we are all in this together" and, unlike David Cameron, we are able to demonstrate that.'

Tibbert says: 'We've worked to help people understand and access the money and benefits they already have but don't make the most of. For example, we explain the value of

their pension, as people often undervalue this benefit. We've introduced salary sacrifice schemes, health and well-being and discount programmes.' With the purse strings tight in Hertfordshire, career development was identified as a key motivator in the staff survey. 'We've maintained our training budget throughout the organisation. We are focusing on the skills we will need in the future that people really value.'

Jonathan Trevor, lecturer in HR and organisational behaviour at Cambridge Judge Business School, says employers could go even further to get more value from their reward strategy. 'First, stop using consultants and spend the money on management development and people training. Second, simplify pay. If people can't understand pay, they won't value it. Third, reduce HR's admin burden and place the emphasis on the line manager to explain the pay and reward message – they manage the experience of employment, not HR. They can either be the advocates of the system or its strongest critics.'

Trevor says line managers should 'have a say on pay' and HR and the line managers need to work closely together to enable workers to perform to their maximum potential. But while rewriting the narrative around pay can help redefine the terms of engagement with staff in difficult times, there is always the danger that pay freezes are born of the CFO's natural desire to contain cost rather than economic necessity.

Duncan Brown, principal for reward and engagement at consultancy Aon Hewitt, argues: 'Corporate profits in some sectors are at record levels, with evidence on both sides of the Atlantic of a decline in the share of profits going to the workforce. Companies are making profits but they're just not spending it – they're hoarding it. Is it right that we're not giving pay awards that at least match inflation?'

Charles Cotton, reward adviser at the CIPD, also questions the prevailing wisdom on pay: 'Pay rises lag the cost of living, and that can be a hard sell for employers if employees are finding it difficult to juggle costs. Communicating the rationale for pay decisions can be more challenging in organisations sitting on piles of cash.'

Citing the example of Jaguar Land Rover, which negotiated a real-terms pay cut to ride out the economic storm, Brown says: 'I'm not sure it's right to assume it's a good thing to "get away" with a low increase. If you took pay cuts for the survival of the business, you could take that for a year or maybe two. Jaguar were lucky things picked up... But the situation with low pay awards is wearing a bit thin. If employees agree to share in the pain, when it picks up they should share in the gain.'

For Tibbert, 'there's a lot of pressure from the government to keep pay low. But sometimes you can't get the calibre of people if you do that.' There is no easy solution to remove disaffection over pay. And there's certainly no light at the end of the economic tunnel to suggest the arguments over pay freezes are likely to dissipate any time soon. But at least by being open and honest, empowering line managers and making the most of benefits, HR has a fighting chance of keeping staff motivated against the odds.

'It'll just be our little secret'

The tricky politics of rewarding high performers

When an organisation faces a pay lockdown, one of the key fears is that star employees will find themselves picked off by rivals with deeper pockets. How can you keep them happy?

Share options can be offered to high performers below board level, and more employers are considering this. If the organisation isn't publicly listed, you can open a 'phantom share plan', which operates like a profit share scheme.

Higher employer pension contributions can be used to favour those on a 'fast track' scheme, which also offers significant tax advantages.

Corporate ISAs for select individuals have become increasingly popular.

Enhanced training opportunities can be better for staff retention than a lump sum. Every year, the US restaurant chain Olive Garden sends 14 top employees to Tuscany for an all-expenses paid Italian cookery masterclass. It found participants were far less likely to leave.

A mentoring programme can promote informal succession planning, as well as help high performers feel valued. But all fast-track schemes carry a risk: criteria and selection must be openly communicated and open to all, to avoid creating resentment.

Churchard (2013)

Reprinted with kind permission of *People Management*.

Questions

1 What is the overall perspective on approaches to reward you glean by reading the various views and approaches to reward as explained by the various HR managers, economists and academics?

2 Kerry Smith, head of HR at the Royal Horticultural Society, has a novel approach to salary reviews. If you feel that you deserve a salary increase, you have to put a business case forward. Do you think that this approach is practical? One can imagine a queue of people outside her office door, all with good testaments as to why they should be paid more! Does this approach say something of the people, the culture and the overall approach to people management by the (charitable) society? You may gain some understanding of the organisation by visiting their website and viewing an explanatory video at: **www.rhs.org.uk/about-us**

3 Moog, the engineering specialist company (**www.moog.co.uk**) offers a perspective on reward which focuses on talent management in tough economic times.

Have you a view as to why one of their main considerations should be about retention of staff? You will gain some insight into the issue by reading the article by Foy and Murray Brown (2013).

4   Duncan Brown, principal for reward and engagement at consultancy Aon Hewitt, talking about organisations who negotiate low pay deals during tough economic times: 'Jaguar were lucky things picked up... But the situation with low pay awards is wearing a bit thin. If employees agree to share in the pain, when it picks up they should share in the gain.' What do you think he means by sharing the gain? You will find some guidance on this point by reading the articles by Jones (2008) and King (2013).

12.8 REWARD SYSTEMS

It is necessary for a professional HR specialist to develop an understanding of both traditional and modern reward systems since, at particular times in their career, they may be expected to work effectively with both the old and the new. Also, the point should be made here that although organisations with a modern outlook on reward may have introduced 'new pay' systems, some still use traditional systems in parallel with the new, rewarding different categories of employee appropriately.

The decline in manufacturing in the UK and the complementary increase in 'service' and sedentary types of work has reduced the demand for some of the traditional pay systems. Now, however, there is a demand for new and innovative pay systems, especially in the light of the need to attract, retain and motivate highly skilled staff, even in times of economic stress.

12.8.1 WAGES AND SALARIES

Before exploring the above concept of reward further, it is important to understand the difference between *wages* and *salaries*. Wages are paid weekly to employees. Employees who receive a wage are paid on an hourly or weekly rate, while employees who are on an annual salary are paid less frequently, usually monthly. The older and more traditional pay systems were largely designed to motivate and reward factory-floor wage-earners in manufacturing companies. Basic pay can be paid hourly, weekly, monthly or annually – in other words, it is a *time-rated* pay system, based upon a rate for the job. This type of salary reflects both internal and external relativities and may even involve trade unions in the negotiation, as is the case with teachers, university lecturers and some other public sector bodies. The problem with this type of salary/wage system is that it may not change over time and thus becomes outdated.

12.9 CONTINGENCY PAY

Contingency pay is additional to the basic pay of the employee. This part of the pay is called contingent because it is *at-risk* pay and is therefore, in some way, dependent upon performance. It may consist of a mix of the following:

- performance-related pay (PRP) – dealt with later in this chapter
- bonuses
- some form of incentive pay linked to targets
- commission
- service-related pay, which is pay dependent upon how long the individual has been with the organisation

- skill-based pay
- competence-related pay
- career-related pay, which is linked to increased responsibility
- allowances, perhaps for working in harsh conditions, shift-type working or having extra responsibilities.

KEY CONCEPTS

Total earnings is the sum of basic pay plus additions from variable pay, for example pay dependent upon products manufactured or products sold.

Total remuneration includes the sum of *total earnings* plus benefits and *indirect pay*. (The term *indirect pay* is an alternative term for employee benefits. *Indirect pay* refers to those elements of remuneration, including pensions, health insurance, and benefits in kind, which are made in addition to the basic wage.)

Incentives aim to motivate – so are future oriented.

Rewards are given for achievement – so are associated with past events.

The following section will deal with some of the elements listed above.

12.9.1 INCENTIVE AND EQUITY PAY SCHEMES

Systems of payment may be *incentive-based* or *equity-based*. Incentive-based schemes are designed to motivate a good performance in terms of the quantity and quality of what is produced. Equity systems, for example stock option-based pay schemes, tend to link reward with the importance and value of the job, as well as to the person actually doing it. A stock option scheme allows employees the right to buy a specific number of the company's shares at a fixed price within a certain period of time. Employees who purchase shares (stock options) hope to profit by selling their company shares at a higher price after the minimum time that they must hold them has expired. In this way an employee shares in the success and, of course, failure of the company.

12.9.2 INCENTIVE SYSTEMS OF PAYMENT

It was in the early twentieth century that F.W. Taylor introduced a system of payment that was designed to motivate employees by rewarding their performance fairly. He devised what we now call *work study*. After calculating how much work a human being could achieve in a particular amount of time, he linked employees' pay to their performance. Pay mechanisms such as these came to be referred to as *payment by results*, or PBR, schemes. (Note, you may also see performance-based reward as an alternative interpretation of the acronym.) In organisations where they are now used, such schemes are more sophisticated than those of Taylor, but the basic principle remains the same.

Taylor's main objective was to increase productivity, and it seemed logical to him to simply show the workers how they might increase their rewards: 'the more you produce, the more you will earn.' He claimed that managers were ignorant of what men [sic] could produce, and criticised their lack of effort to find out. He believed that people worked to obtain financial rewards, rather than because they were interested in what they were doing. Clearly, they [the employee] needed a reason to work (in addition to keeping their jobs), and he devised a system of payment by results to provide an attractive incentive. Taylor's view of how people were motivated was based upon economics; people would adjust their work effort in accordance with the way rewards were linked to the task.

12.9.3 PAYMENT BY RESULTS SCHEMES

Payment by results schemes are those in which pay is tied to actual performance. The idea of pay being tied to actual performance is illustrated simply by *piecework*. This is where employees, whose job it is to produce a certain number of items daily or weekly, are paid in accordance with an agreed rate per item for the number of items produced. When this kind of system was introduced, almost a hundred years ago, it worked in a totally direct fashion, that is, 'no work, no pay'. Figure 12.2 shows a simplified diagram of a piecework scheme which links productivity to pay. Practically there would be a requirement for an employee to produce some work in return for the minimum wage.

Figure 12.2 Example of a piecework scheme

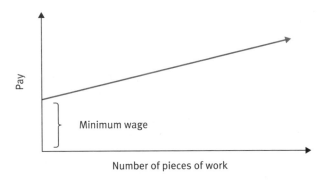

Where this system is still in use it has been modified to provide for a guaranteed basic wage, in which the worker receives at least the minimum wage. Beyond the guaranteed wage level, workers are given targets which, when exceeded, makes them eligible for a piece-rate bonus (see Figure 12.3).

In Figure 12.3, note the angle of the curves: they are actually straight lines beyond the 'guaranteed' point. Through the bargaining process, managers and workers negotiate what they call the steepness or flatness of the scheme. In a 'steep' scheme fewer items may be produced to obtain a high bonus, whereas in a 'flat' scheme a greater number of items would have to be produced to achieve the same bonus. Figure 12.3 shows two possible schemes.

Criticisms of piecework include the notion that it places the productivity effort in the hands of the workers, instead of the managers, and that the 'money-motivated' rush for quantity adversely affects the quality of the product. Also, workers tend, informally, to standardise productivity beyond the guaranteed point, and trouble may arise when the need for productivity reduces. Discontent may occur because, in the medium to long term, employees become accustomed to receiving regular weekly piece-rate bonuses, and unconsciously incorporate the extra cash into their 'guaranteed regular income'. When they are asked to reduce productivity, the inevitable slimmer pay packet comes as a shock.

Obviously, workers who are paid in this way have an advantage over the support workers, such as clerks and administrators, who have less control over what is in their pay packets. This sometimes creates dissatisfaction among the support workers, and many companies have successfully minimised the discontent by introducing organisation-wide bonus schemes, based upon how the organisation has performed. In this way all workers benefit from the profitability produced by their efforts, whether they are classed as 'direct' or 'support' employees.

Figure 12.3 Guaranteed wage plus piece-rate bonus

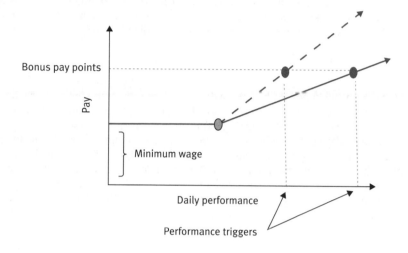

12.9.4 FIXED INCREMENTAL PAY SCALES

Some organisations, particularly those in the public sector, have fixed incremental pay scales. Within each job there is a scale through which the job-holder may progress in an annual 'step-up' fashion (see Figure 12.4).

In most organisations that use this system, the regular and unquestioned 'step up' has been replaced, so that now managerial discretion, usually based on performance ratings, may be used to reduce or increase the value of each increment.

Figure 12.4 Example of a fixed incremental scale

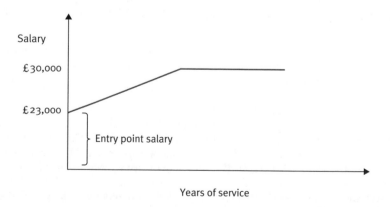

12.9.5 BONUS SCHEME

This is a company-wide scheme in which all employees are rewarded with an annual or bi-annual bonus on the basis of the organisation's productivity as a whole. The reward is usually a percentage of each person's annual pay. With this kind of scheme the productivity measure selected would have to be one that genuinely reflects whether or not the employees exceeded a previously agreed productivity standard over the relevant period. In this way, the amount of bonus paid is directly related to employee performance. The rationale for this kind of scheme is that employees will co-operate with each other and with the managers to achieve as high a bonus as possible.

12.9.6 MEASURED DAYWORK

It was noted above that PBR schemes have been criticised because they place the control of productivity in the hands of the employees. One approach to solving this problem was to introduce measured daywork schemes, which became popular in the 1950s and 1960s when there were a large number of mass production factories in the UK.

The measured daywork scheme is a system that fixes employees' pay based upon the understanding that employees will maintain a specified level of performance. Pay does not fluctuate in the short term with an individual's performance, as it would with a piecework scheme, because performance is averaged out over a period of time. Measured daywork provides an incentive for the employee to perform at a required level. This puts the employee under an obligation to meet that level since the incentive is guaranteed in advance.

12.9.7 TEAM REWARD SCHEME

Reputedly, this is a simple concept, but it can be extremely difficult to administer. The idea is that an incentive-based pay system that rewards teams by reinforcing desired behaviour should lead to effective teamwork.

Armstrong (2012a, p.293) suggests that five criteria need to be met in order for a team reward to be effective:

- The teams have to be clearly defined and have defined targets.
- The teams should have a certain amount of autonomy in how they work.
- There should be an interdependence of work between one team member and the next. Jobs should not be stand-alone.
- The teams do not change over time; membership is relatively stable.
- The teams are mature and used to working, as he says, 'flexibly', perhaps by having an interchangeability of roles.

He acknowledges that the above are exacting requirements: 'If they can be met then there might be a case for team pay. But the fact that they are so demanding explains why it has never taken off, in spite of the powerful arguments in favour of it' (Armstrong, 2012a, p.293).

For team remuneration systems to work, all of the team members should share the rewards equally. In this case the assumption must be that all team members have put in an exactly equal contribution to the effort that earned the reward! The work of Bamberger and Levi (2009) suggests that rewarding team members using equality norms {meaning – everyone received the same reward}, rather than using equity norms encouraged teamworking behaviours. Equity theory, attributed to Adams (1972), is based upon how people feel they have been treated in comparison with others. If they feel they have contributed more to a team's effort and they receive less than a colleague, they will feel that they have not been treated fairly. It has its roots in *social exchange theory*.

Rewarding teams is complex and fraught with problems because it has the same difficulties as trying to predict how individual employees may react to a reward system plus the added complexity of the problems of trying to predict an individual's feelings associated with equality of treatment, receiving the same reward as a co-worker, and equity of treatment, that is, receiving a reward based upon team contribution or seniority. As Bamberger and Levi (2009, p.319) write, when discussing their findings in relation to how team members may feel if they hold back or limit help to a colleague, 'For example, help providers may be concerned that the help-seeker will reciprocate such "ungracious" behavior in the future when roles are reversed with today's help-seeker becoming tomorrow's help provider.' In essence, part of the motivational drive of a team member may be associated with not wishing to be seen as negative because they may, in turn, require assistance with their part of a team task at some time in the future!

PAUSE FOR THOUGHT

Equality or equity?

Adams' (1972) work on equity in reward focused on people's feelings on and about how they were rewarded. Consider the following example:

Take two recently recruited technician engineers: both had studied at the same college, both achieved the same qualification and both had good-quality work experiences before joining the company in which they were now working. Rajvinder had attended her interview two weeks before Barney. Raj and Barney had been recruited by different HR advisers; the regular adviser had been on leave when Barney had been recruited and so a stand-in from another division of the company had made him the offer of employment and set his salary.

A senior technician, Alexa, had volunteered to mentor both technicians. Alexa was having a meeting with Raj and Barney and they were talking about opportunities for promotion. Alexa indicated that it was probable that within two years they would be in a position to apply for a senior technician's role, provided the business continued to expand. Alexa was happy to divulge what salary she was receiving. Although over £4,000 per annum more than the salary either Raj or Barney were receiving, they thought this satisfactory because Alexa had significantly more experience and responsibilities. In other words, there was an equity {meaning –

fairness} because the salary differential could be explained. Neither Raj nor Barney expected their salaries to be equal to the salary of Alexa. Balance and harmony remained.

Later, after the discussion about promotion opportunities from Alexa had finished, Barney and Raj were talking over a cup of tea. Raj was saying that she was feeling good and was going out that evening to celebrate with her partner; she was taking him for a meal to celebrate her new job. Barney indicated he was feeling good but the job change hadn't made that much difference to his take-home pay. It wasn't long before Barney found out that the salary Raj had been offered was £1,500 per annum more than the salary he had been offered and accepted – and they were both doing the same job! The balance of harmony had been disturbed. Barney considered that there was a distinct inequity between their salaries. He kept 'his cool' and continued his conversation with Raj but later in the shift he went to see his supervisor...

Using the above story to explain the concept of equity, in the context of reward, is too simplistic if only the one perspective, that of Barney, is considered. Barney's psychological state, his feelings of unfairness, of inequity, is driven by a perceived belief that he is being under-rewarded for his efforts *when compared with Raj*. Until he realised that Raj was a higher earner than himself, he had no comparator and he was content with his situation. Raj, who is a very good friend of Barney, also has a feeling of inequity. In Raj's situation, her emotional state of inequity is driven by her feelings of being over-rewarded for her efforts *when compared with Barney*.

In a similar way to Barney, Raj was happy with her effort-wage exchange, that is, until she found out that she was, for the same work, receiving a better rate for the job. She then felt a sense of guilt.

The purpose of exploring the above example is to demonstrate that decisions on rewarding people are not straightforward but impact upon employees in many ways. The outcome of a pay decision in the story affected both Barney and Raj. Rather than getting on with the job and accepting that Raj had been lucky or perhaps a better negotiator of her salary, the concern is that Barney becomes pre-occupied with the perception of his 'unfair treatment'.

The above discussion deals with the feelings – psychological state – when Barney and Raj have some form of internal comparator which creates disharmony and feelings of inequity. However, the world is interconnected and quite easily the comparator can be from outside the organisation. This would be the case if a competitor company, employing similarly skilled people, was offering better rates of pay for similar roles. The 'savvy' employer should be aware of this type of threat to the stability of the workforce; it is not difficult to monitor the external market. Such threats can be mitigated by employers by engaging with their employees, perhaps by publishing total reward statements (TRS), which express, in detail, the pay, benefits and privileges that company employees receive. Employees are then, in a subtle way, helped to consider and reflect upon the total remuneration package rather than individual aspects; and so perhaps make a balanced decision whether to leave or to stay.

Theories, especially about HR topics, are just that, theories: they have been tested during research and links have been made about a hypothesis {meaning – a supposition} which perhaps links one thing to another. Equity theory considers the feelings of people and how they perceive things. No one person is the same as the next, so no one individual will react exactly the same as their neighbour to a situation, and so may not react at all as predicted. Overpayments which are made to people tend to be accepted more readily than underpayments; there is a greater tolerance to accept an overpayment. Robbins et al (2010, p.157), calling on the (1987) research of Huseman et al, reflect upon the previous point: 'It's pretty damaging to a theory when one-half of the equation (how people respond to overreward) falls apart. Second, not all people are equity sensitive.'

Further reading and case examples about equity theory can be found in Chapter 11, 'Employee Motivation and Performance'. Also, Robbins et al (2010) deal with Adams' equity theory in a very detailed manner and discuss, in the context of reward, the range of choices of outcome that an employee can make.

12.9.8 JUSTICE IN REWARD

Closely linked to equity theory is the notion of justice in terms of reward. 'Justice in reward' is linked to the feelings and emotions associated with how an employee perceives the equity or fairness of a reward. The employee makes comparisons of reward received and efforts made by others when measured against one's own situation. Employees also, consciously or subconsciously, consider the following:

- the process of how rewards are made – procedural justice
- the fairness of how rewards are or have been allocated – distributive justice.

Bearing the above two concepts in mind, it becomes almost a common-sense precept {meaning – *maxim or moral instruction*} that the methodology for making decisions about rewards needs to be transparent. During the annual appraisal and pay round, the level of reward that individuals receive, bonuses, pay increase or promotions will quickly be knowledge, if not common knowledge. How fair or unfair the decisions have been will be reconciled in the minds of friends and colleagues based upon the knowledge of a co-worker, their competence, entrepreneurial abilities, commitment, and so on.

In terms of pay satisfaction there are a number of studies which support the notion that both procedural and distributive justice influence how employees feel. Kalayanee (2011) points to studies by Jones, Scarpello and Bergman that indicate 'that pay satisfaction is likely to be higher when employees believe they have the opportunity to appeal and modify pay decisions, and when pay decisions are clearly communicated and justified to employees' (ibid, p.161).

Comparing how procedural justice impacted upon an employee's perceptions of pay satisfaction compared with distributive justice, Kalayanee cited further research which compared the perceived impact of the two concepts:

> Tremblay, Sire, and Balkin (2000) found that distributive justice perceptions were better predictors of pay satisfaction; however, this result was reversed for benefit satisfaction. The conclusion that procedural justice was generally a better predictor of benefits satisfaction than distributive justice was also drawn by Arnold and Spell (2006). (Kalayanee, 2011, p.161)

12.9.9 UNINTENDED OUTCOMES

A reward system should encourage the behaviours which an organisation wishes to see in its employees. The Law of Unintended Consequences, very much in the vein of Murphy's Law, states that it is not always possible to predict the results of purposeful action. Reality is frequently too complicated and unpredictable and when decision-making is done without the totality of relevant information, it is not surprising that an intended outcome brings with it other positive or negative consequences. For example, the demilitarised zone between North and South Korea has become a wildlife sanctuary, which is positive for the local fauna and flora. However, not all such outcomes are positive.

The economic crash of 2008 arguably was as a direct result of the way investment bankers were paid. Large bonus payments were intended to reward high-achievers but, as an unintended consequence of the system, it also encourages risk-taking in the investment banking field as well as in the housing market, which led to the approval of mortgages that were, in the medium to long term, unaffordable for the applicants. The following is from *The Times* of 9 February 2009:

> Bonus payments are a standard part of senior bankers' remuneration. They also extend to quite junior employees. Bankers are typically paid a basic salary and an annual bonus that is intended to reflect firm-wide profitability and individual contribution. With more junior staff, the aim is to reward effort, progress and potential. ... Even though bankers' bonuses will be substantially lower than in previous years – and will probably remain so for a long time – they will not adequately reflect the imprudent risks that the banks took on in the boom years. Bankers are paid for generating returns higher than those of the overall market. . .

ACTIVITY 12.4

The argument about bankers' bonuses continues. Hosking (2013) writes in *The Times*:

> A new criminal offence of reckless banking punishable by jail is one of the most eye-catching proposals from the Parliamentary Commission on Banking Standards being published today. MPs and peers on the commission said that while they had no illusions about the difficulty of securing a conviction for such an offence, the threat 'would give pause for thought to the senior officers of UK banks'.

Are the teeth with which the Government is proposing to bite bankers who transgress real or illusory? As Hosking writes (ibid), 'Nobody in Britain has been prosecuted over any of the bank failures of 2008, while many of the most senior people in charge at the time have quit with huge pensions and no attempt to claw back past rewards.'

Consider the following questions:

- Should bankers have their bonus payments capped? The country relies heavily upon the revenue generated by the banking sector and to cap bankers' bonuses is likely to drive not only 'banking talent' into the arms of overseas institutions but the banking institutions would likely relocate their investment arms overseas as well.

- On what basis would you reward bankers? The Chancellor of the Exchequer, as recently as 26 September 2013, has warned that capping bankers' bonuses would 'hurt the City of London'. It is possible to obtain context about this quote by reading Griffiths (2013).

- You have been asked, as head of remuneration for a logistics company, to consider developing a bonus system for drivers who will be involved in delivering cars. The cars arrive at the docks from Japan and South Korea. They are then transported by road to a main storage and pre-dealership preparation facility some hundred miles away. Except for a 50-mile stretch of motorway, the route runs through built-up areas of the suburbs of two cities or winds its way through rural countryside.

- Your management is keen to capture a long-term contract with the vehicle manufacturer so wishes to show that it can deliver the vehicles on time and within budget. It has been suggested that you develop a bonus system based on the number of cars delivered per driver over a seven-day period:

  1 What issues are likely to arise with this type of incentive?

  2 What are the likely intended and unintended outcomes/consequences?

  3 Can you think of a better system?

PAUSE FOR THOUGHT

Whenever a group or team is formed, a leader appears. The leader may be one that is appointed by the organisation (a *formal leader*), or one that has emerged by mutual consent to represent the team (an *informal leader*). Leaders report to the people who put them where they are. A group, therefore, may have two leaders. The question that arises is: which leader decides on the amount of work effort that is *actually put in*, and thereby controls the value of the bonus?

12.10 JOB EVALUATION SCHEMES

Why conduct a job evaluation? According to Acas (2010, p.5), job evaluation is 'a method of determining on a systematic basis the relative importance of a number of different jobs'. Job evaluation schemes are used as the basis for fair pay systems. With these types of scheme, jobs are compared with each other and then graded according to their values yet, at the same time, trying to maintain some sort of process that allows for a competitive pay structure, which enables the organisation to recruit from the external market. While the grades do not constitute a payment system, they do provide the basis for valuing one job against another and thus the process is integral in the development of a pay structure.

Job evaluation allows for internal relativities of jobs to be determined. Job evaluation structures are developed/suggested by job evaluators and approved by a job evaluation committee or panel. Any job evaluation scheme should provide a hierarchy of jobs that is free from discrimination and has a 'buy-in' from all management and also those affected. Employees should perceive the system as 'felt to be fair'.

There are several approaches to job evaluation, some of which are 'non-analytical' and some 'analytical'. The non-analytical approach does not offer a defence against equal value pay claims (Equality and Human Rights Commission at: **www.equalityhumanrights.com/advice-and-guidance/tools-equal-pay/step-2-additional-information/what-is-job-evaluation**).

Three approaches to job evaluation will be discussed; the first two are non-analytical and have been included for completeness:

- job ranking
- job grading or job classification
- points rating.

12.10.1 JOB RANKING

This is a non-analytical process that simply compares whole jobs with each other without breaking them down into their component parts. The whole process centres on assessing the comparative worth of jobs. Evaluators, usually managers who know the jobs, identify the positions of jobs and rank them hierarchically in order of their size. Jobs that are perceived to be of equal value are placed into groups.

A major criticism of job ranking is that it is a subjective process. There are no reputed standards for assessing the sizes of the jobs. Those employees who see their jobs ranked positively, that is, above or at least equal to the ranking of other jobs, will regard the system as fair. Those who have their jobs ranked lower than other jobs will perceive the system as skewed and unfair. In a sense, however, job evaluation in general may be seen as a subjective process since, as we shall see, even analytical systems are ultimately based on the consensus of a panel of evaluators.

CASE EXAMPLE 12.2

NON-ANALYTIC JOB EVALUATION

Job ranking

In this example, which relates to a large and independent retail store, four jobs have been selected and job descriptions written:

- administrative assistant
- accountant
- office supervisor
- section manager.

We can see immediately that some of the jobs are likely to have a different value.

Other office jobs are then ranked alongside the administrative assistant, slightly higher jobs alongside the accountant, and so on. It is a rather crude and basic form of job evaluation, and it is sometimes necessary to grade certain jobs individually, since not all jobs fit neatly, even into broad categories, on the hierarchy. Some jobs 'stick out' as isolated entities, as might be the case if the store employed just one 'fashion buyer'.

12.10.2 JOB GRADING/CLASSIFICATION

Job grading, or job classification as it is often called, is another non-analytical approach. It is similar to job ranking except that the evaluators decide on the groupings or pay grades in advance; after which a general job description is produced for all of the jobs in each group. A typical individual job is then identified and used as a benchmark. Finally, each job is compared with the general job description and the benchmark job, then placed in an appropriate grade. This can be useful in times of change, since new or redesigned jobs can be assessed according to the criteria and placed at the appropriate level. On the other hand, modern thinking about organisational design tends to favour lean and flattened structures with a reduced number of levels, which can produce difficulties when categorising jobs in a scheme such as this.

An alternative approach to job grading is to categorise the jobs according to the criteria without considering their potential hierarchical position. In this way, criteria are related more directly to the actual work itself, so that the levels of knowledge, skills and competences required to do the work are taken into account, along with responsibilities and the importance of the decisions the job-holder takes. This approach has some advantages because it does not rely upon, for example, the number of other positions which report into a job position as an indicator of the job's worth or weight, but rather on criteria which the organisation has identified as important and thus, eventually, will pay for.

The process reveals a similarity between the methods of job grading and those of job ranking, in so much as when the committee is making comparisons, it treats jobs as whole entities. The job evaluation committee makes its decisions by reaching a consensus. Decisions are open to consider appeals from employees who feel that their jobs have been unfairly or inappropriately graded. In some organisations, appeals are considered by independent panels.

As mentioned above, because the process is non-analytical, it does not offer a defence against equal pay challenges by employees and so the approach is not recommended.

12.10.3 POINTS RATING METHOD

This is an *analytical method* and probably the most commonly used. The principal feature of points rating is that instead of comparing the value of whole jobs, as in *non-analytical* approaches, it analyses and compares jobs on the basis of elements of a job, called *factors*.

Factors, according to the Equality and Human Rights Commission, are clearly identifiable aspects of jobs that can be defined and measured and which provide the basis for assessing and comparing the relative overall worth of different jobs. Factors can be: qualifications and competences required, degree of responsibility, customer contact, job complexity, technical complexity, working conditions and also physical requirements. However, if physical requirements are used, the requirement has to be thought through very carefully so as not to, unnecessarily and perhaps illegally, discriminate against one group of people. For example, if a factor (job characteristic) is identified as physical strength, this might automatically discriminate against a significant number of female employees. If the job can be shown to be achievable using a mechanical aid, strength can no longer be used as a factor which helps to define the role.

Each of the factors carries a number of points, and the number apportioned to each job is determined by the degree to which the factors are present within it. A hierarchical structure is produced on the basis of the points rating of each job. Pay for a particular job is determined according to the number of points it carries.

Job analysis is an essential precursor to a points rating system. When the factors mentioned above have been identified, job descriptions and specifications need to be reviewed, revised and, where necessary, completely rewritten. The ultimate scheme has to be seen to be fair, and since the differences between jobs are measured in accordance with the degree to which the selected factors are present, great care must be taken over the analysis. In all systems the 'volume of work' does not play a part in the value that is placed on a job. If the volume of work is large, more people are employed to do the work!

Deciding how many points to allocate to each factor is a well-known problem in points rating. The factors vary in their importance to each job, and the most complex or most important are allocated the greatest number of points. This is called the *weighting* of factors. The factors are placed in order of importance and complexity, and weighted according to a maximum number of points, bearing in mind the degree of importance that each factor has in a particular job. Each job is then graded according to the level at which the factors are present. See also the discussion below, which addresses equality and reward.

12.10.4 MANAGEMENT CONSULTANTS' SCHEMES

Several management consultancy firms can provide 'tailor-made' job evaluation schemes (which are usually analytical). Alternatively, the organisation can commission the consultancy to custom-build a scheme.

As a 'do-it-yourself' exercise, the development of a job evaluation scheme can be costly and time-consuming, and it may ultimately be more cost-effective to engage a consultancy and to use a proprietary system of job evaluation, such as the Hay method.

Wright (2006, p.55) offers the following comments about proprietary and tailor-made schemes:

The advantages of proprietary schemes are that they offer:

- expertise from consultants in setting up and using job evaluation
- access to quality pay information
- the possibility of using the same scheme as well-known companies.

The advantages of tailor-made schemes might be:

- control over development of the scheme in-house to suit highly specific organisational environments
- possibly cost-effective, depending on which staff might be involved in developing a new scheme and how their time is accounted for
- opportunity for internal HR staff and managers to gain detailed knowledge of the scheme – its drawbacks as well as its advantages.

12.10.5 JOB EVALUATION AND EQUAL VALUE

The Equality and Human Rights Commission (EHRC) says the following about equal pay for equal value of jobs:

The term 'like work' means work which is the same or broadly similar. Unless differences can be objectively justified, jobs which are the same or broadly similar should have the same pay, irrespective of whether they are done by a man or by a woman, by a white employee or by one from a different ethnic background, by an employee with a disability or by one with no disabilities.

If similar jobs are not to be regarded as like work, the differences must be of practical importance. Apparently dissimilar jobs can be seen as like work: Lecturers of different subjects within the same employment; Cleaner and a Porter.

Pay means not just basic pay but also access to overtime, holidays, a company car and all other components of the pay package. (EHRC: **www.equalityhumanrights. com/advice-and-guidance/tools-equal-pay/checklists-equal-pay-in-practice/2-equal-pay-for-like-work/** [Accessed 27 December 2013])

It therefore makes sense for employers to opt for job evaluation as a basis for a grading and pay structure. A job-evaluated system will also assist in providing a defence to an equal pay claim and greatly facilitate carrying out an equal pay audit.

According to the EHRC (*Job Evaluation Defence*) the Equal Pay Act 1970 gives job evaluation schemes two roles:

(a)   A woman can claim equal pay on the ground that a scheme has rated her job, although different, as equivalent to that of a man (this is known as a 'work rated as equivalent' claim).

(b)   An employer can defend a claim for equal pay for work of equal value if a non-discriminatory analytical job evaluation scheme rates the woman's job as lower in value than her male comparator's job. This is known as the job evaluation defence.

> A good job evaluation scheme should involve employee representatives and be thorough in its approach to finding out about the jobs to be evaluated and, once an approach to the evaluation has been agreed, then the methodology should be communicated to those involved because it is important that the system is not only managed in a transparent and logical and open manner but that the system is one that is 'felt fair' by all whom it impacts upon. (adapted from Acas, 2010)

When working through the dimensions of an analytical scheme, the factors that are chosen must be done so that they cannot be construed to have any reference to discriminatory factors that are or can be construed to be sex-, age-, ethnicity-related, religious based, and so on, but should be solely on neutral grounds.

The job should be thoroughly researched to ensure that all relative factors are included, for example someone working in a crèche should have the caring nature of the role included. The weighting of factors should also be carefully assessed to ensure that inappropriate weighting is not given to those factors that are typical of a man's job. For example, the physical effort that a miner may be required to exert compared with the applied knowledge or skill with the use of medical instruments that a nurse may be required to have should not be overrated. The problem of weighting the factors used in an analytical scheme is recognised to be notoriously difficult.

CASE EXAMPLE 12.3

ANALYTICAL JOB EVALUATION SCHEME

Consider Table 12.2a, which compares the relative merits of a professional engineering position to that of an HR adviser role.

Professional engineer:

- Required education (minimum): undergraduate degree in appropriate discipline, Level 6 (National Qualifications Framework – NQF), Second Class, Div. I.
- The position demands that the holder must have chartered membership of a relevant professional institution.
- Subordinate staff = 20.
- Location: office-based, plus the role demands work in chemically hazardous environments and may, at times, be in the open and so exposed to adverse weather. There is an expectation that the incumbent could be away from home for several days each month.
- Budgetary responsibility is circa £2 million.

HR adviser:

- Required education (minimum): Level 3 (NQF), or equivalent (3 A-level at C grade or BTEC Diploma in Business) plus a Certificate in HR Practice.

- The position demands that the holder must have Associate Membership of the Chartered Institute of Personnel and Development (CIPD).
- Subordinate staff = 1.
- Location: office-based, plus travel to sites in the UK. There is an expectation that the incumbent could be away from home for several days each month.
- Budgetary responsibility is circa £20,000.

The maximum rating for each factor is variable and is given in Table 12.2a.

Table 12.2a Factor analysis – professional engineer versus HR adviser

Factor	Senior (professional) engineer	Senior HR adviser	Max of Range Weighting
Entry qualification	15	5	20
Professional body registration	10	10	10
Experience required (max 5 years)	20	20	30
Application of specialist knowledge	25	20	30
Use of specialist equipment (computer systems/software packages)	15	10	25
Interpretation of data	10	5	15
Analytical ability	20	15	25
Impact of advice given on the business	20	20	25
Conditions of work (good – low score)	10	5	20
Planning/co-ordinating	15	10	20
Co-ordinating contractor activity	20	15	25
Knowledge updating	15	15	15
Budgetary responsibility	15	5	20
Responsibility for subordinate staff	20	10	30
Total	230	160	310

Fictitious data, for illustration purposes only

In the above example, the senior HR adviser's job, predominantly a female role, would be rated at a lower value than that of the senior engineering role. This, in itself is not a problem, so long as the factors have been fairly developed and truly reflect the demands of the roles.

The grade values for the two jobs above would be reviewed in bands, against which pay ranges would be allocated. Based upon the scores in Table 12.2a for the two positions, it would be unlikely that the grades allocated would be equivalent.

Graded bands could be grouped (as an example):

Points: 151 to 175, 176 to 200, 201 to 225, etc.

or with wider bands as:

Points: 151 to 200, 201 to 250, 251 to 300, etc.

A review of the agreed factors, and initial scoring, raised some concerns with the job evaluation panel. Recognising that it is important that all relevant factors are included and none are duplicated the panel reconsidered their initial factor matrix and analysis of the two positions.

It is arguable that 'Planning/co-ordinating' is duplicated by 'Co-ordinating contractor activity' and so artificially skewing the evaluation towards the male-dominated job. After some discussion, it was agreed that 'Co-ordinating contractor activity' is still an important constituent of the role but the overall maximum should be reduced to 10 points; in essence, the overall weighting of the factor had to be reduced. Similarly, 'Use of specialist equipment' was considered not to be of significant importance because, in the main, it is the engineering contractors and consultants who use the specialist computer software packages. After discussion this factor was removed because it was not a substantive part of the role.

The scoring of the 'Conditions of work' were re-evaluated for both roles and it was considered that the senior engineering position should be scored at 12 points and the HR adviser 8 points, which better reflect the anti-social hours away from home.

Reflecting upon the HR advisor staff role, the company decided that the role should take on a more pronounced profile and become more strategic in nature. The incumbent would need to be aware of and be influenced by HR research. This change in the role profile demands an improvement in the overall quality of the HR cadre *{meaning - a small group of people specially trained for a particular purpose or profession}*. The new requirement is for all HR advisers to be Chartered Members of the CIPD. This change also impacts upon the scoring in Table 12.2a. It changes the points allocated to both the education and also the professional membership factors of the HR adviser. The reason is that to meet the Chartered Member professional requirements of the CIPD, the educational requirements are that members are required to have a postgraduate diploma in HRM or HRD, which equates to 'Level 7' within the National Qualifications Framework.

Concern was expressed about the use of 'Responsibility for subordinate staff' as a factor. The concern was about the overall weighting, rather than the exclusion of the factor; it was decided that the maximum points should be reduced to 10. It was felt that some roles, although not having many direct reports, have a significant impact upon the working lives of company employees. It was agreed to include a factor called 'Impact upon staff' to compensate for this omission. For example, the outcome and influence of decisions made by the HR adviser may affect a significant number of employees, for example when developing a reward package.

The updated factor and analysis is shown in Table 12.2b.

Table 12.2b Factor analysis – professional engineer versus HR adviser

Factor	Professional engineer	HR adviser	Max of Range Weighting
Entry qualification	15	15	20
Professional body registration	10	10	10
Experience required (max 5 years)	20	20	30
Application of specialist knowledge	25	20	30
Interpretation of data	10	5	15
Analytical ability	20	15	25
Impact of advice given	20	20	25

Conditions of work (good – low score)	12	8	20
Planning/co-ordinating	15	10	20
Co-ordinating contractor activity	10	3	10
Knowledge updating	15	15	15
Budgetary responsibility	15	5	20
Responsibility for subordinate staff	7	4	10
Impact upon staff	5	10	15
Total	199	160	265

Fictitious data, for illustration purposes only

With the above challenges and subsequent modifications, it can be seen that the relationship between the two roles changes significantly. Depending upon how the banding is structured, the two roles may or may not be graded alike.

 ACTIVITY 12.5

In groups, draw up a comparative analytical job evaluation scheme for a nurse and an AA patrol technician. Which role would you rate as warranting the higher rate of pay? Go to the Acas website or access the NHS Job Evaluation Handbook website to see the factors they recommend when conducting job evaluations.

Guidance can be found on the following websites:

- Acas: **www.acas.org.uk/index.aspx? articleid=682**
- NHS Job Evaluation Handbook: **www. nhsemployers.org/Aboutus/Publications/ Documents/ NHS_Job_Evaluation_Handbook.pdf**
- Equality and Human Rights Commission, guidance on equal pay in *The Statutory Code of Practice on Equal Pay*: **www. equalityhumanrights.com/uploaded_files/ EqualityAct/equalpaycode.pdf**

12.11 PERFORMANCE-RELATED PAY (PRP)

The bases for performance-related pay (PRP) are fairness and equity. While the idea is to reward good performance, it is hard to resist the notion that once PRP is established in an organisation, it also provides an incentive to perform well, that is, making contribution which is beyond what would be termed 'good performance'. *Merit* pay is a similar performance-based idea which originated in the early twentieth century, which was an attempt to provide satisfactory rewards for the exercise of ability and current performance. According to Tyson and York (1996), 'Merit increases are ... given to show recognition and to imply the kinds of actions and attitudes which the company wishes to reward.' The same principle applies with PRP, in which it is fair to reward various levels of performance differentially.

PRP has been through varying levels of popularity and unpopularity over the years. For PRP to influence behaviour, the level of the reward, for good or very good performance, has to be meaningful. In times of high inflation, as was the case in the 1970s, when the cost of living and wage inflation was running in double figures, the percentage increases that were awarded within PRP schemes were meaningless. This was because the value of any performance-related reward became insignificant compared with pay increases that were given to employees simply to maintain their salaries in line with living costs.

There has been a growth in the use of performance-based schemes. Such schemes are used to reward both managerial and non-managerial staff. Table 12.3 shows data on the use of individual performance-related rewards as depicted by the CIPD (2013e) *Reward Management* survey. Taking all sectors of employment into consideration, 59.8% reported using individual bonus schemes and 56.4% reported using some form of merit-based individual performance-related scheme. The fixed to variable amount of an employee's salary, where some form of PRP scheme is operated, averages at approximately 90:10. Private sector employers, when questioned about the split between non-performance- and performance-related pay indicated that they would like to see a ratio change in favour of the performance-related element, so that the balance is 80:20 or 70:30 (CIPD, 2013e, p.4).

Table 12.3 Incidence of individual performance-related reward by sector (2013)

Sector	Individual bonus	Merit pay	Sales commission
Manufacturing	51.8%	57.1%	35.7%
Private sector services	69.7%	55.7%	53.3%
Public services	48.8%	51.2%	4.7%
Not for profit (voluntary, community)	45.0%	70.0%	5.0%

CIPD (2013e, p.17) *Reward Management* annual survey report. Reproduced with kind permission of the CIPD.

There are arguments which are both for and against PRP as a motivator. As Perry et al (2009, p.40) point out, PRP is based upon expectancy theory, which itself assumes that 'individuals will exert effort if they expect it will result in an outcome that they value'. Without entering into the detail of the arguments here, in broad terms, surveys have indicated that while there is general support for the principle of PRP, most respondents did not believe that it had improved their motivation (Marsden and French, 1998). Other research has suggested that PRP is actually demotivating staff, rather than encouraging them (Bevan and Thompson, 1991).

12.11.1 INFLUENCE OF INDIVIDUAL DIFFERENCES IN RELATION TO PERFORMANCE-RELATED PAY (PRP)

Individually different perceptions of these schemes and of the purposes of reward in general have a strong influence on the results of such surveys. Some people, for example, adopt a particular profession because they feel naturally drawn to it, and while clearly they have to maintain a particular standard of living, it is the work itself that motivates them, rather than what they receive for carrying it out. Perry et al (2009) pick up on this point when they argue that PRP has not, in the public sector (of the USA), delivered its intended outcomes:

> Although research has identified occasional performance pay successes, the programs typically have fallen short of intermediate and long-term expectations. We argue, however, that our findings are less cause for despair than for caution and more strategic thinking. The reasons for the persistent failure of performance-related pay are more likely its incompatibility with public institutional rules, proponents' inability or unwillingness to adapt it to these values, and its incompatibility with more

powerful motivations that lead many people to pursue public service in the first place. (Perry et al, 2009, p.45)

On the other hand, Taylor's assumption (1911, 1947) that people work exclusively for money was based on his perception of entirely different types of worker. According to Goldthorpe (1968), manual workers are motivated almost entirely by 'extrinsic' rewards. In other words, they see it as the means by which they are able to sustain a particular living standard.

Armstrong (2012a, p.92) writes, 'It is interesting to note that 11 out of the 15 positive findings [*on the effectiveness of PRP usage – author's note*] relate to research in the United States while four negative reports are based on UK data.' He reflects that PRP schemes have probably failed in a UK context because of the way they were introduced; for example, assuming that private sector PRP schemes could simply be transferred into public sector use.

Key to any PRP scheme being effective is that it should be a bespoke design. The scheme should clearly reflect the desired outcomes of the business strategy and, for it to work, all those involved should have an understanding of the detail. Managers who implement the scheme and perform staff appraisals should have specific training in its operation.

ACTIVITY 12.6

1   In your organisation, or one with which you are familiar, identify three job-holders who you believe would be motivated mostly by financial reward and three who would be motivated mostly by the work itself.

2   Do you think that PRP has a place in a not-for-profit organisation such as a charity, for example the RSPCA or the RNLI? Read the article in *People Management* (Arkin, 2002) entitled 'Tides of change'.

12.12 GUIDELINES TO ACHIEVE ACCEPTANCE

A set of guidelines for action designed to achieve a positive attitude towards a PRP scheme might include:

- integrative bargaining for the optimal scheme
- the selection or creation of a scheme in which all employees may participate
- the onus of responsibility to identify the level of an employee's performance in relation to the minimum standard being placed firmly on the manager
- managers who operate the scheme being trained to do so, and given a thorough understanding of the spirit as well as the letter of its regulations
- steps being taken to ensure that all employees are provided with an explanation of the scheme and access to further explanatory information and advice
- employees being given the right of reassessment by request.

Perry et al (2009, p.43), citing a study by Greiner (1977), suggested that PRP schemes 'in which goals were clear, compensation was adequate, and a significant amount of support for merit pay plans existed, performance-related pay resulted in positive outcomes'.

12.12.1 HOW PERFORMANCE-RELATED PAY WORKS

The in-job performance of employees is appraised and there is a mechanism through which overall performance levels are identified. The gradings might be as follows:

- Level 1 – Excellent: has exceeded all standards and objectives.
- Level 2 – Good: has met standards and achieved objectives.
- Level 3 – Average: has met most standards and achieved objectives.
- Level 4 – Poor or unsatisfactory: has failed to meet standards or objectives.

The company must first of all agree what 'bonus pot', that is, how much capital, it will allocate to the annual exercise. This will of course be dependent upon the performance of the company and the organisation's current ability to pay and how it sees contingent pay supporting the overall organisation's strategy. One may decide to put further restrictions on management as to how they can award bonuses, for example only 10% of the workforce can be rated as Level 1; 30% as Level 2; 60% as Level 3; and of course one would hope that no one falls into the Level 4 banding, which would be associated with failure to meet the performance standard. Apprentices and other trainees would probably be excluded because, by definition, 'they are not yet competent'. This type of *forced distribution* would have to then be fed into the appraisal process. The outcome of the exercise would then look something like Table 12.4.

Table 12.4 Bonus table

Level	Bonus as a percentage of salary
Level 1	10%
Level 2	7%
Level 3	3%
Level 4	0%

In the above example, an employee on £20,000 would receive a bonus based upon the organisation's performance and their own personal performance in the following way. Assume that the organisation has agreed an overall performance bonus plus a cost of living increase of 2.5% (of base salary) and the employee, as a level 2 performer, has a personal bonus of 7% (of base salary), the overall bonus would be, for the year's work, 9.5% of £20,000 = £1,900.

The question then arises as to whether the above bonus should be included as part of a new base salary (£21,900), and therefore pensionable if the company was operating a final salary pension scheme, or paid as a one-off lump sum. Paying the bonus, and then to include the bonus amount as part of the new base salary, for the following years, is attractive for the employee but from the employer perspective this is seen as *salary creep* and as such continues to reward individuals, year on year, for past performance.

As with any system of payment, a PRP scheme must be handled with care and continuously monitored for its fairness, effectiveness and transparency of implementation. The attitudes of the managers and employees towards a particular scheme are of critical importance, and if the basis on which the scheme is founded is perceived as flawed, or the approach to assessment is regarded as biased, the scheme will fall into disrepute.

Rewarding people, if taken as a process, cannot be divorced from the emotive relational part of the employment relationship and so has links to such concepts as the psychological contract, which is dealt with in Chapter 3, 'Human Resource Management'.

ACTIVITY 12.7

Read the following article from *People Management*, entitled: 'Don't tell people what to do.' The article is an edited discussion between Dan Pink and *People Management* reporter Claire Warren:

The old command-and-control model doesn't work anymore, says management guru Dan Pink. It's easy to blame the relentless economic gloom and the constant tide of corporate scandals for the crisis of trust and engagement in Britain's businesses, but the truth is employees' confidence in their employers was in decline long before the banking sector brought the economy to its knees. That's because we are relying on outdated management techniques and rewarding people for short-term thinking, says Dan Pink, best-selling author of *Drive: The surprising truth about what motivates us*. As he teams up with the CIPD to deliver a range of workshops (see below), *People Management* asked him about the right balance of carrot and stick.

Why are businesses having so much trouble engaging their staff?

We tend to think that management has always been here, but it is just something some guy invented in the 1850s. It's a brilliant technology but it is designed to get compliance. What we have is a set of motivational mechanisms that were good for 19th century work and not bad for 20th century work. But they have outlived their usefulness for most 21st century work. If you ask people when they were most engaged at work, they don't say: 'I was so engaged when my boss told me exactly what to do.' So the challenge – and it's one that the CIPD is grappling with – is to prepare people for the workforce of now rather than the workforce of yesterday.

How could we improve motivation?

There's a certain kind of reward we use in organisations, I call it an 'if-then' reward – if you do this, then you get that. Social science tells us that if-then rewards are effective for

simple, short-term technical work but are less effective for jobs that require more creativity. If-then rewards narrow people's vision and time horizons. You can't see the fundamental systemic changes if your focus is narrow and short term. Kodak was so focused on objectives that it met all its targets – and made a brilliant job of being in the wrong business [making camera film]. The world changed underneath it. Dell hit all its numbers until people stopped buying PCs and bought tablets instead. This is what happens if you don't have a wider vision.

Does that mean we should ditch performance-related pay and stop giving people bonuses?

There isn't an easy answer to that. Money narrows your vision but the problem with if-then rewards isn't the money, the problem is the if-then part. That is a form of control and people don't do their best in complicated tasks under conditions of control. Money matters a heck of a lot, yet people can think about the work more if they are not thinking about the money.

If we can't rely on financial carrots, how can we motivate people?

What we do now is to use if-then rewards where the science tells us they work and go to another mechanism where they don't work. That mechanism is typically built around three key ideas – autonomy, mastery and purpose.

The first is the principle of self-direction – the way that human beings get engaged is by getting there under their own steam. The second one is mastery – one of the most powerful human motivators out there is getting better at something. People do this all the time in non-work realms such as sport. The final one is purpose. Purpose with a capital 'P' is 'let's change the world'; purpose with a small 'p' is more important – it's 'does what I do matter?' I think a lot of people have doubts about that and in that case they disengage.

What will happen if we don't change the way we motivate and reward people?

Ultimately, the system is unsustainable. You can run an old operating system on a new computer but it is going to crash. I still think it's amazing that if I want to know the population of, say, Liverpool, I can find it on my phone in seconds, but my kids' attitude is 'that's just how it is'. So you have this whole new generation of people who have lived their lives with rich, robust, meaningful feedback. Then we stick them in organisations and even the enlightened ones give feedback only twice a year.

Do you think businesses are up to the challenge?

I don't think there is much of a choice. What's interesting now, as we crawl slowly out of this recession, is that it offers us an opportunity to do some serious rethinking. The way we do that isn't necessarily to wave a magic wand: we just need to run our businesses a little better. Everybody has the capacity to be more innovative and creative. When we look at somebody who is passive and inert in the workplace, we tend to think that's how they are but I'm convinced that is learned behaviour. You are not going to take someone who is sluggish and inert and suddenly get them inventing the next iPad Mini – but you can help that person become a bit more autonomous.

A lot of young companies are embedding autonomy, mastery and purpose from the beginning. You also see initiatives such as 'ShipIt Days' taking hold in some bigger companies – one day of intense, undiluted autonomy, where people can work on whatever they want for a day, provided they show what they've created to their colleagues 24 hours later. No rewards, no punishments, no million-dollar bonuses for coming up with a good idea. What this does is to give people an island of autonomy in an otherwise somewhat controlling environment. Over and over again, people do creative conceptual work when they have a certain measure of autonomy and freedom.

What's HR's role in this?

The most important thing any individual HR professional can do is to challenge orthodoxy. Are if-then rewards the best way to motivate? Are yearly performance reviews the best way to provide feedback? Some of those orthodoxies are going to hold up, yet in many cases they are not. Rejecting all the orthodoxies is in some ways foolhardy, but the idea that just simply continuing to do something because that's how we've always done it is very dangerous. We also need to change the lens through which we look at the workforce. There is a lot of inertia behind certain kinds of work practices. The CIPD can be that outside force that explains to business why we need to point in a different direction.

Think Pink

Autonomy

- Look for opportunities for staff to set their own schedule.
- Focus on whether work is getting done, not how.

Mastery

- Work with your team to identify steps each member can take to improve.
- Ask people to identify how they will know they are making progress.

Purpose

- When giving instructions for a task, share the why as well as the how.
- Think about how people can experience the organisation's purpose directly.

Source: Warren (2013a) 'Don't tell people what to do'. *People Management*. 18 April.

Reproduced with kind permission of *People Management*.

Questions relating to the above article:

1   Dan Pink's thinking is quite radical. How much management do you think business requires?

2   Do you think, in reality, Pink is suggesting that organisations should phase out management or simply redefine what is meant by management in *their* specific organisation?

3   How could you visualise that the management of your business could change by redefining what managers do? The above article refers to 'ShipIt Days'. Atlassian, an American software house,

invites its employees to develop something, anything. Management do not have any influence on what an employee does, so long as they do something!

The following extract is from the Atlassian website at **www.atlassian.com**:

'Every quarter, we give employees the chance to work on anything that relates to our products, and deliver it during ShipIt Day, our 24-hour hackathon. *Been wanting to build that plugin, redesign that interface, or completely rethink that feature that's been bugging you? You've got 24 hours ... go!*

'Why? – Foster creativity – When there's no rules, anything's possible. Scratch

itches – Every employee has something that bugs them about our products, and ShipIt is the time to tackle it. Get radical, dude – ShipIt gives a spotlight and traction to radical ideas that might not normally be prioritized.

'Have fun! – Traditions like ShipIt Day help make Atlassian a more fun place to work.

'What? – Some of the projects from ShipIt Day are turned into features that go into production like FishEye's side-by-side diffs. Others were built for fun and learning like Atlassian Invaders....'

4   Do you think that your organisation would encourage or even allow 'ShipIt Days'?

12.13 OTHER FACTORS IMPACTING UPON REMUNERATION

12.13.1 LEGISLATION

All organisations have to bear in mind the provisions of the legislation on pay, for example the National Minimum Wage and discrimination laws. When developing and administering a payment scheme, therefore, the organisation has to conform to the minimum standards, which include the provisions of:

- the Employment Rights Act 1996
- the National Minimum Wage Act 1998
- the Equality Act 2010 – the Equality Act became law in October 2010. It replaces previous legislation (such as the Race Relations Act 1976 and the Disability Discrimination Act 1995) and ensures consistency by defining equality requirements within the workplace. For further information on this topic, refer to Acas guidance at: **www.acas.org.uk/index.aspx?articleid=3017**

12.14 TOTAL REWARD

Previous discussion has centred on monetary reward, the exchange between labour and pay for services rendered. However, this is not by any means the full picture, especially when one considers the totality of the factors that impact upon motivation in the workplace. When we consider all the factors that motivate people, it is important to include the non-monetary rewards such as praise and career development; the reward equation must include both tangible and intangible rewards. According to Armstrong (2012a), total reward is made up of:

Financial reward + Non-financial rewards = Total reward

Armstrong suggests (2012a) that the rewards in Figure 12.5b can also be characterised as a mix of *transactional* reward, that is, those which include the work, pay exchange, and others, which are *relational* in nature and thus depend upon how they, the employees, are engaged by the line manager and organisation in general. The mix and how the above factors are managed impact heavily upon the psychological contract.

For a fuller treatment of total reward, refer to Rumpel and Medcof (2006).

Figure 12.5a Total reward

Figure 12.5b Elements of 'total reward'

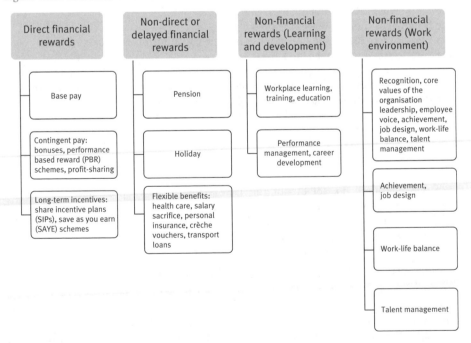

Adapted from Armstrong 2012a, p.109.

ACTIVITY 12.8

Discuss why you think that reward is one activity – perhaps the most significant and critical – within the HR armoury that impacts upon the relationship between the organisation and the individual employee.

12.15 CONTEMPORARY ISSUES

12.15.1 PENSIONS

Pensions, in the context of reward, have been dealt with earlier in the chapter in 'Pause for Thought – The Cost of Getting Old' and Activity 12.1. Space for discussion on this topic has also been found within this section because it is of significant national concern. The Government is encouraging everyone to have some form of private pension. Auto-enrolment is a means of starting the 'saving' process across the UK. It is not without its problems. Recently highlighted and placed high on the list of government priorities is to tackle the high pension administration charges levied by some pension providers.

The current value (May 2014) of the state pension is £113.10 per week, £5,881.20 per annum. It increases by the Cost of Living Index (CPI) each year, which, as of May 2014, was 2.5% (**www.gov.uk/state-pension/overview**).

This £5,881 annual income is clearly not one which would sustain a lifestyle. It just about covers the essentials of life. With the average dual-fuel energy bill in the UK at around £1,470 per household, add to this house rental, food and other basic living costs such as transport, the state pension is not one to support extravagant living. The Government's message is clear: we need to prepare for retirement because, even with a mixture of 'non-means-tested' and 'means-tested' income support, it will become a struggle to 'make ends meet' for many people after retirement. As previously discussed, the Government is encouraging, through 'auto-enrolment', employees to join a work-based pension scheme.

As well as being concerned that people are not preparing for their retirement, the Government is concerned that pension fund management organisations, which manage pensions on behalf of organisations, are charging too much for their services. Some pension fund management organisations charge as much as 2.3% to look after an employee's pension pot. Coupling these charges with inflation, the net amount the individual receives after retirement can be significantly reduced.

In response to the above concerns, and as a means to show that there is both interest and concern that those saving for retirement under the new auto-enrolment pension system get a fair deal, the Government is looking into capping the management fees which pension providers charge. The proposed cap is between 0.75% and 1% of a person's pension pot (Collinson and Watt, 2013).

To demonstrate the impact of management charges, the Government gives the example of a person paying £100 a month into their pension pot over their working career of 46 years. The effect of charges would reduce their pension pot by the following:

- around £170,000 if the annual charge was 1%; or
- around £230,000 if the annual charge was 1.5%.

The following websites give useful advice on preparing for retirement:

- Pensions Advisory Service: **www.pensionsadvisoryservice.org.uk**
- Money Advisory Service: **www.moneyadviceservice.org.uk/en/articles/protecting-your-retirement-income**
- See Steve Webb, the government minister responsible for pensions, talking about pension management organisations. Available at: **www.bbc.co.uk/news/business-24736960**

The CIPD offers advice to organisations on 'auto-enrolment' compliance to meet the Government's requirement that they offer their staff a work-based pension at: **www.cipd.co.uk/podcasts/_articles/_Pension-auto-enrolment-the-practicalities.htm**

12.15.2 EMPLOYEE VALUE PROPOSITION (EVP)

The green shoots of improvements to the UK economy have rekindled concern about the recruitment and retention of quality staff. There is a pressing need for organisations to think about how they are going to hold on to talented individuals and how to recognise and attract future talent.

Total reward has strong links to the notion of *employer branding* and the *employee value proposition* (EVP). The concepts are not new but they have relevance as a means of giving focus to those things that employees value.

Reward, in all its various facets, is one of the key features which can influence how an employee perceives the value of working for their organisation. Other aspects, such as culture, engagement, involvement, the organisation's core values, and so on, may inform opinion. The nature of the EVP will change from organisation to organisation. Clearly, therefore, the only absolute way to find out what employees value is to ask them. Many organisations conduct annual surveys of their employees. Distilling from this type of survey the relevant information which relates to the employee value proposition and, above all, using the insights gleaned to inform reward practice is a powerful tool to improve employer-employee linkages and the employer brand.

- See how Deloitte portrays its EVP to potential employees at: **www.youtube.com/watch?v=qDXWYzz7cHM** and **www.youtube.com/watch?v=XyQnILVaoI0**
- See what the Australian Strategist Group, a commercial organisation, has to say about employer branding at: **www.youtube.com/watch?v=dN8CNZ78syg**
- View Malcolm Gladwell discussing 'Choice, happiness and spaghetti sauce' at: **www.youtube.com/watch?v=iIiAAhUeR6Y&list=PLr0D4AII35YTI1yUa-5W0Z075QiS9_Ljk**

How does Gladwell's video narrative relate to the employee value proposition?

ACTIVITY 12.9

Soldiers from the British Army, sailors from the Royal Navy and Royal Air Force men and women all go into harm's way at the bequest of our political leaders, yet they are not incentivised to do so. They may receive remuneration for the harsh conditions they endure while on active service but not for putting their lives at risk. They perform their duties diligently and with good humour. Can industry learn from the military? Perhaps the advertisements for military jobs do not offer a true picture of what 'service' is about. On the other hand, we are all aware of the loss of life and terrible injuries suffered in Iraq and Afghanistan. So what motivates people to join?

Discuss why people should be prepared to put their lives at stake for relatively little reward.

Advertisements for the Army and Royal Marine Commando can be found at:

- Royal Marine Commando: **www.youtube. com/watch?v=OhahiQJhfTo**

- British Army: **www.army.mod.uk/Join/ StepUp/default.aspx/? campaigncode=N13X00200A&referrer= N13X00200BPPC01&gclid=COXbwbevxro CFSrJtAodd1UA8g**

12.15.3 EQUAL PAY REVIEWS

The Fawcett Society in their 4 March 2012 campaign poster on equal pay offer the following damning comment on the state of pay parity between men and women:

> Over 40 years after the Equal Pay Act came into force in the UK women still face a stark gap in their earnings compared to men's and experience one of the highest pay gaps in the EU.

> In 2012, comparing all work, women earned 18.6% less per hour than men. Comparing those in full-time work, women earned an average of 14.9% less per hour than men – this means that for every £1 a man takes home, a woman takes home 85p.

> The pay gap varies across sectors and regions, rising to up to 33% in the City of London and 55% in the finance sector. (Fawcett Society, 2012, **www.fawcettsociety. org.uk**)

In its 2009* *Reward Management* annual survey report, the CIPD advises '…that overall, 52% of respondents have already carried out, or plan, an equal pay review (EPR)'.

*Note, the CIPD (2009) survey as indicated above is the most recent the author has sourced on the topic.

Why is it good practice to carry out an EPR? The Equality and Human Rights Commission (EHRC, n.d.) argues that:

> The Equality Act 2010 (the Act) gives women (and men) a right to equal pay for equal work. It replaces previous legislation, including the Equal Pay Act 1970 and the Sex Discrimination Act 1975, and the equality provisions in the Pensions Act 1995.

> Under the Equality Act (2010) employees may claim equal pay with colleagues of the opposite sex where they are in the same employment and are doing equal work. Equal work can be:

- The same, or broadly similar (known as like work)
- Different, but which is already rated under the same job evaluation scheme as equivalent to hers (known as work rated as equivalent)
- Different, but which would be assessed as equal in value in terms of demands such as effort, skill and decision-making (known as work of equal value)

> …the same principles apply in equal pay cases in relation to race, disability, age and whether employees are full-time or part-time.

The Code of Practice on Equal Pay, which emanates from the Equality Act (2010) came into force in April 2011. It was developed by the EHRC. Its main purpose is to provide a detailed explanation of the equal pay provisions in the Equality Act 2010. It will assist courts and tribunals when interpreting the law and help those who need to apply the law and understand its technical detail; it applies to England, Wales and Scotland.

The Equality and Human Rights Commission recommends that all employers regularly review and monitor their pay practices, although this is not a formal legal requirement. Involving trade unions or other employee representatives can help make pay systems more transparent. This code (Part 2) suggests that equal pay audits may be the most effective means of ensuring that a pay system delivers equal pay (Equality and Human Rights Commission, 2011, p.9).

The EHRC (2011, p.50) also advises that employers should ensure that their pay systems are transparent. They indicate that:

> ...a number of common pay practices, listed below, pose risks in terms of potential non-compliance with an employer's legal obligations:

- Lack of transparency and unnecessary secrecy over grading and pay
- Discretionary pay systems (for example, merit pay and performance-related pay) unless they are clearly structured and based on objective criteria
- Different non-basic pay, terms and conditions for different groups of employees (for example, attendance allowances, overtime or unsocial hours payments)
- More than one grading and pay system within the organisation
- Long pay scales or ranges
- Overlapping pay scales or ranges, where the maximum of the lower payscale is higher than the minimum of the next higher scale, including 'broad banded' structures where there are significant overlaps
- Managerial discretion over starting salaries
- Market-based pay systems or supplements not underpinned by job evaluation
- Job evaluation systems which have been incorrectly implemented or not kept up to date
- Pay protection policies.

EHRC (2011, p.50)

The Statutory Code of Practice on Equal Pay is available at: **www.equalityhumanrights.com/uploaded_files/EqualityAct/equalpaycode.pdf**

It is also worth looking at the Hay Group's (HR consultancy) website to see their advice on equal pay audits: **www.haygroup.com**

 ACTIVITY 12.10

Why do you think that the EHRC (reference the above list of pay practices) does not recommend that organisations use the above in their pay practices? Can you explain the linkage between, for example, managerial discretion over pay practices and long pay scales and potential unfair pay practice? Some of the linkages are more transparent and easy to explain than others.

 ACTIVITY 12.11

Using the advice given by the EHRC (2011, pp.47–57) website **www.equalityhumanrights.com/uploaded_files/EqualityAct/equalpaycode.pdf**, explore how an equal pay audit should be conducted. Do you consider that there are jobs or groups of jobs within your organisation that would be shown to be under- or over-valued when compared with others that are staffed mainly by female employees?

12.15.4 NATIONAL MINIMUM WAGE (NMW)

Workers are entitled to be paid at least the level of the statutory National Minimum Wage (NMW) for every hour they work for an employer. The level of the wage is reviewed by the Low Pay Commission on an annual basis (for further information go to Chapter 16).

12.15.5 THE LIVING WAGE

The Joseph Rowntree Foundation defines an 'adequate income' as:

> It is based on what members of the public think is enough money to live on, to maintain a socially-acceptable quality of life. (Joseph Rowntree Foundation: **www. jrf.org.uk/topic/mis?gclid=CIXgidKDu74CFbShtAodlHAA5g**)

Hirsch (2013, p.4) suggests that the Minimum Income Standard (MIS) budget, '. . .a single person requires £201 a week, excluding rent, up from £193 in 2012. This requires a wage of £16,852 a year (based on assumptions about minimum housing costs).' Hirsch's MIS calculator proposes an hourly rate of £8.62 for a single person and £9.91 per hour each for a couple with two children.

The Joseph Rowntree Foundation publishes details of what they consider to be the minimum annual wage (JRF call it the minimum wage standard). They provide an online calculator where people can assess their own income against the minimum standard, available at: **www.minimumincome.org.uk**

Warner, writing in the *Telegraph* of 17 January 2013 about public opinion and 'bankers' bonus payments', the growth in the economy and related topics, comes to the conclusion that there is in fact a case for the 'living wage'. He writes,

> . . .the great bulk of internationally competitive business in Britain already pays living wages. It is in the low-skilled, service areas of the economy that the problem largely lies.

> Set high enough, a living wage would obviate the need for in-work benefits – one of the biggest areas of growth in welfare spending; it would significantly add to demand in the economy; and it would substantially boost tax receipts, ... (Warner, 2013)

He believes that the concept is not yet ready to be adopted, but 'the banking crisis has turned much conventional thinking on its head. This may be an idea whose time will yet come' (ibid).

12.16 SUMMARY

As indicated earlier in this chapter, success of the organisation is ultimately determined by the performance of its employees. It follows, therefore, that an organisation needs to recruit and retain people who are appropriately skilled and flexible in their outlook. From this, it follows that the reward systems must support the overall business strategy, indeed they should flow from it, and that pay should be commensurate with employees' contributions to the positive outcomes of the organisation.

The chapter discusses and explains what is meant by reward in its widest sense. Reward is a mix of financial and non-financial factors that, when managed in a holistic manner, are seen as contributing to how an individual is compensated for their efforts.

E.E. Lawler (1990) and Schuster and Zingheim (1992) were the first to put their names to the concept of 'new pay'. The focus of this concept is that reward should be linked to performance. Perry et al (2009, p.45) argue, though, that PRP, especially in the public sector, has not delivered the intended outcomes; it has provided more rhetoric than reality. It does, however, have its roots in fairness and equality. In some cases, within the private sector, where the conditions have been appropriate and there has been care over communication of its aims, it has had some limited success.

How someone is remunerated is a mix of base pay, contingent pay, which is dependent upon some deliverable outcome, and benefits. Contingent pay can be based upon some form of incentive, that is, upon the successful delivery of a completed item, or alternatively the incentive could be based upon a measure of quality. Payment schemes, especially in manufacturing, have developed over the years and can be based upon rate per item completed or perhaps a base pay with bonuses paid for items completed over and above a threshold level. Schemes have also been designed that reward the achievement of competences.

Part of the package of reward is made up of benefits; the benefits package can be fixed so that all within the organisation receive the same, or it can be flexible, in which case employees can choose and even swap cash for benefits or even buy supplementary benefits. The benefits package, especially if it is tailored to the needs of the organisation, can be powerful in the retention of employees. The CIPD gives advice on the most common range of benefits offered by organisations.

Total reward is a concept that brings all elements of reward into the equation, including non-financial reward. Savvy organisations consider how they link, in a joined-up manner, base pay, contingent pay, benefits and non-financial rewards (recognition, leadership and so on – Herzberg's motivators) and how they wish to position themselves in context to the employees' perception of the organisation. Total reward has strong links to the notion of *employer branding* and the *employee value proposition* (EVP). Some organisations are offering what is termed *total reward statements* (TRS). The TRS provides personalised information about the value of an individual's employment package. It includes details about remuneration and the benefits provided by the employer.

Reward is an emotive subject because the process of rewarding people is as important as the level of reward or the size of a bonus payment. Employees seek to reassure themselves that they have been rewarded fairly compared with others in a similar situation, that is, that there is an equity of reward and that there has been due regard to distributive justice. Employers are advised to operate systems of rewarding people that have due regard to procedural justice, that is, a transparency, a clarity of how the decisions on bonus levels have been made. Having some form of appeal emphasises that there is a process which can be logically defended.

REVIEW QUESTIONS

1 How would you define 'reward'?

2 What are non-financial rewards?

3 Why does an organisation offer particular benefits and facilities? What is in it for the organisation?

4 Define the following:

- total earnings and total remuneration
- incentives and rewards.

5 Why do you think E.E. Lawler, and Schuster and Zingheim, proposed what they term 'new pay'? What are the key differences between 'new pay' and 'old pay'?

6 What are the constraints and obligations (or pressures) that influence the formulation of reward strategy? (You may wish to go onto the Towers Watson website at **www.towerswatson.com** to see what advice they offer on reward strategy.)

7 Incentive schemes are so called because they are designed to have a positive influence on future performance, but what does a PRP scheme reward?

8 Why do you consider that PRP is more likely to work in private than in public sector organisations?

9 What do you understand by the term EVP? Why is it so important? In what way does it link to the concept of employer brand?

10 The gender pay gap is still with our society. Read the Office for National Statistics (2013) *Patterns of Pay: Results from the Annual Survey of Hours and Earnings, 1997 to 2012*. Available at: **www.ons.gov.uk/ons/ dcp171766_300035.pdf**. Particularly access the graph on page 19, 'Gender pay gap for median full-time hourly earnings (excluding overtime) by major occupation group, UK, April 2012', and reflect upon why in some occupations the gender pay gap is more pronounced than in others, for example Managers v Professional Occupations. What other information would you need to be able to make some logical decisions as to why the pay gap should vary?

11 Go to the website of the Low Pay Commission and see what they have to say about the levels of the National Minimum Wage. What are the current levels?

12 What is the difference between the National Minimum Wage and the Living Wage? You will get some idea of what this means by accessing the 'Living Wage Foundation' website at: **www.livingwage.org.uk**

EXPLORE FURTHER

BOOKS

ARMSTRONG, M. (2012) *Armstrong's handbook of reward management practice [online]*. 4th ed. London: Kogan Page. [Accessed 1 November 2013]. Available at: www.dawsonera.com

Any suggested further reading list is not complete without mention of Michael Armstrong's text on reward management. Armstrong writes in an authoritative yet easy to understand style. His text covers all aspects of reward and is one of those books that an HR professional should have on their bookshelf, ready for easy access should the need arise.

The above text, as indicated, is available online through ebook resources (Dawsonera).

VIDEO DISCUSSION

Listen and watch

A very funny, yet serious video clip of a presentation by Frans de Waal about equality, 'Fair pay for monkeys'. Available at: **www.youtube.com/watch?v=-dMoK48QGL8**

Dan Pink discusses why performance-related pay should not be used and why people should not be managed! The video is available at: **www.youtube.com/watch?v=rrkrvAUbU9Y#t=24**

John Bremen, Managing Director, Talent and Rewards, The Americas, Towers Watson, discusses three things successful employers are doing with their total rewards programmes to maximise the value to employees – the idea of Employee Value Proposition (EVP), available at: **www.youtube.com/watch?v=ABtIOvw4uCU**

A video which offers some insights into the gender pay gap as explained by the European Union: **www.youtube.com/watch?v=hoAWOlL2RIo**

See what Towers Watson Consulting has to say about 'total reward', available at:

www.youtube.com/watch?v=fGfemoNZUIc

The Office for National Statistics discussion on work at: **www.ons.gov.uk/ons/rel/ lmac/women-in-the-labour-market/2013/video-summaey.html**

USEFUL DOCUMENTS

The Statutory Code of Practice on Equal Pay: **www.equalityhumanrights.com/ uploaded_files/EqualityAct/equalpaycode.pdf**

Reward and pay: an overview (CIPD Factsheet): **www.cipd.co.uk/hr-resources/ factsheets/reward-pay-overview.aspx**

Office for National Statistics (2013) *Patterns of Pay: Results from the Annual Survey of Hours and Earnings, 1997 to 2012*: **www.ons.gov.uk/ons/dcp171766_300035.pdf**

WEB LINKS

The CIPD offers a number of factsheets and surveys dealing with reward issues: Reward podcast, Reward and Diversity, Reward Management annual survey, Reward Strategy, Rewarding Performance and Rewarding Work: The vital role of line managers [in the reward process]. These can all be found at: **www.cipd.co.uk/ onlineinfodocuments/atozresources.htm**

Other useful web links

Acas: **www.acas.org.uk**

Department for Business, Innovation and Skills: **www.gov.uk/government/ organisations/department-for-business-innovation-skills**

Equality and Human Rights Commission: **www.equalityhumanrights.com**

Fawcett Society (not for profit): **www.fawcettsociety.org.uk**

Hay Group (consultants): **www.haygroup.com**

Living Wage Foundation: **www.livingwage.org.uk**

Low Pay Commission: **www.lowpay.gov.uk**

Pensions Management Institute: **www.pensions-pmi.org.uk/home/**

Schuster-Zingheim and Associates (consultants): **www.paypeopleright.com**

Towers Watson (consultants): **www.towerswatson.com**

UK Acts of Parliament: **www.legislation.gov.uk**

Unison (union): **www.unison.org.uk**

World at Work (consultants): **www.worldatwork.org**

CHAPTER 13

The Employment Relationship

LEARNING OBJECTIVES

After studying this chapter you should:

- be able to define the employment relationship and understand its legal framework
- understand the psychological contract
- be able to differentiate between the unitarist, pluralist and Marxist perspectives on the employment relationship
- understand how the multiple agencies and organisations impact upon the employment relationship
- understand the role of trade unions
- be aware of the role played by Acas in employment relations
- understand one of the key areas of employment relations: absence management.

13.1 INTRODUCTION

The aim of this chapter is to provide an understanding of the employment relationship and the elements that shape its formal and informal structure. The term employee relations (ER) tends to have taken over from 'industrial relations', mainly because of the decline in 'industry' and the move towards service and knowledge economies. There has also been a general move away from collective bargaining towards a more individualised approach (see Chapter 12, 'Employee Reward', for more on pay). In 1979, the trade unions represented and spoke for over 13 million employees, compared with around 6 million today. Industrial relations (IR) often inferred all sorts of negative connotations, such as disputes, strikes and an 'us and them' mentality. In today's world, attitudes have mostly changed with more focus on engagement and 'working together for the same goals'. 'Employee relations' tends to have a wider remit – it is that part of human resource management that deals with the whole of the relationship between management and employees.

'Employment relations', then, not only applies to any collective agreements between unions and management, but also includes the contractual and statutory rights and obligations of the employer and the employee; the importance of the psychological contract within the employee relationship; and the rules and procedures that are put in place to manage the employment relationship collectively and at individual level.

KEY CONCEPT: THE EMPLOYMENT RELATIONSHIP

Blyton and Turnbull (cited in Rose, 2008, p.7) define the employment relationship as being 'the context within which intricate interactions between employees, who may be unionised or nonunionised, and employers, are conducted, both collectively and individually'.

13.2 THE EMPLOYMENT RELATIONSHIP

It can be argued that the 'interactions' are framed by the relationship between employer and employee. There is of course a contractual relationship but one where there is plenty of scope for filling in gaps with meaningful and constructive discussion and negotiation.

Employee relations is about this relationship between the employer and the employee. There are formal and informal aspects to the relationship and both parties have rights, obligations and expectations. The formal side is regulated through the provisions of the *contract of employment*, and in the UK legislation sets common standards for the conduct of the relationship. In very broad terms it can be said that the informal side of the relationship is governed by what is known as the *psychological contract*.

KEY CONCEPT: THE PSYCHOLOGICAL CONTRACT

This is a contract that is based upon the employee's subjective expectations of, and beliefs about, the relationship between themselves and the organisation. It is tacit, not negotiated, and includes subjective assumptions made by both sides.

> A major feature of psychological contracts is the concept of mutuality – that there is a common and agreed understanding of promises and obligations the respective parties have made to each other about work, pay, loyalty, commitment, flexibility, security and career advancement. (Pointon and Ryan, 2004, p.520)

With the exception of pay, all of these promises and obligations are items you would not find in the formal employment contract, but they are important determinants of behaviour.

It was Edgar Schein who first identified the concept and used the term 'psychological contract'. He said that 'the notion of a psychological contract implies that there is an unwritten set of expectations operating at all times between every member of an organisation and the various managers and others in that organisation' (Schein, 1965).

It is within the reciprocal spirit of the psychological contract that people are motivated to work, gain satisfaction from what they do, develop feelings of job security, belongingness and commitment, and enjoy a culture of trust and mutual respect. All of this implies that the *exchange* aspect of the psychological contract is about mutual expectations and the satisfying of needs.

13.2.1 BREACHING THE PSYCHOLOGICAL CONTRACT

The psychological contract needs to be handled with care. As with any other kind of contract, it is capable of – and even susceptible to – being breached. Where it is breached by the organisation it seriously affects employee morale. Goodwill is one of the mainstays of a positive relationship between employer and employee. It leads to mutually advantageous informal employee behaviour, such as carrying out tasks that are not on the list of duties. Such behaviour should be fostered, since if everyone did exactly what was on their job descriptions and nothing else, you would never get everything done. Goodwill can take a long time to establish, yet it can be destroyed with a single thoughtless act.

PAUSE FOR THOUGHT

Do you feel as if you have a psychological contract with your employer? What do you expect from your employer that is not in your employment contract? What do you think your employer expects from you? Additionally,

what about your tutors at the university or college you attend? Is there a psychological contract between you and them? What are the unwritten expectations of both parties?

13.3 DIFFERENCES BETWEEN CONTRACTS

As is discussed in detail in Chapter 16, all employees have a contract of employment. The contract is based on what both parties have agreed to be a *fair exchange* (the employee's time and skill in exchange for a salary or wage), that is, the notion of wage/effort or pay/performance bargaining. However, as well as the formal contract of employment there is a relationship, hopefully positive, which has developed between the employer and the employee. This relationship, although not bound by a formal agreement, is of equal importance because it can influence how far the employee is prepared to exercise discretionary behaviour, sometimes called organisation citizenship behaviour (OCB) (as also discussed in detail in Chapter 3), and work beyond the formal contract of employment. The way that line managers handle the relationship between themselves and their staff is key to how employees feel about and thus are prepared to engage in their work. As Kinnie et al (2005) write, '...employee attitudes are influenced not so much by the way these policies [meaning HR policies] are intended to operate as by the way they are actually implemented by line managers and team leaders on a day-to-day basis'.

ACTIVITY 13.1

Discretionary behaviour

Access the CIPD's factsheet *How to ... Unlock Discretionary Effort*, available from **www.peoplemanagement.co.uk/pm/articles/2006/10/howtounlock.htm**. Compare and contrast what is said in this article with the

view on discretionary behaviour expressed by John Philpott in his *People Management* article 'By the book' (Philpott, 2004, p.26).

What can be done realistically in order to encourage discretionary behaviour?

13.4 PERSPECTIVES ON THE EMPLOYMENT RELATIONSHIP

In the previous section we learned about the psychological contract and the unwritten expectations associated with this concept. However, there are other perspectives on the relationship between management and their employees. The previous concept, the idea of building a positive psychological contract, leads to goodwill and positive employment relations, but there are other ways to view the employment relationship. Examples of these perspectives are the unitary and the pluralistic perspectives and the rather less relevant Marxist perspective.

13.4.1 THE UNITARIST PERSPECTIVE

The unitarist perspective (refer also to Chapter 3) sees the organisation as one big happy family, where everyone shares similar goals and objectives, rather than having diverse interests which may lead to antagonistic behaviour. The unitarist view sees conflict as being negative and disruptive – that is, something to be avoided. This approach, whereby employees are expected to be loyal, sees trade unions' role being more as a moderating force rather than taking an aggressive stand against management.

Reward for effort comes only if the organisation functions efficiently and effectively enough to achieve its economic and growth objectives. The philosophy of HRM, with its emphasis on commitment and mutuality, is based on the unitary perspective; the basis of HR policies should be to unify effort, motivate and inspire employees with reward systems designed to foster loyalty and commitment.

13.4.2 THE PLURALIST PERSPECTIVE

This is the opposite view to unitarism: pluralism expects that there will be diverse groups who represent a range of interested parties, all with *differing* views, objectives, rules and loyalties. Groups may include trade unions, shareholders, employees, management and other stakeholders. Pluralism relies on managing by consent, rather than by right. Conflict is seen as natural and unavoidable – and even as a good thing, in that it brings about challenges to traditional thinking and encourages innovation and change.

13.4.3 THE MARXIST PERSPECTIVE

Rather dated now, but still occasionally in evidence, the Marxist philosophy has in the past played an important part in industrial relations. It sees inequality in wealth and power as emanating from capitalism and that management have an interest in retaining this imbalance of power: trade unionism therefore is essential in helping to avoid this exploitation.

 PAUSE FOR THOUGHT

Think of your own organisation or one that you have frequent business contact with:

- List all types of people or organisations that may be involved with and impact upon the employment relationship.

- How many of these organisations or actors impact upon the day-to-day relationship, and which affect the relationship infrequently?

ACTIVITY 13.2

Think about how your organisation (or one with which you are familiar) is managed. How do you think employees are/were regarded by the managers? What does the managerial style indicate to you? What needs do the employees have in common with the employer? What needs do employees have that are in direct opposition to the employer's wishes? In light of what is said above, do you regard it as a unitary or a pluralistic organisation?

13.4.4 HRM AND PLURALISM

There are aspects of HRM, such as *individual* commitment and *mutuality of interest* in the success of the organisation, which are in sympathy with the unitary concept, and therefore in conflict with a pluralistic philosophy. However, employers and employees do indeed have different interests – which fits the pluralistic view.

According to Armstrong (2014, p.415): 'The nature of the employment relationship is strongly influenced by HR actions.' He suggests that one of the ways in which HR can contribute to the development of a positive and productive employment relationship is by 'adopting a general policy of transparency', so that employees know what is happening in the organisation and how that impacts on their employment, development and prospects. The CIPD survey report on Employment Relations (CIPD, 2011a) states that '55% of respondents describe the relationship between management and unions as positive or very positive' – which is an encouraging indicator of the state of ER.

13.4.5 EMPLOYEE ENGAGEMENT

Employee relations today focuses on employee commitment, involvement and engagement. Part of the role of HR is to increase this involvement and enable employees to participate in workplace decisions, thus giving workers an opportunity to really engage with their employment – which fits in with the unitarist approach mentioned above. It also links with the notion of the psychological contract – in that those who are engaged and involved with their work and workplace are likely to have a positive psychological contract.

MacLeod and Clarke (2009, p.75) suggest that one of the four drivers of engagement is employee voice, the others being leadership, engaging managers and integrity. On employee voice they say this means:

> An effective and empowered employee voice is where employees' views are sought out; they are listened to and see that their opinions count and make a difference. They speak out and challenge where appropriate. A sense of listening and responsiveness permeates the organisation, enabled by effective communication.

So today many employers have increased their efforts in communicating directly with employees, rather than through trade unions. There has been a rise in employer-sponsored forms of employee participation and representation: over the past 25 years there has been a large increase in the proportion of workplaces using non-union mechanisms to give employees a 'voice'. Willman et al (2009) suggest that appetite for employee participation and representation has not diminished, but rather shifted away from the forms involving unions.

ACTIVITY 13.3

Read the Acas (2012c) 'Future of Workplace Relations' discussion paper *Voice and Participation in the Modern Workplace: challenges and prospects* (March 2012), available at: **www.acas.org.uk/index.aspx? articleid=4701&q=voice**

What are your thoughts – do these newer types of communication with the workforce exist in organisations that you are aware of? Do they actually work in increasing engagement? Do they replace trade unions?

13.5 PARTIES IN THE EMPLOYMENT RELATIONSHIP

Taking a pluralist perspective, there are a number of parties who are part of the wider employment relationship; the obvious ones are employers and employees, and trade unions, who act on behalf of employees. At a higher level there are other institutions that impact on the way in which employment relations are carried out, such as the Confederation of British Industry (CBI), which is the body that represents the interests of employers at a government level, and the Trades Union Congress (TUC).

ACTIVITY 13.4

Before looking at Figure 13.1, see what institutions you can think of which have an impact on the employment relationship at a policy-making level. Make a note, then check

your answers with the ones given in Figure 13.1. (Organisations relating to the trade union institutions are given later in the chapter.)

13.5.1 CONFEDERATION OF BRITISH INDUSTRY (CBI)

The CBI, as they say on their website, '. . .deliver results by lobbying and campaigning . . . to keep business interests at the heart of policy in Westminster' and 'speak for more than 240,000 companies of every size'. Their aim is to represent views of UK business and try to influence the UK Government and international legislators throughout the world. They take a stance, on behalf of their business members, and then represent this view to government, whether this is in the UK or overseas. They are a member of BusinessEurope.

13.5.2 BUSINESSEUROPE – THE CONFEDERATION OF EUROPEAN BUSINESS

BusinessEurope describe themselves as 'the leading advocate for growth and competitiveness at European level, standing up for companies across the continent and campaigning on the issues that most influence their performance. A recognised social partner, we speak for all-sized enterprises in 35 European countries whose national business federations are our direct members' (**www.businesseurope.eu**).

On behalf of its European members (of which the CBI is one), BusinessEurope deals with the following policy areas: economic and financial affairs; international relations; social affairs; industrial affairs; legal affairs; entrepreneurship and small and medium-sized enterprises (SMEs); and the internal market. BusinessEurope has a voice on the European Union's European Economic and Social Committee (EESC), which is itself a consultative body of the European Union, acting as 'an advisory body which helps to ensure that

European policies and legislation tie in better with economic, social and civic circumstances on the ground' (**www.eesc.europa.eu**).

Figure 13.1 Some key players in the employment relationship

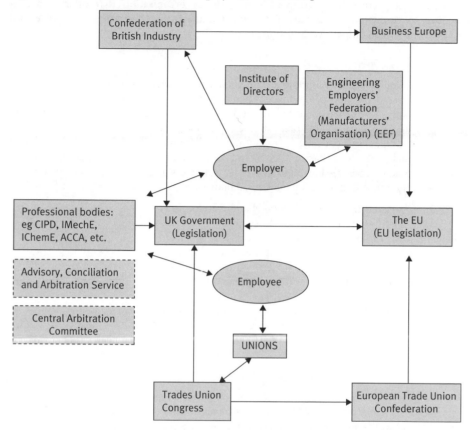

Note: Lines and arrows indicate where there is influence and/or lobbying.

Groups such as the CBI, through BusinessEurope, trades union representative bodies such as the European Trade Union Confederation (ETUC), consumers, and so on, all have a place at the European Union's table, where their voice can be heard and taken into consideration when policy and legislation is developed.

13.5.3 INSTITUTE OF DIRECTORS (IOD)

The IOD are an independent association of business leaders. Their aim is to support businesses and encourage entrepreneurial activity and responsible business practice for the benefit of the business community and society as a whole.

They exert influence through direct discussion with local MPs, civil servants, by writing responses to consultation documents and by producing research and policy papers.

The IOD have around 34,500 members and are non-political. As well as acting as a lobbying organisation on behalf of its members, they offer guidance and advice to directors to help them run their businesses.

13.5.4 ENGINEERING EMPLOYERS' FEDERATION (MANUFACTURERS' ORGANISATION) (EEF)

The EEF – as well as being a lobbying organisation that represents the manufacturing industries' perspective at government level – is an organisation that offers practical guidance to its members. Its aim is to help manufacturing companies to evolve and compete in today's competitive environment.

13.5.5 PROFESSIONAL BODIES

Professional bodies represent employees in their chosen profession and set standards of professional behaviour and competence. They offer training and often have their own set of qualifications. The professional bodies, on behalf of their members, will take a view on developing policy issues and present them to interested bodies, which could be government or government-related organisations. They also, through research and best practice models, seek to influence their members to adopt certain practices and thus, in turn, these practices will feed through into organisational standards of member groups.

Some of the more well-known professional bodies are:

- CIPD – Chartered Institute of Personnel and Development
- IMechE – Institution of Mechanical Engineers
- IChemE – Institution of Chemical Engineers
- CIMA – Chartered Institute of Management Accountants
- ACCA – Association of Chartered Certified Accountants
- ILM – Institute of Leadership and Management.

13.6 UNIONS AND THE ROLE OF UNIONS

KEY CONCEPT: TRADE UNION

A trade union as defined in law, by the Trade Union and Labour Relations (Consolidation) Act 1992, 'consists wholly or mainly of workers of one or more descriptions and whose principal purposes include the regulation of relations between workers of that description or those descriptions and employers or employers' associations'.

PAUSE FOR THOUGHT

The role of the trade union

Are you a member of a trade union? What benefits are there to you as a member? What is the relationship between your employer and your union? Does this fit with the unitarist or the pluralist approach?

13.6.1 TRADE UNION MEMBERSHIP

Unions are, themselves, organised in many different ways – occupational, craft-based, general, and so on – but there has been a recent trend towards mergers to create super unions, a development that, in itself, will shift the dynamics of the relationship.

Trade union membership accounts for just over a quarter (26%) of the workforce (Department for Business, Innovation and Skills, 2012). The WERS survey 2011 shows that only 10% of workplaces have a majority of their workers who are union members. This continues the slow decline of union representation – in 2004, 14% of workplaces had a majority of their workforce in a union. There are now just less than 6 million members of TUC-affiliated unions, which is less than half the number just 30 years ago; peak figures reached just over 13 million members in 1979. The two largest unions are UNITE and UNISON (TUC, 2014).

The decline of the manufacturing sector accounts for some of the drop in numbers: in 1995, there were around 1.5 million union members in the manufacturing sector. Some 17 years later, the numbers had reduced by a third to around 0.5 million.

Public sector union members accounted for an increasing proportion of overall union membership in the period up to 2010, with rising membership until 2010, but because of the effects of the recession and fiscal consolidation, membership declined sharply between 2010 and 2011 and levelled off between 2011 and 2012. Private sector membership did the reverse: dropping from 1995, but then slightly increasing from 2011 (see Department for Business, Innovation and Skills, 2012).

Trade union members are increasingly older employees. About 36% of trade union member employees were aged over 50 in 2012, compared with 22% in 1995 (Department for Business, Innovation and Skills, 2012).

ACTIVITY 13.5

Trade union membership

The Department for Business, Innovation and Skills and Office for National Statistics are responsible for publishing the national statistics on trade union membership. Go to **www.gov.uk/government/publications/trade-union-statistics-2012** and look at the documents on trade union membership statistics.

In addition to an Excel document giving detailed statistical figures, you will also find a statistical bulletin which gives an analysis on membership trends and characteristics. The commentary on how things have changed since the 1970s makes an interesting read.

- What appear to be the reasons for the drop in membership?
- Which groups of employees are most likely to be in a union?
- Does being in a union make a difference to your pay? (see page 9 of *Trade Union Membership 2012: Statistical Bulletin* for answers to this).

13.6.2 WOMEN IN TRADE UNIONS

Female employees are more likely to be members of a trade union. In 2012 the proportion of female employees who were in a trade union was around 29% (3,613,000 women) compared with 23% of male employees (3,142,000).

Fifty-five per cent of union members were female in 2012, up from 45% in 1995 (Department for Business, Innovation and Skills, 2012).

ACTIVITY 13.6

Unionisation of women

There are more women than men in trade unions: 3,613,000 women as opposed to 3,142,000 men (Department for Business, Innovation and Skills, 2012).

● Can you think of reasons why union membership of women has increased?

13.6.3 CHANGES IN THE ROLE OF TRADE UNIONS

Workplace relationships are on the whole very different from how they were in the 1970s and early 1980s, where unions represented the workforce and spoke for employees collectively (39% of the workforce were in a union in 1989 compared to 26% in 2012). Nowadays, with less collective bargaining (29% of employees are covered by collective agreements) and a greater focus on individualism, the employment relationship has changed. Unions do still work towards making their members' lives at work better, but much of the antagonism has gone. Strikes still occur, but at much lower frequency than historically. In the 1970s the number of strikes averaged between 2,000 and 3,000 every year, peaking in 1979 when almost 30 million working days were lost due to industrial action. In 2012 this had dropped to 131 stoppages of work with 248,800 working days lost through labour disputes. The actual number of stoppages is fairly evenly split between the public and private sector, but the public sector accounts for 79% of days lost. The majority of cases centre on wage disputes (Office for National Statistics, July 2013).

ACTIVITY 13.7

Labour disputes

Look at the Office for National Statistics' *Labour Disputes Annual Article 2012*, available at **www.ons.gov.uk/ons/rel/bus-register/labour-disputes/annual-article-2012/art—labour-disputes–annual-article-2012.html**

● In which industries/sectors were the most disputes? (See Table 3 Industrial analyses.) Are you surprised at this?
● What were the main causes for disputes? (See Tables 6 and 7.)

As we can see, then, the role of trade unions is changing. There is less need to fight for rights and pay (although the need still exists, as can be witnessed by the large number of employment tribunal cases). But, much of the historical campaigning for rights has led to the huge advances in UK employment legislation, and today unions focus more on working together with employers to achieve results.

13.6.4 FUNCTIONS OF TRADE UNIONS

If the unions' main function is not to negotiate pay, then what is their role? One is as a campaigner for employment rights and improvement of working conditions. Today's unions are listened to by government and employers and act as an influential voice in the wider areas of health and safety, for example. Another role is to support members at tribunal cases, for example in claims for unfair dismissal, improper deductions from wages, discrimination cases, and so on. In 2012 unions won a record £330 million compensation for their members through legal action. They won £1 million in equal pay claims – an average of £15,000 per member. In the best workplaces employers and unions have put behind them outdated ideas of confrontation and work together in partnership (TUC website, 2013).

A union looks after the interests of employees at work by:

- negotiating agreements with employers on pay and conditions
- discussing big changes such as large-scale redundancy
- discussing members' concerns with employers
- going with members to disciplinary and grievance meetings.

(**www.gov.uk**, Joining a Trade Union)

ACTIVITY 13.8

Role of unions

Read the Acas discussion paper '*What role for trade unions in future workplace relations?*' available at **www.acas.org.uk/index.aspx?articleid=4701&q=role+for+trade+unions**

- What do you think the role of unions will be in future?

13.6.5 TRADE UNION REPRESENTATIVES

Trade union representatives (or workplace representatives) are not employed by the trade union, but are employees of the company, who are allowed time off to carry out union activities. This might include such tasks as representing members at a disciplinary hearing, assisting with a grievance or negotiating over conditions of employment. Trade union representatives are elected to the position and represent employees in a particular department or section of the organisation. There may also be a senior representative (a 'convenor'), who spends all of their time on union business and may be paid either by the employer or by the union.

Unions are made up of local branches, which may comprise workers in one organisation, or several in one geographical area. Above the branch there is usually an 'area' or 'regional office', which is staffed by employees of the union.

13.6.6 UPHOLDING EMPLOYEE RIGHTS

One of the aims of a trade union is to represent and assist people who feel they have been treated unfairly in the workplace. There were 191,541 claims which went to employment tribunals between April 2012 and March 2013, of which there were 49,036 cases of unfair dismissal (Ministry of Justice, 2012/13).

A union may help with employment tribunal cases on a whole range of issues such as disability discrimination, equal pay, race discrimination, age discrimination and detrimental treatment/unfair dismissal connected with pregnancy.

The presence of a union in the workplace acts as a brake on possible management actions because of the collective power that union membership offers (the pluralistic perspective on the relationship between management and their staff). The role of the union goes further than representation of rights, in terms of contractual pay and conditions. The presence of a union gives a voice to the workforce, a voice that has, through its privileged position, a right to be heard. Trained union members can be asked to accompany employees at disciplinary hearings and, for example, trade unions have to be included in the safety management of the organisation; smart employers work with rather than against their trade union.

13.6.7 TRADE UNIONISM AND THE LAW

The key areas of legislation controlling the operation of trade unions and rights of their members are as follows:

- Trade Union and Labour Relations (Consolidation) Act 1992 (c. 52)
- Trade Union Reform and Employment Rights Act 1993 (c. 19)
- Employment Rights Act 1996
- Employment Relations Act 1999 and 2004
- Employment Act 2002.

There is, of course, a mass of other legislation but the above Acts of Parliament cover some of the key themes associated with trade unions and trade union membership.

13.6.8 THE TRADES UNION CONGRESS (TUC)

Most unions are members of the TUC, although it is not obligatory. As its website (**www. tuc.org.uk**) indicates, the TUC 'is the voice of Britain at work'. It campaigns for a fair deal at work and for social justice, building links with political parties, business, local communities and wider society. It currently has 54 unions affiliated to it, representing 6.2 million working people. Not all unions are members of the TUC: these include the Police Federation, which is barred by law from affiliating to the TUC.

The remit of the TUC is broad in terms of its activities. As an organisation it brings Britain's unions together to draw up common policies, helps unions develop new services for their members and lobbies the Government to implement policies that will benefit people at work. In addition, it carries out research on employment, runs extensive training and education programmes for union representatives and helps to avoid clashes between unions. It also has links worldwide in its endeavour to promote unionism.

 ACTIVITY 13.9

TUC campaigns

Access the TUC website – **www.tuc.org.uk** - and determine the range of issues that they get involved in. Were you aware of the range of TUC activity?

The policy-making body of the TUC is the annual Congress, which meets for four days each year during September. Each affiliated union can send delegates to Congress – the larger the union, the more delegates it can send. At Congress, 'motions' (resolutions for debate) are proposed and discussed. These form the basis of the TUC's work for the next year. The campaign for 2013 covered five areas:

1 jobs, growth and a new economy

2 fair pay and a living wage

3 good services and decent welfare

4 respect and a voice at work

5 strong unions.

The TUC's European counterpart is the European Trade Union Confederation (ETUC).

13.6.9 THE EUROPEAN TRADE UNION CONFEDERATION (ETUC)

The **European Trade Union Confederation** (**ETUC**) defines itself as 'a united, pluralist organisation' which 'represents all workers at European level'. It was set up in 1973 to promote the interests of working people at European level and to represent them in the EU institutions. In order for unions to defend and bargain for their members effectively at national level, they must co-ordinate activities and policies across Europe. The ETUC enables them to act collectively at European level to influence the economy and society at large (**www.etuc.org**).

The ETUC defends fundamental social values such as solidarity, equality and cohesion. The ETUC aims include the right to high-quality jobs, the right to a high level of social protection, gender equality, equal opportunities for all, social cohesion and inclusion, and the right to health and safety at work.

The ETUC exists to speak with a single voice, on behalf of the common interests of workers, at European level. It currently comprises 85 national trade union confederations in 36 countries, plus 10 European trade union federations.

The ETUC is based in Brussels and brings together thinking from its partner organisations from around the EU, for example the UK's Trades Union Congress. Because of its geographic location and because it is formally recognised as one of the social partners that has an entitlement to have its voice heard at the European Commission and Council of Ministers, it, in part, reflects the social dimension to the European Union. The Council of the European Union represents the individual member states and the European Commission seeks to uphold the interests of the EU as a whole. The ETUC would automatically be included, and thus have a voice, on matters that relate to employment legislation, which of course would impact right across all the EU member countries.

Some areas in which the social partners have impacted include:

- parental leave (1996), revised in 2009
- part-time work (1997)
- fixed-term work (1999)
- telework (2002)
- work-related stress (2004)
- harassment and violence at work (2007)
- inclusive labour markets (2010)

(ETUC, 2014).

13.6.10 UNIONLEARN

One of the growing areas of union involvement and activity is in learning and education. 'Unionlearn' is the learning and skills organisation of the TUC. It works to assist unions in the delivery of learning opportunities for their members as well as managing the Union Learning Fund (ULF) (see more at **www.unionlearn.org.uk**).

It has been responsible for helping hundreds of thousands of learners at all levels, from basic numeracy and literacy to degree-level qualifications. More than 30,000 union learning representatives (ULRs) have been trained and more than 220,000 people are being given training and learning opportunities through their union every year. Union learning representatives analyse learning or training needs, provide information and advice about learning or training matters and arrange learning or training for members.

Time off for learning, although it cannot be guaranteed to occur at specific times, is, however, a provision of legislation, particularly the Trades Union and Labour Relations (Consolidations) Act 1992 and the Safety Representatives and Safety Committee Regulations 1977. This legislation gives trade union and safety representatives a legal right to reasonable time off, with pay, to attend courses that are approved by the TUC or a recognised union. The common-sense approach is that the 'reasonable time off' to attend a course is negotiated with management; it cannot just be taken. In the past, many ULRs have had difficulty in obtaining time off from employers to carry out their duties and to train for them. That is why the TUC and its unions persuaded the Government to introduce statutory recognition that gives learning representatives similar rights to union representatives as a whole. The Employment Act 2002 gives rights to paid time off to ULRs provided they are in independent unions – such as those affiliated to the TUC – or they are in workplaces where unions are recognised by the employer for collective bargaining purposes.

All in all, the aspirations of Unionlearn are extensive and carry on the long traditions of union activities.

PAUSE FOR THOUGHT

Reflect on all you have read above about the roles of trade unions. Are their activities and interests broader than you thought?

13.6.11 ADVISORY, CONCILIATION AND ARBITRATION SERVICE (ACAS)

Acas is a fair, unbiased and professional public service which offers free advice to employers and employees on employment legislation and employment relations issues. It is independent of government but is still part of the Civil Service. It has been operating, in its present form, since 1975 but has a history dating back to 1896 when the Government launched a voluntary conciliation and arbitration service, which also gave free advice to employers and unions on industrial relations and personnel problems (Acas, n.d.[a]). The advice and services it offers are impartial, neither favouring employers nor employees. It supplies up-to-date information, independent advice and high-quality training, as well as working with employers and employees to solve problems and improve performance. Its main aim is 'to improve organisations and working life through better employment relations' (Acas, n.d.[a]).

Acas gives advice and guidance via its telephone helpline to 800,000 callers a year and promote good practice through training. It also works with individual companies in partnership with employer/employee/trade union groups to find lasting solutions for their workplace disputes. Although more recently it has been significantly involved in dealing with issues in colleges and universities, local government, the NHS and the fire brigade, much of its conciliation work is now focused on individual complaints to employment tribunals. These complaints are passed to Acas and at present 75% are settled or withdrawn without ever reaching a tribunal hearing (Acas, 2014). From 6 April 2014, anyone thinking about making an employment tribunal claim must contact Acas first.

KEY CONCEPT: CONCILIATION

'Collective conciliation is a specific term used to refer to talks aimed at resolving disputes between representative groups (most typically trade unions) and employers – or, less frequently today, groups of employers – facilitated by an independent third party' (Acas, 2009).

KEY CONCEPT: ARBITRATION

'Arbitration involves an impartial outsider being asked to make a decision on a dispute. The arbitrator makes a firm decision on a case based on the evidence presented by the parties. Arbitration is voluntary, so both sides must agree to go to arbitration; they should also agree in advance that they will abide by the arbitrator's decision.

'Arbitration is often used for collective employment related disputes or it can be used to settle individual disputes.'

It may be used to solve pay disputes between unions and employers, as the arbitrator will make an independent and impartial decision. Or it may be used to deal with individual cases, perhaps to avoid the stress and expense of having to go to a tribunal. Arbitration is carried out in private and can be seen as an alternative to a court of law. The arbitrator asks the questions and, unlike a court, there is no formal cross-examination or swearing of oaths.

Acas's arbitration services should not be used until all attempts at resolving a dispute using internal procedures have been exhausted.

(Adapted from Acas, n.d.[b]) © Acas

13.6.12 CENTRAL ARBITRATION COMMITTEE (CAC)

The CAC is a permanent independent body with statutory powers whose role is to resolve disputes in England, Scotland and Wales under legislation relating to:

- recognition and derecognition of trade unions
- disclosure of information for collective bargaining
- information and consultation of employees
- European works councils
- European companies and cooperative societies, and cross-border mergers.

(**www.cac.gov.uk**)

As Rose (2008, p.19) points out, '. . .CAC will arbitrate directly in an industrial dispute . . . as well as receiving requests from Acas.'

The chairperson and the members of the CAC are appointed by the Secretary of State.

 ACTIVITY 13.10

Read the Acas policy discussion paper 'The alchemy of dispute resolution – the role of collective conciliation' (**www.acas.org.uk/index.aspx?articleid=2988**) for a better understanding of how Acas becomes involved in dispute resolution.

- How important do you think the role of Acas is?

 ACTIVITY 13.11

Research by Meadows (2007) into the economic impact of Acas identified that the collective conciliation service alone provides benefits worth £159 million a year to the national economy. This establishes collective conciliation as the most cost-effective of the range of services provided by Acas. Overall, Meadows found that in addition to a short-term direct impact of its activities worth nearly £800 million, Acas's activities contribute to a reduction in absenteeism in the UK and an increase in foreign direct investment, both of which add hundreds of millions of pounds to national output.

Have a look at her report (Meadows, 2007) for details on how these benefits were calculated.

- Were you aware of the economic benefits that Acas offer?
- Where are the key areas of impact?

13.7 COLLECTIVE BARGAINING

Where trade unions or staff associations are recognised by organisations, collective bargaining is the means used to address conflicting issues between the organisation and its employees. It is concerned with making and delivering agreements on all aspects of employment practice, such as terms and conditions of employment, pay, changes in working hours and practices, redundancies and training. Collective bargaining also takes place when there are disputes between managers and employees at national level, in organisations such as local government and higher education institutions.

Twenty-nine per cent of employees are covered by collective agreements (64% of whom are in the public sector). Larger workplaces are more likely to negotiate pay through collective bargaining; in 2012 the proportion of employees who had their pay affected by a collective agreement was around 42% in larger workplaces, compared with 16% in workplaces with fewer than 50 employees (Office for National Statistics, 2012).

13.7.1 TYPES OF COLLECTIVE BARGAINING

Although we have seen that the role of unions is far greater than wage negotiation, the role of unions in collective bargaining still exists. There are two types of collecting bargaining, which may be referred to as distributive and integrative bargaining:

Distributive bargaining assumes there is a fixed amount of value (a 'fixed pie') to be divided between the parties, so the more one party gains, the less is available for the other; a 'win-lose' situation. One side will make an offer and the other side will make a counter-offer.

Integrative bargaining often attempts to create value in the course of the negotiation, that is, to 'expand the pie'. The objectives are about 'an area of common concern'. It often involves a higher degree of trust and the forming of a relationship and can also involve creative problem-solving that aims to achieve mutual gains, that is, achieving a 'win-win' situation.

13.8 PRODUCTS OF COLLECTIVE BARGAINING

Pay, working time and holiday entitlements are typical issues that are resolved through distributive bargaining. These are generally referred to as substantive issues: the outcomes alter employees' terms and conditions of employment. Agreements that are reached in this way are referred to as *substantive agreements*.

The agreements that are reached through integrative bargaining are referred to as *procedural agreements*, because the parties are engaged in 'how we shall go about doing things'. Typical internal issues are related to health and safety procedures and procedures that form part of the *internal justice system*, such as those for handling grievances and dealing with matters of discipline.

13.9 THE INTERNAL JUSTICE SYSTEM

All organisations have an internal justice system (IJS), which on the one hand enables organisations to take action against individuals whose conduct at work is not acceptable and on the other enables the individual to seek a solution to perceived unfairness or ill treatment. In this way, both sides of the employee relationship have access to a system through which redress may be sought. The formal processes of the IJS are managed through a *disciplinary procedure* and a *grievance procedure* (see Chapter 16, 'Understanding Employment Law', for further discussion).

The use of these procedures tends to be psychologically negative, since the disciplinary rules, for example, define unacceptable behaviour, ranging from minor indiscretions to comparatively serious offences, which are referred to as 'gross misconduct'. Additionally, through the grievance procedure, employees seek solutions to negative situations. Circumstances in which one party or the other is not satisfied by the outcomes of the process may lead to recourse to internal mediation and perhaps external institutions, such as employment tribunals, Acas or the courts.

13.10 MANAGING A KEY EMPLOYMENT RELATIONS ISSUE

13.10.1 ABSENCE MANAGEMENT

This is one of the most costly and serious concerns to managers. The CBI report on Absence and Workplace Health (CBI/Pfizer, 2013) suggests that 160 million working days were lost in 2012, costing the UK economy £14 billion, with non-genuine absences costing £1.7 billion. Imagine how much money organisations could save if they reduced their staff absence rate.

As well as employee wages, other costs must be included:

- line manager costs in finding a temporary replacement or rescheduling work
- the actual cost of the temporary employee
- costs related to showing a temporary employee what to do
- costs associated with a slower work rate or more errors from a temporary employee
- costs of contracts not being completed on time.

In addition, there is the cost of lower morale and higher stress amongst staff who have to take on extra work in order to cover for the absent person. The impact on customer satisfaction and thus on business success is a real threat. As Acas state in their managing absence guidance, 'High levels of unauthorised absence, including sick leave can cause lost or delayed production, low morale and reduce the standard of service within an organisation' (**www.acas.org.uk/index.aspx?articleid=1566**).

From April 2014, employers can no longer reclaim sick pay from the Government. The Government will invest instead in a new Health and Work Service. The new service aims to provide support that will benefit employers by enabling employees on sickness absence to return to work more quickly (where possible). The intention is to assist employers to manage sickness absence in a better way.

 KEY CONCEPT: POLICY ON ABSENCE

According to the CIPD, 94% of organisations who responded to their *Absence Management* survey (2013) have a written absence/attendance management policy. Employees have the right, under the Employment Rights Act 1996, to be provided with information about 'any terms and conditions relating to incapacity for work due to sickness or injury, including any provisions for sick pay'.

13.10.2 MANAGING AND CONTROLLING ABSENCE

Considerable attention has been paid to the problems related to absenteeism, and this has resulted in the use of management control systems, some of which are linked to the disciplinary procedure. On the other hand, the objective in setting up an absence management system is to head off the need to use the disciplinary procedure. For an employee to be of use to the organisation they have to be present, no matter how competent or willing they may be. The CIPD's 2013 *Absence Management* annual survey report indicates that average absence is 7.6 days per employee, per year. Levels are highest in the public services sector (8.7 days per employee per year) and lowest in the manufacturing and production sector (6 days per employee per year). The report indicates that the average cost of absence is about £595 per employee per year (CIPD, 2013k). In recognition of the impact that absence has on the business, 'organisations with higher levels of absence are most likely to have a target in place to reduce it. On average, organisations' target was 2.3 days (per employee per year)' (CIPD, 2013k, p.5).

If we look at the incidences of absence caused by, or relating to, the actual workplace, the Health and Safety Executive (HSE) has some chilling figures:

- **78,000** injuries to employees were reported under the Reporting of Injuries, Diseases and Dangerous Occurrences Regulations 1995
- **175,000** over-7-day absence injuries occurred (Labour Force Survey)
- **1.1 million** working people were suffering from a work-related illness (2011/12)
- **27 million** working days were lost due to work-related illness and workplace injury (2011/12).

(HSE, 2012/13)

13.10.3 REASONS FOR ABSENCE

According to the CIPD *Absence Management* survey report (2013k, p.20), there are many reasons that people take time off work. Short-term absences can be categorised as, in order of frequency:

- minor illnesses, such as colds and flu, headaches and migraine
- musculoskeletal injuries
- back pain
- stress.

One of the features of this list is that some of the reasons given are predictable, and therefore easier to manage since they can be planned for ahead of time. On the other hand, unapproved absence is unpredictable and difficult to manage. Importantly, the former does not cause a reduction in productivity, whereas the latter does. Non-genuine illness is among the most common causes of short-term absence: manual workers, 26%; non-manual, 21%. This is reportedly more common in the private than public sector (CIPD, 2013k).

ACTIVITY 13.12

Long-term absence

Access the 2013 CIPD *Absence Management* annual survey report from **www.cipd.co.uk/hr-resources/survey-reports/absence-management-2013.aspx** and determine the reasons for long-term absence.

13.11 MEASURING ABSENCE

Managers know when there are absences from their daily contact with the staff, but only monitoring absence and measuring its frequency will reveal the true extent of the problem. If the problem is serious, the task is to identify the causes and decide what to do about it. Persistent and widespread absence may be found in a particular department, in which case the departmental issue needs to be investigated to discover the cause. It might have been caused by unpopular changes in the work systems, the style with which the manager leads and communicates with the staff, or an increase in the workload.

On the other hand, absenteeism may be endemic across the whole organisation; it might be taken for granted that staff take unapproved time off, such as a 'duvet day'. In some cases, it is almost as if it is an entitlement.

Return-to-work interviews and trigger mechanisms to review attendance are ranked among the most effective approaches for managing short-term absence, while occupational health involvement is most commonly among organisations' most effective methods for managing long-term absence (CIPD, 2013k).

13.11.1 THE BRADFORD FACTOR

There are several systems available for measuring absence. The Bradford factor is probably the most well known and is used by many organisations. The system is designed to identify persistent short-term absences by measuring the number of spells of absence. It is calculated according to the formula: S x S x D, where S = the number of spells of absence by an individual over a rolling period of 52 weeks; and D = the total number of days of an individual's absence in 52 weeks.

CASE EXAMPLE 13.1

THE BRADFORD FACTOR

- Ten one-day absences = 10 x 10 x 10 = 1,000
- One ten-day absence = 1 x 1 x 10 = 10
- Five two-day absences = 5 x 5 x 10 = 250
- Two five-day absences = 2 x 2 x 10 = 40

The involvement of the line manager is key to the success of the steps that are taken to reduce absenteeism. First, the manager needs to keep a record of the frequency of the spells of absences and the number of days taken in each spell. The actual calculations for the Bradford factor are usually done centrally via the human resources information systems (HRIS) and feedback from this is given to the manager. When the causes have been identified, the next task is to decide what to do about it. The effectiveness of the action that they take is determined by their leadership skills, since only as a last resort should the disciplinary procedure be invoked.

13.11.2 RETURN-TO-WORK INTERVIEWS

These have proved to be an effective intervention on the part of the line manager. They give the line manager the opportunity to talk to staff about the underlying causes of absence. Training line managers to conduct effective return-to-work interviews and developing their capability to manage absence is most likely to have a positive impact on absence (CIPD, 2013k).

13.11.3 FIT NOTES

The introduction of the 'Fit Note' has not had the impact hoped for. The idea was that Fit Notes would outline what employees could do, rather than be signed off sick completely by a doctor. The intention was to help more people stay active in work, rather than drift into long-term sickness absence. However, 72% of employers, according to the CBI/Pfizer report on Absence and Workplace Health, 2013, say that Fit Notes have not helped employees to return to work earlier. The report says that employers feel that this is partly due to doctors not being trained to use the Fit Note as intended and also that many doctors have a limited understanding of workplace health.

CASE EXAMPLE 13.2

Alan Whistler has had several days off with a migraine. In the last six months he has had two days off every month with the same complaint. His sickness record is poor, with a multitude of minor illnesses: colds, stomach upsets and headaches.

His manager calls him in for yet another return-to-work Interview. During the interview Alan states that his doctor has advised that he reduces the amount of time spent on the computer as this could be the cause of his headaches. Alan is also under pressure at work and says he is constantly stressed.

His manager is keen to do something to help and realises that it would be beneficial to Alan if his workload is reviewed and changes made. They discuss the issues and agree that Alan will change his duties so that he is not working on the computer screen all day. They also arrange for a health and safety audit of his computer screen and equipment to ensure that his workstation is ergonomically sound.

Three months later, Alan has had no recurrences of his headaches and feels much better about the work situation. He also feels better because he knows his manager has listened to him and he feels valued.

13.11.4 MANAGING ABSENCE: SOME CONCLUSIONS

Managing absence in the workplace is a key ER issue, an issue that is fraught and charged with emotion.

Problems occur in many forms and with many subtleties. Consider the person who has a long-term illness, who wants to work but every three or four months has to undergo treatment at hospital as an outpatient, which takes them away from their workplace for three or four days, maybe more, at a time. Their Bradford score goes sky high on an equally regular basis. How is this managed? What are the implications for management? Should they make a special case in respect of this person? Should the treatment of the individual be completely different and the person be taken out of the Bradford system for these episodes?

There are a number of areas where an employer can impact on managing absence. These include the quality of management, working relationships, job design, employment relations, communication of information and flexible working arrangements (Acas, 2013c). Probably the most important action is to convey the message to employees that absence will be investigated; if workers know that their absence will be noticed, they are less likely to take time off work unnecessarily. Keeping individual attendance records to monitor absence and lateness, holding return-to-work interviews and training managers to handle absence will all help to reduce the absence problem.

13.12 SUMMARY

Employment relations, in simple terms, means exactly what it says: that there is a relationship between the employer and the employee. There are formal and informal aspects to the relationship and both parties have rights, obligations and expectations. As well as the written contract of employment there is a relationship that is built between the employer and the employee, which is based upon the subjective expectations of, and beliefs about, the relationship between the employee and the organisation. Breaching this 'psychological contract' can happen easily, through promises made and not kept, but rebuilding it can be very difficult.

The chapter addresses the idea of the unitarist and pluralist perspectives on the employment relationship. Managers who take the unitarist view regard themselves as the only legitimate source of power and authority, which they value and protect. On the other hand, those who take the pluralist perspective allow and actively foster freedom of expression and the development of groups, which establish their own norms and elect their own informal leaders. HRM follows the unitarist approach, but the reality is that with so many differing groups at work, there are bound to be a variety of interests – that is, pluralism.

There are many parties in the employment relationship, ranging from line managers and employees, who have daily contact between each other, as well as with organisations such as unions and management organisations (for example the Confederation of British Industry). These types of organisation are indirectly involved in the worker-management interface yet can, from time to time and over time, influence the nature of the relationship. The chapter also addresses the role of the union and how it provides a formal negotiating body between management and employees during disputes or when an employee needs representation at a disciplinary hearing. It also addresses the focus of unions on learning, with the establishment of 'Unionlearn', which aims to help unions support 220,000 members a year to access and progress through lifelong learning.

For more on the relationship between employer and employee in terms of grievance and disciplinary hearings, see Chapter 16, 'Understanding Employment Law'.

The chapter has also looked at one of the key employment relations issues – absence management – and suggested some ways of measuring and managing absence.

REVIEW QUESTIONS

1 Why is the term 'employee relations' more widely used today rather than the older 'industrial relations' title?

2 What is the difference between a 'unitarist' and a 'pluralist' approach?

3 What is the main function of the CBI?

4 If the trade unions' main task is no longer to perform collective bargaining, what is their main function in today's workplace?

5 What other roles do trade unions undertake?

6 How would you describe 'Unionlearn'?

7 Name three ways in which Acas can help an employer with employment relations.

8 How much does employee absence cost the UK economy?

9 What is the formula for the Bradford factor? What does the Bradford system seek to achieve in the monitoring of employee absence?

10 Using the CIPD annual Absence Management survey report, find out what organisations do to improve the management of sickness absence.

EXPLORE FURTHER

BOOKS

GENNARD, J. and JUDGE, G. (2010) *Managing employment relations*. London: CIPD.

ROSE, E. (2008) *Employment relations*. 3rd ed. Harlow: Pearson Education Ltd.

These are texts which give a solid grounding in the area of employment relations. They offer a detailed analysis of the employment relations scene and are essential reading for students who have aspirations of furthering their careers in this field.

WEB LINKS

The CIPD factsheet is a good place to start. As with all CIPD factsheets, it gives the basics of employee relations and explains it in a straightforward manner: **www.cipd. co.uk/hr-resources/factsheets/employee-relations-overview.aspx**

The Advisory, Conciliation and Arbitration Service, Acas (**www.acas.org.uk**) is of particular relevance to this subject and offers all kinds of guidance and information. See in particular the 'Trade Union Representation in the Workplace' booklet.

The TUC website (**www.tuc.org.uk**) offers a good insight into what unions can be involved with in a wider environment.

For more on Unionlearn see **www.unionlearn.org.uk**

Organisations with an impact on the employment relationship:

Central Arbitration Committee: **www.cac.gov.uk**

Confederation of British Industry (CBI): **www.cbi.org.uk**

Engineering Employers' Federation (Manufacturers' Organisation)(EEF): **www.eef.org.uk**

Institute of Directors (IOD): **www.iod.com**

Find out about the EU: **http://europa.eu/index_en.htm**

Links to some of the professional institutes:

Association of Chartered Certified accountants: **www2.accaglobal.com/uk/**

Institution of Chemical Engineers: **www.icheme.org**

Institute of Leadership and Management: **www.i-l-m.com/**

Institution of Mechanical Engineers: **www.imeche.org**

CIMA (Chartered Institute of Management Accountants): **www.cimaglobal.com**

Information on absence management:

CIPD *Absence Management* survey: **www.cipd.co.uk/hr-resources/survey-reports/absence-management-2013.aspx**

The Acas 'Managing attendance and employee turnover' booklet provides excellent advice: **www.acas.org.uk/index.aspx?articleid=1183**

CBI/Pfizer (2013) *Fit for Purpose – Absence and Workplace Health 2013*: **www.cbi. org.uk/media-centre/press-releases/2013/07/work-absence-at-record-low-but-still-costs-economy-£14bn-a-year-cbi-pfizer-survey/**

Health and Safety Executive: **www.hse.gov.uk**

Some interesting and useful case studies on absence management can be found at: **www.hse.gov.uk/sicknessabsence/experience.htm**

CHAPTER 14

Health, Safety, Well-being and Work-life Balance

LEARNING OBJECTIVES

After studying this chapter you should:

- understand the role of the HR practitioner in health and safety at work
- be able to make meaningful contributions to the organisation and administration of health and safety at work
- be aware of the legislation on workplace health and safety and understand the organisation's obligations and responsibilities
- be aware of and understand the initiatives to identify current and future threats to workplace health
- understand the concepts and importance of employee well-being and work-life balance.

14.1 INTRODUCTION

Whenever the conversation turns to health and safety at work, people usually talk about the organisation's obligations under the law. Undoubtedly, conformity to the provisions of the law is of paramount importance, but there is also a strong business case for providing a healthy and safe working environment. After all, if the organisation is good at attracting the right people, it is more likely to retain them if it looks after their health and safety and takes whatever steps are necessary to ensure their well-being while they are at work.

In this chapter the relationships between health and safety are explored and explained in the context of the work environment and its links to good people management practices. Relevant legislation is examined, and since the HR practitioner has a significant administrative and advisory role, there is guidance on how the provisions of the law may be implemented.

Beyond the essential control and good practices, which are associated with health and safety measures in the workplace, increasing importance is being placed upon employee well-being and work-life balance. Both of these concepts can be considered from an employee and employer perspective. In the two sections of this chapter which tackle these issues, perspectives are offered from the key stakeholders in the work relationship: the employer, the employee, the Government, employer representative bodies, such as the Confederation of British Industry (CBI) and the Institute of Directors (IOD), as well as employee representatives, the Trades Union Congress (TUC) and charitable organisations. There is overlap, in terms of content and theory, between work-life balance and employee well-being and this will be evident when reading the chapter.

14.2 HEALTH AND SAFETY

14.2.1 THE LAW

Historically, the UK's long-term record for ensuring the health and safety of employees is poor. During the Industrial Revolution little was done to protect employees, visitors, local residents or passers-by from the hazards that arose from an organisation's activities. Those most likely to be the victims of health and safety risks were the employees, and this is still the case.

Consider the well-known phrase 'mad as a hatter', which has been used in conversation to refer to a crazed person. The origins of the phrase lie in the early hat manufacturing industry. Mercury was used in the production of felt, which was in turn used in the manufacture of hats in the eighteenth and nineteenty century. Employees in the hat factories were exposed, over a period of years, to small yet cumulative doses from the vapours emitted from the heavy, liquid metal. The dementia-like condition, suffered by the hatters, is correctly called Korsakoff's syndrome.

Mercury, in its various forms, is dangerous to humans. The US Government Environmental Agency says the following of mercury poisoning:

> Symptoms include these: tremors; emotional changes (e.g., mood swings, irritability, nervousness, excessive shyness); insomnia; neuromuscular changes (such as weakness, muscle atrophy, twitching); headaches; disturbances in sensations; changes in nerve responses; performance deficits on tests of cognitive function. At higher exposures there may be kidney effects, respiratory failure and death. (**www. epa.gov/hg/effects.htm**)

Several Factories and Shops Acts were passed in the early twentieth century, but most employee protection was derived from what is termed common law. Until 1949 there was no such thing as legal aid, and employees had to rely on the goodwill of their 'masters' to compensate them for injuries or health problems that were attributable to conditions in the workplace.

14.2.2 THE HEALTH AND SAFETY AT WORK ACT 1974

The Health and Safety at Work Act (HASAWA) 1974 places an obligation on everyone involved in an organisation's endeavours to produce goods or offer a service, to maintain standards in the health, safety and well-being of people throughout the workplace. This responsibility extends not only to fellow employees but also to visitors or members of the general public passing by or living close to the premises. The responsibility includes protecting and securing people's safety and preventing environmental pollution of any kind.

14.2.3 THE HEALTH AND SAFETY EXECUTIVE (HSE)

The HSE is the primary delivery agent for the Department for Work and Pensions' (DWP) strategic objective of improving health and safety outcomes. The Health and Safety Executive is a 'non-departmental public body' (NDPB) (see **www.hse.gov.uk/ aboutus/howwework/management/dwphse.pdf**).

The framework document between the DWP and the Health and Safety Executive states that (HSE, n.d.[a], p.2):

> The Secretary of State for Work and Pensions agreed that the HSE's aims should be to:
>
> i. continue to deliver its mission of preventing death, injury and ill health to those at work and those affected by work activities; and
> ii. deliver any targets agreed for work-related health and safety.

The HSE will also

i. protect the health and safety of workers and minimise risks from work to members of the public; and

ii. ensure that the major hazard industries (such as nuclear, petrochemicals and offshore oil and gas) manage and control the risks around their work to a high standard which enhances assurance and allows these industries to operate with a high degree of public acceptance.

The framework document between the DWP and the HSE also sees the HSE as having an influencing role and an investigative role:

- to embrace high standards of health and safety;
- promote the benefits of employers and workers working together to manage health and safety sensibly;
- investigate incidents, enquire into citizens' complaints and enforce the law.

The full rights and responsibilities that the HSE has can be found at **www.hse.gov.uk/aboutus/howwework/management/dwphse.pdf**

HSE inspectors have the right to *enter premises without notice and examine records*. They can issue *enforcement notices* and prosecute serious and persistent offenders. The point should be made, however, that HSE inspectors have these powers in case they need them, rather than to fill the courts with minor and accidental offenders. HSE inspectors advise organisations on health and safety at work, and persuade them to behave responsibly.

14.2.4 WHAT ORGANISATIONS MUST DO

There are particular steps an organisation must take to conform to the law. One way to explain this is to imagine that you have just set up a new organisation. There are 11 actions (steps) you must take to provide your organisation with a sound basis for health, safety and well-being, as listed below:

1 Appoint someone who is responsible for health and safety matters.

2 Write a *health and safety policy*. This means deciding how you are going to manage health and safety.

3 Set up a *risk assessment system*. Decide what could cause harm to people and how to take precautions. They must also keep records of the findings of the risk assessments.

4 Consult employees on health and safety matters. Most organisations have a *health and safety committee*.

5 Provide free health and safety training for your workers so they know what hazards and risks they may face and how to deal with them and provide them with personal protective equipment (PPE).

6 Provide the appropriate welfare facilities, washing facilities and drinking water for all of your employees, not forgetting those with disabilities. These are the basic health, safety and well-being needs.

7 Make arrangements for first aid, accidents and ill health.

8 Display the health and safety law poster or provide a leaflet containing similar information.

9 Buy *employers' liability insurance* and display the insurance certificate in your workplace. If you employ anyone, you must do this.

10 Keep up to date on health and safety matters. This can be achieved by engaging a professional who can give you *competent advice* to help you to meet your health and safety duties. Advisers can be an organisation's own workers, external consultants or a

combination of these. If an organisation recognises a trade union in any part of the business, then the Safety Representatives and Safety Committees Regulations 1977 (as amended) will apply. If the organisation does not recognise a trade union, the Health and Safety (Consultation with Employees) Regulations (as amended) will apply. Both of these regulations set out the duty of the employer in respect of how they must treat their safety representatives.

11 Report particular work-related accidents, diseases and dangerous events. You must also report if you are starting a construction project. RIDDOR stands for the Reporting of Injuries, Diseases and Dangerous Occurrences Regulations 1995; in the context of RIDDOR, the Health and Safety Executive requires organisations to report work-related illnesses and accidents to them.

It used to be a general requirement that all organisations register with the HSE or local authority. However, this has now changed. From 6 April 2009, employers no longer have to register the factories, offices and shops in which their employees work with the relevant health and safety authority.

Some businesses will still have to register and submit forms under other regulations. This will depend on the type of business and the regulations that govern it. For example (HSE, 2008):

● Food and catering businesses must continue to meet food standards registration and other requirements, which local authorities enforce.
● Businesses producing, storing, using, and/or transporting substances defined under major hazard legislation, must continue to meet major hazard requirements, which the HSE enforces.

14.3 HEALTH AND SAFETY POLICY

First, this is a statement of how the organisation intends to manage the health, safety and well-being of its employees, visitors and the general public. Second, it describes how health and safety will be organised and how the high standards that have been set will be achieved through the involvement of everyone, at all levels, throughout the organisation. Third, the statement includes details of how the policy will be implemented.

PAUSE FOR THOUGHT

Have you read your organisation's health and safety policy? Can you remember what it contains? Does it make you feel that the organisation is committed to providing a healthy and safe working environment?

What would you put into a health and safety policy? You will find help from:

● *Write a Health and Safety Policy for your Business*, available at: **www.hse.gov.uk/simple-health-safety/write.htm**
● HSE (2011), *Health and Safety Made Simple: The basics for your business*, available at: **www.hse.gov.uk/pubns/indg449.pdf**

14.4 RISK ASSESSMENT

Risk assessment is about the identification of current and potential hazards, analysing the possible attendant risks and making recommendations for the removal or reduction of the risks. The HSE (2006) says that health and safety is about preventing people from being harmed or becoming ill through work; a *hazard* is anything that can cause harm or make people ill. *Risk* is the chance, high or low, that someone will be harmed by the hazard. The HSE (2011a, p.1) says:

> A risk assessment is an important step in protecting your workers and your business, as well as complying with the law. It helps you focus on the risks that really matter in your workplace – the ones with the potential to cause real harm. In many instances, straightforward measures can readily control risks, for example ensuring spillages are cleaned up promptly so people do not slip, or cupboard drawers are kept closed to ensure people do not trip. For most, that means simple, cheap and effective measures to ensure your most valuable asset – your workforce – is protected.

> The law does not expect you to eliminate all risk, but you are required to protect people as far as 'reasonably practicable'. This guide tells you how to achieve that with a minimum of fuss. (HSE, 2011a)

14.4.1 STATUTORY REGULATIONS AND CODE OF PRACTICE

Risk assessment is regulated by the Management of Health and Safety at Work Regulations 1999, regulation 3, which offers guidance on risk assessment. The regulations say that the employer must 'carry out a risk assessment of the workplace and make all necessary changes to bring property, practices and procedures up to the required standard'. Specifically it says the following:

> Every employer *[and self-employed person – author's comment]* shall make a suitable and sufficient assessment of-

> (a)   the risks to the health and safety of his employees to which they are exposed whilst they are at work; and

> (b)   the risks to the health and safety of persons not in his employment arising out of or in connection with the conduct by him of his undertaking, . . .

(Management of Health and Safety at Work Regulations 1999)

14.4.2 CARRYING OUT A RISK ASSESSMENT

If you employ five or more people, your risk assessments must be recorded. Clearly, then, an employer who fails to carry out risk assessments is breaking the law, and the penalties can be severe. The HSE, for example, points out various tasks and situations in which typically high-risk hazards are found:

- manual handling:
  receipt of raw materials, for example lifting, carrying
  stacking and storage, for example falling materials
- movement of people and materials, for example slips, trips and falls, collisions
- harmful substances:
  processing of raw materials, for example exposure to toxic substances
- maintenance of buildings, for example roof work, gutter cleaning, working in confined spaces
- maintenance of plant and machinery:
  lifting tackle
  installation of rotating equipment and repairing machinery
  installation, maintenance and cleaning of pressurised equipment
- using electricity, for example using hand tools, extension leads
- operating machines:
  for example operating without sufficient clearance or at an unsafe speed; not using safety devices

using equipment which has excessive vibration levels

using or in proximity to equipment with high radiation levels, for example communication equipment

● failure to wear protective equipment, for example protective (hard) hats, boots, clothing

● dealing with emergencies, for example spillages, fires, explosions

● health hazards arising from the use of equipment or methods of working, for example visual display units (VDUs), repetitive strain injuries from badly designed workstations or working practices.

(*The Health and Safety Toolbox: How to control risks at work*, available at: **www.hse.gov. uk/toolbox/index.htm**)

14.4.3 FIVE STEPS TO RISK ASSESSMENT

The HSE (2011a, p.2) explains the risk assessment process in five steps:

● Identify the hazards.
● Decide who might be harmed and how.
● Evaluate the risks arising from the hazards and decide whether existing precautions are adequate or if more should be done.
● Record findings and implement them.
● Review the assessment periodically and update if necessary.

When carrying out the evaluation of risk, those involved should assess the level of risk in relation to each separate hazard. The severity of hazards may be classified on a short scale of, for example, 'slight risk', 'medium risk' and 'high risk'. Holt and Andrews (1993) proposed a severity rating scale as given in Table 14.1.

Table 14.1 Risk assessment: Severity rating

1 Catastrophic	Imminent danger exists, hazard capable of causing death and illness on a wide scale
2 Critical	Hazard can result in serious illness, severe injury, property and equipment damage
3 Marginal	Hazard can cause illness, injury or equipment damage, but the result would not be expected to be serious
4 Negligible	Hazard will not result in serious injury or illness, remote possibility of damage beyond minor first aid case

Source: Holt and Andrews (1993)

Risk is a mixture of the severity of the risk and the frequency. Specifically the HSE offer the following guidance:

Risk = Severity of harm x Likelihood of occurrence

Where **severity** is rated according to:

(**3**) **Major** – Death or major injury or illness causing long-term disability
(**2**) **Serious** – Injuries or illness causing short-term disability
(**1**) **Slight** – All other injuries or illnesses

The **likelihood** of harm may be rated according to:

(**3**) **High** – Where it is certain that harm will occur
(**2**) **Medium** – Where harm will often occur
(**1**) **Low** – Where harm will seldom occur

(HSE, n.d.[b])

The risk assessment process is not complete until action has been taken to eliminate any hazards found in the assessment and analytic process. Many organisations have staff members who are experts in the relevant fields, and the organisation's safety manager/officer will play a significant role in the whole process and in ensuring that appropriate action is taken. Where it is needed, however, specific advice is also obtainable from the HSE.

The reviews may be regularly undertaken, say annually or bi-annually, but special reviews may be necessary when change takes place, such as the introduction of new technology, new equipment or a reallocation of jobs. In essence, a common-sense approach is required. If something has changed within the organisation's environment – equipment, buildings, products, fresh people have been recruited into the organisation, there are pregnant women, young or vulnerable or disabled people – a risk assessment may be required.

Specifically, the HSE offers the following advice:

> In terms of what they require of duty-holders, HSE considers that duties to ensure health and safety so far as is reasonably practicable ('SFAIRP') and duties to reduce risks as low as is reasonably practicable ('ALARP') call for the same set of tests to be applied. (HSE, n.d.[c])

ACTIVITY 14.1

A friend who owns a hairdressing salon asks if you would help perform a risk assessment on his premises. You will get some advice by:

- Accessing the HSE website and review their advice on risk assessment in *Five Steps to Risk Assessment*, from: **www.hse.gov.uk/risk/fivesteps.htm**
- Reading the guidance offered in the HSE's document entitled *Example risk assessment*

for a hairdressing salon, available at: **www.hse.gov.uk/risk/casestudies/pdf/hairdressers.pdf**
- Accessing the risk assessment Word template at: **www.hse.gov.uk/risk/theory/alarp1.htm**
- Looking at the TUC's guidance about risk in their 'Unionlearn' publication, 'Risk Assessment', which can be downloaded from: **www.tuc.org.uk/sites/default/files/extras/riskassessment.pdf**

According to the HSE (2011b, p.47), the factors that cause workplace risks are as follows:

- skin contact with irritant substances, leading to dermatitis, etc.
- inhalation of respiratory sensitisers, triggering immune responses such as asthma
- badly designed workstations requiring awkward body postures or repetitive movements, resulting in upper limb disorders, repetitive strain injury and other musculoskeletal conditions
- noise levels that are too high, causing deafness and conditions such as tinnitus
- too much vibration, for example from hand-held tools leading to hand-arm vibration syndrome and circulatory problems
- exposure to ionising and non-ionising radiation including ultraviolet in the sun's rays, causing burns, sickness and skin cancer
- infections ranging from minor sickness to life-threatening conditions, caused by inhaling or being contaminated by micro-biological organisms
- stress causing mental and physical disorders.

14.5 ACCIDENTS AT WORK

References to accidents at work may evoke a variety of recollections ranging from those of our own individual experiences of witnessing or being personally involved in minor accidents or 'close shaves' to those major incidents that remain in our minds forever, such as large-scale factory fires, explosions and fires in chemical plants. For example:

- Over a period of several days during December 2005 there raged a massive fire and explosions which occurred at the Buncefield oil storage depot (Hemel Hempstead) (**www.buncefieldinvestigation.gov.uk**). Forty people were injured but happily there were no fatalities.
- In June 2010 a large fish tank which weighed 200kg crushed the leg of a 59-year-old man at the Alloy Bodies Ltd business in Miles Platting near Manchester. The 2m wide tank fell off a fork-lift truck as it was being loaded on to the back of a van. The tank crushed and broke both legs of the worker. He now has a pin in his right leg and has to wear a prosthetic limb on his left leg because it had to be amputated.
  The Health and Safety Executive prosecuted the company under the Health and Safety at Work Act (1974). The case came to trial in December 2013 and lasted six days. Alloy Bodies Ltd were fined £30,000 and ordered to pay £56,621 in costs.

> 'Speaking after the hearing, HSE Inspector Alex Farnhill said: "This was an entirely preventable incident which resulted in an employee having to have part of his leg amputated. His whole life has been affected by the shortcomings of this company. No effort was made to plan the work in advance, despite it being a highly unusual activity for employees at the factory. The firm should have considered the risks and found a safe way of moving the fish tank"' (Slater, 2013)

For more details about this accident see Slater (2013) and HSE (2013g).

Discovering the causes of accidents is an extremely important aspect of accident prevention. The causes identified through accident investigations may lead to appropriate preventive measures. Explanations for accidents are many and varied and attempts have been made to categorise them. These include: (i) environmental, (ii) behavioural and (iii) physiological (Molander and Winterton, 1994).

It is important to regard the three sources of explanation as interrelated. For example, individuals' responses to the environment and the factors within it are both behavioural and physiological. Also, particular types of behaviour, such as alcohol or drug abuse, cause perceptive and physiological disorders that produce a negative and often dangerous psychological state.

14.5.1 ENVIRONMENTAL CAUSES

The working environment is extremely important, especially in industries that clearly are very hazardous, such as working on railways, at sea on ships and oil rigs, chemical factories, and building and mining operations. In such industries, however, both organisational and employee awareness of risk is high, and significant progress has been made in training and the provision of safety equipment.

While this high level of safety consciousness has resulted in fewer accidents, such industries are still regarded as high risk, although industries which clearly are less hazardous, by their nature, have a higher incidence of minor accidents. With many people, environmental causes of accidents are thought of as 'factory floor' phenomena, but the point has to be made that an office environment, with carelessly laid extension leads across the floor, faulty electrical fittings and insufficient working space, lighting and ventilation, can also be a dangerous place.

People will attempt to make minor repairs and adjustments to their electrical equipment, lighting and so forth, without switching off the power supply and without the use of appropriate steps or ladders to reach the area in which they think there is a fault. Thus we find people standing on chairs to reach ceiling fittings, bending under desks to fiddle with connection boxes and so forth. Often, even the chairs they sit on are unsafe in one way or another.

14.5.2 BEHAVIOURAL CAUSES

Particular aspects of social learning are responsible for accidents at work. This refers to learning that has not been developed through formal education or training, but picked up from copying the behaviour of others, conformity to 'norms' and through trial and error. With good safety policies in place and a positive safety culture, one would hope that any informal learning would be to reinforce good safety habits. Sadly, however, not all organisations have positive safety cultures that discourage bad practice in the workplace.

Bad practice breeds bad practice and encourages unsafe behaviours. A new employee, for example, may notice that to achieve particular productivity levels, which may carry extra pay, some workers breach health and safety regulations by removing machine guards or engaging in other unsafe practices. The opportunities to learn bad behaviours are limitless: the use of ropes and slings for lifting heavy equipment which grossly exceeds the safe working load of the slings and ropes; using inappropriate tools for a job of work, standing on a stool, rather than seek out a step ladder to reach files placed on high shelves; running up and down stairs; not wearing personal protective equipment in a designated industrial work area ... the list goes on. Accidents occur unnecessarily just to enable people to achieve a short-term goal.

Also, people experiencing stress undergo changes in behaviour. When worried about, for example, marriage, home and family, job security and career prospects, people have a tendency to think about these things when they should be concentrating on the job at hand. It has long been known that 'daydreaming' is a cause of accidents at work.

14.5.3 PHYSIOLOGICAL CAUSES

In addition to those referred to above, there are several specific physiological causes of accidents. Poor eyesight, colour blindness, poor hearing, a limited sense of smell and other physiological problems can cause slow reactions to situations and might turn a prospective 'near miss' into an accident. Not everyone is fit and healthy, and managers and supervisors should be aware of their employee's state of health and fitness in relation to the nature of the work that they assign to them. This especially applies to young people who may not be aware of safety procedures and may be easily influenced by others, as previously mentioned, who have bad safety habits.

14.6 MANAGING HEALTH AND SAFETY IN THE WORKPLACE

The HSE are shifting their approach to one of:

- Plan
- Do
- Check
- Act.

The objective is to 'achieve a better balance between the systems and behavioural aspects of management. It also treats health and safety management as an integral part of good management generally, rather than as a stand-alone system' (HSE, 2013, 2013b).

14.6.1 PLAN

There needs to be a planned and systematic approach to the development and implementation of the health and safety policy through an effective health and safety management system. The aim is to minimise risks.

Risks have to be identified and a good starting point is to both consider where there have been accidents or near-misses and, if record-keeping is non-existent or shoddy, some form of recording mechanism needs to be introduced.

Risk assessment methods are used to decide on priorities and to set objectives for eliminating hazards and reducing risks. Wherever possible, risks are eliminated through selection and design of facilities, equipment and processes. If risks cannot be eliminated, they are minimised by the use of physical controls, barriers, guards, and so on, or, as a last resort, through systems of work. A 'system of work' is a co-ordinated and carefully thought through set of procedures underpinned by rules and regulations to control how things should be done in the workplace. The procedures would also define the type and usage of personal protective equipment (PPE).

The plan also involves the development of an effective health and safety policy. This, as previously indicated, is a legal requirement if an organisation employs more than five people. The health and safety *policy* sets a clear direction for the organisation to follow, a strategy of how health and safety is to be managed. It contributes to all aspects of business performance as part of a demonstrable commitment to all aspects of continuous improvement. The HSE (2011b, p.7) advises that, 'Stakeholders' expectations in the activity (whether they are shareholders, employees, or their representatives, customers or society at large) are satisfied. There are cost-effective approaches to preserving and developing physical and human resources, which reduce financial losses and liabilities.' In short, there is a business and moral case in recognising health and safety issues and to take steps to put in place preventative or remedial measures to eliminate or reduce risks to an acceptable level. The objective is to promote a positive health and safety culture.

Good planning is thinking of the future and setting standards to be achieved based upon the present situation. Thought needs to be given to measuring how well safety is being managed, for example how many lost- and no-lost-time injuries have occurred within a given time period. Performance measures should be agreed with all who are affected by a process or activity. As the HSE (2013) advises, 'Think about ways to do this that go beyond looking at accident figures – look for leading as well as lagging indicators.' Fire and emergency plans need to be included in the plan as do safety issues which arise because an organisation may share its premises with others. However, the plan will remain a plan unless there is someone responsible for its implementation.

In terms of *organising* there needs to be an effective management structure in place that is committed to safety through staff involvement and communication. In fact, the HSE uses the four 'Cs' of *Control*, *Co-operation*, *Communication* and *Competence*, which are necessary to deliver workplace safety. It can clearly be seen that management's role is to ensure that there is effective control over how work is done safely – that their beliefs are communicated, that they enlist the co-operation of their staff and treat them as equals in the context of safety. It is also important to recruit and develop competent staff who are capable of understanding the need for, and therefore who are able to deliver, a safe working environment for the good of all.

The manager's role is central in the process of communicating effectively the values of the organisation. The HSE notes the following about how the behaviour of managers is interpreted by their staff:

Managers, particularly senior managers, can communicate powerful signals about the importance and significance of health and safety objectives if they lead by example. Equally, they can undermine the development of a positive health and safety culture through negative behaviour. Subordinates soon recognise what their superiors regard as important and act accordingly. (HSE, 2011b, p.29)

14.6.2 DO

Doing, in the sense that the HSE considers the word, means assessing the key risks in the workplace, they call it, 'identifying the risk profile'. Logically one would approach this problem by analysing the types of risks and the extent of harm they can cause to individuals and equipment. The levels of risk can be ordered and thus an action plan put in place to systematically reduce the levels of risk, working from the most damaging to the least.

The aim is to minimise risks. Risk assessment methods, as previously indicated under PLAN, are used to decide on priorities and to set objectives for eliminating hazards and reducing risks. Wherever possible, risks are eliminated through selection and design of facilities, equipment and processes. If risks cannot be eliminated, they are minimised by the use of physical controls, barriers, guards, and so on, or, as a last resort, through systems of work, meaning rules and regulations as to how things are done in the workplace, and the use of personal protective equipment (PPE).

The best way to tackle the problem is to involve those who have to work in or around the risk; they are best placed to understand the issues and to offer advice on how to reduce the risk to zero or to mitigate its effect. Candour, on the part of management, rather than taking a defensive stance on health and safety matters helps develop a positive culture on these matters.

Providing adequate resources, appropriate tools, advice and specialist help is important to either reduce or eradicate the risk and to demonstrate management's commitment and concern about health and safety issues. And finally, no action is complete without a follow-up phase – to check whether the risk has been effectively controlled. The 'DO' phase brings the 'PLAN' to life.

ACTIVITY 14.2

Do you think it is too difficult to develop a safety management system in your organisation?

View how the American Federal Aviation Administration offers advice on safety

management systems at **www.youtube.com/ watch?v=bxrbwBhuNbU** and reflect on how you might introduce the principle explained in the video to develop or improve the safety management system in your organisation.

14.6.3 CHECK – MEASURE SAFETY PERFORMANCE

Safety performance needs to be measured against agreed standards to reveal when and where improvement is needed. *Active* self-monitoring reveals how effectively the health and safety management system is functioning. *Active* measurement systems review the planning of new equipment and plant that is to be installed into the workplace or the design of new ways of working. It is also addresses how effective safety systems are working and reviews their operation against plan. *Reactive* measurement, on the other hand, monitors incidents, accidents and incidences of ill-health. Measuring how health and safety is operating in the workplace, which is the process of checking how effective safety systems are operating, is an opportunity to involve staff and so reinforce the safety culture of the organisation.

What the above means in practice could be interpreted as, for example, the organisation and execution of regular safety audits of parts of the organisation by senior management and safety representatives and also the conducting of staff surveys (HSE, 2013b, p.6).

14.6.4 ACT

The HSE recommends that a formal boardroom review of health and safety performance is essential. It demonstrates commitment to safety and:

> It allows the board to establish whether the essential health and safety principles – strong and active leadership, worker involvement, and assessment and review – have been embedded in the organisation. It tells you whether your system is effective in managing risk and protecting people. (HSE, 2013b, p.7)

As the HSE points out, many organisations report upon health and safety performance in their annual reports. Stakeholders, both inside and outside an organisation, have an interest in how safely the operation of a manufacturing plant, factory, fuel storage depot, large warehousing facility, tyre or plastics recycling facility is managed.

The HSE offers this advice for large private and public sector organisations:

> Larger public and private sector organisations need to have formal procedures for auditing and reporting health and safety performance. The board should ensure that any audit is perceived as a positive management and boardroom tool. It should have unrestricted access to both external and internal auditors, keeping their cost-effectiveness, independence and objectivity under review. (HSE, 2013b, p.7)

PAUSE FOR THOUGHT

Good health and safety practice makes good sense in many ways. The following was reported in the *Lancashire Telegraph* on 13 December 2007. It reports into the appeal of a judgement under the Health and Safety at Work Act against the directors of Ruttle Contracting Ltd and Chargot Ltd in connection with the death of Shaun Riley, a driver for the company.

Appeal over workman death conviction fails

TWO companies and a director who were fined over the death of a workman who was buried beneath a mound of earth have had their convictions and sentences upheld. George Henry Ruttle, Ruttle Contracting Ltd – which he directed – and Chargot Ltd were all convicted of Health and Safety offences at Preston Crown Court in November last year over the death of 31-year-old Shaun Riley. Father-of-three Mr Riley died while driving a dumper truck at Heskin Hall Farm, near Chorley, in January 2003. Chargot Ltd was fined £75,000, Ruttle Contracting was hit with a £100,000 fine, and Mr Ruttle was fined £75,000. All three defendants were also left with heavy legal costs bills.

The Health and Safety Executive points out that the Health and Safety at Work Act (HASAWA) 1974 sets out the responsibilities of employers and employees with regard to safety in the workplace and the penalty for breaching the act can be unlimited if a case goes to Crown Court. Specifically they offer this advice:

> Section 2(1) of the HSAWA states: 'It shall be the duty of every employer to ensure, so far as is reasonably practicable, the health, safety and welfare at work of all his employees.'

Section 3 (1) of the HSAWA states, 'It shall be the duty of every employer to conduct his undertaking in such a way as to ensure, so far as is reasonably practicable, that persons not in his employment who may be affected thereby are not thereby exposed to risks to their health or safety.' (HSE, 2006)

14.7 NON-ACCIDENTAL HEALTH PROBLEMS

Not all health and safety problems are accident-related. When we think of accidents we think of events that cause physical injuries or even death. Serious damage to health, however, can be caused in the workplace by inhaling noxious gases or ingesting certain substances, perhaps caused by a failure to use safety equipment, or alternatively caused by carelessness – carelessness in the movement of goods around a factory or warehouse, incorrect storage of materials or faults in production machinery and equipment. For example:

- Office workers may experience visual and musculoskeletal problems when using computer terminals.
- Repetitive strain injury (RSI) is the result of overuse of the same part of the body for too long a period, for example typing.
- Vibration 'white finger' is numbness in finger joints caused by continuous exposure to a vibration source such as a pneumatic road drill or a vibrator plate used for compacting hardcore.

Prevention of the above type of health problem is by regular communication to staff, perhaps by incorporating discussion of health and safety issues and practice as the first item on the agenda of departmental meetings, use of 'toolbox talks', displaying posters, and good-quality health and safety training.

> Toolbox talks The HSE offers some useful resources to help guide supervisors to develop their 'toolbox talk' techniques: **www.hse.gov.uk/construction/resources/ toolboxtalks.htm**

14.7.1 HEALTHY WORKPLACE INITIATIVES

Healthy workplace initiatives began in 1992, when the national initiative *The Health of the Nation* was introduced in a white paper published by the Department of Health. The white paper recognised that the increasing concern of employers and their workforces over health issues provided opportunities to intensify health promotion in the workplace.

14.7.2 TASKFORCE SURVEY

A taskforce was appointed to examine and expand this activity. The taskforce carried out a nationwide survey and the results were set out in a report, *Health Promotion in the Workplace*, published by the Health Education Authority (HEA), which has been replaced the Health Development Agency (HDA), which is part of the National Institute for Health and Care Excellence (NICE). The survey was designed to gather information about the nature and frequency of 'health at work' activities, in terms of track record, the present situation and future plans. In total, 1,344 organisations were examined.

Many aspects of workplace activity were covered, including:

- smoking and tobacco products
- alcohol and sensible drinking
- healthy eating
- weight control
- exercise/fitness/activity

- stress management and relaxation
- health screening
- cholesterol testing
- blood pressure control
- drugs/substance abuse
- back care
- HIV/AIDS
- heart health and heart disease
- breast screening
- cervical screening
- lifestyle assessment
- repetitive strain injury
- eyesight testing
- hearing
- women's health.

The Beaumont and Thomas (2012) report published by the ONS, *Measuring National Well-being, Health, 2012*, indicates that cancer was still the most common cause of death in the UK in 2011, followed by heart disease, diseases of the respiratory system and then brain-related conditions such as strokes. Treatment of mental health conditions has seen little improvement from the beginning of the new millennium to the end of the first decade of the twenty-first century. The G8 Public Health Dementia Summit, which was hosted by the UK Government on 11 December 2013, was aimed at addressing this major concern by attempting to bring the weight of the world's wealthy nations to commit to co-operation by focusing research funding to combat this terrible illness. Prime Minister David Cameron made the following statement:

> One of the greatest challenges of our time is what I'd call the quiet crisis, one that steals lives and tears at the hearts of families, but that relative to its impact is hardly acknowledged.

> We've got to treat this like the national crisis it is. We need an all-out fight-back against this disease; one that cuts across society. (Prime Minister David Cameron, speaking at the Alzheimer's Society Conference, March 2012)

Further information on the G8 Dementia Summit can be found at **http://dementiachallenge.dh.gov.uk/category/g8-dementia-summit/**

Obesity, smoking and drinking, which includes binge drinking, is still of significant concern. The causal link between smoking and lung cancer was established over 50 years ago. In the UK tobacco consumption is now recognised as the single greatest cause of preventable illness. Cancer UK have identified that over 100,000 deaths were linked to smoking during 2009.

In terms of managing workplace health, the collection of statistics plays a vital part. Knowing where problems exist and, above all, how being able to quantify the size of the problem and thus the cost to the economy is important when deciding upon priorities. The Office for National Statistics (ONS), on behalf of the Government, maintains a database of key health and mortality statistics for the whole of the UK.

14.7.3 SICKNESS ABSENCE IN THE LABOUR MARKET

Table 14.2 illustrates in 'millions of days lost from work' the conditions which keep people away from work.

Table 14.2 Total days lost (millions) due to sickness absence

United Kingdom		
Reason	**2010**	**2011**
Musculoskeletal problems	38.3	35.0
Minor illnesses	36.2	27.4
Other	15.4	18.1
Stress/Depression/Anxiety	11.8	13.3
Gastrointestinal problems	10.9	10.3
Prefers not to disclose	4.0	5.8
Respiratory conditions	7.8	5.3
Genito-urinary problems	3.2	5.0
Heart/Blood pressure	2.9	4.5
Ear/ Nose/Throat/ Dental/Eye	2.6	3.8
Headaches and migraines	3.4	1.6
Serious mental health	0.7	0.7
Diabetes	n/a	0.4

Source: Office of National Statistics, Data Sets. Available at: www.ons.gov.uk/ons/dcp171776_265016.pdf

Reproduced from the Office for National Statistics licensed under the Open Government Licence v.1.0

ACTIVITY 14.3

Explore how sickness absence rates vary according to age, gender, demographic location and sector by accessing the ONS report:

● *Sickness Absence in the Labour Market*, April 2012, available at: **www.ons.gov.uk/ons/dcp171776_265016.pdf**

and the video, also produced by the ONS:

● **www.ons.gov.uk/ons/rel/lmac/sickness-absence-in-the-labour-market/2012/video-summary.html**

The data presented in Table 14.3 highlights the significant causes of work-related absence caused by work or a deterioration in the condition caused by work-related activities. The information, although presented by the Health and Safety Executive, has been gathered by the Labour Force Survey.

[Note: This is how the UK Data Service {*slightly modified – author comment*} describes the Labour Force Survey (LFS): It is a unique source of information. It uses standard international definitions of employment and unemployment and economic inactivity, together with a wide range of related topics such as occupation, training, hours of work and personal characteristics of household members aged 16 years and over. Available at: **http://discover.ukdataservice.ac.uk/catalogue/?sn=6727&type=Data%20catalogue**]

Table 14.3 Estimated days lost due to work-related illness or injury (self-reported cases) (2011–2012)

Type of complaint	Estimated Days Lost × 1,000
All illness	22,681
Musculoskeletal disorders	7,503
Breathing or lung problems	667
Stress, depression or anxiety	10,378
Infectious disease (virus, bacteria) – Sample size less than 40	316
Other type of complaint	2,468
All injury	4,320
All illness and injury	27,001

Source: Labour Force Survey, cited by the HSE. Available at: www.hse.gov.uk/statistics/lfs/index.htm#stress

Reproduced in modified form; contains public sector information published by the Health and Safety Executive and licensed under the Open Government Licence v1.0.

As can be seen from Tables 14.2 and 14.3, there are, not unexpectedly, similarities between the two sets of information. Musculoskeletal disorders and stress feature prominently as reasons why people are absent from work. Collecting and accessing this type of information helps the Government, business and the health sector focus its activities both on research, health provision, occupational health and the guidance services.

ACTIVITY 14.4

Using the HSE website at **www.hse.gov.uk/statistics/lfs/index.htm#illness** explore how:

● The 'lost days off work' for 2011–12 are reported when plotted against 'age' and

'gender'. Which age and gender group are more likely to be absent from work?

● Which group, by occupation in the year 2011–12, was most likely to be affected by musculoskeletal problems?

14.8 HEALTH AND SAFETY AUDITS

Organisations should carry out health and safety audits, involving as many as possible of those directly concerned with health and safety issues. This may include health and safety officers and advisers, HR specialists, managers and trade union representatives. The purpose of such an audit is defined by Saunders (1992):

A safety audit will examine the whole organisation in order to test whether it is meeting its safety aims and objectives. It will examine hierarchies, safety planning processes, decision-making, delegation, policy-making and implementation as well as all areas of safety programme planning.

The audit should include practical and quantitative issues, such as the adequacy and implementation of the organisation's health and safety policies and procedures, and safety practices such as the efficiency and effectiveness of risk assessments and accident investigations. Additionally it should cover attitudinal and qualitative issues such as commitment to all aspects of health and safety at work and the level of seriousness adopted by involved groups, such as the health and safety committee.

As with all audits, the purpose of a health and safety audit is to identify problems and areas for improvement, and ensure that appropriate action is taken to resolve problems and improve the relevant areas.

The law that applies to this is as follows:

● Management of Health and Safety at Work Regulations 1999

The HSE have provided guidance on interpreting the legislation at: **www.hse.gov.uk/ toolbox/index.htm**

● Safety Representatives and Safety Committees Regulations 1977
● Health and Safety (Consultation with Employees) Regulations 1996

The HSE offers guidance on both the 1977 and 1996 regulations (see HSE, 2008a, 2012, 2013c).

 ACTIVITY 14.5

Next time you are walking through the workplace, university, college campus or school, keep an eye open for posters and other notices about health and safety. Count how many there are and note what they say.

14.9 THE PRIORITIES FOR OCCUPATIONAL SAFETY AND HEALTH RESEARCH

The following narrative highlights some, but not all, of the substances and work practices which are likely to impact significantly on people at work in the future.

14.9.1 OCCUPATIONAL HEALTH AND WORKING PRACTICES

There is a continuous drift towards a knowledge- and service-based economy. The jobs it provides are a mix of the highly skilled, especially in the field of information technology, but also low-paid jobs, with people working unsocial hours, some in poor working conditions and others effectively on-call 24/7. This creates a stressed environment and a high emotional load. There is an increasing requirement to research the outcomes associated with this type of working.

14.9.2 OCCUPATIONAL HEALTH AND RECYCLING

The waste we produce and assiduously {*meaning – persevere*} recycle is likely to cause its own problems with respect to occupational health. The waste management and recycling is one of the fastest growing green economy sectors in terms of employment. However, the materials we recycle, both from industrial plants and the homes in which we live, may contain biological agents which can be both toxic and provoke allergic reactions. There is a need to assess the way waste is recycled to reduce the harm to those involved in the process.

14.9.3 OCCUPATIONAL HEALTH AND AMBIENT INTELLIGENCE (AMI)

This refers to the new ranges of equipment with which we play, for example the head-mounted glasses (spectacle) type technology, and how we communicate using information displays. Military and commercial airline pilots have been using 'head-up displays' for many years but within the home their use is only now starting to be introduced.

The negative impact of their use is little known, insufficient time has passed for data to be collected; but probably the negative effects are likely (potentially) to be associated with mental workload. However, the technology may offer a potential to help the elderly and some with specific disabilities.

14.9.4 OCCUPATIONAL HEALTH AND ELECTRO-MAGNETIC FORCES (EMF)

The EMF and electro-magnetic radiation from many of the devices which we use in our everyday lives is harmless. However, the use of resonance imaging scanners and transmitting antennae in hospitals and similar environments may expose workers to serious risk such as cancers. The research into this field needs to clear some of the contradictory evidence about the effect of such devices. The *Independent* on 20 May 2014 used the following headline: 'Thousands of London teenagers recruited to study how mobile phones affect their brains'. The article said the following,

> From today, more than 160 secondary schools in the capital will be invited to take part in the study, with scientists hopeful of securing 2,500 year seven pupils whose mobile phone use will be tracked for three years, ... researchers said that there was a lack of reliable evidence on the impact of mobile phones, and other wireless technologies, on the brains of young people. (*Independent*, available at: **www. independent.co.uk/life-style/health-and-families/health-news/thousands-of-london-teenagers-recruited-to-study-how-mobile-phones-affect-their-brains-9398597.html**)

14.9.5 OCCUPATIONAL HEALTH AND DISEASE

Across Europe the number of work-related fatalities due to accidents is reducing but fatalities linked to work-related diseases is increasing. There is increased exposure to chemical and biological agents, exposure to which may, at least, cause some form of sensitisation and allergic reactions but, at worst, may be fatal. For example, members of the public who have been exposed to Legionnaire's Disease have suffered serious illness and in some cases have died.

Further research is needed on the new range of chemicals and biological agents used in processes and the link with some types of cancer. Similarly, the use of nanomaterials in the food, transport and other industries is far ahead of the research into the harmful effects of such materials. Research into how these materials can be safely disposed is lagging behind their usage.

For further reading on the direction of research into potential health and safety issues read the policy paper published by the European Agency for Safety and Health at Work (2013).

14.10 STRESS-RELATED ILL-HEALTH

The word *well-being*, rather than *welfare*, is used in this chapter because it covers the services that one associates with welfare, but it also refers to individuals' physical and mental health, which implies that employees should be working in a physically safe and stress-free environment. Well-being is also concerned with employees' problems, such as their working hours, work overload, financial, home and marriage situations, susceptibility to stress and their general health and lifestyle.

14.10.1 WORKPLACE STRESS

The main emphases in this section are on the causes of stress, the nature and identification of the symptoms, and the steps that can be taken by the organisation and the individual concerned.

KEY CONCEPT: STRESS

It is sufficient for our purposes to say that stress occurs when an individual is pushed or pressurised beyond the limits of their normal coping capacity; when a person's perception of a situation induces tension and anxiety at a level that is beyond their normal experience.

14.10.2 THE SIZE OF THE STRESS PROBLEM

The HSE offers the following depressing statistics, which reflect the nature and extent of occupational illness linked to work place stress.

> The Labour Force Survey (LFS) estimated that the main work activities causing work-related stress, or making it worse (averaged over 2009/10–2011/12) were:
>
> i. Workload (incl. tight deadlines, too much work, pressure or responsibility) with an estimated prevalence of 186,000 cases;
>
> ii. Lack of managerial support with an estimated prevalence of 61,000 cases;
>
> iii. Violence, threats and bullying with an estimated prevalence of 54,000 cases.
>
> The total number of cases of stress in 2011/12 was 428,000 (40%) out of a total of 1,073,000 for all work-related illnesses.

(HSE, 2013d)

- Depression and anxiety are the most common stress-related complaints seen by GPs, affecting 20% of the working population of the UK.
- On average, each person suffering from a stress-related condition took 21 days off work. This is one of the highest average days lost per case figure amongst the recognised health complaints covered in the Labour Force Survey (LFS), see: **www.hse.gov.uk/statistics/lfs/swit1.xls**
- The occupations with the highest estimated prevalence rate of work-related stress in GB, averaged over the period (2009/10 – 2011/12) were: nurses, teaching and education professionals and welfare and housing associate professionals.

 KEY CONCEPTS

(Taken from HSE 2009a, p.24)

The **Labour Force Survey** (LFS) is a survey of 50,000 households each quarter which provides information on the UK labour market. The HSE's annual questions in the LFS are used to gain a view of work-related illness and workplace injury based on individuals' perceptions. The analysis and interpretation of these data are the sole responsibility of HSE. Further details about the LFS, and more specifically the HSE-commissioned questions, are available from: **www.hse.gov.uk/statistics/lfs/technicalnote.htm**

Self-reported work-related illness (SWI): These are incidences of ill-health reported by people who have conditions which they think have been caused or made worse by their current or past work, as estimated from the LFS. The estimates of self-reported ill-health include long-standing as well as new cases; these 'incidences' comprise those who first became aware of their illness in the last 12 months. HSE has carried out SWI surveys, linked to the LFS, periodically since 1990 and have done, annually, since 2003/04.

14.10.3 THE LEGAL CASE: WHAT THE LAW REQUIRES

As discussed earlier in this chapter, employers have duties under:

● Management of Health and Safety at Work Regulations 1999: to assess the risk of stress-related ill-health arising from work activities
● Health and Safety at Work Act 1974: to take measures to control that risk.

The HSE expects, as previously discussed, organisations to carry out a suitable and sufficient risk assessment for stress and to take action to tackle any problems identified by that risk assessment. Assessing the risk in terms of stress, a psychological illness, which can be triggered or made worse by work or working conditions, is no different from the requirement to assess a work site or working practices which might physically harm an employee. Refer to the HSE's guidance (HSE, 2011a).

14.10.4 SOURCES AND CAUSES OF STRESS

Sources of stress are those areas of life in which stressors are active. Research shows that there are six main areas of stress:

1   *The workplace:* workload, work schedule etc.

2   *Interpersonal relationships:* difficulties with a supervisor, co-workers, patients, relatives.

3   *Changes at work:* reduction in resources which includes staff, changes in work content, capability problems, changes in management, company takeover.

4   *Personal development:* redundancy or threat of redundancy, job insecurity, examinations, training courses.

5   *Home-work interface:* family responsibilities, pregnancy, health problems (physical), severe event such as a death of friend or relative.

6   *Traumatic event:* violence at work, accident, disciplinary action.

14.10.5 STRESS AS A COMMUTER

The effects of stress that originates in one of the areas listed above stay with people as they commute from one area to the next. For example, people take their workplace stress home with them, where its effects are communicated to the family. If there are additional pressures at home, perhaps concern over finances, the accommodation itself, or 'neighbours from hell', they will be added to the load like a rolling snowball and carried to the other areas, including the workplace. In a severe case the load becomes too much to bear and ill-health follows.

14.10.6 STRESS AND PRODUCTIVITY

Stress adversely affects productivity. The HSE (2013e) advises that 10.4 million working days are lost annually through stress-related factors, such as sickness absence and reduced work performance. It is worth bearing in mind that these losses are 30 times greater than those associated with industrial relations problems. An anomaly emerges when one compares the national and corporate investments that have gone into industrial peace with those dedicated to addressing stress problems.

14.10.7 THE HUMAN FUNCTION CURVE

This provides an explanation of what can happen when an individual is expected to cope with end-to-end emergencies, a continuously high workload or an excessive amount of time spent in the workplace. It is often said that 'a little stress is good for you' and that work performance increases as the pressure rises. However, there is a difference between stress and pressure. Stress is detrimental and can cause long-term health problems if not dealt with effectively. We all need some pressure, 'it gets the adrenalin running,' they say, 'and you experience an energy boost.' There is a 'line' when pressure, which can be energising, becomes stress and at this point the stress experienced *actually reduces* one's ability to cope with the job, which in turn creates further stress (see Figure 14.1).

Figure 14.1 The human function curve

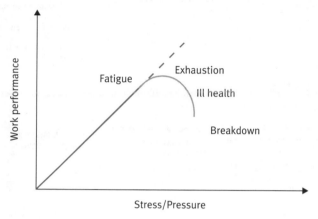

In Figure 14.1, the point at which *fatigue* appears on the curve will vary from one individual to the next, but the general principle is the same for everyone. In cases of severe stress, the employee is not always aware that their work performance is being affected in the way that is indicated in Figure 14.1.

14.10.8 DYNAMICS OF WORK STRESS

It was once thought that work-related stress was experienced mainly by company executives who claimed that time was their primary concern: always dashing about, attending breakfast meetings in the London boardroom and lunch meetings in Geneva. According to Smith et al (1978) and McLean (1979), stress-induced illnesses are not confined to either high- or low-status workers.

Regardless of how one job may compare with another in terms of stress, it is helpful to recognise that every job has potential stress agents (stressors). Additionally, it is helpful to note that an event or situation that one person may regard as stressful might be seen by another as an interesting challenge or even part of their development. Furthermore, stress affects different people in relatively different ways. Some people find it easy to cope with pressure, while others have great difficulty.

14.10.9 ORGANISATIONAL CAUSES

As we have seen from earlier discussion, the HSE has identified a number of common causal factors which impact upon the individual and cause them to be stressed (stressors). Common to all jobs, these factors vary in the degree to which they are found to be causally linked to stress in each job and to the illnesses that may result from the experience of stress. Refer to Figure 14.2 for a pictorial representation of how these factors are linked to the outcomes of stress.

Figure 14.2 Picturing workplace stress

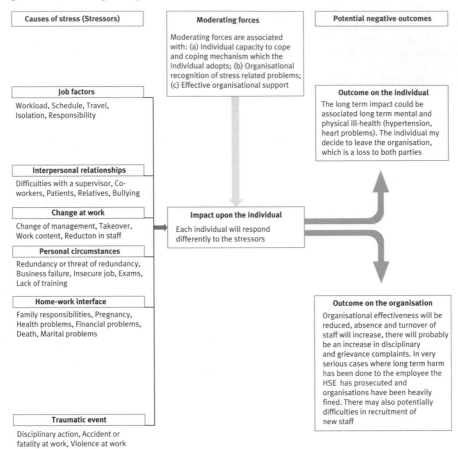

14.10.10 THE ROLE OF THE ORGANISATION

What can the organisation do to alleviate these problems? It was noted above that there are strong business reasons for an organisation to recognise the effects of stress and take action to alleviate it. There are also legal reasons. And finally organisations have a social and moral responsibility for the quality of life at work. Clearly, there is likely to be some stress in any job. There is a level which is required to create a sense of urgency and importance but, as can be seen from Figure 14.1, there is a limiting level at which further stress causes damage to the individual.

Stress has been classified as *transient*, *post-traumatic* and *chronic*, all of which are related to the timing of the events that caused them:

- **Transient stress:** occurs at the same time as its cause and is a short-term experience. For example, it may be experienced by emergency services workers when they are dealing with events such as public disorder, accidents, fires and a variety of other types of incident.
- **Post-traumatic stress disorders (PTSD):** occurs after a shock caused by a critical life event, such as involvement in a serious traffic accident, sustaining severe personal injury, perhaps being mugged or fighting in a war zone.

- **Chronic stress:** occurs as a result of continuous pressures being experienced by the individual for a period of time that is too long for the person to endure.

14.10.11 MANAGING STRESS

In this section, for the purposes of explanation, a distinction is drawn between *stress management* and *coping* with stress. Stress management consists of the arrangements that organisations, and others, make to minimise workplace stress, whereas coping with stress refers to the steps that an individual might take to moderate or eliminate their own personal stress.

Many organisations try to moderate the effects of stress by setting up an *occupational support service* (OSS). This type of service can either be provided from within the organisation or bought in from a specialist provider. Depending upon an organisation's policy, employees can either self-refer or request to be referred when they are or have experienced the effects of stress. Typically the scope of the service offered by an OSS is determined by the number of employees and the kind of work in which the firm is engaged. A small to medium-sized organisation, for example, may arrange to access the skills of a nurse, an occupational psychologist and/or a stress counsellor, who can be called on as and when required. On the other hand, a large organisation might employ such experts and set up the OSS as a special department.

14.10.12 THE GOVERNMENT'S RESPONSE TO THE PROBLEM OF WORKPLACE STRESS

Because of the size of the problem of workplace stress, the UK Government, through the HSE, has introduced *The Management Standards for Work Related Stress*. The standards consider and define the culture of how best to manage workplace stress. Particularly, as the website indicates (HSE, 2013f), the management standards for work-related stress help:

- identify the main risk factors for work-related stress
- employers focus on the underlying causes and their prevention
- provide a yardstick by which organisations can gauge their performance in tackling the key causes of stress.

The management standards for work-related stress cover six areas of work that are recognised to be stressors: the *demands* of the job, for example workload; how much *control* someone has over their work; the *support* by management that people receive; the quality of *relationships* in the workplace; the understanding of the work *role*; and how organisational *change* might be affecting people.

The management standards (HSE, 2013f) offer a tool with which to assess the state of the mental health of the organisation. The process that the HSE recommends is a five-step process:

1   Identify stress risk factors.

2   Decide who might be harmed and how.

3   Evaluate the severity of the risk.

4   Record the findings of the investigation.

5   Monitor and review progress.

As with many work-related issues, the process of risk assessment with respect to workplace stress can be effective only with the active support of senior management and engagement with and support of the employees and employee representatives.

 ACTIVITY 14.6

How would you advise the management of an organisation to plan for and conduct a 'workplace stress audit'?

Go to the HSE's (2007) publication, *Managing the Causes of Work-related Stress: A step-by-step approach using the Management Standards* and see how they suggest that a risk assessment on workplace stress should be conducted. You can access the publication from: **www.hse.gov.uk/pubns/priced/hsg218. pdf**

The document is long but the key themes of how to go about a workplace stress-related risk assessment can quickly be determined. There is also a quick guide (HSE, 2009) called *How to Tackle Work-related Stress: A guide for employers on making the Management Standards*. This guide can be accessed from **www.hse.gov.uk/pubns/indg430.pdf**

14.10.13 THE 'CARING' ORGANISATION

Some managers are reluctant to offer advice and assistance to employees on developing a healthy lifestyle. They regard lifestyle as a very personal issue and think that 'interference' by the organisation may be regarded as an unwarranted intrusion. Within the organisation, however, they have an opportunity to set an example by promoting a 'healthy workplace' by taking the following initiatives:

- **Smoke-free work areas**: It is now illegal to smoke in a confined public place. This also includes vehicles operated by an organisation. The onus is on management to police this piece of legislation. Messages are important when managing health and safety related issues. Having a no-smoking policy and turning a blind eye to smoking in company cars, vans and lorries sends mixed messages about the sincerity and intent of management.
- **Consulting the workforce** about the kinds of food that are served in the staff restaurant. This is best achieved by agreement and having a food policy.
- **Providing employees with information** about healthy living, including information on physical activity, healthy eating, generally looking after oneself. Employees with health problems and disabled employees may need to consult a physician before adopting the advice.
- **Providing facilities**, where possible, for employees to engage in physical activity, and encouraging them to participate in sports.
- **Providing annual health checks:** there are 'well man' and 'well woman' schemes in which all occupational physicians are versed.
- **Creating and managing** a work environment that is physically safe and generally conducive to good health.

Ahmed was happy in his work and generally conscientious. He had been with the company for seven years. Ten months ago he had been moved onto shift working as a supervisor, which meant greater responsibility for the work. He worked in a large distribution warehouse. His job was to make sure that large articulated trucks were loaded with the correct goods and dispatched on time. Some of the materials handled were hazardous and needed special care when being transported from their secure storage onto the waiting trucks. The new job was quite pressurised because many of the commercial businesses (customers) that his company provides goods for operate a 'just-in-time' stock control system. If goods from Ahmed's warehouse fail to arrive on time, their production lines stop.

He had never managed a team of people before and coping with the work and personal issues, which naturally people bring to work with them, was something alien to him. But he tried and continued to try to cope with both demands without complaining. He was surprised that he had been given no preparatory training for the people management part of the job. He had been promoted on his technical competence, which he had gained en route to becoming a key warehouse worker. He could drive or manipulate all the warehouse equipment and was competent in the use of the computer systems which controlled the workflow; he also applied his intellect to solving problems.

He was finding the night shift particularly problematic; there was no other manager on duty and so he could not share or ask advice on how to handle some situations. He didn't have a mentor who he could contact and simply talk through how *he* was feeling or from whom to receive good advice. His life appeared to revolve around the problems of others and the pressure to get the next load out of the warehouse!

Lately the night shift supervisors were also being asked to attend mid-week planning and progress meetings. He was finding this particularly problematic because Ahmed has sleeping difficulties during the day. Once awake, and having attended a 2pm meeting, there was no point in going home to rest because he was also responsible for collecting his daughter from nursery at 5pm.

Work has not been going well; Ahmed had been late for some night shifts and some key deliveries had been delayed leaving. The day shift foreman had to complete some of the night shift's tasks before the delayed truck or, in some cases, trucks were ready to leave. He found this embarrassing; Ahmed is a proud man.

After one mid-week planning and progress meeting he was asked to stay behind to meet with his manager, Dave, a fair but blunt individual. Dave made it very clear that Ahmed was, as he quite bluntly explained, 'not cutting the mustard'. In short, Ahmed was not performing and would be put onto a performance improvement programme if he did not 'get a grip on his team' and his job. Dave indicated that he expected much more from Ahmed.

Questions about the case

1   What was wrong with Dave's approach?

2   If, as an HR adviser, you were approached by Dave for advice on how to proceed with the case, what would you propose? Bear in mind that Dave is all for 'putting Ahmed on performance improvement and then managing him out of the organisation'.

3   What factors would you consider?

4   What would you propose as a way forward?

Discussion about the case

Before making any recommendations, it is appropriate to thoroughly investigate the context, the facts and any substantive issues which would bear upon any decision that a disciplinary hearing could take.

The following factors and facts are noteworthy:

1 How is Ahmed feeling at this moment in time? What is his perception of the problems? Understanding how Ahmed feels is vital to a competent investigation. Although other shift supervisors may not be feeling the stress of the role, it is how he feels that is important. Learning how to do a new job is like learning to drive. There are so many knobs, levers, pedals and switches to press, push, turn, and all while the car is going at an amazingly fast 20mph!

2 Ahmed has had very little training or coaching in his new role. Assuming that a key worker can be promoted and perform as a good supervisor is illogical. Good players do not always make good coaches. However, there is no indication that Ahmed could not rise to the challenge given appropriate training and development and perhaps mentoring.

3 The organisation has not helped Ahmed's situation because they have been requiring him to visit the workplace during his 'off-time'.

4 'Night workers who deal with special hazards or whose work involves mental or physical strain cannot work longer than 8 hours in any 24-hour period. Special hazards and work involving mental or physical strain should be identified as part of risk assessments. They may also be set out in collective or workforce agreements.' Refer to **www.gov.uk/ night-working-hours** for further advice on this topic.

5 Perhaps as a way forward, Ahmed could be temporarily taken off shift working and placed alongside a day supervisor. He could, while in this 'training role', be released to attend an introductory course on supervision. Allocating Ahmed a mentor, an experienced coach who has the ability to empathise with Ahmed's concerns, would provide the essential support those new to supervising require.

6 The organisation needs to review its practice of calling in shift supervisors to attend progress and planning meetings; thought should be given to alternative ways and means of conducting these important meetings.

14.11 EMPLOYEE WELL-BEING

There are a range of approaches to achieving the holy grail of employee well-being. On the one hand there is a mix of encouragement and enforcement, which government offers; on the other hand there is the provision of family-friendly policies and employee assistance programmes adopted by organisations.

ACTIVITY 14.7

Working in small groups, discuss what you consider is meant by health and well-being in the workplace.

Earlier in this chapter well-being was discussed in the following terms:

'Well-being, as well as being associated with an employee's physical and mental health, is also concerned with their associated problems, such as their working hours, work overload, financial, home and marriage situations, susceptibility to stress and their general health and lifestyle.'

You will find some good ideas on this subject by accessing the Acas booklet, *Health, work and wellbeing*, and discussion paper, *The future of health and wellbeing in the workplace*, which are available at:

● **www.acas.org.uk/media/pdf/3/t/Health-work-and-wellbeing-accessible-version.pdf**

and

● **www.acas.org.uk/media/pdf/7/k/The_future_of_health_and_wellbeing_in_the_workplace.pdf**

14.11.1 GOVERNMENT ENCOURAGEMENT

The origins of the government initiatives on employee well-being were in 2005 when the Government launched its health, work and well-being strategy. The Government focus was, and is, on the improvement of well-being for people of a working age and getting those who:

● have some protracted illness which is keeping them away from work, back to work
● are out of work and in receipt of some form of social benefit, into work.

The thinking about and around well-being is currently, from a governmental perspective, multi-departmental, linking the Department for Work and Pensions, Department of Health and the Health and Safety Executive, of which much has been discussed in this chapter. Following on from its early beginnings, on 25 November 2008, Dame Carol Black, who headed up a government initiative on well-being, presented a review of the health of Britain's working age population (Black, 2008). Her review was conducted against three principles (ibid, p.9):

1   prevention of illness and promotion of health and well-being

2   early intervention for those who develop a health condition

3   an improvement in the health of those out of work, so that everyone with the potential to work has the opportunity they need to do so.

Dame Carol, in her review, justifies the Government's initiative by pointing out that 175 million working days were lost to illness in 2006 – this equates to over 5.7 days of work lost for each person employed per year. Further, she argues that on average the days lost to ill-health do not compare favourably with most other countries. Critically, the cost to the country of ill-health and worklessness amounted to over £100 billion annually (Black, 2008, p.10), which the review points out is equivalent to the total GDP of Portugal. Dame Carol gives the main causes of the problem in the following way (Black, 2008, p.10): 'mental health problems and musculoskeletal disorders are major causes of sickness absence and worklessness due to ill-health'. The figures, quoted by the Office for National Statistics (ONS), for 2013 show that there has been a decrease in working days lost due to illness, down to 131 million days, which equates to 4.4 days of work lost for each person employed per year (ONS, 2014).

As a direct result of the Black (2008) report, the Government introduced two initiatives:

- Pump-priming funding *{meaning – initial but limited funding}* was awarded to eleven 'Fit for Work Services' until March 2011 and a further seven until March 2013.
- Occupational health advice services for small businesses and GPs.

The 'Fitness for Work' programme aimed to offer a one-stop-shop mainly for small to medium-sized enterprises (SMEs). The provision focused on employees who had been ill and their illness had caused them to be away from work for more than four weeks. The extent of the provision depended upon geographical area but generally covered: 'fit note' solutions, phased return to work, restricted duties, flexible working, changes to job role, finding alternative employment, and so on. In some cases the support extended to advice and support for social concerns including finance, housing, family, carer issues, occupational management interventions including workplace risk factor assessment and modification. (**http://webarchive.nationalarchives.gov.uk/20110202185534/http:/dwp.gov.uk/health-work-and-well-being/our-work/fit-for-work-services/**)

The concern with the number of people out of work or away from work through illness has remained a government priority. Government is tackling the issue through a broad front of initiatives:

- Introducing measures to give Jobcentre Plus flexibility in helping people back to work:

  Helping young unemployed people gain work experience: this part of the programme is centred primarily on 18–24-year-old jobseekers. The initiative seeks to overcome the problems of 'landing a job' through work experience placements lasting two to eight weeks which is available through the Youth Contract.

- Providing training, work experience and a guaranteed interview in sectors with high local vacancies. This initiative targets individuals who are claimants of:

  ○ Jobseeker's Allowance
  ○ Employment and Support Allowance (work-related activity group).

- Helping people who want to start their own business. This initiative is supported by what is termed the 'New Enterprise Allowance'. The scheme is not open to all but is specifically targeted at those who are unemployed, aged 18 or over and crucially receive:

  ○ Jobseeker's Allowance
  ○ Income Support as a lone parent
  ○ Employment and Support Allowance, if you're in the work-related activity group.

- The support offered is a mix of loans or a weekly allowance up to a capped figure; as of April 2014 the total allowance is £1,274 paid over 26 weeks.
- Encouraging people who want to become self-employed to share their experiences through what are termed 'Enterprise Clubs'. 'Enterprise Clubs are clubs set up and run by local businesses and partnerships for people who are out of work and who are considering starting their own business or becoming self-employed' (JobCentrePlus, 2012).
- Encouraging people who are out of work to share skills and experience through 'Work Clubs'.
- Promoting volunteering to improve employment prospects.

- Introducing flexibility for some people in full-time training to remain on Jobseeker's Allowance:

The Government has introduced limited flexibility into the administration of Jobseeker's allowance in so far as, if a claimant has been in receipt of Jobseeker allowances for 6 months or more, they may attend full-time training without losing their allowance. This is in preference to transferring individuals to a training allowance. As with all these schemes there are time caveats which are applied to control the benefit.

The Government's focus on well-being is driven by economics. In short, people who are not in work are not contributing to either their own or the country's wealth.

ACTIVITY 14.8

1   Access the ONS report *Sickness Absence in the Labour Market, February 2014* and explore what the situation was in 2013 in respect of absence differentials between the public and private sector, where the highest absence rates occur in the public sector and the rates of absence of those who are self-employed compared with salaried workers. You will find the report at: **www.ons.gov.uk/ons/rel/lmac/**

sickness-absence-in-the-labour-market/ 2014/rpt—sickness-absence-in-the-labour-market.html

2   Go to the Government website sponsored by the Department for Work and Pensions at **www.gov.uk/government/topics/ welfare** and explore the initiatives that the Government is sponsoring to help encourage more people into work.

14.11.2 THE GOVERNMENT AND WELL-BEING LEGISLATION

Organisations are responsible for the well-being of their employees while they are working on their behalf; the organisation is said to have a 'duty of care' for its employees. Today, it is becoming commonplace for employees, or ex-employees, to take legal action against their ex-employers for breaching their duty of care.

Increasingly, the kind of UK legislation that is related to employee well-being has been introduced as a result of European directives that have been enacted in all of the member countries of the European Union (EU). The EU, as well as bringing together countries within an economic entity, has also a social dimension to political philosophy. The bases of EU policies are: (i) equal treatment for all, (ii) fairness at work and (iii) family-friendliness. It is important to bear in mind that much of this legislation is directed at non-work areas, as well as the area of employment.

ACTIVITY 14.9

Working in small groups, explore and discuss what family-friendly legislation means in practice.

You will find some guidance from:

- the TUC document: *Family Friendly Rights: Transforming Britain's Workplaces*, available at: **www.tuc.org.uk/sites/default/ files/extras/familyfriendlyguide.pdf**

Although Chapter 16 deals with how employment legislation impacts upon the workplace, it would be remiss of us here if there were no mention of how legislation has sought to influence, through controlling measures, the link between work and a healthy workplace and a healthy work environment, both physical and mental. The previous section of this chapter sought to address how the Government, through the HSE, is seeking to influence behaviours in the workplace to encourage organisations to adopt healthy work practices, in the broadest sense.

Legislation surrounding health and well-being has been included on the 'statute books' in the UK since the late 1990s. Specifically we refer to the Working Time Regulations, the Work and Families Act 2006 and the Health Act (England) 2006.

The Working Time Regulations address, as the name implies, among other things: the length of the working week, rest breaks and holiday entitlements. The essence of this piece of legislation is on the specification of the minimum standards with which all organisations must comply, in the context of the duration of work.

The Work and Families Act (WFA) sought to remove some of the pressures that impact upon new parents. The law gives rights to parents to claim statutory maternity pay, take leave, upon the arrival of their new child, and also to request (not demand) flexible working. The law, though, on parental leave will be changing from 2015. Acas states that:

> ...once a mother has taken two weeks' maternity leave, the remaining 50 weeks can be shared flexibly with her partner. The plans allow them to take the leave in turns, in blocks or together, but for no more than 12 months in total and with no more than 9 months at statutory pay. (Acas, 2014c)

The right to request flexible working (see Chapter 16) originally offered the opportunity for certain groups of people, that is, those with children under six years of age (as of April 2009 the qualifying age was increased to under 17 years), those with a disabled child under 18 years of age or those with caring responsibilities to *request* flexible working. However, primarily because the Government, which came to power in 2010, was a coalition between Conservative and Liberal Democrats, there has been a mix of business-focused, hard-headed economics-driven legislation and also socially driven legislation around family-friendly policies. In 2012 the Government announced that it would allow parental leave to be shared, as discussed above, from 2015 and the right to *request* flexible working open to all, from June 2014, subject to them being employed for a minimum of 26 weeks with an organisation. Only one request is allowed within a 12-month period (Childrens and Families Act, 2014).

Finally, the Health Act (England) 2006 deals specifically with the health issues associated with smoking in the workplace. The impetus for this Act of Parliament focused upon the right of employees to work in an unpolluted, smoke-free environment, given that the dangers of passive smoking are substantial. In practice if an employer does not ensure that the workplace is pollutant-free, as would be the case if someone smoked in the office or company transport, the employer would be breaking the implied terms of the employment contract, which is that they must provide a safe working environment – and clearly a smoke-laden environment would not be healthy!

It can be seen that the Government, through various Acts of Parliament, regulations and initiatives, is encouraging employees to adopt healthy lifestyles and for employers to work towards creating healthy workplaces with a focus on both the healthy mind and the healthy body. The welfare system will have its focus on supporting people to work or enabling them to be able to work.

In the context of health, safety and well-being, the Coalition Government's concern and attention has been mixed and actions have been across a number of areas:

- As previously discussed, getting those people who cannot work because of illness back into work.
- By improving and extending certain family-friendly legislation, for example extending the scope of the right to request flexible working. Acas signalled the proposed changes as follows:

> On 30 June 2014 the Flexible Working Regulations will be amended. This will mean that the right to request flexible working will be extended to cover all employees after 26 weeks' service, rather than only those with children under the age of 17 (or 18 if the child is disabled) and certain carers. (Acas, 2014b)

- Following a report (*Common Sense Common Safety*) written by Lord Young of Graffham, the focus turned to where it was considered health and safety legislation inhibited or restricted good business. Further to Lord Young's report, the Government published on 21 March 2011 *Good Health and Safety, Good for Everyone*. The document laid a blueprint for reforms as to how business could both access good and accurate health and safety advice and how the Health and Safety Executive 'polices' HSE within organisations. The Government will:

  - launch an Occupational Safety and Health Consultants Register to ensure that businesses have access to competent and ethical advice
  - move health and safety enforcement activity away from businesses that do the right thing and concentrate on high-risk areas and dealing with serious breaches of health and safety rules
  - simplify health and safety legislation and guidance and in doing so ease the burden on business.

www.gov.uk/government/publications/good-health-and-safety-good-for-everyone
www.gov.uk/government/uploads/system/uploads/attachment_data/file/214613/dwp-worklessness-codesign-ir.pdf

14.12 ORGANISATIONAL HEALTH AND WELL-BEING

The business focus on employee well-being centres on provision of benefits such as: counselling services, employee assistance programme, provision of free fruit, subsidised gym membership, private healthcare and stop smoking support (CIPD, 2013j).

The CIPD (2013j) *Employee Outlook Survey: Focus on Employee Well-being* does not make good reading. The survey findings paint a picture of half of the 2,229 employees surveyed indicating:

> ...they have noticed an increase in workloads in their organisation over the last 12 months. This figure increases to 63% in the public sector. Just under half of employees said they have seen an increase in stress over the past year, which is again more common in the public sector (60%). People working longer hours and an increase in pressure to meet targets were reported by 35% of survey respondents. (CIPD, 2013j, p.3)

The pressures that people indicated that they felt when asked what caused them to go into work when feeling unwell were associated with: the pressure of work, the demand for presenteeism and 'personally felt' pressure not to let one's team members down.

The majority of the Government's drivers for changing well-being employment legislation are, as mentioned above, economic. From an organisation's perspective, the equation which surrounds employee well-being is complex; much depends upon whether the organisation considers its people as assets, which can be grown and developed – this concept has strong linkages to the McGregor's Theory Y and the best practice approach to strategic HRM. Alternatively, the organisation may consider employees simply as a resource, to be used; in this respect the perception of an employee's motivation to work could be viewed from the McGregor Theory X perspective in the context of their perceived attitude to work.

Those organisations which take the X perspective would want to have controls in place:

- Employees would more than likely to be at their place of work on all occasions even though working remotely might be more beneficial.
- Presenteeism would be the order of the day.
- Activities, absences, and so on, are likely to be tightly controlled.
- Trust would be low, impacting negatively upon the psychological contract.

The alternate perspective, Theory Y, is refreshing. Trust is high and control is with the individual. However, this approach brings with it pressures and concerns. As mentioned previously, in the CIPD (2013j, p.4) *Employee Outlook Survey: Focus on Employee Well-being*, 'The most common reasons for going into work ill were: not wanting to let your team down, having deadlines to meet, being worried colleagues would have to pick up the work of absent colleagues as well as their own, and not being sure if you were ill enough to stay off work'.

In reality, whether an organisation's culture, views and perspectives of its employees are negative (the cup is half-empty) or positive (the cup is half-full), there is a strong case to consider their well-being. The picture of what organisations offer, in terms of well-being initiatives, is varied. The CIPD (2013j) survey found that:

> Around two in five (44%) people we surveyed said their organisation does not promote health and well-being. Just 28% of employees said they know what well-being benefits are on offer and how to access the services/take part. Overall, the public sector is more active than the other sectors in promoting employee health and well-being. (CIPD, 2013j, p.4)

 ACTIVITY 14.10

Working in small groups, discuss whether you think that extending family-friendly legislation, as discussed previously, is driven by the social political leanings of the Liberal Democrat part of the Coalition Government or whether it is more about family-friendly policies bringing a positive impact on the ability to do business – that is, the business case.

To get some idea as to how to approach this question, read the following extract from a statement made by the chief executive of CarersUK. You can also access their and other websites given below to see what various organisations have to say about family-friendly employment legislation:

'According to Carersuk (**www.carersuk.org/ Home**) there are 6.5 million carers in the UK, which equates to one in eight adults, of whom 3 million are working. The stress associated with both caring for and finding the time to care for someone is immense. The right to request flexible working goes some way to mitigating the stress that this role causes employees and so may assist them to be able to remain in the workplace. Helena Herklots, Chief Executive of CarersUK said the following about the Government's decision to extend the right to request flexible working to all:

> Extending the right to request a more flexible working pattern is very welcome and should make it easier for families to share caring responsibilities alongside work, as well as normalising flexible working across the workforce. The Deputy Prime Minister has rightly highlighted the cost and availability of childcare as a major obstacle to women returning to work. However, our work shows that care for older and disabled loved ones is as important as childcare in enabling carers, and particularly women, to work. To support and boost the number of women in work, we also need services, including quality care and support for older and disabled people, which support caring over a life course – and which deliver a range of flexible affordable care from childcare through to eldercare. (Herklots, 2012, speech available at: **www.carersuk. org/northernireland/news-ni/action-on-social-care-needed-alongside-flexible-working-progress**

Consider what 'mumsnet' has to say about family-friendly legislation in the context of women with children and the opportunities to work: **www.mumsnet.com/jobs/flexible-working.** In an interview with the *Guardian* (19 November 2013), Justine Roberts talks candidly about her experiences of when she left work to go on maternity leave. You can read her comments in the *Guardian Professional* [online] at: **www.theguardian. com/women-in-leadership/2013/nov/19/ justine-roberts-maternity-leave-mumsnet**

The question, of course, for organisations is, what to do? What is possible to deliver that, on the one hand, meets the needs of employees and, at the same time, gives returns for the organisation? Some companies with available financial resources, such as Citigroup, invest heavily in the well-being of their workforce. The Confederation of British Industry (CBI), the voice of British industry, published the results of a survey they conducted in 2011, *Healthy returns? Absence and workplace health survey 2011*. The survey covered employers of all shapes and sizes and overall employed more than 1 million people. The editorial note by the CBI Chief Policy Director Katja Hall effectively sums up the position of the CBI, which centres upon absence management, that is, the development of processes which can help reduce high levels of absence, such as the fit note and employee capability. When discussing the employee well-being findings, the CBI (2011, p.32) offers the following:

- Almost nine out of ten organisations (89%) operate stress management policies.
- Counselling and occupational health support are the most widely used arrangements, followed by flexible working
- Three-quarters of employers (74%) consider improving employee well-being to be a priority over the next year.
- Approaches to improving employee well-being take many forms, the most widespread including some directly linked to health such as occupational health advice (74%) and others focused on day-to-day management actions such as praise for a job well-done (61%).

When employers were asked whether they would be improving employee well-being, the response was as follows:

> The survey asked employers whether they considered improving employee wellbeing to be an HR priority for their organisation in the next 12 months. ... Close to three quarters of employers (74%) said it was an HR priority, with a third (30%) identifying it as a top priority for their organisations. One in five employers (22%) said that they viewed improving employee wellbeing as desirable in the longer-term, but they had more urgent issues to address in the next 12 months. (CBI, 2011, p.34)

According to the CIPD's *Absence Management* survey (2013k),

> Overall, just two-fifths (41%) of organisations report they have a well-being strategy (or similar), comparable with previous years once size differences in the samples are taken into account. Smaller organisations are less likely to have a well-being strategy. ... Public sector organisations are twice as likely to have a well-being strategy as their counterparts in other sectors. (CIPD, 2013k, p.48)

ACTIVITY 14.11

Access the CIPD's annual *Absence Management: Annual Survey 2013*, p.49, and examine the range of initiatives and benefits that companies offer to their staff. How would you choose what to offer in your organisation if you were asked to consider what well-being initiatives your company should offer?

14.12.1 HELP FOR SMALL BUSINESSES

What to include in the well-being strategy has always been a problem for employers, especially the small to medium-sized organisations. The Government initially tackled this problem by providing some guidance to small business through a project called NHS Plus. The project was closed in 2013 and in its place is the 'Health for Work' website and advice line, which gives free advice to businesses that have health issues which affect their organisation (**www.health4work.nhs.uk/**).

CASE EXAMPLE 14.2

Consider the following article that appeared in *People Management* in 2012, which deals with how a large business, from a strategic perspective, dealt with the issue of employee well-being.

Well-being programme at Carlsberg 'focuses on the healthy'

Encouraging staff to make even small improvements to their basic health can help increase engagement in the workplace, the CIPD's Well-being for High Performance conference heard this morning.

Julian Daley, reward manager for Carlsberg UK, explained that there had been no pressing business need to introduce a well-being programme as sickness absence levels were low and consistent, and engagement scores more favourable than the UK average.

But the company believed that healthier staff 'would be more engaged and productive at work', said Daley, adding

'sometimes you just have to do the right thing by your employees.'

Delegates heard that Carlsberg had taken the more unconventional step of focusing its well-being strategy on the healthier 80 per cent of its workforce – rather than the least healthy 20 per cent – as this approach was felt to offer the greatest impact within the budget available.

The brewer – which employs 1,700 staff across 15 UK sites – rolled out an annual well-being day in November 2010. This saw 70 per cent of workers attend to have their basic health assessed – including blood pressure, heart rate, body mass index and hydration.

Results indicated that blood pressure, hydration and body fat content among the workforce were generally worse than the norm, so the company focused its efforts on 'nutrition, hydration and exercise'.

Carlsberg invested £860,000 in improving dining and kitchen facilities, and worked with its catering firm to improve the nutritional value of menus, move to healthier cooking techniques and re-position healthy snacks on food counters, so individuals were encouraged to make healthy choices.

A 'nutrition wheel' was developed with diet experts to give staff an accurate idea of the number calories they should aim to consume for their age, height and activity levels of their job role.

Water coolers were repositioned in the workplace to enhance access, while discounted gym memberships, a cycle to work scheme and walking routes outside the sites were introduced.

Daley said that absence management rates had remained steady and engagement levels were increasing year-on-year.

Many employees had been motivated to register an improvement on their results the following year, and some staff had completely altered their lifestyles. 'Just by raising people's awareness you can change people's mindset and their health,' he explained.

Daley added that as a beer company, Carlsberg was particularly aware about promoting responsible drinking both to the general public and internally, and that 'a real culture change' around healthy drinking levels had taken place in the firm in recent years.

Offering some advice to delegates on devising well-being programmes, Daley said it was important to make initiatives fun and engaging to involve the target audience.

'Ensure all stakeholders have the right messages before the [well-being] day and when running the programme, and understand what you are trying to achieve,' he explained. 'Find the metrics that work for you and start to measure them – you will not be able to focus your efforts or measure success without them.'

Source: Stevens (2012)

Reprinted with kind permission of *People Management*.

ACTIVITY 14.12

Read and reflect upon the article in Case Example 14.2. Notice that it was the 'reward manager' who presented the paper at the CIPD Well-Being Conference.

Consider the following questions:

● What do you perceive were the aims of Carlsberg's focus on the 'healthy'?

● What 'paybacks' do you consider the company were seeking by introducing their well-being initiative?

● Were the 'paybacks' just monetary or does introducing this type of programme have a wider effect upon employee relations?

14.12.2 EMPLOYEE ASSISTANCE PROGRAMMES

Larger organisations may operate their own occupational health schemes, but others, including some SMEs, may opt to buy into *employee assistance programmes* (EAPs). An EAP is an external agency commissioned by the organisation to manage facets of employee well-being on its behalf. The external agency is staffed by experts such as psychologists and counsellors. There may also be access to other experts such as solicitors, accountants and doctors, whose services might be required, depending upon the cause of stress experienced by an employee. EAPs are seen as an alternative to occupational support schemes. There are arguments for and against each of the two kinds of employee service.

Employees have greater confidence in an EAP, since they may be somewhat suspicious of the in-house *occupational support service* (OSS) worker, who might be seen as a manager's informant. As an external agency, the EAP has the added advantage of objectivity and, 'having no internal political axe to grind', may be totally candid when it tells managers where there is room for improvement in the way they handle staff.

It has been noticed that organisations that avail themselves of such external services are well placed to demonstrate that they have a caring attitude towards their employees. Demonstrating that the employer has done its best to mitigate health issues by providing an EAP service would be beneficial in a tribunal should an employee, for example, decide to take legal action on the grounds of a stress-related cause of illness and loss of employment.

In addition to the above, organisations may decide to offer a range of benefits, from gym membership to yoga classes. Boyd (2009, p.1) has a word of caution, quoting Spooner from the University of Technology, Sydney, when she says, 'Staff who are healthier, both physically and psychologically, can grow productivity but free trips to the gym or massages at work will do little to make those suffering from illness or from dread of work refrain from taking sick leave.' Spooner sees a more 'productive' approach by, for example, having flu inoculations at work as being better targeted. To further muddy the waters, in the same article, Professor Don Iveson points out that Coors, the US beer company, has, through a cardiac rehabilitation scheme, got heart attack sufferers back to work earlier and worked with them to help them to a fuller life.

Making the right choice of what to do when introducing a well-being set of benefits or a full wellness programme, as an employer, is a crucial one. A knee-jerk reaction to introduce, for example, gym membership as a benefit, although administratively an 'easy' option, may not be the best overall approach to the problem for the company and its employees; and it may be perceived by the more cynical employee as tokenism. A better approach would be to involve those concerned and to ask their views.

14.13 WORK-LIFE BALANCE

In light of the increase of stress in the workplace, it is pertinent to consider the concept of work-life balance as this can have an effect on stress, employee well-being and thus on motivation in the workplace.

An attractive work-life balance policy, which has been constructed with the co-operation of, and contributions from, the staff will demonstrate the organisation's commitment to its employees' quality of life.

KEY CONCEPT: WORK-LIFE BALANCE

In the context of work-life balance, 'work' relates to paid employment, 'life' refers to all of the non-work aspects of people's total lifestyle, and 'balance' to the reasonableness with which everything in their life fits together. For most people, work provides the central structure of their lives, while everything else is organised around it. Work-life balance involves time management, deciding what the priorities are, in terms of work, the needs of others – such as a spouse/partner and children – and making time and provision for personal interests, hobbies and leisure pursuits.

14.13.1 LONG-HOURS CULTURE

Many employees in the UK work longer hours than the Working Time Regulations (WTR) limit of 48 hours a week allows. In December 2012, the TUC estimated that a record 5.26 million people worked unpaid overtime during the previous year. According to the TUC:

> Long hours cause stress; are bad for our health; wreck relationships; make caring for children or dependents more difficult; and tired, burnt-out staff are bad for business. Evidence suggests that it is increasingly difficult for people to get their jobs done in their contractual hours and that there is a mismatch between the hours that people would like to work and the jobs available. (TUC, 2013)

This is a phenomenon that takes many forms:

- Working voluntarily beyond the contracted time. 'The tendency to stay at work beyond the time needed for effective performance on the job is known as "presenteeism"' (Simpson, 1998).
- Taking work home.
- Time spent talking and thinking about work.
- Low-paid employees may have to work overtime simply to earn a reasonable living.

 PAUSE FOR THOUGHT

How much time do you spend thinking about work when you are not there? Do you constantly check your work phone or emails? Does work impinge on your home life?

The practice of supplying employees with laptop computers and hand-held devices that can deal with mobile telephone calls and emails remote from the place of work all add further pressures on individuals to be working outside what we take to be normal office hours. Couple this with the ability of these devices to communicate on a global basis it further adds to the pressure to 'just answer this email' and so further reduce the time available for 'self'.

According to the CIPD's autumn 2013 *Employee Outlook* report (CIPD, 2013l), employees' satisfaction with their work-life balance has seen a slight increase to 58%, compared with 57% in spring 2013. The report goes on to say that those contracted to work between 1 and 24 hours per week were most likely to be satisfied with their work-life balance while only 37% of those on more than 40-hour contracts were satisfied with working their contracted hours. This suggests that working long hours has a detrimental effect on satisfaction.

14.13.2 THE BUSINESS CASE FOR WORK-LIFE BALANCE

Work-life balance is not only an issue of interest to employees. The CIPD (2013m) suggests that there are benefits to employers of introducing policies to underpin work-life balance issues:

- higher productivity and competitiveness
- increased flexibility and customer service, for example to cover for absence and holidays
- raised morale, motivation, commitment and engagement
- reduced absenteeism
- improved recruitment and retention of a diverse workforce

- wanting to become an 'employer of choice'
- meeting legal requirements.

(CIPD, 2013m)

Clutterbuck (2003) suggests that it is important to measure outcomes to show clear and positive impacts for employees and the organisation. He suggests measuring not only hard returns such as cash, return on investment or share prices, but also retention, corporate reputation, productivity quality, creativity and customer service, as these are where much of the success of work-life balance policies can be seen.

Clearly, employers will know what they wish to achieve in terms of their core business requirements, but if they regard the long-term well-being of the employees as important, the employees, along with their representatives (trade unions), need to be consulted about what they too wish to achieve. The employer should:

- take the lead in demonstrating a commitment to work-life balance
- explain any changes to employees and keep them abreast of regulatory changes, for example the right for parents to request flexible working (see Chapter 16).

PAUSE FOR THOUGHT

Work-life balance is a relative concept: there is no universally acceptable level of work-life balance. What is appropriate for one person might be inappropriate for another. Do you consider that you have the right 'work-life balance'? It is easy to lose a sense of reality, in terms of the hours committed to work,

when one's job is both interesting and demanding. Sometimes it takes a gentle nudge from one's partner or friend to indicate that work is becoming too great a part of life – the trick is to listen and not ignore but to heed the advice. This is easier said than done.

14.13.3 SO WHAT CAN EMPLOYERS DO?

It is unlikely that an individual will achieve a satisfactory work-life balance without the co-operation and assistance of others. The employer has a significant role to play in this. Clutterbuck (2003) suggests that most people have complex lives with many choices, opportunities and demands available to them. He states that organisations need to recognise that having work-life balance policies alone will not be sufficient unless the culture is supportive. He says that organisations need to consider the following:

- **Processes for work organisation** – how are work and responsibilities divided up?
- **Technology** – for example, can people work from home using mobile technology?
- **HR systems** – how can HR processes such as appraisal, recruitment, succession planning and training support (or act as barriers to) work-life balance?

In addition, Clutterbuck (ibid) considers that training is important so that: senior managers demonstrate their commitment; line managers learn how to allocate work effectively; teams avoid issues relating to conflict of needs; and individuals receive help in planning their work-life balance.

14.13.4 ACHIEVING WORK-LIFE BALANCE

Acas (2013d) suggests that 'Employers have a "duty of care" to protect employees from risks to their health and safety. These risks might include stress caused by working long hours or not being able to balance work and home life. Flexible working can help to improve the health and well-being of employees and, therefore, improve their levels of attendance.'

Gradually, employers are becoming more flexible and understanding of their employees' commitments, and there is also legislation that requires employers to assist in particular circumstances.

14.14 FLEXIBLE WORKING

One of the main ways of achieving work-life balance is through flexible working. According to the CIPD (2012a) survey report on *Flexible Working Provision and Uptake*, the vast majority of employers (96%) offer some form of flexible working. There is no universal prescription for a satisfactory work-life balance for individuals; all organisations are different from each other and have different situations in terms of what can be offered. There are many different forms of flexible working; it can relate to the place we work – such as homeworking – or the kind of contract we have – such as a temporary or part-time contract. See also the previous discussion in the 'Employee Well-being' section of this chapter.

Common kinds of flexible working include flexitime, job-sharing, working shifts and part-time working. Flexible working can also help organisations to reduce absenteeism and increase productivity, employee commitment and loyalty. The most common forms are laid out below.

14.14.1 TELEWORKING/HOMEWORKING

This permits employees to work all or part of their working week at a location remote from the employer's workplace. The great advantage is not having to commute, but drawbacks include the lack of social contact and networking. The number of people working from home has increased by 13% in the last five years to just over 4 million, according to TUC analysis of Labour Market Force statistics (TUC, 2013).

14.14.2 JOB-SHARING

Two people share the responsibility for a job between them and split the hours, usually on an equal basis, for example each person works eighteen and a half hours, making a 37-hour week.

14.14.3 PART-TIME

This means working less than full-time hours either by working fewer days or shorter days, perhaps to fit in with school hours, for example.

14.14.4 TERM-TIME WORKING

The contract hours are as normal, except that employees on this type of contract would not be expected to work during school holidays. This type of contract is attractive for anyone with school-age children.

14.14.5 COMPRESSED HOURS

Compressed hours means working full-time hours but over fewer days. For example, working the normal 37.5 or 40 hours that would constitute a week's work, but worked over four days. Some organisations work a nine-day fortnight, where the normal ten working days, over a two-week period, is compressed into nine days. Each alternate week gives employees a long, three-day weekend, Friday, Saturday and Sunday. There is no reduction in hours worked: time at work is reallocated into fewer, but longer days.

14.14.6 FLEXITIME

Normal length of working week (for example 37.5 hours, or 18.5 hours if part-time, say), but the employee chooses when to start and end work (within agreed limits). There is usually a requirement to be present during 'core hours', for example 9.30am to 4pm, but with flexibility to start work perhaps between 8am and 9.30am and to finish early at 4pm or work later until 6pm. Hours can sometimes be accrued so that extra days' leave can be accumulated.

14.14.7 ANNUALISED HOURS

The employee has to work a certain number of hours over the year but they have some flexibility about when they work them. There are sometimes 'core hours' which the employee regularly works each week, and they work the rest of their hours flexibly or when there is extra demand at work. It gives employers some flexibility so they can call staff in when they are needed, but not have them in work when times are quiet.

14.14.8 CAREER BREAKS

Career breaks, or sabbaticals, are extended periods of leave – normally unpaid – of up to five years or more. These are usually taken by workers who want to spend time with family or studying for a qualification.

14.14.9 ZERO-HOURS CONTRACTS

Workers are not contracted to work any set number of hours, but are called in to work whenever the employer needs them. There is no obligation for employers to offer work, or for workers to accept it. Zero-hours contracts are used to provide a flexible workforce to meet a temporary need for staff – perhaps for a one-off event, or a sudden need for more staff.

Zero-hours contracts have attracted a bad press. They can be abused and some MPs have called for them to be banned for being exploitative. The Work Foundation report (2013) states:

> The UK labour market currently supports a wide variety of flexible working arrangements. Moreover, zero hours contracts can suit some people and there may be some circumstances where work is so erratic that it would be hard for an employer to offer the work on any other basis.

Properly used, zero-hours contracts can offer flexibility to some individuals and allow employers to offer work that would otherwise not be available.

The CIPD's *Employee Outlook* (autumn 2013j p.16) suggests that 'those on zero-hour contracts were more likely to agree or strongly agree that they achieve the right balance between work and home life, even when they worked more than 40 hours per week, suggesting that they were more in control of accepting or declining additional working hours'.

PAUSE FOR THOUGHT

What situations can you think of where a zero-hours contract could be useful? What are the advantages for an employer? Do you think there are advantages for the employee? To help you think about this topic, consider the following articles and videos:

1   The Government (Department for Business, Innovation and Skills, 2013) published a consultation paper on zero-hour employment contracts, available at: **www.gov.uk/government/uploads/ system/uploads/attachment_data/file/**

267634/bis-13–1275-zero-hours-employment-contracts-FINAL.pdf

2   The *Guardian* (5 May 2014): 'Jobseekers being forced into zero-hours roles', available at: **www.theguardian.com/uk-news/2014/may/05/jobseekers-zero-hours-contract**

3   Watch Ed Miliband, the Leader of the Labour Party, discuss zero-hours contracts at: **www.bbc.co.uk/news/uk-27152757**

4   Watch Christian May, representative of the IOD (Institute of Directors), discuss zero-hours contracts at: **www.youtube.com/watch?v=drL363Ei2Uo**

14.14.10 THE LAW AFFECTING WORK-LIFE BALANCE

The current law is explained and discussed in Chapter 16 (under 'Family friendly rights') – much of which affects work-life balance.

For ease of reference, the key areas are summarised below:

- **Part-time work:** Part-timers are entitled to the same hourly rate of pay and the same entitlements to annual leave and maternity/parental leave as full-timers but on a pro rata basis. Part-timers must also have the same entitlement to contractual sick pay and no less favourable treatment in access to training.
- **Annual leave:** From 1 April 2009, all employees are entitled to a minimum of 28 days' paid annual holiday. Bank holidays can be counted towards this entitlement. Those working on part-time contracts receive the 28 days of leave adjusted pro rata as the percentage of the holiday entitlement received by a comparable full-time worker.
- **Working time:** There is a limit of an average 48 hours a week on the hours a worker can be required to work, though individuals may choose to work longer by 'opting out'. The Working Time Regulations also provide for minimum rest periods and make special provision for night work.
- **Parental leave:** There is a right to 18 weeks' unpaid parental leave for men and women at any time up to the child's fifth birthday (18 if disabled). There is a limit of four weeks per year for each child. Parental leave applies to *each child*, not to an individual's job.
- **Time off for dependant care:** This is the right to take unpaid time off to deal with family emergencies (for example concerning an elderly parent, partner, child or someone who depends on you for care). You are allowed a 'reasonable amount' of time – there is no set limit, as it depends on the situation (refer to the Chapter 16, 'Understanding Employment Law', for more detail).
- **Maternity leave:** Under the Children and Families Act (2014) working parents will have much greater flexibility about how they 'mix and match' their maternity or adoption leave. From April 2015 mothers, fathers and adopters can opt to share parental leave around their child's birth or adoption placement. This gives families more choice over taking leave in the first year – dads and mothers' partners can take up to a year, or parents can take several months at the same time.
- **Right to request flexible working:** The Children and Families Act (2014) means any worker with six months' continuous service is now able to request to work flexibly after 30 June 2014. This includes working from home, working compressed weeks, doing a job-share, or other forms of flexible working.

14.14.11 REQUESTS AND ENTITLEMENTS

When studying employee rights in these respects, it is important to distinguish between situations in which the employee has a 'right to request' and those in which there is a clear 'statutory right'. Every one of the rights listed above is related to attendance, and it has to be borne in mind that to survive, develop and attend to customer demands, organisations have business needs and priorities that, at times, may conflict with the needs of employees.

14.14.12 CONSULTATION

In any organisation, the strategy for work-life balance has to be specifically tailored to meet both business and individual needs. It involves more than simply conforming to the law; it means finding out directly from the employees about their personal needs and priorities, then considering how they can be met in ways that positively support business needs and priorities.

14.14.13 VOLUNTARY MEASURES

There are several benefits that an employer may offer above and beyond the legal standards that may help employees to achieve a satisfactory work-life balance. Some of these are beneficial to the organisation as well as the employee. They may include unpaid career breaks, paid sabbatical schemes and financing educational and training courses. Additionally, there are more informal benefits such as allowing the occasional paid or unpaid day off to attend to an important, but non-urgent, matter at home or in the community. Furthermore, the minimum standards set down in legislation for maternity, paternity and other matters could be enhanced by offering higher pay and/or longer leave.

Such schemes not only give employees a great measure of control over how their working lives fit in with everything else they do, they also foster goodwill, loyalty, motivation and commitment.

14.14.14 HR CONTRIBUTION

The HR contribution to the formulation of a feasible work-life balance policy is probably more significant than any other. The objective is to ensure that the organisation encourages a healthy balance between work and non-work commitments among its employees. The task is eased if the top managers genuinely value their employees and are open to suggestions about a way forward. In the first instance, there are several steps that can be taken:

1   Organise a meeting with the employees and managers to tell them about business changes, intentions and find out from employees where they think improvements might be made.

2   Gather relevant information about the business needs and identify how the implementation of a policy will contribute to the achievement of business objectives.

3   Formulate a work-life strategy that will benefit both the business and the employees. The essence of the strategy should clearly be about organisational needs but should also reflect the needs of its employees, so further embracing the concept and reality of working in a mutually beneficial partnership.

4   Consider the arrangements that will be needed to cover for absence, to preserve goodwill with customers and between the employer and employees.

5   Draft a feasible and cost-effective action plan to accompany the strategy.

6   Take the package to the top managers and explain to them how and why the right work-life balance policy will benefit the organisation and its employees.

The package should include:

- policies that match operation needs
- reward and performance measures based on staff effectiveness in terms of results
- clear guidelines about the proposal, particularly for the line managers

- details of a meeting with staff to explain the new policies
- arrangements to have a joint meeting with staff to hear their views, discuss any ideas they may have for further improvement
- arrangements to have regular meetings with staff to advise them on any changes and listen to their ideas
- a monitoring system to check progress and identify and correct faults.

While it is the line manager who is in the best possible position to observe employees and identify those in need of assistance, it is primarily the role of HR to advise and assist in the development of a workplace culture that is supportive of employees striving to achieve a satisfactory work-life balance (WLB). Clutterbuck (2003, p.4) maintains that:

> ...only HR can make a convincing case for the business impact of investing time and money in promoting good work-life balance; only HR can craft and sell in to top management viable strategies for taking advantage of the competitive potential that a proactive approach to WLB brings; only HR can design and integrate the wide portfolio of policies needed; and only HR can develop and implement the processes for measuring progress against WLB goals.

It is important to involve staff in developing work-life balance policies rather than to decide for them in a paternalistic manner. Including discussion of work-life balance issues in the annual appraisal process is a way to find out the concerns of individuals that can be factored into future policy development or in fact form the basis of immediate action. Focus groups and staff surveys all form part of the process by which information about staff views on flexible working and work-life balance can be determined.

14.15 SUMMARY

This chapter discusses the concept of health and safety at work and the importance it plays in the employment relationship. The Health and Safety Executive (HSE) is introduced as the overarching body that has been set up by the Government to deliver its mission of preventing death, injury and ill-health to those at work and those affected by work activities, and also, from a wider governmental perspective, to deliver targets agreed for work-related health and safety. The HSE is instrumental in developing and enforcing workplace legislation.

There are certain things that an employer must do: appoint someone who is responsible for health and safety matters; write a *health and safety policy*; set up a *risk assessment system*; *consult employees* on health and safety matters; provide *free health and safety training* for workers; provide employees with *personal protective equipment*; provide the appropriate *welfare facilities*; make arrangements for *first aid, accidents and ill health*; display the *health and safety law poster* or provide a leaflet; buy and display an *employers' liability insurance policy*; *keep up to date on health and safety matters*; and *report accidents*.

An employer must be aware of these requirements and not implementing them is a failure in their duty to the employees. It is for this reason that the key health and safety legislation is addressed within the chapter, particularly:

- Health and Safety at Work Act (HASAWA) 1974
- Safety Representatives and Safety Committees Regulations 1977
- Health and Safety (Consultation with Employees) Regulations 1996
- Management of Health and Safety at Work Regulations 1999.

HR has a role to play in the health and safety of an organisation's employees because good health and safety practice is inextricably linked to behaviour in the workplace and is therefore a matter for the HR department.

According to the HSE, managing a safe working environment can be done by a four-pronged strategy based upon:

- plan
- do
- check
- act.

Clearly, with the best will in the world there are those within the workplace who will either take shortcuts in work processes and expose themselves or others to dangers – for example driving a heavy articulated lorry above the speed limit in a built-up area or perhaps using a mobile phone while driving – and so there needs to be legislation that acts both as a deterrent and as a punishment. This chapter therefore explores some, not all, of the legislation that applies in the workplace.

A significant proportion of this chapter is devoted to stress in the workplace because it is one of the major causes of workplace ill-health. Stress is an invisible enemy but managers have no excuse if they do not recognise the signs exhibited by employees or perhaps signs that may indicate that stress is being more widely experienced within the organisation.

We can see that there has been a growth in the interest in the subject of work-life balance and also employee well-being and that it is not only of interest to employees, but also makes good business sense. There are opportunities for employers to accommodate their workers' need for flexibility, with options such as allowing part-time working, job-share or homeworking, but it is important to remember that it is not always possible. However, if an employer can facilitate employees' needs in terms of work-life balance, it is one way of reducing stress and of demonstrating the employer's commitment to the employees' quality of life.

REVIEW QUESTIONS

1 What should an organisation's health and safety policy contain? (You will find help by accessing the Health and Safety Executive's website at: **www.hse.gov.uk/simple-health-safety/write.htm**)

2 What are the main purposes of carrying out risk assessments? Where would you find information on how to carry out a risk assessment in the workplace?

3 How are the three main categories of accidents at work classified?

4 When should a risk assessment be undertaken?

5 What do the acronyms SFAIRP and ALARP stand for? Why are they important?

6 What is the purpose of a health and safety audit?

7 What does the HSE approach of 'plan, do, check, act' mean? You will find guidance at **www.hse.gov.uk/managing/plan-do-check-act.htm**

8 Why should the organisation offer support and assistance to employees with non-work-related problems?

9 What are the key factors that cause stress in the workplace?

10 How would you define stress? What is a stressor?

11 Give the three reasons why organisations should seek to reduce the stress on those employees affected by high levels of stress.

12 What types of worker are the most susceptible to stress?

13 What are the management standards for work-related stress?

14 What are the characteristics of a healthy workplace?

15 What can the HR department do in its role to promote a positive health and safety environment and culture?

16 In what circumstances might the Working Time Regulations be ineffective?

17 What are the negative effects of working long hours?

18 How would you set up a health and safety management system? You will find guidance by accessing **www.hse.gov.uk/pubns/priced/hsg65.pdf**

19 What do you understand by 'employee well-being'?

20 Why should employers consider introducing 'well-being' programmes into the workplace?

21 How has the Government facilitated employee well-being through its focus on family-friendly employment legislation?

22 Why does work-life balance make good business sense?

23 Name three ways of offering flexible working.

24 Name some of the key legislation affecting work-life balance.

EXPLORE FURTHER

BOOKS

PILBEAM, S. and CORBRIDGE, M. (2010) *People resourcing and talent planning: HRM in practice.* Harlow: Pearson Education Ltd.

Pilbeam and Corbridge's text provides a very good introduction to the management of health and safety in the workplace.

CLUTTERBUCK, D. (2003) *Managing work-life balance: a guide for HR in achieving organisational and individual change.* London: CIPD.

Although dated, this textbook has a wealth of information on work-life balance.

JOURNAL ARTICLES

MCCARTHY, A., DARCY, C. and GRADY, G. (2010) Work-life balance policy and practice: understanding line manager attitudes and behaviors. *Human Resource Management Review.* Vol 20, No 2, June. pp.158–67.

MAIN SOURCE MATERIALS

The Health and Safety Executive website provides a reservoir of high-quality advice, guidance and statistical information on health and safety issues. The information is generally free to access. Available at: **www.hse.gov.uk**

Similarly, the European Agency for Safety and Health at Work's website offers the following information about the role of the organisation:

Campaigning – We raise awareness and disseminate information on the importance of workers' health and safety for European social and economic stability and growth.

Prevention - We design and develop hands-on instruments for micro, small and medium-sized enterprises to help them assess their workplace risks, share knowledge and good practices on safety and health within their reach and beyond.

Partnership - We work side-by-side with governments, employers' and workers' organisations, EU bodies and networks, and private companies. Our voice is multiplied by occupational safety and health networks represented by a dedicated focal point in all EU Member States, EFTA countries and candidate and potential candidate countries.

Research – We identify and assess new and emerging risks at work, and mainstream occupational safety and health into other policy areas such as education, public health and research *(sic)*.

The European Agency for Safety and Health at Work. Available at: **https://osha.europa.eu/en**

WEB LINKS

General

Acas points out on its website that work can have a positive impact on the health and well-being of employees that impacts upon business performance. They have produced a booklet entitled *Advisory booklet: Health, work and wellbeing*, Acas (2013d), which deals with, as they say on their website, 'the relationships between line managers and employees, the importance of getting employees involved in job design, flexible working and the use of occupational health'. Their booklet can be downloaded from **www.acas.org.uk/index.aspx?articleid=693**

For practical advice on managing health and safety in the workplace, the Health and Safety Executive publish a series of books that are written in a very easy-to-understand style and deal in a practical way with the essentials of safety and health management in the workplace.

The HSE book *Essentials of Health and Safety at Work* can be found at: **http://books.hse.gov.uk/hse/public/saleproduct.jsf?catalogueCode=9780717661794**

Advice and an explanatory case study on safety management systems can be found at: **www.youtube.com/watch?v=bxrbwBhuNbU**

Acas: **www.acas.org.uk**

Anxiety UK: **www.anxietyuk.org.uk**

UK Government: **www.gov.uk/browse/working**

Carers UK: **www.carersuk.org/Home**

Charlie Waller Memorial Trust (Raising awareness about depression): **www.cwmt.org**

Department for Work and Pensions: **www.dwp.gov.uk**

Depression Alliance: **www.depressionalliance.org**

UK Acts of Parliament from 1267 to the present day at: **www.legislation.gov.uk/ukpga**

The Work Foundation: **www.theworkfoundation.com**

The UK Data Service is a comprehensive resource funded by the Economics and Social Research Council (ESRC) to support researchers, teachers and policy-makers who depend on high-quality social and economic data. Available at: **http://ukdataservice.ac.uk/get-data/key-data.aspx**

Health and Safety Web sources

European Agency for Health at Work: **www.osha.europa.eu/en/topics/whp/**

European Agency for Safety and Health at Work (2013), available at:

https://osha.europa.eu/en/publications/reports/priorities-for-occupational-safety-and-health-research-in-europe-2013–2020

Health and Safety Executive: **www.hse.gov.uk**

Health and Safety annual statistics: **www.hse.gov.uk/statistics**

Health and Safety Executive's role:

www.hse.gov.uk/aboutus/howwework/ management/dwphse.pdf

HSE: *Managing the causes of work-related stress: A step-by-step approach using the Management Standards*:

www.hse.gov.uk/pubns/priced/hsg218.pdf

Institute of Directors guide 'Leading Health and Safety at Work':

www.iod.com/intershoproot/eCS/Store/en/pdfs/hse_guide.pdf

Well-being resources and work-life balance

Acas (2013d) *Booklet on Flexible working and work-life balance*. The booklet provides an excellent guide to flexible working. Available at: **http://acas.ecgroup.net/Publications/Flexibleworking.aspx**

The DTi, CBI and TUC produced a report – *Practical ways to reduce long hours and reform working practices* – which has some useful tips on introducing changes to long working hours: **www.bis.gov.uk/files/file14239.pdf**

The EHRC also produce *Working Better: A managers' guide to Flexible Working* (2009), which contains useful case studies: **www.equalityhumanrights.com/advice-and-guidance/working-better/a-managers-guide-to-flexible-working/**

The Equality and Human Rights Commission (EHRC) also produced a *Short Guide to Flexible Working* (2009), which is full of information and tips on how to make it work for your business. Available at: **www.equalityhumanrights.com/advice-and-guidance/here-for-business/guidance-for-businesses/a-short-guide-to-flexible-working/**

The Government's health and work initiative: **www.workingforhealth.gov.uk/default.aspx**

The 'Fit note': **www.gov.uk/government/collections/fit-note**

Health for Work – Adviceline – is a free service that provides small business managers with the expert advice and support they need to help team members experiencing ill-health. The Adviceline is available for both employers and employees working in any organisation based in England. The advice is restricted to health issues. Available at: **www.health4work.nhs.uk/**

The Health Foundation is an independent charity working to improve the quality of healthcare in the UK. Available at: **www.health.org.uk/areas-of-work/research/qualitywatch/?gclid=CN_DgrO5oLsCFWmWtAod7wwA5g**

International Stress Management Association: **www.isma.org.uk**

MIND (national association for mental health): **www.mind.org.uk**

NHS Choices – Your health, your choice. NHS Choices includes links to hundreds of external websites. These links are provided to give users quick access to the widest possible range of high-quality information resources on health and social care. Available at:

England: **www.nhs.uk/LiveWell/workplacehealth/Pages/workplacehome.aspx**

Scotland: **www.scotland.gov.uk/Topics/Health/Healthy-Living**

Wales: **www.healthyworkingwales.com/**

NHS Choices also hosts a video library on various health issues. Available at: **www. nhs.uk/Video/Pages/Kidneyfailurerealstory.aspx**

Office for National Statistics video 'Sickness Absence in the Labour Market 2012'. Available at: **www.ons.gov.uk/ons/rel/lmac/sickness-absence-in-the-labour-market/2012/video-summary.html**

Public Health England: **www.gov.uk/government/organisations/public-health-england**

Rethink Severe Mental Illness: **www.rethink.org**

Small business help for those that have health issues which affect their organisation. The 'Health for Work' website and advice line gives free advice: **www. health4work.nhs.uk**

The American Institute of Stress: **www.stress.org**

The Samaritans: **www.samaritans.org**

There is an excerpt from the TUC's *Hazards at Work* book online, available at: **www. tuc.org.uk/workplace-issues/working_time.cfm.** The full textbook, *Hazards at Work: Organising for safe and healthy workplaces – 2013 edition,* is available by order from the TUC website: **www.tuc.org.uk/publications/hazards-work-organising-safe-and-healthy-workplaces-2013-edition**

CIPD resources on well-being

All of the resources listed below can be accessed via **www.cipd.co.uk/ atozresources** unless otherwise indicated.

CIPD report: *What's Happening with Well-being at Work?* This report provides case study examples of how organisations have introduced well-being initiatives into their organisations.

CIPD factsheet: *Stress and Mental Health at Work*

CIPD research insight: *Preventing Stress: Promoting positive manager behaviour.*

CIPD *Employee Outlook* autumn 2013 covers a section on work-life balance: **www. cipd.co.uk/hr-resources/survey-reports/employee-outlook-autumn-2013.aspx**

CHAPTER 15

Diversity and Equality

LEARNING OBJECTIVES

After studying this chapter you should:

- understand what is meant by diversity and equality and the implications for the organisation
- be able to define the key terms of diversity, equality, discrimination and prejudice
- recognise the 'protected characteristics' named in the legislation
- be able to understand the business case for diversity
- be aware of the law on discrimination and the provision of equal opportunity
- understand the role of the HR practitioner in the implementation of policies on equality and the management of diversity
- be aware of the meaning of bullying and harassment and their implications in the workplace.

15.1 INTRODUCTION

Diversity has become one of the important issues and challenges in the workplace. With increasing globalisation, workers coming in to the UK from the European Union, an ageing workforce and the ever increasing raft of anti-discrimination law, it is a topic that requires careful consideration.

The aims of this chapter are to provide an understanding of diversity and equality, including how it is managed in the organisation, its influence on the nature of social interaction and the general workplace culture. We also look at some of the legislation and its impact on employment.

While legislation continues to be the driver for equal opportunity, there is much more to diversity than compliance. The law (embodied in the Equality Act 2010) says that we must not discriminate on the grounds of what are now called the *protected characteristics* of *age, disability, gender reassignment, race, religion or belief, sex, sexual orientation, marriage and civil partnership and pregnancy and maternity* and it is essential that employers and employees conform to that. However, the main root of discriminatory behaviour is prejudice – which is far harder to eradicate or even to detect. We must ensure that not only do our policies and procedures fall in line with anti-discriminatory practice, but also that we try to bring about a culture that encourages diversity and diminishes prejudice. Legislation is therefore only part of the solution to discrimination, and it is important to recognise this and consider what else can be done.

As Jo Swinson, Minister for Women and Equalities, states in the foreword to the Department for Business, Innovation and Skills paper *The Business Case for Equality and Diversity* (2013), 'We need to move away from diversity being a "human resources" issue to realising that companies can prosper by making the most of the diversity and flexibility of their workforce and customers.'

KEY CONCEPTS: DIVERSITY, EQUALITY, DISCRIMINATION

Diversity

Generically the word *diversity* means variety. The term *organisational diversity* refers to the range of differences between the individuals and groups among employees.

Equality

Equality is about 'ensuring that every individual has an equal opportunity to make the most of their lives and talents, and believing that no one should have poorer life chances because of where, what or whom they were born, what they believe, or whether they have a disability. Equality recognises that historically, certain groups of people with particular characteristics for example race, disability, sex and sexuality, have experienced discrimination' (Equality and Human Rights Commission, 2013).

Discrimination

Unlawful discrimination occurs when someone is treated 'less favourably' than another person because of a 'protected characteristic' they have or are thought to have. It is important to note that it is discrimination on the *grounds of a protected characteristic* that is unlawful. We can 'discriminate' or 'make choices' when selecting a candidate for a job, for instance – but these choices must be on *justifiable* grounds – such as better qualifications, wider experience of the job, and *not* based on a person's age, gender or religious belief, for example.

15.1.1 INDIVIDUAL DIFFERENCES

All individuals are different from each other; they are different psychologically, physically and behaviourally. The chance of finding two people who are exactly alike is the same as that of finding two people who have matching fingerprints. Individuals have their own personal values, beliefs, feelings and attitudes that have developed from their long-term perceptions and interpretations of the world around them. Wherever people go, from one country to another, from one organisation to another, their unique personality characteristics travel with them.

Differences between people become apparent when you watch them work. Everyone has their own unique way of learning and of developing and using their knowledge, talents and skills. No two people work in exactly the same way. Even people who do the same job have their own peculiar way of doing it. All of this can be summarised in one word: *diversity*.

15.2 ORGANISATIONAL DIVERSITY

The general use of the word 'diversity' in relation to the make-up of an organisation's workforce is comparatively recent, but diversity itself is as old as humankind. The original concept is based upon individual differences, and since every individual is unique, organisations always have had diverse workforces. In modern terms, however, diversity tends to relate to differences between groups of different ethnic backgrounds, religious groups, sexual orientation, gender, marital status, disability and age: that is, the 'protected characteristics' referred to by the equality legislation.

KEY CONCEPT: PROTECTED CHARACTERISTICS

There are nine 'protected characteristics' which, according to the legislation, must not be used as grounds for discrimination:

Age: this refers to a person belonging to a particular age (for example 32-year-olds) or range of ages (for example 18–30-year-olds).

Disability: a person has a disability if they have a physical or mental impairment which has a substantial and long-term adverse effect on that person's ability to carry out normal day-to-day activities.

Gender reassignment: the process of transitioning from one gender to another.

Marriage and civil partnership: marriage is defined in the Equality Act 2010 as a 'union between a man and a woman'. (Note: since legislation in 2013, same-sex couples can now marry and presumably this definition of marriage will be amended.) Civil partners must be treated the same as married couples on a wide range of legal matters.

Pregnancy and maternity: pregnancy is the condition of being pregnant or expecting a baby. Maternity refers to the period after the birth, and is linked to maternity leave in the employment context. In the non-work context, protection against maternity discrimination is for 26 weeks after giving birth, and this includes treating a woman unfavourably because she is breastfeeding.

Race: refers to a group of people defined by their race, colour, nationality (including citizenship), ethnic or national origins.

Religion and belief: religion has the meaning usually given to it but belief includes religious and philosophical beliefs including lack of belief (for example atheism). Generally, a belief should affect your life choices or the way you live for it to be included in the definition.

Sex: a man or a woman.

Sexual orientation: whether a person's sexual attraction is towards their own sex, the opposite sex or to both sexes.

(Equality and Human Rights Commission, 2013b)

15.2.1 THE INFLUENCE OF DEMOGRAPHIC CHANGES

The demographic changes that have taken place in the UK population in recent years are reflected in the workforces of organisations. Today's organisations employ people who come from a range of national, religious, social, cultural and ethnic backgrounds. In addition, there are differences in age, gender and physical and mental ability, including disability. Some examples of the changing demographics are that:

- Over the period 1985–2012, the number of people aged 65 and over in the UK increased by 26% to 10.8 million; in 2012, 17% of the population were aged 65 and over (Office for National Statistics website, **www.statistics.gov.uk/hub/population/ageing/older-people**).
- There were 3.63 million 16–24-year-olds in employment (22% of whom were in full-time education), up 50,000 from April to June 2013.
- 7.97 million women work full-time, up 68,000 from April to June 2013.
- 2.15 million men work part-time, up 41,000 from April to June 2013.
- The number of non-UK-born people in employment in the UK increased by 112,000 (September 2012 – September 2013) to reach 4.38 million.

(Office for National Statistics, November 2013)

These demographic changes have broadened the diverse structure of the UK population, especially in terms of group types. In organisations, this has focused attention on the need to recognise diversity, to learn how to manage it and how to avoid unfair discrimination. It is unlikely, however, that discrimination will ever be totally eliminated. The point was made above that discrimination is born of prejudice, which is a personality characteristic that causes particular individuals to discriminate against others simply on the grounds of their differences. We can perhaps change people's behaviour (we can make them refrain from asking discriminatory questions in an interview, for example), but changing what they think (their attitude) is much more difficult.

PAUSE FOR THOUGHT

How do people treat each other in your organisation or in your university or college? Do they all respect each other's beliefs and values? Or are there those whose prejudices show through now and again? Do you think it is important that people respect each other regardless of their background? Why?

15.2.2 WHAT ORGANISATIONAL DIVERSITY IS ABOUT

According to Daniels and MacDonald (2005), diversity is:

> ...about recognising this range of differences in people and valuing people as individuals, respecting their differences and their different needs. It is also about accommodating differences wherever possible so that an individual can play a full part in the working environment.

The CIPD says that diversity is about 'valuing everyone as individuals, as employees, customers and clients' (CIPD, 2012). Bloisi (2007) says that diversity is about 'recognising that people are different and that these differences should be valued and used to enhance the workplace'.

15.3 PREJUDICE

In generic terms, *prejudice* means the holding of an unreasonable opinion or like or dislike of something. Heery and Noon (2008, p.201) say that in the context of workplace discrimination, prejudice means holding negative attitudes towards a particular group, and viewing all members of that group in a negative light, irrespective of their individual qualities and attributes.

Prejudicial attitudes are towards groups, because they are different, and towards individuals, because they are members of those groups.

We tend to think of prejudice as being against a member of one of the 'protected characteristic' groups (gender, race/ethnicity, religion, disability, age and sexual orientation, for example). However, Heery and Noon (2008, p.201), make the very pertinent observation that

> prejudice extends much further, and is frequently directed at other groups based on features such as accents, height, weight, hair colour, beards, body piercings, tattoos and clothes. It is extremely rare to find a person who is not prejudiced against any group – although most of us are reluctant to admit our prejudice.

KEY CONCEPT: STEREOTYPING

Stereotyping is the act of judging people according to our assumptions about the group to which they belong. It is based on the belief that people from a specific group share similar traits and behave in a similar manner (Heery and Noon, 2008, p.443).

15.3.1 STEREOTYPING

Such biased perceptions occur when people rely on the stereotyped image and ignore factual information concerning individuals. For example, stereotypes might be that an elderly person will have outdated ideas; young drivers are reckless; men cannot multi-task; and women are not good drivers. A glance at the facts, however, will tell you that none of these assumptions is true of all members of those groups. However, not all stereotyping results in creating negative images: the preconception can also be positive. For example, it might be believed all Welsh and Italian people are good singers.

Prejudice is often against individuals because of a group that they belong to. But it can also be because of being *perceived to* belong to a certain group.

ACTIVITY 15.1

Read Case Example 15.1, which refers to a case of 'perceived' membership of a group and the bullying that was linked to it. This was described as a landmark case by the Equality and Human Rights Commission.

CASE EXAMPLE 15.1

English v Thomas Sanderson (British and Irish Legal Information Institute EWCA Civ 1421 [2008])

A 56-year-old married man was repeatedly taunted at work about being gay because he lived in Brighton.

Stephen English suffered years of abuse and insinuation from colleagues at Thomas Sanderson Blinds, based near Portsmouth, where he had worked in sales.

Mr English told the tribunal that he 'regularly had to endure remarks such as "faggot" at national sales meetings, team meetings at my home and regional managers' meetings.'

'These comments caused considerable distress both to myself and to my family, who were at home on occasions when I held team meetings and overheard comments referring to my perceived sexual orientation.'

Mr English brought a claim against them for harassment on grounds of sexual orientation under regulation 5 of the Employment Equality (Sexual Orientation) Regulations 2003. He won his case at the Court of Appeal.

In his judgement, Lord Justice Sedley said:

'You cannot legislate against prejudice. You can set out in specified circumstances to stop people's lives being made a misery of it.'

The Court of Appeal said that protection should be extended to victims of homophobic abuse at work, even when the perpetrators are aware that the victim is not gay, but the abuse is motivated by homophobia and associated stereotypes.

John Wadham, Group Legal Director of the Equality and Human Rights Commission, said:

'Bullying is unacceptable, whatever your background – gay, straight, black or white.

'The fact that Stephen English's colleagues knew he wasn't gay does not excuse their behaviour nor should it prevent him from enjoying the same rights to dignity and respect at work – the harassment he suffered was distressing.

'Until now, victims of this type of abuse had little or no legal protection. By supporting Mr English's case, the Commission has helped to clarify the law to protect those who suffer harassment based on old-fashioned stereotypes.'

ACTIVITY 15.2

Think of groups of people you know, for example students, British people on holiday, teenagers. What stereotypes come to mind? Do the people you know in these groups fit the stereotype? If you are a member of one of these groups (for example student), how does it feel to be viewed in this way?

It would be rare to find a person who does not attribute particular characteristics to members of diverse groups. Problems of discrimination arise when we base our impressions of people on stereotype alone.

PAUSE FOR THOUGHT

How do you think you would react if you were presented with new information about an individual that contradicts your stereotyped image of them? Would the information cause you to alter your attitude towards that person? Or would you ignore the new information in order to maintain your original view? How dangerous is it to view people via stereotypes?

15.3.2 WHY BE CONCERNED WITH EQUALITY AND DIVERSITY?

There are two sets of arguments relating to why equality and diversity are important: 'the social justice case' and the 'business case'.

The social justice case

The social justice case relies on the premise that we have a 'moral obligation to treat employees with fairness and dignity' (Beardwell and Claydon, 2010, p.201).

The CIPD (2012) states that the social justice argument is based on the belief that 'everyone should have a right to equal access to employment and when employed should have equal pay and equal access to training and development, as well as being free of any direct or indirect discrimination and harassment or bullying. This can be described as the right to be treated fairly.'

The business case

Diversity and provision of equal opportunities make good business sense. The Department for Business, Innovation and Skills and the Government Equalities Office's report *The Business Case for Equality and Diversity* (2013) gives the following reasons for having a diverse workforce:

External Business Benefits arise when firms better represent the world (and legislative environment) around them. For instance, having staff with roots in other countries and cultures can help a business address its products appropriately and sensitively to new markets. Consumers are becoming more diverse and firms may need to reflect this or risk losing out in important markets.

Internal Business Benefits arise from improving operations internal to the firm. For example, a diverse workforce which includes a range of perspectives can improve creativity and problem-solving, resulting in better decisions. Also a diverse workforce can offer greater flexibility.

So we should encourage diversity not only because it is 'a good thing to do', but also because of the business benefits.

ACTIVITY 15.3

Consider your own workforce – how diverse is it? Make a list of all the benefits to your organisation of having a diverse workforce. Could it be improved by having more diversity?

PAUSE FOR THOUGHT

Have you ever worked in an 'all-male' or 'all-female' team? Have you noticed any differences in the way they work together? Does being in a mixed team affect how people work together?

15.3.3 RECOGNISING DIVERSITY – THE ADVANTAGES TO BUSINESS

The primary purpose of an organisation is to survive and develop so that it can continue to provide the best possible service for its public, or to provide the highest possible return to its shareholders. To achieve those ends, the organisation needs a knowledgeable and competent workforce. A diverse workforce can mean that you have access to a wide range of people, with a variety of views, abilities and outlooks – all of which can enhance your business, by bringing different ideas and attitudes that may add to your competitive advantage.

Employing 'clones' will lead to less challenging attitudes and 'more of the same'. Having a diverse workforce brings variety, which may lead to creativity and innovative ways of working. This attitude is one that recognises the potential benefits that diversity can bring to the organisation. Your customers are likely to be a diverse group – it makes sense for your employees to reflect this diversity too. The more diverse the range of people and ideas in the organisation, the more likely that the organisation will accommodate changes and survive in a recession or compete in boom times. Diversity in the workforce encourages flexibility and adaptability – which are important to any successful business that wishes to stay ahead of its competitors.

Organisations may demonstrate an interest in promoting social equality as one way to attract good employees. Part of an 'employer brand' might be about being an equal opportunity employer, as this sends the message that the organisation cares about their employees and thus is a 'good' employer. As we know, attracting the right kind of employees is vital in achieving a competitive edge, so being attractive to prospective employees is a real advantage. Equal opportunities and diversity is all too often considered from a legislative point of view – 'we must ensure we don't break the law', but the business case for diversity is equally important.

The paper on *The Business Case for Equality and Diversity* by the Department for Business, Innovation and Skills and the Government Equalities Office (2013) states, 'There is no single approach that all businesses can adopt to ensure equality and diversity are beneficial. To be effective, equality and diversity need to be embedded in the business strategy, not treated as an ad-hoc addition.'

15.3.4 EQUALITY BODIES

The Equality and Human Rights Commission (EHRC)

Set up in 2007, the fundamental objectives of the Equality and Human Rights Commission (EHRC) are to help organisations and individuals comply with the law and follow the highest standards of practice. But in addition to mere legal compliance, it aims to bring about a society that understands and respects equality and human rights – by shaping and influencing attitudes and behaviours. Its public leadership and advocacy role aims to create a consensus which recognises that equality and human rights are central to a fair society. Key to this is an understanding of the challenges that organisations face in embedding equality and human rights in their activities. One clear objective is to build confidence and understanding of equality and human rights across the private, public and voluntary sectors. In addition, the EHRC plays a major role in protecting individuals from discrimination and human rights violation.

The Government Equalities Office

Set up in 2007, the Government Equalities Office has lead responsibility for equality strategy and legislation for the UK Government, together with a responsibility to provide advice on all other forms of equality (including age, race, sexual orientation and disability) to other UK government departments. Their work involves taking action on the Government's commitment to remove barriers to equality and helping to build a fairer society, leading on issues relating to women, sexual orientation and transgender equality.

The Equality and Diversity Forum (EDF)

The Equality and Diversity Forum (EDF) is a network of national organisations committed to equal opportunities, social justice, good community relations, respect for human rights and an end to discrimination based on age, disability, gender and gender identity, race, religion or belief, and sexual orientation. The EDF works towards 'a society in which everyone can fulfil their potential, everyone is treated with respect regardless of background or circumstances, and diversity is celebrated' (EDF, 2013).

CASE EXAMPLE 15.2

BESPOKE SOLUTIONS FOR AN EAST OF ENGLAND INDEPENDENT GARAGE

Andy's Cars is a local family-run garage that services and repairs cars. It has also been recognised with a Remploy 'Leading the Way' Award for its efforts in enabling disabled people to realise their working potential. Andy Kent, the owner, explained the benefits of his focus on equality: 'Far too many businesses make the excuse of cost. There's a gain, rather than a cost, if only they would think about it … the benefits are you get extreme loyalty from staff. So that in itself has a knock-on effect to the customers as well, because if you have good staff who enjoy what they're doing and doing it because they want to do it, then you get more customers, and we get more customers because they tell their friends and they travel from further distances as well. As a business, 50% of our customers come from the fact of what we do, I'd say. One of our biggest customers actually brings vehicles into us from all over the country now just because of what we do. If we didn't do it, we wouldn't have the rapport with the particular sector, so we wouldn't understand the customer's need.'

(With kind permission of Andy's Cars and the Equality and Diversity Forum, 2013)

15.3.5 EQUAL OPPORTUNITY AS A LEGAL OBLIGATION

As we have seen above, having a diverse workforce is advantageous to the business. Getting managers and employees to adopt an equal opportunities approach should provide benefits both internally and externally to the organisation.

However, no discussion of equality in the workplace would be complete without addressing the legal side. The adoption of equal opportunities is a legal obligation; organisations must conform to the law and have acceptable policies and procedures in place.

15.4 LEGISLATION

Discrimination is a subjective term when used in normal daily life. When people make choices about what food or clothes to buy, they *discriminate* in favour of some things and against others. Such decisions reflect people's tastes and opinions. In such contexts discrimination is perfectly legitimate. In some other contexts, however, discrimination has been made unlawful – that is, where we discriminate on grounds that are not fair, for example if we base our decision on whether to appoint someone because of their race or their gender, or any of the 'protected characteristics' named in the legislation, rather than on their ability to do the job. So we need to be aware of current legislation in order not to discriminate unfairly.

The law on discrimination is complex and extensive. The legislation protects you at work, in education, as a consumer, when using public services, when buying or renting property and as a member or guest of a private club or association. For the purposes of this chapter, the emphasis is on employment law.

15.4.1 IMPLICATIONS FOR EMPLOYERS

The legislation carries widespread implications for employers. The areas that are most affected are:

- **Recruitment and selection**, in which every stage and action, from drafting a job requisition through to making the selection decision, is subject to the law.
- **Employment contracts**, including the terms and conditions of employment.
- **Training and development**, in which there should be an equal opportunity to undertake courses, not forgetting longer-term courses financially sponsored by the organisation and involving attendance at a local college or university. Training also should be provided to ensure that staff understand the importance of equality issues.
- **Promotion**, in which, again, equal opportunities must be given.
- **Flexible working,** whereby different forms of flexible working should be considered – such as job-sharing, part-time working, flexible hours, homeworking and annualised hours.
- **Pay, benefits, facilities and services** such as pension schemes, medical care, help with long-term sickness and counselling services, in which equal access must be available.
- **Severance**, including terms and conditions for share options, selection for redundancy and redundancy payments, in which the criteria must be fairly applied.
- **Bullying and harassment, discipline and grievance.** There should be clear management commitment to prevent unacceptable behaviour at work. Equality policies should state that any breaches of the policy will be dealt with through the disciplinary procedure.

VOLUNTEERS DENIED EMPLOYMENT RIGHTS

CASE EXAMPLE 15.3

The current economic climate has led to an increase in interns and volunteers looking for ways to enhance their prospects of obtaining permanent employment, which in turn has prompted a flurry of cases about their employment rights.

In the latest case on this, *X v Mid-Sussex Citizens Advice Bureau* (2012 UKSC 59), the Supreme Court has ruled that true volunteers do not have rights when it comes to discrimination.

Facts

The claimant was a volunteer at a Citizens Advice Bureau (CAB) and signed a contract to volunteer for four to five hours a week which stated that it was 'not a contract of employment or legally binding'.

When the CAB asked the claimant to stop volunteering (she had been unable to attend around 25% of her appointed times owing to ill-health), she brought a claim for disability discrimination under the Disability Discrimination Act 1995 (DDA), the provisions of which have been substantially replicated in the Equality Act 2010.

Decision

The DDA provided protection to those in employment; those whose complaint relates to recruitment arrangements (job applicants, in a wide sense); and those on work placements.

The Supreme Court found on the facts that the claimant was not in employment, as she was not obliged to provide any services to the CAB, or undertaking a work placement, as her arrangement continued indefinitely and was not for the purpose of vocational training.

And she was not volunteering for the purpose of being selected for a permanent position either, so did not fall within the protection of the DDA.

The Supreme Court also considered whether the claimant could rely directly on the EU directive which the Equality Act 2010 implements.

The court decided there was no evidence that the European Commission intended the directive to cover volunteers.

Comment

Whether or not an intern or volunteer will have the right not to be discriminated against, or any other employment-status-related right (such as the right to the National Minimum Wage), will depend on how the relationship operates in practice.

The usual tests for employment (such as mutuality of obligation between employer and the individual, degree of control by the employer, and the requirement for the individual to provide a service personally) will apply.

As a general rule, if there is no element of training and no remuneration, it is unlikely that volunteers will be able to argue they fall within the protection of the Equality Act 2010.

(Source: CIPD/HR-Inform, January 2013. Used with kind permission of *People Management*)

15.5 THE EQUALITY ACT 2010

The Equality Act 2010 has been the culmination of a stream of legislation, codes of practice and regulations (nine equality laws and around a hundred smaller pieces of legislation!) on many forms of discrimination since 1970 which have aimed to address equality issues; commencing with the Equal Pay Act in 1970, then in 1975 the Sex

Discrimination Act, followed by the Race Relations Act in 1976. The Disability Discrimination Act came a little later, in 1995, and then age discrimination legislation followed in 2006. The 2006 Equality Act brought much of this together by establishing the Equality and Human Rights Commission (EHRC) in 2007 to replace the Equal Opportunities Commission, the Commission for Racial Equality and the Disability Rights Commission to deal with all aspects of equality under one umbrella. In addition to sex, race and disability discrimination, the Act covered discrimination on the grounds of religion or belief, sexual orientation, and imposed duties relating to sex discrimination on persons performing public functions.

The Equality Act 2010 consolidated all of the existing discrimination legislation, extended protection to a wider range of workers (including job applicants who never start work, former employees and the self-employed) and introduced new safeguards. The Act made it unlawful to discriminate against persons in any of the 'protected characteristics' groups, that is, *age, disability, gender reassignment, race, religion or belief, sex, sexual orientation, marriage and civil partnership and pregnancy and maternity*. It also provided protection for the first time from discrimination by 'association' or 'perception' and introduced rules on gender pay reporting, pay secrecy and brought in a ban on pre-employment health questions.

Note that in addition to the Equality Act there is also the Trade Union and Labour Relations (Consolidation) Act 1992, which made it unlawful to discriminate on the grounds of trade union membership, although the Act focused on protecting the rights of trade union members and not just discrimination.

The Equality Act applies to all workers, including office-holders, police, barristers, partners in a business and members of the armed forces. The Act covers anyone who applies to an organisation for work, or who already works for the organisation, whether directly employed or working under other kinds of contracts. Organisations are also responsible for someone else on their premises, for example someone from a different organisation repairing a piece of equipment Amend to (Acas, 2011b).

Despite all of this activity, discrimination in the workplace still occurs. In terms of providing equal opportunities in the workplace, the rights of individuals have become well known, and yet there still are gaps in some employers' understanding of the moral, ethical and legal aspects of managing diversity and the provision of equal opportunities.

The rest of the chapter looks at some of the implications of the Equality Act in more detail.

15.6 DISCRIMINATION

Workplace discrimination has been illegal since 1970, when the provisions of the Equal Pay Act became law. Since then, as we have seen above, increases in the amount and complexity of legislation and case law decisions have provided managers with the daunting task of keeping the organisation within the law and struggling to control discriminatory behaviour, not only in the implementation and interpretation of policy, but also on the part of employees.

15.6.1 INDIVIDUAL DISCRIMINATION

This occurs when, for example, in employment selection assessment and decision-making, selectors allow their prejudices to influence their decisions. Also, when in employment, members of minority groups are often denied the opportunity to be trained and developed, or to gain opportunities for promotion.

15.6.2 LEGAL POINT

If a person wishes to show that they have been discriminated against, they must also show that the treatment received was different from that offered to other employees in a similar situation. A lesbian woman, for example, would have to show that she was treated differently than a heterosexual man or woman would have been treated in a similar situation.

15.6.3 GROUP DISCRIMINATION

If there are a lot less of one type of group in your workforce (for example women, disabled people, and so on), that group might be considered to be 'disadvantaged'. If there are very few ethnic minorities in the workplace, for example, they may be classed as a 'disadvantaged group'.

Group discrimination occurs on national and organisation-wide bases. For example, on a national basis, statistical information shows that in April 2013 hourly rates for men working full-time were £13.60, compared with only £12.24 for women (Office for National Statistics, December 2013). There is a gender pay gap (as measured by the median hourly pay excluding overtime) of around 10% for full-time employees.

ACTIVITY 15.4

In your own organisation, how many women managers are there? Do women reach their full potential? What is your experience of discrimination – have you ever felt that you were unfairly treated?

15.6.4 INSTITUTIONAL DISCRIMINATION

Discrimination against groups may become institutionalised. Sometimes the way the organisation operates is fundamentally discriminatory. Discriminatory behaviour becomes part of the culture. This kind of culture might be demonstrated by staff making jokes about certain racial groups or about disabled people, for example, and that becomes an accepted way of behaving. If it does become part of the culture, it may not be reported, since the employees may feel that their complaints, particularly of sex and race discrimination, will not be investigated thoroughly. Organisations such as the police have made great efforts to avoid institutionalised racism, for example, by changing their procedures and their culture and by training staff.

Public sector equality duty

The public sector equality duty came into force across Great Britain on 5 April 2011. It means that public bodies have to consider all individuals when carrying out their day-to-day work – in shaping policy, in delivering services and in relation to their own employees.

It also requires that public bodies:

- have due regard to the need to eliminate discrimination
- advance equality of opportunity
- foster good relations between different people when carrying out their activities.

(Gov.uk Guidance, 2013. Available at: **www.gov.uk/equality-act-2010-guidance**)

CASE EXAMPLE 15.4

Central Manchester University Hospitals NHS Foundation Trust v Browne UKEAT/0294/11/CEA

The Manchester University NHS Foundation Trust was ordered to pay £933,115 in 2012 in compensation to a former manager after an employment tribunal concluded that he had been subjected to race discrimination and unfairly dismissed. Unite, the trade union which represented Browne in the tribunal, called for the trust to 'tackle its culture of institutionalised racism'.

PAUSE FOR THOUGHT

When making a selection decision 'to recruit, promote or to select' someone for a special project, selectors have to discriminate in favour of one candidate and against the others. However, the grounds on which such selection decisions are made are clearly prescribed by law. What approach do you think the selectors might adopt to ensure that such decisions are made without prejudice? What role can an HR adviser play in this type of process?

In Activity 15.4, disproportionate results (the lack of women in high-level jobs) might be attributable to employment selection and internal promotion procedures. Written policy statements usually demonstrate good intentions in legal and ethical terms, but implementation through the related procedures does not always reflect those good intentions. Interviewers may not ask overtly discriminatory questions, but may still harbour prejudice and discriminatory attitudes. These prejudices are not unlawful until they turn into behaviour where they are used to discriminate against someone.

15.7 CATEGORIES OF DISCRIMINATION

Discriminatory decisions and behaviour may occur on the grounds of protected characteristics, as we saw earlier in the chapter. Such decisions and behaviour may be categorised as direct discrimination (possibly via associative discrimination or perception discrimination), indirect discrimination and victimisation.

KEY CONCEPT: DIRECT DISCRIMINATION

Direct discrimination occurs when someone is treated less favourably than another person because of a protected characteristic they have, or are thought to have, or because they associate with someone who has a protected characteristic. So if person A treats person B less favourably than they treat (or would treat) others because of a protected characteristic, section 13 of the Equality Act defines that as 'direct discrimination'.

It is possible to place various interpretations on the term 'less favourably'. For example, a person who is treated differently from others might regard that treatment as less favourable than the treatment the others received. It might be, however, that the complainant's employment circumstances were just *different* from those of the other employees; different treatment is not always less favourable treatment.

CASE EXAMPLE 15.5

DIRECT SEX DISCRIMINATION

Debbie, who is a lesbian, is not promoted because Mark, the manager, believes the team that she will work with are homophobic. Mark thought that Debbie's sexual orientation would prevent her from being able to fit in with the team and work effectively with them. This is direct discrimination on the grounds of sexual orientation against Debbie.

KEY CONCEPT: ASSOCIATIVE DISCRIMINATION

This is direct discrimination against someone because they associate with another person who possesses a protected characteristic.

CASE EXAMPLE 15.6

Alison works as a supervisor and would like to further her career with the organisation.

However, after she tells her manager that her mother, who lives at home, has developed a long-term debilitating illness and will need looking after, she was not considered for promotion. This may be discrimination against Alison because of her association with a disabled person.

KEY CONCEPT: PERCEPTION DISCRIMINATION

This is direct discrimination against an individual because others think they possess a particular protected characteristic. It applies even if the person does not actually possess that characteristic.

CASE EXAMPLE 15.7

Arshad is 40 but looks as if he is in his early twenties. He is not allowed to work on a lucrative project dealing with important clients because the director thinks that he is too young. Arshad has been discriminated against on the perception of a protected characteristic.

 KEY CONCEPT: INDIRECT DISCRIMINATION

Indirect discrimination can occur when you have a condition, rule, policy or even a practice in your organisation that applies to everyone but particularly disadvantages people who share a protected characteristic. It appears therefore to be non-discriminatory but *does* actually apply to more members of disadvantaged groups compared with other groups.

Indirect discrimination can be justified if you can show that you acted reasonably in managing your business, that is, that it is 'a proportionate means of achieving a legitimate aim' (see Case Example 15.9). A legitimate aim might be any lawful decision you make in running your business or organisation, but if there is a discriminatory effect, the sole aim of reducing costs is likely to be unlawful (Acas, 2011b)

 INDIRECT SEX DISCRIMINATION

CASE EXAMPLE 15.8

In the case of *Price v The Civil Service Commission*, indirect sex discrimination was demonstrated when a maximum age limit of 28 years was imposed on entry to the 'executive officer' grade. It was argued that under this ruling, women were considerably disadvantaged since they were often raising a family at that age, and that the imposed limit constituted indirect discrimination. This was not regarded as discrimination on grounds of age; the ruling given was that the imposed age limit constituted indirect discrimination.

(*Price v. Civil Service Commissioner* [1978] 1 All ER 1228.)

 ACTIVITY 15.5

Examine the definition of indirect discrimination then study Case Example 15.8. The person who brought the legal action was a woman, so she was a member of the disadvantaged group. Can you think of other examples of rules which may constitute indirect sex discrimination?

CASE EXAMPLE 15.9

INDIRECT DISCRIMINATION: LEGITIMATE AIM

A company needs its accounting staff to work on a Friday to deal with urgent price information. Some of the staff would like to go early on Friday afternoon in order to be home before sunset – a requirement of their religion. They want to make up the hours at an alternative time in the week. The company cannot agree because the need for the figures is urgent and there is no one else who can perform the work. The requirement to work on Friday afternoon is not unlawful indirect discrimination as it meets a *legitimate business aim* and there is no alternative means available.

15.7.1 VICARIOUS LIABILITY

Vicarious liability refers to a situation where someone is held responsible for the actions or omissions of another person. In a workplace context, an employer can be liable for the acts or omissions of its employees, provided it can be shown that they took place in the course of their employment.

Employers should ensure that they have taken all reasonable steps to prevent such acts or omissions from occurring. For example, maintaining an up-to-date equal opportunities policy and providing anti-discrimination training to staff serve to demonstrate an active commitment on the part of the employer towards combating discriminatory practices in the workplace. This would then reduce the likelihood of an employer being held vicariously liable for any discriminatory acts committed by its employees. (Acas, 2012, *Understanding what vicarious liability means for employers*)

15.7.2 OCCUPATIONAL REQUIREMENTS

Employers may be exempt from observing the provisions of the Equality Act for jobs that have particular requirements, which are known as *occupational requirements*. The purpose of this is to maintain public decency and/or to meet certain expectations. For example, it is lawful to employ a person of one specific sex in certain jobs, such as an actor, where the role demands a certain age, gender or nationality, or where decency or privacy needs to be maintained, for example a shop assistant providing a bra-fitting service.

CASE EXAMPLE 15.10

Halal butcher

If a butcher has to prepare halal meat (meat that has been prepared in a way that is consistent with the Muslim faith), it might be justified to insist that this role is performed by a Muslim.

Religious organisations

An organisation whose work is based on a specific religion or belief may be able to use this rule. A Catholic care home might be able to show that its carers should be Catholic because their work will involve them meeting a client's spiritual needs. But they might not be able to make the same claim for their reception staff, who do not need to provide spiritual leadership or support the clients.

(Equality and Human Rights Commission, 2013a)

15.7.3 VICTIMISATION

Victimisation occurs when an employee is treated badly because they have made or supported a complaint or raised a grievance under the Equality Act; or because they are suspected of doing so. The Equality Act (2010) amended the definition 'victimisation', so that there is no longer a need to point to a comparator.

15.7.4 POSITIVE ACTION

The Equality Act allows you to take 'positive action' if you think that employees or job applicants who share a particular protected characteristic suffer a disadvantage connected to that characteristic, or if their participation in an activity is disproportionately low.

The Act allows you, if you want to, to take a protected characteristic into consideration when deciding who to recruit or promote. So for example, if there are not many women in your workforce (that is, they are disproportionately under-represented in your workforce) and you have two candidates who are equally as good, you could appoint the woman, providing she is 'as qualified as' the male candidate. This does not mean she has to have *exactly* the same qualifications as the other candidate; it means that your selection assessment on a range of criteria rates her as equally capable of doing the job. You would also need some evidence to show that people with that characteristic (in this case, 'being a woman') face particular difficulties in the workplace or are disproportionately under-represented in your workforce or in the particular job for which there is a vacancy. In these circumstances, you can choose to use the fact that a candidate has a protected characteristic as a 'tie-breaker' when determining which one to appoint. If a man and a woman are equally good candidates, you can appoint the woman. You cannot just appoint her 'because she is a woman and you would like to have more women in the workforce' – she must still be equivalent to the best candidate.

You must not have a policy of automatically treating job applicants who share a protected characteristic more favourably in recruitment and promotion. This means you must always consider the abilities, merits and qualifications of all of the candidates in each recruitment or promotion exercise.

Quotas: It should be noted that it is unlawful to select a person for a job on the basis of their gender or race in order to achieve a fixed quota of employees of that gender or race.

(adapted from Acas, 2011b. © Acas, Euston Tower, 286 Euston Road, London NW1 3JJ)

 CASE EXAMPLE 15.11

The Pinkglass glazing company wishes to take positive action to improve disabled people's chances of being selected for its vacancies. Therefore it offers guaranteed interviews to disabled people to encourage them to apply. In order to identify the disabled candidates, it asks on the application form whether the candidate has a disability, and makes it clear why the question is being asked. This is so that applicants know that the company has a positive approach towards employing disabled people.

The use of guaranteed interviews should help to create a better opportunity for the disabled applicants to give them a chance of demonstrating their ability to do the job.

15.7.5 SEX DISCRIMINATION

The Equality Act makes it unlawful to treat individuals less favourably on the grounds of sex or marital status and prohibits unjustified differences in pay and contracts: that is, the terms and conditions of employment, which must be the same for men and women doing like work or 'work of equal value'. Equal work can be:

- the same, or broadly similar (known as 'like work')
- different, but which is already rated under the same job evaluation scheme as equivalent (known as 'work rated as equivalent')
- different, but which would be assessed as equal in value in terms of demands such as effort, skill and decision-making (known as 'work of equal value').

It is important to note that under this Act men and women have equal rights to protection, although the number of legal actions brought by women is far greater than those brought by men. It is also unlawful to discriminate in pay arrangements and other terms of employment in relation, for example, to race, disability, sexual orientation, and the same principles would apply.

 CASE EXAMPLE 15.12

Michalak v Mid Yorkshire Hospitals NHS Trust ET/1810815/08

In *Michalak v Mid Yorkshire Hospitals NHS Trust*, the employment tribunal awarded former NHS consultant Eva Michalak one of the largest ever discrimination payouts of just under £4.5 million.

Dr Michalak brought claims for unfair dismissal, sex and race discrimination. The employment tribunal upheld all of her claims. They considered the events leading to her dismissal were a 'concerted campaign' to terminate her employment.

 ACTIVITY 15.6

Visit the XpertHR site at **www.xperthr.co.uk/ law-reports/in-the-employment-tribunals- december-2011/111368/#michalak? cmpid=ILC|PROF|HRPIO-2012-XHR_Freel 58719&sfid=701200000004Zsc** for an overview of the *Michalak* case.

- What do you think could be done to avoid a repetition of this sort of case?
- What impact might the case have on other staff?

15.8 GENDER REASSIGNMENT

A transsexual person is someone who proposes to, starts or has completed a process to change his or her gender. The Equality Act does not require a person to be under medical supervision in order to be protected – so a woman who decides to live as a man but does not undergo any medical procedures would still be covered.

It is discriminatory to treat transsexual people 'less favourably for being absent from work because they propose to undergo, are undergoing or have undergone gender reassignment than they would be treated if they were absent because they were ill or injured' (Acas, 2011b).

It has been estimated that there are about 18,000 people in the UK who have sought gender reassignment treatment, but the number is increasing at over 20% per annum. Organisations should assume that 1% of their employees and service users may be experiencing a significant degree of gender variance, although few of them have so far sought treatment (Gender Identity Research and Education Society, 2013).

More detail can be found by visiting the Gender Identity Research and Education Society website at **www.gires.org.uk**

15.9 SEXUAL ORIENTATION

Under the Equality Act 2010 it is unlawful to discriminate against workers because of sexual orientation.

Sexual orientation is defined as:

- orientation towards people of the same sex (lesbians and gay men)
- orientation towards people of the opposite sex (heterosexual)
- orientation towards people of either sex (bisexual).

The Act makes it unlawful on the grounds of sexual orientation to:

- discriminate directly against anyone and to treat them less favourably than others because of their actual or perceived sexual orientation
- discriminate indirectly – to apply a criterion, provision or practice which disadvantages people of a particular sexual orientation, unless it can be objectively justified
- subject someone to harassment – harassment is unwanted conduct that violates a person's dignity or creates an intimidating, hostile, degrading, humiliating or offensive environment
- victimise someone because they have made or intend to make a complaint or allegation in relation to a complaint of discrimination on the grounds of sexual orientation

(Acas, 2011d. © Acas, Euston Tower, 286 Euston Road, London NW1 3JJ)

CASE EXAMPLE 15.13

SEXUAL ORIENTATION

Lustig-Prean and Beckett were British naval personnel who were dismissed from the Royal Navy due to their homosexuality. Lustig-Prean and Beckett alleged that the investigations into their homosexuality and their discharge from the Royal Navy on the sole ground that they were homosexual violated their rights under Article 8 of the European Convention on Human Rights (ECHR). The ECHR found that their rights had been breached. The UK Government immediately suspended discharging homosexuals and within months changed the law. This is seen as a pivotal case on sexual orientation discrimination.

(*Lustig-Prean and Beckett v the United Kingdom* 31417/96; 32377/96 [1999] ECHR 71 (27 September 1999) British and Irish Legal Information Institute.)

15.10 RACIAL DISCRIMINATION

Under the Equality Act, race includes:

- colour
- nationality
- ethnic or national origins.

The CIPD (2013r) makes the very pertinent comment that:

> Managing diversity and inclusion successfully is essential to good people management because everyone is different. Different views, perspectives, experiences and ideas challenge 'group think', stimulate creativity and innovation and contribute to better business performance. Failure to deal with prejudice, stereotyping and unconscious bias regarding issues of personal identity results in unfair decisions about the recruitment, development, retention and release of talent and flawed approaches to the development and promotion of products and services to diverse markets.

As with other types of discrimination, 'occupational requirements' may apply to recruitment, selection, training or promotion for certain types of work, for example to work in a Chinese restaurant for the sake of authenticity. However, discriminatory treatment in the terms and conditions of employment is not permitted.

 INDIRECT DISCRIMINATION

CASE EXAMPLE 15.14

Aina v Employment Service [2002] DCLD 103D

A Black African employee applied for the post of equal opportunities manager in his organisation. He was assessed as having the skills and ability for the job. However, his application was rejected because, unknown to him, the post was open only to permanent staff at higher grades than his. Monitoring data showed that the organisation had no permanent Black African employees at the grades in question.

The employment tribunal held that there was no justification for the requirement and that it amounted to indirect discrimination on racial grounds.

(Equality and Human Rights Commission, n.d.)

15.11 RELIGION AND BELIEF

According to the Equality Act, 'religion' means any religion and does not give a list of religious and belief groups that are covered. It does, however, also include 'not having any religion' – so if someone were to be discriminated against because they have no religion, this would be unlawful.

'Belief' means any religious or philosophical belief and a reference to belief includes a reference to a lack of belief.

'Occupational requirements' apply here too, as with sex and race: an example might be a hospital or school chaplain or, in the Islamic faith, a halal butcher must be Muslim.

15.11.1 BELIEFS

Care needs to be taken over the interpretation of the word 'belief ', since the beliefs that some people hold may not be religious. Many people believe in particular causes and they confer virtue upon what those causes are designed to achieve. Some such beliefs are political, while others may be environmental. To fall under the Act, a belief must usually satisfy a number of criteria, including that it is an important aspect of the way in which a person behaves in conducting their life.

It is important to appreciate that diversity in religious belief is not a static concept. There are changes over time in the ways in which religions expect their members to behave. Within individual religions, different groups and individuals also have different standards of orthodoxy and devoutness, and may consider themselves to be bound by their religion to observe different forms or standards of behaviour.

 KEY CONCEPT: PREDOMINANT FORCES

The UK is a secular country and the most powerful influences over the way we live come from secular institutions, including industry. Christianity is the established religion in the UK, although different denominations predominate in different areas and among different sectors of the population. However, there are many non-Christian religious minorities, some of them very sizeable, such as Muslims and Jews. The law requires organisations in the UK to respect the customs of adherents to all accepted religions, and not just to Christianity.

15.11.2 IMPLICATIONS FOR THE ORGANISATION

The criteria for religious and belief discrimination are virtually the same as those for discrimination on grounds of race. While it is essential for employers, and particularly HR practitioners, to develop an understanding of the law in these respects, sound employment policies and practices are the real answer to ensuring the effectiveness of a diverse workforce. The degree of success in this respect is attributable to the culture of the organisation and how culture is managed.

Contrary to common assumption, the variety of religions and beliefs in the community has only slightly increased. The more obvious effect is the raising of the profile of particular religions and beliefs through a marked increase in their membership. This, of course, is reflected in workforces across the UK.

Employers should screen policies and working practices to remove unfair discrimination and bias as part of a coherent diversity strategy (CIPD, 2013r). Any kind of discrimination case can be costly, as we have seen from the earlier case examples.

15.12 DISABILITY

15.12.1 HISTORICAL PERSPECTIVE

The initial legislative attempts to provide disabled people with protection from discrimination were the Disabled Persons (Employment) Acts of 1944 and 1958. These original Acts were aimed at helping those who were disabled during the Second World War and introduced a 3% workforce quota of disabled employees on employers who had more than 20 staff on their payroll. The protection provided by these Acts was generally regarded as inadequate, and those representing disabled people actively campaigned for improvements. Their efforts eventually paid off when the Disability Discrimination Act 1995 (DDA95) was passed. The DDA95 came into force in 1996 and provided disabled people with discrimination law in line with sex and race discrimination and abolished the 3% quota on the premise that disabled people should be treated fairly and not be subject to a 'quota'. The legislation founded in the DDA95 has now been subsumed into the Equality Act 2010.

15.12.2 EQUALITY ACT: MAIN PROVISIONS FOR DISABILITY

The Equality Act 2010 provides disabled people with protection from discrimination in the workplace. The Act states that it is unlawful to

> discriminate against workers because of a physical or mental disability or fail to make reasonable adjustments to accommodate a worker with a disability.

CASE EXAMPLE 15.15

An employer has two employees who are starting work as checkout operators. Both will be doing the same job. If the employer decided to pay one of them less because they were a disabled person, this would almost certainly be unlawful discrimination because of disability.

KEY CONCEPT: DEFINITION OF DISABILITY

A person is classified as disabled if they have:

'a physical or mental impairment which has a substantial and long-term adverse effect on their ability to carry out normal day-to-day activities' (Equality Act 2010)

- 'substantial' is more than minor or trivial – for example it takes much longer than it usually would to complete a daily task, like getting dressed
- 'long-term' means 12 months or more – for example a breathing condition that develops as a result of a lung infection
- 'Normal day-to-day activities' refers to the activities that most people carry out as normal parts of their lives, including things such as using a telephone, reading a book or using public transport. It does not refer specifically to the day-to-day activities that are involved in the individual's job.

(**www.gov.uk/definition-of-disability-under-equality-act-2010**)

For more guidance on definitions, see the 'Equality Act 2010 – Guidance on matters to be taken into account in determining questions relating to the definition of disability', published by Office for Disability Issues: **http://odi.dwp.gov.uk/common/publications-index.php**

Examples of disability include cancer, diabetes, multiple sclerosis and heart conditions; hearing or sight impairments, or a significant mobility difficulty; and mental health conditions or learning difficulties. 'Invisible' disabilities are also included, for example diabetes and depression, and temporary illnesses or injuries, for example severe back disorders.

The Equality Act also forbids discrimination against someone because they had a disability in the past.

Certain impairments are explicitly excluded, for example seasonal allergic rhinitis (hay fever), tattoos and ornamental body piercing, and various anti-social personality disorders, for example a tendency to set fire, to physical or sexual abuse, to voyeurism or exhibitionism.

CASE EXAMPLE 15.16

Four years ago, a woman experienced a mental illness that had a substantial and long-term adverse effect on her ability to carry out normal day-to-day activities, so it met the Act's definition of disability. She has experienced no recurrence of the condition, but if she is discriminated against because of her past mental illness she is still entitled to the protection afforded by the Act, as a person with a past disability.

(Office for Disability Issues, 2011)

15.12.3 REASONABLE ADJUSTMENTS

For employers, probably the most pertinent part of the law is the duty to make 'reasonable adjustments' to accommodate a worker with a disability. This means that, where workers are disadvantaged by workplace practices because of their disability, employers must take reasonable steps in order for them to be able to carry out their job.

This might mean adjusting hours or duties, providing wheelchair access, adjusting, modifying or repositioning equipment, buying or modifying equipment or allowing time off.

Recruitment and selection procedures may be changed to make it possible for a disabled person to apply for a job in the first place. This may include modifying the design of documents, for example large print, and a willingness to accept job applications by email or other suitable media.

CASE EXAMPLE 15.17

Ushma needs special software to help her read documents on her computer. Providing the cost is not prohibitive and could be considered as being 'reasonable', the employer would be expected to provide this with no cost to Ushma herself.

The Equality Act also makes it more difficult for disabled people to be unfairly screened out when applying for jobs, by restricting the circumstances in which employers can ask job applicants questions about disability. You can ask health-related questions to help you to decide whether you need to make any reasonable adjustments for the person to the selection process. However, questions about reasonable adjustments needed for the job itself should not be asked until after a job offer is made (unless relating to a function which is intrinsic to the job).

CASE EXAMPLE 15.18

The KVD Fastening factory is recruiting for a warehouse worker. Applicants are asked by HR whether they require any reasonable adjustments to the interview process to ensure that they are not disadvantaged during the selection procedure. However, this information is not taken into account when deciding who to employ. The job requires a lot of heavy manual handling, so a candidate with a mobility impairment could be asked whether they could manage handling heavy goods. However, the person could not be asked how their impairment would affect them in getting to the workplace, because this is not something that is intrinsic to the job itself.

15.13 AGE DISCRIMINATION

The Equality Act makes it unlawful to discriminate against employees, job-seekers and trainees because of their age. This includes direct and indirect discrimination, harassment and victimisation. The Act removed upper age limits on unfair dismissal and redundancy.

In addition, it is illegal to discriminate against someone, in certain circumstances, after the working relationship has ended or to compulsorily retire an employee unless it can be objectively justified.

Objective justification means that differences of treatment on the grounds of age can sometimes be justified; objective justification is a test that employers will have to use to substantiate any exemptions to the laws.

Note that since the Act originally came into force, the default retirement age (DRA) has latterly been scrapped (in 2011 through the Employment Equality (Repeal of Retirement Age Provisions) Regulations 2011 (SI 2011/1069)) so employers are able to set their own retirement age, provided they can justify it. Employees may agree to retire at a certain age, but employers can now only enforce dismissal of an older worker by following a fair dismissal procedure and relying on one of the fair reasons for dismissal. It is still theoretically possible for an organisation to have a specific retirement age, but this has to be objectively justified, which is extremely difficult for most employers to establish.

The CIPD states:

The CIPD is committed to the removal of age discrimination in employment because it is wasteful of talent and harmful to both individuals and organisations. The use of age, age bands and age-related criteria reduces objectivity in employment decision-making and increases the likelihood of inappropriate decisions which can harm organisational performance and damage corporate reputation if legal claims are brought. (CIPD, 2013s)

The concept is discussed further in Chapter 17, 'Ending the Employment Relationship'.

The National Minimum Wage is still related to age, as is the basic award used when calculating unfair dismissal awards (which is the same as statutory redundancy payments).

15.14 HARASSMENT AND BULLYING

Bullying or harassment is behaviour that makes someone feel intimidated or offended, usually meaning something has happened to someone that is unwelcome, unwarranted and that causes a detrimental effect. Bullying itself isn't against the law, and while employers used to be held responsible for third party harassment under the Equality Act, the Enterprise and Regulatory Reform Act 2013 repealed this liability from October 2013 on the grounds that this imposes additional liabilities on employers, hindering business growth and economic recovery.

However, a sound bullying and harassment policy is still a good idea. Bullying is difficult to define – what one person sees as bullying, another may consider to be fair management prerogative. There are perhaps some common behaviours which we see happening that are not always construed as bullying: the CIPD in its 2012 factsheet give 'shouting and bawling' as an example of bullying – which sadly is often seen as being acceptable behaviour by managers. Of course, it may not just be managers who bully – it could be other colleagues.

Bullying and harassment may take a variety of forms – name-calling, jokes, spreading malicious rumours, unfair treatment, picking on someone, regularly undermining a competent worker, or denying someone's training or promotion opportunities. Other examples include failure to safeguard confidential information, setting impossible deadlines and displaying of offensive or obscene material. This also includes sending such material by email – so beware of any 'rude jokes or pictures' that might be circulating – they may be construed as harassment.

Bullying and harassment can have a serious effect on the health and well-being of individuals, who can become stressed, demotivated and unproductive. Since the results may lead to a rise in grievance cases, absenteeism, stress, lost productivity and an increase in staff turnover, we can see why it is so important to take any cases seriously. It can, however, be a difficult issue to deal with because people do not always wish to report it and feel intimidated about doing so.

 KEY CONCEPT: BULLYING

Note that there is no legal definition of bullying. The Health and Safety Executive (HSE) says that bullying involves negative behaviour being targeted at an individual, or individuals, repeatedly and persistently over time. Behaviour such as:

- ignoring or excluding you
- giving you unachievable tasks or 'setting you up to fail'
- spreading malicious rumours or gossip
- giving you meaningless tasks or unpleasant jobs
- making belittling remarks
- undermining your integrity
- withholding information deliberately
- making you look stupid in public
- undervaluing your contribution – not giving credit where it is due.

(HSE, 2013h)

Acas gives the following useful interpretation:

'Bullying may be characterised as offensive, intimidating, malicious or insulting behaviour, an abuse or misuse of power through means intended to undermine, humiliate, denigrate or injure the recipient.' (Acas, *Bullying and Harassment at Work: Guide for managers and employers*, 2013)

KEY CONCEPT: HARASSMENT

The Equality Act 2010 defines harassment as:

'Unwanted conduct related to a relevant protected characteristic, which has the purpose or effect of violating an individual's dignity or creating an intimidating, hostile, degrading, humiliating or offensive environment for that individual.'

Employees are also protected from harassment because of perception and association: they are now able to complain of behaviour that they find offensive even if it is not directed at them, and the complainant need not possess the relevant characteristic themselves.

For behaviour to count as harassment in equality law, it has to be one of three types:

Type 1: unwanted behaviour related to the nine protected characteristics named in the Equality Act

Type 2: sexual harassment

Type 3: less favourable treatment because of submission to or rejection of previous sex or gender reassignment harassment.

(Equality and Human Rights Commission, *Avoiding and Dealing with Harassment*, 2013)

15.14.1 HARASSMENT

As noted above, liability by employers for third party harassment has now been repealed from the Equality Act. However, there are other ways to complain about harassment:

- via a claim for 'direct discrimination', where the employer failed to act because of a protected characteristic, which results in less favourable treatment of the employee concerned when compared with how others were (or would have been) treated; or
- via a claim of 'harassment', on the basis that the employer's inaction amounts to unwanted conduct related to a protected characteristic that violates the employee's dignity or creates an intimidating, hostile, degrading, humiliating or offensive environment for the employee; or
- claim constructive dismissal on the grounds that the employer has ignored third party harassment; or
- call the police if they feel an offence has been committed under the Protection from Harassment Act 1997.

(Javaid, M. (2013) Third party harassment provisions repealed. *People Management*. 1 October)

CASE EXAMPLE 15.19

A female employee, Ms H, who works in a club, has been sexually harassed by a customer. She has now complained to her employer, Mr B, who needs to take action to prevent further harassment occurring. Action Mr B could take might include putting warning notifications of unacceptable behaviour in the reception area, entrances, notice boards and company website. He could also train staff in dealing with instances of harassment by members of the public. He might also speak to the person who has harassed Ms H to tell them their behaviour was not acceptable. It may be appropriate to stop the person visiting the club in future to make sure the staff are protected.

15.14.2 CYBER-BULLYING

There have been many cases of bullying and harassment taking place online – so-called 'cyber-bullying'. These may be via blogs or comments on social network sites. An employee may not even be aware that they are being discussed online, behind their back. Access to these sites via email and smart phones brings problems for the employer, as it may be done outside of work hours and the workplace – when is it the employer's responsibility?

Employers need to make sure that their bullying and disciplinary policies include guidance on the use of social media – for example, clearly stating what behaviour is unacceptable. If an employer wishes to monitor emails or online activity (in the case of a complaint about online bullying, for instance), it must be done with the full knowledge of those employees being monitored.

PAUSE FOR THOUGHT

Have you ever heard someone spreading malicious gossip about another person, or seen someone being ridiculed by others at work? Did it occur to you that this might be constituted as bullying or harassment? Often this kind of behaviour is ignored or seen as 'usual'. People may fail to do anything about it because they may be thought of as over-reacting.

Facts do not cease to exist just because they are ignored or brushed aside, but it is possible for the top managers of the organisation not to be aware of what is going on at middle and junior levels.

15.14.3 SEXUAL HARASSMENT

Sexual harassment is unwelcome physical, verbal or non-verbal conduct of a sexual nature. It includes unwelcome sexual advances – touching, standing too close, display of offensive materials, asking for sexual favours, or questioning a person about their sex life. It may also include making decisions on the basis of sexual advances being accepted or rejected – *'I will promote you if you sleep with me'*

Since workplace banter might include jokes of a sexual nature, care needs to be taken not to be committing sexual harassment inadvertently. The key to sexual harassment is that it is *unwelcome.*

It is important to note that it is possible for two people to develop a relationship at work that is warm and friendly, without being sexual. If the relationship does develop further and it is welcome on both sides, that is acceptable. However, it might lead to sexual harassment if only one of the parties to the relationship persists in trying to take the relationship further, while to the other, such advances are clearly unwelcome.

KEY CONCEPT: THE ROLE OF CRIMINAL LAW

Individuals are further protected against harassment by other laws that make harassment a criminal offence: for example, the Criminal Justice and Public Order Act 1994 and the Protection from Harassment Act 1997. Under the Criminal Justice and Public Order Act, it can be a criminal offence for an individual to deliberately harass another person.

15.14.4 WHAT SHOULD EMPLOYERS DO ABOUT BULLYING AND HARASSMENT?

Employees are encouraged to sort out the problem informally first if possible. If they can't, they should talk to their manager, to HR or their trade union. Mediation by a neutral third party can often be helpful in resolving difficult issues.

If the informal route is not successful in resolving the problem, it will be necessary to follow a formal complaints procedure.

Acas suggests that a formal policy is important. This shows that there is serious commitment from management about not tolerating this kind of behaviour in the organisation. The policy should be linked to discipline and grievance procedures so that people understand the importance of bullying behaviour and how to act in the case of a complaint. It should also include examples so that people know what constitutes bullying – as we saw earlier, bullying behaviour may be seen as acceptable or even normal, perhaps a joke, but may not be perceived like that by the person receiving the bullying.

As with many issues relating to people management, it is also important to train managers to deal with these areas and make sure that they have the skills to deal with them. Any investigations must be done promptly and objectively. As a result of the investigation, it may mean that counselling needs to be provided for the person being bullied – and possibly for the accused as well. Another useful option is to bring in an independent mediator who can help to resolve the situation.

It is suggested that employers should make sure they do the following:

- check that their anti-harassment policy expresses zero tolerance
- inform third parties that harassment will not be tolerated, for example, by including it as a term in commercial contracts, displaying public notices, and so on
- require managers to intervene if they observe harassment by third parties and ask employees to report any such behaviour
- promptly investigate any complaint of harassment by a third party and act upon it.

(Javaid, M. (2013) Third party harassment provisions repealed. *People Management.* 1 October)

ACTIVITY 15.7

Find out if your organisation or university or college has a policy on harassment and a procedure for dealing with it. If it does, ask if you may read the relevant documents. What do the documents contain? Do they cover training for managers and HR specialists in dealing with harassment? Does the organisation provide access to counselling in cases of severe distress caused by harassment or bullying?

15.15 EMPLOYMENT TRIBUNALS

Employment tribunals (ETs) are independent judicial bodies who determine disputes between employers and employees over employment rights. They hear claims about matters to do with employment, such as unfair dismissal, redundancy payments, wages and other payments and discrimination. Any appeals go to the Employment Appeal Tribunal (EAT).

In 2011/12 there were 230,000 jurisdictional complaints accepted by employment tribunals in the UK. The average compensatory award given for a case of race discrimination was £173,408, for sex discrimination, £9,940, and for disability, £22,183.

The maximum compensatory award in 2011/12 was £4,445,023 for the *Michalak v Mid Yorkshire Hospitals NHS Trust* case we saw earlier in the chapter.

We have seen how costly it can be to defend a case of discrimination through the courts. It is not only the compensation itself that costs, though. The sheer time taken in investigating a case, the resources used in preparation and the emotional worry of having to defend one's actions in front of a tribunal make the whole process one to be avoided if at all possible.

HOW TO PUT DIVERSITY AND TALENT MANAGEMENT INTO PRACTICE

CASE EXAMPLE 15.20

Building a workforce that is fully reflective of the community at NHS Tower Hamlets

Deborah Clarke is Director of Human Resources and Organisation Development for NHS Tower Hamlets. Their key aim is to improve the health and well-being of local people living in Tower Hamlets in east London.

She comments:

We want to reduce inequalities in health and improve services for local people. We are focused on all six strands of equality – race, authenticity, gender, disability, religion, sexual orientation and age – and they all inter-relate with each other. We have a set of targets and priorities for each of these areas. There is a very lively discussion currently going on in the organisation about how each of these strands relate to one another. A key issue is having a workforce that is fully reflective of the community that we serve.

What is talent management and diversity about from Tower Hamlets' perspective?

I view talent and diversity as completely linked.

It is not correct to say that they are at odds with each other because having a diverse workforce is the same as having a talented workforce and having a talented workforce must be diverse, so the two go together hand in hand. What I say to people in Tower Hamlets is that we want to recruit the very, very best talent that is available and we want to recruit the widest range of different kinds of people and local people and those two things aren't mutually exclusive. They are the same thing.

The targets and measures we use

Some of the measures/targets we use are part of the local government regime that is called 'best value' – all local authorities have got targets around gender, race and disability, and so with those we aim to get ourselves into the upper quartile in comparison with other local authorities. If that is not really a relevant comparison, we look at what's in the community that we are serving and we match ourselves to that.

The council's cabinet has a report on progress every six months. It's very high profile and the elected members of the council are very committed to achieving progress against the targets. They are younger than average, very diverse, more likely to be in full-time employment and very community focused. They understand what the issues are about. The NHS board is similarly committed and interested, and looking for evidence of progress.

We track how many of our employees live locally, we capture their postcode, we capture promotions, we capture the profile of our workforce against the six equality strands, and we track the people who applied, how many from each area were shortlisted and how many were appointed.

Talent and diversity initiatives/programmes

Career café – We recently held a big event for about 150 of our diverse leaders' network who have been through our talent programmes. We called it a 'career café' and the purpose was to get them to take a bit more responsibility for managing their own careers. We had speakers who gave examples of what they have done in their lives and also from some high-powered headhunters who described what they are looking for, how you need to evidence your experience and the tools to move up the organisation.

Keep diverse talent warm

We are currently partnering with another organisation to identify people that we would want to recruit into Tower Hamlets even if we haven't got a job for them at the moment. We make contact, give them a tour of the borough, introduce them to some of the leading figures and keep them warmed and informed about what's going on in Tower Hamlets. This means that when a job comes up they think, 'I know that they are diversity friendly, I understand what they are about, I can apply for this job.'

Talent programmes

We have a host of different talent and diversity schemes, such as the Hamlets Youth Scheme and different graduate programmes linked to professional career paths. We also have positive action programmes for aspiring leaders and middle managers. We have also recently held a 'career café' for 150 of our diverse leaders' network aimed at getting them to take more responsibility for managing their own careers and to think about what is needed to move up the organisation.

Developing internal talent

We try to fill most senior posts from the talent that we have already got internally because we are a very diverse workforce. We've trained people up, we have identified the stars, we give them opportunities to act up, so if you are a betting person you are probably going to say that it is going to be an internal promotion. However, we still have to try to identify what talent out there would help us to achieve our targets while not compromising on having the very best that's available. We advertise nationally for roles but we also always advertise locally.

Although we are focused on getting local people into employment we are also focused on getting the very best people that we can – we try and do the two together.

In summary, Deborah's advice is:

1   Philosophically reconcile yourself to the fact that talent and diversity must be interlinked.

2   Be really clear about what you want to achieve and have a really practical plan to get you there.

3   Get the buy-in and commitment of your leadership team.

4   Recognise that talent and diversity are business imperatives and have to be driven by the business.

5   Monitor your progress – know where you are and where you want to get to.

(Source: CIPD. (2010) *Opening up talent for business success – Integrating talent management and diversity*. With kind permission of CIPD Publishing.)

15.16 SUMMARY

We have seen an enormous amount of legislation covering discrimination in the UK. Most of this has been embedded into the Equality Act 2010, which covers the 'protected characteristics' of *age, disability, gender reassignment, race, religion or belief, sex, sexual orientation, marriage and civil partnership and pregnancy and maternity.*

In this chapter we have seen the results of unfair discrimination in the courts: the *Michalak* case awarded £4.5 million compensation. In addition to the moral rights and wrongs of the case, the threat of having to pay such large amounts of compensation should act as a deterrent to discriminatory behaviour in organisations.

But being an 'equal opportunity employer' is not just about complying with legislation. Diversity in an organisation makes good business sense. Not only is it good for employees to feel valued and to be treated fairly, and that customers can feel confident that the organisation reflects the diversity that exists in society (the social justice case), but also that the talents of everyone are being used to best advantage (the business case).

Despite the legislation, we have seen that prejudices still exist and that stereotyping can work against the creation of a diverse workforce. For those who do contravene the legislation, it can be a costly affair. With compensatory awards running into thousands of pounds, there is good reason to ensure that equality policies are not only in existence, but are understood and implemented.

Acas (2011a) suggests that employers should ensure they have policies in place which are designed to prevent discrimination in:

- recruitment and selection
- determining pay
- training and development
- selection for promotion
- discipline and grievances
- countering bullying and harassment.

(Acas, 2011a. © Acas, Euston Tower, 286 Euston Road, London NW1 3JJ)

HR should ensure that organisations have policies in place that deter unfair discrimination and encourage a culture of welcoming diversity. It is important that these policies are also put into practice!

REVIEW QUESTIONS

1 How would you define the basic concept of unlawful discrimination?

2 What is meant by 'diversity' in relation to an organisation's workforce?

3 How would you distinguish between the 'business case' and the 'social justice case' for recognising and respecting diversity?

4 What factors in an individual or group might arouse a person's prejudices?

5 Name the protected characteristics under the Equality Act 2010.

6 It has been suggested that we should examine to what extent our impressions of others are based upon stereotyping. What is stereotyping and what are the dangers of referring to stereotypes?

7 How do we distinguish 'direct' from 'indirect' discrimination?

8 What is 'associative discrimination'?

9 What might constitute an 'occupational requirement'?

10 Under disability discrimination, what do you understand by the term 'reasonable adjustment'?

11 What is positive action?

12 What options are open to an employee if they are being harassed at work?

13 What should employers do about instances of bullying and harassment?

14 What is the role of an employment tribunal?

EXPLORE FURTHER

BOOKS

KUMRA, S. and MANFREDI, S. (2012) *Managing equality and diversity: theory and practice*. Oxford: Oxford University Press.

OZBILGIN, M.F., MULHOLLAND, G., TATLI, A. and WORMAN, D. (2008) *Managing diversity and the business case*. London: CIPD.

THOMPSON, N. (2011) *Promoting equality: working with diversity and difference*. Basingstoke: Palgrave MacMillan.

WEB LINKS

Acas offers excellent advice on equality (as on most other employment-related issues). Start at **www.acas.org.uk/index.aspx?articleid=1363** and then see their other specific pages and guides:

Acas *Delivering Equality and Diversity* advisory booklet: **www.acas.org.uk/index. aspx?articleid=818**

Acas (age discrimination): **www.acas.org.uk/index.aspx?articleid=1841**

Acas (bullying and harassment): **www.acas.org.uk/index.aspx?articleid=797**

The CIPD has a page of frequently asked questions on discrimination: **www.cipd.co. uk/hr-resources/employment-law-faqs/discrimination.aspx**

The annual statistical report of the Employment Tribunals Service makes very interesting reading as it lists the number of cases taken to tribunals (ETs and EATs) for unfair dismissal, discrimination, and so on. Perhaps most interestingly, it gives data on the amounts of compensation awarded for the various cases. A scary read – but excellent evidence for demonstrating why we need to follow anti-discrimination policies: **www.gov.uk/government/uploads/system/uploads/attachment_data/ file/218497/employment-trib-stats-april-march-2011–12.pdf**

The Equality and Diversity Forum (EDF) **website (www.edf.org.uk/blog/)** is useful. Their report by Frances McAndrew (2010) *Workplace equality: turning policy into practice* contains a number of sound recommendations for employers.

Equality and Human Rights Commission: **www.equalityhumanrights.com** See in particular their guidance information 'What equality law means for you as an employer. Pay and Benefits': **www.equalityhumanrights.com/uploaded_files/ equalpay/employers_pay_and_benefits.pdf**

They also have a useful guide to the new legislation on same-sex marriages and its implications for employers and employees: **www.equalityhumanrights.com/advice- and-guidance/marriage-same-sex-couples-act-2013-guidance/**

The Government Equalities Office booklet, *The Equality Act, making equality real*, provides a light and very simple overview (it states that is an 'easy read' – always a plus when referring to legal documents!): **www.cquality-law.co.uk/downloads/ GEO_-_Equality_Act_easy_read.pdf**

They also have a variety of individual guidance documents to help with the Equality Act. See **www.gov.uk/government/publications/equality-act-guidance**

The Gender Identity Research and Education Society (GIRES) is a registered charity with a focus on people who experience atypical gender identity development: **www. gires.org.uk/grp.php**

The Office for Disability Issues leads in driving delivery of the Government's vision for disabled people: **http://odi.dwp.gov.uk/**

The document *Equality Act guidance: guidance on matters to be taken into account in determining questions relating to the definition of disability* gives useful clarification and case examples. Download it (or any of their other publications) at **http://odi.dwp.gov.uk/common/publications-index.php**

For disability and employment issues, see the Shaw Trust: **www.shaw-trust.org.uk**

For age discrimination information, see: **www.agediscrimination.info/Pages/Home. aspx**

CHAPTER 16

Understanding Employment Law

LEARNING OBJECTIVES

After studying this chapter you should.

- be able to find employment law legislation using the 'legislation.gov.uk' website
- be able to define the employment relationship and understand its legal framework
- understand the contract of employment and the main statutory provisions that contribute to the regulation of the employment relationship
- understand employees' contractual and statutory rights
- understand the origins of: equal pay, family-friendly, disciplinary and grievance, and health and safety legislation
- be able to define the role of the Information Commissioner in the context of the Data Protection Act (1998) and the Freedom of Information Act (2000)
- understand the extent and requirements of the Data Protection Act (1998) for the organisation
- understand the differences between the Data Protection Act and the Freedom of Information Act (2000).

16.1 INTRODUCTION

The aim of this chapter is to provide an understanding of the employment relationship and the elements that shape its formal and informal structure. This includes the contractual and statutory rights and obligations of the employer and the employee. As indicated in the summary to this chapter, it is not intended to be a definitive guide and should not to be used as a means to replace good-quality employment law advice.

16.2 THE EMPLOYMENT RELATIONSHIP AND LEGISLATION

The UK's employment legislation sets the formal framework within which the employer and an employee conduct their business. Employment legislation sets responsibilities for both the employer and the employee and also gives rights to the employee in the context of the employment relationship.

16.3 DIFFERENCES BETWEEN CONTRACTS

As previously mentioned in Chapter 13, 'The Employment Relationship', there is a contract of employment between the employee and employer. The employment contract can be of defined duration or be continuous (permanent). Whether it is defined or continuous, the employer and employee are still governed by the legal statutes, regulations and directives that are in force.

All employees have a contract of employment. While it is based on what both parties have agreed to be a *fair exchange* (the employee's time and skill in exchange for a salary or wage), it is different from a commercial contract, such as, for example, the sale and purchase of a car or house. Such contracts have completion dates and terms and conditions that are an integral part of the agreement. Unless the duration is specified at the outset, an employment contract is of continuous duration, in that both parties intend that it should go on until one side or the other wishes to terminate the relationship.

The concept of when a worker is recognised as an employee is a topic which has exercised many legal minds. The law, the Employment Rights Act 1996, Ch III, Section 230 defines an employee. However, the definition is open to some interpretation. The following seeks to identify more specifically how an employee can be defined.

The UK Government indicates that if a 'worker' enjoys the following rights or has to perform the following duties or is restricted by certain limitations on whether they perform a duty for an employer then they are *likely* to be an employee. Importantly the word used is *likely* rather than *is* an employee:

- They're required to work regularly unless they're on leave (for example holiday, sick leave or maternity leave).
- They're required to do a minimum number of hours and expect to be paid for time worked.
- A manager or supervisor is responsible for their workload, saying when a piece of work should be finished and how it should be done.
- They can't send someone else to do their work.
- The business deducts tax and National Insurance contributions from their wages.
- They get paid holiday.
- They're entitled to contractual or Statutory Sick, Maternity, or Paternity Pay.
- They can join the business's pension scheme.
- The business's disciplinary and grievance procedures apply to them.
- They work at the business's premises or at an address specified by the business.
- Their contract sets out redundancy procedures.
- The business provides the materials, tools and equipment for their work.
- They only work for the business or if they do have another job, it's completely different from their work for the business.
- Their contract, statement of terms and conditions or offer letter (which can be described as an 'employment contract') uses terms like 'employer' and 'employee'.

www.gov.uk/employment-status/employee

Lewis and Sargeant (2013, pp. 55–6) deal with the thorny issue in some depth.

How the employment status of an individual is defined can have significant implications for both the individual and the 'employing organisation'. Being defined as an employee, as indicated above, gives a number of rights to the individual. Similarly, an individual who was genuinely employed as a contractor by an organisation, and who later claims that they are or have been an employee, can have significant implications, in terms of income tax liabilities in respect of the 'new' employee for the 'employing organisation'. A contractor is normally responsible for their own income tax liabilities. The unscrupulous contractor can, by claiming an employer/employee relationship, transfer the income tax and National Insurance burden from themselves to the employing organisation. Once an individual becomes an employee they assume a number of employment rights, for example rights associated with holiday entitlement, maternity, paternity, adoption leave, redundancy, and so on.

The good HR practitioner can add value to the organisation by making sure that the nature of any relationship between their organisation and an individual is clearly defined by the contract that the individual signs.

16.3.1 THE COMPONENTS OF A CONTRACT

A contract contains four main elements:

- an offer
- an acceptance
- consideration
- the intention to form a legal relationship.

ACTIVITY 16.1

A contract of employment or a contract of service

To understand the difference between a contract of employment and contract of service go to 'Employment Contracts' at **www.gov.uk/employment-contracts-and-conditions**

The HM Revenue and Customs website offers a handy 'Employment Status Indicator' (ESI) for employers to test whether an individual or group of individuals who have similar terms of service are employees or are self-employed.

The ESI can be found at **www.hmrc.gov.uk/calcs/esi.htm**

CASE EXAMPLE 16.1

ESM7180 – Case Law: *Secretary of State for Employment v McMeechan* [1997] IRLR 353

Point at issue

Mr McMeechan was on the books of an employment agency, Noel Employment Ltd, as a temporary catering assistant for about a year. When the agency became insolvent, he sought to recover from the Redundancy Fund, under Section 122 of the Employment Protection (Consolidation) Act 1978, the unpaid earnings due to him in respect of his last engagement. This had been with a client, Sutcliffe Catering, and he was claiming the sum of £105. The underlying matter to be decided was whether Mr McMeechan had been an employee of the agency during the course of this particular engagement.

Facts

Mr McMeechan had worked for a number of clients of the agency for varying periods during the year to March 1993. He had produced a job sheet to the industrial tribunal which contained the terms and conditions of his service with Noel Employment Ltd for the period with Sutcliffe Catering.

Decision

The Secretary of State for Employment refused Mr McMeechan's claim on the grounds that he was not an employee. This refusal was upheld by an industrial tribunal but this was overturned by the Employment Appeal Tribunal (EAT).

Finally, the Court of Appeal decided that, looking at all the terms of the single engagement, it gave rise to a contract of service.

Commentary

The Court of Appeal concentrated on the criterion of mutual obligation and Waite LJ stated:

'The principle which it enshrines is that if there be an absence on the one side of any obligation to provide work and an absence on the other side of any obligation to do such work..., then that provides a powerful pointer against the contract...being one of service.'

However, he went on to say that temporary or casual workers pose a particular problem of their own in that there are often two engagements to consider. There is the general engagement, under which sporadic tasks are performed, and the specific engagement, which begins and ends with the performance of any one task.

The judge stated that 'each engagement is capable, according to its context, of giving rise to a contract of employment'.

In considering the single engagement claim by Mr McMeechan, Waite LJ looked at the conditions in the written agreement and concluded:

'When it comes to considering the terms of an individual self-contained, engagement, the fact that the parties are not to be obliged in future to offer – or to accept – another engagement with the same, or a different, client must be neither here nor there.'

He then went on to weigh the other conditions that applied, in relation to the single assignment with Sutcliffe Catering, and came to the conclusion that that assignment gave rise to a contract of service between Mr McMeechan and Noel Employment Ltd.

In this case the Court of Appeal confirmed the principle established in earlier cases that, as regards casual or temporary workers, there are often two engagements which employment tribunals have to look at: firstly, the general engagement which involves a number of single engagements and, secondly, the specific engagements which make up the general engagement. The reason for doing so is that individual engagements may not be of sufficient duration to found a claim for unfair dismissal (there must be one year [two years prior to 1 June 1999] of continuous service), redundancy, and so on.

In considering the existence of a general engagement, the courts will look to see whether there is a global or umbrella contract of service. They will therefore have regard to all the terms and conditions which apply whether written, oral or implied and also to the conduct of the parties. They will then step back and view the whole picture from a distance. One of the important factors they will look at in considering the general engagement is 'mutuality of obligation'.

In a general engagement, there must be an obligation on the part of the engager to offer work, when it is available, and an obligation on the part of the worker to personally perform that work when it is offered.

However, in considering a single engagement, the mutual obligation, which must exist for there to be a contract of service, is that the engager agrees to provide the work offered and the worker agrees to perform the work personally. There is no need for there to be an obligation to offer and accept future work as there is only one engagement to consider.

The important point to bear in mind is that where you have a general engagement you consider the overall contract in determining employment status. Where there is a single engagement, it is the contract for that specific engagement that forms the starting point.

Acknowledgement

The authors acknowledge that this material is available from the HM Revenue and Customs website at **www. hmrc.gov.uk/manuals/esmmanual/ esm7180.htm** and 'contains public sector information licensed under the Open Government Licence v1.0'.

Comment: From Case Example 16.1 it can be seen that deciding upon whether an individual is an employee or temporary 'worker' can be complex in the extreme. Key to the outcome of the above tribunal and Court of Appeal cases was the fact that even when considering the event for which the subject of the case was contracted to provide work, that event in itself did not provide the starting point for an employment relationship. There was no mutuality of agreement for the organisation to have offered further work nor for the individual to have accepted it.

ACTIVITY 16.2

Access the Lexisnexis case law database at **www.lexisnexis.com** and study the case of *Massey V Crown Life Insurance Co.*

The facts

Mr Massey was the manager of a branch of the respondents' insurance company. He was treated as an employee and the respondents deducted tax, National Insurance contributions, and so on, from his wages. In 1973, Mr Massey was advised by his accountant to change his relationship with his employer and become self-employed. The company agreed to this and a new agreement was entered into with almost identical duties, but with Mr Massey being paid as an independent contractor. The Inland Revenue approved the arrangement and permitted Mr Massey to be taxed under Schedule D.

In November 1975, Mr Massey's employment was terminated. He claimed unfair dismissal compensation. An industrial tribunal and the Employment Appeal Tribunal both held that as Mr Massey was not at the time of his dismissal an employee of the respondents, he was ineligible to claim unfair dismissal compensation.

Comment

The case demonstrates once again the difficulty of deciding when an individual is an employee or a worker providing a contract of service. The outcome of such cases has implications not only in the context of whether an individual can claim unfair dismissal at a tribunal and thus receive a compensation award or perhaps the organisation is required to 're-engage the employee', but may also involve tax liabilities for either the individual or organisation involved.

16.3.2 PERMANENT CONTRACT OF EMPLOYMENT

Permanent contracts of employment are enduring, in the sense that there is nothing specified as to when the employment relationship should end, as in the case of the 'fixed-term' contract of employment, see below. People with employment contracts, whether full- or part-time, receive the following from their employer (**www.gov.uk/contract**):

- a written statement of employment or contract
- the statutory minimum level of paid holiday
- a payslip showing all deductions, for example National Insurance contributions (NICs)
- the statutory minimum length of rest breaks
- Statutory Sick Pay (SSP)
- maternity, paternity and adoption pay and leave.

The employer must also:

- make sure employees don't work longer than the maximum allowed
- pay employees at least the minimum wage
- have employer's liability insurance
- provide a safe and secure working environment
- register with HM Revenue and Customs to deal with payroll, tax and NICs
- consider flexible working requests

- avoid discrimination in the workplace
- make reasonable adjustments to your business premises if your employee is disabled.

More information on the above can be found at: **www.gov.uk/contract-types-and-employer-responsibilities/fulltime-and-parttime-contracts**

16.3.3 FIXED-TERM CONTRACT

This kind of contract always has a clearly specified duration, spelling out the start and finishing dates. People are engaged on a fixed-term contract when they have come into the organisation to carry out a specific project or, for example, to stand in for a permanent employee who is away on maternity/paternity leave, absent because of a long-term illness or on an external secondment or perhaps to meet seasonally driven workloads.

16.3.4 ZERO-HOURS CONTRACT

With this kind of contract the worker is not guaranteed any paid work at all. The worker must be available, however, to be called upon when there is a need. While it may not appeal to many workers, a retired teacher or nurse may find it attractive since it provides an opportunity to earn a little extra cash. For example, they might be called upon to cover for a sick employee. Zero-hours contracts are also offered to shop assistants to do casual work at busy periods such as Christmas and the January sales. Other organisations, such as theme parks, seaside shops and stalls, offer so-called 'seasonal' contracts which are, in effect, zero-hours contracts. Supply teachers, who are employed by an agency and who 'fill in' when a permanent school teacher is unavailable for work, are also, in effect, on zero-hours contracts.

Currently, as this book is being written (May 2014), there is much discussion and debate about the morality of zero-hours contracts. The issue is dealt with, in some depth, in the 'Work-life balance' section of Chapter 14.

16.3.5 CONTRACTS OF EMPLOYMENT – GENERAL CONSIDERATIONS

As an employee, whether on a permanent or some form of temporary contract of employment, the individual enjoys some of the rights of a permanent employee, such as equal pay and pension provision. Additionally, the employer is not allowed to require or request the worker to waive their right to protection against unfair dismissal or redundancy.

An employer cannot ask an employee to sign away a statutory right. If an employer were to dismiss someone for refusing to sign an agreement to waive their right to holiday pay (this is an extreme example!), the employee may have grounds for an unfair dismissal claim, providing they have sufficient service. For employees who started in employment before 6 April 2012, sufficient service is 12 months; for employees starting new employment on or after 6 April 2012, this has been extended to two years.

16.3.6 A NEW FORM OF CONTRACT: EMPLOYEE SHAREHOLDER CONTRACT

An employee shareholder is someone who works under an employee shareholder employment contract. It is a form of employment status which became available in September 2013. The idea behind the concept is that the employee shareholder has a stake in the company and that this leads to a feeling of greater responsibility towards the company compared with someone who is simply an employee.

The employee shareholder must receive shares in the employer's company or employer's parent company to a minimum value of £2,000. There are certain tax liabilities associated with owning shares; the HM Revenue and Customs website at **www.hmrc.gov. uk/employeesharcholder** gives detailed advice on how tax liabilities are handled.

The employee shareholder still has many employment rights, such as:

- statutory sick pay
- statutory maternity, paternity and adoption leave and pay
- unfair dismissal rights where they are classed as automatically unfair reasons, where dismissal is based on discriminatory grounds and in relation to health and safety
- minimum notice periods if their employment will be ending (for example if an employer is dismissing them)
- time off for emergencies
- collective redundancy consultation
- TUPE (TUPE means the 'Transfer of Undertakings (Protection of Employment) Regulations') – the regulations apply to organisations of all sizes and protect employees' rights when the business they work for transfers to a new employer. The TUPE Regulations apply when a business is sold, activities are outsourced or brought in-house (Acas, 2014))
- national minimum wage
- not to have unlawful deductions from wages
- paid annual leave
- rest breaks
- the right not to be treated less favourably for working part-time or on a fixed-term contract
- not to be discriminated against.

However, there are some 'down-sides' to being an employee shareholder. The Department for Business, Innovation and Skills offers the following guidance to potential employee shareholders:

> Both the individual and the employer must understand which rights an employee shareholder will not have, as this must be communicated in the written statement. These are:

- unfair dismissal rights (apart from the automatically unfair reasons, where dismissal is based on discriminatory grounds and in relation to health and safety)
- rights to statutory redundancy pay
- the statutory right to request flexible working except in the 2 week period after a return from parental leave
- certain statutory rights to request time off to train.

(The author recognises that the above is adapted from the Department for Business, Innovation and Skills and 'contains public sector information licensed under the Open Government Licence v1.0'.)

Further information on the above can be found at **www.gov.uk/employee-shareholders**

The aim of the Government was to try to remove what they saw as some of the red-tape which was burdening business and to encourage organisations to be less reticent {meaning – *not to hold back from*} to recruit, by removing some of the perceived risks associated with hiring and of firing individuals during uncertain economic times.

ACTIVITY 16.3

Finding employment legislation

The Government has, conveniently, placed all its legislation on an easily accessible website, **legislation.gov.uk** Go to this website and enter into the 'Title' and 'Year' fields: 'employment rights' and '1996'. Press the 'Go' button with your mouse and you should be offered Employment Rights Act 1996 as the first choice on the retrieved list of legislation.

1   Click on the Act and read what the legislation has to say in Section 1,

'Statement of initial employment particulars'. Specifically, what information does the employer have to provide to the new employee within two months of starting work?

2   Using the same process as above, find the Employment Act 2002. This Act has modified sections of the Employment Rights Act 1996 [ERA96]. Specifically, what has the 2002 Act amended in the ERA96?

PAUSE FOR THOUGHT

Study what is said above about different types of contract, identify your own type of contract of employment and find out if it is different from those of your friends, co-workers or student colleagues.

BUYING A CAR

CASE EXAMPLE 16.2

Have you ever bought a second-hand car? What happened? The car was for sale, you liked it and started to negotiate a price. Eventually, you made an *offer* for it. Your offer may have been a sum that was less than the original asking price but the person selling the car *accepted* your offer. They accepted it in *consideration* of your offer, as an agreed purchase price. A contract is drawn up and you both sign it. You hand over the money

and the seller hands over the car and the legal documents are completed. The car is now yours; end of *legal relationship*; end of contract.

Unlike the type of contract described in the above example, in which the terms and conditions were agreed on a once-and-for-all basis, the terms and conditions related to the employment contract are subject to continuous renegotiation and change.

16.3.7 TERMS AND CONDITIONS OF THE EMPLOYMENT CONTRACT

These fall into three categories:

1   **Express terms and conditions:** this is the list of the terms and conditions that govern and specify the details of the contract, which is given to the employee in writing usually shortly after joining the organisation. The expressed terms may be incorporated in a collective agreement, that is, with trade unions who are recognised

by the employer or with the whole workforce. The CIPD factsheet on contracts of employment (2009a) states that these could, in many cases, be terms that meet minimum standards required by law, in areas such as the right to:

- paid holidays
- receive at least the National Minimum Wage
- receive statutory notice of termination
- daily and weekly rest breaks.

2   **Implied terms and conditions:** these are integral parts of the contract, although they are not usually given in writing. It is assumed, for example, that the employer will be fair and reasonable and provide a healthy work environment. The terms implied at common law affect both the employee and employer.

Duties of the employee are to:

- render personal service – the employee has no right without the employer's consent to absent themselves from the place of work
- obey lawful and reasonable orders
- act honestly and in good faith – for example, to use the company's computing systems only for the purpose they were intended and not, for example, to use them for personal business or to download pornography
- act with reasonable care
- render accounts – this refers to employees who handle money. They are expected to maintain accounts through which expenditure can be traced
- act in a spirit of co-operation and trust.

Duties of the employer are to:

- pay the wages of the employee
- provide work for the employee
- provide a safe system of work – this is now underpinned with the various Health and Safety Acts, and especially the Health and Safety at Work Act 1974
- act in a manner showing co-operation, reasonableness and trust towards their employees.

3   **Statutory terms and conditions:** the employer should abide by the provisions of employment legislation which, for example, lay down standards for health and safety, working time, data protection, discrimination and statutory notice periods when terminating one's employment.

PAUSE FOR THOUGHT

If you have a part- or full-time job, try to distinguish between the three types of terms and conditions in your contract. The *express* terms and conditions should be easy to identify, but can you identify the *implied* and *statutory* terms and conditions?

Note: you cannot negotiate on the statutory terms and conditions of a contract!

16.4 EMPLOYEES' STATUTORY RIGHTS

While employees have rights under the terms of the employment contract they have with the organisation, they also have rights that are created by legislation in the form of Acts of

Parliament, such as those for equal pay, data protection and discrimination. A large proportion of this legislation has its roots in European Union directives and regulations.

The UK legislation covering employee rights is the Employment Rights Act 1996 (ERA96). Before this Act, employees' rights were provided by employment protection legislation, most of which was enacted in the 1970s and 1980s. The ERA96 consolidates the provisions of the earlier legislation and includes additions. The ERA96 is a very powerful piece of 'employment law' legislation and bestows on UK citizens many rights of employment. It should be borne in mind that the legislation relating to employee rights lays down minimum standards and that many organisations enhance those standards, for example with a view to retaining valued staff. The Employment Rights Act 1996 (ERA96) was amended, in part, by additions predominantly associated with changes to parental leave to include *paternity leave* entitlements, which are defined in the Employment Act 2002. Subsequent amendments to both the ERA96 and the Employment Act 2002 are included in the Children and Families Act 2014.

The Children and Families Act 2014 covers many social areas of legislation, but amongst other changes and additions to the law, specifically extends the *right* to request flexible working to all and gives parents, who qualify, the opportunity to share parental leave.

Agreement over enhancing certain rights may be reached through collective bargaining. In this book, space limitations prevent the coverage of all statutory rights; those explained below are the main rights. The meaning of a contract, in the context of the Act, is given on the legislation.gov.uk website (Employment Rights Act 1996, Ch. III, s230): '"contract of employment" means a contract of service or apprenticeship, whether express or implied, and (if it is express) whether oral or in writing'.

16.4.1 STATEMENT OF TERMS AND CONDITIONS

One of the most important rights of an employee is to receive a statement of the terms and conditions of employment within two months of joining the organisation. The details that the Act (ERA96) requires to be included in the statement are:

- the names of the parties to the contract (the employer and employee)
- date of commencement of period of continuous employment
- hours of work
- location of the workplace and an indication if there could be a requirement to work elsewhere
- details of pay: the rates of pay, how it is calculated and frequency of payment, for example weekly, monthly
- job title or a brief description of the duties and responsibilities
- holiday entitlements
- arrangements about sick pay and sick leave
- details of the pension scheme
- entitlement to receive notice of termination of employment and obligation to give notice
- date of termination if it is a fixed-term contract
- any terms of a collective agreement that affects working conditions
- the contract must specify any disciplinary rules
- the person with whom the employee can seek redress of any grievance procedure.

There are also specialist terms that will not be covered here but would apply if the employee were to be asked to work outside the UK for a period of time exceeding one month.

ACTIVITY 16.4

Go to the Employment Rights Act 1996 (ERA96), which is available at **www.legislation.gov.uk/ukpga/1996/18/contents** and read what the Act has to say about:

- disciplinary procedures (Section 3)
- the right not to suffer unauthorised deductions from wages (Section 13)
- time off for dependents (Section 57A).

16.4.2 CHANGING TERMS AND CONDITIONS OF EMPLOYMENT

The ERA96 also deals with changes to terms and conditions of contract. Employers may change terms and conditions of employment but employees have certain rights if the changes are made. For example, a sudden reduction in pay rates that is made without consultation and an agreement represents a serious breach of the contract. Similarly, the contract would be breached if unilateral changes (changes made without any consultation) were made to other terms and conditions of employment, such as the number of hours required of the employee to work, the times required to work and holiday entitlements and company pension contributions.

The essence of the ERA96, as its name implies and as previously mentioned, is to give rights to employees. Although other legislation may enable employees, for example, to request flexible working (the original regulations were the Flexible Working (Eligibility Complaints and Remedies) Regulations 2002 SI 2002/3236), it is the Employment Rights Act 1996 (s80F) that gives a statutory right to employees to actually make the request as a change in terms and conditions in respect of working hours, working time or place of work. Thus the ERA96 would be the legislation that enables any agreement between the employer and employee on the change of working time because of a request made under the Flexible Working Regulations 2002 or subsequent legislation on this subject. The Children and Families Act 2014 has repealed some of the limitations associated with requests for flexible working, for example: ERA96, section 80F,1b, and as from 30 June 2014 all *employees* can request flexible working, with a duty on employers to consider requests in a *reasonable* manner.

ACTIVITY 16.5

Access section 80G of the Employment Rights Act 1996 and read what the duties of the employer are when they receive a request for flexible working from an employee. Is the employer duty-bound to agree to the employee's request to, for example, modify their hours of work?

You will find the relevant legislation at: **www.legislation.gov.uk/ukpga/1996/18/part/8A** and also **www.legislation.gov.uk/ukpga/2014/6/contents/enacted**

16.4.3 COMPANY HANDBOOK

Most medium-sized and large organisations issue a copy of the company handbook to all employees on joining or direct them to an online copy, which would be on the company's intranet. Most of the items listed above are included in the handbook, as are copies of the disciplinary and grievance procedures. The company handbook may or may not form part of the main contract of employment; much depends upon the detail and preciseness that the handbook deals with employment relations and employment rights issues.

16.4.4 RIGHTS TO TIME OFF

There is a long list of rights to time off, some of which are given below as examples and all of which are rights that are given in the ERA96:

- The Children and Families Act 2014 has changed how parental leave can be taken. The Government says this about the new rights:
  From April 2015, mothers, fathers and adopters can opt to share parental leave around their child's birth or placement. This gives families more choice over taking leave in the first year – dads and mothers' partners can take up to a year, or parents can take several months at the same time.
  From 1 October 2014, prospective fathers or a mother's partner can take time off to attend up to two antenatal appointments.
  Adoption leave and pay will reflect entitlements available to birth parents from April 2015 – no qualifying period for leave; enhanced pay to 90% of salary for the first six weeks; and time off to attend introductory appointments. Intended parents in surrogacy and 'foster to adopt' arrangements will also qualify for adoption leave and pay (**www.gov.uk/government/news/landmark-children-and-families-act-2014-gains-royal-assent**)

For more information on the regulations the Gov.UK website at **www.gov.uk/parental-leave/eligibility** gives detailed information as to eligibility.

- Time off for public duties – employees who hold certain public positions are entitled to reasonable time off – which is paid – to perform the duties associated with them. For example, someone who is a member of: a local authority, a statutory tribunal, a police authority, a board of prison visitors or a prison visiting committee, a relevant health body, a relevant education body, or the Environment Agency or the Scottish Environment Protection Agency.
- An employee who is an official of an independent trade union must be allowed reasonable time off with pay to carry out those duties.
- Employees with more than two years' continuous service who have been given notice of redundancy are allowed paid time off to seek alternative employment and to arrange training.
- An employee is entitled to be permitted by their employer (ERA96 section 57a) to take a reasonable amount of time off during the employee's working hours to take action that is necessary:

  ○ to provide assistance on an occasion when a dependant falls ill, gives birth or is injured or assaulted
  ○ to make arrangements for the provision of care for a dependant who is ill or injured
  ○ in consequence of the death of a dependant (note: the term 'dependant' is clearly defined in the ERA96)
  ○ because of the unexpected disruption or termination of arrangements for the care of a dependant
  ○ to deal with an incident that involves a child of the employee and that occurs unexpectedly in a period during which an educational establishment that the child attends is responsible for them.

16.4.5 TERMINATION OF EMPLOYMENT

This refers to the amount of notice of termination given by both the employer and the employee.

KEY CONCEPT: TERMINATION OF CONTRACT BY THE EMPLOYER

Once again it is the Employment Rights Act 1996 (s86) which specifies the minimum requirement for notice:

1 'The notice required to be given by an *employer* to terminate the contract of employment of a person who has been continuously employed for one month or more –

(a) is not less than one week's notice if his period of continuous employment is less than two years,

(b) is not less than one week's notice for each year of continuous employment if his period of continuous employment is two years or more but less than twelve years, and

(c) is not less than twelve weeks' notice if his period of continuous employment is twelve years or more.

2 The notice required to be given by an *employee* who has been continuously employed for one month or more to terminate his contract of employment is not less than one week.

3 ...but this section does not prevent either party from waiving his right to notice on any occasion or from accepting a payment in lieu of notice.'

Termination of employment, as a subject, is discussed in detail in Chapter 17, 'Ending the Employment Relationship'.

16.5 FAMILY-FRIENDLY RIGHTS

16.5.1 MATERNITY RIGHTS

It is the ERA96 that gives the right for maternity or adoption leave, but subsequent legislation – in particular the Work and Families Act 2006 and the Children and Families Act 2014 – extended further the rights of employees in relation to maternity and adoption leave and pay, flexible working and paternity leave and pay.

In terms of antenatal care the right is for pregnant employees to be granted reasonable time off work to attend medical appointments connected with a pregnancy, without loss of pay. Section 55 of the ERA96 states: 'An employee who is permitted to take time off under section 55 is entitled to be paid remuneration by her employer for the period of absence at the appropriate hourly rate.' The Children and Families Act 2014 enables: 'from 1 October 2014, prospective fathers or a mother's partner can take time off to attend up to 2 antenatal appointments.'

All pregnant employees are entitled to a period of 26 weeks' Ordinary Maternity Leave (OML) regardless of length of service. Women are now entitled, irrespective of length of service, to an additional 26-week leave, termed Additional Maternity Leave (AML), giving her 52 weeks in total. The changes in terms of the removal of the qualifying period for AML were introduced as a result of the Work and Families Act 2006 (WFA).

The Children and Families Act 2014 has brought in the following changes which impact upon how parents can take and share leave, either after the mother has given birth or the parents have adopted a child. The changes have been detailed previously (see 'Rights to Time Off'), but the essential information is repeated here:

● From April 2015, during the first year, mothers, fathers and adopters can opt to share parental leave around their child's birth or placement.

● Provision is made, from October 2014, for prospective fathers and mothers to attend two antenatal appointments or if adopting, up two introductory appointments.

- Adoption leave and pay will reflect entitlements available to birth parents from April 2015 – no qualifying period for leave; enhanced pay to 90% of salary for the first six weeks.

All women who qualify for maternity leave must take two weeks' Compulsory Maternity Leave (CML) for the two weeks after giving birth or four weeks if a factory worker.

An employee qualifies for Ordinary Maternity Leave if she notifies her employer at least 15 weeks before the baby is due and provides proof that she is pregnant and to provide proof of pregnancy 21 days before the date on which she intends her Ordinary Maternity Leave to qualify for the statutory maternity pay. The specific requirements are to provide the following information:

- that she is pregnant
- the expected week of childbirth – she must also provide a medical certificate that confirms this if the employer requests it
- the date she intends to start her Ordinary Maternity Leave.

(**www.gov.uk/employers-maternity-pay-leave/entitlement**)

A woman cannot return to work within the first two weeks after her child has been born. If the employer allows this to happen it would be considered a criminal offence.

During the 26 weeks' leave a woman is entitled to benefit from all of her normal terms and conditions of employment except for pay; this is termed Ordinary Maternity Leave (OML). She should continue to receive benefits such as holiday entitlement and car allowance and, if receiving contractual maternity pay or statutory maternity pay (SMP), pension contributions. At the end of it she has the right to return to her original job. If the job no longer exists, the employer must offer her a suitable alternative, but if this is not possible, she may be entitled to redundancy pay.

ACTIVITY 16.6

Use your web browser to access the Children and Families Act 2014, available from **www. legislation.gov.uk/ukpga/2014/6/section/ 117/enacted** The Act was introduced: to make provision for statutory rights to leave and pay in connection with the birth or adoption of children; to amend s80F of the Employment Rights Act 1996; and to make provision for workers' entitlement to annual leave.

Access the Act using the web address given above and see what it has to say about:

- sharing of parental leave and the statutory rights to leave and pay (Part 7).
- the right to request a 'contract variation' flexible working (Part 9).

16.5.2 RIGHTS UNDER THE WORKING TIME REGULATIONS 1998

Regulations to implement the European Working Time Directive came into force in October 1998. The regulations apply to all workers, including most agency and freelance workers. The regulations place limits on working hours and provide certain entitlements such as rest breaks and annual leave. The Working Time Regulations are available at **www.legislation.gov.uk/uksi/1998/1833/contents/made**

The Working Time Regulations specify a range of rights, in terms of length of the working week, hours of work and regulated minimum breaks to which each and every employee is entitled. For example, the maximum working week, aggregated over seven days, is limited to 48 hours.

The daily rest that employees are entitled to enjoy is not less than 11 consecutive hours in each 24-hour period during which they work for their employer. Currently, as a result of the Working Time (Amendment) Regulations 2007, there is an entitlement to, since 1 April 2009, 5.6 weeks' annual leave (28 days), which can include the nationally nominated bank holidays (8 days). Where a worker's working time is more than six hours, they are entitled to a rest break of not less than 20 minutes.

There are usually special requirements for young workers, and the Working Time Regulations entitle young people to take a 30-minute rest away from their workstation after 4.5 hours' work.

Clearly, as well as having impact under the heading of 'family-friendly regulations', the Working Time Regulations have an impact in the field of health and safety because they restrict practices that encourage employees to overwork, become tired and so more likely to make mistakes and have accidents.

ACTIVITY 16.7

Access the Working Time Regulations 1998 at **www.legislation.gov.uk/uksi/1998/1833/contents/madehtm**

● Identify how the Government 'specifies' a young person. You will find the definition in Part 1 General, Section 2 (Interpretation) of the Statutory Instrument.

● Why do you think the authorities go to so much effort to be specific about definitions? You will also find some useful information about the Working Time Regulations at **www.hse.gov.uk/contact/faqs/workingtimedirective.htm**

16.5.3 RIGHTS TO FLEXIBLE WORKING

Since April 2003, the right to request flexible working has been available to qualifying employees who care for a child or children under the age of six (this has since been extended – see below), or in the case of a disabled child, under 18. However, these regulations have since been updated:

● The Children and Families Act 2014 has, from 30 June 2014, extended the right to *request* flexible working to all qualifying employees. Employers have a duty to consider all requests in a reasonable manner; however, organisations will have the flexibility to refuse requests on business grounds.

Acas (2013c) offers the following on the subject of flexible working:

There are many forms of flexible working. It can describe a place of work, for example, home-working, or a type of contract, such as a temporary contract. Other common variations include: part-time working, flexitime, job sharing and shift working. (Acas, 2013c)

PAUSE FOR THOUGHT

Consider the following:

Many employers argue that such measures (as the right to request flexible working) would add substantially to their costs and make them less competitive internationally. There is also evidence of discontent about such measures from employees who do not have families, and a fear that too much legislation, rather than helping women's employment prospects, is acting as a 'disincentive to hiring women of prime child bearing age' (Lea, cited in Torrington et al, 2008, pp.766–7).

Read what the manufacturers' organisation the EEF has to say about the proposed

changes to flexible working at: **www.eef.org. uk/releases/uk/2011/EEF-comment-on-flexible-parental-leave-and-right-to-request-flexible-working.htm**

Do you consider that the Government has gone too far with this kind of legislation and is making the UK a nanny state rather than a competitive state?

See and hear the Government's and Acas' approach to opening up the right to request flexible working to all qualifying employees with greater than 26 weeks' service at **www. acas.org.uk/index.aspx?articleid=1616**

16.6 EQUALITY LEGISLATION

The Equality Act 2010 is a critical piece of legislation. It brings together previous discrimination legislation. It establishes two key concepts:

- the concept of protected characteristics, which are: age, disability, gender reassignment, marriage and civil partnership, pregnancy and maternity, race, religion or belief, sex and sexual orientation
- the definitions of direct discrimination and indirect discrimination.

The Equality Act 2010 replaces a raft of previous anti-discrimination legislation (see the following list), thus bringing together a series of legislative instruments and Acts which have been developed over time into one concise document:

- Equal Pay Act 1970
- Sex Discrimination Act 1975
- Race Relations Act 1976
- Sex Discrimination Act 1986
- Disability Discrimination Act 1995
- Equality Act 2006 – not all sections
- Employment Equality (Religion or Belief) Regulations 2003 (SI 2003/1660)
- Employment Equality (Sexual Orientation) Regulations 2003 (SI 2003/1661)
- Disability Discrimination Act 1995 (Pensions) Regulations 2003 (SI 2003/2770)
- Employment Equality (Age) Regulations 2006 (SI 2006/1031)
- Equality Act (Sexual Orientation) Regulations 2007 (SI 2007/1263)
- Sex Discrimination (Amendment of Legislation) Regulations 2008 (SI 2008/963).

The Act is wide ranging and covers more than employment legislation, for example it makes it unlawful to discriminate against a person when providing a service (which includes the provision of goods or facilities) or when exercising a public function. In terms of employment legislation, sections 23–27 of the Act make it unlawful to discriminate against, harass or victimise a person at work or in employment services. The Act also contains provisions relating to equal pay between men and women; pregnancy and maternity pay;

provisions making it unlawful for an employment contract to prevent an employee disclosing their pay; and a power to require private sector employers to publish gender pay gap (the size of the difference between men and women's pay expressed as a percentage) information about differences in pay between men and women. It also contains provisions restricting the circumstances in which potential employees can be asked questions about disability or health. Refer also to: Chapter 15, 'Diversity and Equality'.

(Equality Act 2010, Part 2 and Part 5 including Schedules 6, 7, 8 and 9. Note: Content is available under the Open Government Licence v2.0.)

All organisations have to bear in mind the provisions of the legislation on pay, for example the National Minimum Wage and discrimination laws. When developing and administering a payment scheme, therefore, an organisation has to conform to the minimum standards, which include the provisions specified in the following Acts:

- Equal pay as defined in the Equality Act 2010
- Employment Rights Act 1996
- National Minimum Wage Act 1998.

CASE EXAMPLE 16.3

Use the Internet to explore the equal pay for equal value at work for female Birmingham City Council workers. You will be able to see and hear how a group of 174 former council workers, all female, won a Court of Appeal decision on equal pay claims.

- BBC News (Birmingham and Black Country): **www.bbc.co.uk/news/uk-england-birmingham-15935274**
- Video link: **www.youtube.com/watch?v=z1n5floKiOQ**

16.6.1 PART-TIME WORKERS AND EQUAL RIGHTS

In 2000, another milestone in terms of pay equality entered the statute books when the Part-time Workers (Prevention of Less Favourable Treatment) Regulations 2000 (SI 1551) came into force. These regulations give rights to part-time workers to receive equal treatment in respect of their contract of employment when compared with full-time workers. Subsequent regulations (2002, SI 2035), amending the 2000 regulations, establish that it does not make a difference as to whether the part-time worker is on a fixed-term contract or one of enduring length. In practice this means that part-time workers' pay should be pro rata for hours worked when compared with full-time workers and that they should be entitled, for example, to join a company pension scheme if full-time workers enjoy these benefits.

PAUSE FOR THOUGHT

Think of the contract of employment that you are employed under. What benefits, other than pro rata pay, would part-time workers who work for your organisation be eligible to enjoy?

16.6.2 MONITORING AND COUNTERING DISCRIMINATION

The Equality Act 2006 set up the Equality and Human Rights Commission (EHRC). The Commission became effective from October 2007. The Equality Act 2010 also repealed parts of the 2006 Act. Prior to this time the policing of discrimination was handled by a number of commissions, each dealing with their own specific area of discrimination, for example: the Commission for Racial Equality (CRE), the Disability Rights Commission (DRC) and the Equal Opportunities Commission (EOC).

The Equality and Human Rights Commission (EHRC) monitors human rights, protecting equality across nine grounds – age, disability, gender, race, religion and belief, pregnancy and maternity, marriage and civil partnership, sexual orientation and gender reassignment. The EHRC is an executive non-departmental public body of the Department for Culture, Media & Sport. (**www.gov.uk/government/ organisations/equality-and-human-rights-commission**)

PAUSE FOR THOUGHT

Take time out to read how employers proactively tackle the issue of gender discrimination in the workplace in the 'Stonewall Top 100 Employers 2013' at **www.stonewall.org.uk/documents/ final_wei_2013_booklet.pdf**

16.7 EMPLOYMENT AND PAY

16.7.1 EMPLOYMENT RIGHTS ACT 1996 (ERA96)

As mentioned previously, this legislation consolidates employees' statutory rights into a single Act of Parliament. It affects employees' pay in that it prescribes (lays down rules about) unwarranted deductions from pay unless such deductions are made in particular circumstances. The Act therefore legitimises deductions if any of the following circumstances apply:

- when deductions are authorised by law, such as income tax, National Insurance contributions or court orders, such as for payment of maintenance to an ex-spouse
- when there is a statement in the employee's written contract which specifies that certain deductions may be made from wages and when the employee has already given written consent, for example when agreed deductions are made as a result of poor performance or rule-breaking, such as unacceptable attendance times
- accidental overpayment of wages, or of expenses, even though this is likely to be the fault of the employer
- when the employee has been absent because they are taking industrial action
- in retail companies, to make good any cash deficiency in a till or a shortfall in the stock (though certain conditions apply, for example not exceeding 10% of the gross wages on any pay day).

16.7.2 NATIONAL MINIMUM WAGE ACT (NMWA) 1998

Workers are entitled to be paid at least the level of the statutory National Minimum Wage (NMW) for every hour they work for an employer. 'Workers' are entitled to be paid the NMW provided they have reached school-leaving age and work, or ordinarily work, in the

United Kingdom. Employers are required to keep records of all those to whom they pay the NMW and employees on the NMW have the right to view these records.

The National Minimum Wage Act is available at **www.legislation.gov.uk/ukpga/1998/39/contents**

The National Minimum Wage is not static and tends to be reviewed on an annual basis, in October, by the Low Pay Commission. Should an organisation fail to pay the NMW, in the most serious cases of non-compliance, they will be tried in a crown court, which will have the power to impose, effectively, an unlimited penalty.

ACTIVITY 16.8

To understand how the Government tackles in a strategic manner the National Minimum Wage and influences the thinking of the Low Pay Commission, it is worth reading the 'Final Government Evidence for the Low Pay Commission's 2014 Report'. Specifically the small section on agency workers and the use of zero-hours contracts is worth considering when trying to understand how the Government investigates the use, impact and possible abuses of atypical working practices on employees.

The report, which is published on behalf of the Department for Business, Innovation and Skills, is available at **www.gov.uk/government/uploads/system/uploads/attachment_data/file/273665/bis-14–533-national-minimum-wage-government-evidence-for-the-low-pay-commission-2014.pdf**

ACTIVITY 16.9

Access the Low Pay Commission website at **www.lowpay.gov.uk** and determine the following National Minimum Wage rates:

- adult rate (aged 22+)
- development rate (ages 18–21)
- 16–17-year-old rates.

You can also find out information about the NMW by accessing the Gov.UK website at **www.gov.uk/browse/working/tax-minimum-wage**

- If an employee agrees to accept a wage that is less than the NMW, is the person's employer breaking the law if the employer pays less than the NMW? (Hint: you will find information about this question by accessing the Gov.UK website.)
- Is a foreign worker from outside the UK, but someone *legally* working in the UK, entitled to the NMW?
- Which groups of workers are exempt from the NMW?

16.8 GRIEVANCE PROCEDURES

Although how grievances are handled is not defined within legislation, it is legislation that transfers responsibility for developing disciplinary and grievance codes of practice to Acas. The code for handling discipline and grievance issues is issued under section 199 of the Trade Union and Labour Relations (Consolidation) Act 1992.

Grievances are concerns, problems or complaints that employees raise with their employers (Acas, 2014d, p.40).

The grievance process is based, as specified by the Employment Act 2008, on the Acas code of practice that came into force on 6 April 2009 but has since been updated (March 2014) (Acas, 2014d).

The type of concern or issues that may give rise to an employee raising a grievance are as follows:

- terms and conditions of employment
- health and safety
- work relations
- bullying and harassment
- new working practices
- working environment
- organisational change
- discrimination.

(Acas, 2014d, p.41)

The formal grievance procedure provides a channel through which employees can have their grievances heard by managers. Most grievances take the form of dissatisfactions and complaints. The procedure has a structure that comprises, in effect, a number of stages, so that if an aggrieved employee does not obtain satisfaction at one stage, the process can move on to the next. In the event of repeated dissatisfaction, or if the issue is beyond the manager's control or authority, the grievance is heard at successively higher levels, ranging from the supervisor to a board member, such as the managing director or HR director. Each stage takes the form of an interview between the manager and the employee, who may be accompanied by a trade union representative or colleague.

Note: from 'Structure of a grievance procedure' as discussed in the following section, it is clear that the HR department does not get involved at the initial stage. Experience shows that most grievances are resolved at supervisory or line manager level. Speed and fairness to all concerned are said to be the most essential ingredients of a good procedure. At any time during the process the issue may be resolved by introducing a third party who can mediate in the situation and help the two sides involved reach a conclusion. The mediator's job is not to find the solution but to help facilitate the two groups to reach a workable resolution to the problem.

If, at the close of the final stage, the matter still remains unresolved, a solution is sought through the organisation's disputes procedure, in which conciliation and arbitrative approaches are used. If the relevant trade union representatives feel strongly enough about the issue, they may take a vote for industrial action, although this is normally delayed until all possible avenues have been exhausted.

Personnel Today offer a ten-step guide for conducting a grievance hearing: **www. personneltoday.com/hr/a-10-step-guide-to-preparing-for-and-conducting-grievance-hearings/**

16.8.1 STRUCTURE OF A GRIEVANCE PROCEDURE

Preamble: This is an informal stage in which the employee airs the grievance to their immediate manager/supervisor and an attempt is made to resolve the issue informally.

Initial stage: This takes place if the issue was not resolved at the preamble and usually involves a more senior manager. The grievance, at this stage, must be made in writing. The employee states the grievance and an attempt is made to resolve it. At this more formal stage there is a right to be accompanied.

Mediation: This can be introduced at any stage.

KEY CONCEPT: GRIEVANCE HEARING

For the purpose of this chapter a grievance hearing is a meeting at which an employer deals with a complaint about a duty owed by them to a worker, whether the duty arises from statute or common law, for example contractual commitments (Employment Relations Act 1999, section 13). However, good practice suggests that the employee should be allowed to be accompanied at the hearing by a colleague or a suitably qualified union representative. The employee must make a 'reasonable request' to exercise this right. The companion may put the worker's case, sum up the case, respond on the worker's behalf to any view expressed at the hearing and to confer with the worker during the meeting (Acas, 2014d, p.49).

ACTIVITY 16.10

Access the Acas *Guide on Disciplinary Grievances at Work* at **www.acas.org.uk/index.aspx?articleid=2179** and determine who can accompany an employee who has raised a grievance or who is involved in a disciplinary hearing.

You will find that one of the possible candidates to be a 'companion' at a hearing is: 'a workplace trade union representative'. However, the guide suggests that, in particular, this person should have had formal training on the process and has some form of authentication to confirm that the training has been followed. Why do you think such a requirement is placed specifically on a companion who is also a workplace trade union representative?

The Acas Guide (2014d, p.50) suggests that once the grievance has been heard, the meeting should be adjourned to allow reflection before a judgement is made. The decision should be communicated in writing.

The appeal: This takes place if the issue was not resolved at the previous stage and involves a more senior line manager and perhaps the HR manager. The grievance receives a full hearing and an attempt is made to resolve it.

A final appeal: In normal circumstances the grievance is resolved at this stage but there may be a final appeals process in a large organisation, for example. If the employee is allowed a second appeal, the grievance remaining unresolved, a meeting is held involving the employee, a senior director and, where appropriate, an area/regional union officer.

Few grievances reach the *final appeal* stage. Most are resolved at 'stage 1' and many at 'stage 2'. In extreme circumstances, however, special panels may be set up, including the involvement of experienced external conciliators or arbitrators, where appropriate, in attempts to resolve serious or complex grievances.

16.8.2 THE INITIAL GRIEVANCE INTERVIEW

Individuals may feel aggrieved for a variety of reasons. Grievances vary in their complexity and so, therefore, do the interviews. The initial interview has two purposes: first, for the employee to state the grievance, and second, for the manager to analyse what is being said, identify the cause and, where possible, eliminate or in some way resolve the issue.

16.8.3 PREPARING FOR THE INTERVIEW

Employees are usually well prepared for such events and the manager should also prepare. The person raising the grievance must state their grievance in writing; this helps to clarify what the real reason is behind the grievance. Before the interview, the manager should obtain an understanding of the problem which lies at the root of the grievance. In a small organisation, the employee is probably well known to the manager and, indeed, may be known to be an inveterate *{meaning – long established}* griper. In large organisations, however, where it is not possible to get to know everyone personally, it is a good idea to check such matters with associates and take a look at the employee's record. In all cases it is important that managers involved should maintain an open mind.

Making enquiries will provide the manager with several perceptions of the individual and of the circumstances, so that when the employee's version of the grievance is expressed at the interview, the manager can put the complaint into some kind of context, taking care not to jump to conclusions and taking care to base decisions on fact.

16.8.4 CONDUCTING THE INTERVIEW

At the interview, the manager should listen attentively and allow the person to speak freely. There is no better way of getting the employee's perception of the situation. After the manager has heard the grievance and established mutual agreement with the employee over its nature, both parties can adopt a joint problem-solving approach in which the employee is encouraged to suggest solutions to the problem. Some suggestions may be impracticable, or outside the limitations of the organisation's policies, but the manager can offer the employee guidance about the possibilities. It may be that the meeting is adjourned for the manager to investigate matters by speaking to relevant people. If agreement is reached over the solution to the problem, it is important for the manager to follow this up and ensure that any agreed action is taken.

Those who draft procedures try to write them in language that makes them watertight, so that the possibility of misinterpretation is reduced to a bare minimum. On the other hand, every case is different, and where a grievance has been shown to be justified, it is often possible for the manager to apply discretion to be fair to the employee and any others who may be involved.

16.9 WORKPLACE DISCIPLINARY RULES

Standards of behaviour in organisations are regulated by systems of rules, codes of practice and procedures. The rules classify and define offences of which the organisation disapproves. While they vary from one kind of organisation to another, they may, for example, refer to:

- **General conduct**, such as violence, threatening/abusive behaviour and fooling around, such as horseplay.
- **Punctuality**, including arriving at and leaving the workplace at the agreed working times, being on time for meetings.
- **Personal appearance** - this is particularly important where the employee is in a customer-facing role; however, most organisations have minimum standards of dress code. The standards, of course, should be clearly communicated to employees in their induction and be written down in the employee handbook. A common-sense approach is taken where staff wish to wear and display religious symbols.
  Usually a compromise can be reached where the symbol to be worn is discreet and, unless there is conflict with health and safety requirements. For example, the wearing of earrings would not be allowed in a food processing plant because of the risk that a piece of the metal fastening may fall into a batch of the food which is undergoing processing.
- **Absenteeism**, including regular attendance – this refers not only to arriving and being in the workplace, but also to the employee's actual workstation.

- **Health and safety** - this covers use of safety equipment on every occasion that the task demands and handling the equipment in a responsible manner so that no one is placed at risk.
- **Drug and alcohol abuse** - being on the premises while under the influence of drugs and/or alcohol.
- **Stealing**, including the removal of any of the company's property from the place it normally occupies, unless written permission has been given.
- **Bringing the organisation into disrepute** - this includes behaviour within and outside the organisation that throws a negative light on the reputation of the employer.
- **Discriminatory behaviour** - this includes behaviour that indicates dislike or hatred of members of the opposite sex or people of a particular colour or ethnic background.
- **Use and abuse of social media platforms** – this includes improper use of an organisation's information technology systems, making defamatory comments about the organisation on social media, using social media to bully co-workers or publish sensitive information about the organisation.

Offences may be classified and action taken according to their seriousness, as follows:

- **minor offence**, such as arriving slightly late for work on several occasions, for which the employee may receive a reprimand or an oral warning
- **serious offence**, such as neglecting or misusing health and safety equipment, for which the employee may be given a written warning
- **gross misconduct**, such as violence, stealing, serious defamation of the company's name or brand, flagrant disregard of health and safety rules and procedures, deliberate and knowing misuse or abuse of safety equipment, for which the penalty is usually dismissal without compensation.

The aim of the above section is to provide examples of disciplinary rules, show how they are classified and the typical actions that are taken when the disciplinary procedure is invoked.

16.10 DISCIPLINARY PROCEDURES

Disciplinary procedures are usually compiled by the HR department, approved by the senior managers and agreed with the trade unions, in workplaces where a union is recognised. The organisation should have a separate procedure for dealing with matters of capability, which includes poor performance and cases of ill-health. The Advisory, Conciliation and Arbitration Service (Acas) updated its code of practice in March 2014 (Acas, 2014d). The updated code, entitled *Discipline and Grievances at Work: The Acas Guide*, is a set of guidelines on the content and process of these procedures.

16.10.1 WHAT THE DISCIPLINARY PROCEDURE SHOULD SET OUT TO ACHIEVE

The Acas code outlines the structure and content of a disciplinary procedure as follows, saying that it should:

- be in writing
- specify to whom it applies
- be non-discriminatory
- provide for matters to be dealt with without undue delay
- provide for proceedings, witness statements and records to be kept confidential
- indicate the disciplinary actions that may be taken
- specify the levels of management that have the authority to take the various forms of disciplinary action
- provide for workers to be informed, in writing, of the complaints against them and, where possible, all relevant evidence before any hearing, including witness statements

- provide workers with an opportunity to state their case before decisions are reached
- provide workers with the right to be accompanied
- ensure that, except for gross misconduct, no worker is dismissed for a first breach of discipline
- ensure that disciplinary action is not taken until the case has been carefully investigated
- ensure that workers are given an explanation for any penalty imposed
- provide a right of appeal – normally to a more senior manager – and specify the procedure to be followed.

16.10.2 USEFUL LETTERS TO USE DURING A DISCIPLINARY PROCESS

Acas offers guidance in terms of the documentation which could be used when inviting employees to attend a disciplinary hearing or advising them of the result of the disciplinary investigation. They are available at **www.acas.org.uk/media/pdf/l/c/ Discipline-and-grievances-Acas-guide.pdf**

16.10.3 HANDLING THE DISCIPLINARY PROCEDURE

The aims of a disciplinary procedure are to guide the handling of the disciplinary process fairly and speedily. Because of its ultimate implications, a disciplinary procedure has to be seen to be fair to all who are involved. Fairness and justice should prevail and the approach, rules and practice surrounding the procedure should reflect this.

The Act of Parliament that provides for the individual rights of employees is the Employment Rights Act 1996 (ERA96). Employees will need to qualify (as an employee) before they can make a complaint to an employment tribunal. The law states that the employee must have at least one year's continuous service, for employees in employment before 6 April 2012, and two years for employees starting employment on or after 6 April 2012. There is no length of service requirement in relation to 'automatically unfair dismissal grounds'.

Disciplinary procedures generally have been formulated with the law on unfair dismissal in mind. The structure that will be familiar to most practitioners provides for repeated offences and has a number of stages. The next section outlines a suggested structure for use when conducting a disciplinary process. Good practice would be to involve employees – in a unionised environment involve the union representative – in developing the company's procedure.

16.10.4 APPEALING TO AN EMPLOYMENT TRIBUNAL

Acas says the following about making an appeal to an employment tribunal:

> The Employment Tribunals are an independent judicial body established to resolve disputes between employers and employees over employment rights. . . .

> Employment Tribunals are less formal than a court, for example no one wears a wig or gown. However, like a court, tribunals cannot give out legal advice, almost all hearings are open to the public, and evidence will be given under oath or affirmation. . . .

> Before lodging an Employment Tribunal claim, Acas must be notified first and this can be done through Early Conciliation. An independent, impartial Acas Conciliator will then attempt to help both parties to resolve their differences . . . (**www.acas.org.uk/index.aspx?articleid=1889**)

16.10.5 STRUCTURE OF A DISCIPLINARY PROCEDURE

1   An employee may be given an informal warning for committing a minor offence. The warning may be delivered orally or in writing; usually it is given orally. However it is given, it must advise the employee of the nature of the offence they have committed and of the possible consequences of repeating the offence. What Acas says about the informal process is as follows:

> If informal action does not bring about an improvement, or the misconduct or unsatisfactory performance is considered too serious to be classed as minor, employers should provide employees with a clear signal of their dissatisfaction by taking formal action. (Acas, 2014d, p.10)

2   If the employee continues with their misconduct or poor performance or commits a more serious offence, the process must become more formal. The individual should be advised, *in writing*, of the nature of the problem and the facts surrounding the issue should be thoroughly investigated without delay.

- The individual should then be called to a meeting, where they can be supported by a colleague or a qualified union representative. The request to attend the meeting should be in writing, stating why the meeting has been called. Employers should include copies of any written evidence and inform the employee of their right to be accompanied at the hearing. What is said at the meeting should either be recorded by a 'note-taker', someone not involved in the disciplinary process, or electronically recorded and transcribed. All parties should have access to a copy of the 'minutes of the meeting'.
- The manager conducting the process should listen to the employee's side of the argument and be prepared to call on any witnesses that the employee has indicated they may wish to use to present evidence in support of their case. If the employee is found to have committed the misdemeanour, they can be issued with a warning, which should always be given in writing, stating the time, date, place and nature of the offence. Again, the possible consequences of repeating the misdemeanour should be pointed out and, in particular circumstances, the employee may be referred for counselling. Of course, the employee has a right to appeal the result of the disciplinary findings.
- The sanction, for example a written warning, may also be supplemented with counselling or perhaps training, all with a view of trying to help prevent further occurrences of the problem.
- If an employee does not attend a disciplinary meeting after being called a number of times – without good cause – the employer can make a decision in their absence on the evidence available to them.

3   Further poor conduct, within the period of the initial warnings, could put the employee in danger of receiving a severe penalty and this should be made very clear by the individual's manager. But once again, should the individual digress into further unacceptable behaviours, while a warning is still active, the process should be repeated as previously detailed, with an investigation, a hearing – where the accused may, if they wish, be accompanied – and, if the case is proven, appeal against the decision.

- The removal of privileges, suspension or even dismissal could result from a repeated offence after a final written warning.

4   *If again the individual repeats the offence or commits a more serious misdemeanour,* the form of hearing would probably be by a panel of senior managers, including the HR manager or director, but only after the case has been thoroughly investigated; *process* in these types of situation is very important. After the hearing, decisions are

made about the culpability of the employee and, where appropriate, the penalty to be applied. Most often at this stage the penalty is dismissal.

If the cause of a problem is very serious and could be classed as gross misconduct, it is possible that the process would start at the final stage, where dismissal is a distinct possibility. One could imagine that this could be as a result of flouting safety regulations, for example smoking in a restricted area while working in a petroleum refinery or, perhaps, vandalising company property.

ACTIVITY 16.11

1   How long would a:

- first written warning remain on an employee's record?
- final written warning remain on an employee's record?

2   Subject to provisions in the contract of employment, what sanctions, other than dismissal, can an employer use if a disciplinary case against an employee is proven?

You will find some guidance on answering these questions by looking at Acas (2014d).

16.10.6 RECORD-KEEPING

The foreword to the code of practice (Acas, 2014d) advises employers to keep a written record of any disciplinary or grievance cases they deal with.

Records should include:

- the complaint against the employee
- the employee's defence
- findings made and actions taken
- the reason for actions taken
- whether an appeal was lodged
- the outcome of the appeal
- any grievances raised during the disciplinary procedure
- subsequent developments
- notes of any formal meetings.

 MISUSE OF COMPANY PROPERTY

CASE EXAMPLE 16.4

One man and his van

Satvinder is 28 and is a carpenter, working for AtHomeService (AHS), a service company which provides electrical, plumbing and general home repair services to the general public. His role allows him, effectively, to work from home, where he keeps the company van. He is competent in his work. He always calls in on time when he starts work and there have never been any customer complaints.

However, the office administrator has noticed that the fuel and mileage log of the van while it has been allocated to 'Sat' shows double the mileage and fuel consumption when compared with other vehicles used by the company's technical staff doing a similar job.

There have been rumours, but no concrete information, that some staff have been using company vehicles on non-company business. However, a letter had been received from a member of the public noting that the writer had heard that AHS would hire out their vans, with a driver, to move small items of furniture locally. The female writer had seen the AHS van doing a delivery to her next-door neighbour. She understood that the rates were very competitive and wanted to know how she could book a van to take some old furniture to the local waste and recycling centre. Satvinder only lived around the corner from the letter's author.

What issues does this case example raise? As Satvinder's line manager, how would you handle the problem?

16.10.7 THE STRUCTURE OF THE DISCIPLINARY MEETING

The Acas guide (2014d, p.20) offers the following advice when conducting disciplinary meetings and points out that the meetings may not proceed in neat, orderly stages, but it is good practice to:

- introduce those present to the employee and explain why they are there
- introduce and explain the role of the accompanying person if present
- explain that the purpose of the meeting is to consider whether disciplinary action should be taken in accordance with the organisation's disciplinary procedure
- explain how the meeting will be conducted.

It is important that the meetings are seen to be transparent, to all interested parties, in terms of process and documentation. It is usually advisable to keep matters formal and ensure that due process is followed, ensuring that the employee has the opportunity to clarify points, discuss issues with the person accompanying them and that the process is conducted in a logical and transparent manner, with care that a factual record of events is made.

16.10.8 HR'S ROLE IN THE DISCIPLINE PROCESS

The role of the HR practitioner in disciplinary matters varies from one organisation to another, but usually it is to ensure that corporate policy and procedures are followed and that employment legislation is strictly adhered to. In cases where a dismissal looks possible, the matter should be referred to a senior manager to gain approval for the proposed action. Normally managers and supervisors have some authority in disciplinary matters, but in the absence of a senior manager, it is recommended that HR practitioners do not dismiss the person, even in cases of gross misconduct. The procedure should allow for an employee to be accompanied by a trade union representative or colleague when the formal warning is issued, and the manager too is advised to issue them in the presence of another manager or an appropriate HR specialist.

It is important that a thorough inquiry is carried out at every stage of the procedure, and all of the facts are collected, witnesses interviewed and the evidence recorded, along with details of what happened, as explained in 'Record-keeping' above. If the dismissal of an employee results in an employment tribunal, one of the first questions from the bench is to check whether a thorough and fair investigation has been carried out.

16.10.9 INVOKING THE DISCIPLINARY PROCEDURE

Managers and supervisors should not be too quick to invoke the procedure. Often, a manager under pressure making a superficial assessment of the situation does not get the whole story. For example, being late for work is an offence in most organisations, but if an employee who has a good record for punctuality suddenly starts arriving late, the manager should investigate the cause, rather than go straight for the rule book.

CASE EXAMPLE 16.5

COMMON SENSE IN SOLVING WORKPLACE PROBLEMS

Late again, Price!

Joe Price was a section leader in the IT department. He had been with the organisation for six years, his performance was good and he was normally reliable and punctual. Makpal Dospanbetova, the IT manager, noticed that on several days in the past two weeks Joe had been arriving late, sometimes by as much as 45 minutes, so she called him into her office to ask for an explanation.

It turned out that Joe's wife had left him. He now had his two children to look after, which included getting them ready in the mornings and taking them to school. His mother sometimes did this for him, but she was unable to do it every day and those were the days on which he was late. After school, a reliable neighbour picked up the children and looked after them until Joe got home.

Makpal's solution was to alter Joe's hours so that he started and finished work an hour later and that solved the problem. It was to be a temporary solution until Joe got himself sorted out. The idea of taking disciplinary action did not occur to Makpal.

Except in cases where flagrant breaches of the rules occur, disciplinary processes should begin with a *preamble*, in which the manager and the employee get together to discuss the reasons why a rule has been broken. This gives the manager an opportunity to discover any problems, assess the employee's attitude towards their behaviour and to decide what action might be taken.

Good workers are hard to find, and if a manager can counsel an employee, or guide them towards the solution to, say, a personal problem, a good worker can be turned into an even better, more loyal and motivated worker. The manager's first step, therefore, should be to ask for an explanation.

16.10.10 CONFLICT MANAGEMENT IN THE WORKPLACE

Conflict in the workplace has its place. It can be good if it is focused on business issues where people air their views and argue their positions on issues with a view to improving the status quo, business processes, helping to define strategies, and so on. However, conflict can – if it's through poor or weak management, inappropriate working cultures, fractious relationships – suck the life blood away from an organisation. Conflict diverts energy away from the core organisational tasks and instead is expended seeking to redress grievances. Table 16.1 shows the types of mechanism which have been used to manage conflict in the workplace according to the CIPD (2011b.)

Table 16.1 Use of different methods of dealing with workplace conflict over two years (2009–2011)

	Increased %	Decreased %	Stayed the same %
Disciplinary action	49.5	8.6	41.9
Grievance procedures	47.7	1.3	42.1
Internal or external mediation	49.4	3.5	47.1
Independent arbitration	10.3	6.6	83.1
Early neutral evaluation	7.5	8.3	81.2
Training line managers to handle difficult conversations	61.5	6.9	31.6
Troubleshooting by HR department	65.3	7.3	27.5

CIPD (2011b, p.2) *Conflict Management: Survey Report*, March 2011. Reproduced with kind permission of the CIPD.

From the same report the CIPD report the following:

> The survey findings confirm that the scale of workplace conflict is remarkable and has increased in the recession. Table [16.1] shows significant increases in most forms of managing conflict, internal and external.
>
> Of those who used each method, almost half say their organisation has increased its use of disciplinary action (49.5%), grievance procedures (47.7%) and mediation (49.4%) in the last two years. The high proportion of respondents saying that their organisation makes more use of mediation is encouraging, but is overshadowed by the proportion making increased use of training line managers in handling difficult conversations. (CIPD, 2011b, p.2)

16.10.11 MEDIATION

The Government sees workplace mediation as a means of reducing the use of formal and time-consuming processes to deal with conflict and grievances at work. Acas says the following about mediation:

> Mediation is where an impartial third party, the mediator, helps two or more people in dispute to attempt to reach an agreement. Any agreement comes from those in dispute, not from the mediator. The mediator is not there to judge, to say one person is right and the other wrong, or to tell those involved in the mediation what they should do. The mediator is in charge of the process of seeking to resolve the problem but not the outcome. Mediators may be employees trained and accredited by an external mediation service who act as internal mediators in addition to their day jobs. Or they may be from an external mediation provider. They can work individually or in pairs as co-mediators. Mediation distinguishes itself from other approaches to conflict resolution, such as grievance procedures and the employment tribunal process, in a number of ways.

Mediation is:

- Less formal
- Flexible
- Voluntary
- Morally binding but normally has no legal status
- Confidential
- (Generally) unaccompanied
- Owned by the parties.

(Acas/CIPD, 2013, p.8)

To find out more about mediation and the models of mediation, the following sources offer some insightful guidance:

- Acas (2008) *How Can Acas Help: Mediation explained [online]*. London: Acas. Available at: **www.acas.org.uk/media/pdf/t/g/Mediation_Explained_Dec_2008.pdf**
- Acas/CIPD (2013) *Mediation: an approach to resolving workplace issues [online]*. London: Acas and CIPD. Available at: **www.acas.org.uk/media/pdf/2/q/Mediation-an-approach-to-resolving-workplace-issues.pdf**

ACTIVITY 16.12

Disputes and grievances in the workplace can be resolved in a number of ways. Using the CIPD *Conflict Management* survey report (CIPD, 2011b), the Acas/CIPD *Mediation: An approach to resolving workplace issues* (2013) report or information from other sources, develop a response to the following questions:

1   What is a compromise agreement and in what conditions is it used?

2   Mediation is a very useful process to facilitate the resolution of workplace grievances. The mediation can be delivered by internal (to the organisation) or external personnel. Explore the advantages and disadvantages of the two approaches.

16.11 HEALTH AND SAFETY LEGISLATION

The law that applies to this is as follows:

- Health and Safety at Work Act 1974
- Reporting of Injuries, Diseases and Dangerous Occurrences Regulations 1995 (RIDDOR): require employers to notify certain occupational injuries, diseases and dangerous events
- Health and Safety (Consultation with Employees) Regulations 1996
- Employment Rights Act 1996
- Health and Safety (Consultation with Employees) Regulations 1996
- Management of Health and Safety at Work Regulations 1999 (risk assessment)
- Corporate Manslaughter and Homicide Act 2007.

The Health and Safety Executive offers a complete listing of the various Acts of Parliament and regulations which affect safe working. It is free to download at **www.hse.gov.uk/legislation/statinstruments.htm** The above listing is some of the key legislation which affects how we manage and keep people safe.

Health and safety legislation, in the form we know it today, came to life with the Health and Safety at Work Act 1974 (HASAWA). Prior to 1974 the limited health and safety legislation was focused on standards in the workplace, that is, sanitation and protecting people from hurting themselves on machinery. However, the introduction of the HASAWA heralded a move from the focus on hardware to a focus that also brought into view people and improving their behaviours.

The HASAWA gave general duties to employers to 'ensure, so far is reasonably practicable, the health and safety and welfare at work of all his employees' (HASAWA 1974, s2). The Act also made reference to maintenance of plant (equipment and machines) but only in broad terms. Key also to improving the workplace safety environment was that specific mention was made of the requirement for training and supervision of the workforce. An important requirement of the Act was to require the employer to make a written policy statement with respect to health and safety in the workplace (s3), thus recognising that all those who go to a place of work are involved in its safe operation. The Act also introduced a mandatory requirement to involve recognised workplace trade unions in the safety process with a demand that management recognise a union-nominated safety representative. The Act gave true voice, through the union, to workers in the context of health and safety. The Act, crucially (s10), set up the Health and Safety Commission and the Executive in 1974; both bodies, since 2009, have merged into the Health and Safety Executive.

ACTIVITY 16.13

Access the HASAWA at **www.legislation.gov.uk/ukpga/1974/37/contents**

What does the Act have to say about the:

- duties of employees (s7)?

- duties of others involved in the workplace (s4)?
- powers of inspectors (s20)?

The Employment Rights Act 1996 provides a sense of joined-up legislation, for example linking with HASAWA, because, for example, it protects safety representatives from unlawfully being penalised in any way for involving themselves in safety matters. Another example of this joined-up thinking would be in the case of a whistle-blower in the context of health and safety legislation. To dismiss someone because they have raised an issue that their employer would rather 'brush under the carpet' because it causes real difficulties and may be an expense for the employer would be classed, automatically, as unfair dismissal.

In the context of the Health and Safety (Consultation with Employees) Regulations 1996 (No. 1513), the employer is required to consult employees, making sure the workforce knows who their safety representatives are and advised:

- in good time about matters relating to their health and safety that might significantly affect their safety while at work
- about the introduction, including the planning, of new technologies into the workplace.

If there is not a recognised union, employees should be consulted directly or a representative should be nominated by the workforce. The regulations (s4), when discussing persons to be consulted, say the following:

> in respect of any group of employees, one or more persons in that group who were elected, by the employees in that group at the time of the election, to represent that group for the purposes of such consultation (and any such persons are in these Regulations referred to as 'representatives of employee safety'). (Health and Safety (Consultation with Employees) Regulations 1996 (No. 1513))

ACTIVITY 16.14

The TUC and health and safety

To find out what the Trades Union Congress (TUC) has to say about consulting with safety representatives, go to **www.tuc.org.uk/sites/default/files/extras/safetyrep_1b.pdf** and download the TUC *Safety Representatives Resource* at: **www.tuc.org.uk/workplace-issues/health-and-safety/safety-representatives/safety-representative-resources/safety.** (You will also find similar information about safety representatives by consulting the Unite Union website at **www.unitetheunion.org/uploaded/documents/UniteHealth&SafetyGuideNov201311-7504.pdf**)

- After reading the literature, how serious do you think the Trades Union Congress is about the appointment of a safety representative?
- How comprehensive is the literature they have produced on the above?
- Could someone take on the role without specialist training?
- What criteria could be used to determine how many safety representatives would be needed within an organisation?

The Health and Safety Executive gives further information about employee involvement in health and safety in the workplace at **www.hse.gov.uk/involvement/membership.htm**

The regulations specifically require the health and safety representatives to raise issues about health and safety of the premises and equipment, on behalf of the employees. This puts an onus on the employee representative, as well as management, to respond to such concerns (under HASAWA). The Act also gives a right to employee representatives to take time off with pay for consultation and training purposes. In essence, the whole focus of the Health and Safety Executive is on *dialogue, shared rights and responsibilities and worker involvement.*

The Management of Health and Safety at Work Regulations 1999 (risk assessment) introduce the requirement for an organisation to introduce risk assessments and employee health surveillance where risks have been identified. This could be, for example, where an organisation has to use chemicals that may be, if not contained properly, hazardous to health.

The regulations also identify special categories of people, such as employees employed under a fixed-term contract, expectant mothers and young employees, for special mention. Some of these groups, because of their ignorance of the work and required safe working practices, may be exposed to potential dangers. These categories of people should not be exposed to potentially harmful environments or complex machinery without having had appropriate training or perhaps being under close supervision – we all have to learn! In the case of temporary contract workers, they have to be informed of any special qualifications required for the work they are to be engaged to carry out. Expectant mothers are singled out as a priority case because of the obvious need to protect not only the mother but also her unborn baby. In essence, the employer needs to carry out a risk assessment; the regulations state the following:

> [if] the work is of a kind which could involve risk, by reason of her condition, to the health and safety of a new or expectant mother, or to that of her baby, from any processes or working conditions, or physical, biological or chemical agents, ... on the introduction of measures to encourage improvements in the safety and health at work of pregnant workers and workers who have recently given birth or are breastfeeding. (Management of Health and Safety at Work Regulations 1999, s16).

The Health and Safety Executive, in developing the legislation, also went further and recognised that, in many cases, two or more employers share a workplace. In these cases the employers must work together on safety matters that cross over and affect the shared premises, in terms of the various activities that occur in and around the shared area. For example, this could apply to the sharing of information about potentially harmful chemicals stored on part of the premises; it could also apply to the planning of fire drills together.

16.11.1 CORPORATE MANSLAUGHTER

The following is a narrative from Westlaw about the offence of corporate manslaughter:

> The new (sic) offence provides that an organisation will be found guilty of corporate manslaughter if: the way in which its activities are managed or organised causes a death; and this amounts to a gross breach of a relevant duty of care to the deceased; and a substantial part of the breach arose from the way activities were managed by a senior manager.
>
> The new (sic) offence is intended to complement existing health and safety legislation and as such organisations can be prosecuted for corporate manslaughter as an alternative to, or in addition to, existing health and safety offences. The Act provides for indictment to carry both corporate manslaughter and offences under the Health and Safety at Work etc. Act 1974.
>
> There is no liability for individuals (including company directors and managers) under the Act and an individual also cannot be convicted of aiding, abetting counselling or procuring the commission of the new offence (s.18). (Ponting, 2013)

The Act enables the Crown to prosecute an organisation; there is no liability for individuals (including company directors and managers) but individuals can still be liable under the common law offence of gross negligence manslaughter.

The *Telegraph* (2011) says the following about the Corporate Manslaughter Act:

> The Corporate Manslaughter and Corporate Homicide Act 2007 creates a means of accountability for deaths caused by very serious management failings. ... Prior to the act coming into force, it was possible for a corporate entity, such as a company, to be prosecuted for a wide range of criminal offences, including the common law offence of gross negligence manslaughter   The offence is concerned with corporate liability and does not apply to directors or other individuals who have a senior role in the company or organisation. (*Telegraph*, 2011)

The new law widens the scope of how not only individuals but also organisations can be brought to account for encouraging or specifying work practices which can lead to employees, customers or members of the general public being harmed. A company can be convicted if it can be proven that there was a gross breach of duty of care by 'senior management,' instead of just one individual.

Corporate manslaughter has to prove the failure of an organisation rather than an individual, and the failure must be by senior management. It carries an unlimited fine, the starting point for which is expected to be 5% of a company's turnover. Companies could also find themselves on the receiving end of a 'publicity order'.

16.12 LEGAL ASPECTS OF RECORD-KEEPING

Many managers are reluctant to allow employees access to the information about themselves that is on record. Most employees feel that they are entitled to have access to information about themselves, even if only to check that the information is correct. The Data Protection Act 1998 (DPA98) provides a legal entitlement for employees to access their own personal records and, indeed, any information about themselves.

KEY CONCEPT: RIGHT OF ACCESS TO PERSONAL INFORMATION

The Data Protection Act 1984 (DPA84) provided people with the right to examine information about them that was stored electronically. The DPA98 extends this by providing right of access regardless of how it is stored.

Data protection is a critical aspect of record-keeping and this is discussed later in this chapter.

16.12.1 CONFIDENTIALITY

Confidentiality is a two-way issue. Most people would object to their personal information being disclosed to others unless it was clear that it was needed for legitimate purposes. However, there can be little harm in communicating collective and anonymous data in statistical form to internal and external third parties who, for example, are generally looking for information, such as absence or accident rates. This type of data-gathering is normally acceptable. The really sensitive area is in passing on information from which people can be identified.

As a broad rule, therefore, the release of blocks of statistical data is normally acceptable, while the release of personal information about individual employees is not – at least not without the express permission of the employee concerned.

CASE EXAMPLE 16.6

The NHS have been planning to share patient medical data, held within primary care trusts (doctors' surgeries), with interested research groups. This is not a new idea. Patient data from hospitals has been shared with groups that wish to advance the understanding of and possibly develop cures for life-threatening diseases. Smyth (2014) in *The Times* writes that:

'Plans to share the private medical data of NHS patients have been shelved for at least six months after health chiefs conceded that they had failed to explain the scheme properly and needed to restore public confidence.

'In an embarrassing climbdown, NHS England has promised to ask doctors, patients and charities how best to explain the project, which will take information from GP records and link it with existing data from hospitals.

'Tougher scrutiny of who is given access to the information has also been promised, after accusations that it would put patient confidentiality at risk. The health service is under pressure to undertake a national TV advertising campaign and to write to every patient individually.' (Smyth, 2014)

There is concern that the 'care.data' scheme has been launched in a manner which has not effectively engaged with the general public whose data is to be shared. Government has legislated that the scheme be launched so that the public have to 'opt out' rather than 'opt in' to the release of their data. There is concern over the ability of large bodies, such as the NHS, to manage the release of confidential data.

There are always differing views on topics. Consider the following perspectives:

1   To read and watch a video of what the NHS has to say about the subject: **www.nhs.uk/NHSEngland/ thenhs/records/healthrecords/ Pages/care-data.aspx**

2   The perspective of the Patients Association, 19 February 2014, can be found at: **www.patients-association. com/Default.aspx? tabid=81&Id=1149** Quoting from the website:

Katherine Murphy, Chief Executive of the Patients Association said: 'We welcome the delay to the start of the care.data scheme. Numerous patients have contacted our Helpline to express their concerns about how safe it is to keep patient data in one place and who will have access to the records, as well as from patients who are confused about what the scheme means.'

3 Triggle (2014), the BBC's health correspondent, offers his insight at: **www.bbc.co.uk/news/health-26239532** 'The information made available on the database will be stripped of identifiable data – although it will include the gender, age band and area a patient lives in.

However, concerns have been raised about the prospect of keeping all the information in one place, with campaigners saying that it could lead to privacy problems and data breaches.'

4 Kirby and Pickover (17 February 2014), in the *Independent on Sunday*, share the concerns of some doctors to the roll-out of the new scheme, reporting that, 'Last week, the Royal College of GPs (RCGP) warned of a "crisis of public confidence" in the new care.data system.' The full article is available at **www.independent.co.uk/life-style/health-and-families/health-news/doctors-raise-fears-over-sharing-nhs-patient-records-9133807.html**

16.12.2 AUTHORISED ACCESS TO INFORMATION

With properly run computerised systems it is difficult for an unauthorised person to access information to which they are not entitled, although illegally 'hacking in' to systems, a process whereby unauthorised users gain access, is always possible. There are a variety of ways in which systems may be made secure from 'intruders'. The most frequently used of these is the 'password' system, in which authorised employees are given a personal password, which is unknown to others and which will provide them with access to the information to which they are entitled.

 KEY CONCEPT: RELEASING INFORMATION

The release of personal information without the express permission of the employee concerned is actionable in law. HR records are confidential and should be kept under very tight control. A 'safety first' maxim in this respect is: 'if in doubt, hold back.'

Legislation provides for the protection of individuals and usually relates to information rather than the keeping of records, but if the data is kept in secure systems, maintained and updated regularly, the information that results is more likely to be lawful, accurate, useful and reliable. It can be accessed speedily and presented clearly and attractively.

16.12.3 LEGISLATIVE REQUIREMENTS

In addition to the above details, legislation demands that particular records are kept. For example, under health and safety law, there is a requirement to keep records of accidents, injuries sustained by employees, the training they have received to enable them to use equipment safely, and a host of other measures. Other legislative measures that demand record-keeping include the following:

- Employment Rights Act 1996 (ERA96)
- Working Time Regulations 1998 (WTR98)
- National Minimum Wage Act 1998 (NMWA98)

- Health and Safety at Work Act 1974 (HASAWA)
- Data Protection Act 1998 (DPA98)
- Equality Act 2010.

Bearing in mind the provisions of the legislation listed above, organisations feel the need to protect themselves by keeping records that include accounts of relevant incidents and events that might lead to complaints of:

- race or sex discrimination
- unfair dismissal
- imposing unreasonable working hours on employees
- offering wages and salaries that are below the legal minimum limit
- breaching health and safety regulations
- refusing to allow justifiable access to individual records
- challenges in respect of unfair recruitment practices
- failing to provide equality data on the issue of employment contracts.

HR records contain information that may be used in evidence if an employee makes a claim that leads to an employment tribunal or other legal proceedings. Employers try to avoid such circumstances, not only because of the cost but also because the organisation's reputation as an employer and product brand may be at stake.

16.13 DATA PROTECTION

The Data Protection Act (DPA98) – which has its origins in the European Union Data Protection Directive – came into full effect in March 2000. The DPA98 replaced the DPA84 and the Access to Personal Files Act 1987. Space prevents us from going into the greater detail of the DPA98, but there are points of which the HR practitioner should be aware, especially since this is an area of the law that is having an important impact on how organisations are managed, although data protection is yet to become an issue at the management/trade union negotiating table.

Those who are familiar with the vocabulary of the DPA84 will need to understand two minor points on which the new Act differs from the old one:

1   The DPA98 changed the Data Protection Registrar's title to Data Protection Commissioner and in January 2001 the name was further changed to the Information Commissioner's Office and the 'Commissioner' was given the added responsibility of the Freedom of Information Act 2000.

2   The *registration* system under the DPA84 is replaced under the DPA98 by the *notification* system.

16.13.1 INDIVIDUAL RIGHTS

In the DPA98, the person about whom the information is held is referred to as the *data subject*. This Act defines data and refers to a *relevant filing system*.

 KEY CONCEPT: RELEVANT FILING SYSTEM

Any 'set' of information relating to individuals to the extent that the set is structured by reference to individuals or by reference to criteria relating to individuals in such a way that specific information relating to a particular individual is readily accessible.

Any information falling into the category of a relevant filing system constitutes data. The new Act also distinguishes between *personal data* and *sensitive personal data*.

KEY CONCEPT: PERSONAL DATA (DPA98, S1)

Information about a living person who can be identified from that information.

 KEY CONCEPT: PROCESSING PERSONAL DATA (DPA98, S7)

Any individual employee is entitled to:
- receive a copy of any data – including manually stored data – processed by reference to them
- know what data is being processed
- know why the data is being processed
- know who might receive the data
- be told the source of the data – except in limited circumstances
- where data is processed automatically, and is likely to form the sole basis for any decision significantly affecting the individual, the right to know the logic involved in that decision-making and not to have significant decisions based on results of automatic processing
- prevent processing likely to cause damage and distress.

 KEY CONCEPT: SENSITIVE PERSONAL DATA (DPA98, S2)

In this context, the HR practitioner is the 'guardian' of this kind of information, which the DPA98 defines as:
- racial or ethnic origin
- political opinions
- religious or similar beliefs
- membership of trade unions
- physical or mental health
- the person's sexual life
- commission or alleged commission of offences
- data relating to criminal offences, ongoing proceedings, or the decision of courts in respect of proceedings.

16.13.2 SENSITIVE DATA

There are other types of data that it is inadvisable (although not illegal) to process. For example, results of occupational or psychological tests may be misinterpreted if accessed by someone who is not an expert in testing and does not understand how and why particular inferences are drawn from test results. Most employers provide the test subjects with hard (paper) copies of their results.

Incidentally, a word of caution to all aspiring HR practitioners who may believe that the records they hold in the department are the only records that refer to employees: they are not. In all probability managers and supervisors will be holding data, which would be classed as personal data, on members of their staff!

KEY CONCEPT: PROCESSING OF DATA

Under the DPA98, the processing of sensitive data is forbidden unless:

- The 'data subject' provides explicit consent.
- It is necessary for the exercise or performance of a right or legal obligation in connection with employment. This could be in the processing of a payroll.
- It is necessary in connection with any legal proceedings or for obtaining legal advice.
- It is necessary for the administration of justice, or for the exercise of functions conferred by statute.
- It is in the data subject's vital interests.
- It is done for medical reasons by a health professional.
- It is processing of data on racial or ethnic origin needed to monitor equal opportunity.

KEY CONCEPT: THE DATA CONTROLLER

A data controller is any person who determines the purposes for which, and the manner in which, any personal data are or are to be processed. Many employers will be data controllers. All data controllers must provide a notification to the Information Commissioner and be included on the register of data controllers.

There is a notification fee structure for data controllers, who will fall into one of two tiers depending on business financial turnover and number of staff. The notification fee for controllers in Tier 1 is £35 and £500 for those in Tier 2 as of March 2014.

LOSING SENSITIVE INFORMATION

CASE EXAMPLE 16.7

Being absent-minded is no excuse when dealing with confidential information

Karim, a manager in a Manchester company, was involved with a review of six employees who were being considered for promotion. The candidate profiles were stored in the company's HR information system (HRIS) and had been shared with all managers and HR staff involved in the review process.

The data shared included information about each of the promotion candidates. It gave the previous three performance appraisals, absence records, their experiences and roles within the company, and the application letter that each candidate was asked to write in support of their application.

Karim decided to finish work early on Thursday and to take the candidate

information home with him, so that he could work in peace and quiet and review the data ready for the selection interviews on Friday. He quickly transferred the information onto his 'tablet' computer, left the office and bought a newspaper, which he read on the tram home. It was only when he got home, with the newspaper under his arm and no tablet, that he realised that he had left his tablet computer on the tram. He never saw his tablet again; it was a 'hard pill' to swallow. To make matters worse, he had never got around to password-protecting the device.

Task

What are the implications of Karim's action in losing his 'tablet' computer, containing personal data of employees? Assuming the role of the HR manager, write a brief paper outlining the action that you would take. Specifically, what is the implication for:

- the organisation?
- Karim?
- the people whose information has been lost?

You will get some advice on this subject by accessing:

- the Information Commissioner's (ICO) website at **http://ico.org.uk/ for_organisations/data_protection/ security_measures**
- specifically, the Information Commissioner's Office (ICO) website at

http://ico.org.uk/for_organisations/ data_protection/lose
- the CIPD employment law frequently asked questions webpages at **www. cipd.co.uk/hr-resources/employment-law-faqs/Data-protection-sensitive-personal-data.aspx**
- the CIPD factsheet on 'Retention of HR Records' at **www.cipd.co.uk/hr-resources/factsheets/retention-hr-records.aspx**
- the Gov.UK website (Data protection and your business) at **www.gov.uk/ data-protection-your-business**

Case Example 16.7 is representative of what does happen. Consider the article written by Greenhill in the *Daily Mail* on 19 May 2014 about Nick Robinson, the political editor of the BBC:

> During an unfortunate incident as he attended a football match, Nick Robinson lost his mobile phone containing personal contacts for everyone from the Prime Minister down.
>
> Mobile numbers for 'most of the Cabinet', Downing Street officials and key civil servants were stored on the phone, sources said.
>
> Now the loss of the treasure trove of government contacts is being treated as a 'serious security breach' by No.10.
>
> It is also being investigated by the data watchdog the Information Commissioner, it is understood. (**www.dailymail.co.uk/news/article-2633202/PMs-number-BC-Nicks-lost-mobile-Number-10-treats-misplaced-handset-security-breach-went-missing-attended-football-match.html**)

16.13.3 EMPLOYERS' OBLIGATIONS

Employers are obliged to notify the Information Commissioner (**www.ico.gov.uk**) if they process personal data. The individual must give consent for the personal data to be *processed*, unless it is necessary for certain specified circumstances.

ACTIVITY 16.15

The role of the Information Commissioner

1   Access the Information Commissioner's (ICO) website at **www.ico.gov.uk** and find out what the role comprises and encompasses. You will find that the Information Commissioner has much more responsibility than just looking after data protection issues.

2   The Data Protection Act 1998 requires every organisation that processes personal information to register with the Information Commissioner's Office (ICO), unless they are exempt. Failure to do so is a criminal offence. How does the DPA98 define the data controller? Is it a person or organisation?

KEY CONCEPT: PROCESSING DATA

Processing is defined as: organising, adapting, altering, retrieving, using, disclosing, combining, blocking or erasing data and calling up data on a computer screen.

There is a list of eight criminal offences relating to data protection, which are:

- processing without notification
- failure to notify the Commissioner of changes to notification register entry
- failure to comply with an enforcement or information notice
- making a false statement in response to an information notice
- obstructing or failing to assist with the execution of a search warrant
- obtaining or disclosing personal data without permission from the data controller
- selling or offering to sell unlawfully obtained data
- making a person supply a copy of their personal data, unless required or authorised by law or in the public interest.

KEY CONCEPT: REQUIREMENT OF THE DATA PROTECTION ACT

As mentioned in the previous activity, the Data Protection Act 1998 requires every organisation processing personal data to register with the ICO, unless they are exempt. Further information can be found at **http://ico.org.uk/for_organisations/data_protection**

ACTIVITY 16.16

You work as an HR administrator and have been approached by a supervisor in the marketing department's administrative section. She has asked for information, specifically absence records and records of disciplinary warnings, concerning one of the company's employees. How would you deal with his request if the supervisor's request was for information about:

- one of her direct reportees?
- a member of the company's staff working in another department?

16.13.4 DATA PROTECTION POLICY

Managers are advised to formulate and actively implement clear policies and procedures that will ensure that all employees understand the organisation's approach to compliance with the data protection laws. Employers, in their efforts to conform to the data protection laws, should as a minimum adopt the following eight data protection principles, which are recommended in the Data Protection Act (1998). Data should be:

- processed fairly and lawfully and shall not be processed unless certain conditions are met
- obtained only for specified and lawful purposes
- adequate, relevant and not excessive in relation to the purposes for which it is processed
- accurate and up to date

- kept for no longer than is necessary
- processed in accordance with the rights granted under the DPA98
- kept securely
- not transferred to a country without adequate data protection. [*Authors' comment:* The Information Commissioner's Office requires that individuals should be informed if processing of information is to be done outside the European Economic Area.]

This might necessitate programmes of training for particular employees, such as personnel practitioners, middle managers and team leaders. Also, there should be a system for monitoring the effectiveness of the procedures, which will be designed to ensure that the data protection principles are followed.

PAUSE FOR THOUGHT

The Information Commissioner has teeth!

The following is from the Information Commissioner's Office (ICO, no date).

We have a statutory power to impose a financial penalty on an organisation if the Information Commissioner is satisfied that:

- there has been a serious breach of one or more of the data protection principles by the organisation; and
- the breach was likely to cause substantial damage or distress

The power to impose a financial penalty only applies if:

- the breach was deliberate; or
- the organisation knew (or should have known) that there was a risk of a breach which was likely to cause substantial

damage or distress, but failed to take reasonable steps to prevent it.

The Information Commissioner will take account of the circumstances of each case when he decides the amount of any financial penalty. The maximum penalty he can impose is £500,000. For more on financial penalties, see the 'Information Commissioner's guidance about the issue of monetary penalties' on our website.

(*The Guide to Data Protection: How much do I need to know about data protection? A little, a lot, nothing, don't know.* Available at: **http:// ico.org.uk/Global/~/media/documents/ library/Data_Protection/ Practical_application/ THE_GUIDE_TO_DATA_PROTECTION.ashx**)

16.13.5 WHAT STEPS MIGHT ORGANISATIONS TAKE?

The CIPD has developed an extensive factsheet on data protection (CIPD, 2013g), which includes a list of statutes that are concerned with the privacy of the individual, and access to and disclosure of information in the public interest that employers need to consider. All those collecting data have to ask themselves why it is being collected, how it is going to be used and who will have access to it. The list includes:

- Public Interest Disclosure Act 1998
- Human Rights Act 1998
- Freedom of Information Act 2000
- Telecommunications (Lawful Business Practice) Regulations 2000.

The eight principles of data protection (see previously and also the ICO website at **http:// ico.org.uk/for_organisations/data_protection/the_guide/the_principles**)   give   some guidance as to how data should be managed. It would be common sense to use the eight principles as a guide to develop a 'compliance' audit programme for an organisation based upon the following ideas:

- Consider the appointment of a person to be in charge of all aspects of information, including the Freedom of Information Act.
- Audit information systems – find out who holds what data, and why.
- Consider why information is collected and how it is used. Issue guidelines for managers about how to gather, store and retrieve data.
- Ensure that all information collected now complies with the Data Protection Act 1998.
- Check the security of all information stored.
- Check the transfer of data outside the European Economic Area.
- Check the organisation's use of automated decision-making.
- Review policy and practice in respect of references.
- Review or introduce a policy for the private use of telephones, email and post, company social media, and web-based intranet and extranet systems.
- Review or introduce a procedure for reporting under the Public Interest Disclosure Act.

The above has been developed from CIPD, Acas and ICO sources.

It is worth watching the video on how the Information Commissioner's Office advises management of data on a day-to-day basis (**www.youtube.com/watch?v= CdYWoLC7TNI&feature=youtu.be**).

The CIPD offers a 'Frequently Asked Questions' guide on the interpretation of the DPA98 and the Freedom of Information Act at **www.cipd.co.uk/hr-resources/employment-law-faqs/data-protection-legislation.aspx**

16.13.6 THE FREEDOM OF INFORMATION ACT 2000

Operating hand in glove with the operation of the Data Protection Act 1998 is the Freedom of Information Act 2000. Both the Freedom of Information Act and the Data Protection Act come under the heading of 'information rights' and are regulated by the ICO.

As discussed above, the Data Protection Act 1998 deals with how personal information should be handled and it gives a right to individuals to access their *own personal* data.

The Freedom of Information Act 2000 offers the following to anyone who requires information from a *public authority*. The Information Commissioner advises that:

> The Act covers any recorded information that is held by a public authority in England, Wales and Northern Ireland, and by UK-wide public authorities based in Scotland. Information held by Scottish public authorities is covered by Scotland's own Freedom of Information (Scotland) Act 2002. (**http://ico.org.uk/for_ organisations/freedom_of_information/guide/act#what-is-the-freedom-of-information-act-1**)

As the ICO indicates (ibid), the default position in terms of providing information, unless there is 'good reason', is that it is politically healthy for people to have a right to know about what is happening in, and the activities of, public authorities. Part VI of Schedule 1 of the Act defines what is termed a *public authority*.

The ICO advises that public authorities should be proactive about publishing relevant information, for example: policies and procedures, minutes of meetings, annual reports and financial information.

Any person making a request, which must be in writing, for information to a public authority is entitled:

1   to be informed in writing by the public authority whether it holds information of the description specified in the request, and

2   if that is the case, to have that information communicated to him/her.

The request for information must include the name of the person requiring the information and the address for correspondence.

The Information Commissioner offers the following advice as to which bodies are covered by the Freedom of Information Act:

- Companies wholly owned by public authorities in England, Wales and Northern Ireland. These include:
  - government departments
  - local authorities
  - schools and universities
  - NHS
  - GPs and dentists
  - police forces
  - health authorities.

(ICO (Requesting Information from Public Bodies), at: **http://ico.org.uk/Global/faqs/ requesting#f5FB1B1EE-57CC-4F41-B205–92B9C5F41E89**)

Schedule 1 of the Freedom of Information Act 2000 lists all bodies, of which there are many. Only a token few have been identified in this narrative. For example, in addition to those listed on the ICO website, the armed forces of the Crown, except the following units, are affected by the legislation:

- the special forces, and
- any unit or part of a unit which is for the time being required by the Secretary of State to assist the Government Communications Headquarters in the exercise of its functions.

There is no fixed fee for requesting the information. The government body from whom the information has been requested can refuse to supply the information if the cost to research the data is (currently) above £600 for government departments and £450 for public authorities. The only charges that can be passed on to the person requesting the information are those incurred for providing the information, which would include photocopying and postage.

To read what the Freedom of Information Act does, visit: **http://ico.org.uk/ for_organisations/freedom_of_information/guide/act#what-is-the-freedom-of- information-act-1**)

16.14 SUMMARY

This chapter has introduced a basic overview of the legislation relating to employment. As more and more legislation appears, the HR practitioner needs to be aware of the implications of the changes in the law as it affects the business and its employees. The chapter is not a definitive guide and should not to be used as a means to replace good-quality employment law advice. Neither is it designed to develop the reader into a law expert, but it is designed to highlight some of the key pieces of employment legislation that impact upon day-to-day lives at work.

The chapter has explored the employment contract and employees' statutory rights, together with family-friendly legislation: maternity rights, Working Time Regulations and the right to flexible working.

In addition to the various Acts of Parliament, the chapter has touched upon issues surrounding the management of discipline and grievance, based on the Acas code of practice on discipline and grievance as well as the guidance literature published by Acas. It is important for the practitioner always to review the code of practice to ascertain whether any amendments have been made.

The final part of the chapter discusses the legal aspects of record-keeping. One of the roles of HR is to keep employment records, and indeed the law requires HR to keep a large amount of data on such things as health and safety, accident records, training and so on. HR is responsible for holding personal information and this is covered by the Data Protection Act – there are rules on how and where data is held and processed.

Any textbook is quickly out of date when it comes to the law, so do make sure you access websites that will keep you informed of changes.

Those who work for public authorities and those organisations which can be required to provide information under the Freedom of Information Act need to know the extent of information that should be provided and how a response should be made to a legitimate request made under the Freedom of Information Act 2000. All of us need to understand how personal information should be managed and the extent to which one needs to go to ensure that such information is safeguarded and thus our responsibilities under the Data Protection Act 1998.

REVIEW QUESTIONS

1 How is the status of an employee defined? What employment rights do they enjoy that a contract worker for the organisation does not?

2 Identify the key legislative employment instruments which govern how people are employed.

3 When can an individual legitimately claim time off work? Which piece of legislation gives these rights?

4 Explain the differences between compulsory maternity leave (CML), ordinary maternity leave (OML) and additional maternity leave (AML).

5 What are the main purposes of the Employment Rights Act 1996 (ERA96)? Explore the Act and find under what circumstances it is legitimate for an employer to make deductions from an employee's pay.

6 What considerations should an employee write about and address to their employer when they are requesting flexible working? You will find some guidance by referring to section 80F(1) of the Employment Rights Act 1996.

7 Who can request flexible working? What are the qualifying criteria? What changes to a role could flexible working entail?

8 What are the three categories of the National Minimum Wage (NMW)? To whom should complaints about the NMW be made?

9 When conducting a formal disciplinary or grievance procedure, what record of events should be kept?

10 Who can accompany an accused employee to a discipline or grievance hearing? What is the role of the person who accompanies the employee to such a meeting? Can they speak for the accused employee? When would it be appropriate to suspend someone, with pay, during a disciplinary investigation?

11 What happens if an employee raises a grievance while they are subject to a disciplinary hearing?

12 Taking the role of an HR adviser, you are coaching one of your students who is following a CIPD Certificate in HR Practice course. You work in a petrochemical plant. She asks you:

(a) What constitutes gross misconduct in the workplace?
(b) Could someone found smoking in the office be disciplined in accordance with the company's gross misconduct procedures?

(c) What would happen if an employee was observed smoking in or around the petroleum refining equipment?

(d) You will find guidance on these questions by accessing *Discipline and Grievance at Work: The Acas guide* (Acas, 2014d).

13 What is the role of a mediator in a disciplinary or grievance case? Who can take on the role of the mediator? Is the outcome of a case, where both parties have agreed to mediation, binding?

14 What is meant by 'personal or sensitive data'?

15 For how long should personal or sensitive data be held?

16 What type of information processing is exempt from the DPA?

17 What is meant by the data protection principles?

18 What steps might the organisation take to ensure compliance with the data protection principles?

19 What is a 'data access request'? You will find information by accessing the Information Commissioner's website at **www.ico.gov.uk** Which Act of Parliament enables an individual to access data about themselves?

20 Under which Act of Parliament can I request a copy of my personal data from my employing organisation?

21 What is the role of the data controller in an organisation? You will get some ideas on this topic by:

(a) reading how the ICO defines the data controller at **www.ico.gov.uk/ for_organisations/guidance index/~/media/documents/library/ Data_Protection/Detailed_specialist_guides/data_controllers_ and_data_processors.ashx**

(b) accessing the Information Commissioner's website at **http://ico.org. uk/for_organisations/data_protection/the_guide/key_definitions**

(c) reading *Guidance: Identifying 'data controllers' and 'data processors'* at **http://ico.org.uk/news/current_topics/~/media/documents/library/ Data_Protection/Detailed_specialist_guides/data-controllers- and-data-processors-dp-guidance.pdf**

22 As an HR manager, what do you have to do if you receive a 'data access request' from one of your employees for a copy of their personal data? You will find guidance at **http://ico.org.uk/for_organisations/data_protection/ subject_access_requests**

23 As a private citizen, how does one go about making a freedom of information request to a public body? You will find guidance at **http://ico. org.uk/Global/faqs/requesting#f6F077BED-9486-4B1F-998D- ED5045CB85DF**

EXPLORE FURTHER

BOOKS

BELL, A.C. (2012) *Nutshell employment law*. Andover: Sweet and Maxwell.

DANIELS, K. (2012) *Employment law: an introduction for HR and business students*. London: Chartered Institute of Personnel and Development.

LEWIS, D. and SERGEANT, M. (2013) *Essentials of employment law*. 12th ed. London: Chartered Institute of Personnel and Development.

This is another book suitable for those studying and practising HR.

WEB LINKS

Government legislation: **www.legislation.gov.uk**

For employment rights:

- Acas: **www.acas.org.uk**
- Citizens' Advice Bureau: **www.Adviceguide.org.uk**
- Law Centres Federation: **www.lawcentres.org.uk**
- Government advice website: **www.gov.uk**

Specifically for maternity/paternity information, useful guidance can be found:

- Equality and Human Rights Commission: **www.equalityhumanrights.com**
- HM Revenue and Customs: **www.hmrc.gov.uk**
- Health and Safety Executive (HSE): **www.hse.gov.uk/mothers/law.htm**
- NHS Healthy Working Lives: **www.healthyworkinglives.com**
- Working Families: **www.workingfamilies.org**

For discipline and grievance don't forget to visit the Acas website. It is well worth browsing for sound advice on all kinds of HR issues: **www.acas.org**

- Information Commissioner: **www.ico.gov.uk**
- Low Pay Commission: **www.lowpay.gov.uk**
- Pay and working rights: **http://payandworkrightscampaign.direct.gov.uk/index.html**
- Trades Union Congress (safety representatives): **www.tuc.org.uk/extras/brownbook.pdf**
- TUC website: **www.tuc.org.uk**
- Unite union: **www.unitetheunion.org.uk**
- Worksmart (from the TUC): **www.worksmart.org.uk/rights/viewsection.php?**

PODCASTS

Listen to the CIPD's podcast on 'Dispute Resolution': **www.cipd.co.uk/podcasts/_articles/_dispute-resolution-podcast-69.htm?link=title**

VIDEO LINKS

Acas Senior Policy Adviser, Adrian Wakeling, talks about social media in the workplace: **www.youtube.com/watch?v=JhWBnOEyGyc**

CIPD Discussion on Flexible Working and Working Time Regulations: **www.youtube.com/watch?v=i5h9zxuTF0g**

eBay and Flexible working: **www.youtube.com/watch?v=kpBXK2XhapE**

Flexible working (2013–2014), the Acas view: **www.youtube.com/watch?v=vczXA9wyNB0**

Watch how the Information Commissioner's Office and Orbit Social Housing discuss how a breach of the Data Protection Act was managed: **www.youtube.com/watch? v=S2QOwYSBBFY**

Watch a video on how the Information Commissioner's Office advises how to manage your data on a day-to-day basis: **www.youtube.com/watch? v=CdYWoLC7TNI &feature=youtu.be**

CHAPTER 17

Ending the Employment Relationship

LEARNING OBJECTIVES

After studying this chapter you should:

- be able to describe the different ways in which the employment relationship might end
- understand the meaning of fair and unfair dismissal
- be aware of the legislative implications of redundancy
- understand that redundancy has an impact upon both those made redundant and those who survive the process and thus consideration needs to be given to both sets of individuals
- understand the legislative changes which have impacted upon retirement as a means of ending the employment relationship.

17.1 INTRODUCTION

Ultimately the employment contract comes to an end, and there are a variety of circumstances in which this might happen. The most common reasons fall into two categories:

- the employer may terminate the contract of employment
- the employee may terminate the contract of employment.

In this chapter we will also consider the management of redundancy and retirement as a means of ending the employment relationship. Since the financial crisis of 2008, redundancies have been used as a means of cutting overheads. However, even in buoyant times, organisations may still need to restructure and re-form to maintain their competitive advantage in a global economy, thus possibly giving rise to redundancies. The role of HR in handling redundancies is key – both in communicating with staff involved in the process and in ensuring that the legal due processes are followed.

17.2 TERMINATION OF CONTRACT

17.2.1 TERMINATION BY THE EMPLOYEE

There are a wide range of reasons why an employee may decide to terminate the relationship with their employer. Largely, these are either personal or career-related, and several typical examples of each are listed below.

Personal reasons

- to take care of a sick relative
- to care for children or grandchildren or an elderly parent

- to move to another area or country
- to escape from a hostile culture or unfriendly co-workers
- to take a career break
- to retrain or improve educational qualifications
- to retire.

Career-related reasons

- resigning to take up a post with another employer
- to undertake a full-time course
- a desire for a career change.

It is important to find out reasons for the termination, especially if there is high labour turnover in the organisation. Part of HR's role would be to investigate reasons for leaving; this might be done by the use of exit interviews.

KEY CONCEPT: EXIT INTERVIEWS

Exit interviews may be used with several purposes in mind. The data that is gathered is useful to both those who manage the employment relationship and to HR planners. The objective of the exit interview is to try to find out the reasons for leaving. This may be difficult, as leavers may not always be truthful about their real reasons for quitting. For instance, they may not admit to having had difficulties with their manager and believe they may, at some later date, need a reference or perhaps simply wish to leave all options open because returning to work for the organisation at a later date may be a possibility.

ACTIVITY 17.1

Conducting exit interviews

Considering the issues raised in the above Key Concept (Exit Interviews):

- Who do you think should carry out exit interviews?

- How can the true reasons why someone has left an organisation be determined?
- Are exit interviews the best way of finding out why people decide to leave an organisation?

17.2.2 TERMINATION BY THE EMPLOYER

There are a number of reasons why an employer might terminate the contract:

- **Disciplinary dismissal:** Employees who persistently break the rules risk being dismissed, subject to the outcome of a disciplinary hearing and depending on the severity and frequency of the offence. For example, inappropriate behaviour may be considered to constitute 'gross misconduct'. This could be, for example, the misuse of an organisation's information technology by downloading inappropriate material such as pornographic images or data which could be related to terrorist activity onto a company computer, tablet or mobile device. It could also be the disregard of or breaking of health and safety regulations which might put colleagues or members of the public at risk. Any of these activities could fall into the category of gross misconduct. The nature of what is, and what is not, gross misconduct would be defined in an organisation's procedures documentation, which in turn forms part of the contract of employment. The dismissed employee may have grounds for appeal to an employment tribunal for unfair dismissal.

- **Lack of capability:** It is legitimate for the organisation to dismiss an employee on the grounds that the person has shown themselves to be grossly unsuitable for the job; this may relate to attitude or aptitude. Admittedly the organisation will have had the opportunity to test an individual's knowledge, competence and personality prior to engagement, but the law recognises that errors can occur.

- **Redundancy:** This occurs when the organisation no longer requires a job, or group of jobs, to be carried out at a particular venue. With this kind of severance, the employee has a statutory entitlement to compensation. The employee may have grounds for an appeal to an employment tribunal for *unfair selection for redundancy*. Where redundancy is concerned, it is important to remember that it may not be the current 'job-holder' who is made redundant. A number of jobs may be grouped together as part of determining a 'redundancy pool'. The organisation can then select, for example on competency-related grounds, the 'weakest' person(s), in terms of their contribution to the organisation, to be dismissed through the redundancy process.

- **A statutory duty or restriction** prevents the employment from being continued. This could relate to having recruited an individual who does not have the right to work in the UK.

- **Retirement** is, in the main, when an *employee* chooses to finish working, to retire. The default retirement age, which was 65 years of age, has been phased out.

- Employers can set a compulsory retirement age *if they can underpin their decision with a business case*. Retirement is dealt with more fully later in this chapter.

17.3 EMPLOYEE STATUS

The law on fair and unfair dismissal applies only to workers who are employees of an organisation. Defining what an employee is appears straightforward. However, because there are so many rights associated with the status of an employee, the definition of who is and who is not an employee has exercised legal minds and there have been many examples of case law which have tried to put some clarity on what is and what is not an employee.

All employees are workers, but not all workers are employees.

ACTIVITY 17.2

Consider the following questions:

- How would you define a worker?
- How would you define an employee?
- What characteristics does the role of an employee have that a worker does not have?

All employees are workers, but an employee has extra employment rights and responsibilities which do not apply to workers who are not employees.

Having a clear understanding of what is and is not an employee is important. For example, one of the rights which an employee 'enjoys' is that, if they believe that they have been unfairly dismissed from their job, they can take their case to an employment tribunal. A worker, for example a consultant working for an organisation, would not be able to go to an employment tribunal if their 'employing organisation' decided to dispense with their services.

The concept of what is an employee and how an employee is defined in law is dealt with in Chapter 16, 'Understanding Employment Law'.

17.4 DISMISSAL

Dismissal procedures are subject to the Acas (2014d) *Code of Practice on Discipline and Grievance*. The code does not apply to redundancies. The Code was issued under section 199 of the Trade Union and Labour Relations (Consolidation) Act 1992 and was laid before both Houses of Parliament on 9 December 2008.

According to Acas:

> A failure to follow the Code does not, in itself, make a person or organisation liable to proceedings. However, employment tribunals will take the Code into account when considering relevant cases. Tribunals will also be able to adjust any awards made in relevant cases by up to 25 per cent for unreasonable failure to comply with any provision of the Code (Acas, 2014d, p.1)

17.4.1 UNFAIR DISMISSAL

Not everyone can claim unfair dismissal, for instance those who are not employees, such as independent contractors or freelance agents. The relationship between the employee and their 'employer' is important to establish, because this will determine the employee's actual employment status. Only those who are employed are entitled to claim unfair dismissal.

If an employee feels that they have been unfairly dismissed, they can take their case to an employment tribunal. This has to be done within three months of the effective date of termination of employment.

In most circumstances employees will need to qualify before they can make a complaint to an employment tribunal:

- at least one year's continuous service for employees in employment before 6 April 2012
- two years for employees starting employment on or after 6 April 2012.

(Acas, n.d., and **www.gov.uk/dismissal**)

For people working as employees in Northern Ireland, the qualifying period is still normally one year.

Since 25 June 2013, there is no qualifying period if an individual has been dismissed because of their political opinions or affiliation. They will automatically have the right to go to an employment tribunal (Gov.UK, 'Dismissal Your Rights', available at **www.gov.uk/dismissal/what-to-do-if-youre-dismissed**).

There is no length of service requirement in relation to 'automatically unfair grounds'. *Automatically unfair* reasons include:

- **pregnancy:** including all reasons relating to maternity
- **family reasons:** including parental leave, paternity leave (birth and adoption), adoption leave or time off for dependants
- **representation:** including acting as an employee representative as well as trade union membership grounds and union recognition
- **part-time and fixed-term employees** [*This applies to dismissal on the **grounds** that the person was part-time or on a fixed term contract. If an employee naturally comes to the end of a short-term contract, this is fair.*]
- **discrimination:** including protection against discrimination on the grounds of age, sex, race, disability, sexual orientation and religion or belief
- **pay and working hours:** including the Working Time Regulations, annual leave and the National Minimum Wage.

(Acas, 2010b; also refer to the Employment Rights Act 1996)

ACTIVITY 17.3

1   What circumstances would lead to an employee's dismissal being deemed to be unfair?

2   Can a police officer or member of the armed services make a claim for unfair dismissal?

You will find some help to answer the above questions by exploring the websites of the following organisations: Acas, Citizens Advice Bureau (CAB), Age Concern, TUC and Gov.UK. The above list is not complete. The Government website is at **www.gov.uk/ dismissal/unfair-and-constructive-dismissal**

How do people fare if they take a claim to an employment tribunal? An idea of what happens when someone takes the step to go to an employment tribunal if they consider they were unfairly treated in some way at work, perhaps in relation to discrimination or perceived unfair dismissal, can be gleaned by examining the statistics which the Ministry of Justice provides about the working of the Tribunal Service.

During the period 2011–12, on the list of claims handled by employment tribunals, claims associated with unfair deductions from wages are at the top, with 51,200 claims. Second in the list are claims associated with unfair dismissal. In 2011–12 there were 46,300 claims for unfair dismissal which were accepted by employment tribunals.

Not all claims are heard by a tribunal; many are settled using conciliation, using the services of Acas. In 2011–12 Acas conciliated 76,200 claims, which is 33% of all claims. Over a quarter of all claims were withdrawn prior being considered by the tribunal service (62,000). Of the original 230,000 claims, 56,100 cases proceeded to a final hearing. Compared with the total number of original people who made a claim to a tribunal, 12% (26,900) were successful at a hearing (Ministry of Justice, 2012).

In terms of 'unfair dismissal', 11,200 claims proceeded to a hearing. Of the 11,200 claims, 5,100 were successful. If, after investigation at an employment tribunal, a dismissal is found to be unfair, there are three options that the tribunal may recommend:

● reinstatement
● re-engagement
● compensation.

From the 5,100 successful claims, five employees were re-engaged or reinstated, 2,300 received awards, but 2,600 received no award. The maximum award was £173,408 and the median was £4,560. The limit for *unfair dismissal* is, as of April 2014, £76,574.

ACTIVITY 17.4

Employment tribunals

Access the website **www.justice.gov.uk/ tribunals/employment** Determine the latest statistics relating to employment tribunals.

For those students who are employed in the HR sector:

1   Consider how many employment tribunals that staff from your organisation have to attend in a year. By reducing the number of tribunals an organisation has to attend, significant savings could be made.

2   How much does it cost an organisation to go to a tribunal? (Think of all the costs that attending a tribunal incurs: the wages of the staff who have to attend; the opportunity costs associated with productivity losses while staff are away from their jobs; the costs of the solicitor who will represent the case.)

Specific statistics about tribunals can be found at **www.gov.uk/government/ collections/tribunals-statistics**

17.4.2 FAIR REASONS FOR DISMISSAL

There can be many reasons for fair dismissal. These can include: poor performance, misconduct, redundancy, the ending of a fixed-term contract. A dismissal is fair if the employer had reason for the dismissal and acted reasonably in doing so.

As from 1 October 2011, employers can no longer issue forced retirement notices to their employees. This is the end for the Default Retirement Age (DRA) of 65. As previously discussed, an employer would have to justify requiring an employee to retire at 65, but if they cannot make such justification an employee would have a claim of unfair dismissal on the grounds of age discrimination. Read the section later entitled 'Retirement' for the government perspective on this topic.

Cases of 'gross misconduct', such as theft, downloading Internet pornography, serious insubordination, breach of confidence, for example to denigrate {*meaning – to blacken, to 'rubbish'*} the company on Facebook, could be considered as fair dismissal, which could result in immediate termination of the contract without notice.

In a case where an employee has been dismissed, they may still have to work a period of notice or receive 'payment in lieu of notice'.

17.4.3 CONSTRUCTIVE DISMISSAL

If an employee resigns from their job because of an employer's behaviour, it may be considered to be constructive dismissal. The employee would need to show that:

- their employer has committed a serious breach of contract
- they felt forced to leave because of that breach
- they could not have done anything to suggest that they have accepted the breach or a change in employment conditions.

Examples of constructive dismissal might be where an employee has been psychologically bullied by a co-worker or their boss, or their conditions of work have been changed unacceptably, for example putting the employee on to shift work without consultation and agreement. The Government recommends that:

> If you do have a case for constructive dismissal, you should leave your job immediately – your employer may argue that, by staying, you accepted the conduct or treatment. (**www.gov.uk/dismissal/unfair-and-constructive-dismissal**)

 ACTIVITY 17.5

Constructive dismissal

Can you think of any other reasons for constructive dismissal? Carry out some research, for example using the Gov.UK or Citizens Advice Bureau websites. Interrogate the sites about constructive dismissal.

Read what the Trades Union Congress has to say about the change in the qualifying time before an employee can claim unfair dismissal at: **www.tuc.org.uk/workplace-issues/ employment-rights/unfair-dismissal-reforms-will-leave-three-million-workers-without**

17.5 REDUNDANCY

There are a number of Acts of Parliament that relate to the detail of the management of redundancy, including (but not exhaustive):

- Chapter II, sections 188–198 of the Trade Union and Labour Relations (Consolidation) Act 1992 as amended by section 34 of the Trade Union Reform and Employment Rights Act 1993
- the Collective Redundancies and Transfer of Undertakings (Protection of Employment) (Amendment) Regulations 1995 (SI 1995 No 2587) and 1999 (SI 1999 No 1925)
- Employment Rights Act 1996.

The Employment Rights Act 1996 simply defines redundancy in the following manner, where:

- an employer ceases to carry on the business
- an employer ceases to carry on the business *in the place where the employee was employed*
- the requirements of the business for employees to *carry out work of a particular kind have ceased or diminished* and where the employee is employed to carry out that work.

(Employment Rights Act 1996, s139)

17.5.1 HANDLING OF REDUNDANCY

Employers normally deal with redundancies in one of the following three ways:

- **an ad hoc approach** whereby there are no formally established arrangements, with the practice varying according to the circumstances of each redundancy
- **a formal policy** setting out the approach to be adopted by management when faced with making redundancies. In such cases the agreement of trade union or employee representatives with the contents of the policy will not have been obtained
- **a formal agreement** setting out the procedure to be followed when redundancies have to be considered. The contents of such a procedure will be the result of negotiation and agreement between management and trade union or employee representatives

Acas offers this advice about redundancy and its impact upon employees' rights to claim redundancy payments:

> Although an employee will need 2 years' service for a redundancy payment, dismissal due to redundancy can happen at any point, the fairness of a dismissal may be challenged if an employee has at least one year's continuous service for employees in employment before 6th April 2012 or two years for employees starting employment on or after 6th April 2012, however if the redundancy dismissal was due to asserting a statutory right e.g. requesting flexible working, then no fixed length of service is required. (Acas, n.d.)

It is advisable to have a formal policy or procedure on redundancy. How redundancy is handled will depend on the numbers involved. If there are 20 or more to be made redundant, there is a requirement to consult with the relevant unions or workforce representatives within a given timeframe and to notify the projected redundancies to the Department for Business, Innovation and Skills.

The minimum timeframe for notification is as follows:

- 45 days (for 100 employees or more over a period of 90 days or less)
- 30 days (for 20–99 employees over a period of 90 days or less).

Acas (2013a), in their booklet 'How to manage collective redundancies', offers very useful practical advice and guidance to HR specialists on this subject. It is available at **www.acas. org.uk/media/pdf/o/i/How-to-manage-collective-redundancies.pdf**)

PAUSE FOR THOUGHT

HR managers may wish to take advice when deciding upon how to handle large-scale redundancies. Consider the following article from *People Management* (13 September 2013):

Government wins right to appeal Woolworths redundancy ruling

Union slams decision to re-visit case which set a new legal precedent

A court has given the go-ahead for the government to appeal the landmark ruling on collective redundancy made earlier this year.

The Employment Appeal Tribunal (EAT) has granted the Department for Business, Innovation and Skills (BIS) the right to appeal against a decision, which offered compensation to workers affected by collective redundancy when their employers failed to follow the proper consultation procedures.

In May this year, thousands of former employees of Woolworths and Ethel Austin won payouts after the EAT ruled that the companies' administrators did not consult fully with representatives over job losses when the businesses were going into administration.

Around 1,200 Ethel Austin staff and 3,200 Woolworths workers had missed out on compensation awarded to their colleagues, because fewer than 20 staff had been affected in the stores where they worked. This meant that, technically, they were not covered by legislation around collective redundancy.

However, the EAT's decision in May created a legal precedent where collective redundancy consultations would not be limited to lay-offs 'at one establishment', and the judge ruled that these three words should be deleted from the law. This meant that the affected staff would be entitled to up to eight weeks' pay at Woolworths and 12 weeks' pay at Ethel Austin.

Shopworkers' union Usdaw, which campaigned for the workers to receive compensation over the lack of consultation, is angry at the EAT's decision to let BIS appeal.

John Hannett, Usdaw's general secretary, said: 'It is particularly galling that the government lodged an appeal after not bothering to attend the EAT hearing. These were mass redundancy situations because the businesses were closing down and it is no fault of the individual workers how small the store was that they worked in.'

'The government should concentrate on encouraging administrators to focus on keeping businesses open, not supporting their failure to properly consult with workers, as required under law.'

Catherine Wilson, head of employment at law firm Thomas Eggar, said: 'We are surprised that this is happening now and that the government did not react to this earlier, given the importance of the EAT case and its implications.'

'Employers now have to aggregate all of their possible redundancies across all of their establishments, which can be logistically difficult. We advise employers to take a cautious view and an inclusive approach if considering redundancy, considering how many people will be going across the business rather than focusing on one department.'

She added that if the government was successful in overturning the EAT's decision to compensate the workers, the legal situation would revert to as it was before. The 'at one establishment' rule would apply, and fewer than 20 redundancies at one branch or office would not require a formal consultation process.

(Faragher, 2013. Published with kind permission of *People Management*.)

Discussion

The above ruling has far-reaching implications for those organisations that employ people doing similar jobs across a number of locations. As an example, consider the dilemma of a major roads service contractor which has responsibility for the maintenance of roads across a number of counties.

Consider the situation if one of the councils decides to cut back on its road repairs. The contractor responds to the reduction in work by deciding to cut two of its repair teams of 13 people per team, a total of 26 employees. Because more than 20 people are likely to be made redundant, the implication of the Woolworths decision is that the contractor would probably have to include all its people in its teams across several counties as being potentially part of the redundancy pool and so advise all of them of the possibility of redundancy.

Common sense suggests that consultation should be as soon as possible in the case of dismissals involving redundancies. Consultation must be completed before any notices of dismissal are issued to employees. Details of the consultation arrangements with any trade union or employee representatives should be made available. This might include details of any relocation expenses, details of the appeals procedures and information on the selection criteria to be used where redundancy is unavoidable, together with details of the severance terms.

Employees will be concerned about job losses so the organisation's policy on redundancy should also give reassurances about maintaining job security wherever possible and particularly any measures for minimising or avoiding compulsory redundancies. The policy should also include details on the support the business is prepared to give to redundant employees to help them to obtain training or search for alternative work.

The management of redundancies of fewer than 20 people is now defined by case law, known as the *Polkey* decision. Polkey (*Polkey v AE Dayton Services Ltd*, 1987) was a van driver who appealed against his redundancy when his employer reduced the number of vans required in his business from four to three. The appeal against redundancy went to the House of Lords after going through the employment tribunal and appeal stages.

In essence the *Polkey* decision indicated that if there was any significant procedural irregularity in the way in which a case was dealt with by the employer, there was an entitlement to a finding of unfair dismissal. If it was only a technical matter, however, the tribunal could decide that, despite the procedural irregularity and the consequent unfair dismissal, the compensation could be set at nothing or very low.

Prior to the *Polkey* judgement, where there was a procedural irregularity in an otherwise fair dismissal – for example, failure to consult before a redundancy – but if it could be shown that carrying out the proper procedure would have made no difference to the final decision, the employment tribunal would be able to find the dismissal fair. This was held to be wrong in the *Polkey* judgement, so although the decision could be defined as unfair, compensation could be reduced.

After two reversals of the *Polkey* judgement, the Employment Act 2002 restored the pre-*Polkey* position. The law was later repealed back to the *Polkey* position by the Employment Act 2008, that is, that there is the need to demonstrate procedural fairness. This means that procedural failings will normally render a dismissal unfair, but compensation can be reduced in proportion to the likelihood that the dismissal would have occurred had a fair procedure been followed. Whether the reasons for a redundancy are fair, though, is still set out in the Employment Rights Act 1996.

In essence, the employer should consult and communicate fully with the employee on the following:

- warning should be given about impending redundancy (job loss)
- an idea of how selection for redundancy will be carried out
- the employee must have an opportunity to communicate their feelings and concerns
- consideration of alternatives (redeployment?).

One may of course finally say that the individual may challenge the need for any redundancy at all.

CASE EXAMPLE 17.1

The above discussion is exemplified in the following *People Management* article of 29 November 2012:

Procedurally flawed redundancy is fair

In *Ashby v JJB Sports*, the Employment Appeal Tribunal [EAT] held that the dismissal of a senior employee for redundancy was fair, even though there had been no consultation.

At the time of his redundancy, Ashby was an associate director of JJB Sports and head of human resources and payroll. A new CEO was brought in, who created a new role of HR director. A significantly more highly qualified person was hired for that role and Ashby, who was not aware of the restructuring of the company, was then made redundant without any form of consultation. He claimed unfair dismissal.

The employment tribunal decided, and the EAT subsequently agreed, that the dismissal fell within the limited number of situations where consultation would have made no difference to the outcome. The EAT held that this was far from an ordinary case of redundancy, in view of the company's need to implement a radical and urgent reorganisation to protect itself from insolvency. It considered it reasonable that Ashby was not involved in 'highly sensitive commercial decisions' and the company's decision not to appoint him to the role of HR director was held not to be unfair, particularly as it was clear that the other candidate possessed superior experience and skills.

The EAT stressed that this case was unusual but, even so, employers should treat it with enormous caution, perhaps verging on suspicion. It is difficult to see why the EAT came to the decision it did, particularly with regard to its conclusion that the circumstances of this particular case can be described as 'exceptional', simply because they involved a senior employee and a substantial reorganisation of the business.

The 'futile' exception identified in *Polkey* is rarely successfully argued and employers would be wise not to assume it can be relied on. For the time being at least, and notwithstanding this case, consultation remains a fundamental feature of a fair redundancy process.

(Mander and Henry, 2012)

Published with kind permission of *People Management*.

17.5.2 DISCLOSURE OF INFORMATION

Acas suggests that the following information is given in the course of the consultation:

- the reasons for the proposals
- the numbers and descriptions of employees it is proposed to dismiss as redundant
- the total number of employees of any such description employed at the establishment in question
- the way in which employees will be selected for redundancy
- how the dismissals are to be carried out, including the period over which the dismissals are to take effect
- the method of calculating the amount of redundancy payments to be made to those who are dismissed.

(www.acas.org.uk/index.aspx?articleid=4256)

The Information and Consultation of Employees Regulations 2004, commonly called the 'ICE Regulations', gives employees the right to be informed about the business's economic situation and also to be informed and consulted about employment prospects and about decisions that may lead to substantial changes in work organisation or contractual relations, including redundancies and transfers. As from 2008 these regulations apply to organisations that employ 50 or more staff.

17.5.3 REDUNDANCY PAY

Redundant employees are entitled to redundancy pay as compensation for loss of their job, security and career prospects. The redundancy payment due to each employee under the statutory redundancy payment scheme depends on their age and length of service, up to a maximum of 20 years. This determines the number of weeks' pay due, which is then subject to a limit on weekly pay – see the Department for Business, Innovation and Skills website (**www.gov.uk**).

Consider the following example:

> If you are 37, have been with your employer for 9 years and are paid £500 a week, you could be entitled to £4,176 redundancy pay.
>
> This is: 9 (weeks' pay) x £464 (the maximum weeks' pay for the calculation).

The rules that the Government uses to calculate redundancy pay are:

- half a week's pay for each full year you were under 22
- 1 week's pay for each full year you were 22 or older, but under 41
- 1 and half week's pay for each full year you were 41 or older.

(**www.gov.uk/redundant-your-rights/redundancy-pay**)

There are circumstances where employees may not be entitled to compensation – for instance, if the employer has made a 'suitable' offer of alternative employment and the employee has unreasonably rejected it.

There is a maximum statutory limit relating to a week's pay (£464, May 2014). The BIS website offers a calculator for a table to determine the statutory amounts of redundancy pay: **www.gov.uk/calculate-your-redundancy-pay/y/2014–04–01**

ACTIVITY 17.6

Using the above, calculate the statutory redundancy payment for your own job or a job of someone you know. Alternatively, calculate the redundancy payment for a 30-year-old employee with 12 years' service, currently earning £29,530 per annum.

17.5.4 VOLUNTARY SEVERANCE

The above payments are the statutory minimum that every employee is entitled to receive if they have two or more years of continuous service. However, many employers choose to encourage staff to leave the organisation voluntarily by offering an enhanced severance package. The individual makes the choice to leave and so does not have to go through a traumatic exercise of selection for redundancy.

17.5.5 SELECTION FOR REDUNDANCY

The selection procedure must be, and be seen to be, fair and non-discriminatory. Criteria used should be designed to retain the best employees who will take the organisation forward in a competitive world. This might mean considering both present and future skills and knowledge required by the organisation as well as past work performance – information which could be accessed from appraisal and training records. Discipline and absence records could be used as objective criteria within the process. Care should be taken not to use any criteria that could be construed as being discriminatory, for example years' service. In the past, organisations have used 'last in, first out' (LIFO) as a means of selection, but this is now considered discriminatory in the light of age discrimination legislation. However, the case of *Rolls Royce v Unite the Union* at the Court of Appeal (*Rolls Royce plc v Unite the Union*, Court of Appeal, 2009 EWCA Civ 387) suggests that length of service, particularly *when coupled with other selection criteria*, does *not* constitute discrimination because it 'was proportionate to achieving the legitimate aim of rewarding loyalty and creating a stable workforce in the context of a fair redundancy' (Beale, 2013, section 25).

Brittenden (2013) points to the following in the context of a fair system of selection:

> **Fair System Of Selection**: In the recent authority of Morgan v Welsh Rugby Union [2011] I.R.L.R. 376 the EAT set out the following guidance: where an employer has to decide which employees from a pool of existing employees are to be made redundant, the criteria will reflect a known job, performed by known employees over a period of time. Where, however, an employer has to appoint to new roles after a re-organisation, the employer's decision must of necessity be forward-looking. It is likely to centre upon an assessment of the ability of the individual to perform in the new role.

The objective when deciding on the criteria on which to base decisions of redundancy is to be as objective as is possible: 'The fact that selection criteria used to decide which employees from a pool are to be made redundant requires a degree of judgement on the employer's part does not necessarily mean that they cannot be assessed objectively or dispassionately' (ibid).

Relying solely on devised 'objective criteria' without giving managers opportunity to contribute to the selection of individuals to be made redundant can in itself lead to problems. In *Mental Health Care v Biluan*, the Employment Appeal Tribunal (EAT) on 19 October 2012 had to consider whether a redundancy selection exercise was fair where capabilities were assessed primarily on exercises designed for recruitment, and where managers found the results 'surprising' given the employees' past performance.

> The Employment Appeal Tribunal commented that the employer had taken a lot of trouble over the redundancy selection exercise ... But in doing so, an elaborate and HR-driven method had been chosen which deprived the employer of the benefit of input from managers and others who actually knew the staff in question and which, by its very elaborateness, was liable to be difficult to apply consistently. Where an experienced manager was surprised by the outcome, but felt he had to accept the situation even if he disagreed with the results, ... (Javaid, 2013)

CASE EXAMPLE 17.2

A manufacturer of smart phones has been affected by the change in market demand and has cause to reduce its UK head office staff by 110 people. The reduction in staff is planned to take place over a period of approximately three and a half months, 105 days.

The HR team recognise that consultation should take place at least 45 days before the first dismissal takes effect if 100 or more employees are to be made redundant at one establishment over a period of 90 days or less. Although the period over which the redundancies occur is greater than the 90 days, it was considered good practice that negotiations about the redundancies start early to maintain, at a difficult time, some semblance of regard which the company has for its staff; employee relations have always been good.

Clearly the company is required to notify the Government that there are over '100' possible redundancies. A consultation period with the representatives from the trade unions is planned.

HR needs to consider a range of options to deal with the impact of these redundancies.

These might include:

- Meet with affected management staff.
- Meet with the trade unions and/or employee representatives to inform them of the reasons for the redundancies and numbers involved, followed by further meetings on the terms and conditions of the redundancies.
- Meet with the workforce initially to present to them the nature and extent of the planned changes. This would include informing the rest of the workforce of the situation, initially through the 'works council' and then through a series of briefings, to allay any fears. A series of questions and answers is to be placed on the company intranet to assist in this communication.
- Arrange meetings with individuals and management to discuss personal issues and concerns.

It is important to consider the needs of the employees because the company takes the view that people are important and are a valued asset. This is a message that the company wishes to give to the remaining employees in other sections of the business – so it is important to treat those facing redundancy well and with respectful care.

To these ends, HR is planning to put the following processes in place:

- Contract a counselling consultant to provide 24-hour telephone counselling for those who are finding the whole issue hard to cope with.
- Contract an outplacement provider who will help with CVs, skills analysis, advice on retraining and interview skills. Facilities for email, fax, printing and telephone communication are to be provided to help the employees in their job search.
- Time off for employees to seek other jobs, for instance attending an interview.
- Support employees with opportunities for retraining and redeployment into other areas of the business. Employees with suitable skills will be guaranteed an interview for any relevant vacancies within the company.
- Agree to release staff who gain new employment without them having to work their contractual notice.
- Advice on financial issues to be provided by an independent financial adviser.

Useful information about collective or multiple redundancies

For further information about collective redundancies, see **www.gov.uk/staff-redundant/redundancy-consultations**

Before a consultation starts, contact the Insolvency Service Redundancy Payments Service (RPS) by filling out form HR1. Instructions on where to send it are on the form at **www.bis.gov.uk/assets/insolvency/docs/forms/redundancy-payments/hr1pdf.pdf**

The Insolvency Service website is moving during 2014 to **www.gov.uk/government/organisations/insolvency-service**

See Acas, *How to Manage Collective Redundancies*, at **www.acas.org.uk/media/pdf/c/n/How-to-manage-collective-redundancies.pdf**

There is some guidance and discussion in *HR Magazine* about outsourcing agencies and the issues that the HR professional might wish to consider when selecting an agency if faced with the need to help their employees find alternative employment after redundancy: **www.hrmagazine.co.uk/hr/features/1075824/outplacements-model**

ACTIVITY 17.7

Taking the role of an HR manager, reflect upon how you might expect a line manager to approach and advise a member of her staff that their job is at risk and they might face redundancy. What type of skills do you think that the manager might need? How could you help her in this task? Acas suggests that an organisation which is facing large-scale redundancies over a protracted period of time might consider training a 'downsizing envoy'.

You will get some ideas by reading and watching the following Acas literature and video material and also by listening to the CIPD podcast on redundancy:

- 'Breaking Bad News at Work', Acas guidance. Available at: **www.acas.org.uk/index.aspx?articleid=4103**
- Acas 'Breaking Bad News at Work' video. Available at: **www.acas.org.uk/index.aspx?articleid=747**
- CIPD Podcast, Number 29, Part One and Part Two, Managing Redundancy. Available at: **www.cipd.co.uk/podcasts/_articles/_managingredundancy.htm** and **www.cipd.co.uk/podcasts/_articles/_managingredundancy2.htm**

17.5.6 DEALING WITH SURVIVORS

Those employees who remain with the organisation after a compulsory redundancy exercise are likely to feel a range of emotions: shock, fear (of what may yet happen), anger and guilt. Alternatively, they may feel elation – that they have kept their jobs!

The effects of redundancy may also mean that there is more work to be undertaken by those who remain. This could have a negative effect on morale, counteracting the positive feelings of having escaped being made redundant.

Redman and Wilkinson (2009, p.394) emphasise the above when they write, 'employees are more likely to have low morale and increased stress levels, be less productive and less loyal, with increased quit levels. Sennett (1997, p.125), describes survivors as behaving as though "they lived on borrowed time, feeling they had survived for no good reason".'

There is a need to communicate with employees about what has happened. The impact of any traumatic event on those involved means that there may be a need to counsel both those who are directly affected by redundancy (that is, having lost their jobs) and also those employees who are impacted indirectly by the whole exercise. Line managers and HR both have a role to play in ensuring that the impact is minimised and the organisation continues to function efficiently. This would mean that the message needs to be communicated that redundancy was a last resort and that all alternatives were (and would be in the future) exhausted before relying on job cuts as a means of reducing costs. This is of course based on the premise that organisations take a 'best practice' approach to HRM.

Having gone through a careful selection process, designed to identify and keep the best staff, the last thing the business wants is to then lose its best people, possibly to a competitor. It is important to ensure that the business does not lose valuable staff who have the skills and knowledge that are essential to the future of the enterprise. Honest communication is therefore of vital importance. There is no point in giving empty hope, but expressing the truth of the economic situation is more likely to inspire confidence and maintain trust at a time when rumours will be rife.

In addition to communication, HR can support the situation by focusing on learning and development activities for the survivors, which will improve employee engagement and help them to feel valued, thus reducing uncertainty.

In medium- to large-scale redundancies, there will probably be a need to reorganise the work; this should be seen as an opportunity to involve all those impacted and so be part of the confidence-rebuilding process.

Jobs can be restructured to use skills to best advantage. It would make sense to undertake a skills audit and training needs analysis to enable effective utilisation of staff. If survivors can see that they have an opportunity for training and development, they will be more likely to become engaged and committed, and therefore motivated to move the organisation forward.

17.5.7 WAYS TO AVOID REDUNDANCY

From a 'best practice HR' approach redundancies should be avoided as far as is possible. This might be achieved by forward thinking and undertaking human resource planning. Chapter 5 offers a discussion on this activity.

If it is not possible to avoid redundancies altogether, efforts should be made to protect the core workforce. So one step may be to release temporary staff. There should be a freeze on recruitment and it is common sense to retrain and redeploy affected staff, as vacancies occur, throughout the business. Further steps would be to reduce overtime and, perhaps more drastically, move to short-time working and even pay cuts.

One option used by some employers during a recession is to use the spare work time for training, rather than lay people off or make them redundant.

The reality of redundancy can be felt by reading David Johnson's article in the *Sentinel*, Stoke-on-Trent's local newspaper, about the problems faced by JCB during the dark days of the recession in 2008, *Digger giant tells staff to stay at home* (Johnson, 2008).

17.6 RETIREMENT

This is what the Government says about retirement:

> Default retirement age (formerly 65) has been phased out – most people can now work for as long as they want to. Retirement age is when an employee chooses to retire. Most businesses don't set a compulsory retirement age for their employees. If an employee chooses to work longer they can't be discriminated against. However, some employers can set a compulsory retirement age if they can clearly justify it. It's an employee's responsibility to discuss when and how to retire with their employer. This could include phasing retirement by working flexibly. . . .

> Employers may or may not be able to agree requests. If an employee is unhappy with their employer's decision, they can challenge this at an employment tribunal. (**www.gov.uk/retirement-age**)

Acas, when discussing retirement, offers the following advice:

> Unless it can be objectively justified it is not permissible to dismiss someone on the grounds of retirement. Older workers can voluntarily retire at a time they choose and draw any occupational pension they are entitled to. Employers cannot force employees to retire or set a retirement age unless it can be objectively justified, for example posts in the emergency service that require a significant level of physical fitness. (**www.acas.org.uk/index.aspx?articleid=4620**)

ACTIVITY 17.8

Taking the role of an independent HR consultant, what help and advice could you give to an older employee who wishes to stay on with his current employer but feels that his role, in terms of commitment, is getting to be too much for him?

You will get some good advice by reading through:

● Department for Work and Pensions (2012) *Employing older workers: An employer's guide to today's multi-generational workforce*. Available at: **www.gov.uk/government/uploads/ system/uploads/attachment_data/file/142751/employing-older-workers.pdf**
● CIPD (2012) *Managing a Healthy Ageing Workforce: A National Business Imperative*. Available at: **www.cipd.co.uk/binaries/5754ManagingageingworkforceWEB.pdf**
● Acas (2011) *Future of Workplace Relations* discussion paper series. Available at: **www.acas. org.uk/media/pdf/e/p/The_Employment_Relations_Challenges_of_an_Ageing_Workforce. pdf**
● See also: **www.ageuk.org.uk/work-and-learning/looking-for-work/the-rise-of-the-older-worker/**

17.7 SUMMARY

This chapter has covered the various ways of ending an employment contract: for example fair and unfair dismissal, redundancy and the changes to retirement law. The *Polkey* decision has been highlighted to demonstrate the need to conduct the dismissal process by following an approved process. There has also been discussion about exit interviews and how important they can be in ascertaining why people leave; and how difficult it is to ascertain the real reasons why someone might have left an organisation.

The issue of redundancy has been addressed in some detail (something commonplace in times of recession), giving an outline of how to manage the redundancy process fairly and effectively. Selection for redundancy, pay and consultation have all been discussed. The idea of managing survivors of a redundancy situation is also an important HR process. How an organisation thinks and acts about how a redundancy situation affects all staff reflects, in some part, on how it views its employees. It is important to ensure that those who remain within the organisation are not demotivated and will continue to give their best, so that when times improve, the business is in a state of preparedness to compete and to succeed.

Ending the contract can be messy and difficult, which is why dealing with it fairly and equitably is paramount. HR must handle the issues sensitively and with great care. There are a great many employment tribunal cases around redundancy issues and unfair dismissal. Many of these could have been avoided if they had been dealt with professionally, using correct procedures. The need to follow a logical process is vital – many a tribunal case has been lost because the process was not carried out properly. By reading and understanding this chapter, you should now have a basic knowledge about how to choose people for redundancy in a professional and fair manner.

Finally, consideration has been given to the subject of retirement and the Employment Equality (Repeal of Retirement Age Provisions) Regulations 2011, which abolish the UK retirement age of 65. Only if an organisation can demonstrate an objective requirement can retirement be used by an employer as a fair means of dismissal.

REVIEW QUESTIONS

1 What is the purpose of an exit interview?

2 What is meant by fair dismissal?

3 What constitutes 'automatically unfair' dismissal?

4 How has the case law as defined by the *Polkey* decision and subsequent changes to employment law legislation impacted upon how dismissals should be conducted?

5 What are the conditions under which you can take a case of unfair dismissal to an employment tribunal?

6 What do you understand by 'constructive dismissal'?

7 How much notice has to be given if you are making fewer than 20, more than 30 or 120 employees redundant within a 90-day period?

8 What criteria can be used to select people for redundancy?

9 How can an organisation improve morale for the survivors of a redundancy exercise?

10 What is the function of an outplacement agency?

11 What are the options for avoiding or reducing redundancies?

12 Can an organisation request employees to apply for voluntary redundancy without being accused of constructive dismissal?

13 What legislation has impacted on the UK retirement age?

14 What objective reasons might an employee use to have a default retirement age?

15 If an employer had a default retirement age for one group of workers, for example people who might be involved in heavy manual labour, would this mean that they would have to have a default retirement age for all employees?

16 What does it cost an individual to apply to an employment tribunal in respect of a claim associated with:

(a) unpaid wages

(b) redundancy payments

(c) an employer refusing you time off to go to antenatal classes

(d) unfair dismissal

(e) age or sex discrimination complaints

(f) whistle-blowing.

You will find some useful information by reading the relevant section in Chapter 16, 'Understanding Employment Law' and reading **www.gov.uk/government/uploads/system/uploads/attachment_data/file/254326/T435_1113.pdf**

EXPLORE FURTHER

BOOKS

LEWIS, D. and SARGEANT, M. (2013) *Employment law: the essentials*. 12th ed. London: CIPD.

An accessible text, written for the HR practitioner, dealing with issues of employment law.

JOURNAL ARTICLES

ASHMAN, I. (2012) Downsizing envoys: A public/private sector comparison. Acas. Available at: **www.acas.org.uk/media/pdf/7/1/Downsizing-envoys-a-public-private-sector-comparison-accessible-version.pdf**

ASHMAN, I. (2012) 'The nature of bad news infects the teller': The experiences of envoys in the face to face delivery of downsizing initiatives in UK public sector organisations. Research Paper [online]. Norwich: Acas. [Accessed 24 December 2013]. Available at: **www.acas.org.uk/media/pdf/k/s/ 0312_Downsizing_envoys_Ashman-accessible-version-Apr-2012.pdf**

McNICHOLAS, C. (2010) A fair selection process. *Employers' Law*. November, pp18–19.

ROBERTSON, N. and LAST, M. (2012) How to cut the cost of redundancies. *Employers' Law*. November. pp14–15.

IRS (2009) Managing the survivor syndrome during and after redundancies. *IRS Employment Review*. No 921, 26 May. 11pp.

WEB LINKS

Acas (on redundancy): **www.acas.org.uk/index.aspx?articleid=3619**

Citizens Advice Bureau (guidance on dismissal): **www.adviceguide.org.uk/wales/ work_w/work_work_comes_to_an_end_e/dismissal. htm#h_step_one_who_cannot_claim_unfair_dismissal**

Government advice on age discrimination (retirement information): **www.dwp.gov. uk/docs/legislation-20-facts.pdf**

Government UK: **www.gov.uk**

Employment tribunals: **www.justice.gov.uk/tribunals/employment**

VIDEO RESOURCE

View senior employment law advisers from XpertHR discussing collective redundancies: **www.youtube.com/watch?v=nXEl-9Ron7s**

CHAPTER 18

Change Management

LEARNING OBJECTIVES

After studying this chapter you should:

- understand the concept of the drivers and triggers of change
- understand and describe how the planned approach to change is designed to work
- understand and describe the emergent approach to change
- be able to describe Lewin's three-stage model of change
- be able to explain the role of the change consultant
- be able to identify and explain how some of the techniques of the change consultant are used.

18.1 INTRODUCTION

Burnes (2011, p.448), in an introductory article inviting contributions as to why change fails, makes the following comment:

> Whether one likes it or not, organizational change plays a signicant role in our lives. In our own organizations, it affects the nature of our jobs, or even if we have a job. In our everyday life, it impacts on the cost, quality, and availability of the services and goods we rely upon. In the broader scheme of things, the ability of organizations to manage change successfully may have profound implications for global warming, and the availability and cost of energy, food supplies, and other vital raw materials.

18.2 TRIGGERS (DRIVERS) FOR CHANGE

Burnes (2009) suggests that organisations should not become involved in planned change unless the change is significant. He argues that change should not be considered unless:

- The company's vision/strategy highlights the need for change or improved performance.
- Current performance or operation indicates that severe problems or concerns exist.
- Suggestions or opportunities arise (either from the area concerned or elsewhere) that potentially offer significant benefits to the organisation.

If one or more of the above circumstances arises, this should trigger the organisations to assess the case for change (Burnes, 2009, p.448).

18.2.1 THE NEED FOR CHANGE

The need for change often arises from changes in the external environment, especially market demands and the activities of competitors. Sometimes changes are needed urgently, induced perhaps by a crisis, and they have to be implemented as quickly as possible, but there is a limit to what can be done in the short term. Experience shows that the most effective and enduring changes take place when they have been carefully planned and introduced in gradual, incremental stages. To develop a culture that is conducive to the achievement of objectives, the envisioned culture and the organisation's future plans should be considered concurrently *{meaning – at the same time}*, from the beginning of the change process.

18.2.2 CHANGE FACTORS

Four of the major factors that have influenced and will continue to influence change, particularly as they affect HR, are:

- new and amended laws that affect employment, many of which, to a significant degree, have their origins in European directives
- the continuous advances in technology, especially in information technology
- human resource management (HRM), as a system that influences how the whole organisation is run, especially in terms of the internal structure, culture, development, human performance and the general working climate within organisations.
- the forever growing interconnectedness of world economies and business.

Christine Lagarde, Managing Director, International Monetary Fund, gave the Richard Dimbleby Lecture on 3 February 2014. She chose as her theme, 'A New Multilateralism for the 21st Century'. She said the following:

> For one thing, world trade has grown exponentially. We are now in a world of integrated supply chains, where more than half of total manufactured imports, and more than 70 percent of total service imports, are intermediate goods or services. A typical manufacturing company today uses inputs from more than 35 different contractors across the world.
>
> Financial links between countries have also grown sharply. In the two decades before the crisis in 2008, international bank lending—as a share of world GDP— rose by 250 percent. And we should expect this to rise further in the future, as more and more countries dive into the financial nexus of the global economy.
>
> We are also living through a communications revolution. It has produced a starburst of interconnections, with information traveling at lightning speed from limitless points of origin. The world has become a hum of interconnected voices and a hive of interlinked lives. (Lagarde, 2014)

Lagarde's point was that the people of the world are becoming ever more reliant and affected by each other and that we are moving from an 'industrial age to the hyperconnected digital age', (Lagarde, ibid). Emphasising her theme she further noted that, 'In such an interwoven labyrinth, even the tiniest tensions can be amplified, echoing and reverberating across the world—often in an instant, often with unpredictable twists and turns.' One only needs to consider how the large-scale default on mortgage payments coupled with the development and packaging of complex financial products brought the world to its knees with the 2008 financial crisis.

18.2.3 EVOLUTION AND REVOLUTION

The four change factors that are mentioned above are probably the most visible to those who manage organisations, but change has several perspectives. Handy, for example, talks about two types of change: *continuous* and *discontinuous*. In an analogy that describes continuous change, he says:

If you put a frog in cold water and gradually turn up the heat, the frog will eventually let itself be boiled to death. Similarly, if we don't actively respond to the radical way the world is currently changing we will not survive. (Handy, 1989)

The CIPD suggests in its factsheet on change management (February 2014) that:

Change management matters because, although change is taking place at an ever-increasing pace, there is evidence that suggests that most change initiatives fail. For example, CIPD research suggests that less than 60% of re-organisations met their stated objectives, which are usually bottom-line improvement. This is consistent with other published research.

The impact of failures to introduce effective change can also be high: loss of market position, removal of senior management, loss of stakeholder credibility, loss of key employees, and reduction in engagement. . .. (CIPD, 2014)

 ACTIVITY 18.1

How long have you been with your current employer? Look back to when you first joined and reflect upon what it was like to work there then. Now compare that with the way things are now. Try to identify exactly what has changed and, above all, why it has changed.

What Handy describes as *discontinuous* change is more revolutionary than evolutionary. This type of change imposes sudden, large-scale changes, such as the implementation of a major new policy, a merger with another organisation or the privatisation of a public authority, or the changes brought about by the banking collapse of 2008, which reduced the money supply to organisations across the world; but there are yet other evolutionary changes. Champy and Nohria (1996) claim that three major drivers are stirring organisational change faster than ever before:

- **technology:** particularly IT, which is transforming businesses in dramatic ways
- **government:** rethinking its role in business, with all governments on a worldwide basis initiating deregulation, privatisation and increasing free trade
- **globalisation:** companies from all parts of the globe are competing to deliver the same product or service, anytime, anywhere, at increasingly competitive prices, which is causing organisations and companies to organise themselves in radically different ways.

If we consider the introduction of new technology as an example, this can have both positive and negative outcomes.

On the positive side, it enables the organisation to:

- enhance the productivity rate and the quality of its goods and services, for example by the introduction of computer-aided design and robotic manufacturing systems
- broaden and deepen its range of goods and services
- increase the efficiency and effectiveness of administration and the speed at which administrative tasks are carried out
- communicate internally and externally almost instantaneously
- carry out some of its functions more cost-effectively by transferring them to overseas locations, for example call centres.

On the negative side:

- The initial capital outlay for new technology can be prohibitively high.
- The rate at which technology is developing means that further advances are made before the organisation has had a full return on its capital outlay.
- Advances in technology affect the types of knowledge and skill requirements, and often require costly, wide-ranging training and retraining programmes.
- Its installation may cause the organisation temporarily to lose its day-to-day effectiveness.
- Employees may be negatively affected by the 'threat' of technological change and concerned over job losses.

The above forces for change, as described by Champy and Nohria, are largely external forces to the organisation. However, other forces can bring about change which are largely factors of the internal organisation, such as the need to restructure, moving from one organisational type to a matrix organisation to improve control, efficiency and teamworking (refer to Chapter 1, 'Organisations').

But there are alternative views.

Hughes (2007, p.40) suggests typical forces for change might include:

- competition
- government changes
- new senior management
- IT development.

Huczynski and Buchanan (2013, p.620) offer the following as internal triggers for change:

- new product and service design innovations
- low performance and morale, high stress and staff turnover
- appointment of a new senior manager or top management team
- inadequate skills and knowledge base, triggering training programmes
- office and factory relocation, closer to suppliers and markets
- recognition of problems, triggering reallocation of responsibilities
- innovation in the manufacturing process
- new ideas about how to deliver services to customers.

ACTIVITY 18.2

Listen to the CIPD's Podcast No. 85, which discusses ways in which social and digital technologies can and increasingly will have a real impact on the world of work: **www.cipd. co.uk/podcasts/_articles/social-business-podcast-85.htm?link=title**

- Have any of the changes discussed impacted upon your organisation or one you know of?
- If so, in what way?
- If not, why not?

ACTIVITY 18.3

How does one start a movement? To create the impetus to overcome the initial inertia which prevents change to happen? Watch the Ted Video on how to start a movement: **www.ted.com/ talks/derek_sivers_how_to_start_a_movement**

Derek Sivers from the Boston Consulting Group suggests that it is the first followers who make the difference when starting a movement. Do you think his analysis of the situation is correct? What factors help bring about what Sivers call the *tipping point*, which makes it acceptable for others to join the movement? How does industry, and in particular advertising, use the ideas offered by Sivers in the video clip?

In a similar manner as Derek Sivers introduces the concept of leaders and followers in the context of creating the basis of a 'movement', Seth Godin picks up on the notion of tribes as *movements* as a means of bringing about change. He argues the Internet has ended mass marketing and revived a human social unit from the distant past: tribes. Founded on shared ideas and values, tribes give ordinary people the power to lead and make big change: **www.ted.com/talks/seth_godin_on_the_tribes_we_lead**

PAUSE FOR THOUGHT

Competition drives change

In today's economy it is simply not enough for businesses, especially if they are quoted on the stock exchange, to make a profit. It is the three-monthly comparative figures as well as the annual, current end of year to last year, figures which are also of importance. The ever present pressure is on managing directors not only to make a profit but also to maintain a healthy financial position relative to past performance as well as to do well against the market competitors.

Consider the following example of how these types of pressures – triggers – have caused the large UK supermarkets to engage in a price war to maintain their market position. Intense media scrutiny of the situation further intensifies the situation for the supermarkets' chief executives.

High-street supermarkets are coming under pressure to cut costs. A number of pressures are causing the big supermarkets to consider their cost base, with a view to giving customers a better deal. The pressures on supermarkets are immediate: their sales are monitored on a quarterly basis. The pressures, the 'triggers for change', at the moment (March 2014) are coming from two directions. For Tesco and Sainsbury's they have both been impacted by a downturn in sales, as has Morrisons. Tesco's problem is not new but Sainsbury's and Morrisons have suffered since December 2013. Morrisons' management has also had to do some 'catch-up' because their business model had not included online grocery shopping. Luckily Ocado, the online grocer, was seeking a

partner with which to develop its online business. Ocado had the warehousing and infrastructure to deliver the goods to homes but needed a high-profile partner, which it found with Morrisons. The situation is not yet rosy for either Ocado or Morrisons:

> Morrisons reports its full year results tomorrow and is expected to reveal that pre-tax profits slumped as much as 20 per cent following a dreadful Christmas, with cash-strapped customers deserting the company in droves for the likes of discount chains Aldi and Lidl.

> ...The lack of a profit for the online-only Ocado continues to be a problem for the business, especially since Tesco revealed last month that it took a trading profit of £127 million from its online operation. ...Shares in Ocado slipped back on the results today...' (Neville, 2014)

James Davey of Reuters [online], under a headline banner of 'Morrisons boss waives bonus after profit warning', wrote: 'Earlier this month the Bradford, northern England, based firm said profit before tax and one-off items dropped to 785 million pounds in the year to February 2 and warned that underlying profit in the 2014–15 year would be in the range of 325–375 million pounds.'

'The firm also sparked talk of an industry price war by saying it would invest 1 billion pounds in price cuts over three years in a bid to recover' (Davey, 2014)

The problems for Tesco, Sainsbury's and Morrisons are also being compounded by the growth of Lidl and Aldi. The bad news (for the existing supermarkets) does not stop there. In the *Sunday Times* Business Section (23 March 2014), Sir Philip Green, owner of BHS, is vowing to undercut food prices in the supermarkets by 10% when he introduces food sales into his BHS chain of stores (Shah, 2014). The following is a sample of what the papers are saying about the pressures on the big supermarkets:

> **Tesco** boss Philip Clarke is expected to signal next week that the scale of the investment needed to win back disaffected UK shoppers will mean sacrificing the industry-leading levels of profitability that once made the supermarket chain one of Britain's most admired companies.
>
> Clarke will update investors and analysts about his turnaround plan on Tuesday. Tesco performed poorly over Christmas and, based on recent market data, has suffered a further deterioration since. (Wood, 2014)

Sainsbury's sales have fallen for the first time in nine years in what the supermarket group said was the slowest market for almost a decade.

Sales at stores open a year fell 3.1%, excluding fuel, in the three months to 15 March and sales at all stores dropped 1%, ending a run of 36 quarters of growth under departing chief executive Justin King.

> King, who leaves in July after leading Sainsbury's for 10 years, admitted the sales fall was 'disappointing' and that Sainsbury's had been caught out by shoppers' restraint and late Easter shopping. (Farrell, 2014).
>
> Embattled grocer **Morrisons** sent a shiver down the High Street after issuing another profit warning that also wiped 8 per cent off the shares of rival Sainsbury's and 4.9 per cent off Tesco.
>
> Britain's fourth-biggest supermarket chain fell 12 per cent after declaring a price war, investing £1billion in cuts to compete with discount chains Aldi and Lidl.

Investors fear the battle will leave all of the big supermarket players licking their wounds. (Steiner, 2014)

You may wish to explore the media to see if similar scrutiny affects how other large organisations react to similar reporting of their financial situations.

 ## ACTIVITY 18.4

All change at school (and college?)

This activity is in two parts. Answer Part 1 before tackling, as a group, Part 2.

Part 1

Think about how your college or university works. What factors external to the organisation and what changes internal to the organisation could cause it to change what it does? For example, in the provision of undergraduate or postgraduate courses. (Hint: you could consider doing a PESTLE (STEEPLE) analysis.)

Part 2

The following narrative is the introductory message from Massachusetts Institute of Technology (MIT) President L. Rafael Reif, welcoming Internet browsers to the MIT Open Courseware (OCW) website.

In the spring of 2001, the world greeted MIT OpenCourseWare as a brave experiment. The brainchild of MIT faculty members, OCW drew on a tradition of open sharing at MIT that stretched back at least to the 1950s. But no previous project could match OCW for scope, ambition or elegance. It was a bold new strategy for sharing knowledge and increasing opportunity—but no one knew how well it would work.

Today, OCW is a flourishing MIT institution and a global model for open sharing in higher education. This Institute-wide undertaking has touched more than 125 million people in every country on Earth. (L. Rafael Reif, 2014. Available at: **http://ocw.mit.edu/about/ presidents-message/**)

Questions to reflect upon:

- Why do you think MIT are making the majority of their courses free to view online?

- Can you find by reading material on the MIT OpenCourseWare website whether MIT reaps any immediate financial gain?
- Has what you have found in the above (Part 2) caused you to think whether the MIT experiment will impact upon the UK education scene and cause colleges and universities to rethink the way they deliver and charge for courses?

18.3 TYPOLOGIES OF CHANGE – SOFT AND HARD CHANGE PROBLEMS

Change can broadly be categorised into 'hard' or difficult change situations and 'soft' or messy problems.

The 'hard' type of problems are those which can be resolved by logical means, for example, by resolving complex problems which lend themselves perhaps to a systems approach. The installation of a complex array of conveyors which sort, carry and deliver baggage from the check-in desk of an airport, as was the case when the new Terminal 5 was commissioned for British Airways in 2008, is an example of 'hard' change. Because a definitive answer can be developed it does not mean that the problem is any easier. Consider the following article from *Computer Weekly* in May 2008. The human interface, where problems become 'messy', cannot be ignored:

Terminal 5 is one of the most technologically advanced airport terminals in the world, but MPs described its opening as a 'national humiliation'. During the first five days, BA misplaced more than 23,000 bags, cancelled 500 flights and made losses of £16m.

The Transport Select Committee called in Willie Walsh, BA's chief executive, Colin Matthews, airport-owner BAA's chief executive, and Nigel Rudd, a non-executive chairman of the board, to face some tough questions earlier this month.

Willie Walsh revealed that IT problems and a lack of testing played a large part in the trouble. But he said the airline could have coped if IT had been the only issue. (British Airways reveals what went wrong with Terminal 5. (2008) *ComputerWeekly.Com [online]*. 14 May. Available at: **www.computerweekly.com/ news/2240086013/British-Airways-reveals-what-went-wrong-with-Terminal-5**)

'Soft' change problems are the ones which will be considered in this chapter. 'Soft' or messy problems tend not to be bounded by a clear time-frame, there are implications for and involve those employed and touched by the change. The desired outcome in terms of cost reduction, efficiency or behavioural change may be understood, but the structure, numbers of people, power bases, areas of influence, which emerge from the change process is ill defined; hence the term 'messy'. The process is likely to be stressful for those involved and likely to be impacted by the change. The reason for the change may not be accepted by everyone and so techniques from the study of organisation development (OD) are likely to be used to effect the change.

18.4 RESISTANCE TO CHANGE

The chief preoccupations of managers when they are planning and implementing change are usually related to the cost and technical aspects of the change process. This can be a complex and testing set of disciplines to handle. Mistakes can be costly, but the key factor and certainly the most essential ingredient to a successful change process is the way in which the employees are taken through it. It is hard to imagine a more stringent test of managers' leadership skills.

When, for example, technological innovation triggers change, many of the long-serving employees fear it. Their skills have served them well in terms of their performance and earning capacity, but they feel abandoned and redundant when their previously valued abilities are no longer needed by the organisation. They might resist change for several reasons, since to them it might mean:

- a threat to their stability and may make their jobs redundant
- a change of routines, which can be frustrating
- being moved into jobs they fear they may not understand
- a change in status
- a change in pay structure and other rewards
- having to work in a new area with previously unknown colleagues
- having to work for a new and unknown boss
- having to work for a boss who is known, but is generally not liked
- a change in working hours
- changing to a job that is insufficiently challenging.

As Hughes (2007, p.11) says, 'Organisational change and transformations involve the redistribution of power, information, resources, status, authority, and influence. Therefore, individuals' rights, dignity and privileges can be at risk.'

Erwin and Garman (2010, p.45), citing a 'self-reported' survey on individuals' resistance to change conducted by Oreg (2006) within 177 American firms operating in the defence industry:

> ...he [Oreg] examined resistance based upon employees' concerns about the impact of the change on their job security, intrinsic rewards (e.g. autonomy, flexibility, and challenge), and how their power and prestige were affected. Oreg found that concerns about job security were strongly related to emotional reactions, changes in intrinsic rewards were related to both emotional and cognitive reactions, and threats to power and prestige were significantly related to cognitive reactions.

Change is happening all the time and so employees must change and learn to cope with the changes that are, in many cases, forced upon them. It is not easy to cope with change, especially if, as Erwin and Garman (ibid) indicate, it affects the individual in the organisation. The fact that change is forced, or is in some way inevitable, may cause the individual to resist the changes. Not all employees respond in the same way to change. Individual differences have a profound effect on how employees perceive change. Intelligence and motivational factors may frustrate retraining, and age differences may inhibit more mature employees when it comes to their routines being disrupted and perhaps separating them from their long-term work colleagues. For these reasons, therefore, change may raise the staff turnover rate and lead to redundancy and recruitment programmes. Change has significant implications for the HR role.

Organisations can be thought of as socio-technical systems. Changing the way work is organised, how people are redeployed in the workplace or the disrupting shift routines in the cause of drives for efficiency and 'better ways of working' will have an impact upon both individuals and work-groups of employees. Trist and Bamforth (1951), referred to in Chapter 3, deal with the issues associated with social groups in the workplace.

18.4.1 DEALING WITH RESISTANCE

Encountering resistance may be used as an opportunity to examine how the change proposal is being handled. If the nature of the change has not been fully explained to employees, the prophets of doom, from the ranks of the employee body, will step forward and rumours, especially negative ones, about the proposed change will become widespread. Resistance, however, can be turned around and made constructive if it causes managers to interact more frequently with their staff, for example when they explain the nature of the proposed change in detail.

The proposed change should be explained to employees from the very outset. If it is not, it will create uncertainty among employees about what their future holds, which may lead to personal feelings of insecurity on the part of individuals. The approach to delivering news of change should be a consultative one, in which managers elicit employees' feelings and opinions. This kind of approach has been known to cause managers to explore alternative ways of meeting the desired objective. It may be that the alternatives proposed by the employees represent an improvement on the original proposal. If the employees are asked to think about the change, they will get to know more about it, which will serve three possible ends: first, to allay any rumours; second, to produce an improved proposal; and third, to reduce or even eliminate resistance to the proposed changes. A positive outcome to a consultative approach may confer upon employees feelings of 'ownership' of the change and also engage them in the change process, which naturally leads towards commitment to the change.

To involve employees and ensure that they engage with the change process, it may be worth considering the work of Tannenbaum and Schmidt (1973), cited in Mullins (2013, pp.377–8), who suggest that there is a continuum of leadership and involvement, ranging from telling, selling, consulting and joining. There is a danger that if the management make all the decisions and simply 'tell' the employees about the change, there will be no 'buy-in' from staff.

Alternatively, at the other end of the continuum, if managers involve employees in the decision-making process, that is, 'join' with them, there is more likely to be commitment and engagement to the change and in the change process. Often managers settle for the mid-way approach of 'selling' the benefits of the change or maybe going as far as 'consulting' staff. The optimum situation for gaining commitment from employees is, of course, to 'join' with them, thus allowing the employees to exercise 'employee voice' and to be fully involved with the change activity and embrace the changes positively.

18.4.2 USING A FORCE FIELD ANALYSIS TO OVERCOME RESISTANCE TO CHANGE

One method of trying to manage a change process in the context of overcoming the resistance to change is to perform a force field analysis. This examines the key drivers and key resistive forces to a particular change situation. One can imagine a change problem to be like a large and unwieldy block of material on rollers that has forces trying to push it forward and resistive forces trying to prevent it from moving (Figure 18.1).

It can be seen that not all the forces are of the same magnitude; the width of the arrows gives some indication of this. Also, there may not necessarily be the same number of forces for the change as there are against the change. The art is in trying to identify all the relevant forces and then finding ways of increasing the strength of the forces for change and reducing the forces that are resisting change so that the heavy block on rollers, which represents the change process, moves to the right.

Figure 18.1 Forces for and against change

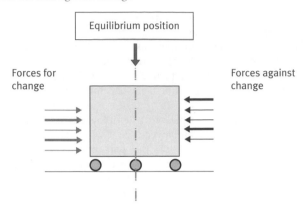

The work on the force field analysis was first conducted in the 1950s by K.Z. Lewin and is still relevant today. Force field analysis provides a model for examining the forces that influence a situation, originally in the field of social sciences. The following seven steps, after Senior (2002, p.254), can be used when conducting a force field analysis:

- **Step 1:** The problem is defined in its present situation, with its strengths and weaknesses, and then the situation that the organisation would like to achieve is defined.
- **Step 2:** The forces for and against the situation are listed. These can be associated with people (who may be in positions of authority and so can impact upon the change positively or negatively), finances (and other resources), time factors, internal and external political factors, technical issues, competitor positions, what is the status quo with accepted and rigid ways of doing things – in fact, a mini PESTLE (STEEPLE) analysis can be conducted on the situation.
- **Step 3:** The forces are rated against a scale of 1 to 5; say, a force of 1 being weak and 5 being strong.
- **Step 4:** A diagram is drawn, as in Figure 18.1, which has all relevant forces indicated.
- **Step 5:** Analyse each of the forces in turn, especially the strong forces, and think of ways that the forces 'for' can be improved and strengthened and the forces 'against' weakened.
- **Step 6:** After identifying the forces and the relative strengths, an action plan has to be agreed. It may be that if it is a person who is causing significant resistance to change, they can be 'turned' to work for the change by explaining to them issues and possible consequences of which perhaps they were not aware. Alternatively, as a final resort, they can be moved to another section or department of the organisation.
- **Step 7:** Identify the resources that will be needed to bring about the changes. Usually for large-scale changes a member of the senior management team (SMT) is identified as a 'change champion'. This person will have the necessary authority to approve actions, budgets, make decisions and so on, to enable change to be effected.

Senior and Swailes (2010) later modified their approach by adding an eighth and ninth step, which were to identify resources needed to effectively bring about the change and to develop an action plan.

FORCE FIELD ANALYSIS

CASE EXAMPLE 18.1

Keep on 'truckin', or is it 'bussin'?

Hilborough Horizons is a profitable tour bus company. It has 40 coaches and services a significant area covering a number of towns in the Black Country and into and around Birmingham. It has been in existence since 1936 when James Hilborough bought his first, but second-hand, 'charabanc' – really an extended car with a 'soft top' (fabric roof).

The business model of Hilborough Horizons is based upon:

1 A mix of British and European travel holidays, which are in the main planned to occur during the summer months.

2 Contracts which the company has with the local councils to provide school bus services. This work predominantly is the typical morning and evening 'school runs'; taking children, who live in rural communities, to and from school. This work constitutes 50% of its business.

3 A small contract with a local long-stay car parking company to provide a circular bus service from their car parks to Birmingham Airport.

Alfred Hilborough, a descendant of James, has recently taken over the business. He considers that the business has reached a plateau, in terms of economic development, and unless it changes it will either wither or be taken over by a more aggressive rival or, at best, plod on as it is. He considers that Hilborough coaches have too few eggs in too few baskets. In essence, he considers that the company should diversify by taking advantage of its strengths to generate more business. The financial strain, as imposed by government on councils, is likely to continue for the foreseeable future. He considers that the financial squeeze will be passed on to its contractors, such as the like of

Hilborough Horizons, as demands on council resources force contractors to cut profit margins.

All the staff in Hilborough Horizons have been recruited locally; many have worked for the company for 20 years, some significantly longer. The management team consists of Alfred, as the CEO, his mother, who has always taken an interest in the business but does not take an active part in its management, the chief finance officer and an operations manager. The chief finance officer, Satvinder, is one of the business's stalwarts; he worked with Alfred's father, has his values and is a family friend. Alfred's mother has always 'taken council' from 'Sat'. The operations manager, Jenni, is a relatively new team member, having joined the company after completing her degree as a mature student. Alfred recognised her abilities very quickly and promoted her to the small management team; she is an innovative person and enjoys both solving the immediate problems that the family business offers but also can think strategically. It was a discussion with Jenni that caused Alfred to think about the company's present situation.

The company's current premises lie in the centre of the city and they are at their maximum capacity. The building is an old tram station and, for a number of reasons, has passed its true usefulness. Vehicular exit and entrance over the years has become increasingly more difficult for drivers to manoeuvre their coaches in and out because the town has slowly grown and so encroached on the old tram station. The coaches have grown in size. The building is listed and so cannot be significantly changed; in short, it cannot take any more coaches and so is an impediment for expansion of the current business.

Alfred, together with Sat (the chief finance officer) and Jenni (his operations manager), conducted a SWOT analysis on the Hilborough Horizons business and they consider that the company could diversify, perhaps into haulage, removals as well as heavy vehicle maintenance – maybe not all at once but staged over a period of five years. In fact, they consider that it would be a good idea to have a rolling five-year plan. The company's financial balance sheet is strong; business has been good and money has been spent prudently to develop the business to where it is today. Although a very logical person, Sat is ultra-cautious and although supportive in the discussion, Alfred is not sure whether he (Sat) would actually back such a 'revolutionary' plan. The very nascent *{meaning – the act of being born}* plan would develop new strands to the business: removals and heavy haulage as well as maximising the use of its dedicated mechanics. Brief and confidential discussions with the head of the vehicle workshop reinforced that there is a market in vehicle servicing and testing; she believes that she can undercut the main dealer outlets on both servicing and repair costs.

Alfred has also done an analysis of the regional market and sees an opportunity for long haulage into Poland, where a number of local and significant Birmingham-based businesses have supply sources.

One of the concerns which Alfred has lies in the fact that the business will have to move at least 15 miles from its current location. He has already scouted a business park which has good links to the M5 and M6 and has planning permission for bespoke buildings as well as room to expand. If he took an initial lease, he would have 'first refusal' on any adjoining plot should another company come along and wish to lease land alongside. The local council is eager to encourage companies to develop by giving rate reductions for the first two years of operation. His staff all live within a short distance of the present premises and are quite set in their ways; big

change is when someone buys a new jacket and that will be the focus of conversation for the following week! However, the staff are committed and they have skills which Alfred would find difficult to replace. Good-quality people are becoming increasingly difficult to find as the Birmingham economy starts to pick up. Problematic in the development is Alfred's mother, who he loves dearly. Although not active in the business, she does hold significant shares. She has very conservative views and is generally risk-averse. She has pointed out that when many similar companies were buying coaches through bank finance deals, she and her husband always self-financed purchase of new stock. Many of the former companies went broke when, after the 2008 financial collapse, banks started to call in debt, but they remained healthily solvent. Sat's views and support are clearly also important to any new venture. To effect the move the company would have to borrow significant monies from the bank, a first for Alfred and Hilborough Horizons. The sale of the old tram station would, to a certain extent, offset the cost of moving. It is a prime property for conversion into city centre flats.

Key to Alfred's thinking is that nothing is definite about the immediate or long-term future except that there is no opportunity to grow the business as it is presently operated.

Task

Question 1: Is the proposed change likely to be a *hard* or *soft* model of change?

Question 2: What are the drivers for change in the above case study?

Question 3: Using a force field analysis technique, how would you, as Alfred, go about bringing the desired change? Draw the relevant force fields, with forces for and against, and develop an action plan of how you would overcome the (potential) resistance to change and develop the business as Alfred envisages.

You will find further guidance on how to handle these questions at:

- KOTTER, J.P. and SCHLESINGER, L.A. (2008) Choosing strategies for change. *Harvard Business Review [online]*. Vol 86, No 7/8. pp.130–39 [Accessed 26 March 2014]. Available at: **www.web.a. ebscohost.com**

- SENIOR, B. and SWAILES, S. (2010) *Organisational change.* 4th ed. Harlow: Prentice Hall, pp.270–72.

Note: 'Hilborough Horizons' is a purely fictitious company and every effort has been made to check whether there is an organisation operating with the same name.

18.5 CHANGING THE CULTURE

As we have previously seen, the foundations of the culture of any organisation are in its history. The traditions that have built up over time, including its methods of operating, tend to remain evident for as long as the organisation continues to succeed. What is done and how it is done are reinforced by success, and an 'if it ain't broke, don't fix it' attitude emerges. The facts have to be faced, however; things do change. Competition becomes more fierce, market demands change as technological innovation continues to progress, people (customers) have become more discerning and price-conscious, and living standards are raised continually – at least, that is the case in the more advanced countries. Sometimes, however, the more senior members of the organisation may be inclined to place a high value on tradition, as Case Example 18.2 shows.

CASE EXAMPLE 18.2

IN CHANGE MANAGEMENT

What you can learn from RSA: The happy couple

When an insurance giant's financial woes saw engagement hit rock bottom, an ambitious – and award-winning – pairing stepped in

Imagine the fusty interior of an insurance company office, bedecked with polished dark wooden panels and green leather. For Royal and Sun Alliance, that was home at the start of the 21st century. A global giant headquartered in Berkeley Square, London, its mindset – like its HQ – was more reminiscent of the 18th century.

In the first nine months of 2002, the company posted pre-tax losses of £156 million. Even after an emergency rights issue, it burned through £146 million the following year. Things looked dire.

'The business was struggling,' says Jeremy Phillips-Powell, group HR strategy and development director. 'Andy Haste

was brought in as CEO in 2003 with a mandate: bring the business back from the brink and turn it around.'

The change programme that followed was enormous. 'We went from 70,000 people to 20,000 in a couple of years, sold off the US business, sold off the life business; it completely transformed the group,' says Phillips-Powell. 'When you go through a change programme of that magnitude and lose that many people in that space of time it leaves quite a deep impact. People felt pretty battered and bruised.'

By 2007, now re-housed in an ultra-modern building in the City of London, the company (soon to be renamed RSA) needed a turnaround of another kind. Phillips-Powell, along with Oliver Strong, group director of internal communications and engagement, was tasked with transforming levels of employee engagement.

'Morale was low,' admits Phillips-Powell, recalling press speculation when he joined (in 2005) about who might be buying the company. 'It was just rumours,' he says. 'But when you start seeing that kind of thing every day it is unsettling. There was a sense of... has this organisation got a future?'

The first step was to find out just how engaged the staff were. As it turned out, not very. The first of many Gallup Q12 questionnaires put RSA in the 38th percentile of all the firms in Gallup's dataset globally – well below average.

Phillips-Powell says: 'Gallup explained "In our experience companies of your size with these results in year one take five years to get to world class." So we said "That's great, we'll do it in three." And we did.'

RSA went on to scoop the top prize in the 2012 CIPD People Management Awards, and debuted sixth in the *Sunday Times* 25 Best Big Companies to Work For survey. All this took place during the global economic downturn – and despite in 2009 having to lose 15 per cent of the workforce, shut an entire office in Bristol, and close the defined benefit pension scheme. How did the company keep its engagement scores rising throughout?

Hold people to account

The bulk of engagement happens at a team and leader level, says Strong. '"Do I come to work and have a really great boss who inspires my performance?" You need leadership accountability for that, but also team accountability.' Addressing accountability among line managers was the best starting point to drive engagement, adds Phillips-Powell. In year one, he says, it was about: 'If you're a leader, you're going to be held accountable for improving [engagement] and we're going to start looking at how engaged your team is when we're looking at leaders for promotions and bonuses.'

The language in the organisation also changed – 'managers' became 'leaders', which helped to further embed

accountability and, importantly, pride. But crucially, says Strong, it wasn't just about holding leaders accountable, it was about giving them the tools to get results.

Fix your priorities

While the ambition was for cultural transformation, it was necessary to first identify 'priority leaders', says Phillips-Powell – leaders who were low scoring in terms of team engagement and/or had an important population of people. 'For example, if it's a big growth area or customer-facing, that's a priority unit for us,' he says. From that list, about 40 leaders were identified as needing additional coaching support. 'You need to get people's immediate environment right first and then you build on that,' he says.

Be rigorous

Phillips-Powell has one word that sums up turning employee engagement around in only three years: rigour. 'Someone said to me "You're running an engagement programme with the rigour that someone would run a business with",' he says. 'I thought that was hugely complimentary.'

For each leader, the engagement survey results were just the start, adds Strong: 'After that comes analysis, advice on what to do and what a really great action plan looks like. We also introduced a half-year "pulse check" to ensure people followed through on the action plans.'

Data analysis showed engaged staff in RSA's call centres spent 35 per cent less time between calls; a 0.36 correlation between teams' engagement levels and customer satisfaction; and a 0.6 correlation between engagement levels and new business growth. The call centre figure caused ripples, says Phillips-Powell. 'It means that for every eight engaged people you have in your team, you get an extra member of staff for nothing. Say that to somebody who runs a 500-person operation and they can see why this is a good thing to do.'

Coach your leaders

Coaching was extended to 300 leaders across the global business, with the coaches mainly chosen internally. 'It could be a leader from somewhere else in the business; it could be someone from HR,' says Phillips-Powell.

The team engagement scores of those in the coaching programme went up six times more than average. 'If there's one thing I've learned that a company should do to raise its engagement,' says Strong, 'it's probably this [coaching]. People in management may have got there because they're technically great, but you need to invest in their leadership capability.'

Celebrate success

All this focus on accountability and rigour could have become a bit humourless. Phillips-Powell recalls: 'I was going through all the plans and Andy [Haste, then CEO] just asked "What are we going to do to make it more fun around here?"'

The leaders with the highest team engagement scores, and the most improved, were taken for a celebratory meal – an event that is now annual. And in 2010, the company's 300-year anniversary provided 'a great excuse for a big party', says Phillips-Powell. For the insurer of the journeys of the RMS Titanic, Charles Darwin and Captain Cook, it was a time to reflect on the company's history and take pride in it, says Strong. This was coupled with a focus on CSR and volunteering. 'Our team went and worked together painting a duck house at a city farm this year,' says Strong.

Take it to the next level

The Gallup scores on engagement rose steadily at RSA from 3.75 out of 5 in 2008, to 3.94 in 2009, 4.17 in 2010 and 4.30 in 2011. In 2012, the scores plateaued. The goal is no longer to raise them, but to drive performance. 'The thinking we've come to now is about where we channel this energy,' says Strong. 'We're now at quite an exciting stage, moving from generic engagement – or engagement for engagement's sake – to more transformational engagement.'

(Smedley, 2013) Reprinted with kind permission of *People Management*.

In making sense of the methodologies which were adopted to bring around the changes within RSA in the Smedley (2013) article, it is worth reading the following:

Strebel (1996) is worth reading because it details the issues which the CEO of Phillips Electronics managed when needing to bring about widespread change in a very large 'multi-domestic' electronics company which was moving towards difficulty, although employees were not prepared to acknowledge the dangers which lay ahead.

Margolis and Stoltz (2010) consider some advice for managers when dealing with situations that they have not met before and perhaps feel beyond their capacity to cope. Many of us have been in this situation. Margolis and Stoltz (ibid) identify the following characteristics of leadership behaviour in difficult times:

Psychological resilience – the capacity to respond quickly and constructively in a crisis – can be hard to muster when a manager is paralysed by fear, anger, confusion, or a tendency to assign blame.

Resilient managers – shift quickly from endlessly dissecting traumatic events to looking forward, determining the best course of action given new realities. They understand the size and scope of the crisis and the levels of control and impact they may have in a bad situation.

Coaching resilience – often even the most resilient managers run into trouble trying to coach direct reports in crisis. They react with either a how-to pep talk delivered utterly without empathy or understanding, or a sympathetic ear and reassurance that things will turn out okay. Neither response will equip your team members to handle the next unforeseen twist or turn. Instead, you should adopt a collaborative, inquisitive approach that can help your direct reports generate their own options and possibilities. (Margolis and Stoltz, 2010, pp.4–5)

18.5.1 MAKING THE CHANGE: CAN IT BE DONE?

In Chapter 2 references are made to the work of several eminent writers on culture, and from these you will have seen that culture is made up of relatively stable characteristics. From reading Part 1 of the following discussion, you will see that changing an organisation's culture appears to be an extremely difficult task. We hope, however, the evidence from the second part of the discussion will indicate to you that cultures can be changed.

18.5.2 PART 1: DON'T ROCK THE BOAT

The long-held beliefs and deeply rooted values to which the employees of an organisation are strongly committed motivate them to maintain the culture. In mechanistic organisations (highly structured organisations with centralised policies, rigid hierarchical ranks, a strong emphasis on administration), that is, those organisations typically servicing a stable market (see Chapter 1 for a fuller explanation), there are forces that combine to reinforce the importance of adhering to the cultural norms. These include written policies, mission statements and philosophies that emanate from the top, the infrastructural design, the buildings, the hardware, the structure, the beliefs and styles of leadership, the general climate of the place, the policies on recruitment, selection, training and promotion, the rituals and historic myths about the organisation and its key people.

Historically, mechanistic organisations have always attracted employees who seek stable and structured positions. Senior managers are selected on the grounds that they are the most likely people to perpetuate 'the way things are'. Strebel's article (1996) explains these exact circumstances as they impacted upon the Phillips Electronics giant in the 1990s.

18.5.3 PART 2: CATALYSTS OF CULTURE CHANGE

If, in the organisation-wide sense, the culture matches the values and philosophies of those at the top, there is an overall cohesiveness that makes for a strong culture, which is the most difficult type of culture to change. In any organisational scenario, the culture change process presents a daunting prospect, but research and experience shows that it can be done.

In particular circumstances, organisations are vulnerable to culture change when a severe crisis arises, such as when a competitor suddenly and unpredictably launches a new major product on the market, as happened when the Android-type phones superseded the then market-leading BlackBerry mobile phone organiser system in cost, operating flexibility (they could take reasonable photos, play music, and so on) and adaptability – in so much as the 'architecture' of the new Android devices allowed downloads of mobile phone 'Apps' (Application Packaging Standard) which were starting to appear. Alternatively, if, for example, there is a critical financial downturn such as happened with the banking collapse of 2008, organisations would be driven to critically review their business models, how they conduct business, cost and profit centres. A shock – as explained in the two examples previously given, the advent of Android technology and the banking collapse – can form the catalyst and a solid reason why things need to be done differently. In such cases, organisations usually bring in a new chief executive. However, sometimes the shock can come too late for management to effectively turn around a failing situation.

Sometimes failure can be so catastrophic that it impacts upon a whole industry; this was the case when Mid Staffordshire NHS Hospital Trust failed in its duty to safeguard and effectively treat between 400 and 1,200 patients who unnecessarily died (see Chapter 3, 'Human Resource Management'). On 26 March 2014, Jeremy Hunt, the Health Secretary, visited Virginia Mason Hospital in Seattle, USA, which has become a model of safety, quality and health throughout the world. The Government said this about the NHS in anticipation of Hunt's speech at the Seattle hospital:

A new ambition to reduce avoidable harm in the NHS by half over the next three years, cut costs and save up to 6,000 lives has been outlined by Jeremy Hunt. In a speech at Virginia Mason Hospital in Seattle, the Secretary of State has announced details of how NHS organisations can work together to improve patient safety and save money. (**www.gov.uk/government/news/halving-avoidable-harm-and-saving-up-to-6000-lives**)

In his speech the Health Secretary, Jeremy Hunt, said:

It is my clear ambition that the NHS should become the safest healthcare system anywhere in the world. I want the tragic events of Mid Staffs to become a turning point in the creation of a more open, compassionate and transparent culture within the NHS.

We now have a once in a generation opportunity to save lives and prevent avoidable harm – which will empower staff and save money that can be re invested in patient care. Hospitals are already 'signing up to safety' as part of this new movement – and I hope all NHS organisations will soon join them.' (**www.gov.uk/government/news/halving-avoidable-harm-and-saving-up-to-6000-lives**)

Templeton and Gilliespie, in the *Sunday Times* (23 March 2014, News, p.18) write under a dramatic headline banner of 'Hunt likens Mid Staffs to Chernobyl' that:

Hunt will point to international disasters such as Bhopal, which claimed 8,000 lives, the radioactive leaks at Three Mile Island in America and Chernobyl – where 14,000 people had to evacuate the city – and the oil pollution from Piper Alpha and Exxon Valdez, as moments that heralded a profound change in their industries.

In the case of Mid Staffordshire Hospital NHS Trust, an enquiry was set up under Sir Robert Francis QC (**www.gov.uk/government/publications/mid-staffordshire-nhs-ft-public-inquiry-government response**), who made a series of recommendations for patient health care and the training of hospital staff which will have a significant impact upon the NHS and how it recruits and trains its staff. See Chapter 7, where we deal with values-based selection as a first step in the journey to identify the type of people the NHS wants within its ranks to treat and give care to its patients

As part of the 'turn-around strategy' for Mid Staffordshire Hospital NHS Trust, it is to lose specialist services and come under the control of new management, Jeremy Hunt, the Health Secretary, has announced:

The trust will be dissolved, with Stafford coming under the University Hospital of North Staffordshire trust, and its sister hospital in Cannock Chase becoming part of the Royal Wolverhampton hospitals' trust. But Support Stafford Hospital campaigners want to keep more important services, arguing that patients may have to travel up to 18 miles on poor roads for acute services. They are particularly worried that patients will be reluctant to use a downgraded obstetrics and maternity unit. (Meikle, 2014)

In public sector organisations it is not uncommon when part of the organisation is seen to be failing that a rebranding exercise is undertaken. Typically when an organisation is perceived to be failing, staff start to leave and it becomes increasingly difficult to recruit. Schools which have been put in 'special measures' by OFSTED inspectors and, after successive evaluations by inspectors, have still not met the required standards may be closed and then re-opened under new management and perhaps be rebranded with a new name. Because the previous entity (school) has closed, jobs can be advertised and not all who had previously worked at the 'old' school will be recruited by the new leadership.

When a long-established and successful organisation sets up a new major division or a subsidiary company in order to fulfil a major contract, the new organisation is ripe for the development of a culture that is conducive to success. In such a case, the top managers may instil new values, demonstrate new rituals and generally make the employees aware of the kind of behaviour that is expected of them.

In these circumstances, however, sometimes the managers and specialists needed for the new organisation are drawn from the main company, and if the new set-up is put together as a matrix, it will need to draw upon the expert and administrative services of the main company. In other words, the new employees' contacts will be those who espouse the old culture.

The new organisation will be more likely to succeed by shifting the way the organisation works, from a cultural operating perspective, along the *mechanistic-organic* dimension (see Chapter 1). Rather than carrying with them the old way of working, structures and cultures, the new managers purposefully develop a culture that is appropriate for the central task. It is important to note that if nothing is done about defining and developing a fresh culture, one will evolve anyway.

An option which is sometimes used when innovative products have been developed is to create a spin-off company. Chynoweth writes in the *Sunday Times* (23 March 2014):

> Some companies invest a lot of time and money in the hope that their staff will come with profitable ideas. It doesn't necessarily mean that they should develop those ideas themselves.

> Instead of pursuing innovations in-house, it might be better to spin them off into new businesses, or even let them leave the company entirely...

Spinning off a business opportunity has a number of advantages. The culture of the parent company may not be the most appropriate to bring the new idea or product to fruition but instead stifle the energy of a true new, young, energetic and innovative company which is free 'of existing corporate formats' (Chynoweth, 2014).

Further, as Hege, cited in Chynoweth's article (ibid), indicates, there are three distinct advantages:

1 It can minimise the potential for discontent because those involved have a stake in its success by bringing their 'brain child' into the world.

2 The parent company 'won't have to worry about complaints from other staff that the entrepreneurs are getting special treatment'.

3 Innovation is recognised and thus truly incentivised because the innovators have the opportunity to share in the success of their ideas

(Chynoweth, 2014, [Appointments, p.3])

The parent company, which has provided the 'nursery of innovation', will want a stake in the new venture, yet without management oversight. This is possible by taking shares in the new venture. Seed capital will be required to fund the development from prototype to a marketable product, or by 'royalties on the transferred intellectual property or opportunities to be a supplier to the new business' (Chynoweth, ibid).

18.5.4 IDENTIFYING THE CULTURE GAP

In an organisation that has been established for several years, the managers may feel that the current culture is inappropriate for the achievement of corporate objectives. In such a case, the managers' first task is to envision the kind of culture that would be most appropriate for the foreseeable future. Second, they have to analyse and identify the true make-up of the current culture (see above and also the discussion of Johnson and Scholes, cultural web, in Chapter 2), which will enable them to compare the old against the new in order to identify the culture gap; at which stage they can develop a culture-change strategy that deliberately and systematically moves the organisation from an old to a new operating paradigm *{meaning – the way things are done}.*

According to Armstrong (2011, p.221), culture change programmes can focus on particular aspects of the culture. The examples he cites include 'the ability to deliver, performance standards, quality, customer service, teamworking and flexibility, which indicate the need for people with different attitudes, beliefs and personal characteristics'.

18.6 ORGANISATION DEVELOPMENT

Organisation development (OD) is the term used to describe a process through which, using the principles and practices of behavioural science, a change programme is applied in the organisation, often on an organisation-wide basis. OD is driven by the ultimate purpose of creating an effective organisation by altering the structure and changing employees' attitudes, beliefs and values. It is concerned not with *what* is done but with the *way* things are done, and with creating a new culture of cohesiveness, interdependence and mutual trust.

KEY CONCEPT: ORGANISATION DEVELOPMENT

French and Bell (1990) defined OD as: 'a planned systematic process in which applied behavioural science principles and practices are introduced into an ongoing organisation towards the goals of effecting organisational improvement, greater organisational competence, and greater organisational effectiveness.'

The CIPD (2012c) says the following about organisation development (OD). The definitions of OD may vary in emphasis, but there are common features:

OD applies to changes in the strategy, structure, and/or processes of an entire system, such as an organisation, a single plant of a multi-plant firm, a department or work group, or individual role or job.

OD is based on the application and transfer of behavioural science knowledge and practice (such as leadership, group dynamics and work design), and is distinguished by its ability to transfer such knowledge and skill so that the system is capable of carrying out more planned change in the future.

OD is concerned with managing planned change, in a flexible manner that can be revised as new information is gathered.

OD involves both the creation and the subsequent reinforcement of change by institutionalising change.

OD is orientated to improving organisational effectiveness by:

- helping members of the organisation to gain the skills and knowledge necessary to solve problems by involving them in the change process, and
- promoting high performance including financial returns, high-quality products and services, high productivity, continuous improvement and a high quality of working life.

(CIPD, 2012c)

The focus is on organisations and their improvement, or to put it another way, *total systems change.* The orientation is on action – achieving desired results as a result of planned activities. Once the areas and aspects that require change have been identified, the next step is to introduce the ideas to the employees. Employees vary in their attitudes to significant change. In general terms, the longer-serving employees, who have a need for job security, may fear that they will lose their jobs, and therefore they tend to resist it more than the younger employees, who may see it as an interesting challenge. The earlier part of this chapter deals with this problem and it will be helpful to your understanding if you study the sections on 'Resistance to change' and 'Dealing with resistance'.

18.7 LEWIN'S THREE-PHASE MODEL OF CHANGE

Lewin's (1951) three-phase model consists of:

- unfreezing
- moving or changing
- refreezing.

18.7.1 UNFREEZING

Unfreezing the current behaviour is about getting employees to think about changing what they do, rather than being frozen in traditional ways. This is the period of time when the current circumstances are explained to those involved with the change. The situation is made difficult because the picture of the future is less secure and uncertain. It could be that a vision of competitor penetration into the market, in which an organisation has been operating almost as a single source (monopolistic), and the situation is about to change – because there is a need to change. The competitor is known to be entrepreneurial and is likely to change pricing, the nature of the product and is ready to market their goods. Management make it clear that 'things have to change'; if not, the company is likely to have to downsize, because the company cannot compete, and perhaps even go out of business. The idea is to try to create the mood among staff such that they will more readily be open to ideas that will bring about efficiencies, changes to ways in working, and so on.

A critical event, as previously discussed, which is either within or outside the control of the organisation, may also be the catalyst which both stimulates the necessity to change and also rationalises and justifies that change must happen. This was the case with the situation in the NHS caused by the Mid Staffs NHS Trust patient care crisis of which the reverberations as to what needs to change – which range from nurse to patient ratios, record-keeping, cleanliness of wards and patients, the dignity and care of patients and the selection criteria used to identify staff who have appropriate attitudes – are still being felt.

Consulting employees

It is at this time that engagement with employees starts with a view to soliciting ideas of what type of change could occur and how they can contribute to the overall process. While the total change process is introduced and driven by the managers, employee groups should be consulted about specific changes that affect their areas of work. Management-led group discussions will help to clarify the nature of and the reasons for the changes, and should be carried out in a way that confers a significant degree of ownership on the employees. This is achieved by seeking employees' opinions, particularly about how the change process should be handled. Their advice should be considered seriously and their experience will be valuable, since they are the people at the work interface. The bonus from this is that when ownership of the change is felt by employees, they are less likely to resist and more likely to ensure that it succeeds.

The key to success is employee involvement. One way of eliciting employee involvement is through workshops where those involved are asked to consider the facts about the need to change and then to depict the change in the form of a cartoon or cartoons. The forces resisting the change being shown as crocodiles or monsters, each suitably labelled, while the forces and effects allowing/enabling the change being depicted as other, more benevolent animals or symbols. While this may seem frivolous or childish, it can evoke a sense of fun and ensure staff are on board with the ideas. They see it as less of a threat.

Communication is important at all levels, from team talks through to senior management. Typical communication processes are open forums, podcasts and use of the company intranet to answer frequently asked questions.

18.7.2 MOVING OR CHANGING

At this stage the ideas of what can happen and what management has approved to happen all start to occur. New departments and sections are created, new equipment is installed, new work practices start to be introduced and old practices are discarded. Where jobs are to be reduced it is at this stage that people are redeployed and perhaps, as a final change, some people may be made redundant. The Lewin process does not necessarily require redundancies to happen, but in today's cost-efficient and cost effective world, either voluntary or compulsory redundancies are usually 'on the cards'. Voluntary redundancy is of course a preferred way of, euphemistically, *losing people* because this has both a minimum effect on those that go – they have chosen to go – and also it is easier to manage the survivors: those that remain.

It is at this stage that a change champion may also have to become involved; this role is likely to be assumed by a senior director who has the muscle, the authority, to approve problematic changes to operational practice and to make things happen. It may also be that it is their financial authority that is required to approve an expense or perhaps the approval to make the changes as to how a department is structured – even perhaps the staffing levels within a department. This of course may trigger work for the HR department, perhaps starting a redundancy process or changing the terms and conditions of employment of staff. For example, if the change requires shift-working to start, where before the operation was traditional day-working (nine to five), this will involve significant changes to how people work and therefore a change in the contract of employment, which will be part of a negotiation process.

Change levers

A change lever is a process which can be used to help reinforce change – for example, introducing appraisals which focus on and assess customer care behaviours. If the outcome of an employee appraisal is coupled with how bonus payments are awarded, the employee will quickly recognise the benefits of exhibiting the behaviours towards customers that the business requires. A change lever is a process which helps and facilitates the introduction of new behaviours or ways of working.

Some of the change levers described by Armstrong (2006, p.316) include:

- **performance:** the introduction of performance-related or competence-related pay schemes, performance management processes, leadership training, skills development
- **commitment:** communication, participation and involvement programmes, developing a climate of co-operation and trust; clarifying the psychological contract
- **customer service:** customer-care programmes
- **teamwork:** team-building, team performance management, team rewards
- **organisational learning:** taking steps to enhance intellectual capital and the organisation's resource-based capability by developing a learning organisation
- **values:** gaining understanding, acceptance and commitment through involvement in defining values, performance management programmes and employee development interventions.

The OD approach, which underpins culturally bound organisation change, has five elements at its core: respect for people, trust and support, power equalisation, confrontation and participation (Robbins et al, 2010, pp.526–7).

18.7.3 REFREEZING

In this part of the process it is necessary to fix the changes to make sure that the old ways of working are not reintroduced. In its simplest form this could be the removal from computers of an old software program that staff could revert to using, thus forcing the use of new systems as all involved with the changes get to grips with and get over the teething problems of introducing a new software system. In terms of how people work, getting them to accept and embed new practices may be difficult because of a level of comfort with and knowledge of the issues and foibles of the old ways of working. The new strategies and structure and lines of reporting within the organisation should, to some extent, prevent old habits from reappearing (Senior, 2002) and, 'Once strategy, structure and systems have been changed it is equally important to reinforce the changes through symbolic actions and signs such as change of logo, forms of dress, building designs and ways of grouping people to get work done' (Senior and Swailes, 2010, p.324).

HR processes such as recruitment, selection and development through promotion can be used to reinforce the essential changes. As indicated by Senior and Swailes (ibid), one could envisage, for example, moving managers who are seen not to have embraced the new ideas or ways of working, and transferring into the section, managers who have accepted the new practices. Redistribution of authority and responsibilities, which are embodied in this type of action, sends strong messages to all involved because it will be perceived as a result of conscious management thought. The signals sent out, when employees see changes in management and management responsibilities, will have an impact upon how people think and behave. The implicit messages which are sent, when those who have clearly embraced the new concepts and ideologies are promoted, underline what people need to do and the behaviours that are required to 'get on' in the organisation.

In essence, while working on these change levers, the positive aspects of the old culture should be emphasised and reaffirmed, while the new values should be stated clearly and frequently. Employee behaviour that is conducive to the success of the change programme should be rewarded.

Schein (1985) listed five mechanisms for embedding and reinforcing the culture:

- what leaders pay attention to, measure and control
- leaders' reactions to critical incidents and crises
- deliberate role-modelling, teaching and coaching by leaders
- criteria for allocation of rewards and status
- criteria for recruitment, selection, promotion and commitment.

18.8 THE OD CHANGE MODEL

The OD model of change is a process-driven model and is logical in its working. The fact that it is process driven is also given as a criticism of the model; because change does not always happen in a logical and systematic manner. Change may happen because of a financial crisis, and so happen quickly and without planning, discussion, negotiation, implementation and review.

As can be seen from Figure 18.2, the OD model of change is very systematic in its operation. In fact, this is a criticism of the model because it can be argued that change, because of its nature, means the organisation, or that part of the organisation which is in change, is moving and in flux and therefore cannot be controlled in a systematic way. However, using the OD process as a model, one can see how change can be brought about. It gives us certain 'anchors' on which we can base our thoughts and actions.

The process starts by defining the current status of how the organisation or part of the organisation is operating, identifying the advantages of how it works as well as the disadvantages. The outcome of the deliberations is that the management team should have a clear vision of what the future should hold and what the organisation should be. There is a requirement to consider how internal and external forces may cause the organisation to change and how much it should change.

It is at this stage that there is a:

'...need for a more detailed examination of such things as:
- Organisational purposes and goals
- Organisation structure and culture
- Prevailing leadership styles
- Recruitment practices, career paths and opportunities
- Reward structures and practices
- Individuals' motivation and commitment to their work organisation
- Employee training and development provision
- Intra- and inter-group relationships.'

(Senior and Swailes, 2010, p.329)

Figure 18.2 The OD model of change

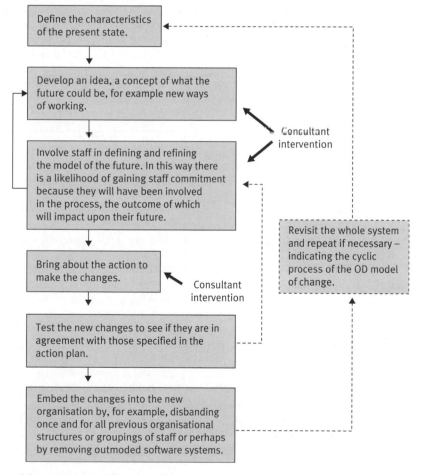

Adapted from Senior and Swailes, 2010.

The next step is to develop an idea, a concept, of how the business could operate, perhaps by introducing new structures to reflect how the competition operates their organisation, or part of their organisation, and also how the structure may need to be improved to fit better with how new technology operates and how new customer interfaces are envisaged. At this stage employees should be intimately involved in how the new structures could be shaped and how perhaps new ways of working could better influence the shape and structure of the business. It is a time of honesty and fidelity {meaning – *strict conformity to the truth*}; because, if the new structures and new ways of working may lead to job losses, this should be stated 'up front'. However, this should not deter from the overall focus of the OD process, which is on staff involvement, with the objective of developing staff commitment to the changes. There needs to be a process at this stage to check back with the original concepts and reasons for changing as the developing ideas are becoming more concrete in nature. This checking back and refining is called an iterative process: improving things for the better little by little.

Once the ideas and model of the future become more concrete, changes have to be made. Once again, as the changes are made there should be a process of checking back to the 'blueprint' to see if the changes are in line with the original proposals.

Finally, as all the new parts of the jigsaw start to fit into place, they need to be embedded to prevent the whole new organisation slipping back into its previous state. As previously discussed, this could mean removing software systems from employee computers to prevent their use. The age old problem, with the introduction of new systems, is simply one of unfamiliarity. More significant changes have to be embedded by making sure that old organisational structures and groupings of employees are disbanded or those who have resisted areas of change are perhaps moved to new locations, where they have no historical context.

18.9 THE ROLE OF THE CHANGE CONSULTANT

A characteristic of the OD model of change is the intervention, within the process of change, by an internal or externally recruited consultant, sometimes called a 'change agent'. In this context we are defining the change consultant or change agent as being different from the change leader.

The change leader is someone who has the responsibility to bring about the change in the organisation, probably a senior manager who is very close to the day-to-day operations and so will have difficulty standing back and not getting involved with issues because of personal preferences and alliances.

The change consultant can be from within the organisation or recruited from outside. There are disadvantages and advantages for taking either route. Using someone from within the company, preferably someone respected as being able to take a logical stance on issues, has the advantage that they will know and understand the culture, people, processes and structures. However, no matter how they may try not to be partisan {meaning – *not having a leaning to or preference of an approach*} when issues arise and require resolving, they may be seen to be part of a particular camp or 'persuasion'. On the other hand, resourcing someone from outside the organisation has the advantage that they have no baggage with which to be burdened but they neither know the culture nor the people or processes; this of course can be perceived as an advantage.

The change consultant or change agent can act in a number ways. Ideally they should have no particular allegiance in the context of what the outcome of the change may be but should be an 'honest broker' in terms of reviewing ideas and perhaps offering suggestions for a way forward, not necessarily solutions because the solutions should come from those who are and will be working with the new systems and in the new structures. The change consultant should try to facilitate those involved with the process to get to the most appropriate solutions. They can also act as a mediator between competing groups in which negotiations and discussion have led to an impasse with progress stifled. They may offer different ways to view problems and thus energise staff to overcome issues.

Paton and McCalman (2008, p.232) offer the following as the skills of an effective change agent:

1   To help the organisation define the problem by asking for a definition of what it is.

2   To help the organisation examine what causes the problem and diagnose how this can be overcome.

3   To assist in getting the organisation to offer alternative solutions.

4   To provide direction in the implementation of alternative solutions.

5   To transmit the learning process that allows the client to deal with change on an ongoing basis by itself in the future.

The role of the change agent will depend upon whether the change is planned, as in the (OD) model discussed, or is emergent; different skills are involved.

18.9.1 THE TOOLS OF THE CHANGE CONSULTANT (CHANGE AGENT)

Huczynski and Buchanan (2013) and Senior and Swailes (2010) offer a number of tools that the change agent can deploy when working with groups on a change process:

- **Survey feedback:** Consultants can use surveys to determine opinions and attitudes of groups of staff, to form a benchmark of 'where we are now' so that similar surveys can be conducted in the future to determine what changes, if any, have taken place. Surveys also give some idea of the temperature of parts of the organisation and where there are issues and thus problems to be resolved.
- **Organisational mirroring:** Using this technique, groups are defined, with one group becoming the host or home group. Other groups that interface with their operations and systems, which they 'own', are invited to comment. The idea is that the host group is not there to defend how they work but to learn how their way of working, in the context of relationships, impacts upon others. The consultant's skills can sometimes be sorely tested trying to prevent open hostility! There needs to be clear ground rules, and the consultant has to be very competent and professional when engaging with what could be very emotive issues – especially when the host group is listening to criticisms of the way they have been perceived to interact! Once one group has been the focus of the other groups in the process, places are exchanged.
- **Inter-group development:** Inter-group development is about addressing the functional boundaries that exist between groups. It may be that systems of operation cause clashes; for example, engineers need to spend money quickly to resolve technical problems, whereas accountants need authorisation before they can release money. In this case it is the different criteria for control and success that cause the conflict or disharmony between the groups. Inter-group development, as its name implies, is all about finding out about the barriers between groups that cause the business to falter and work in an inefficient manner. This activity is sometimes called inter-group confrontation.
- **Role negotiation:** Role negotiation is similar to organisational mirroring in terms of its intentions. The focus is on the relationships between individuals and why they are, as a small team or an interfacing part of the business, dysfunctional. The idea is to allow one person to air their perceptions of the other person, then to reverse the role, and thus, from the learning gained, some mutual understanding is arrived at with a view to improving the relationship and ways of working.
- **Quick wins:** Success breeds success and so if one can publish quick wins, where one part of a change programme has been successfully implemented, the hope is that the advantages seen, by publicising the outcomes of a successful component part of the overall change process, will encourage and give hope to others to work through their part of the change initiative (Kotter, 1996).

- **Team-building:** As the change progresses and new structures and groupings appear, there is a need to build internal morale. Especially where colleagues may have left under redundancy circumstances, there is a need to support those who are left through group activities that are designed to improve that all-important morale. The most common form that many of us have experienced or have seen on television are the outward-bound activities that cause people to work together to overcome obstacles that are placed in their (their team's) path. The objective is to create situations where people become reliant on their peers; it is also about building, in a 'forced manner', relationships that otherwise may take months or years to develop.

18.10 CRITICISMS OF THE PLANNED APPROACH TO CHANGE

There are many criticisms of the planned approach to change. Burnes (2009, p.346) points out that the planned approach infers that the change can be controlled, moving the organisation from one state to the next, but this does not recognise that organisations are dynamic and subject to external and internal turbulence. The planned approach to change neither recognises that transformational change is sometimes required nor that organisations are political systems. Burnes (2009, 349), citing Dawson (1994), Hatch (1997) and Wilson (1992), also points out, ' … that the Planned change approach is based on the assumption that common agreement can be reached, and that all parties involved in a particular change project have a willingness and interest in doing so.' In reality those in power may not act in what one might term a logical rational manner, that is, they may not have the best interests of the organisation at heart.

18.11 THE EMERGENT APPROACH TO CHANGE

In organisations today, minor day-to-day changes take place that are made as a result of 'on the hoof' decisions by managers and others. These changes go unnoticed at the time, such as a minor modification to a work system or a gradual change in the style of communication. This is evolutionary change in which organisations change gradually and evolve in ways that enable them to continue to meet the needs of the internal and external environments. It is also one of the ways in which organisations respond to the factors that are brought to light by a SWOT or PESTLE (STEEPLE) analysis.

In this case change is not a discrete, one-off activity. For those who are the proponents of the emergent approach to change, they consider change to be happening all the time in some part of an organisation as a response to emerging threats and changes in how work is done and people interact.

Burnes (2009, p.368), using Weick's words, explains that:

> Emergent change consists of ongoing accommodations, adaptations, and alterations that produce fundamental change without a priori intention to do so. Emergent change occurs when people re accomplish routines and when they deal with contingencies, breakdowns, and opportunities in everyday work. Much of the change goes unnoticed, because small alterations are lumped together as noise in otherwise uneventful inertia. . . .

 ACTIVITY 18.5

All change

Think of some of the things that have changed in your workplace, college or university. Have the changes been planned or has something happened that has caused an activity or work to be done differently?

As Burnes (2009) suggests, change is not driven by recipes, but the essence of change is that work exists because of interactions between people, whether these be groups or individuals. By considering change as emergent and having a political dimension, the concept of change as an activity becomes more real if one compares this with the planned approach to change, which does not incorporate 'the political nature of change into the more traditional [planned approach] and more prescriptive literature on change' (Burnes, ibid, p.368).

In essence, what emergent change recognises is that there are power and political dimensions to an organisation that must be managed.

There are a number of factors that can influence how people act and react when change opportunities occur. Burnes (2009) suggests that the nature and type of organisational structure, organisational learning, managerial behaviour, power and politics within an organisation can impact upon the readiness and ability of people, at all levels within the organisation, to become involved with change.

ACTIVITY 18.6

Factors that impact on change

Can you explain how the factors cited above – organisational structure, organisational learning, managerial behaviour, power and politics – impact upon the ability of an organisation to engage with change?

You will get some help by accessing Burnes (2009, p.376) at: **www.dawsonera.com**

18.12 ROLE OF HR IN SUPPORTING THE MANAGEMENT OF CHANGE

CIPD research (summarised in its factsheet) on change management (CIPD, 2014) has also identified that HR's involvement in various aspects of change can make the difference between successful and less successful projects by, for example:

- involvement at the initial stage in the project team
- advising project leaders in skills available within the organisation – identifying any skills gaps, training needs, new posts, new working practices, and so on
- balancing out the narrow/short-term goals with broader strategic needs
- assessing the impact of change in one area/department/site on another part of the organisation
- being used to negotiating and engaging across various stakeholders
- understanding stakeholder concerns to anticipate problems
- understanding the appropriate medium of communication to reach various groups
- helping people cope with change, performance management and motivation.

HR has a clear role and responsibility to ensure that issues such as organisation (re) design, due process, employee voice, access to clear communications and so on are appropriately and effectively addressed as part of change management. Learning and development (L&D) professionals also have a critical role to play in ensuring the long-term sustainability of a change, through effective design and delivery of learning initiatives. The key for HR and L&D is to build credible relationships throughout the organisation which enable them to anticipate change and be involved from the beginning (CIPD, 2014).

18.13 MAKING CHANGE WORK

Kotter (2007) points out that,

> A few … corporate change efforts have been very successful. A few have been utter failures. Most fall somewhere in between with a distinct link towards the lower end of the scale. … The most general lesson to be learned from the more successful cases is that the change process goes through a series of phases that in total, usually require a length of time. Skipping steps creates only an illusion of speed and never produces a satisfying result. (Kotter, 2007, p.96)

Kotter (ibid) offers advice in terms of identifying the errors which are typical in change programmes which have failed through:

1 Not establishing a sufficient sense of urgency.

2 Not creating a powerful enough guiding coalition.

3 Lacking a vision – effective change programmes should have a vision of the future which can be communicated in relatively simple terms to all.

4 Under-communicating the vision by a factor of ten.

5 Not removing obstacles to the vision – this infers that such things as departmental structures which might negatively impact upon change should be dismantled, thus empowering those who have been energised by the change to move forward. This is where a change champion or change agent (the role has many names), who has the 'organisational clout' to make things happen, can unlock the 'barred gates to change'.

6 Not systematically planning for and creating short-term wins.

7 Declaring victory too soon.

8 Not anchoring changes in the corporation's culture – this is analogous to Schein's 'refreezing' stage, where the new ways of working and behaviours are reinforced to prevent a relapse.

The above points have been distilled from:

> KOTTER, J. (2007) Leading change. *Harvard Business Review.* Vol 85, No 1. pp.96–103. The article is a reprint of Kotter's original paper under the 'Best of HBR', which appeared in 1995 and, in the editor's words, 'A decade later his work on leading change remains definitive.'
> Reprinted with permission from 'Leading Change: Why Transformation Efforts Fail' by John P. Kotter. *Harvard Business Reveiw*, January 2007.

18.14 CHANGE AND EMPLOYEE BEHAVIOUR

Each and every employee of an organisation will not necessarily respond the same way, both in terms of their emotions and reactions, to the change process. There will be some who will see their world being turned upside down and fear the change. They may see their territories, their status and zone of comfort all being threatened. Some, potentially, could delay or try to prevent the change from happening. It is with these people that time and effort will need to be spent communicating the need for the change and consequences of *not* changing. It may be, though, that they will never accept the need for the change. This has consequences for those who are managing change. One of the problems with change is that the outcome cannot be predicted accurately in all its facets; there will always be some uncertainty until the major part of the process is complete (is change ever complete?).

On the other hand, there will be those in the organisation who have been restricted in their work because of archaic and old-fashioned practices and processes and who will be extremely enthusiastic about the opportunities that new changes may bring. These will be the people who can be used as ambassadors for change, especially in their part of the organisation, and so help the process of change progress positively. They can be used to demonstrate and to advertise where the change process has resulted in beneficial outcomes.

It is important that communication with employees is frequent and honest. If the change process is likely to result in job and therefore people losses, through gains in efficiency, this should be communicated early and thought given to how potential redundancies (see more on this in Chapter 17) are handled, perhaps in the first instance through voluntary severance or redeployment.

Where change happens on a frequent basis, employees may tire of the whole repetitive process. Even those who have previously embraced change in a positive way may find the experience draining and will not wish to engage.

18.15 SUMMARY

Change can have a severe impact upon people, both in a positive and negative sense. In other words, there is an ethical dimension that should be considered when significant change is planned. Hughes (2007, p.11), citing Weiss, says that there are 'potential ethical dilemmas of change management. Organisational changes and transformations involve the redistribution of power, information, resources, status, authority, and influence. Therefore, individuals' rights, dignity and privileges can be at risk.'

To effectively manage change, the discussion touches on the need to consider the sensibilities of those who are impacted by the change and also the survivors of the change process.

REVIEW QUESTIONS

1 What are the possible consequences of allowing an out-of-date culture to persist at a time of significant external change?

2 What are the main drivers for change in an organisation?

3 What are the main forces that cause resistance to change?

4 Give some advantages and disadvantages of technology as a driver for change.

5 What constitutes and underpins organisation development (OD) as a process?

6 What is the role of the:
   (a) change leader?
   (b) change consultant or change agent?

7 What do you understand by:
   (a) organisational mirroring?
   (b) survey feedback?
   (c) team-building?

8 Discuss what is meant by the term 'change lever' or 'lever for change' and give some examples.

9   What is meant by the emergent approach to change? How does the concept of 'emergent change' differ from the 'planned approach to change'?

10 What are the major criticisms of the planned approach to change?

11 What is the role of HR in supporting change?

12 Why is there an ethical dimension to be considered during a process which involves significant change?

EXPLORE FURTHER

JOURNAL ARTICLES

The Kotter and Schlesinger (2008) article below was first published by the *Harvard Business Review* in 1979. The editor of the *Harvard Business Review* (HBR) points out that many things have changed, 'but one thing has not. Companies the world over need to change course.' The Kotter and Schlesinger (2008) paper is one of HBR's 'Best of HBR' classic articles which they believe is still relevant in today's business world.

KOTTER, J.P. and SCHLESINGER, L.A. (2008) Choosing strategies for change. *Harvard Business Review [online]*. Vol 86, No. 7/8. pp.130–39. [Accessed 26 March 2014]. Available at: **www.web.a.ebscohost.com**

STREBEL, P. (1996) Why do employees resist change? *Harvard Business Review [online]*. Vol 74, No 3. pp.86–92. [Accessed 26 March 2014]. Available at: **www.web.a.ebscohost.com**

ORGANISATIONAL CHANGE CASE STUDIES

CIPD (2011) *Developing organisation culture: six case studies [online]*. London: CIPD [Accessed 27 March 2014]. Available at: **www.cipd.co.uk/binaries/Transforming%20culture%20(PROOF).pdf**

BOOKS

SENIOR, B. and SWAILES, S. (2010) *Organizational change*. Harlow: Pearson Education Ltd.

Senior and Swailes' text covers a broad spectrum of change issues. The book addresses the nature of organisational change and how structure, culture and leadership impact upon change as well as the politics of change in the context of organisations. They also offer strategies for managing change. It is a solid, well-written text on change and the material is accessible to the student who is meeting the theory of change management for the first time.

CAMERON, E. and GREEN, M. (2012) *Making sense of change management: a complete guide to the models, tools and techniques of organisational change*. 3rd ed. London: Kogan Page.

VIDEO

Professor Mike Bourne, Cranfield School of Management, is interviewed about understanding some of the key issues which impact upon the management of change: **www.youtube.com/watch?v=tosiBRHKbIU**

Professor Rosabeth M. Kanter, Harvard Business School, discusses 'Six keys to leading to positive change' at a TEDx Talk: **www.youtube.com/watch? v=owU5aTNPJbs**

PODCASTS

CIPD Podcast 31 – Making change work – part one: **www.cipd.co.uk/podcasts/ _articles/_makingchangeworkpart1.htm**

CIPD Podcast 31 – Making change work – part two: **www.cipd.co.uk/podcasts/ _articles/Makingchangework_part2_episode_31.htm**

CIPD Podcast 81 – Changing values and culture in the City: **www.cipd.co.uk/ podcasts/_articles/_changing-values-and-culture-in-the-city-podcast81.htm? link=title**

A look at how culture and values in the City's *{The City of London}* financial sector are starting to change. We explain how some of the City's leading financial organisations can demonstrate these changes and how HR can play a lead.

CIPD Podcast 86 – Look ahead to 2014: **www.cipd.co.uk/podcasts/_articles/_look-ahead-to-2014-podcast86.htm?link=title**

In 2014 Mark Beatson and Peter Cheese, chief executive of the CIPD, considered some factors that may have an impact on the world of work in 2014. How effective do you think they were in analysing the future? Did their analysis offer an improved economic view that enabled HR professionals to think more strategically?

WEB LINKS

Also worth a read is the CIPD (2014) factsheet on change management. The CIPD looks at why organisations change and 'change strategies', and considers HR's role in change and how change can be managed more effectively. The factsheet can be found at: **www.cipd.co.uk/subjects/corpstrtgy/changemmt/chngmgmt.htm**

The CIPD produces some help and guidance to help organisations manage the potentially stressful outcomes of workplace change programmes. Together with AXA PPP Healthcare, the CIPD has produced the following article:

CIPD/AXA PPP HEALTHCARE. (2013) *Supporting employees to manage change [online]*. London: CIPD. [Accessed 27 March 2014]. Available at: **www.cipd.co.uk/hr-resources/axa/supporting-employees-manage-change.aspx**

CHAPTER 19

Handling and Managing Information

LEARNING OBJECTIVES

After studying this chapter the student will be able to:

- understand the difference between the needs for strategic, tactical and operational information
- define what is meant by information in the context of human resource management
- identify the differences between types and usage of HR information systems (HRIS)
- analyse, make and prepare comparative types of data information
- understand information in bar chart and pie chart formats.

Note: 'understand the operation of the Data Protection Act 1998 and Freedom of Information Act 2000' is dealt with in Chapter 16, 'Understanding Employment Law'.

19.1 INTRODUCTION

This chapter is about information used in the context of human resource management. To help you understand this, it includes a number of practical exercises in handling and managing information. As you go through the chapter, you may complete various activities to help you understand how to use information in order to make decisions about human resources.

A case study looks retrospectively at the resolution of issues, through the application of data analysis techniques, which affected the fictional (case study) company (EPRO Oil and Gas) over its operational lifetime from the 1990s to 2014. Using data analysis, as a starting point, and coupling this with HR initiatives, which attempted to make sense of the underlying reasons for high staff turnover, it is possible to understand how recommendations for improvement were developed and subsequently implemented. Because the data tables of recruitment and turnover cover a broad time span, it is possible to see the impact of the recommended changes. The idea behind the case study is to allow you to manipulate figures in order to grasp how things change over time and what the impact can be.

19.2 INFORMATION COLLECTION

Appropriate identification of types of information and storage is a valuable tool for the HR practitioner. The majority of people reading this text will not have to decide upon what information to collect but will, from time to time, have to manipulate information.

Information can be classified, in terms of its usage, into three broad areas:

- strategic
- tactical
- operational.

19.3 WHY IS INFORMATION COLLECTED?

Information is collected for a number of reasons. The needs range from legal requirements, for example the need to keep work-related accident statistics, to the need to have a background of data against which future plans can be made. In general, information-gathering can be considered against the following headings:

- **Recording** – in the case of HR this could be: (a) diversity data: gender, age, ethnicity mix of the organisation; diversity data during recruitment activities, development and training information, promotions and disciplinary cases; (b) data associated with health and safety requirement reporting; (c) payroll information: job groups, salary levels, pension information, flexible benefits options.

- **Planning** – this activity is closely linked with 'recording' because it is the data from the previous activity which would be used, for example in planning the development of those employees who have been identified as the 'talent' of the organisation. Consider the case of a multinational organisation which must develop its talent to eventually be able to take the role of a company director at some time in the future. These individuals would need to be exposed to a number of challenging environments, both in the UK and essentially overseas, to develop the breadth of overview and capacity to take on such a demanding international role.

- **Measuring** and **monitoring** – data collected from: the annual appraisal exercise, turnover statistics, absence statistics, accident and near-miss statistics, costs to hire, time to hire, days of training per employee, cost of training as a percentage of staff costs or operating budget, operating budget spend, training budget spend, overtime hours and costs – the list is endless.

- **Controlling** – this type of data is used to determine progress or lack of it. Controlling is strongly linked to the task of measuring and monitoring. Not all the parameters {meaning – the factors} measured will be used immediately to help make decisions, or to trigger actions, but some will. Consider the case of expenditure on salaries against planned expenditure. If staff costs become a factor, overtime costs would probably come under intense scrutiny. Once overtime salary costs hit a set maximum figure for the month, this might trigger cuts in overtime.

- **Decision-making** – decision-making can occur at the three levels initially discussed: the operational, the tactical and the strategic. The data required for each level recedes in detail as one moves from operational to strategic requirements.

19.3.1 STRATEGIC INFORMATION

In this case the information should be provided in broad or summarised terms, for consumption by the board of directors of the organisation. They need information to make strategic decisions that can inform the direction the company will take on issues. The data should not be detailed but rather kept to the figures which represent an overview of the parameter which is being monitored.

Information which would fall into this category would be, for example: the profitability of the business as a whole, the profitability of part of the business, key issues which might affect profitability. In the case of the latter example, many of the major banks have had to allocate significant budgets to meet claims for their mis-selling of personal protection insurance (PPI). The size and level of the information surrounding PPI is of importance because the magnitude of the mis-selling in past decades has been such that the total claims have accumulated to several tens of millions of pounds and therefore have impacted upon the profit and loss account of the bank.

Many organisations have significant deficits in their final salary pension funds (defined benefit fund). The deficits are increasing because employees, who have retired, are living longer and more employees, the baby boomers born after the Second World War, are increasingly joining the ranks of the retired, so adding further strain to the pension fund. As a result of the increased financial burden placed on organisations, many chief executives see no option but to close down the final salary pension schemes to new, and sometimes existing, employees and to offer instead a 'defined contribution' pension scheme. This type of scheme is less attractive for employees. Defined contribution schemes are less attractive because the final annual pension will depend upon what the individual's accumulated pension pot will buy, in terms of a pension fund, on retirement. However, the defined contribution type funds are more attractive for the employer because their ongoing contribution to a fund is clearly defined, in terms of a monthly amount, and thus predictable and the organisation has no responsibility for the pension which an employee ultimately receives.

For an organisation's management team, information about the health of the pension scheme, if it is of the defined benefit type, is of vital importance because if the scheme is in deficit the organisation has responsibilities to the scheme, which can impact upon the organisation's profit and loss account.

19.3.2 TACTICAL INFORMATION

Information of a tactical nature is for use by middle management. From a financial perspective the HR manager will need to budget, on an annual basis, for the running of their department. This means that the major cost areas have to be identified and values, that is, budget projection figures, attributed to those areas. It is the type of information that might be required to put a plan together or to justify a course of action.

Let us consider these needs. Assuming that budgets for all activities have been devolved to each department of the organisation, let us assume that 'HR' holds the budget for:

- salaries budget for the HR department
- pension budget for the HR department
- office management cost, which includes the stationery and equipment costs for the HR department
- staff training budget for the whole organisation (this might be split by cost of safety training, 'ICT' training, production specialist training, training for finance staff, and so on)
- staff development budget for the whole organisation
- operational maintenance costs for the HR information system (HRIS)
- operational maintenance costs for the payroll management system.

Knowing the above information, the annual operating costs for the HR department can be identified and cost metrics developed.

Data requirement

The data held by the HR department will be a mix of information on human resource activities it requires for its own use and also for senior management in other functional departments. For example, data held for the whole organisation might include, by department and section:

- recruitment data, which includes: vacancies filled, time to recruit, ethnicity data of people interviewed
- staff turnover

- absence data
- training and development data on individuals: type, length, cost, duration, and so on
- training and development data for the organisation: type, cost, length, location, and so on.

Some data may be required for regulatory reasons, for example:

> Safety training, such as: permits for fork-lift truck drivers; permits for domestic electricians (called the Part P – Electrical Safety); working with scaffolding requires inspection by a qualified person to inspect scaffolding before use [Construction Industry Scaffolders Registration Scheme (CISRS)]; and so on.

Some data may be required by managers to decide upon the cost-effectiveness of training. For example, if the production department wishes to know how much it costs to 'provide' one day of training for a member of their department, this information could perhaps be provided either as an average cost per day of training or a cost per day for a specific course (based upon past data).

Some of the tactical data may of course be used to furnish information for strategic decision-making. From the human resource information system (HRIS), data can provide such information as: total days of training, total training costs, training cost as a percentage of staff budget or percentage of operational costs, and so on. Early decisions as to what type of data is held for tactical reasons can influence the type and quantity of information which can be provided for strategic purposes. Knowing what is required in terms of data is very important when developing the initial specification for any HRIS.

In terms of tactical needs, information will be required for managers to be able to determine the level of budget they need in order to operate their part of the business. The HR manager, for example, will need to know, or at least have some guidance on, the level of the recruitment and training and development activity, the number of staff typically who have received training – which can give some indication of likely future demands, new business developments within the organisation which will stimulate specific training requirements, and so on. All this complex mix of past data, which is used to predict future demands, and planned cross-organisation activities will go into the HR manager's annual budget planning exercise.

19.3.3 OPERATIONAL INFORMATION

Operational activities occur at the level of the business: the day-to-day operation, perhaps the output from a part of the business. For example, the training manager will need a monthly update of the training budget expenditure so that he can monitor the budget, so ensuring that the organisation does not agree to training or development that it cannot afford.

When dealing with an absence case, the department manager will require information about the absence record of the member of staff involved so that an informed decision can be made about a course of action. Operational information would also include information on the training received by a staff member. Before deciding whether or not to agree to sponsor an employee for a development course, information on the past history of the employee in terms of attendance, success and application of previous sponsored training and development might be useful to inform a decision as to whether to sponsor the individual or not at this time.

EPRO Oil and Gas is an international company that has its UK headquarters in Aberdeen, Scotland. It both explores for oil and gas in the North Sea, as well as building fixed platforms from which it produces the oil and gas to pump to onshore refineries and gas plants where the oil and gas is converted into petrol, diesel, tars and 'consumer gas' to pump into the National Grid to warm and provide heat for cooking in UK homes.

It employs approximately 3,000 people in its onshore offices and gas plants and offshore platforms and drilling rigs.

The company takes pride in its people management practices. HR business partners are responsible for its internal staff planning process as well as for providing a generalist HR service: recruitment, advice on development and training of staff, taking care of dismissals and activities such as advising on discipline and grievance cases, as well as handling personnel issues that flow into tribunal cases. There is a small corporate HR team which offers guidance on policy and other corporate issues; corporate HR also manages the payroll for the company.

The HR business partners also manage the staff planning side of the business, linking the business plan to staffing requirements, which involves the traditional areas of recruitment, selection and development.

The company has had a number of staffing problems during its operational life. A major area of concern for a number of the business partners was the relatively high turnover of staff between 2007 and 2010. The senior management of the organisation, at the time, asked for an analysis of the figures. They wished to understand why the overall turnover figures had grown from 10.2% in 2005 to 12.1% in 2010.

Consider Tables 19.1a, 19.1b and 19.1c. These three tables are typical of the type of information an organisation would keep about its resourcing activities. They show the key departments and the respective staff numbers, staff turnover (raw numbers) and percentage turnover numbers (see the 'Note' on labour turnover below Table 19.1c and also Chapter 5 for an explanation of how these numbers are calculated) on a year-by-year basis from 2005 to 2013.

Clearly there must have been some recruitment activity to maintain overall numbers in each department.

Table 19.1a EPRO – Staffing numbers by department (2005–2013)

EPRO Staff numbers

	2005	2006	2007	2008	2009	2010	2011	2012	2013
Production & Maintenance Dept	1725	1715	1740	1755	1759	1760	1760	1770	1769
Project engineering	525	500	495	490	530	480	490	495	496
Logistics	495	500	470	495	503	492	496	497	496
Finance department	169	170	175	175	175	175	175	173	176
HR department	33	31	30	28	27	27	26	27	26
Law	10	12	11	11	12	12	11	12	11
Public relations	5	5	5	5	5	5	4	4	4
Totals	**2962**	**2933**	**2926**	**2959**	**3011**	**2951**	**2962**	**2978**	**2978**

Table 19.1b EPRO staff – Turnover statistics 'raw data' (2005–2013)

EPRO Turnover numbers

	2005	2006	2007	2008	2009	2010	2011	2012	2013
Production & Maintenance Dept	208	205	200	204	206	204	190	189	185
Project engineering	52	52	72	84	93	102	80	45	35
Logistics	32	42	36	29	24	27	22	22	24
Finance department	5	9	14	16	19	24	16	5	4
HR department	2	1	1	1	2	1	1	2	0
Law	1	0	1	0	0	0	1	0	1
Public relations	1	0	0	0	0	0	1	0	0
Total Turnover	**301**	**309**	**324**	**334**	**344**	**358**	**311**	**263**	**249**

Table 19.1c EPRO staff – Turnover statistics % (2005–2013)

EPRO % Turnover

	2005	2006	2007	2008	2009	2010	2011	2012	2013
Production & Maintenance Dept	12.1%	12.0%	11.5%	11.6%	11.7%	11.6%	10.8%	10.7%	10.5%
Project engineering	9.9%	10.4%	14.5%	17.1%	17.5%	21.3%	16.5%	9.1%	7.1%
Logistics	6.5%	8.4%	7.7%	5.9%	4.8%	5.5%	4.5%	4.4%	4.8%
Finance department	3.0%	5.3%	8.0%	9.1%	10.9%	13.7%	9.1%	2.9%	2.3%
HR department	6.1%	3.2%	3.3%	3.6%	7.4%	3.7%	3.8%	7.5%	0.0%
Law	10.0%	0.0%	9.1%	0.0%	0.0%	0.0%	8.7%	0.0%	8.7%
Public relations	20.0%	0.0%	0.0%	0.0%	0.0%	0.0%	22.2%	0.0%	0.0%
Overall % turnover	**10.2%**	**10.5%**	**11.1%**	**11.3%**	**11.4%**	**12.1%**	**10.5%**	**8.9%**	**8.4%**

$$\textbf{Labour Turnover} = \frac{\text{Number of leavers in a set period}}{\text{Average number employed in the same period}} \times 100$$

Strategic information management

From a **strategic perspective**, management could see, from the percentage turnover figures, that there had been little increase, over the years 2005–10, in the turnover in the Production and Maintenance Department, but it is apparent there had been a growing increase in the turnover in both the Project Engineering and the Finance Departments.

The above tabulated information was collated by the HR business partners and given to the HR director, who presented the data to the EPRO Oil and Gas management team. Although the turnover in the Production and Maintenance Department had not increased significantly over time in real terms, the absolute value of the turnover was a concern. Particularly the *increase* in turnover in the Project Engineering and Finance Departments was, at that time, a worry.

In light of the above analysis, and after a meeting of the company's management team, a strategic decision was made to:

1   Start an apprentice scheme, linked to a local college, for production and maintenance technicians. EPRO's intention was to fund the scheme on an equal share cost basis with local government for a five-year (renewable) term. Although no guarantees would be given to the scheme's recruits, EPRO would offer offshore and onshore 'training placements'. The intention was to 'cherry-pick' the best technician trainees for its operations.

    The approach to develop a training scheme was initially justified on the basis of the high staff turnover figures for 2005–10. Further justification of the strategic decision to introduce a training scheme was found when the recruitment figures for the years 1990–2004 were unearthed and calculations were made, showing that £25.3 million was 'wasted' on recruitment activities for the Production and Maintenance Department. This was based upon the cost of recruiting 4,134 persons over the 20-year period (1990–2010), with cost data taken from the CIPD *Recruitment, Retention and Turnover* survey figures for 2009, which gave an average cost of £6,125 per employee recruited. Note: Average median recruitment costs from the CIPD *Resourcing and Talent Planning* survey 2013 range from £6,500 per senior manager/director (Manufacturing and Production) to £1,750 for other roles (Manufacturing and Production). Average recruitment costs have been driven down over the years largely due to the growth of online recruitment – a cheaper and more cost-effective option when compared with traditional recruitment advertising.

    By forming early links with high-quality 'potential' technicians, it was envisaged that a strong cultural bond would reduce the turnover in the Production and Maintenance Department.

2   Introduce a professional engineering development scheme for project engineers, for recently qualified graduates, linked to universities within and around the Aberdeen area. This decision was made in advance of the outcome of recommendation 4 below.

3   Consider the introduction of a mentoring system for new employees who have been identified to join the organisation's talent development programme.

4   To recommend that an investigation be conducted into why there has been a consistent increase in 'churn' [turnover] in the Project Engineering and Finance departments.

Tactical information management

Tables 19.1b and 19.1c show that turnover in the Finance Department increased from a figure of 5.3% in 2006 to 13.7% in 2010. Clearly something happened to cause this unacceptable increase in turnover. Turnover increased during a period of time when the economy was going through troubled times and jobs, particularly outside the petroleum sector, were generally at risk; yet people were leaving EPRO Oil and Gas!

From a tactical perspective a decision was taken jointly by the Finance, Engineering and HR directors to investigate the cause of the increase in turnover. Three considerations came to mind:

1   Had there been some change in the Finance and Engineering Department in the context of:

    (a)   operational demands?
    (b)   management?
    (c)   job content, workload, and so on?

2   To conduct a review of the effectiveness of the induction programme to determine whether or not it was still fit for purpose.

3   Review the effectiveness of the exit interview process. The data obtained from exit interviews conducted by line staff was of limited use. It was thought that the methodology – that is, how the system operated, who conducted the interviews, when they are conducted, how and if the information from the interviews was (if at all) fed back into the review process and so on – needed to be reappraised.

A survey, plus semi-structured interviews with staff and their managers, was conducted in an attempt to understand what was causing the increase in staff turnover in the two departments.

Operational information management

From an operational perspective, the information in Tables 19.1a, 19.1b and 19.1c is not of much use. What is more important at an operational level would be access, for example, to the personnel files of staff. As examples of the need to keep information on employees, consider the following list:

Operational data would include information on individuals such as:

- contact details for emergency call-out purposes
- next of kin details (NOK)
- department in which they work
- location of their workplace
- courses attended, for example if the employee has attended induction, first aid training, or perhaps a management and leadership training course
- qualification attained – for example these may range from academic, NVQ-type qualifications to being recognised and recorded as being competent as a fork-lift truck driver or whether staff had passed the safety (survival) courses to be able to fly offshore in a helicopter
- current study – this is relevant if the employee is following a course of study: open learning, or perhaps at a local college or university
- level of skill – the employee may be rated as competent to train people on the job they do in the organisation
- specialist skills – the employee may have training and mentoring skills that can be used to mentor newly recruited people into the organisation
- preferred options for career development
- personal development plans (PDPs)
- training requirements, which may include mandatory health and safety training
- absence management information.

ACTIVITY 19.1

Employee turnover

Initial investigations showed that there had been no change in the management of either the Finance or Engineering Departments.

Prior to setting up the investigation into why the turnover had increased over a number of years in the Finance and Engineering Departments, the HR team brainstormed ideas, as per points 1 and 2 in Case Example 18.1,

as to what they considered to potentially be causing people to leave.

1   What other factors would you consider to be influential in causing competent staff to leave the organisation (any organisation)?

2   How would you go about finding out why employees were leaving an organisation?

We will return to this discussion later in the chapter.

ACTIVITY 19.2

Consider your own organisation, or an organisation you know. List the type of information about an employee you would wish to have access to for operational or legal purposes. Do not simply list information, but rather think how you would make use of the information once you have access to it.

Note: the Data Protection Act (1998) (see Chapter 16, 'Understanding Employment Law')

advises that information on people should be held only if it is essential and should be held for only as long as it is needed by the organisation or required by law. Read the 'eight data protection principles' at: **http://ico.org.uk/for_organisations/data_protection/the_guide/the_principles**

19.4 THE RANGE AND EXTENT OF HR INFORMATION HELD WITHIN AN HRIS

The above list of information (operational level) is focused on the employee. However, some information useful to HR and the organisation as a whole is not about one individual, but may be about:

● meeting targets
● information about groups of people which may have to be presented to management, for decision purposes or simply for briefing purposes.

Management will certainly be interested in budgets and whether they have been under- or overspent; they will also be interested in such diverse matters as ethnicity monitoring within the organisation and the outcomes of staff satisfaction surveys and recruitment campaigns. Some of this information will be aggregated from individual records, for example data on ethnicity and absence, but data on staff satisfaction surveys will have to be inputted once the survey has taken place and the data analysed.

Some data may have to be inputted manually but wherever possible data should be handled (in totality if at all possible) by electronic transfer for items such as staff satisfaction surveys; much depends on whether or not the data collection can be done online.

As mentioned above, one can think of information as being 'personal information', that is, about people, age, date of birth, gender, home contact information, next of kin, contractual arrangements, learning and development, induction and general training records, and so on. However, to use an HRIS and all its computing power simply to store this type of information is to under-use the system. An HRIS can be incorporated into, and form a key element of, the knowledge management processes of the organisation.

Information gleaned from focus groups, client interviews, projects with (internal as well as external) client groups, the extent to which service-level agreements have or have not been maintained, and the learning gained from the experience of success or failure of a project all contribute to the wealth of knowledge that can be shared with others who will access the systems in future. Figure 19.1 shows a skeleton diagram of an HRIS.

Figure 19.1 Skeleton of an HR information system (HRIS)

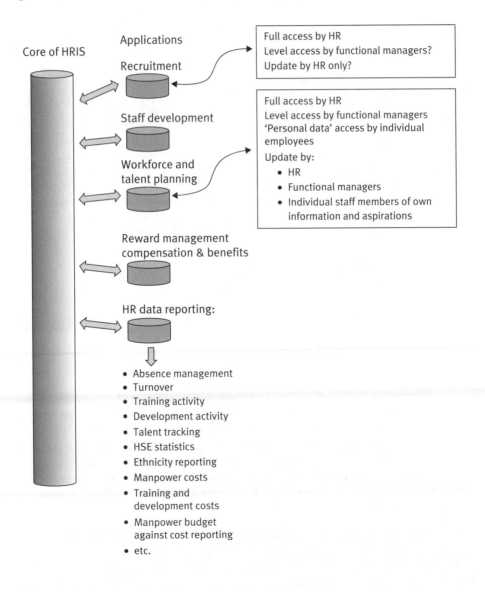

ACTIVITY 19.3

Designing an HRIS

An HRIS is only as good as the quality of the product in terms of reliability and capacity to compute, manipulate and provide information and to interface with other operational systems.

Given the task of developing an HRIS for an organisation, consider the following questions:

1   What type of information would you consider such a system should hold?

2   How and what type of information might be manipulated, for example to provide turnover statistics?

3   How might that information be eventually presented in terms of reports, letters, presentation formats?

The above is a task that should be thought about well before an organisation commits to purchase such a product and will determine its viability and ultimate usefulness to the HR department and organisation as a whole.

ACTIVITY 19.4

Accessing HRIS data

Using your own organisation, one that you are familiar with or the skeleton system in Figure 19.1, consider what information should be uploaded and accessed by:

● HR staff only
● functional managers
● all employees (for their own records).

In Figure 19.1 some levels of access have been suggested. Start from the position that all employees have access to all information. If, in the course of your analysis, you restrict access to one or two groups of people, for example HR staff or HR staff + functional managers, you must justify your position.

When thinking about Activity 19.4, consider the following. The reasons why information is restricted can be argued from a number of positions. It may be that information is 'organisationally sensitive' and so would give competitors a commercial advantage, or it is simply sensitive in the context that the organisation would not wish the data to be in the public domain. It could be that information is personal and so only the individual concerned plus certain authorised staff who have need to see that information – to be able to make decisions about the individual – should have access. On the other hand, one could also argue that to restrict information unnecessarily is paramount to not having trust in the organisation's employees. Arguably the best person to maintain a personal record is the individual to whom the record appertains. Adopting this approach builds an 'adult-adult' relationship between organisation and the involved individual rather than a 'parent-child' relationship. Ask yourself: which type of relationship with your employer would be your preference? The degree to which employee self-service (ESS) is allowed is, as Weeks (2012, p.41) suggests, important and a strategic consideration.

19.5 TYPES OF HR SYSTEM

Initially, many HR information systems (HRIS) were simply used as data banks and, as Ball, cited in Torrington et al (2007, p.809), found, 'HRISs were still being used primarily for administrative rather than analytical ends and exploitation remains painfully slow and patchy. One of the key attractions for technology for the HR function is that it can reduce time on administrative chores to free up this time for strategic activities.' In a similar way, Bandarouk and Ruel (2009, p.504) argue that, 'as one of the early IT adopters in 1980s, HR functions used to employ IT for administrative processes, primarily payroll processing, with little attention being paid to so-called transformational HR practices'.

KEY CONCEPT: HR INFORMATION SYSTEMS AND E-HRM

Haines and Petit (1997, cited in Bandarouk and Ruel 2009, p.506) 'considered HRIS as a system used to acquire, store, manipulate, analyze, retrieve, and distribute pertinent information about an organization's human resources'.

Bandarouk and Ruel (2009, p.507) define 'e-HRM as: an umbrella term covering all possible integration mechanisms and contents between HRM and Information Technologies aiming at creating value within and across organizations for targeted employees and management'.

The second definition expands on the first definition because its outlook is broader, recognising that all 'e' type channels of information can feed into and out of a system, thus enabling scope for manipulating data sets from different sources.

Human resource information systems can be used to store and manipulate HR management data, as previously described in this chapter. This is extremely useful as data is at one's fingertips; the key is making use of it. According to Reddington, cited in Torrington et al (2008), the primary drivers for using HR information systems are a mix of:

- 'operational' (that is, improving cost-effectiveness by reducing the cost of service and headcount)
- 'rational' (that is, improving its services to employees and line managers who are increasingly demanding)
- 'transformational' (that is, addressing the key strategic drivers of the organisation).

(Torrington et al, 2008, p.809)

There has been a growth in HRIS that allows employees to store and share information that aids personal development and career planning. This type of system may be used as a general data-sharing medium, similar to YouTube; it may have parts 'sectioned off' that are used as specialist areas where wikis are set up to allow staff, perhaps working from different geographical locations, to share information on their specialist subject through the organisation's intranet. One can imagine the different functions within the business having dedicated sites within the HRIS where essential information, gleaned from working for and with clients, is held, thus forming a critical part of the organisation's knowledge management capacity. Having ready and secure access to this type of information both supports current employees, who may be working with clients, but also forms a platform to be used when preparing bids for future business.

Human resource information systems are also very useful when employees are working towards in-house qualifications. Tutors in remote locations can monitor the progress of their 'students' because they (the students) can upload work within their own work-area site and then tutors can access and assess the information, grade it and return it with comments. Within this type of system areas can also be allocated to groups for blogging about their work; once again this is all focused around knowledge and human capital (people) management and development.

The move is to enterprise resource planning (ERP) systems where, as Bandarouk and Ruel (2009, p.504) write, 'for example, e-HRM applications are no longer "stand-alone" tools but mostly a part of more complicated ERP systems, where e-HR modules are integrated with financial or other modules'. In this way data from the HRIS can be integrated with financial data, manipulated and used by cross-functional teams for decision-making purposes. Bandarouk and Ruel (ibid) point out, though, that there is not much evidence to suggest that organisations have become more strategic in their use of the information that an HRIS offers. In fact, they argue that e-HRM was primarily used in support of routine administrative HR tasks. Although, there are obvious advantages of a professional HRIS: ready, secure and remote access to various data sources, distributed access to data by different classes of user, management as well as employees, and the fact that the majority of HRISs are not bespoke causes a convergence in their use. If many organisations have the same access to similar technology, there is nothing, in 'innovative technological terms', to harness to make any distinguishable difference between organisations and how they can operate. In short, there is nothing to give one organisation the competitive edge over the other. What can make a difference, though, is their innovative use.

A recurring theme about HR information systems is, as Weeks (2013, p.36) writes: 'The lack of strategic or operational functionality has been cited as a recurring problem with current HRIS. Insufficient integration with other systems within the organization, complication of the system, inflexibility, and lack of a user-friendly interface.' Weeks (ibid) makes the point that to get the most out of an HRIS, which has been costly to install and has been time-consuming and expensive to train staff in its use, is to develop and encourage its use in what is termed a portal for both managers and employees to access, to store key data and also as a vehicle to communicate with vendors and other approved parties. The future of HRIS is probably in its development as an 'expert system' in the vein of 'ICIT' systems, which have been developed and are being introduced into the world of medicine.

ACTIVITY 19.5

HR information systems

Access the websites for the following HRISs:

● PebblePad: **www.pebblepad.co.uk/default. asp**
● ORACLE – PeopleSoft Enterprise Human Capital Management: **www.oracle.com/hcm** or **www.oracle.com/us/products/ applications/peoplesoft-enterprise/ overview/index.html**
● Watch the PeopleSoft video at: **www. youtube.com/user/PSFTOracle**
● Watch Morepayhr at: **www.youtube.com/ watch?v=hKC8mhIo-lc#t=13**

Browse through the applications to view the range of activities that each of the systems offer. Many HRIS providers offer access through 'cloud' computing systems, especially for small to medium organisations.

1 Why, do you consider, is it advantageous for small to medium-sized organisations to use a 'cloud-based' HRIS?

2 What are the disadvantages of a 'cloud-based' system?

19.6 USING INFORMATION TO BEST ADVANTAGE

When presenting information the tendency is to try to encapsulate a significant amount of data into one figure. A simple measure, quite often used, is the 'average' or 'mean'. What we do by using an average is to give one measure of commonality and particularly what is termed 'centrality' of a set of data. The average is a single figure that, in a very simplistic way, represents the data set; for example, quite often quoted is the average height of women or men or perhaps the average age of a class of students. In the examples used it gives some idea of what to expect when considering the age or height of a group of people. Other common measures of centrality are the median and mode. None of the three terms mentioned – mean, median or mode – give information either about how closely the data is grouped together, that is, the spread of data, or the range of the data, that is, the maximum or minimum values.

19.6.1 THE MEAN (AVERAGE)

The mean is easy to calculate: simply add up the individual values of all the numbers and divide by the total number in the set. Consider the examination grades of the following 15 students given in Table 19.2.

Table 19.2 Mean examination grade

The Mean or Average

The mean is just the average of the numbers.
It is easy to calculate: add up all the numbers, then divide by how many numbers there are.

Let us consider a class of 15 students whose examination marks are as follows:

Name	Grade
Student 1	75 %
Student 2	56 %
Student 3	98 %
Student 4	36 %
Student 5	45 %
Student 6	50 %
Student 7	87 %
Student 8	85 %
Student 9	60 %
Student 10	60 %
Student 11	65%
Student 12	75 %
Student 13	30 %
Student 14	53 %
Student 15	57 %

Mean (Average)	=	Sum of values divided by number in sample or group
Sum of values	=	(75%+56%+98%+36%+45%+50%+87%+85%+60%+ 60%+65%+75%+30%+53%+57%)
Sum	=	932%
Number	=	15
Mean	=	932% / 15 = **62%**

From the data the mean score in the examination is 62% – actually, 62.13%, but this level of accuracy was not required. The 'mean' as a measure gives neither information about the minimum nor the maximum scores in the examination.

19.6.2 WHEN NOT TO USE THE MEAN

The mean should not be used when there are significant values which are near to or at the minimum or maximum possible values of the data set. Consider the following example where data on the salaries of employees is being considered. The number of employees on which there is salary information available is 15. The data shows that of the 15 staff members, there are 13 who earn £30,000 (£30k) or less. However, two earn above £90k. If the mean of the salaries is calculated it would give a figure of £28,867, which in the context of the data set is meaningless. The mean is artificially 'lifted' because two employees earn significantly more than most of the employees in the data set. Refer to Table 19.3 and the accompanying figure to see how this data appears pictorially.

Table 19.3 When not to use the mean (average)

No.	Name	Grade
1	Employee 1	£10,000
2	Employee 2	£11,000
3	Employee 3	£16,000
4	Employee 4	£17,000
5	Employee 5	£17,500
6	Employee 6	£18,000
7	Employee 7	£18,500
8	Employee 8	£19,000
9	Employee 9	£20,000
10	Employee 10	£21,000
11	Employee 11	£22,000
12	Employee 12	£26,000
13	Employee 13	£27,000
14	Employee 14	£90,000
15	Employee 15	£100,000

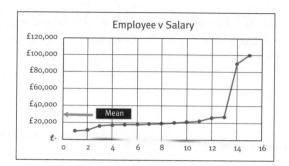

Total salary	=	£433,000
Number employees	=	15
Mean	=	£28,867

The mean is being skewed by the two large salaries. Taking the *median* would be a better measure of central tendency in this situation.

19.6.3 THE MEDIAN

The median is probably one of the simplest statistical measures. The median is the number which 'sits' in the middle of an *ordered list*. Consider the two examples which are shown in Table 19.4.

Table 19.4 Median

Example 1 'Odd' numbers in the batch. The median is the 'middle number' (in a sorted list of numbers).														
Consider the following list of numbers, note there are 15 in the set. The median is the 8th in the ordered list.														
List not in order	5	4	24	32	57	23	15	15	14	47	65	23	69	32	36
In order	4	5	14	15	15	23	23	**24**	32	32	36	47	57	65	69
Median = 24														

Example 2 'Even' numbers in the batch.																
Consider the following list of numbers, note there are 18 in the set. The median is the average of the 9th and 10th numbers																
List not in order	3	4	24	34	56	23	15	15	14	47	65	23	65	32	35	42	66	70
In order	3	4	14	15	15	23	23	24	**32**	**34**	35	42	47	56	65	65	66	70
Median = 33																

Therefore, if the *median* value is taken for the salary data which is presented in Table 19.3, the eighth salary value, in the *ordered list*, would represent the median and would in the example return a value of *£19,000*. This is far more representative than the mean which was calculated to be £28,867.

The example in Table 19.4 is simple because there is very little data to manipulate. A more realistic example, again using salary data, is if there are more employees in the data set and a number are on the same salary or grade point. Consider the data in Table 19.5.

Table 19.5 Pay versus frequency of employees on same grade point

No. Employees – Cumulative Frequency	Frequency	Salary	Salary Bill per Grade Point
5	5	£11,000	£55,000
14	9	£13,000	£117,000
32	18	£14,000	£252,000
48	16	£15,000	£240,000
63	15	£16,000	£240,000
77	14	£17,000	£238,000
90	13	£18,000	£234,000
100	10	£20,000	£200,000
109	9	£21,000	£189,000
116	7	£23,000	£161,000
121	5	£32,000	£160,000
125	4	£35,000	£140,000
128	3	£40,000	£120,000
131	3	£45,000	£135,000
No. Employees =	131		
Total Salary Bill =	£2,481,000		

The data in Table 19.5 is presented as a cumulative frequency data set. Reading from the top of the table, the frequency column tells us that there are five employees being paid at £11,000 per annum, nine employees being paid at £13,000 per annum, and so on. The cumulative frequency column simply adds up the number of employees in each grade to those in the next, progressively down the column.

Incorporating a table of cumulative frequencies when analysing lists of data is very useful because it gives, at a glance, a significant amount of information. For example, simply by reading off from the cumulative frequency column, we can glean the following:

- 48 employees were paid £15,000 or less
- alternatively, knowing that there are 131 employees, we can easily work out that 83 employees earn more than £15,000
- 116 employees were paid £23,000 or less, and so on
- 131 employees were in the cohort {group} analysed.

All of the above is useful information because it helps to tell a story about the data set; don't let us lose sight of the fact that the words 'data set' in reality indicate what people are earning. From the above information, the *mean* can also be readily calculated by taking the total wage bill of £2,481,000 and dividing this by the number of employees = £18,939 (to the nearest £).

Using Excel, or some similar spreadsheet tool, this allows for automatic calculation of the above values. Excel also allows, once the data has been put in tabular form, for graphs to be drawn automatically; see Table 19.6, which takes the above statistical information and also provides the data in a graphical format.

Table 19.6 Pay versus frequency of employees on same grade point with graphical representation

No. Employees - Cumulative frequency	Frequency	Salary	Salary bill per grade point
5	5	£11,000	£55,000
14	9	£13,000	£117,000
32	18	£14,000	£252,000
48	16	£15,000	£240,000
63	15	£16,000	£240,000
77	14	£17,000	£238,000
90	13	£18,000	£234,000
100	10	£20,000	£200,000
109	9	£21,000	£189,000
116	7	£23,000	£161,000
121	5	£32,000	£160,000
125	4	£35,000	£140,000
128	3	£40,000	£120,000
131	3	£45,000	£135,000

No. Employees = 131

Total salary bill = £2,481,000
Mean = £18,939
Mode – £14,000
Median = £17,000

Note: Median = 66th Salary point

Skewed Distribution

The above data table (19.6) and graph shows that the 'distribution' {spread} of salaries is skewed. The highest peak of the graph gives the *modal* value, which is the most frequently occurring value. In the above case, this is easily obtained either directly from the data table or the chart. The data table shows that the most frequently occurring salary is £14,000, with 18 occurrences. The salary value where the graph peaks is also the salary *mode*. Thus from the data table and by means of calculation in the case of the *mean*, the following information can be obtained:

- **Mean** = £18,939 [Total salary bill of £2,481,000 divided by 131 employees]
- **Median** = £17,000 [66th salary value in the data set]
- **Mode** = £14,000 [as discussed above]

For data which produces a skewed chart, as above, the median is generally taken as being representative of the data set. Table 19.6 is typical where high values, that is, in this case 'high earners', skew the data set so that the mean no longer is representative in terms of the centrality of the data.

19.6.4 THE MODE

In the previous example the concept of the *mode* was introduced. The mode is quite simply the number which appears most often in a list of numbers. Table 19.7 is a list of salaries, frequency rates and cumulative frequencies and, once again, the *Salaries versus Frequency* are shown in graphical form.

Table 19.7 Pay versus frequency salary structure

Cumulative frequency	Frequency	Salary	Salary bill per grade point
1	1	£10,000	£10,000
4	3	£13,000	£39,000
8	4	£14,000	£56,000
19	11	£15,000	£165,000
25	6	£16,000	£96,000
31	6	£17,000	£102,000
34	3	£18,000	£54,000
36	2	£20,000	£40,000
38	2	£25,000	£50,000
40	2	£30,000	£60,000
42	2	£35,000	£70,000
44	2	£36,000	£72,000
46	2	£40,000	£80,000
47	1	£45,000	£45,000

Salary v Frequency

No. Employees	= 47	Total Salary Bill	= £939,000	
Mean	= 19,979	Mode	= £15,000	Median = £6,000 [Equals the 24 salary value in the ordered salary data set]

In Table 19.7, the mode is easily identifiable because, quite simply, it is the salary value, £15,000, which correlates to the peak in the representative curve as previously explained. It shows that there are 11 employees 'sitting' at this salary point. This information could as easily have been gleaned from the 'Salary versus Frequency' table, but the graphical representation really emphasises the mode.

19.6.5 MULTIPLE MODES

It is quite possible that a data set could have more than one mode. For example, it could be quite possible that as well as there being 11 employees on the £15,000 salary point, there could be 11 employees at the £18,000 salary point. In this case, the data set is bi-modal.

19.6.6 INTERPRETING INFORMATION

Statistics should be about making our lives easier rather than simply considered to be an extension of mathematics that one needs to learn to pass an assessment. So how can the three concepts of *mean*, *median* and *mode* help us to understand information?

Once again consider Table 19.7, which, using Microsoft Excel, is used to give a simple graph of *Salary versus Frequency* of the data set which sits alongside.

Taking the position of an HR professional with this data set representing the salaries of employees within the part of the organisation for which you have HR responsibility, what can be gleaned from this simple data set and accompanying graph? From an HR perspective the graphical representation should start to ring 'alarm bells' because there are a significant number of employees 'stuck' at one salary point. The data simply represents, in an easy to interpret manner, what is happening in the organisation. It does not give any 'richness' as to why something may be happening but it at least shows anomalies and allows the professional HR person to ask the question why? The answer can only be found by carefully and systematically interpreting the reality of what the data represents.

To begin to answer the question as to the reason why there are a number of people resting on the same salary point, the following information about the group would be useful:

- Who are the group's members: names, ages, gender, and so on?
- Is there something which links the individuals? For example, are they all from the same department?
- Why have the members not progressed within their salary range? For example, are they waiting to take a progression-linked examination?

In essence, the data gives an idea of 'what' is happening, but does not give the 'why'.

CASE EXAMPLE 19.2

Each year the CIPD produces a number of survey reports which are designed to reflect what is happening in human resource management across a range of sectors and organisational size. The surveys cover topics such as: employment law; health, safety and well-being; learning and development; reward; resourcing and talent planning, and so on.

From an HR practitioner's perspective, the information contained within the surveys is useful because, in general terms, the information can be used as a 'rough and ready' benchmark against what is happening within their own organisation. Trends might be identified as well as 'hotspots', for example the highlighting of where similar organisations are experiencing recruitment difficulties with a profession or specialism.

In Table 19.8, the data shows the number of short- and long-term vacancies which organisations have had to resource (fill) during 2012 (CIPD/Hays, 2013, p.8).

Table 19.8 Recruiting employees

Median number of short-term and permanent vacancies organisations tried to fill in 2012 by size of organisation and sector

No. of permanent staff employed in UK	Private sector		Public sector		Not for profit	
	Short term vacancies	Permanent vacancies	Short term vacancies	Permanent vacancies	Short term vacancies	Permanent vacancies
1–40	0	3	0	0	2	3
50–249	2	15	5	13**	5	18
250–999	10	44	22	40*	20	70
1,000–9,999	40	250	78	105	40**	106**
More than 5,000	250	550	500	775	75*	1850*

Base: 422. * Fewer than 5 respondents in this category: ** Fewer than 10 respondents in this category
CIPD/Hays (2013, p.8)
Reproduced with kind permission of the CIPD.

It is important that, when interpreting any type of statistical data, such as when trying to make some sense and meaning of the data in Table 19.8, that the basis on which the data has been collected and presented is understood.

Table 19.8 is presented exactly how the CIPD/Hays have presented the table in the 2013 *Resourcing and Talent Planning* survey report. So, what can be gleaned from the information that is presented in the table?

- **Measure of centrality:** Importantly, the figures that represent how many vacancies there are for temporary and permanent staff are given as median values. From the earlier work in this chapter the median value is that of the middle number in an ordered data set. The median, in preference to the mean, has been used probably because there are some very low and very high values in the number of short- and long-term vacancies. These extreme values would artificially increase or decrease the mean value. In other words, the mean would not represent what was generally happening in an organisation or group of organisations; hence the median was used.

- **Organisational representation:** The survey's authors have recognised that the type of organisation is important and so have given a broad split of organisation by public, private and not-for-profit. The size of the organisation is also considered to have relevance to potential readers. One might argue that splitting the private sector into business types: manufacturing, mineral extraction, and so on, might also have been useful; much depends upon what the authors wish to highlight and emphasise and what they perceive that their reader population will deem useful.

- **Information to be treated with caution:** It is noticeable that two of the values presented under *public sector* and four values in the *not-for-profit* sector have been identified by either one or two asterisks. Here the survey's authors have deemed it important to highlight that the values, as some form of central and representative measure, were reported by fewer than five (one asterisk) and ten (two asterisks) respondents in the categories. The message is clear: 'treat the information with some caution'.

Even when a set of data is presented in a relatively simple and easy-to-read format, as it is in Table 19.8, it is useful to put some narrative around the findings to add a certain 'richness' to the hard numbers. The narrative is the author's way of sharing some insights that they have obtained through the course of their detailed analysis of the results. For example, the authors of the CIPD/Hays (2013) survey write the following about some of the results which are relevant to the public sector:

> The median number of short-term vacancies was highest in the public sector, where it was double that of the private sector for all organisation size categories. Moreover, the ratio of short-term vacancies to permanent vacancies was much higher in the public than private sector, reflecting the ongoing funding cuts as part of the Coalition Government's measures to reduce the budget deficit. (CIPD/Hays, 2013, p.8)

However, not all the information about the survey, which might inform and influence the interested reader, is immediately available. Further 'digging' into the report is necessary. Activity 19.6 will help uncover some useful information about the survey.

    ACTIVITY 19.6

Interpreting data

Access the 2013 CIPD/Hays *Resourcing and Talent Planning* annual survey report at **www.cipd.co.uk/hr-resources/survey-reports/resourcing-talent-planning-2013.aspx**

On page 8 of the survey you will find Table 19.8 as presented earlier (in the CIPD/Hays survey it is Table 2). The information contained here gives some useful insights about vacancies that organisations have approved to be resourced during a period which might be indicative of the UK coming out of recession. However, Table 1 (p.7 of the survey) is perhaps more beneficial from this perspective because it gives a time-lined indication of the vacancies on a year-by-year basis over a period after the 2008 financial 'meltdown' up to and including 2012.

Questions

1   When reading and making sense of, say, Table 1 or Table 2 of the *Resourcing and Talent Planning 2013* survey report, what information, about the collation of data for these tables (and others in the survey), do you think is necessary to fully understand how representative and relevant the data presented is of UK organisations?

2   What definitions are provided in the 'Background to the Survey'?

Hint: pages 46–8 of the survey give some useful background about how the report was compiled, from where data was collected and how many organisations contributed to the findings.

ACTIVITY 19.7

Interpreting data

Consider the Tables 19.9, 19.10 and 19.11, which have been taken from the CIPD *Annual survey report supplement 2013: Aligning strategy and benefits.*

Table 19.9 Benefits less likely to be offered by organisations with employee absenteeism difficulties

Benefit	% of all respondents offering benefit	% of respondents that have experienced absenteeism difficulties to a greater extent offering benefit	% difference
Tea/coffee/cold drinks free	64.6	32.4	32.2
Christmas party/lunch	66.0	45.9	20.1
Paid study leave	45.9	29.7	16.2
Flexible/homeworking	43.2	29.7	13.5
Training and career development	82.9	70.3	12.6
Death in service/life assurance	66.7	54.1	12.6

Questions

1   Before reading the narrative which immediately follows, in small groups decide what sense and what conclusions can be drawn from the above information?

2   What conclusions *cannot* be drawn from the data?

Table 19.10 Benefits less likely to be offered by organisations with employee recruitment difficulties

Benefit	% of all respondents offering benefit	% of respondents that have experienced recruitment difficulties difference to a greater extent offering benefit	% difference
Flexible/homeworking	43.3	20.5	22.3
Enhanced paternity/maternity leave	55.8	43.2	12.5
Paid leave for military service activities	48.5	36.4	12.1
Pension schemes	82.5	70.5	12.0
Training and career development	82.7	72.7	10.0
Cycle to work scemes and loans	45.6	36.4	9.2

Table 19.11 Benefits less likely to be offered by organisations with employee retention difficulties

Benefit	% of all respondents offering benefit	% of respondents that have experienced retention difficulties to a greater extent offering benefit	% difference
Flexible/homeworking	43.5	16.7	26.8
Training and career development	82.6	66.7	15.9
Paid study leave	45.8	31.0	14.8
Pension schemes	82.6	69.0	13.6
Christmas party/lunch	65.9	52.4	13.5
Death in service/life assurance	66.6	54.8	11.8

CIPD (2013i, p.23)
Printed with kind permission of the CIPD.

The following is what the CIPD says when interpreting the information. The tables show benefits:

> ...which are less likely to be offered by organisations which have experienced absenteeism (Table 19.9), recruitment (Table 19.10) and retention (Table 19.11) difficulties in the past 12 months. There are some intriguing findings here: flexible/homeworking and training/career development feature on all three lists; pension schemes and Christmas parties – while opposite ends of the scale in terms of employer investment – are equally well represented. Speculating about the reasons for these results, it is perhaps helpful to think of the absence of these benefits as characteristic of organisations experiencing these employee problems rather than as cause and effect equations. It would be erroneous, for example, to deduce that the lack of free tea or

coffee at work leads to absenteeism difficulties. However, we could expect that organisations experiencing recruitment and retention difficulties would be less likely to agree to flexible working requests if they were already under-staffed. Overall, we get a picture of organisations perhaps unable to offer certain benefits because of employee problems, which in turn makes them less attractive places to work, which exacerbates the problems and so on. (CIPD, 2013i, pp.22–3)

Note: table numbers in the original document have been amended to fit in with the tabular values of this chapter

In the above narrative one of the key sentences is:

Speculating about the reasons for these results, it is perhaps helpful to think of the absence of these benefits as characteristic of organisations experiencing these employee problems rather than as cause and effect equations. (CIPD, 2013i, p.23)

The CIPD goes to significant lengths to point out that one cannot make a 'cause and effect' comparison between the absence of a benefit and high absenteeism, but rather that the omission of particular benefits is probably symptomatic of a type of organisation. The final sentence sums up the likely scenario. The challenge for HR in these circumstances would be to find a way out of the downward spiral.

ACTIVITY 19.8

Exercise in calculating mean, median and mode – EPRO oil and gas revisited

Returning to the EPRO case study from earlier in the chapter, consider Table 19.12, which shows the recruitment activity for the EPRO Production and Maintenance Department. It is useful to analyse the data to get some idea of the extent (volume) of work, for example in terms of recruitment activity that the HR department has to manage on a regular basis.

Table 19.12 EPRO recruitment: 1991–2013 (Production and Maintenance Department)

Year	1991	1992	1993	1994	1995	1996	1997	1998	1999	2000	2001	2002
Recruitment	202	198	200	214	215	216	208	203	204	202	198	208

Year	2003	2004	2005	2006	2007	2008	2009	2010	2011	2012	2013
Recruitment	199	205	198	230	215	208	207	204	200	188	186

Using the above data, calculate the *mean*, *median* and *mode* for the recruitment figures from 1991 to 2013. The answers are given below, but to understand how the formulae work it is better to work them through yourself:

- **Average** or **mean** (of people recruited per year) – this is the total number of people recruited divided by the number of years = 4708/23 = 205 – rounded up from 204.7 people recruited each year; it is not possible to have 0.7 of a person.
- **Median** – this is the value halfway along the *ordered* data set. In our case this would be 204, that is, the twelfth value. If the number count in the data set was an even number, remember to calculate the value halfway between the two middle values.
- **Mode** – this is the most frequently occurring value. In the case of Table 19.12 there are two modes: 198 and 208, which both occur three times. When using Excel the MODE.MULT function would have to be used to check for and return more than one mode.

All of the above functions are available in Microsoft Excel.

19.6.7 RECRUITMENT AND TURNOVER AT EPRO OIL AND GAS PRODUCTION DEPARTMENT

Perhaps of greater use is if information is presented in a graphical fashion. Consider Figure 19.2, which presents in diagram format the data in Table 19.12 (extended back in time to 1991), which has been obtained using Microsoft Excel. Using a bar chart immediately presents the data in a way that is easily understandable and, perhaps of some importance, can be used in a PowerPoint presentation to highlight issues in a very visible manner.

Figure 19.2 Production and maintenance recruitment data (1991–2013)

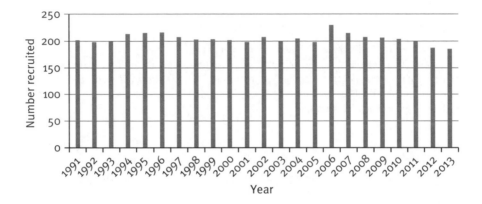

The type of presentation in Figure 19.2 clearly shows that recruitment has largely remained at or around the average of 205 recruited per annum from 1991 to 2005. There is a peak of 216 recruited in 1996. The planned population of the Production and Maintenance Department from 1991 through to 2006 was 1,740 staff. From the figure it is apparent that there is a spike in the recruitment in 2006 of 230 employees taken on payroll. What could be the explanation of this deviation? It is clear that to make sense of the above type of graph, in its fullest sense, there is need for a narrative that helps to explain the changes in the graph's profile.

The deviation (the recruitment spike) is because, from 2007, the workforce staffing plan for the Production and Maintenance Department had changed. The original staffing plan required a staffing complement of 1,740 people. However, a change in the planned target population to 1,770 staff from 2007 was approved by the company's management – the extra recruitment occurring in 2006. The change was as a result of increasing the size of one of the onshore gas plants to accommodate extra capacity in natural gas storage and production – the extra gas capacity coming from natural gas tankers that began transporting liquefied natural gas products from the Middle East, primarily Qatar. In 2007, the tankers began offloading their cargo into the company's gas storage tanks at the coastal gas plant ready for treatment and then injection into the UK's distribution gas pipe network for household and industrial consumption. Once this localised peak in recruitment had occurred, we can see, from 2007 onwards, that the recruitment activity settles down to levels similar level to that between 1991 and 2005; that is, to cope with staff turnover requirements.

In fact, analysis of staff turnover (Table 19.13) shows that turnover has *not* significantly changed between the years of 1991 and 2010. The question, of course, is why had there been no initiatives between 1991and 2010 to try to reduce the waste of time, energy and money recruiting staff simply to cope with such a high rate of average turnover of circa 11.9%.

Figure 19.3 Production and maintenance turnover (1991–2013)

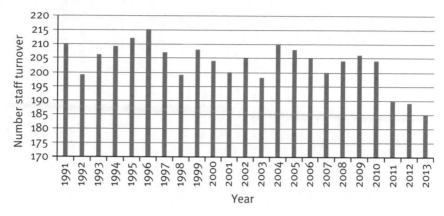

19.6.8 TURNOVER IN THE EPRO OIL AND GAS FINANCE DEPARTMENT

Table 19.13 and Figure 19.4 show the turnover of staff in EPRO's Finance Department. If the profile of the graph of this department is compared with the turnover graph (Figure 19.3) of the Production and Maintenance Department, it is starkly different. Where the graph of the turnover for the Production and Maintenance Department hovers around the average of 206 staff per year, the turnover in the Finance Department changes from a figure of around five per year and starts to 'ramp up' to a turnover, in 2010, of 24 per year. Clearly something was amiss and, whatever had happened to cause the increase in staff deciding to leave the company, happened post-2006. The HR director, together with the head of finance, needed to investigate this phenomenon.

Table 19.13 Finance department: turnover (1991–2013)

Year	1991	1992	1993	1994	1995	1996	1997	1998	1999	2000	2001	2002
Turn-over	5	4	5	4	5	3	5	6	4	5	5	5

Year	2003	2004	2005	2006	2007	2008	2009	2010	2011	2012	2013
Turn-over	5	4	5	9	14	16	19	24	16	5	4

ACTIVITY 19.9

Linking HR reasoning to data analysis

In groups discuss how you would have investigated the causes of, and thus explain, the increase in turnover in the Finance Department during the period 2006–10. As the HR director, how would you approach the finance director with your findings?

Figure 19.4 Finance department: turnover (1991–2013)

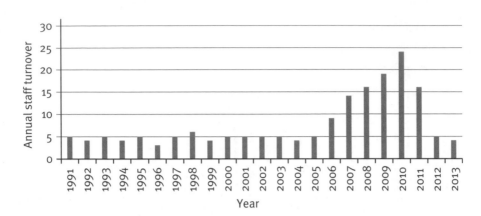

19.6.9 AN INVESTIGATION INTO THE TURNOVER FIGURES: EPRO OIL AND GAS

An investigation into excessive turnover would involve many facets of the work, workload, people interactions, reward and motivation systems, staff engagement, and so on. However, for the purpose of the narrative let us focus on some of the 'not so obvious' factors which might impact upon turnover, engagement, and so on.

The raw data figures for the training budget spend, year-end 2010, for the EPRO Oil and Gas Production Department are presented in Table 19.14.

Table 19.14 Annual training budgets for EPRO departments (2010)

Department	Training budget spend
Production & maintenance department	£5,780,000
Project engineering	£1,400,000
Logistics	£983,500
Finance department	£67,000
HR department	£54,125
Law	£64,800
Public relations	£11,750
Total Training Budget	**£8,361,175**

The information is of course useful but it gives us no comparative measures. It is by making comparisons that judgements can be made. It may be useful to express the training budget expenditure as a percentage of operating expenditure or as a percentage of the department's annual salary budget. The annual salary budget (2010) for the EPRO departments is given in Table 19.15.

Table 19.15 Annual salary budgets for EPRO departments (2010)

Department	Salary budget
Production & maintenance	£79,200,000
Project engineering	£21,600,000
Logistics	£19,680,000
Finance	£7,875,000
HR	£1,215,000
Law	£720,000
Public relations	£200,000
Totals	**£130,490,000**

Using the figures from Tables 19.14 and 19.15, the amount of the annual departmental training budget, as a percentage of the annual departmental salary budget, can be calculated:

[(Annual Training Budget) / (Annual Department Salary Budget)] × 100%

This information is presented in Table 19.16.

Table 19.16 Annual training budget expressed as percentage of departmental annual salary budget (2010)

Department	Training budget as percentage of department salary budget
Production & maintenance department	7.3%
Project engineering	6.5%
Logistics	5.0%
Finance department	0.9%
HR department	4.5%
Law	9.0%
Public relations	5.9%
Total Training Budget	**6.4%**

Table 19.16 is very illuminating because it shows that the total training budget, expressed as a percentage of the annual salary budget, is 6.4% for 2010. With the exception of the Law and Finance Departments, all the other departments' percentage annual training spend, for 2010, hover around this value, give or take one or two percentage points. However, the Law Department has exceeded this value considerably, whereas the Finance Department has significantly underspent. This information can usefully, for presentation purposes, be displayed as a pie chart (see Figure 19.5).

It can be clearly seen from Figure 19.5 that, as previously mentioned, the Finance Department has not been spending, in relative terms, on training compared with other departments. There may of course be very good reasons for this parsimonious behaviour on behalf of the Finance Department's managers but, on the other hand, whatever the reason, this could be contributory to staff deciding to leave the organisation – because of the lack of staff development (for future roles) or skills training.

Figure 19.5 Training budget presented as a percentage of department salary budget (2010)

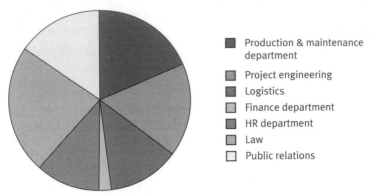

- Production & maintenance department
- Project engineering
- Logistics
- Finance department
- HR department
- Law
- Public relations

Other than keeping records of training expenditure as a percentage of the departments' and EPRO's salary budget, information can be used for comparison purposes and formulated in different ways, for example:

- training days per annum per employee (by department and by the organisation as a whole)
- training expenditure as a percentage of company operating expenditure (OPEX). It would not be meaningful to keep a figure for training expenditure as a percentage of department operating expenditure – because some departments have larger operating budgets than others.

The reason why EPRO Oil and Gas keeps its training expenditure as a percentage of salary budget is so that the international group of companies, to which EPRO belongs, can compare one company with another to determine how each of its operating companies manages its training expenditure. It gives some comparative view, in very broad terms, as to how companies are developing their staff. Similar comparisons, for example with a company's operating expenditure, could be made. Like many statistics, such data does not explain 'why' something has or is happening, as has been previously discussed, but it may cause or create the opportunity for pertinent and sometimes difficult questions to be asked.

As can be seen from the figures in Tables 19.1a, 19.1b and 19.1c, turnover did in fact decrease after 2010, when the investigations into high turnover were made. This may have been as a result of increases in training budget, management changes, increases in salary, or a host of other reasons. The aim of this chapter has been to analyse the information to see where trends lie and where there are spikes in the data. Once we know what the data shows, we can take action to do something about it. This could include training managers, offering better staff development, raising salaries, or any other initiatives which might improve engagement and retention.

19.7 THE LAW AND THE PROCESSING AND FILING OF INFORMATION

19.7.1 DATA PROTECTION ACT 1998 (DPA98)

The Data Protection Act 1998 (DPA98) deals with how data, particularly personal data, should be stored, the geographical limitations from where it can be accessed and sent, how long it can be stored and the limitations upon the manipulation of the data without approval by the 'data subject'. How the Act (DPA98) works is covered in detail, with examples, in Chapter 16, 'Understanding Employment Law'.

19.7.2 THE FREEDOM OF INFORMATION ACT 2000

The above Act of Parliament and how it works and influences our working lives is also dealt with in some detail in Chapter 16, 'Understanding Employment Law'.

19.8 SUMMARY

In this chapter we have considered that there are three types of information, which are differentiated by how they are used:

- strategic information
- tactical information
- operational information.

We have also addressed the issue of the effectiveness of HRISs in terms of how they can be used to maximum effect and how the future of HRISs will be to link with other IT-based systems, such as the organisation's finance department to form what is known as ERP (enterprise resource planning). The future HRIS, once it is integrated with other company-wide systems, will enable data to be manipulated to improve the quality and accuracy of decision-making.

The chapter has also given some examples of the use of information and how it can be used to interpret – using the EPRO Oil and Gas case example – and solve problems that arise. We have also seen how, by using some simple arithmetic measures such as the mean, median and mode, we can, when used together with graphical analysis, interpret and make sense of information. Wherever we are presented with information, whether this be in pictorial, graphical or in a tabular format, there is usually a place for a narrative to qualify and explain what is happening.

REVIEW QUESTIONS

1. What is meant by the following three terms in the context of information management:

   - strategic information?
   - tactical information?
   - operational information?

2. How would you define an HRIS?

3. What is meant by the term wiki?

4. Define the following three terms:

   - mode
   - median
   - average (mean).
   - What is the purpose of the above three measures? What are they indicative of?

ACTIVITY 19.10

Group assignment question

1   Taking the role of an HR manager for a large, high-quality organisation that prides itself on its people management practices, you have been tasked, by the newly appointed HR director, with preparing a report for her on the key people management statistics of your organisation.

- What data would you expect to provide in your report?

2   In anticipation of the introduction of a new HR information system (HRIS), you have been asked, as the HR manager of a medium-sized organisation, by the executive board to present a paper about the key (HR-related) statistics and measures that the company should both monitor and compute.

EXPLORE FURTHER

BOOKS

LANDERS, R.L.N. (2014) *A step-by-step introduction to statistics for business.* London: SAGE.

Visit the SAGE website to sample Chapter 1 of the book: **www.uk.sagepub.com/books/Book237219/title#tabview=samples**

VIDEO LINKS

For some guidance on calculating and understanding *average*, *median* and *mode*, view the following YouTube videos:

www.khanacademy.org/math/probability/descriptive-statistics/old-stats-videos/v/statistics–the-average

www.youtube.com/watch?v=_gbCPPk1KKY

www.youtube.com/watch?v=NZHPVbRbCAY

References

ACAS (n.d.) *Dismissing employees [online]*. Available at: www.acas.org.uk/index.aspx?articleid=1797 [Accessed 21 December 2013].

ACAS (n.d.[a]) *Acas History [online]*. Available at: http://www.acas.org.uk/index.aspx?articleid=1400 [Accessed 26 May 2014].

ACAS (n.d.[b]) *Arbitration [online]*. Available at: http://www.acas.org.uk/index.aspx?articleid=1711 [Accessed 26 May 2014].

ACAS (2009) *The alchemy of dispute resolution – the role of collective conciliation [online]*. Available at: http://www.acas.org.uk/index.aspx?articleid=2988 [Accessed 14 February 2014].

ACAS (2010) *Job evaluation: considerations and risks* [online]. London: ACAS. Available at: www.acas.org.uk/CHttpHandler.ashx?id=922&p=0 [Accessed 26 October 2013].

ACAS (2010b) *Dismissal [online]*. London: ACAS. Available at: http://www.acas.org.uk/index.aspx?articleid=1797 [Accessed 8 January 2010].

ACAS (2011) *What role for trade unions in future workplace relations? [online]*. Available at: http://www.acas.org.uk/index.aspx?articleid=4701&q=role+for+trade+unions [Accessed 31 January 2014].

ACAS (2011a) *Employing people: a handbook for small firms [online]*. Available at: http://www.acas.org.uk/index.aspx?articleid=924 [Accessed 16 September 2013].

ACAS (2011b) *The Equality Act: What's new for employers [online]*. Available at: http://www.acas.org.uk/CHttpHandler.ashx?id=2833&p=0 [Accessed 20 September 2013].

ACAS (2011c) *Personnel data and record keeping [online]*. Available at: http://www.acas.org.uk/media/pdf/c/a/Acas_Personnel_data_record_keeping-accessible-version-July-2011.pdf [Accessed 12 September 2013].

ACAS (2011d) *Sexual orientation discrimination[online]*. Available at: http://www.acas.org.uk/index.aspx?articleid=1824 [Accessed 27 September 2013].

ACAS (2012) *Understanding what vicarious liability means for employers [online]*. Available at: http://www.acas.org.uk/index.aspx?articleid=3715 [Accessed 26 May 2014].

ACAS (2012a) *Voice and participation in the modern workplace: challenges and prospects (March 2012) [online]*. Available at: http://www.acas.org.uk/index.aspx?articleid=4701&q=voice [Accessed 31 January 2014].

ACAS (2012b) *Induction: getting the first few days right [online]*. Available at: http://www.acas.org.uk/index.aspx?articleid=3754 [Accessed 13 September 2013].

ACAS (2012c) *Recruitment and induction booklet [online]*. Available at: http://www.acas.org.uk/media/pdf/l/e/Recruitment_and_induction_%28October-2012%29-accessible-version-may-2012.pdf [Accessed 13 September 2013].

ACAS (2013) *Bullying and harassment at work: guide for managers and employers [online]*. Available at: http://www.acas.org.uk/media/pdf/d/i/Bullying-and-harassment-in-the-workplace-a-guide-for-managers-and-employers.pdf [Accessed 30 September 2013].

ACAS (2013a) *How to manage collective redundancies [online].* Available at: www.acas. org.uk/media/pdf/o/i/How-to-manage-collective-redundancies.pdf [Accessed 22 December 2013].

ACAS (2013b) *Managing absence [online].* Available at: http://www.acas.org.uk/index. aspx?articleid=1566 [Accessed 18 May 2014].

ACAS (2013c) *The right to request flexible working [online].* Available at: www.acas.org. uk/index.aspx?articleid=1616 [Accessed 17th February 2014].

ACAS (2013d) *Booklet on flexible working and work-life balance (2013) [online].* Available at: http://acas.ecgroup.net/Publications/Flexibleworking. aspx [Accessed 17 April 2013].

ACAS (2014) *Changes to TUPE [online].* Available at: http://www.acas.org.uk/media/ pdf/l/1/9908–2901767-TSO-ACAS-TUPE_is_changing-ACCESSIBLE.pdf [Accessed 16 February 2014].

ACAS (2014) *Managing attendance and employee turnover [online].* Available at: http:// www.acas.org.uk/index.aspx?articleid=1183 [Accessed 18 May 2014]

ACAS (2014b) *Handling requests in a reasonable manner to work flexibly: an Acas guide [online].* Available at: www.acas.org.uk/media/pdf/m/9/Handling-requests-to-work-flexibly-in-a-reasonable-manner-an-Acas-guide.pdf [Accessed 22 April 2014].

ACAS (2014c) *Flexible parental leave plans to give working families a boost [online].* Available at: www.acas.org.uk/index.aspx?articleid=4035[Accessed 23 April 2014].

ACAS (2014d) *Discipline and grievances at work: the Acas guide [online].* Available at: www.acas.org.uk/media/pdf/l/c/Discipline-and-grievances-Acas-guide.pdf [Accessed 31 May 2014].

ACAS/CIPD (2013c) *Mediation: an approach to resolving workplace issues [online].* London: Acas and CIPD. Available at: www.acas.org.uk/media/pdf/2/q/Mediation-an-approach-to-resolving-workplace-issues.pdf

ADAMS, J.S. (1961) Towards an understanding of inequity. In: LIKERT, R. (ed.) *New patterns of management.* Maidenhead: McGraw-Hill

ADAMS, J.S. (1972) Inequity in social exchange. In: BERKOVITZ, L. (ed.) *Advances in Experimental and Social Psychology,* Academic Press (1965). Abridged in STEERS, R.M. and PORTER, L.W. *Motivation and work behavior,* 2nd ed. New York: McGraw-Hill

ADLER, N.J. (1986) *International dimensions of organizational behaviour.* Boston, MA: Kent Publishing Company.

ADLER, N.J. (1997) *International dimensions of organizational behaviour.* 3rd ed. Cincinnati: Southwestern.

AGENCY WORKERS REGULATIONS 2010. Available at: www.legislation.gov.uk/uksi/ 2010/93/introduction/made [Accessed 14 August 2013].

ALDERFER, C.P. (1972) *Existence, relatedness and growth: human needs in organisational settings.* New York: Free Press.

ALLEN, D. (2008) Brand aid. *People Management.* 13 November.

ANDERSON, N. and SHACKLETON, V. (1993) *Successful selection interviewing*. Oxford: Blackwell.

ANSOFF, H.I. (1987) *Corporate strategy*. London: Penguin.

ARKIN, A. (2002) Tides of change. *People Management*. 7 February.

ARKIN, A. (2007) Street smart. *People Management [online]*. Available at: www.cipd.co.uk/pm/peoplemanagement/b/weblog/archive/2013/01/29/streetsmart-2007–04.aspx [Accessed 1 October 2013].

ARMSTRONG, M. (1987) Human resource management: a case of the emperor's new clothes. *Personnel Management*. Vol 19, No 8. pp30–35.

ARMSTRONG, M. (1999) *A handbook of HR management practice*. 7th ed. London: Kogan Page.

ARMSTRONG, M. (2006) *A handbook of HR management practice*. 10th ed. London: Kogan Page.

ARMSTRONG, M. (2011) *Armstrong's handbook of strategic human resource management [online]*. 5th ed. London: Kogan Page. Available at: www.dawsonera.com [Accessed 27 February 2014].

ARMSTRONG, M. (2012) *Armstrong's handbook of human resource management practice [online]*. 12th ed. London: Kogan Page. Available at: www.dawsonera.com [Accessed 26 September 2013].

ARMSTRONG, M. (2012a) *Armstrong's handbook of reward management practice [online]*. 4th ed. London: Kogan Page. Available at: www.dawsonera.com [Accessed 1 November 2013].

ARMSTRONG, M. and BARON, A. (1998) *Performance management: the new realities*. London: Chartered Institute of Personnel and Development.

ARMSTRONG, M. and BARON, A. (2004) *Managing performance: performance management in action*. London: Chartered Institute of Personnel and Development.

ARMSTRONG, M. with TAYLOR, S. (2014) *Armstrong's handbook of human resource management practice*. 13th ed. London: Kogan Page.

ARMY (2012) *Transforming the British Army: modernising to face an unpredictable future [online]*. London: Army. Available at: www.army.mod.uk/documents/general/Army2020_brochure.pdf [Accessed 15 August 2013].

ARNOLD. J. with RANDALL, R., SILVESTER, J., PATTERSON, F., ROBERTSON, I., COOPER, C., HARRIS, D., AXTELL, C., DEN HARTOG, D. and BURNES, B. (2010) *Work psychology: understanding human behaviour in the workplace*. 5th ed. Harlow: FT Prentice Hall.

ASHFORD, S.J. and BLACK, J.S. (1996). Proactivity during organizational entry: the role of desire for control. *Journal of Applied Psychology*. Vol 81. pp199–214.

ASHMAN, Dr. I. (2012) *Downsizing envoys: a public/private sector comparison [online]*. Research paper. Norwich: Acas. Available at: www.acas.org.uk/media/pdf/7/1/Downsizing-envoys-a-public-private-sector-comparison-accessible-version.pdf [Accessed 24 December 2013].

ASHMAN, Dr. I. (2012) 'The nature of bad news infects the teller': The experiences of envoys in the face to face delivery of downsizing initiatives in UK public sector organisations [online]. Research paper. Norwich: Acas. Available at: http://www.acas.org.uk/media/pdf/k/s/0312_Downsizing_envoys_Ashman-accessible-version-Apr-2012.pdf [Accessed 24 December 2013].

ASHMORE, R.D., JUSSIM, L.J. and WILDER, D. (eds) (2001) Social identity intergroup conflict, and conflict reduction. Oxford: Oxford University Press.

ATKINSON, J. (1984) Manpower strategies for flexible organisations. Personnel Management. August. pp28–31.

AUSTEN, I. and GELLES, D. (2013) BlackBerry buyout offer raises array of questions [online]. New York Times. 23 September. Available at: www.dealbook.nytimes.com/2013/09/23/blackberry-reaches-4-7-billion-takeover-deal/ [Accessed 23 September 2013].

BALUCH, A.M., SALGE, T.O. and PIENING, E.P. (2013) Untangling the relationship between HRM and hospital performance: the mediating role of attitudinal and behavioural HR outcomes [online]. International Journal of Human Resource Management. Vol 24, No 16. pp3038–61. Accessed via www.search.proquest.com [Accessed 4 September 2013].

BAMBERGER, P.A. and LEVI, R. (2009) Team-based reward allocation structures and the helping behaviors of outcome-interdependent team members [online]. Journal of Managerial Psychology. Vol 24, No 4. pp300–327. Available at: www.search.proquest.com [Accessed 25 October 2013].

BANDAROUK, T.V. and RUEL, H.J.M. (2009) Electronic human resource management: challenges in the digital era. International Journal of Human Resource Management. Vol 20, No 3. pp504–14.

BANDURA, A., ROSS, D. and ROSS, S.A. (1961) Transmission of aggression through the imitation of aggressive models [online]. Journal of Abnormal and Social Psychology. Vol 63, No 3. pp575–82. Available at http://www.ncbi.nlm.nih.gov/pubmed/13864605 [Accessed 16 April 2014].

BANHAM, R. (2011) Forecast 2012: HR experts offer their opinion [online]. HRO Today. Vol 10, No 10. Available at: www.hrotoday.com/content/5028/artful-predictions [Accessed 30 August 2013].

BARNEY, J. (1991) Firm resource and sustained competitive advantage [online]. Journal of Management. Vol 17, No 1. pp99–120. Available at: http://search.proquest.com/ [Accessed 10 June 2014].

BATEMAN, T.S. and ORGAN, D.W. (1983) Job satisfaction and the good soldier: the relationship between affect and citizenship [online]. Academy of Management Journal. Vol 26, No 4. pp587–95. Available at: http://search.proquest.com [Accessed 14 May 2014].

BAUER, T.N. and ERDOGAN, B. (2011) Organizational socialization: the effective onboarding of new employees. In: ZEDECK, S. (ed.) APA handbook of industrial and organizational psychology, Vol 3: Maintaining, expanding, and contracting the organization. APA Handbooks in Psychology. Washington, DC: American Psychological Association, pp51–64.

BEALE, A. (2013) Indirect discrimination: Westlaw.UK, Insights [online]. Westlaw.UK. Available at: www.westlaw.co.uk [Accessed 3 January 2014].

BEARDWELL, I. and CLAYDON, T. (2007) *Human resource management: a contemporary approach.* 5th ed. Harlow: FT Prentice Hall.

BEARDWELL, I. and CLAYDON, T. (2010) *Human resource management: a contemporary approach.* 6th ed. Harlow: Prentice Hall.

BEARDWELL, I. and WRIGHT, M. (2004) *in* BEARDWELL, I., HOLDEN, L. and CLAYDON, T. (eds) *Human resource management: a contemporary approach.* Harlow: Pearson Education.

BEARDWELL, I., HOLDEN, L. and CLAYDON, T. (2004) *Human resource management: a contemporary approach.* Harlow: Pearson Education.

BEATTIE, D. (2002) President's message. *Annual Report 2002.* London: CIPD.

BEAULIEU, C.M.J. (2006) Intercultural study of personal space: a case study [online]. *Journal of Applied Psychology.* Vol 24, No 4. pp794–805. Available at: http://onlinelibrary. wiley.com [Accessed 6 March 2014].

BEAUMONT, J. and THOMAS, J. (2012) *Measuring national well-being, health, 2012 [online].* Newport (Wales): ONS. Available at: www.ons.gov.uk/ons/dcp171766_271762. pdf [Accessed 12 December 2013].

BEER, M., SPECTOR, B., LAWRENCE, P., MILLS, D., and WALTON, R. (1985) *Human resource management: a general manager's perspective.* New York: The Free Press.

BENNETT, R. (2013) Part-timers pay price in lower wages and missed promotions [online]. *The Times.* 8 July. p20. Available at: www.search.proquest.com [Accessed 16 August 2013].

BEVAN, S. and THOMPSON, M. (1991) Performance management at the crossroads. *Personnel Management.* November. pp36–9.

BISWAS, M. and SUAR, D. (2013) Which employees' values matter most in the creation of employer branding? [online]. *Journal of Marketing Development & Competitiveness.* Vol 7, No 1. pp93–102. Available at: www.web.ebscohost.com [Accessed 17 October 2013].

BLACK, C. (2008) *Working for a healthier tomorrow [online].* London: The Stationery Office. Available at: https://www.gov.uk/government/uploads/system/uploads/ attachment_data/file/209782/hwwb-working-for-a-healthier-tomorrow.pdf [Accessed 22 April 2014].

BLAU, D.M. (1990) An empirical analysis of employed and unemployed job search behaviour. *Industrial and Labor Relations Review.* Vol 45, No 4. July. pp738–52.

BLAU, P.M. and SCOTT, W.R. (1966) *Formal organisations.* London: Routledge.

BLESSINGWHITE (2013) *Employee engagement research update (January 2013): Beyond the numbers: A practical approach for individuals, managers, and executives [online].* Princeton, NJ: BlessingWhite. Available at: www.blessingwhite.com/content/reports/ BlessingWhite_Employee_Engagement_Research_Report_2013.pdf [Accessed 21 August 2013].

BLOISI, W. (2007) *An introduction to human resource management.* Maidenhead: McGraw-Hill.

BOUNDS, A. (2013) Jessops returns to the high street: General Retailers [online]. *The Times*. 28 March. p23. Available at: www.search.proquest.com [Accessed 16 July 2013].

BOXALL, P.F. (2007) The goals of HRM. In: BOXALL, P., PURCELL, J. and WRIGHT, P. (eds) *Oxford handbook of human resource management*. Oxford: Oxford University Press, pp48–67.

BOXALL, P., ANG, S.H. and BARTRAM, T. (2011) Analyzing the 'black box' of HRM: uncovering HR goals, mediators, and outcomes in a standardized service environment [online]. *Journal of Management Studies*. Vol 48, No 7. pp1504–32. Available at: www.onlinelibrary.wiley.com [Accessed 6 September 2013].

BOYATZIS, R.E. (1982) *The competent manager: model for effective performance*. New York: John Wiley & Sons.

BOYD, C. (2009) Not all there. *People Management*. 29 April.

BRAMHAM, J. (1994) *Human resource planning*. London: Institute of Personnel and Development.

BRATTON, J. and GOLD, J. (2007) *Human resource management: theory and practice*. 4th ed. Basingstoke: Palgrave Macmillan.

BRATTON, J. and GOLD, J. (2012) *Human resource management: theory and practice*. 5th ed. Basingstoke: Palgrave Macmillan.

BRECH, E.F.L. (1965) *Prejudice: its social psychology*. Oxford: Blackwell.

BREWER, M.M. (2001) Ingroup identification and intergroup conflict: when does ingroup love become outgroup hate? In: ASHMORE, R.D., JUSSIM, L.J. and WILDER, D. (eds) *Social identity intergroup conflict, and conflict reduction*. Oxford: Oxford University Press.

BRITISH PSYCHOLOGICAL SOCIETY (2014) http://www.bps.org.uk/ [Accessed 23 March 2014].

BRITTENDEN, S. (2013) *Redundancy, fair selection: Insight, Section 15 [online]*. London: Thomson Reuters. Available at: www.westlaw.co.uk [Accessed 23 December 2013].

BROCKETT, J (2009) Employer branding still makes its mark. *People Management*. Vol 15, No 6. pp12–13.

BROOKS, I. (2009) *Organisational behaviour: individuals, groups and organisations*. Harlow: Pearson Education Ltd.

BULLA, D.N. and SCOTT, P.M. (1994) Manpower requirements forecasting: a case example. In: WARD, D., BECHET, T.P. and TRIPP, R. (eds) *Human resource forecasting and modelling*. New York: Human Resource Planning Society.

BURNES, B. (2009) *Managing change*. 5th ed. Harlow: Pearson Education Ltd.

BURNES, B. (2011) Introduction: why does change fail, and what can we do about it? [online]. *Journal of Change Management*. Vol 11, No 4. pp445–50. Available at: www.tandfonline.com/loi/rjcm20 [Accessed 24 March 2014].

BURNS, T. and STALKER, G.M. (1966) *The management of innovation*. London: Tavistock.

BUSINESSEUROPE. *[online]* Available at http://www.businesseurope.eu [Accessed 24 January 2014].

CAMPBELL, D. and CRAIG, T. (2012) *Organisations and the business environment.* 2nd ed. London: Elsevier Butterworth Heinemann.

CARLUCCI, D., MARR, B. and SCHIUMA, G. (2004) The knowledge value chain: how intellectual capital impacts on business performance. *International Journal of Technology Management.* Vol 27, No 6/7. p575.

CARRINGTON, L. (2007) Designs on the dotted line. *People Management.* Vol 13, No 21. pp36–9.

CBI/Pfizer (2011) *Healthy returns? Absence and workplace health survey 2011. [online].* Available at: http://www.cbi.org.uk/media/955604/2011.05-healthy_returns_-_absence_ and_workplace_health_survey_2011.pdf

CATTELL, R.B. (1946) *The description and measurement of personality.* New York: World Books.

CBI/Pfizer (2013) *Fit for purpose – absence and workplace health 2013 [online].* Available at: http://www.cbi.org.uk/media-centre/press-releases/2013/07/work-absence-at-record-low-but-still-costs-economy-£14bn-a-year-cbi-pfizer-survey/ [Accessed 14 February 2014].

CENTRAL ARBITRATION COMMITTEE (2014) *[online]* Available at: http://www.cac. gov.uk/ [Accessed 24 January 2014].

CENTRAL MANCHESTER UNIVERSITY HOSPITALS NHS FOUNDATION TRUST v BROWNE UKEAT/0294/11/CEA *[online]* Available at: http://www.employment casesupdate.co.uk/site.aspx?i=ed11465 [Accessed 28 September 2013].

CHAMPY, J. and NOHRIA, N. (eds) (1996) *Fast forward: the best ideas on managing business change.* Boston, MA: Harvard Business School Press.

CHILD, J. (1988) *Organisation: a guide to problem and practice.* 2nd ed. London: Paul Chapman.

CHILDREN AND FAMILIES ACT 2014 [online]. London: Stationery Office. Available at: http://www.legislation.gov.uk/ukpga/2014/6/contents/enacted [Accessed 14 August 2013].

CHURCHARD, C. (2013) HR more worried about the long term than leaders. *People Management.* 22 January. Available at: http://www.cipd.co.uk/pm/peoplemanagement/b/ weblog/archive/2013/01/22/hr-more-worried-about-the-long-term-than-leaders.aspx [Accessed 12 September 2013].

CHURCHARD, C. (2013) No rise, no problem [online]. *People Management.* 25 April. Available at: www.cipd.co.uk/pm/peoplemanagement/ [Accessed 18 October 2013].

CHYNOWETH, C. (2014) When a spin-off is the only answer. *Sunday Times.* 23 March. Appointments, p3.

CIPD (n.d.) *Profession map [online].* London: Chartered Institute of Personnel and Development. Available at: http://www.cipd.co.uk/cipd-hr-profession/hr-profession-map/) [Accessed 12 September 2013].

CIPD (2007) *The changing HR function [online].* London: Chartered Institute of Personnel and Development. Available at: http://www.cipd.co.uk/NR/rdonlyres/9FC78BA5-B992–40B8-85ED-8FA5C3F9FACC/0/chnghrfunc.pdf [Accessed 14 May 2014].

CIPD (2007) *Reward: summary of the research into practice event [online].* Event report. Available at: http://www.cipd.co.uk/subjects/pay/general/_rwrdres07.htm?IsSrchRes=1 [Accessed 23 November 2009].

CIPD (2009) *Performance management in action: current trends and practice [online].* London: Chartered Institute of Personnel and Development. Available at: http://www.cipd.co.uk/hr-resources/survey-reports/performance-management-trends-practice.aspx [Accessed 22 April 2014].

CIPD (2009a) *Contracts of employment [online].* Factsheet. London: Chartered Institute of Personnel and Development. Available at: http://www.cipd.co.uk/EmploymentLaw/empgdprc.htm [Accessed 22 December 2009].

CIPD/Mercer (2010) *Employer branding and total reward [online].* Research report. Available at: http://www.cipd.co.uk/hr-resources/research/employer-branding-total-reward.aspx [Accessed 22 April 2014].

CIPD (2010a) *The talent perspective: what does it feel like to be talent managed [online].* Survey report. London: Chartered Institute of Personnel and Development. Available at: www.cipd.co.uk/binaries/5262_Talent_Perspective.pdf [Accessed 22 February 2014].

CIPD (2010b) *Workforce planning: right people, right time, right skills [online].* Guide. London: Chartered Institute of Personnel and Development. Available at: http://www.cipd.co.uk/hr-resources/guides/workforce-planning-right-people-right-time-right-skills.aspxpdf [Accessed 22 February 2014].

CIPD (2010c) *Opening up talent for business success: integrating talent management and diversity[online].* London: Chartered Institute of Personnel and Development. Available at: http://www.cipd.co.uk/hr-resources/research/talent-business-success-integrating-talent-management-diversity.aspx [Accessed 1 May 2014].

CIPD (2011) *Employee attitudes to pay [online].* Annual survey report. London: Chartered Institute of Personnel and Development. Available at: www.cipd.co.uk/binaries/5738%20Pay%20Attitudes%20(WEB).pdf [Accessed 22 February 2014].

CIPD (2011a) *Employment relations [online].* London: Chartered Institute of Personnel and Development. Available at: http://www.cipd.co.uk/hr-resources/survey-reports/employment-relations-2011.aspx [Accessed 18 May 2014].

CIPD (2011b) *Conflict management [online].* Survey report. London: Chartered Institute of Personnel and Development. Available at: www.cipd.co.uk/binaries/5461_Conflict_manage_SR_WEB.pdf [Accessed 22 February 2014].

CIPD (2012) *Diversity in the workplace [online].* Factsheet. London: Chartered Institute Of Personnel and Development. Available at http://www.cipd.co.uk/hr-resources/factsheets/diversity-workplace-overview.aspx [Accessed 20 September 2013].

CIPD (2012a) *Flexible working provision and uptake [online].* London: Chartered Institute of Personnel and Development. Available at https://www.cipd.co.uk/hr-resources/survey-reports/flexible-working-provision-uptake.aspx [Accessed 27 March 2014].

CIPD (2012b) *Induction [online]*. Factsheet. London: Chartered Institute of Personnel and Development. Available at http://www.cipd.co.uk/hr-resources/factsheets/induction.aspx [Accessed 13 September 2013].

CIPD (2012) *Organisation development [online]*. Factsheet. London: Chartered Institute of Personnel and Development. Available at: www.cipd.co.uk/hr-resources/factsheets/organisation-development.aspx [Accessed 27 March 2014].

CIPD (2013) *Learning and talent development [online]*. Survey report. London: Chartered Institute of Personnel and Development. Available at: http://www.cipd.co.uk/hr-resources/survey-reports/learning-talent-development-2013.aspx [Accessed 21 November 2013].

CIPD (2013a) *Workforce planning [online]*. Factsheet. London: Chartered Institute of Personnel and Development. Available at. www.cipd.co.uk/hr-resources/factsheets/workforce-planning.aspx [Accessed 1 February 2014].

CIPD (2013b) *HR outlook: winter 2012–13 [online]*. Survey report. London: Chartered Institute of Personnel and Development. Available at: www.cipd.co.uk/hr-resources/survey-reports/hr-outlook-winter-2012–13-views-profession.aspx [Accessed 22 February 2014].

CIPD (2013c) *Succession planning [online]*. Factsheet. London: Chartered Institute of Personnel and Development. Available at: www.cipd.co.uk/hr-resources/factsheets/succession-planning.aspx [Accessed 22 February 2014].

CIPD (2013d) *Talent planning [online]*. Factsheet. London: Chartered Institute of Personnel and Development. Available at: www.cipd.co.uk/hr-resources/factsheets/talent-management-overview.aspx [Accessed 22 February 2014].

CIPD (2013e) *Reward management [online]*. Annual survey report. London: Chartered Institute of Personnel and Development. Available at: www.cipd.co.uk/hr-resources/survey-reports/reward-management-2013.aspx [Accessed 22 February 2014].

CIPD (2013f) *Contracts of employment [online]*. Factsheet. London: Chartered Institute of Personnel and Development. Available at: www.cipd.co.uk/hr-resources/factsheets/contracts-of-employment.aspx [Accessed 22 February 2014].

CIPD (2013g) *Retention of HR records [online]*. Factsheet. London: Chartered Institute of Personnel and Development. Available at: http://www.cipd.co.uk/hr-resources/factsheets/retention-hr-records.aspx [Accessed 25 February 2014].

CIPD (2013h) *Teamwork [online]*. Factsheet. London: Chartered Institute of Personnel and Development. Available at: www.cipd.co.uk/hr-resources/factsheets/change-management.aspx [Accessed 9 March 2014].

CIPD (2013i) *Annual survey report supplement 2013: Aligning strategy and benefits [online]*. London: Chartered Institute of Personnel and Development. Available at: www.cipd.co.uk/binaries/6331%20RewMan%20SR%20supplement%20(WEB).pdf [Accessed 11 April 2014].

CIPD (2013j) *Focus on employee well-being: employee outlook: autumn 2013 [online]*. London: Chartered Institute of Personnel and Development. Available at: www.cipd.co.uk/binaries/6381%20EO%20Focus%20on%20well-being%20(WEB).pdf [Accessed 22 April 2014].

CIPD (2013k) *Absence management [online].* Annual survey report. London: Chartered Institute of Personnel and Development. Available at: http://www.cipd.co.uk/hr-resources/survey-reports/absence-management-2013.aspx [Accessed 17 February 2014].

CIPD (2013l) *Employee outlook: autumn 2013 [online].* London: Chartered Institute of Personnel and Development. Available at: http://www.cipd.co.uk/hr-resources/survey-reports/employee-outlook-autumn-2013.aspx [Accessed 18 April 2014].

CIPD (2013m) *Health and well-being at work [online].* Factsheet. London: Chartered Institute of Personnel and Development. Available at: http://www.cipd.co.uk/hr-resources/factsheets/health-well-being-at-work.aspx [Accessed 17 April 2014].

CIPD (2013n) *Employee engagement [online].* Factsheet. London: Chartered Institute of Personnel and Development. Available at: www.cipd.co.uk/hr-resources/factsheets/employee-engagement.aspx [Accessed 13 May 2014].

CIPD (2013o) *Recruitment [online].* Factsheet. London: Chartered Institute of Personnel and Development. Available at: http://www.cipd.co.uk/hr-resources/factsheets/recruitment-overview.aspx [Accessed 25 March 2014].

CIPD (2013p) *Employer brand [online].* Factsheet. London: Chartered Institute of Personnel and Development. Available at: http://www.cipd.co.uk/hr-resources/factsheets/employer-brand.aspx [Accessed 31 May 2014].

CIPD (2013q) *Performance management [online].* Factsheet. London: Chartered Institute of Personnel and Development. Available at: http://www.cipd.co.uk/hr-resources/factsheets/performance-management-overview.aspx [Accessed 22 April 2014].

CIPD (2013r) *Race, religion and employment [online].* Factsheet. London: Chartered Institute Of Personnel and Development. Available at: http://www.cipd.co.uk/hr-resources/factsheets/race-religion-employment.aspx [Accessed 27 May 2014].

CIPD (2013s) *Age and employment [online].* Factsheet. London: Chartered Institute Of Personnel and Development. Available at: http://www.cipd.co.uk/hr-resources/factsheets/age-employment.aspx [Accessed 30 September 2013].

CIPD (2013t) *Competence and competency frameworks [online].* London: Chartered Institute Of Personnel and Development. Available at: http://www.cipd.co.uk/hr-resources/factsheets/competence-competency-frameworks.aspx [Accessed 13 March 2014].

CIPD (2014) *Change management [online].* Factsheet. London: Chartered Institute Of Personnel and Development. Available at: www.cipd.co.uk/hr-resources/factsheets/change-management.aspx [Accessed 24 March 2014].

CIPD/HAYS (2013) *Resourcing and talent planning [online].* Annual survey report. London: Chartered Institute of Personnel and Development. Available at: www.cipd.co.uk/binaries/6226%20RTP%20SR%20WEB.PDF [Accessed 22 February 2014].

CIPD/HR-INFORM (2013) *Volunteers denied employment rights [online]* People Management, HR-Inform. London: Chartered Institute Of Personnel and Development. Available at: http://www.cipd.co.uk/pm/peoplemanagement/p/paymentgateway.aspx?returnURL=/pm/peoplemanagement/b/weblog/archive/2013/01/08/volunteers-denied-employment-rights.aspx&blogid=2&postid=71148 [Accessed 30 September 2013].

CLAYDON, T. (2004) Human resource management and the labour market. In: BEARDWELL, I., HOLDEN, L. and CLAYDON, T. (eds) *Human resource management: a contemporary approach.* 4th ed. Harlow: Pearson Education.

CLEGG, S., KORNBERGER, M. and PITSIS, T. (2011) *Managing and organizations: an introduction to theory and practice.* 3rd ed. London: Sage.

CLUTTERBUCK, D. (2003) *Managing work-life balance: a guide for HR in achieving organisational and individual change.* London: CIPD.

COLLINSON, P. and WATT, N. (2013) Pension scheme charges cap proposed by ministers [online]. *Guardian.* 30 October. Available at: http://www.theguardian.com/money [Accessed 2 November 2013].

COOPER, C.L., COOPER, R.D. and EAKER, L.H. (1988) *Living with stress.* Harmondsworth: Penguin.

COSTELLO, M. (2014) Provider sets ball rolling with £30,000 cash-in move. *The Times.* 21 March. p7.

COUGHLIN, C. (2013) The SAS: a very special force [online]. *Telegraph.* 31 January. p21. Available at: www.search.proquest.com [Accessed 13 June 2014].

COX, A., BROWN, D. and RILEY, P. (2010) Reward strategy: time for a more realistic reconceptualization and reinterpretation? [online]. *Thunderbird International Business Review.* Vol 52, No 3. pp249–60. Available at: www.ebscohost.com [Accessed 7 October 2013].

CURRAN, J. and STANWORH, J. (1988) The small firm: a neglected area of management. In: GOWLING, A.G., STANWORH, M.J.K., BENNET, R.D., CURRAN, J. and LYONS, P. (eds) *Behavioural sciences for managers.* 2nd ed. London: Edward Arnold.

CURRIE, D. (2006) *Introduction to human resource management: a guide to personnel in practice.* London: Chartered Institute of Personnel and Development.

DANIELS, K. and MACDONALD, L. (2005) *Equality, diversity and discrimination.* London: CIPD.

DATA PROTECTION ACT (1998) London: The Stationery Office. Available at: www.legislation.gov.uk/ukpga/1998/29/contents [Accessed 24 February 2014].

DAVEY, J. (2014) Morrisons boss waives bonus after profit warning [online]. *Reuters.* 27 March. Available at: http://uk.reuters.com/article/2014/03/27/uk-morrisons-bonus-idUKBREA2Q28G20140327 [Accessed 24 February 2014].

DEPARTMENT FOR BUSINESS, INNOVATION AND SKILLS (2012) *Trade union membership 2012: statistical bulletin [online]* Available at: https://www.gov.uk/government/publications/trade-union-statistics-2012 [Accessed 31 January 2014].

DEPARTMENT FOR BUSINESS, INNOVATION AND SKILLS (2013) *Guide to apprenticeships [online].* London: Department for Business, Innovation and Skills. Available at: www.gov.uk/apprenticeships-guide [Accessed 19 September 2013].

DEPARTMENT FOR BUSINESS, INNOVATION AND SKILLS (2013a) *Office of the Regulator of Community Interest Companies: Leaflets: Frequently Asked Questions [online].* Cardiff: Office of the Regulator of Community Interest Companies. Available at: https://www.gov.uk/government/uploads/system/uploads/attachment_data/file/223858/13–786-

community-interest-companies-frequently-asked-questions__1_.pdf [Accessed 30 May 2015].

DEPARTMENT FOR BUSINESS, INNOVATION AND SKILLS/DEPARTMENT FOR EDUCATION (2013) *The future of apprenticeships in England: next steps from the Richard Review [online]*. London: Department for Business, Innovation and Skills/Department for Education. Available at: www.gov.uk/government/uploads/system/uploads/attachment_data/file/190632/bis-13–577-the-future-of-apprenticeships-in-england-next-steps-from-the-richard-review.pdf [Accessed 19 September 2013].

DEPARTMENT FOR BUSINESS, INNOVATION AND SKILLS/ GOVERNMENT EQUALITIES OFFICE (GEO) (2013) *The business case for equality and diversity: BIS occasional paper no. 4 [online]*. January. Available at: https://www.gov.uk/government/uploads/system/uploads/attachment_data/file/49638/the_business_case_for_equality_and_diversity.pdf [Accessed 20 September 2013].

DISCLOSURE AND BARRING SERVICE (n.d.) *Guide to eligibility [online]*. Available at: https://www.gov.uk/government/publications/dbs-check-eligible-positions-guidance [Accessed 13 May 2014].

DOVING, E. and NORDHAUG, O. (2010) Investing in human resource planning: an international study [online]. *Management Revue*. Vol 21, No 3. pp292–307. Available at: www.ebscohost.com [Accessed 22 September 2013].

DRUCKER, P. (1977) *People and performance: the best of Peter Drucker on management*. London: Heinemann.

EATON, G. (2012) Police and crime commissioner elections: all you need to know. *The New Statesman*. 12 November. p16.

EATON, M. (2012) Define Britishness? It's like painting wind [online]. *BBC News UK*. 12 March. London: BBC. Available at: www.bbc.co.uk/news/uk-17218635 [Accessed 8 March 2014].

EISENBERG, C. (2006) FIFA 1975–2000: the business of a football development organisation. *Historical Social Research*. Vol 31, No 1. pp55–68. Accessed via: EBSCO Business Source Premier at: www.web.ebscohost.com [Accessed 9 July 2013].

EKMEKCI, O., CASEY, A., ROSENBUSCH, K., CATALDO, C. and BYINGTON, L. (2013) Re-examining the influence of societal culture on organizational identity [online]. *Journal of International Business and Cultural Studies*. Vol 7. pp1–20. Available at: http://search.proquest.com/ [Accessed 9 March 2014].

ELLIOTT, L. (2012) British recessions: a short history [online]. *Guardian*. 7 December. Available at: www.theguardian.com/business/2012/dec/07/britain-recessions-history [Accessed 13 May 2014].

ELLIOTT, F., ALDRICK, P. and SHERMAN, J. (2014) Voters back Osborne's pension revolution. *The Times*. 1 March. p1.

ELLIOTT, L. and WINTOUR, P. (2014) Budget 2014: Osborne targets grey vote with savings and pensions reforms. *Guardian*. 19 March. p1.

EMPLOYMENT EQUALITY (REPEAL OF RETIREMENT AGE PROVISIONS) REGULATIONS 2011 (SI 2011/1069). Available at: http://www.legislation.gov.uk/ukdsi/2011/9780111507735 [Accessed 30 September 2013].

EMPLOYMENT RIGHTS ACT 1996. Available at: www.legislation.gov.uk/ukpga/1996/18/contents [Accessed 15 February 2014].

ENGLISH V THOMAS SANDERSON. EWCA Civ 1421 [2008] Available at: http://www.bailii.org/ew/cases/EWCA/Civ/2008/1421.html [Accessed 23 September 2013].

EQUALITY ACT 2010. Available at: http://www.legislation.gov.uk/ukpga/2010/15/contents [Accessed 28 April 2014].

EQUALITY AND DIVERSITY FORUM (2013) Available at: http://www.edf.org.uk/blog/?page_id=886 [Accessed 27 September 2013].

EQUALITY AND HUMAN RIGHTS COMMISSION (n.d.) Available at: http://www.equalityhumanrights.com/advice-and guidance/your-rights/race/what-is-race-discrimination/what-forms-does-racial-discrimination-take/ [Accessed 28 September 2013].

EQUALITY AND HUMAN RIGHTS COMMISSION (EHRC n.d.[b]) *Work of equal value: equal value checklist [online].* Available at: www.equalityhumanrights.com/advice-and-guidance/tools-equal-pay/checklists-equal-pay-in-practice/3-work-of-equal-value/ [Accessed 27 December 2013].

EQUALITY AND HUMAN RIGHTS COMMISSION. (2010) *What equality law means for you as an employer: pay and benefits [online].* Available at: http://www.equalityhumanrights.com/uploaded_files/equalpay/employers_pay_and_benefits.pdf [Accessed 27 September 2013].

EQUALITY AND HUMAN RIGHTS COMMISSION (2011) *Equal pay statutory code of practice: Equality Act 2010 Code of Practice [online].* Available at: www.equalityhumanrights.com/uploaded_files/EqualityAct/equalpaycode.pdf [Accessed 3 November 2013].

EQUALITY AND HUMAN RIGHTS COMMISSION (2013) *Avoiding and dealing with harassment [online].* Available at: http://www.equalityhumanrights.com/advice-and-guidance/guidance-for-employers/managing-workers/avoiding-and-dealing-with-harassment/ [Accessed 30 September 2013].

EQUALITY AND HUMAN RIGHTS COMMISSION (2013a) *Genuine occupational requirement [online].* Available at: http://www.equalityhumanrights.com/advice-and-guidance/your-rights/religion-and-belief/when-does-the-law-allow-religious-discrimination/a-genuine-occupational-requirement/ [Accessed 27 September 2013].

EQUALITY AND HUMAN RIGHTS COMMISSION (2013b) *Protected characteristics [online].* Available at: http://www.equalityhumanrights.com/advice-and-guidance/new-equality-act-guidance/protected-characteristics-definitions/ [Accessed 20 September 2013].

ERWIN, D.G. and GARMAN, A.N. (2010). Resistance to organizational change: linking research and practice [online]. *Leadership & Organization Development Journal.* Vol 31, No 1. pp39–56. Available at: search.proquest.com [Accessed 24 June 2014].

EUROPEAN AGENCY FOR SAFETY AND HEALTH AT WORK (2013) *Priorities for occupational safety and health research in Europe: 2013–2020 [online].* Available at: https://osha.europa.eu/en/publications/reports/priorities-for-occupational-safety-and-health-research-in-europe-2013–2020 [Accessed 16 December 2013].

EUROPEAN COMMISSION (2003) Commission Recommendation of 6 May 2003 concerning the definition of micro, small and medium-sized enterprises (notified under document number C(2003) 1422) (2003/361/EC). *Official Journal of the European Union [online]*. 20 May. L 124, pp36–41. Available at: http://eur-lex.europa.eu/LexUriServ/LexUriServ.do?uri=OJ:L:2003:124:0036:0041:EN:PDF [Accessed 12 August 2013].

EUROPEAN COMMISSION (2005) *The new SME definition: user guide and model declaration [online]*. Luxembourg: The Publications Office (Enterprise and Industry) of the European Commission. Available at: http://ec.europa.eu/enterprise/policies/sme/files/sme_definition/sme_user_guide_en.pdf [Accessed 18 July 2013].

EUROPEAN COMMISSION (2013) *Enterprise: a new industrial revolution [online]*. Luxembourg: The Publications Office of the European Commission. Available at: http://europa.eu/pol/enter/flipbook/en/files/enterprise.pdf [Accessed 18th July 2013].

EUROPEAN COMMISSION, Enterprise and Industry (2013a) European SME Week [online]. Luxembourg: The Publications Office of the European Commission. [Accessed 18 July 2013]. Available at: http://ec.europa.eu/enterprise/initiatives/sme-week/

EUROPEAN ECONOMIC AND SOCIAL COMMITTEE. Available at: http://www.eesc.europa.eu [Accessed 24 January 2014].

EUROPEAN TRADE UNION CONFEDERATION (ETUC) Available at: http://www.etuc.org [Accessed 24 January 2014].

EUROPEAN UNION PRESS RELEASE (2011) *New EU fundraising rules: boosting venture capital for SMEs and easing access to credit [online]*. 12 July. Available at: http://europa.eu/rapid/press-release_IP-11–1513_en.htm?locale=en [Accessed 18 July 2013].

EUROSTAT, EUROPEAN COMMISSION. *European Social Statistics 2013 edition [online]*. Luxembourg: The Publications Office of the European Commission. Available at: http://epp.eurostat.ec.europa.eu/cache/ITY_OFFPUB/KS-FP-13–001/EN/KS-FP-13–001-EN.PDF [Accessed 18 August 2013].

FARAGHER, J. (2013) Government wins right to appeal Woolworths redundancy ruling [online]. *People Management*. 13 September. Available at: www.cipd.co.uk/pm/peoplemanagement/b/weblog/archive/2013/09/13/government-wins-right-to-appeal-woolworths-redundancy-ruling.aspx [Accessed 22 December 2013].

FARRELL, S. (2014) Sainsbury's sales fall for first time in nine years [online]. *Guardian*. 18 March. Available at: http://www.theguardian.com/business

FAWCETT SOCIETY (2012) *Equal pay: campaign [online]*. London: Fawcett Society. Available at: www.fawcettsociety.org.uk/equal-pay/ [Accessed 3 November 2013].

FAYOL, H. (1949) *General and industrial management*. London: Pitman.

FIFA (no date) *All about the game [online]*. Zurich: The Fédération Internationale de Football Association. Available at: www.fifa.com [Accessed 9 July 2013].

FLEXIBLE WORKING (ELIGIBILITY, COMPLAINTS AND REMEDIES) (AMENDMENT) REGULATIONS 2009. Available at: www.legislation.gov.uk/uksi/2009/595/made [Accessed 17 February 2014].

FOOTE WHYTE, W. (1955) *Street corner society*. Chicago: University of Chicago Press.

FOWLER, A. (1987) When chief executives discover human resource management. *Personnel Management*. January. p3.

FOY, H. and MURRAY BROWN, J. (2013) JLR's success exposes shortage in engineering skills [online]. *FT.com*. 13 June. Available at: www.ft.com/cms/s/0/95ac34ec-d411–11e2–8639–00144feab7de.html#axzz2i9xU2sf [Accessed 25 September 2013].

FRANCIS, H. and KEEGAN, A. (2006) The changing face of HRM: in search of balance. *Human Resource Management Journal*. Vol 16, No 3. pp231–49.

FRANCIS, R. (QC) (2013) *Report of the Mid Staffordshire NHS Foundation Trust Public Inquiry, Executive Summary [online]*. p13. London: The Stationery Office. Available at: www.midstaffspublicinquiry.com/sites/default/files/report/Executive%20summary.pdf [Accessed 3 September 2013].

FREEDOM OF INFORMATION ACT 2000. Available at: http://www.legislation.gov.uk/ukpga/2000/36/contents [Accessed 12 September 2013].

FRENCH, W.L. and BELL, C.H (1990) *Organization development*. Englewood Cliffs, NJ: Prentice-Hall.

FURNHAM, A. and GUNTER, B. (1993) Corporate culture: diagnosis and change. In: COOPER, C.L. and ROBERTSON, I.T. (eds) *International review of industrial and organisational psychology*. Chichester: Wiley.

GENDER IDENTITY RESEARCH AND EDUCATION SOCIETY (2013) Available at: http://gires.org.uk/assets/Research-Assets/Prevalence2011.pdf [Accessed 27 September 2013].

GENERAL MOTORS COMPANY (2010) *This is the new GM. Annual report 2010 [online]*. Detroit, MI: General Motors Company. Available at: www.gm.com/content/dam/gmcom/COMPANY/Investors/Corporate_Governance/PDFs/StockholderInformationPDFs/Annual-Report.pdf [Accessed 26 August 2013].

GENERAL MOTORS COMPANY (2012) *Annual report 2012 [online]*. Detroit, MI: General Motors Company. Available at: www.gm.com/content/dam/gmcom/COMPANY/Investors/Stockholder_Information/PDFs/2012_GM_Annual_Report.pdf [Accessed 26 August 2013].

GIDDENS, A. (1989) *Sociology*. Oxford: Polity Press.

GOFFEE, R. and JONES, G. (2009) *Clever: leading your smartest, most creative people*. Boston, MA: Harvard Business Press.

GOLD, J., STEWART, J., ILES, P., HOLDEN, R. and BEARDWELL, J. (2010) *Human resource development theory and practice*. Basingstoke: Palgrave MacMillan.

GOLDING, N. (2004) Strategic human resource management. In: BEARDWELL, I., HOLDEN, T. and CLAYDON, T. (eds) *Human resource management: a contemporary approach*. 4th ed. Harlow: Pearson Education.

GOLDSTEIN, J. (2013) The time for outsourcing to move from tactical to strategic is now. So why isn't it happening? [online]. *HRO Today*. Vol 12, No 5. Available at: www.hrotoday.com/content/5378/wake-call [Accessed 30 August 2013].

GOLDTHORPE, J.H. (1968) *The affluent worker: industrial attitudes and behaviour*. Cambridge: Cambridge University Press.

GOSS, D. (1996) *Principles of human resource management.* London: Routledge.

GOVERNMENT EQUALITIES OFFICE. Available at: https://www.gov.uk/government/uploads/system/uploads/attachment_data/file/85013/empl oyment-health-questions.pdf [Accessed 25 March 2014].

GOV.UK (2013) *Equality act guidance [online].* Available at: https://www.gov.uk/equality-act-2010-guidance [Accessed 29 September 2013].

GOV.UK (n.d.) *Joining a trade union [online].* Available at: www.gov.uk [Accessed 27 January 2014].

GREENBERG, J. (2013) *Managing behavior in organizations.* 6th ed. Harlow: Pearson Education.

GRIFFITHS, K. (2013) Osborne throws down late legal challenge to bonus cap [online]. *The Times.* 26 September. p33. Available at: www.search.proquest.com

GUEST, D. (1989) Human resource management and industrial relations. In: STOREY, J. (ed.) *New perspectives in human resource management.* London: Routledge.

HALL, E.T. (1959). *The silent language.* New York: Anchor.

HAMPDEN-TURNER, C. (1990) *Corporate cultures: from vicious to virtuous circles.* London: Random Century.

HANDY, C.B. (1976) *Understanding organisations.* Harmondsworth: Penguin.

HANDY, C.B. (1989) *The age of unreason.* London: Business Books.

HANDY, C.B. (1993) *Understanding organisations.* 4th ed. Harmondsworth: Penguin.

HANDY, L., DEVINE, M. and HEATH, L. (1996) *360 degree feedback: unguided missile or powerful weapon?* Berkhamstead: Ashridge Management Group.

HARVARD BUSINESS SCHOOL (2012) *A new vision: Baker Library Historical Collections [online].* Boston: Harvard Business School. Available at: www.library.hbs.edu/hc/hawthorne/anewvision.html#e [Accessed 10 May 2014].

HARVEY NASH (2012) *Onboard and upwards: how an executive's first 90 days can make or break the ones that follow [online].* Available at: http://www.harveynash.com/group/mediacentre/2012/10/a_third_of_executives_consider_quitting_in_their_first_90_days/index.asp [Accessed 8 May 2014].

HEALTH AND SAFETY AT WORK ACT 1974. Available at: http://www.legislation.gov.uk/ukpga/1974/37/contents [Accessed 23 February 2014].

HEALTH AND SAFETY (CONSULTATION WITH EMPLOYEES) REGULATIONS 1996. Available at: www.legislation.gov.uk/uksi/1996/1513/contents/made [Accessed 13 December 2013].

HEERY, E. (1996) *Risk representation and the new pay.* Paper presented to the Buira/Eben Conference. Ethical Issues in Contemporary Human Resource Management. Imperial College, London, 3 April.

HEERY, E. and NOON, M. (2008) *A dictionary of human resource management.* Oxford: Oxford University Press.

HEMP, P. (2002) My week as a room service waiter at the Ritz. *Harvard Business Review.* Vol 80, No 6. pp50–60.

HERSKOVITS, M.J. (1948) *Man and his works.* New York: Knopf.

HERZBERG, F. (1966) *Work and the nature of man.* Cleveland, OH: World Publishing Company.

HERZBERG, F.W., MAUSNER, B. and SNYDERMAN, B. (1957) *The motivation to work.* New York: Wiley

HERZBERG, F., MAUSNER, B. and SNYDERMAN, B.B. (1959) *The motivation to work.* 2nd ed. New York: John Wiley & Sons.

LORD HESELTINE REVIEW (October 2012) *No stone left unturned in pursuit of growth [online].* Available at: https://www.gov.uk/government/publications/no-stone-unturned-in-pursuit-of-growth [Accessed 16 April 2014].

HIGH FLIERS RESEARCH LIMITED (2014) *The graduate market in 2014: annual review of graduate vacancies & starting salaries at Britain's leading employers [online].* Available at: http://www.highfliers.co.uk/ [Accessed 17 March 2014].

HILL, J. and TRIST, E. (1955) Changes in accidents and other absences with length of service. *Human Relations.*

HIRSCH, D. (2013) *A minimum income standard for the UK in 2013: Joseph Rowntree Foundation [online].* 28 June. York: Joseph Rowntree Foundation. Available at: http://www.jrf.org.uk/sites/files/jrf/income-living-standards-full.pdf [Accessed 20 May 2014].

HOFSTEDE, G. (1980) *Culture's consequences: international differences in work-related values.* London: McGraw-Hill.

HOFSTEDE, G. (1991) *Cultures and organisations: software of the mind.* Beverly Hills CA: Sage Publications.

HOFSTEDE, G., HOFSTEDE, G.J. and MINKOV, M. (2010) *Cultures and organizations: software of the mind.* 3rd ed. New York: McGraw-Hill.

HOLT, A. and ANDREWS, H. (1993) *Principles of health and safety at work.* London: IOSH Publishing.

HONEY, P and MUMFORD, A (1982) The Manual of Learning Styles. Maidenhead: P Honey.

HOPE HAILEY, V., FARNDALE, E. and TRUSS, C. (2005) The HR department's role in organisational performance [online]. *Human Resource Management Journal.* Vol 15, No 3. pp49–66. Available at: www.serialsolutions.com [Accessed 1 September 2013].

HOSKING, P. (2013) Reckless top bankers should be jailed, demands commission [online]. *The Times.* 19 June. p36. Available at: www.search.proquest.com [Accessed 25 October 2013].

HR COUNCIL OF CANADA (n.d.) *Strategic HR planning [online].* Available at: www.hrcouncil.ca/hr-toolkit/planning-strategic.cfm [Accessed 25 May 2014].

HSE (n.d.[a]) *DWP/HSE framework document [online].* Available at: http://www.hse.gov.uk/aboutus/howwework/management/dwphse.pdf [Accessed 22 November 2013].

HSE (n.d. [b]) *Risk assessment and management [online]*. Available at: www.hse.gov.uk/quarries/education/powerpoint/topic5.ppt [Accessed 23 November 2013].

HSE (n.d. [c]) *Principles and guidelines to assist HSE in its judgements that duty-holders have reduced risk as low as reasonably practicable [online]*. Available at: www.hse.gov.uk/risk/theory/alarp1.htm [Accessed 23 November 2013].

HSE (2006) *£466,000 in penalties following Lancashire farm death [online]*. Available at: www.hse.gov.uk/press/2006/gnn141432p.htm [Accessed 7 December 2013].

HSE (2007) *Managing the causes of work-related stress [online]*. Available at: www.hse.gov.uk/pubns/priced/hsg218.pdf [Accessed 16 December 2013].

HSE (2008) *Removing premises registration and record keeping requirements – what this change means [online]*. Merseyside: HSE. Available at: www.hse.gov.uk/consult/condocs/cd219-notification.htm [Accessed 22 November 2013].

HSE (2008a) *Involving your workforce in health and safety: good practice for all workplaces [online]*. Available at: www.hse.gov.uk/pubns/priced/hsg263.pdf [Accessed 13 December 2013].

HSE (2009) *How to tackle work-related stress: a guide for employers on making the management standards [online]*. Available at: www.hse.gov.uk/pubns/indg430.pdf [Accessed 16 December 2013].

HSE (2011) *Health and safety made simple: the basics for your business [online]*. Merseyside: HSE. Available at: www.hse.gov.uk/pubns/indg449.pdf [Accessed 22 November 2013].

HSE (2011a) *Five steps to risk assessment [online]*. Merseyside: HSE. Available at: www.hse.gov.uk/pubns/indg163.pdf [Accessed 22 November 2013].

HSE (2011b) *Successful health and safety management [online]*. Available at: www.hse.gov.uk/pubns/priced/hsg65.pdf [Accessed 25 November 2013].

HSE (2012) *Consulting workers on health and safety [online]*. Available at: www.hse.gov.uk/pubns/priced/l146.pdf [Accessed 13 December 2012].

HSE (2012/13) *Statistics [online]*. Available at: http://www.hse.gov.uk/statistics/index.htm [Accessed 17 February 2014].

HSE (2013) *Successful health and safety management (HSG65) is changing [online]*. Available at: www.hse.gov.uk/pubns/books/hsg65.htm [Accessed 26 November 2013].

HSE (2013b) *Leading health and safety at work [online]*. Available at: www.hse.gov.uk/pubns/indg417.pdf [Accessed 6 December 2013].

HSE (2013c) *Consulting employees on health and safety: a brief guide to the law [online]*. Available at: www.hse.gov.uk/pubns/indg232.pdf [Accessed 13 December 2013].

HSE (2013d) *Stress and psychological disorders in Great Britain 2013 [online]*. Available at: www.hse.gov.uk/statistics/causdis/stress/stress.pdf [Accessed 14 December 2013].

HSE (2013e) *Working days lost [online]*. Available at: www.hse.gov.uk/statistics/dayslost.htm [Accessed 16 December 2013].

HSE (2013f) *What are the management standards [online]*. Available at: www.hse.gov.uk/stress/standards/ [Accessed 16 December 2013].

HSE (2013g) Firm sentenced after worker loses leg in fish tank fall [online]. Available at: http://press.hse.gov.uk/2013/firm-sentenced-after-worker-loses-leg-in-fish-tank-fall/ [Accessed 17 December 2013].

HSE (2013h) *Bullying and harassment advice [online]*. Available at: http://www.hse.gov.uk/stress/furtheradvice/bullyingindividuals.htm [Accessed 30 September 2013].

HSIEH, Y.H. and CHEN, H.M. (2011) Strategic fit among business competitive strategy, human resource strategy and reward system [online]. *Academy of Strategic Management Journal*. Vol 10, No 2. pp11–32. Available at: www.ebscohost.com [Accessed 22 August 2013].

HUCZYNSKI, A.A. and BUCHANAN, D.A. (2013) *Organizational behaviour*. 8th ed. London: Pearson Education.

HUGHES, M. (2007) *Change management: a critical perspective*. London: Chartered Institute of Personnel and Development.

ICO (no date) *The guide to data protection: how much do I need to know about data protection? A little, a lot, nothing, don't know [online]*. Wilmslow: ICO. Available at: http://ico.org.uk/Global/~/media/documents/library/Data_Protection/Practical_application/THE_GUIDE_TO_DATA_PROTECTION.ashx [Accessed 25 February 2014].

IDS (2009) *Redundancy dismissal procedures after 6 April*. IDS Employment Law Brief 875 [online]. Available at: www.idsbrief.com [Accessed 8 January 2010].

ILES, P. and ROBERTSON, I. (1989) The impact of selection procedures on candidates. In: HERRIOT, P. (ed.) *Assessment and selection in organisations*. Chichester: Wiley.

INFORMATION COMMISSIONER'S OFFICE. Available at: www.ico.gov.uk [Accessed 26 March 2014].

INGLEHART, R. and WELZEL, C. (2010) Changing mass priorities: the link between modernization and democracy. *Perspectives on Politics*. Vol 8, No 2. p554.

INSTITUTE OF DIRECTORS (IOD) Available at: http://www.iod.com [Accessed 24 January 2014].

INTERNATIONAL TEST COMMISSION (ITC) (2000) International guidelines for test use *[online]*. Available at: www.intestcom.org/itc_projects.htm [Accessed 23 March 2014].

INVESTORS IN PEOPLE. Available at: http://www.investorsinpeople.co.uk/about-iip/applying-framework [Accessed 16 April 2014].

IRS (1996) Performance management. *Management Review*. Vol 1, No 1. London: Industrial Relations Service.

JAVAID, M. (2013) HR's 'blind faith' in process [online]. *People Management*. 21 March. Available at: www.cipd.co.uk/pm/peoplemanagement/ [Accessed 23 December 2013].

JAVAID, M. (2013) Third party harassment provisions repealed [online]. *People Management*. 1 October. Available at: http://www.cipd.co.uk/pm/peoplemanagement/b/weblog/archive/2013/10/01/third-party-harassment-provisions-repealed.aspx [Accessed 27 May 2014].

JOBCENTREPLUS (2012) *Could you run an enterprise club? [online]*. London: Department for Work and Pensions. Available at: www.gov.uk/government/uploads/system/uploads/attachment_data/file/236474/enterprise-club-guide.pdf [Accessed 22 April 2014].

JOHNSON, D. (2008) Digger giant tells staff to stay at home [online]. *Sentinel*. 29 August. Available at: http://search.proquest.com/ [Accessed 24 December 2013].

JOHNSON, J. and SCHOLES, K. (2002) *Exploring corporate strategy: test and cases*. Harlow: Pearson Educational.

JOHNSON, G., WHITTINGTON, R. and SCHOLES, K. (2011) *Exploring strategy*. 9th ed. Harlow: FT Prentice Hall.

JOHNSON, G. WHITTINGTON, R. and SCHOLES, K. (2012) *Fundamental of strategy*. 2nd ed. Harlow: FT Prentice Hall.

JONES, S. (2008) JCB workers take pay cut to avoid layoffs [online]. *Guardian*. 23 October. Available at: www.theguardian.com/business/2008/oct/23/jcb-pay-cut-jobs [Accessed 18 October 2013].

KALAYANEE, K. (2011) Fairness in the workplace: the relative effects of distributive and procedural justice on incentive satisfaction [online]. *The Business Review, Cambridge*. Vol 17, No 2. pp160–66. Available at: http://search.proquest.com/abiglobal/ [Accessed 20 May 2014].

KAMMEYER-MUELLER, J.D. and WANBERG, C.R. (2003). Unwrapping the organizational entry process: disentangling multiple antecedents and their pathways to adjustment. *Journal of Applied Psychology*. Vol 88. pp779–94.

KAPLAN, R.S. and NORTON, D.P. (1996) *Translating strategy into action: the balanced scorecard*. Boston, MA: Harvard Business School Press.

KEW, J. and STREDWICK, J. (2013) *Human resource management in a business context*. 2nd ed. London: CIPD.

KING, A. (2013) JCB staff given pay rise and £500 bonus [online]. *Sentinel*. Available at: www.thisisstaffordshire.co.uk/JCB-staff-given-pay-rise-pound-500-bonus/story-17627697-detail/story.html#ixzz2i9uYFBMS [Accessed 18 October 2013].

KINNIE, N., HUTCHINSON, S., PURCELL, J., RAYTON, B and SWART, J. (2005) Satisfaction with HR practices and commitment to the organisation: why one size does not fit all. *Human Resource Management Journal*. Vol 15, No 4. pp9–29.

KIRKPATRICK, D. L. (1975). 'Techniques for Evaluating Training Programs', in Evaluating training programs D. L. Kirkpatrick (ed.) Alexandria, VA: American Society for Training and Development.

KOEHLER, W. (1959) *The mentality of apes*. New York: Vintage.

KOLB, D.A. (1985) *Experiential learning: experience as the source of learning and development*. London: Prentice-Hall.

KOTTER, J.P. (1996) *Leading change*. Boston, MA: Harvard Business School Press.

KOTTER, J. (2007) Leading change [online]. *Harvard Business Review*. Vol 85, No 1. pp96–103. Available from: Business Source Complete. [Accessed 28 March 2014].

KOTTER, J.P. and SCHLESINGER, L.A. (2008). Choosing strategies for change [online]. *Harvard Business Review*. Vol 86, No 7/8. pp130–39. Available at: www.web.a.ebscohost.com [Accessed 26 March 2014].

KRULIS-RANDA, J. (1990) Strategic human resource management in Europe after 1992. *International Journal of Human Resource Management*. Vol 1, No 2. pp131–9.

LAGARDE, C. (2014) *A new multilateralism for the 21st century: the Richard Dimbleby Lecture [online]*. 3 February. Available at: www.imf.org/external/np/speeches/2014/020314.htm [Accessed 24 March 2014].

LANCASHIRE TELEGRAPH (2007) Appeal over workman death conviction fails [online]. *Lancashire Telegraph*. 13 December. Available at: www.lancashiretelegraph.co.uk/news/1903448.appeal_over_workman_death_conviction_fails/ [Accessed 7 December 2013].

LASHLEY, C. and BEST, W. (2002) Employee induction in licensed retail organisations. *International Journal of Contemporary Hospitality*. Vol 14, No 1. pp6–13.

LAU, S., NEAL, V. and MAINGAULT, V. (2009) Economic trends, buddy systems, receiving criticism. *HRM Magazine*. Vol 54, No 3. pp26–7.

LAWLER, E.E. (1990) *Strategic pay*. San Francisco, CA: Jossey-Bass.

LEATHERBARROW, C. (2014) HRM: the added value debate. In: REES, G. and SMITH, P. (eds) *Strategic human resource management: an international perspective*. London: Sage.

LEGGE, K. (1995) *Human resource management: rhetoric or realities*. London: Macmillan.

LEWIN, K. (1951) *Field theory in social science*. New York: Harper and Row.

LEWIS, D. and SARGEANT, M. (2013) *Employment law: the essentials*. 12th ed. London: CIPD.

LINTON, R. (1945) Present world conditions in cultural perspective. In: LINTON, R. (ed.) *The science of man in world crisis*. New York: Columbia University Press.

LOIZOU, K. (2013) A spoonful of flavouring helped my sales shoot up. *Sunday Times*. 25 June.

LUSTIG-PREAN AND BECKETT V. THE UNITED KINGDOM 31417/96; 32377/96 [1999] ECHR 71 (27 September 1999). Available at: http://www.bailii.org/eu/cases/ECHR/1999/71.html [Accessed 23 September 2013].

MACLEOD, D. and CLARKE, N. (2009) *Engaging for success: enhancing performance through employee engagement. A report to government*. London: Department for Business, Innovation and Skills.

MANAGEMENT OF HEALTH AND SAFETY AT WORK REGULATIONS 1999. Available at: www.legislation.gov.uk/uksi/1999/3242/contents/made [Accessed 23 February 2014].

MANDER, P. and HENRY, A. (2012) Procedurally flawed redundancy is fair [online]. *People Management*. 29 November. Available at: www.cipd.co.uk/pm/peoplemanagement/b/weblog/archive/2012/11/29/procedurally-flawed-redundancy-is-fair-2012–11.aspx [Accessed 22 December 2013].

MANKIN, D. (2009) *Human resource development.* Oxford: Oxford University Press.

MARCHINGTON, M. and GRUGULIS, I. (2000) *International Journal of Human Resource Management.* Vol 11, No 6. pp1104–24.

MARCHINGTON, M. and WILKINSON, A. (2008) *Human resource management at work.* 4th ed. London: CIPD.

MARCHINGTON, M. and WILKINSON, A. (2012) *Human resource management at work.* 5th ed. London: CIPD.

MARGOLIS, J. and STOLZ, P. (2010) How to bounce back from adversity [online]. *Harvard Business Review.* Vol 88, No 1/2. pp86–92. Available from: www.web.a.ebscohost. com [Accessed 26 March 2014].

MARSDEN, D. and FRENCH, S. (1998) *What a performance: performance-related pay in the public services.* London: Centre for Economic Performance.

MASLOW, A.H. (1954, 1972) *Motivation and personality.* New York: Harper and Row.

MATTHEWMAN, L., ROSE, A. and HETHERINGTON, A. (2009) *Work psychology.* New York: Oxford.

MAUND, L. (2001) *An introduction to human resource management: theory and practice.* Basingstoke: Palgrave.

MAYO, E. (1933) *The human side of an industrial civilization.* New York: Macmillan.

MCANDREW, F. (2010) *Workplace equality: turning policy into practice. A report for the Equality and Diversity Forum [online].* Available at: http://www.edf.org.uk/blog/ wp-content/uploads/2010/12/EDF_Report_Narrowing-the-GapFeb11.pdf [Accessed 27 September 2013].

MCCARTHY, A., DARCY, C. and GRADY, G. (2010) Work-life balance policy and practice: understanding line manager attitudes and behaviors. *Human Resource Management Review.* Vol 20, No 2. June. pp158–67.

MCCLELLAND, D. (1961) *The achieving society.* Princeton: Van Nostrand.

MCCORMICK (2014) Warning of worsening in UK skills shortage [online]. BBC News online. Available at: http://www.bbc.co.uk/news/education-25945413 [Accessed 13 March 2014].

MCGREGOR, D. (1960) *The human side of enterprise.* New York: McGraw-Hill.

MCKENNA, E. (1994) *Business psychology and organisational behaviour.* Hove: Lawrence Erlbaum.

MCLEAN, A. (1979) *Work stress.* Reading, MA: Addison-Wesley.

MEADOWS, P. (2007) *A review of the economic impact of employment relations services delivered by Acas.* London: NIESR.

MEIKLE, J. (2014) Mid Staffs NHS trust to be dissolved, Jeremy Hunt announces [online]. *Guardian.* 26 February. Available at: www.theguardian.com/society/2014/feb/26/mid-staffs-nhs-trust-dissolved-jeremy-hunt [Accessed 26 March 2014].

MIGRATION ADVISORY COMMITTEE REVIEW (February 2013) Available at: www. rsc.org/images/mac-report_tcm18–227964.pdf [Accessed 14 May 2014].

MINISTRY OF JUSTICE (2012) *Employment tribunals and EAT statistics, 2011–12, 1 April 2011 to 31 March 2012 [online]*. London: Ministry of Justice. Available at: www.gov. uk/government/uploads/system/uploads/attachment_data/file/218497/employment-trib-stats-april-march-2011–12.pdf [Accessed 21 December 2013].

MINISTRY OF JUSTICE (2012/13) *Tribunal statistics [online]*. Available at: https://www. gov.uk/government/publications/tribunal-statistics-quarterly-and-annual-jan-mar-2013–2012–13 [Accessed 19 May 2014].

MOLANDER, C. and WINTERTON, J. (1994) *Managing human resources*. London: Routledge.

MOORHEAD, G. and GRIFFIN, R.W. (1992) *Organizational behavior*. 3rd ed. Boston, MA: Houghton Mifflin.

MORRIS, S. and CARRELL, S. (2013) Privatisation of UK's search-and-rescue helicopters raises safety and job fears [online]. *theguardian.com*. 31 January. Available at: www. theguardian.com/politics/2013/jan/31/search-rescue-helicopters-privatisation-fears [Accessed 2 June 2014].

MULLINS, L.J. with CHRISTY, G. (2013) *Management and organisational behaviour*. 10th ed. Harlow: Pearson Education.

MUNRO-FRASER, J. (1966) *Employment interviewing*. Plymouth: Macdonald and Evans.

NATIONAL APPRENTICESHIP SERVICE (2014) *Apprenticeship Grant for Employers 16–12 year olds (AGE 16–24): Employers Factsheet: March 2014 (version 16) [online]*. Available at: www.apprenticeships.org.uk/~/media/Documents/AGE16TO24/AGE-Employer-Fact-Sheetv16.ashx [Accessed 25 May 2014].

NEVILLE, S. (2012) G4S had a disastrous Olympics – but the company will barely notice [online]. *Observer*. 22 July. p43. Available at: www.guardian.co.uk or www.search.proquest. com [Accessed 20 July 2013].

NEVILLE, S. (2013) Losses hit £88m for G4S in Olympic security fiasco [online]. *Guardian*. 13 February. p23. Available at: www.search.proquest.com [cited 20 July 2013].

NEVILLE, S. (2014) Ocado on track for first profit in wake of Morrisons deal [online]. *Independent*. 14 March. Available at: www.independent.co.uk/news/business

NEW YORK TIMES (1915) F.W. Taylor, Expert in Efficiency, Dies: On This Day Obituary 22nd March 1915 [online]. *New York Times.com*. The New York Times Learning Network. Available at: www.nytimes.com/learning/general/onthisday/bday/0320.html [Accessed 1 June 2014].

NEXT GENERATION HR. *Time for change – Towards a Next Generation for HR [online]*. London: CIPD. Available at http://www.cipd.co.uk/binaries/5126nextgenthoughtpiece.pdf [Accessed 12 September 2013].

NOE, R.A. (2010) *Employee training and development*. New York: McGraw-Hill.

NSPCC (2014) Available at: http://www.nspcc.org.uk/Inform/research/briefings/Value-based-interviewing_wda95721.html [Accessed 12 May 2014].

OFFICE FOR DISABILITY ISSUES (2011) *Equality Act 2010 Guidance [online].* Available at: https://www.gov.uk/government/uploads/system/uploads/attachment_data/file/85010/disability-definition.pdf [Accessed 29 September 2013].

OFFICE FOR NATIONAL STATISTICS (2012) *Labour Force Survey [online].* Available at: http://www.statistics.gov.uk/hub/index.html [Accessed 31 January 2014].

OFFICE FOR NATIONAL STATISTICS (July 2013) *Labour Disputes Annual Article 2012 [online].* Available at: http://www.ons.gov.uk/ons/rel/bus-register/labour-disputes/annual-article-2012/art—labour-disputes–annual-article-2012.html [Accessed 27 January 2014].

OFFICE FOR NATIONAL STATISTICS (Nov 2013) *Labour market statistics [online].* Available at: http://www.ons.gov.uk/ons/rel/lms/labour-market-statistics/november-2013/index.html [Accessed 19 May 2014].

OFFICE FOR NATIONAL STATISTICS (Dec 2013) *Annual survey of hours and earnings, 2013 provisional results [online].* Available at: http://www.ons.gov.uk/ons/rel/ashe/annual-survey-of-hours-and-earnings/2013-provisional-results/stb-ashe-statistical-bulletin-2013.html [Accessed 28 April 2014].

ONS (2012) *Sickness absence in the labour market: April 2012 [online].* Newport (Wales): ONS. Available at: www.ons.gov.uk/ons/rel/lmac/sickness-absence-in-the-labour-market/2012/index.html [Accessed 12 December 2013].

ONS (2014) *Sickness absence in the labour market: February 2014 [online].* Newport (Wales): ONS. Available at: www.ons.gov.uk/ons/rel/lmac/sickness-absence-in-the-labour-market/2014/rpt—sickness-absence-in-the-labour-market.html [Accessed 8 May 2014].

ORGAN, D.W. (1997) Organizational citizenship behavior: it's construct clean-up time [online]. *Human Performance.* Vol 10, No 2. pp85–97. Available at: www.ebscohost.com [Accessed 14 May 2014].

PAPALEXANDRIS, N. and PANAYOTOPOULO, L. (2004) Exploring the mutual interaction of societal culture and human resource management practices: evidence from 19 countries [online]. *Employee Relations.* Vol 26, No 5.pp495–507. Available at: www.emeraldinsight.com [Accessed 6 March 2014].

PARSONS, T. (ed.) (1964) *Max Weber: the theory of social and economic organisation.* New York: Free Press.

PART-TIME WORKERS (PREVENTION OF LESS FAVOURABLE TREATMENT) REGULATIONS 2000 (SI 1551). Available at: www.legislation.gov.uk/uksi/2000/1551/contents/made [Accessed 17 February 2014].

PATON, R.A. and MCCALMAN, J. (2008) *Change management: a guide to effective implementation.* 3rd ed. London: Sage.

PATEL, P.C. and S. CARDON, M.S. (2010) Adopting HRM practices and their effectiveness in small firms facing product-market competition. *Human Resource Management.* Vol 49, No 2. pp265–90.

PAVLOV, I.P. (1927) *Conditioned reflexes.* Oxford: Oxford University Press.

PEDLER, M., BURGOGYNE, J. and BOYDELL, T. (1997) *The learning company: a strategy for sustainable development.* 2nd ed. London; McGraw-Hill.

PERKINS, S., WHITE, G. and COTTON, C. (2008) A ripping yarn. *People Management.* 30 October. pp28–30.

PERRY, J.L., ENGBERS, T.A. and JUN, S.Y. (2009) Back to the future? Performance-related pay, empirical research, and the perils of persistence [online]. *Public Administration Review.* Vol 69, No 1. pp39–51. Available at: www.search.proquest.com/ [Accessed 1 November 2013].

PESTON, R. (2013) Royal Mail stock market flotation likely in Autumn [Comment] [online]. *BBC News.* 10 July. Available at: www.bbc.co.uk/news/business -23249762 [Accessed 11 July 2013].

PETERS, T. and WATERMAN Jr., R.H. (1995) *In search of excellence: lessons from America's best-run companies.* London: Profile Books.

PFEFFER, J. (1995) People, capability and competitive success [online]. *Management Development Review.* Vol 8, No 5. pp6–10. Available at: www.emeraldinsight.com [Accessed 27 August 2013].

PFEFFER, J. (1998) *The human equation: building profits by putting people first.* Boston, MA: Harvard Business Review.

PFEFFER, J. (2006) When it comes to 'best practices'—why do smart organizations occasionally do dumb things? [online]. *Organizational Dynamics.* Vol 25, No 1. pp33–44. Available at: www.ebscohost.com [Accessed 27 August 2013].

PFEFFER, J. and SUTTON, R.I. (2006) Evidenced-based management. *Harvard Business Review.* Vol 84, No 1. pp62–74.

PHILPOTT, J. (2004) By the book [online]. *People Management.* Vol 10, No 21. p26. Available at: www.peoplemanagement.co.uk/pm/articles/2004/10/ByTheBook.htm [Accessed 18 May 2014].

PIERCY, N. (1989) Diagnosing and solving implementation problems in strategic planning. *Journal of General Management.* Vol 15, No 1. pp19–38.

PILBEAM, S. and CORBRIDGE, M. (2010) *People resourcing and talent planning: HRM in practice.* 4th ed. Harlow: Pearson Education Ltd.

PLIMMER, G., FIFIELD, A. and BLITZ, J. (2013) MoD outsourcing plan stokes US anxiety: Equipment [online]. *Financial Times.* 7 May. Available at: www.search.proquest.com [Accessed 14 August 2013].

POINTON, J. and RYAN, A.J. (2004) Reward and performance management. In: BEARDWELL, I., HOLDEN, L. and CLAYDON, T. (eds) *Human resource management: a contemporary approach.* 4th ed. Harlow: Pearson Education.

PONTING, S. (2013) Corporate manslaughter overview Sections 10–13 [online]. *Westlaw UK, Insight.* Available at: www.westlaw.co.uk [Accessed 23 February 2014].

POP, A.M. (2011) Business buzzwords: rightsizing, downsizing, re-engineering, de-layering [online]. *IDEAS.* Available at: http://ideas.repec.org/a/ora/journl/v1y2011i1p146–152.html#statistics [Accessed 16 June 2014].

PORTER, L.W. and LAWLER, E.E. (1968) *Managerial attitudes and performance.* Homewood, IL: Irwin-Dorsey.

POSTAL SERVICE ACT 2011. Available at: www.legislation.gov.uk/ukpga/2011/5/contents [Accessed 12th July 2013].

POULTER, D. and LAND, C. (2008) Preparing to work: dramaturgy, cynicism and normative 'remote' control in the socialization of graduate recruits in management consulting. *Culture and Organisation.* Vol 14, No 1. pp65–78.

POWELL, I. (2013) The UK must focus on three priority areas in the decade ahead [online]. *Telegraph.* 1 April. Available at: www.search.proquest.com [Accessed 19 September 2013].

PRICE, A.J. (1997) *Human resource management in business context.* London: International Thomson Business Press.

PRYOR, M.G. and TANEJA, S. (2010) Henri Fayol, practitioner and theoretician – revered and reviled. *Journal of Management History.* Vol 16, No 4. pp489–503.

PUGH, D.S., HICKSON, D.J., HININGS, C.R. and TURNER, C. (1968) Dimensions of organization structure [online]. *Administrative Science Quarterly.* Vol 13, No 1. pp65–105. Available at: www.serialssolutions.com [Accessed 13 August 2013].

PURCELL, J. and HALL, M. (2012) *Voice and participation in the modern workplace: challenges and prospects [online].* London: Acas. Available at: www.acas.org.uk/media/pdf/g/7/Voice_and_Participation_in_the_Modern_Workplace_challenges_and_prospects.pdf [Accessed 8 September 2013].

PURCELL, J., KINNIE, N., HUTCHINSON, S., RAYTON, B. and SWART, J. (2003) *Understanding the people and performance link: unlocking the black box.* London: Chartered Institute of Personnel and Development.

PWC (2009) *Insolvency in brief: a guide to insolvency terminology and procedure [online].* London: PwC Business Recovery Services. Available at: http://www.pwc.co.uk/business-recovery/publications/insolvency-in-brief.jhtml [Accessed 16 July 2013].

QUINN, J. (2012) TNT posties take on Royal Mail in London trial [online]. *Telegraph.* 16 April. Available at: www.telegraph.co.uk [Accessed 12 July 2013].

QUINTAS, P. (2001) Managing knowledge in a new century. In: LITTLE, S., QUINTAS, P. and RAY, T. (eds) *Managing knowledge: an essential reader.* London: Sage Publications Ltd.

RACE RELATIONS ACT 1975. Available at: www.legislation.gov.uk/ukpga/1976/74/contents [Accessed 19 February 2014].

RANA, E. (2000) Predictions: enter the people dimension. *People Management.* Vol 6, No 1, 6 January. pp16–17.

RAUSCHENBERGER, J., SCHMITT, N. and HUNTER, J.E. (1980) A test of the need hierarchy concept by a Markov model of change in need strength. *Administrative Science Quarterly.* No 25. pp654–70.

RAY, C.A. (1986) Corporate culture: the last frontier of control [online]. *Journal of Management Studies.* Vol 23, No 3. pp287–97. Available at: http://web.a.ebscohost.com/ [Accessed 11 March 2014].

READ, S. (2012) Are banks getting to grips with our complaints? It doesn't seem so [online]. *Independent*. 29 September. p56. Available at: www.searchproquest.com [Accessed 3 September 2013].

REDFORD, K. (2005) Shedding light on talent tactics. *Personnel Today*. 26 September. p22.

REDMAN, T. and WILKINSON, A. (2009) *Contemporary human resource management: text and cases*. 3rd ed. Harlow: Pearson.

REES, G. and FRENCH, R. (2013) *Leading, managing and developing people*. London: Chartered Institute of Personnel and Development.

REVANS, R. (1982) *The origins and growth of action learning*. Bromley: Chartwell-Bratt.

RICCI, T. (2012) *Biography, Frank Bunker Gilbreth [online]*. New York: ASME. Available at: www.asme.org/engineering-topics/articles/construction-and-building/frank-bunker-gilbreth [Accessed 11 May 2014].

RICHARD, D. (2012) *The Richard Review of apprenticeships website [online]*. London: Department for Business, Innovation and Skills and Department for Education. Available at: www.gov.uk/government/uploads/system/uploads/attachment_data/file/34708/richard-review-full.pdf [Accessed 19 September 2013].

ROBBINS, S.P., JUDGE, T.A. and CAMPBELL, T.T. (2010) *Organizational behavior*. Harlow: Pearson Education.

ROBERTS, I. (2001) Reward and performance management. In: BEARDWELL, I., HOLDEN, L. and CLAYDON, T. (eds) *Human resource management: a contemporary approach*. 4th ed. Harlow: Pearson Education.

ROBERTSON, I.T. and SMITH, M. (2001) Personnel selection. *Journal of Organizational Psychology*. Vol 74. pp441–72.

ROBINSON, M. and HODGEKISS, A. (2013) 1,200 deaths, a damning report on 'failings at every level' and 290 recommendations for reform. Now families of the Stafford Hospital victims and union chiefs call for the head of the NHS to resign [online]. *Daily Mail*. 6 February, updated 31 July. Available at: www.dailymail.co.uk/news/article-2274296/Mid-Staffs-report-Families-head-NHS-resign-damning-scandal.html#ixzz2emwng5r3 [Accessed 13 September 2013].

RODGER, A. (1952) *The seven point plan*. London: National Institute of Industrial Psychology.

ROSE, E. (2008) *Employment relations*. 3rd ed. Harlow: Pearson Education Ltd.

ROSE, J. (2012) Private sector hovers over search and rescue roles [online]. *Financial Times*. 2 August. Available at: www.search.proquest.com [Accessed 14 August 2013].

ROUSSEAU, D.M. (1989). Psychological and implied contracts in organizations. *Employee Responsibilities and Rights Journal*. Vol 2, No 2. pp121–39.

RUMPEL, S. and MEDCOF, J.W. (2006) Total rewards: good fit for tech workers. *Research Technology Management*. Vol 49, No 5. pp27–35.

RUSHTON, K. and WARMAN, M. (2013) Departure means tough choices for Microsoft: new boss must refocus tech giant [online]. *Telegraph*. 24 August. p38. Available at: www. search.proquest.com [Accessed 24 September 2013].

RUSS-EFT, D. and PRESKILL, H. (2005) In search of the Holy Grail: return on investment evaluation in human resource development. *Advances in Developing Human Resources*. Vol 7, No 1. pp71–85.

SAFETY REPRESENTATIVES AND SAFETY COMMITTEES REGULATIONS 1977. Available at: www.legislation.gov.uk/uksi/1977/500/regulation/1/made [Accessed 13 December 2013].

SAISANA, M. (2012) *JRC scientific and policy report monitoring SMEs' performance in Europe: indicators fit for purpose, methodological note [online]*. Luxembourg: The Publications Office of the European Commission. Available at: http://ec.europa.eu/ enterprise/policies/sme/facts-figures-analysis/performance-review/files/ saisana_jrc_sbamethodology_eur25577.pdf [Accessed 18 July 2013].

SAUNDERS, R. (1992) *The safety audit*. London: Pitman.

SCHEIN, E. (1965) *Organisational psychology*. Englewood Cliffs, NJ: Prentice-Hall.

SCHEIN, E.H. (1980) *Organisational psychology*. 3rd ed. Englewood Cliffs, NJ: Prentice Hall.

SCHEIN, E. (1985) *Organisational culture and leadership*. New York: Jossey Bass.

SCHNEIDER, B. (2004) Welcome to the world of service management. *Academy of Management Executive* [online]. 18(2), pp.144–150 [Accessed 1 September 2013]. Available at: www.serialsolutions.com

SCHUSTER, J.R. and ZINGHEIM, P.K. (1992) *The new pay*. New York: Lexington Books.

SCHWARTZ, S.H. (2007) A theory of cultural values and some implications for work [online]. *Applied Psychology: An International Review*. Vol 48, No 1. pp23–47. Available at: www.onlinelibrary.wiley.com [Accessed 6 March 2014].

SCOTT, A. (2012) Dear Prudence [online]. *People Management*. pp36–9. Available at: www.ebscohost.com [Accessed 8 September 2013].

SCOTT, D., MCMULLEN, T. and ROYAL, M. (2012) *Retention of key talent and the role of rewards: A report by WorldatWork [online]* Available at: http://www.worldatwork.org/ waw/adimLink?id=62016 [Accessed 17 September 2013].

SEARS, L. (2011) A new way of seeing: insight-led HR. *People Management*. April. pp34–7.

SENGE, P. (1990) *The fifth discipline: the art and practice of the learning organisation*. London: Century Business.

SENIOR, B. (2002) *Organisational change*. Harlow: Prentice Hall.

SENIOR, B. and SWAILES, S. (2010) *Organisational change*. 4th ed. Harlow: Prentice Hall.

SENNETT, R. (1997) *The corrosion of character*. New York: Norton.

SEX DISCRIMINATION ACT 1975. Available at: www.legislation.gov.uk/ukpga/1975/65/contents [Accessed 19 February 2014].

SHAH, O. (2014) Price war: Green vows to undercut Tesco by 10% with BHS food. *Sunday Times: Business Section*. 23 March. p1.

SIMPSON, R. (1998) Presenteeism, power and organizational change: long hours as a career barrier and the impact on the working lives of women managers. *British Journal of Management*. Vol 9, Issue Supplement s1. September. pp37–50.

SISSON, K. (1995) Human resource management and the personnel function. In: STOREY, J. (ed.) *Human resource management: a critical text*. London: Routledge.

SKILLS FUNDING STATEMENT 2012–2015. Available at: https://www.gov.uk/government/publications/skills-funding-statement-2012–2015 [Accessed 7 December 2013].

SKINNER, B.F. (1953) *Science and human behaviour*. New York: Macmillan.

SLATER, C. (2013) Firm fined £30k after worker loses a leg in fish tank horror: man crushed as it topples off truck [online]. *Manchester Evening News*. 10 December. p7. Available at: www.manchestereveningnews.co.uk/news/greater-manchester-news/manchester-directors-giant-fish-tank-6388176 [Accessed 17 December 2013].

SMEDLEY, T. (2013) What you can learn from RSA: the happy couple. *People Management*. 25 February.

SMITH, A. (1776) *The wealth of nations, Books I-III*. London: Penguin Classics.

SMITH, M., COLLIGAN, M., SKJEI, E. and POLLY, S. (1978) *Occupational comparison of stress-related disease incidence*. Cincinnati, OH: National Institute for Occupational Safety and Health.

SMYTH, C. (2014) NHS chiefs abandon plan for sharing patient data: protests over confidentiality put Major scheme on hold: Patient data plan on hold as NHS agrees to consult [online]. *The Times*. 19 February. p1. Available at: www.search.proquest.com [Accessed 23 February 2014].

STACEY, R. (1996) *Strategic management and organisational dynamics*. 2nd ed. London: Pitman.

STAVROU, E.T., BREWSTER, C. and CHARALAMBOUS, C. (2010) Human resources management and firm performance in Europe through the lens of business systems: best fit, best practice or both? [online]. *International Journal of Human Resource Management*. Vol 21, No 7. pp933–62. Available at: www.ebscohost.com [Accessed 22 August 2013].

STEINER, R. (2014) Morrisons' declaration of £1bn price war with budget stores hammers Sainsbury and Tesco shares [online]. *Daily Mail*. 13 March. Available at: http://www.dailymail.co.uk/money

STEVENS, M. (2012) Well-being programme at Carlsberg 'focuses on the healthy' [online]. *People Management*. 23 February. Available at: www.cipd.co.uk/pm/ [Accessed 23 April 2014].

STEWART, J. and RIGG, C. (2011) *Learning and talent development*. London: Chartered Institute of Personnel and Development.

STOREY, J. (1992) *Development in the management of human resources: an analytical review.* Oxford: Blackwell.

STOREY, J. (1993) The take-up of human resource management by mainstream companies: key lessons from research [online]. *International Journal of Human Resource Management.* Vol 4, No 3. pp529–53. Available at: www.search.serialsolutions.com [Accessed 19 August 2013].

STRACK, R., CAYE, J.M., LEICHT, M., VILLIS, U., BOHM, H. and MCDONNELL, M. (2013) *Boston report: the future of HR in Europe: key challenges through 2015.* European Association for Personnel Management.

STREBEL, P. (1996) Why do employees resist change? [online]. *Harvard Business Review.* Vol 74, No 3. pp86–92. Available at: www.web.a.ebscohost.com [Accessed 26 March 2014].

SY, T. and KEARNEY, A.T. (2005) Challenges and strategies of matrix organisations: top-level and middle-level managers' perspective [online]. *Human Resource Planning.* Vol 28, No 1. pp39–48. Available at: www.search.proquest.com [Accessed 14 August 2013].

TANSLEY, C., TURNER, P.A., FOSTER, C., HARRIS, L.M., STEWART, J., SEMPIK, A. and WILLIAMS, H. (2007) *Talent: strategy, management and measurement.* London: Chartered Institute of Personnel and Development.

TAYLOR, F.W. (1911) *The principles of scientific management.* New York: Harper Bros.

TAYLOR, F.W. (1947) *Scientific management.* New York: Harper and Row.

TAYLOR, S. (2014) *Resourcing and talent management.* 6th ed. London: Chartered Institute of Personnel and Development.

TELEGRAPH (2011) What is corporate manslaughter? Q&A [online]. *Telegraph.* 17 February. Available at: www.telegraph.co.uk/finance/yourbusiness/8331177/What-is-corporate-manslaughter-QandA.html [Accessed 23 February 2014].

THE TIMES (2009) Bankers' pay: the need for reform: ceilings on remuneration would deter talent, but the bonus system must properly reflect and penalise the damage done by irresponsible risk-taking [online]. *The Times.* 9 February. p2. Available at: www.search.proquest.com [Accessed 25 October 2013].

THORNDIKE, E.L. (1913) *The psychology of learning.* New York: Teachers College Press.

TIMES HIGHER EDUCATION (9 May 2013) *Mooc completion rates 'below 7%'* [online]. Available at: http://www.timeshighereducation.co.uk/news/mooc-completion-rates-below-7/2003710.article [Accessed 15 April 2014].

TITCOMB, J (2013) Sorted: answers to key questions raised by the Royal Mail privatisation. *Daily Telegraph.* 11 July.

TORRINGTON, D. and HALL, L. (1998) *Human resource management.* 4th ed. Hemel Hempstead: Prentice Hall.

TORRINGTON, D., HALL, L. and TAYLOR, S. (2007) *Human resource management* [online]. 7th ed. Harlow: Pearson Education. Available at: www.dawsonera.com [Accessed 28 September 2013].

TORRINGTON, D., HALL, L. and TAYLOR, S. (2008) *Human resource management [online]*. 8th ed. Harlow: Pearson Education. Available at: www.dawsonera.com [Accessed 20 April 2014].

TORRINGTON, D., HALL, L., TAYLOR, S. and ATKINSON, C. (2011) *Human resource management*. 8th ed. Harlow: Pearson Education.

TORRINGTON, D., HALL, L., TAYLOR, S., ATKINSON, C. (2014) *Human resource management*. 9th ed. Harlow: Pearson.

TOWERS WATSON GLOBAL WORKFORCE STUDY (2012) *Engagement at risk: driving strong performance in a volatile global environment [online]*. Available at: http://towerswatson.com/assets/pdf/2012-Towers-Watson-Global-Workforce-Study.pdf. [Accessed 17 September 2013].

TRADE UNION AND LABOUR RELATIONS (CONSOLIDATION) ACT 1992. Available at: http://www.legislation.gov.uk/ukpga/1992/52/contents [Accessed 28 April 2014].

TRADES UNION CONGRESS (TUC). Available at: http://www.tuc.org.uk/ [Accessed 27 January 2014].

TREANOR, J. (2014) Bankers and regulators face grilling from Hodge committee over handling of Royal Mail sell-off [online]. *Guardian*. 24 April. p24. Available at: http://search.proquest.com/uknews/docview/1518690667/fulltext/255903C967ED4776PQ/12?accountid=14685 [Accessed 30 May 2014].

TRIANDIS, H.C. (1972) *The analysis of subjective culture*. New York: Wiley.

TRIANDIS, H.C. (1990) Theoretical concepts that are applicable to the analysis of ethnocentrism. In: BRISLIN, R.W. (ed.) *Applied cross-cultural psychology*. Chicago: Sage.

TRIANDIS, H.C. (2002) Subjective culture [online]. *Online Readings in Psychology and Culture, 2:2: International Association for Cross-Cultural Psychology*. Available at: http://dx.doi.org/10.9707/2307–0919.1021[Accessed 6 March 2014].

TRICE, H.M. and BEYER, J.M. (1984) Studying organisational cultures through rites and rituals. *Academy of Management Review*. No 9. pp653–69.

TRIST, E.L. and BAMFORTH, K.W. (1951) Social and psychological consequences of the long wall coal-getting. *Relations*. Vol 4. pp1–38.

TRIST, E.L., HIGGIN, G., POLLOCK, H.E. and MURRAY, H.A. (1963) *Organisational choice*. London: Tavistock.

TRUSS, C., SHANTZ, A. and SOANE, E. (2013) Employee engagement organisational performance and individual well-being: exploring the evidence developing the theory [online]. *International Journal of Human Resource Management*. Vol 24, No 13–14. pp2657–69. Available at: www.search.serialsolutions.com [Accessed 6 September 2013].

TUC (2012) Excerpt from 'Hazards at work: organising for safe and healthy workplaces' [online]. Available at: http://www.tuc.org.uk/workplace-issues/working_time.cfm [Accessed 27 March 2014].

TUC (2013) Home-working on the increase despite the recession [online]. Available at: www.tuc.org.uk/workplace-issues/work-life-balance/04-homeworkers/home-working-increase-despite-recession-says-tuc [Accessed 27 March 2014].

TUC (2014) *Directory [online]*. Available at: http://www.tuc.org.uk/about-tuc/tuc-directory-2014 [Accessed 31 January 2014].

TYSON, S. and YORK, A. (1996) *Human resource management*. Oxford: Butterworth-Heinemann.

UKCES EMPLOYER PERSPECTIVES SURVEY (2012) Available at: http://www.ukces.org.uk/publications/er64-uk-employer-perspectives-survey-2012 [Accessed 24 April 2014].

UK COMMISSION FOR EMPLOYMENT AND SKILLS (2013) *Employer skills survey [online]*. Available at: http://www.ukces.org.uk/ourwork/employer-skills-survey [Accessed 14 May 2014].

UK NATIONAL STATISTICS (n.d.) *Aging in the UK datasets [online]*. Available at: http://www.statistics.gov.uk/hub/population/ageing/older-people [Accessed 1 May 2014].

UK VISAS AND IMMIGRATION. Available at: https://www.gov.uk/government/organisations/uk-visas-and-immigration [Accessed 25 March 2014].

ULRICH, D. (2009) The HR business-partner model: past learnings and future challenges [online]. *People and Strategy*. Vol 32, No 2. pp5–7. Accessed via EBSCO Business Source Complete at www.ebscohost.com [Accessed 28 August 2013].

ULRICH, D. (2012) Ulrich's new dawn for HR [online]. *Training Journal (Change Board Supplement)*. pp41–3. Accessed via EBSCO Business Source Complete at www.ebscohost.com [Accessed 29 August 2013].

ULRICH, D. and BROCKBANK, W. (2005) Role call [online]. *People Management*. Vol 11, No 12. pp24–8. Available at: www.cipd.co.uk/pm/peoplemanagement/b/weblog/archive/2013/01/29/rolecall-2005–06.aspx [Accessed 10 June 2014].

ULRICH, D. and BROCKBANK, W. (2008) *The business partner model: 10 years on – lessons learned [online]*. Available at: http://www.hrmagazine.co.uk/hr/features/1014777/the-business-partner-model-lessons-learned. [Accessed 12 September 2013].

ULRICH, D., YOUNGER, J., BROCKBANK, W. and ULRICH, M. (2012) *HR from the outside in*. New York: McGraw-Hill

ULRICH, D., YOUNGER, J., BROCKBANK, W. and ULRICH, M. (2012) *The six competencies to inspire HR professionals for 2012 [online]*. Available at: http://www.hrmagazine.co.uk/hr/features/1020649/exclusive-the-competencies-inspire-hr-professionals-2012#sthash.1yMcaYYA.dpuf [Accessed 27 May 2014].

UNIONLEARN. Available at: http://www.unionlearn.org.uk/ [Accessed 18 May 2014].

VAN DICK, R., CHRIST, O., STELLMACHER, J., WAGNER, U., AHLSWEDE, O., GRUBBA, C., HAUPTMEIER, M., HOHFELD, C., MALTZEN, K. and TISSINGTON, P. A. (2004) Should I stay or should I go? Explaining turnover intentions with organizational identification and job satisfaction. *British Journal of Management*. Vol 15. pp351–60.

VAN WANROOY, B., BEWLEY, H., BRYSON, A., FORTH, J., FREETH, S., STOKES, L. and WOOD, S. (2011) *The 2011 workplace employment relations study: first findings [online]*. Crown Copyright. Available at: www.gov.uk/government/uploads/system/uploads/attachment_data/file/210103/13–1010-WERS-first-findings-report-third-edition-may-2013.pdf [Accessed 13 September 2013].

VROOM, V.H. (1964) *Work and motivation*. New York: Wiley

WALL STREET JOURNAL (13 January 2014) Available at: http://blogs.wsj.com/moneybeat/2014/01/03/twitter-near-70-valued-at-38-billion-or-49-billion/ [Accessed 5 January 2014].

WARNER, J. (2013) A living wage, or a much higher minimum wage, is worth paying [online]. *Telegraph.* 17 January. Available at: www.telegraph.co.uk/comment/9808681/A-living-wage-or-a-much-higher-minimum-wage-is-worth-paying.html [Accessed 20 May 2014].

WARREN, C. (2013a) Don't tell people what to do [online]. *People Management.* 18 April. Available at: www.cipd.co.uk/pm/peoplemanagement/ [Accessed 1 November 2013].

WARREN, C. (2013b) How to work for Darren Cross: 'We like people who are a little bit theatrical' [online]. *People Management.* 24 July. Available at: www.cipd.co.uk/pm/peoplemanagement/ [Accessed 18 October 2013].

WATSON, J.B. and RAYNER, R. (1920) Conditioned emotional reactions. *Journal of Experimental Psychology.* Vol 3. pp1–14.

WEBER, M. (1964) *The theory of social and economic organisation.* London: Macmillan.

WEEKS, K.O. (2013) An analysis of human resource information systems impact on employees [online]. *Journal of Management Policy and Practice.* Vol 14, No 3. pp35–49. Available at: http://search.proquest.com [Accessed 16 April 2014].

WERS (2011) *Workplace employment relations study [online].* Available at: https://www.gov.uk/government/publications/the-2011-workplace-employment-relations-study-wers. [Accessed 27 May 2014].

WEST, K. (2013) Ejector seats fly off the shelves: inside story: top gun, you're in the seat to survive [online]. *Sunday Times.* 21 July. p1. Available at: www.search.proquest.com

WHIDDETT, S. and HOLLYFORDE, S. (2003) *A practical guide to competencies.* London: Chartered Institute of Personnel and Development.

WHITMAN, D.S., VAN ROOY, D.L. and VISWEVARAN, C. (2010) Satisfaction, citizenship behaviors, and performance in work units: a meta-analysis of collective construct relations [online]. *Personnel Psychology.* Vol 63, No 1. pp41–81. Available at: www.swetswise.com [Accessed 1 November 2013].

WHITTINGTON, R. (1993) *What is strategy and does it matter?* London: Routledge.

WILLIAMS, M. (2000) Transfixed assets. *People Management.* 3 August. pp28–33.

WILLMAN, P., GOMEZ, R. and BRYSON, A. (2009) Voice at the workplace: Where do we find it, why is it there and where is it going? In: BROWN, W., BRYSON, A., FORTH, J. and WHITFIELD, K. (eds) *The evolution of the modern workplace.* Cambridge: Cambridge University Press, pp97–119.

WIN, B. (2013) Leading big change and employer re-branding: 'Is this still a great place to work?' [online]. *People & Strategy.* Vol 36, No 2. pp20–22. Available at: www.web.ebscohost.com [Accessed 17 October 2013].

WOOD, Z. (2014) Tesco under pressure to abandon profit margin targets [online]. *Guardian.* 21 February. Available at: http://www.theguardian.com/business

WOODWARD, J. (1965) *Industrial organization: theory and practice*. Oxford: Oxford University Press.

WORK AND FAMILIES ACT 2006 (SI 3242). Available at: www.legislation.gov.uk/ukpga/2006/18/contents [Accessed 16 February 2014].

WORK FOUNDATION (2013) *Flexibility or insecurity? Exploring the rise in zero hours contracts [online]*. Available at: www.theworkfoundation.com/Reports/339/Flexibility-or-insecurity-Exploring-the-rise-in-zero-hours-contracts [Accessed 27 March 2014].

WORKING TIME REGULATIONS 1998 (SI 1833). Available at: www.legislation.gov.uk/uksi/1998/1833/contents/made [Accessed 16 February 2014].

WORMAN, D. (2013) Is the age of your workforce in shape to deliver your business objectives? [online]. *Impact*. Issue 44. September. pp36–8. Available at: www.cipd.co.uk/impactmagazine [Accessed 28 September 2013].

WRIGHT, A. (2006) *Reward management in context*. London: Chartered Institute of Personnel and Development.

WRIGHT, P., MCMAHAN, G. and MCWILLIAMS, A. (1994) Human resources and sustained competitive advantage: a resource-based perspective. *International Journal of Human Resource Management*. Vol 5, No 2. pp301–26.

YOUNG (LORD OF GRAFFHAM) (2010) *Common sense common safety: a report to the prime minister [online]*. London: The Cabinet Office. Available at: www.gov.uk/government/uploads/system/uploads/attachment_data/file/60905/402906_CommonSense_acc.pdf [Accessed 22 April 2014].

Index